Prentice Hall Brief Review

United States History and Government

Bonnie-Anne Briggs / Catherine Fish-Peterson

Order Information

Send orders to:
PEARSON CUSTOMER SERVICE
P.O. BOX 2500
LEBANON, IN 46052-3009

or

CALL TOLL FREE 1-800-848-9500
(8:00 A.M.-6:00 P.M. EST)

- Orders can be placed via phone
- Price includes shipping and handling

Acknowledgments begin at the back of the text and constitutes an extension of this copyright page.

13-digit ISBN   978-0-13-361222-6
10-digit ISBN   0-13-361222-8

1 2 3 4 5 6 7 8 9 10   12 11 10 09 08

Contents

About This Book

This book has been written to help you, the student, review your United States history and government courses in order to take the New York State Regents Examination. The purpose of this book is to:

- Help you focus on the key facts, themes, and concepts tested on the Regents Examination.
- Familiarize you with the format of the Regents Examination.
- Provide you with the test-taking skills you need to succeed on the Regents Examination.

Content Review Just like the New York State Core Curriculum, this book is organized into seven units.

- The concepts and content that are consistently tested are emphasized in this text.
- Special emphasis has been given to the second unit on United States government and constitutional history to 1865.
- The charts, maps, cartoons, timelines, and graphic organizers in this text will help reinforce your understanding of the content.
- *The Big Idea* notes at the beginning of each section organize the section content at a glance.
- *Key Themes and Concepts* notes summarize important content and link it to the key themes and concepts of United States history and government.

Test-Taking Skills You can practice your test-taking skills on a variety of Regents Examination questions throughout the book.

- Every multiple-choice question has been on a New York State Regents Examination.
- Document-based essay questions, thematic essay questions, and multiple-choice questions are provided in each history and government unit of the book.
- **Six** sample Regents Examinations are provided for additional practice.
- For online test-taking practice, multiple-choice questions and document-based essay questions are available at the Prentice Hall Web site at **www.phschool.com.**
- An extensive Test-Taking Strategies section teaches you the skills and strategies you need for the exam.
- *Preparing for the Exam* notes in the margins help reinforce test-taking skills and strategies.

ABOUT THE AUTHORS

Bonnie-Anne Briggs is a graduate of Nazareth College of Rochester and the State University of New York at Brockport. She retired in June 2002 from her position as teacher and Teacher-in-Charge of Social Studies (department head) at Gates Chili High School in suburban Rochester. She was an adjunct professor in social studies education at the State University of New York at Brockport from 1988 until 2005. Miss Briggs is a past President of the Rochester Area Council for the Social Studies. She is also a past officer of both the New York State Social Studies Supervisory Association and the New York State Council for the Social Studies. Miss Briggs is a recipient of the Rochester Area Council Distinguished Educator Award, the New York State Social Studies Supervisory Association Supervisor of the Year Award, the New York State Council for the Social Studies Distinguished Educator Award, and the Outstanding Alumni Award from Nazareth College of Rochester. She has been inducted into the Gates Chili High School Alumni Hall of Fame, and in 1993, she was a semifinalist for the New York State Teacher of the Year Award.

Catherine Fish Petersen is a graduate of Wellesley College, Harvard University, and the State University of New York at Stony Brook. Ms. Petersen was the consultant to the New York State Education Department on the *Social Studies Resource Guide* and was their social studies consultant for the New York State Academy for Teaching and Learning. She also was an editor for *the State publication, Social Studies Instructional Strategies & Resources PreK-Grade Six.*

Before retirement, she chaired the Department of Humanities (Social Studies and English) in the East Islip School District on Long Island. She has served as the president of the New York State Social Studies Supervisory Association. Until June, 2006 she was the Treasurer and the Executive Secretary of the Long Island Council for the Social Studies and is also a past president of that organization. She has served on the Board of Directors of the New York State Council for the Social Studies. Ms. Petersen has received the Long Island Council for the Social Studies Presidential Leadership Award and its Gus Swift Outstanding Service to Social Studies Education Award, as well as the New York State Social Studies Supervisory Association Supervisor of the Year Award and that organization's Special Service Award. The New York State Council for the Social Studies named her its 1998 recipient of the Distinguished Social Studies Service Award.

Test-Taking Strategies

HOW TO SUCCEED ON THE REGENTS EXAM IN US HISTORY AND GOVERNMENT

This section of the book is intended to help you prepare to take the Regents Examination itself. Other parts of the book review the contents of the course you have studied. This section includes hints about preparing for and actually taking the examination based on test-taking skills you have probably been developing for years in social studies classes. Read and think carefully about all parts of this section as you prepare for the examination.

PREPARING TO TAKE THE REGENTS EXAMINATION

1. **Attend review sessions.** If review sessions are offered by your teacher or school, attend them. You will probably be reminded of something you studied earlier in the year and have not thought of since then. Review sessions also help you bring together the main ideas of the whole course.
2. **Find a study partner.** Two heads can be better than one. Try to review with a friend or a family member who can give you the chance to explain various parts of this course. You will have a better chance of remembering details if you have already explained them correctly to someone else. It has been said that the best way to learn something is to teach it to someone else.
3. **Do not "over-study."** As important as it is to review carefully and over a period of time for your exams, do not make the mistake of "over-studying" or cramming at the last minute. This could leave you exhausted and unable to think clearly during the exam itself. This exam is important enough for you to ask your employer for time off right before the test.
4. **Eat a good meal.** Eat something before the exam so your energy level stays high.
5. **Know the exam site.** Be sure you know the correct time and place of the examination. Arriving half an hour late can make the difference between passing and failing. Be sure someone else at your house has a schedule of your exams.
6. **Be prepared.** Bring several dark ink pens and pencils.
7. **Wear a watch, if possible.** You will need to pay close attention to the time during the exam, and you might be seated where you cannot see a clock.

8. **Stay for the full allotted time.** Come to the exam prepared to stay for the full three-hour examination period. Do not tell someone to pick you up in two hours—you will need all the time allowed. Don't sacrifice a year's worth of work to get outside faster on a nice day.

TAKING THE REGENTS EXAMINATION

1. **Arrive on time.** Use a reliable method of getting to school so you can arrive early in the exam room. This will allow you to get your mind on the task at hand.
2. **Select a seat.** If you are allowed to select your own seat, be sure to choose one with the least distraction. Choose one away from doors or windows.
3. **Dress comfortably.** You will be sitting in one place for a long period of time, so be sure you are comfortably dressed.
4. **Listen to instructions.** Pay full attention to all instructions given by the proctor(s).
5. **Read directions carefully.** Read all directions written on the test booklet as you take the exam. If you have reviewed well, you will be familiar with the terms *discuss, explain, show,* and *describe.* Nonetheless, take the time to read carefully the instructions given to you on the test.
6. **Be an active test-taker.** Become a participant in the exam, not a spectator. You may write on the exam. Underline key ideas. You may write in the margins as you think about the questions. The idea is for you to interact with the exam. Other hints are given as you review the multiple-choice questions from the practice examination.
7. **DON'T leave blanks.** No credit can be given for a blank on either multiple-choice or essay questions. Write something. Write anything, but never leave an answer blank.

THE MULTIPLE-CHOICE SECTION

Part I of the Regents Examination is made up of 50 multiple-choice questions. These questions tend to fall into certain categories that you can identify as you take an examination. The following is about identifying these categories and improving your ability to answer certain types of questions. Samples of these questions come from the June 2000 sample exam.

Data-Based Questions

Data-based questions provide specific information to be used in answering a question or questions. You will probably not be able to answer the question(s) without this information, and you will also need to know some social studies background to help interpret the information. There are several types of data-based questions.

READING PASSAGES Some questions on the practice exam are based on a selected reading passage. These questions often require an ability to recognize opinions expressed in a passage.

If there are words you are unsure of in the selection, try to find a root word you know. Be sure to look for dates or other historical references to help you. You may write notes in the margin near the selection.

EXAMPLE:

"To take a single step beyond these specific [Constitutional] limits to the powers of Congress is to grasp unlimited power.

"The power to create a [national] bank has not, in my opinion, been delegated to Congress by the Constitution. Supporters of the Bank Bill argue that a [national] bank would be a great convenience in collecting taxes. Even if this argument were true, the Constitution allows only for laws which are 'necessary,' not those which are merely 'convenient' for carrying out delegated powers."

The speaker is basing his argument mainly on a strict interpretation of which provision of the federal Constitution?

1 Preamble
2 elastic clause
3 judicial review
4 apportionment of representatives

Answer: The correct answer is 2. The phrase "laws which are 'necessary'" near the end of the reading passage should help you make an association with the elastic clause or "*necessary* and proper" clause. As you read this book, you will find key vocabulary and social studies phrases highlighted throughout.

SPEAKER QUESTIONS Speaker questions present different reading passages by different people on the same topic. When answering speaker questions, follow these steps:

- Determine the theme or topic that all of the speakers are addressing.
- Read the questions before you study the speakers' statements too closely; often you do not have to read each speaker's viewpoint to answer a question.
- Be sure you are reading the correct speaker when answering each question.
- Take your time when answering speaker questions. You will probably need to go back and forth among the readings as you analyze the difference between speakers.

EXAMPLE:

Speaker A: "We cannot make the same mistakes that led to the sinking of the *Lusitania.* Freedom of the seas is important, but we must keep our ships away from possible danger."

Speaker B: "We should encourage Great Britain and France to follow a policy of appeasement."

Speaker C: "Continued isolation is the only alternative. Whichever way we turn in this conflict, we find an alien ideology."

Speaker D: "The future of the free world depends now on the United States and Great Britain. We must not only help win this war, but also ensure that no others occur in the future."

The speakers are most likely discussing the situation facing the United States just before
1 the American Revolution
2 the Spanish-American War
3 World War II
4 the Korean War

Answer: The correct answer is 3, World War II. Underline all hints such as the phrases *mistake of the* Lusitania, *freedom of the seas, Great Britain and France, appeasement, continued isolation,* and *future of the free world.* The correct answer cannot be the American Revolution or the Spanish-American War, because the sinking of the *Lusitania* occurred after both of those wars. The correct answer cannot be the Korean War, because the United States had abandoned its isolationist policy before the Korean War. All of the hints together indicate that these speakers are discussing the situation facing the United States just before World War II.

GRAPHS Graphs may appear in several forms— bar graphs, line graphs, or pie graphs. Some graphs may provide all of the information that you need to answer the question. Others may require you to draw upon your knowledge of social studies to interpret the graph.

EXAMPLE:

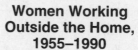

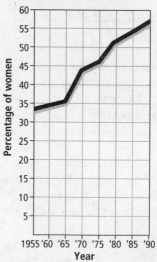

Source: *Statistical Abstract of the United States*

The trend shown in the graph was mainly the result of
1 increases in immigration
2 demands for more schoolteachers
3 a buildup in the defense industry
4 new social attitudes

Answer: The correct answer is 4. The graph indicates a steady increase in the number of women working outside the home between 1955 and 1990. You must draw upon your knowledge of U.S. history to provide the reason for this trend.

TABLES Some questions require you to draw conclusions from information provided in tables. Be *very* careful to base your conclusions only on the information in the table unless the question specifically asks you to do otherwise. Be sure to note the source and date of the information given in the table.

EXAMPLE:

Rural and Urban Populations in the United States		
Year	Rural (thousands)	Urban (thousands)
1860	25,227	6,217
1870	28,656	9,902
1880	36,026	14,130
1890	40,841	22,106
1900	45,835	30,160
1910	49,973	41,999
1920	51,553	54,158

Source: Bureau of the Census

Which statement is best supported by the chart?
1 In the early 1900s, there was an increase in the number of immigrants who became farmers.
2 In the early 1900s, people who lived in cities were more likely to vote than those who lived in rural areas.
3 In 1920, more people lived in cities than on farms.
4 In 1920, there were fewer women working in factories than on farms.

Answer: The correct answer is 3. This question tests your ability to read the table, as well as your understanding of the words *urban* and *rural*. To answer a question such as this, eliminate all possible answers that do not have information given in the chart. For example, answer 1 mentions immigrants, but the table provides no information about immigrants.

POLITICAL CARTOONS Some questions ask you to analyze and interpret a political cartoon. When analyzing a political cartoon, follow these steps:
• Study the caption.
• Look for a date.
• Read all words in the cartoon. Look closely for any small print written on figures or objects in the cartoon.
• Identify the symbolism used by a cartoonist.

EXAMPLE:

According to the cartoon, what was a major contributing factor that led to the collapse of communism in Eastern Europe in the early 1990s?
1 overpopulation   3 democratic elections
2 military force   4 high tax rates

Answer: The correct answer is 3, democratic elections. When analyzing this cartoon, be sure to look very carefully at all parts of the cartoon: the title of the cartoon, the writing on the people's clothing, the symbols used on their clothing, and the words they are saying. The question itself also gives you a good hint about the downfall of communism.

OUTLINES Some questions ask you to complete a hypothetical outline.

EXAMPLE:

In an outline, one of these entries is a main topic and three are subtopics. Which is the main topic?
1 Alexander Hamilton's Economic Program
2 The Rise of National Political Parties
3 The Constitution's First Tests
4 John Adams's Stormy Presidency

Answer: In this question, you are simply asked to determine the main topic. Look for the most general answer. Recognize that the other choices would be subheads on the outline under the main topic. The right choice is 3 because 1, 2, and 4 are examples of the Constitution's first tests.

QUOTATION INTERPRETATION This type of question asks you to explain the idea of a given quotation. Sometimes the date and speaker of the quotation are identified and sometimes not.

EXAMPLE:

"(Sec. 4.) Every person presenting himself for registration shall be able to read and write any section of the Constitution in the English language, and before he shall be entitled to vote, he shall have paid on or before the first day of March of the year in which he proposes to vote his poll tax as prescribed by law for the previous year."

—Public Laws of North Carolina, 1899, chapter 218

The principle purpose of this law was to
1 assure equality of voting rights for all peoples
2 encourage literacy for former slaves
3 prevent African Americans from using their suffrage rights
4 promote the racial integration of southern society

Answer: The correct answer is 3. The date and place of origin of this quotation are important clues, which should remind you that Jim Crow laws were legal in much of the South at the end of the 1800s.

MAPS When maps are given, be sure to look for the following:
• A key explaining any symbols used
• Dates
• Specific place locations
• Compass point for directions

TIMELINES A timeline is a graphic way of showing relationships among events over time. Questions dealing with timelines often ask you to draw a conclusion about a series of events. When answering timeline questions, be careful to focus on the time period shown; do not jump to a different era to answer the question.

Other Multiple-Choice Questions

Many other types of multiple-choice questions appear on the Regents Examination.

"HEADLINE" QUESTIONS In this type of question, you are given a few sample headlines that usually have to do with a common event. Your goal is to determine the connection between the headlines.

EXAMPLE:

"Raise Tariffs!"
"Buy American!"
"Impose Import Quotas!"

Which policy do these slogans reflect?
1 militarism   3 isolationism
2 protectionism   4 détente

Answer: The correct answer is 2. The subject of all three headlines is economics and trade. The words and phrases *tariffs, buy American,* and *import quotas* suggest foreign trade. The only possible answer that deals with foreign trade is protectionism.

RECALL QUESTIONS These questions require you to know specific information about people, events, topics, concepts, and vocabulary studied in the course. Throughout this review book, you will find many suggestions about test-taking strategies, as well as references to the many important people and events covered in this course. There is also a glossary at the end of this book to help you with vocabulary.

EXAMPLE:

At the Constitutional Convention of 1787, a bicameral legislature was proposed as the solution to the disagreement over
1 taxation within each state
2 control of interstate commerce
3 limits on the treaty-making power of a President
4 state representation in the national government

Answer: The correct answer is 4. The key to answering this question correctly is understanding the meaning of the term *bicameral legislature* and the reason for its proposal.

CAUSE-AND-EFFECT QUESTIONS These questions test your understanding of the concepts of cause and effect. A cause is an event or action that brings about another event or action—an effect. Your study of history will have revealed that almost everything is either the cause or result of some event.

EXAMPLE:

Which factor contributed most directly to the settlement and development of the Great Plains after the Civil War?
1 freeing of the slaves in Southern states
2 construction of railroads west of the Mississippi River
3 influx of immigrants from eastern and southern Europe
4 hospitality of the Indian tribes inhabiting the region

Answer: The correct answer is 2. The use of the newly developed railroad as transportation was key to the western development (choice 2). Choice 1 is wrong because the freed slaves did not move west, and 3 is wrong because those immigrants generally stayed in urban areas to work in factories. Note the word *hospitality* in choice 4. Few of the Indian tribes welcomed the arrival of the settlers on the plains.

TIME REFERENCE OR CHRONOLOGY QUESTIONS These are questions that make reference to a particular time period. You rarely need to identify specific dates on Regents exams. However, you often do need to know the time sequence or order of events.

EXAMPLE:

In the period between World War I and World War II, which group made the greatest gains in political rights?
1 African Americans
2 women
3 new immigrants
4 Native Americans

Answer: The correct answer is 2. With a question like this, it is a good idea to write the dates of the period above the question so that you can focus on that specific time. Remember, a condition that was true in one time period may cease to exist in another time period. When answering this question, you should remember that the Nineteenth Amendment granting women the right to vote was passed in 1920 (between the wars). Not until well *after* World War II did the other groups make great gains in their political rights.

GENERALIZATIONS These questions require you to make a general statement about a particular event, time period, or body of information. You are really being asked to draw a conclusion.

EXAMPLE:

A primary aim of the writers of the United States Constitution was to
1 strengthen the power of the central government
2 change from a government based on division of powers to one based on a single power
3 develop a governmental system based on the principle of supremacy of the states
4 weaken the power of the executive

Answer: The correct answer is 1. This question asks you to explain why the Constitution was written. To do so, you need to recall the problems of the Articles of Confederation. Choice 1 is correct because the Constitution does establish a strong central government.

FACT AND OPINION These questions require you to find a statement that is clearly either fact or opinion. If you keep in mind that certain words such as *most important, most significant,* and *greatest contribution* signal opinions, you should have no trouble with this type of question. It is difficult to make true statements that include the words *always, never, all,* or *none.*

SOURCES AND REFERENCES Some questions test your ability to identify a valid source of information. A primary source is one written or told by someone who was present at an event. These sources can be biased, but they can also give a special insight into an event. Secondary sources, such as textbooks, are those that are written after an event.

QUESTIONS ABOUT SOCAL SCIENTISTS Some questions ask about the jobs of certain types of social scientists. These might include the following:

Historian: a person who studies the past and makes judgments about why events happened and how they affected other events

Economist: a person who studies the monetary systems of countries or cultures. The work of economists is important to our understanding of events such as the Great Depression.

Political scientist: a person who studies the workings of government and politics. For example, political scientists analyze the results of elections to determine trends in voting patterns.

THE THEMATIC ESSAY

There will be one thematic essay on your examination. The score on the thematic essay ranges from 0 to 5 points, using a generic scoring rubric. You should become familiar with this rubric as you prepare for the exam, because it will help you learn how to write the most effective essay possible.

You will not have a choice of theme or topic, but you will have many choices within the provided list of suggested examples you may draw upon in writing your essay. You may choose examples that are not on the list of suggestions, but that approach may not be a good idea. The most frequently studied examples are the ones that are usually given in the suggestions.

Blocking Essay Answers

Blocking an essay will help you organize your ideas before you write your answer. Organizing your thoughts before writing will help you earn more points on the essay and avoid leaving out parts of the essay. Experts in helping students prepare for tests know that the more involved you become with a test, the better you will do on it.

STEPS IN BLOCKING AN ESSAY

1. Underline the words that tell you what you need to do: *discuss, describe, explain,* etc.
2. Study the directions next to each bulleted point (•).
3. Use those directions to form headings for your block.
4. Under each section of your block, write facts to help you answer that part of the question.
5. Review to see if you have completed all parts of the *Task.*
6. Check to see that your introduction and conclusion show thought and are not just a repetition of the ones you are given in the question.
7. When you have arranged all your facts in the section of the block, check to be sure you have not left any blocks empty.

SAMPLE BLOCK

This chart blocks the thematic essay that is part of the June 2004 sample Regents examination at the back of this book.

	Two actions	Discuss historical circumstances that resulted in government actions	Discuss influence of a geographic factor (location, physical environment, actions, movement of people, climate resources)	Impact of action on U. S.
Sample answer	Louisiana Purchase	France wanted and needed to sell area much cheaper than U. S. expected to buy; President Jefferson decided the government could purchase the land	U. S. could expand to the west and end French presence on U. S. western border	Gave U. S. chance to double size of territory to allow for future growth and exploration for new resources. U. S. set precedent that it could add additional territory

THEMATIC ESSAY SCORING RUBRIC

SCORE OF 5:
- Thoroughly develops all aspects of the task evenly and in depth
- Is more analytical than descriptive (analyzes, evaluates, and/or creates* information)
- Richly supports the theme with many relevant facts, examples, and details
- Demonstrates a logical and clear plan of organization; includes an introduction and a conclusion that are beyond a restatement of the theme

SCORE OF 4:
- Develops all aspects of the task but may do so somewhat unevenly
- Is both descriptive and analytical (applies, analyzes, evaluates, and/or creates information)
- Supports the theme with relevant facts, examples, and details
- Demonstrates a logical and clear plan of organization; includes an introduction and a conclusion that are beyond a restatement of the theme

SCORE OF 3:
- Develops all aspects of the task with little depth or develops most aspects of the task in some depth
- Is more descriptive than analytical (applies, may analyze, and/or evaluate information)
- Includes some relevant facts, examples, and details; may include some minor inaccuracies
- Demonstrates a satisfactory plan of organization; includes an introduction and a conclusion that may be a restatement of the theme

SCORE OF 2:
- Minimally develops all aspects of the task or develops some aspects of the task in some depth
- Is primarily descriptive; may include faulty, weak, or isolated application or analysis
- Includes few relevant facts, examples, and details; may include some inaccuracies
- Demonstrates a general plan of organization; may lack focus; may contain digressions; may not clearly identify which aspect of the task is being addressed; may lack an introduction and/or a conclusion

SCORE OF 1:
- Minimally develops some aspects of the task
- Is descriptive; may lack understanding, application, or analysis
- Includes few relevant facts, examples, or details; may include inaccuracies
- May demonstrate a weakness in organization; may lack focus; may contain digressions; may not clearly identify which aspect of the task is being addressed; may lack an introduction and/or a conclusion

SCORE OF 0:
Fails to develop the task or may only refer to the theme in a general way; *OR* includes no relevant facts, examples, or details; *OR* includes only the theme, task, or suggestions as copied from the test booklet; *OR* is illegible; *OR* is a blank paper

DOCUMENT-BASED ESSAY QUESTION

There will be one document-based essay question (DBQ) on the examination. The score on the document-based essay question ranges from 0 to 5 points, using a generic scoring rubric. You should become familiar with this rubric as you prepare for the exam, because it will help you learn how to write the most effective essay possible.

The DBQ has two important parts. Part A includes the scaffolding questions in which you examine documents individually and complete short-answer questions. Part B is the essay question in which you draw upon your analysis of the documents and your knowledge of United States history and government to write the essay. You must complete all sections of both parts. There are several steps you should take to ensure success in answering the DBQ:

- **Read the *Historical Context* section carefully.** This sets the time frame in which all parts of the question are set. It also limits the time period that you can write about in your answer. Remember to highlight or underline important data.

- **Read and understand the *Task*.** Read this part carefully to be sure that you complete all parts. Underline any parts of the test that you do not want to forget or overlook.

- **Do not leave any blanks on the scaffolding question section.** Any blanks you leave will cause you to lose points automatically.

- **Keep track of main ideas/block your essay.** As you work through the scaffolding questions, write down the main idea or ideas of each document on your scrap paper. Briefly listing the main ideas of each document will help you organize your thoughts so that you can successfully support your viewpoint in the essay. You may choose to organize the main ideas by creating a simple chart.

Sample Block or Prewriting Outline

The chart on the next page blocks the document-based essay question that is part of the June 2004 sample Regents examination at the back of this book.

Writing the Document-Based Essay Question

Use the list you created while answering the scaffolding questions to help guide the writing of your essay. Using the question from the June 2004 Regents, you should have a list of social, political and economic changes from the given documents. Be sure to note that not all of the changes have to be positive and that some changes definitely had a negative impact on the Untied States.

In your essay, you should take care to draw as much information out of the documents as you can. However, you should also include other information from your knowledge of United States history if that information helps support your viewpoint. In the document-based essay question from the sample Regents examination, for example, you could also include information about other changes that occured such as the work of Martin Luther King, Jr., Rosa Parks, Civil Rights legislation of the 1960's, etc.

Be sure to study carefully the *Guidelines* that are provided in the instructions on writing the document-based essay question. These *Guidelines* will remind you of what you must include in order to score the full five points for the essay.

Document (number and source)	Type of Change (social, political, economic)	Specific Application
1 14th Amendment	political	gave persons natural born or naturalized citizenship
2 F. Douglass	economic	freed slaves that were not given land, money or other assistance to help them get stared as free citizens
3 Senate document	social, political	KKK depriving freed slaves basic human rights, i.e. life, liberty as well as new political right to vote
4 Plantation map	economic	slaves had a right to be tenant farmers, big plantations had been subdivided, therefore change for the old "elite" or Master too
5 Harper's Magazine	economic and social	multiple examples of new types businesses in the south in 1887, iron foundries, cotton mills, train car production
6 separate drinking fountain	social	illustrates separate AND unequal public facilities as recent as the 1950's and 60's
7 Afro-American Council	political	changes did not always happen when they should have, some Southern states made their own laws to deprive African Americans of voting rights
8 NAACP Parade	social, political, economic	shows that in 1917 African Americans were using parades and demonstrations to protest their lack of right to be truly equal (note formal, business dress on marchers)

DOCUMENT-BASED QUESTION ESSAY SCORING RUBRIC

SCORE OF 5:
- Thoroughly develops all aspects of the task evenly and in depth
- Is more analytical than descriptive (analyzes, evaluates, and/or creates information)
- Incorporates relevant information from *at least* **xxx** documents
- Incorporates substantial relevant outside information
- Richly supports the theme with many relevant facts, examples, and details
- Demonstrates a logical and clear plan of organization; includes an introduction and a conclusion that are beyond a restatement of the theme

SCORE OF 4:
- Develops all aspects of the task but may do so somewhat unevenly
- Is both descriptive and analytical (applies, analyzes, evaluates, and/or creates information)
- Incorporates relevant information from *at least* **xxx** documents
- Incorporates relevant outside information
- Supports the theme with relevant facts, examples, and details
- Demonstrates a logical and clear plan of organization; includes an introduction and a conclusion that are beyond a restatement of the theme

SCORE OF 3:
- Develops all aspects of the task with little depth *or* develops most aspects of the task in some depth
- Is more descriptive than analytical (applies, may analyze, and/or evaluate information)
- Incorporates some relevant information from some of the documents
- Incorporates limited relevant outside information
- Includes some relevant facts, examples, and details; may include some minor inaccuracies
- Demonstrates a satisfactory plan of organization; includes an introduction and a conclusion that may be a restatement of the theme

SCORE OF 2:
- Minimally develops all aspects of the task *or* develops some aspects of the task in some depth
- Is primarily descriptive; may include faulty, weak, or isolated application or analysis
- Incorporates limited relevant information from the documents or consists primarily of relevant information copied from the documents
- Presents little or no relevant outside information
- Includes few relevant facts, examples, and details; may include some inaccuracies
- Demonstrates a general plan of organization; may lack focus; may contain digressions; may not clearly identify which aspect of the task is being addressed; may lack an introduction and/or a conclusion

SCORE OF 1:
- Minimally develops some aspects of the task
- Is descriptive; may lack understanding, application, or analysis
- Makes vague, unclear references to the documents or consists primarily of relevant and irrelevant information copied from the documents
- Presents no relevant outside information
- Includes few relevant facts, examples, or details; may include inaccuracies
- May demonstrate a weakness in organization; may lack focus; may contain digressions; may not clearly identify which aspect of the task is being addressed; may lack an introduction and/or a conclusion

SCORE OF 0:
Fails to develop the task or may only refer to the theme in a general way; *OR* includes no relevant facts, examples, or details; includes only the historical context and/or task as copies from the test booklet; *OR* includes only entire documents copied from the test booklet; *OR* is illegible; *OR* is a blank paper

UNIT 1 Geography and the Development of the United States

UNIT OVERVIEW

This unit provides a general review of the physical and cultural geography of the United States. It also reviews some of the ways in which geography has influenced the history of the country. Geographers use five themes to study an area. The five themes are location, place, movement, regions, and human-environment interaction.

These are some of the key questions relating to the nation's geography. Each question relates to one of the five geographic themes:

- Where is the United States located, both absolutely and relatively? How has the country's relative location changed over time?
- What are the physical and human characteristics of the United States?
- How have people, goods, and ideas moved between places?
- How are places within the United States similar to and different from other places?
- How have people in the United States interacted with the natural environment?

KEY THEMES AND CONCEPTS

As you review this unit, take special note of the following key themes and concepts:

Physical Systems How have the nation's systems of mountains and waterways influenced the development of the United States?

Immigration and Migration What have been the major patterns of immigration and movement of people over the course of the country's history?

Places and Regions What different types of regions exist within the United States?

LOCATION

Geographers describe the location of an area in both absolute and relative terms.

Absolute Location

In terms of its absolute location, the United States is located in the Northern and Western hemispheres. With the exception of Hawaii, the country is located on the continent of North America. The country is bordered by the Atlantic Ocean on the east and the Pacific Ocean on the west.

Relative Location

Geographers also consider an area's relative location, or where it is located in relation to other places. For example, the United States is located south of Canada and north of Mexico. California is west of New York.

The relative location of a place can also change over time. For much of the country's history, Americans felt relatively isolated from Europe and Asia. Likewise, people in the West felt relatively isolated from the East.

Changes in transportation and communication technologies changed these perceptions. For example, the number of post offices in the nation leaped from 75 in 1790 to 8,450 in 1830. Regular mail delivery made it easier for people in distant places to communicate with one another. Improved communication and transportation helped tie together different parts of the country as it grew in both size and population.

ANALYZING DOCUMENTS

This map shows the 50 states of the United States.

- Where is New York located in relation to Florida?

- What types of regions are shown on this map?

The United States: Political

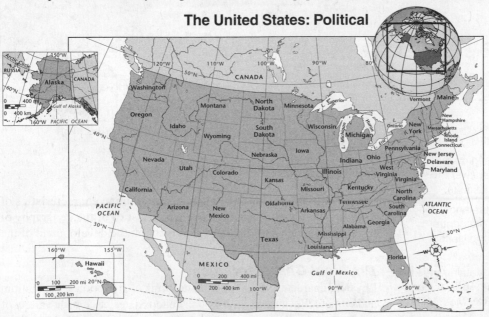

The United States and Canada: Physical

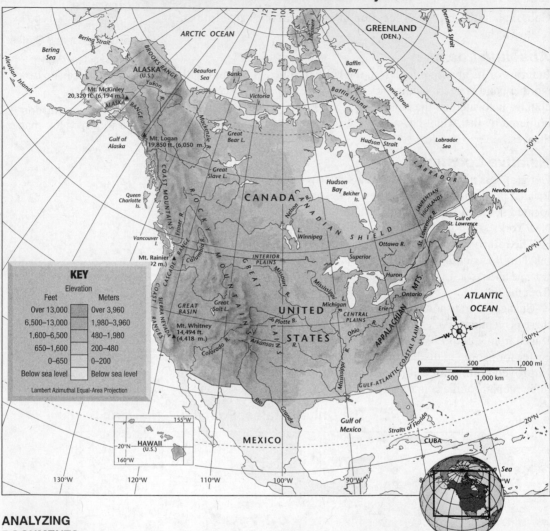

ANALYZING DOCUMENTS

Study the map on this page; then answer the following questions.

- What major landform occupies the central region of the United States?

- Which mountain range is higher, the Appalachians or the Rocky Mountains?

PLACE

Geographers study both the physical and human characteristics of places. Both physical and human characteristics of the geography of the United States have had a huge impact on the development of the country.

Physical Characteristics

Physical characteristics include landforms, water bodies, vegetation, and climate. Because of its size, the United States has a wide variety of landforms. As the map on this page shows, the **Great Plains** and the

Central Plains occupy the central regions of the country, also known as the Midwest. The rich soils and climate of the Midwest encouraged Americans to move to these regions, where they could acquire inexpensive farmland. The **Mississippi River** cuts through the Central Plains as it flows south to the Gulf of Mexico. Boats traveling along the Mississippi allowed farmers and traders to transport their goods to markets throughout the country.

Two mountain ranges run from north to south on either side of the central plains regions. In the east are the lower, older **Appalachian Mountains.** In the west are the **Rocky Mountains.** The Rockies are a cordillera, or a related set of mountain ranges, that stretches from northern Alaska to Mexico, forming the longest mountain chain in North America.

Human Characteristics

Several waves of immigration have created a unique cultural mix of people in the United States. People from every region of the world have settled in the United States. As a result, the region's human characteristics, such as a language, religion, and customs, are varied. About half of all African Americans live in the South. About 9 percent of southern residents are of Latino origin.

In general, population density is greater in the eastern half of the country. The most densely settled region of the country is the Northeast Corridor, which stretches along the east coast from Washington, D.C., to Boston, Massachusetts.

Compared with those in many nations of the world, people in the United States have long life expectancies, high per capita incomes, and high literacy rates.

MOVEMENT

Geographers study the movement of people, goods, and ideas within an area. The movement of people into and within the United States over the course of the region's history can be broken into the following large patterns.

Bering Strait Land Bridge

Geographers believe that during the Ice Ages—between about 20,000 and 12,000 years ago—much of the earth's water was frozen into glaciers and ice sheets. As a result, ocean levels dropped, exposing a flat bridge of land between Alaska and eastern Asia where the Bering Strait is today. Over thousands of years, hunters from East Asia crossed the land bridge and gradually spread out over North and South America. These Paleo-Indians were the first humans in the Americas, ancestors of all the Native American peoples.

ANALYZING DOCUMENTS

The movement of people from east to west put pressure on the government to expand the territory of the United States. Study the map below; then answer the following questions.

- What was the date of the Louisiana Purchase?

- When were the lands of the present-day states of Washington and Oregon added to the country's territory?

- Using the information on this map, describe the acquisition of present-day California.

European Exploration and Slavery

By the 1500s, better ships and navigation methods allowed European explorers to find their way to North America. The first European newcomers, mainly from Spain, settled in what are now Florida, the Southwest, and Mexico. About a century later, people from France and Great Britain set up colonies on the eastern coast of North America. In addition, millions of Africans were enslaved and brought unwillingly to North America.

Migration from East to West

During the 1800s, the promise of land and gold led many Americans of European descent to move westward. Native Americans were forced from their lands to locations even further west. Rivers, wagons, canals, and railroads all played a part in the movement of people to the frontiers of the west. **Manifest Destiny** was the concept that expressed the American belief that the United States was destined to expand across North America.

African American Migration

African Americans moved from the South to the Northeast and Midwest in search of economic opportunities from about 1890 to 1920 and again during the 1940s.

The Rise of the Sun Belt

Beginning around 1950, many Americans moved from the industrial cities of the North and Midwest to the so-called **Sun Belt**—the southern states stretching from Florida to California. Newcomers were attracted by job opportunities and warmer climates.

United States Territorial Expansion, 1783–1853

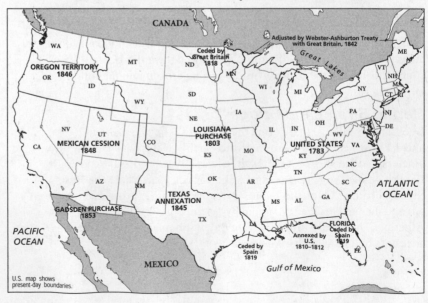

This population shift, along with its corresponding reapportionment of congressional seats, has given the South greater influence in American politics. Once a stronghold for Democrats, the South has become more strongly Republican and conservative.

REGIONS

The continental United States from east to west covers a distance of over three thousand miles. The states of Hawaii in the Pacific Ocean and Alaska in the north Pacific expand the country's geographic dimensions. Given this huge size it is not surprising that geographers can identify hundreds of regions within the country.

Different Types of Regions

Geographers describe regions as places having at least one common characteristic. Regions can be defined by physical characteristics, such as landforms or climate. They can also be defined by cultural characteristics, such as the economy of the area or the political organization of the area. The map on the next page shows regions that share similar economies or land use patterns. Political regions include towns, counties, cities, states, and the United States as a whole.

In the United States, geographers use terms like the Midwest to describe a group of states (Ohio, Indiana, Illinois), or the Northwest (Oregon and Washington) or the Rocky Mountain area. Climatic conditions can cause a region to be identified for its frequency of tornadoes, hurricanes, or snowstorms. The cultural characteristics of people might also designate a region, such as the region around Lancaster, Pennsylvania, where many Amish people live. As you study the history and development of the United States, think about how various immigrant groups gave certain regions distinctive names, for example, New York City's Chinatown.

Regions within New York State

In New York State, some examples of regions include the **Great Lakes** region, the Adirondack Mountains, Long Island, the Finger Lakes, Manhattan, and the Capital District around Albany.

HUMAN-ENVIRONMENT INTERACTION

When studying an area, geographers also examine how people use the environment and how they have changed it. What are the consequences of those changes?

Early Land Use Patterns

From the earliest days of settlement, Americans have been interacting with their environment to survive. When the Europeans began to settle along the Atlantic coast, they faced a range of climatic and geographic

Land Use in the United States

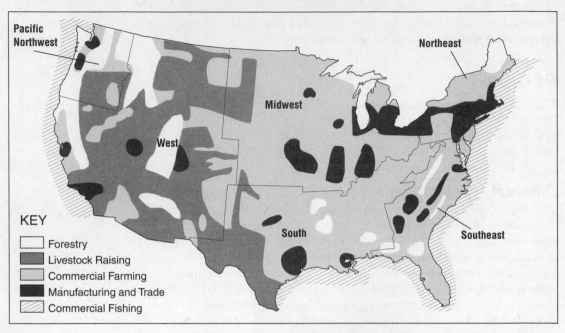

Pacific
Northwest

Northeast

Midwest

West

KEY
☐ Forestry
■ Livestock Raising
▨ Commercial Farming
■ Manufacturing and Trade
▨ Commercial Fishing

South

Southeast

conditions. At various points in this nation's history, these conditions both encouraged and discouraged settlement. In some places, Native Americans assisted the Europeans in adapting to their unfamiliar surroundings.

The great Atlantic coastal plain fostered agricultural development in the Mid-Atlantic region, while further to the south, the long, hot summers gave rise to the tobacco and cotton industries. Settlers of coastal South Carolina drained swamps to create thriving rice plantations. The rocky soil of New England discouraged extensive farming, but the rich coastal waters encouraged the development of fishing and shipbuilding. The waterfalls in the area and elsewhere in the Middle Atlantic states encouraged the development of factories that could benefit from water power. These factories produced goods that were then traded all over the world. Port cities, such as Boston, New York, Charleston, Savannah, and New Orleans developed as centers of this trade.

Tourism and Conservation

In addition to the land use patterns shown on the map above, tourism is another form of land use. The national parks are an example of human-environment interaction in which the landscape and natural resources are preserved for the enjoyment of future generations. Niagara Falls, New York, leads a double life as a tourist attraction for its natural beauty and as a major source of hydroelectric power.

ANALYZING DOCUMENTS

Study the land use map on this page; then answer the following questions.

• What is the major land use activity in the Midwest?

• How do the economic activities of the Pacific Northwest compare with those of the Northeast?

• Where are the most concentrated areas of manufacturing and trade located?

It was only in the late twentieth century that many people began to realize the need to protect and preserve the environment for future generations. Today, geographic issues include waste disposal, air and water pollution, energy sources, energy use, and topics related to demographics, such as the changing composition of the population, the "graying" of America, and the effects of the baby boom generation.

LOOKING AHEAD

As you continue through this review book, you will have many opportunities to utilize the concepts of location, place, movement, regions, and human-environment interaction. Use the maps located in this unit and elsewhere in this text to help you draw conclusions about the impact geography has had and continues to have on the development of the United States.

ANALYZING DOCUMENTS

Study the climate map on this page; then answer the following questions.

- Much of the southwestern United States has a hot, dry, arid climate and receives less than 10 inches of rainfall each year. Many people have been moving to this region in recent decades. How do you think climate affects the human-environment interaction in this region?

- Describe the climate of the southeastern half of the United States.

The United States and Canada: Climate Regions

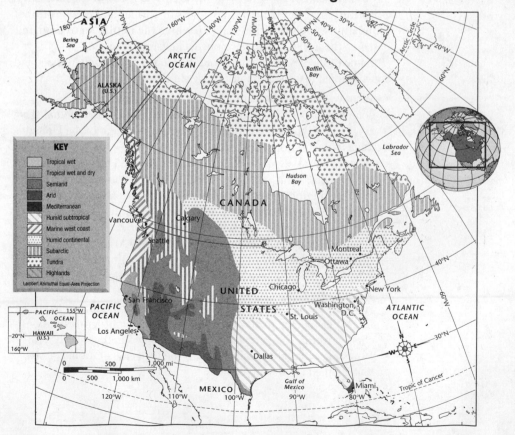

KEY

- Tropical wet
- Tropical wet and dry
- Semiarid
- Arid
- Mediterranean
- Humid subtropical
- Marine west coast
- Humid continental
- Subarctic
- Tundra
- Highlands

Lambert Azimuthal Equal-Area Projection

UNIT 2

Constitutional Foundations for the United States Democratic Republic

Section 1 The Constitution: The Foundation of American Society

Section 2 The Constitution Tested: Nationalism and Sectionalism

UNIT OVERVIEW

Unit 2 covers the period from the first English settlement in 1607 through the end of the Civil War in 1865. The focus of the unit is the Constitution of the United States—its historical and constitutional foundations, including the ways in which the nation's government, based on the Constitution, developed and was then tested.

Some of the key questions about the United States government and constitutional history through 1865 include:

- What was the influence of the colonial settlement pattern, colonists' experience living in the American colonies, colonial slavery, and Enlightenment thought on the development of the United States Constitution?
- What opinions about government were discussed and debated by the Framers? What compromises did they reach in order to create the Constitution and ensure approval by the states?
- What is the structure of the United States Constitution, and how does the government it describes function?
- What are the basic constitutional principles of American democracy? Why were they important when the Constitution was written? Why have they remained critical principles throughout United States history?
- How did the new nation go about putting its constitution into effect? What helped to build nationalism? What conflicting opinions about government were discussed and debated in those early years?
- How did sectionalism and slavery bring on a constitutional crisis that led the nation to civil war?

The Constitution: The Foundation of American Society

SECTION OVERVIEW

For centuries, the only inhabitants of North American were Native Americans. In the 1600s, English settlers arrived to found colonies and were soon joined by other Europeans, as well as Africans brought as slaves. By the mid-1700s, tensions between the colonies and Great Britain increased sharply. The colonies declared independence and won the American Revolution. They established a weak central government under the Articles of Confederation, but in 1787 replaced that with the United States Constitution that is still the guiding document of this nation today.

KEY THEMES AND CONCEPTS

Take special note of the following key themes and concepts:

Diversity In what ways did the Native Americans, Europeans, and Africans who met in North America differ?

Citizenship What led the colonists to rebel against the British government?

Foreign Policy Why did France forge an alliance with the colonists during the American Revolution?

Constitutional Principles How does the Constitution ensure that no single part of the government can gain too much power?

KEY PEOPLE

Be sure you understand the significance of these key people:

John Adams	John Marshall
Samuel Adams	James Monroe
Benjamin Franklin	Baron de Montesquieu
Alexander Hamilton	Jean-Jacques Rousseau
Patrick Henry	Voltaire
Thomas Jefferson	George Washington
John Locke	John Peter Zenger
James Madison	

★ **THE BIG IDEA**
The Constitution is the foundation of American society. The United States

- developed from 13 English colonies.
- developed its political system based on British traditions, Enlightenment thought, and American experience.
- won independence in the American Revolution.
- bases its government on the 1787 U.S. Constitution.

KEY TERMS

French and Indian War
indentured servants
triangular trade
Middle Passage
republic
Enlightenment
natural rights
charter
House of Burgesses
Albany Plan of Union
salutary neglect
Proclamation of 1763
mercantilism
Stamp Act
First Continental Congress
Second Continental Congress
Declaration of Independence
Articles of Confederation
Mayflower Compact

23

GEOGRAPHY IN HISTORY

How did the environment influence the culture of Native Americans?

 PREPARING FOR THE EXAM

On the examination, you will need to have a thorough understanding of important United States historical and governmental terms.

• What is a confederacy?

• What are two examples of confederacies in United States history?

PART 1 THE HISTORICAL FOUNDATIONS OF AMERICAN SOCIETY AND GOVERNMENT

Before examining the Constitution of the United States and the features that make it unique, it is important to understand the roots of the ideas in that document. To do that, we must start with the historical origins of the United States of America.

THE PEOPLES AND PEOPLING OF THE COLONIES

In North America, three different cultures came together—Native Americans (the original inhabitants), Europeans, and Africans brought as slaves.

NATIVE AMERICANS

Native Americans were the first people to occupy the Western Hemisphere. In the late 1400s, they numbered as many as 15 million in North America alone. The way of life of Native Americans was heavily influenced by the environment. The eastern Native American lifestyle was based on agriculture, hunting, and fishing. Trade was an important part of this economic system.

Native American religious beliefs were closely linked to nature. Another feature of their way of life was their strong social organizations based on ties between extended families, with women in positions of some power in some tribes.

The Iroquois Confederacy

The most powerful government of the eastern woodlands' Indians was that of the Iroquois. The Iroquois Confederacy, formed in 1570, was made up of first five and then six Iroquois nations located in central and western New York. At the peak of its power between 1644 and 1700, the Confederacy made it possible for the Iroquois to hold onto its lands against European pressure for almost two centuries.

Trade and Alliances

Relations between colonists and Native Americans often centered around trade and exchange, alliances, or warfare. The survival of the English settlers depended on Indian crops, such as corn and squash. Native Americans' interactions with the settlers led to outbreaks of deadly diseases, such as measles and smallpox.

Patterns of trade developed that influenced later relations between the settlers and Native Americans. For example, the Iroquois wanted control of the fur trade between the Great Lakes region and New York.

In the 1640s and 1650s, the Iroquois fought the Huron and Erie tribes, which threatened French dominance in that region. Wars with France ended only in 1701 when the Iroquois adopted a neutrality policy toward France and England.

The survival of Jamestown, founded in 1607 as the first permanent English settlement in North America, must be credited in part to the food supplied by the many Algonquin tribes that made up the Powhatan Confederacy. Powhatan was motivated by the possibility of the Europeans allying with him in his wars with other tribes.

Different Views and Values

Land control was the central conflict between Native Americans and colonists. Native Americans held land in common and believed it should be used for the good of all. It could not be bought or sold, although the rights to the use of land could be transferred. The English valued individual ownership and had a tradition of buying and selling land.

Secondly, there were cultural and technological differences. The European colonists believed in the superiority of their way of life and acted accordingly. They attempted to convert the Native Americans to Christianity and assumed that they would adopt an English lifestyle.

Warfare

Profitable tobacco farming led settlers to move into Native American

KEY THEMES AND CONCEPTS

Interdependence

Contact between Native Americans and English colonists was not always hostile. The Powhatan Confederacy, for example, provided food to the Jamestown settlers to help them survive. What was their motivation for helping the colonists?

ANALYZING DOCUMENTS

Examine the cartoon, then answer the following questions.

- Which groups do the speakers in this cartoon represent?

- What point is the cartoonist making about immigration to the United States?

ANALYZING DOCUMENTS

"I am now grown old , and must soon die; . . . Why should you take by force that from us which you can have by love? Why should you destroy us, who have provided you with food? . . . What is the cause of your jealousy? You see us unarmed, and willing to supply your wants, if you come in a friendly manner, not with swords and guns, as to invade an enemy."

—King Powhatan, 1609

• What is the answer to Powhatan's question, "What is the cause of your jealousy?"

ANALYZING DOCUMENTS

Examine the timeline below, then answer this question.

• Which event occurred first: the election of representatives to the Virginia House of Burgesses or the signing of the Mayflower Compact?

lands in the Chesapeake area. In 1622, Powhatan's brother attacked, killing about one fourth of the colony's population. Fighting continued for over 20 years, but eventually, the Powhatan Confederacy was destroyed.

In the mid-1670s, an alliance of New England tribes launched King Philip's War. Native Americans were threatened by the growing number of English settlements. Two years of fighting resulted in victory for the settlers. Numerous Indian survivors were sold into slavery in the West Indies. By the mid-1700s, settlers were moving into the interior of the continent.

The **French and Indian War** (1754–1763) was one of many wars between France and England in the 1700s. France and England were great rivals, and when they battled over issues in Europe, their colonists often fought in America. The French and Indian War erupted when the English challenged the French for control of the land that is now Ohio and western Pennsylvania.

The war pitted the English against the French and their Indian allies. (Native Americans tended to support the French because as fur traders, they built forts rather than settlements, as English colonists did.) The Iroquois, influenced by their earlier trade conflict with the French, supported the English toward the end of the war.

THE COLONISTS

The oldest settlement in what is now the United States is Saint Augustine, in Florida (1565). Founded by the Spanish, it did not become part of the United States until the 1800s. What was to become the United States began with the settlement of Virginia in 1607. By 1732, with the charter of Georgia, there were a total of 13 English colonies.

The Colonial Experience, 1607–1732

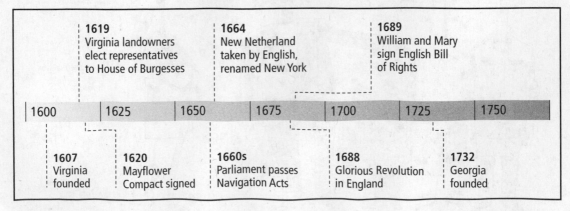

| 1619 | 1664 | 1689 |
| Virginia landowners elect representatives to House of Burgesses | New Netherland taken by English, renamed New York | William and Mary sign English Bill of Rights |

1600 1625 1650 1675 1700 1725 1750

| 1607 | 1620 | 1660s | 1688 | 1732 |
| Virginia founded | Mayflower Compact signed | Parliament passes Navigation Acts | Glorious Revolution in England | Georgia founded |

Who Came to the Colonies

The settlers were a diverse group. They included Africans brought against their will, Scotch-Irish from northern Ireland, Germans, Portuguese, Jews, Swedes, Dutch, French, Welsh, Irish, Scots, Belgians, and Swiss. In the colonial period, a large number of European immigrants came as **indentured servants** who contracted to work as many as seven years to repay the cost of their passage.

Most of each colony's population, however, was English. This fact would greatly affect the nature of the government that developed in the United States.

Why They Came

Just as the colonists represented many ethnic backgrounds, so did their motivations for coming to the colonies vary.

RELIGIOUS REASONS Some colonies were founded for religious reasons, but the colonists represented different religions and had different motivations. Massachusetts, for example, was founded by Pilgrims, or Separatists, who had left the Church of England, and Puritans who wanted to reform it. Colonies controlled by the Puritans allowed no religious freedom. Rhode Island, on the other hand, permitted all religions including Judaism. Pennsylvania was founded as a refuge for Quakers; Maryland for Roman Catholics.

ECONOMIC REASONS Economic motives were a major factor in the founding of Virginia, Delaware, and New Netherlands (later New York), as well as North and South Carolina. Georgia, the last of the colonies to be founded, was settled by debtors.

POLITICAL REASONS Separatists and Puritans came to North America after having fallen into political disfavor because of their objections to the established Church of England and the king who headed it. Quakers, Catholics, French Huguenots, and Jews came to escape religious intolerance and even governmental persecution.

What Influenced Their Experiences

Geography was a primary influence on the colonial way of life. So were the practices colonists brought from their homelands. Ethnic groups tended to settle together. Large distances and difficult transportation encouraged continuing family patterns, gender roles, and farming methods brought from Europe although these were sometimes modified by the new environment. Native American and African cultures also influenced changes in colonial lifestyles.

READING STRATEGY

Organizing Information
Europeans came to the colonies for three major reasons. In the space below, name these reasons and provide examples of each.

1.

2.

3.

Examine the map at right, then answer the following questions.

- How did geography influence colonists' decisions about where to settle and build colonies?

- By 1776, two thirds of the population of the English colonies lived no more than 50 miles from the ocean. Why?

- Which ethnic groups had the largest settlements in 1770? Which had the smallest settlements?

- Which natural harbors in the Thirteen Colonies contributed to the development of **commerce,** or trade between cities, states, and nations?

Colonial Settlement by Ethnic Group in 1770

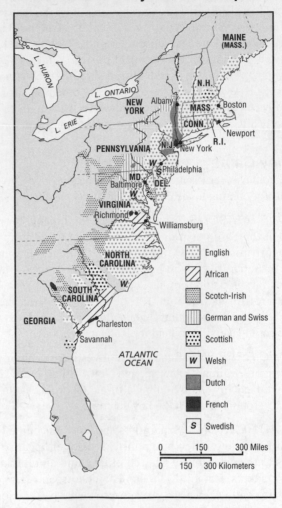

⚷ KEY THEMES AND CONCEPTS

Cultural and Intellectual Life

Founded by Puritans, Harvard College (1636) is the oldest of the nine colonial colleges in existence before the American Revolution.

New England

Every aspect of New England life was influenced by religion in the early colonial period. Church membership was a requirement for participation in government. Strict moral codes were enforced.

The cold climate and poor soil of New England challenged Puritan farmers, who grew crops mostly for their own families' consumption. Only when they reached the Connecticut River valley with its richer soil were they successful at commercial farming.

New England developed a diversified economy. Although farming was the most common occupation, New England also became the center of colonial shipping, with major ports at Boston and Salem. Fishing and ship building were among the related industries. Merchants and professionals made up the wealthiest social class.

The Middle Colonies

The middle colonies had a diverse population, including Dutch, Germans, and Scotch-Irish. These colonies, especially New York and Pennsylvania, benefited from more fertile soil. They exported wheat and corn, and this trade helped build New York and Philadelphia. Large numbers of tenant farmers—who rented rather than owned the land—lived in the Hudson River valley of New York and in New Jersey.

The Southern Colonies

Agriculture flourished in the southern colonies, which had a warmer climate and rich soil. The southern economy was based on crops grown for export, such as tobacco, rice, and indigo. They were cultivated first by indentured servants and then by enslaved Africans.

The wealthiest social class included Chesapeake tobacco planters and the owners of the Carolina rice plantations. The labor of servants and slaves contributed to their growing wealth. By 1775, South Carolina and Georgia had the highest average wealth per free landholder in the colonies.

THE AFRICANS

By 1700, the institution of slavery—involving Africans primarily— already served to highlight the regional differences in the colonies.

Origins of the Atlantic Slave Trade

The first enslaved people in the Americas were Native Americans. In the 1500s, the Spanish and Portuguese forced them to work in mines and on sugar plantations. After the Native American population declined as a result of European diseases, the Spanish, Portuguese, and French began enslaving West Africans. With the growth of tobacco, indigo, and rice plantations, the British colonies also began to participate in the slave trade. By the early 1700s, England controlled the Atlantic slave trade.

For some goods, there was a two-way trade between England and the colonies: grains, fish, fur, wood products, tobacco, indigo, and rice from the colonies were exchanged for English manufactured goods. The slave trade, however, was a **triangular trade.** New England merchants traded rum for slaves in West Africa. The slaves were sold in the West Indies for molasses or sugar, which was shipped to New England to make more rum.

Development of Slavery in the Colonies

The first Africans in the colonies were brought to Virginia in 1619. At this time, most were considered indentured servants and were considered free when their contracts ended.

♀ KEY THEMES AND
♀ CONCEPTS
Places and Regions
Slavery was more common in the southern colonies than in New England. Why?

READING STRATEGY

Organizing Information
Many enslaved Africans found both peaceful and violent ways to resist their enslavement. What are two peaceful ways that slaves resisted?

1.

2.

What are two violent ways that they resisted?

1.

2.

By the middle of the 1600s, large numbers of Africans began to be brought to the colonies as slaves. As the tobacco market grew, planters sought enslaved Africans to work the fields because of a shortage of workers. Free workers were reluctant to suffer the difficult working conditions on tobacco plantations, and indentured servants were now scarce. Soon, a system of permanent slavery was in place.

Slavery

By 1700, a race-based definition of a slave was written into law. Slavery became central to the southern economy. In South Carolina and Georgia, slavery was based on the Caribbean plantation system. The Africans were slaves from the time of their arrival and worked on huge rice plantations. The slave code was the strictest in the colonies.

By the early 1800s, the lower Mississippi Valley contained the greatest number of large plantations—those with 100 or more slaves. Cotton was increasingly important, and profits related directly to the amount of land cultivated. This encouraged the slave system to grow.

In contrast, slavery in the middle and New England colonies was less common, because the diverse economy and smaller farms made the region less dependent upon agriculture. At the end of the colonial period, seven out of every eight enslaved Africans lived in the South. In the North, most slaves worked in agriculture, but in northern cities some slaves worked as skilled tradesmen, domestic workers, and other laborers. The slave codes were also milder in the North.

Slave Resistance

Throughout the period in which slavery was legal, Africans and African Americans resisted their enslavement. On the slave ships during the voyage (called the **Middle Passage**) from Africa to the Americas, some staged revolts. Others chose starvation or drowning over enslavement.

Even in the face of severe punishment, some enslaved Africans attempted escape. Small communities of escaped slaves formed in Spanish Florida, South Carolina, Georgia, and Virginia. Other slaves offered more subtle resistance, such as slowing down at work, pretending illness, or damaging tools and crops.

In colonial America, open rebellion was not very common. Two notable colonial revolts took place in New York City in 1712 and at the Stono River near Charleston, South Carolina, in 1739. Both rebellions were put down by local militia. Most of those slaves who survived were later executed.

The Influence of Africa and African American Culture on Colonial Cultures

The blending of West African cultural traditions with European culture became the basis of a new African American culture. Some African words found their way into the English language, as did certain farming methods, foods, folk literature, and folk art. African building traditions of multiple small dwellings, front porches, and decorative iron work influenced southern colonial architecture. Some African musical styles and instruments, such as the banjo, continued to be incorporated into religious music and work songs. African musical traditions later influenced many forms of American music.

MAJOR HISTORICAL INFLUENCES ON AMERICAN GOVERNMENT

The government of each of the 13 colonies reflected ideas that came from the heritage of Western civilization. Those ideas were then modified by centuries of English thought and practice and by the American colonial experience.

Ideas from Ancient Greece

The concept of democracy, or government by the people, began in the city-state of Athens (in what is now Greece) between 750 B.C. and 550 B.C. Athens had a direct democracy, one in which all eligible citizens participated in government.

Ideas from Ancient Rome

The concept of republican government was established by the ancient Romans. In a **republic,** voters elect representatives who speak and act for other citizens in the business of government. These representatives

♀ KEY THEMES AND
⊩ CONCEPTS
Civic Values
American political rights and governmental institutions had three major sources:

1. British constitutional, political, and historical traditions

2. 17th- and 18th-century Enlightenment ideas

3. American colonial experience

What is an example of how each source influenced the political rights and governmental institutions in the United States?

Foundations of American Rights

Rights	Sources of Rights			
	Magna Carta (1215)	English Bill of Rights (1689)	Virginia Declaration of Rights (1776)	Bill of Rights (1791)
Trial by jury	✔	✔		✔
Due process	✔	✔		✔
Private property	✔			✔
No unreasonable searches or seizures			✔	✔
No cruel punishment		✔	✔	✔
No excessive bail or fines		✔		✔
Right to bear arms		✔		✔
Right to petition		✔		✔
Freedom of speech			✔	✔
Freedom of the press			✔	✔
Freedom of religion			✔	✔

PREPARING FOR THE EXAM

Common law is law that developed from traditional and court decisions in England. It became the basis of English and then United States law.

- Why do you think that the colonists used English common law as the basis for United States law?

READING STRATEGY

Problem Solving

Why is the writ of *habeas corpus* called the "Great Writ of Liberty"?

READING STRATEGY

Reinforcing Main Ideas

Which two rights guaranteed in the U.S. Constitution can be traced directly to the English Bill of Rights?

are supposed to work for the common good. This form of government is sometimes called representative democracy.

Influence of English Events and Documents

Other basic concepts of government and law were established in England before or during the colonial period in America.

MAGNA CARTA In 1215, English noblemen forced King John of England to agree to the Magna Carta, or Great Charter, a document that placed limits on his power to rule. For example, this document established the right to a jury trial—but only for nobles.

PETITION OF RIGHT In 1628, King Charles I signed the Petition of Right. It put in writing certain basic rights and legal traditions, such as a writ of *habeas corpus,* which prevented people from being imprisoned without a trial.

THE ENGLISH BILL OF RIGHTS In 1689, the Glorious Revolution ended a decades-long power struggle between the English Parliament and the monarchy. Parliament overthrew James II and replaced him with William and Mary, who were required to agree to the English Bill of Rights. This established that representative government and the rule of law outweighed the power of any monarch.

17th- and 18th-Century Enlightenment Thought

The framers of the Constitution were also strongly influenced by the ideas of the philosophers of the **Enlightenment.** This intellectual movement held that reliance on reason and experience would lead to social progress.

JOHN LOCKE John Locke believed that people are born free with certain **natural rights,** including the rights to life, liberty, and property. Such rights predate any government and exist in the "state of nature." Locke also wrote about the social contract theory. This theory holds that to protect their natural rights, people agree to form a state and grant to its government the powers necessary to protect those rights. When a government fails to do so, the contract has been broken and the people are free to change or replace that government. This means that governments exist with the consent of the governed.

THE BARON DE MONTESQUIEU The French philosopher Baron de Montesquieu believed that the British political system was successful because the power to govern was divided among the monarch and the two houses of Parliament. This division helped balance political power among the branches, so that no one branch had too much power.

JEAN-JACQUES ROUSSEAU Another French philosopher, Jean-Jacques Rousseau, developed further the idea of a social contract. His arguments in support of government by the consent of the governed influenced our Declaration of Independence.

VOLTAIRE A third important French philosopher, Voltaire, wrote *Philosophical Letters,* praising British institutions and rights. He wrote against religious intolerance and persecution.

THE COLONIAL EXPERIENCE: POLITICAL RIGHTS AND MERCANTILE RELATIONSHIPS

During the colonial period, two important forces helped shape a uniquely American way of life: (1) political ideas based on the English experience and on Enlightenment thinking and (2) the colonists' experience thousands of miles from their home country.

Colonial Charters and Self-Government

Twelve of the 13 original colonies were founded based on charters issued by the British government. A **charter** provided legal authority to companies or individuals to start a colony. Most of the colonies were originally self-governing private enterprises, but by 1730, most became royal colonies. Even after England later centralized control, the colonies remained largely self-governing and independent.

Colonial Principles and Practices of Government

The beliefs that colonists held about the proper role of government had a strong influence over the way they structured their governments.

LIMITS ON GOVERNMENT The colonists believed that the power of government should be limited, in accordance with English laws and traditions. The colonists wrote laws based on the principle that government existed to protect people's natural rights. The rights to life, liberty, and protection of property were most often mentioned. As early as 1641 in Massachusetts, the right to own property and protect it from being illegally seized by the government was written into law. The right to vote helped to protect property rights.

ENFORCEABLE CONTRACTS Colonists believed in the right to enter into contracts. Enforceable contracts between parties can be traced to the idea of a political compact, or contract. After the United States won independence, decisions of the Marshall Court protected individuals' right to enter into contracts.

FREEDOM OF THE PRESS Colonists believed there should be legal limits on government attempts to control what is written. In 1735, John Peter Zenger, a German immigrant to New York, was tried for seditious libel for accusing the governor of the colony of wrongdoing. Zenger's lawyer argued that no crime was committed when what Zenger had printed was true, and the jury found Zenger not guilty. Later, this case helped establish the principle of freedom of the press in the United States.

ANALYZING DOCUMENTS

"We whose names are underwritten . . . covenant and combine ourselves together into a civil body politic, for our better ordering and preservation and furtherance of the ends aforesaid; and by virtue hereof to enact, constitute, and frame such just and equal laws, ordinances, acts, constitutions, offices from time to time as shall be thought most meet and convenient for the general good of the colony; unto which we promise all due submission and obedience."

—Mayflower Compact

- What words indicate that this is a contract or compact?
- Is this to be a limited government?

MAYFLOWER COMPACT In 1620, before landing at Plymouth in present-day Massachusetts, the Pilgrims signed the Mayflower Compact. This was a contract in which the colonists consented to be governed by a government that they created—**self government**.

Colonial Assemblies and Local Governments

The importance of self-government is seen in the colonial assemblies established in each colony. As early as 1619, Virginia colonists took the first step toward republican government when they instituted the colonies' first representative lawmaking body, the **House of Burgesses.** Most colonies established a bicameral, or two-house, legislature modeled after the two-house English Parliament.

Colonists also recognized the need for local governments. The county was the center of local government in most of the colonies. In New England, local government was at the town level, where the **town meeting** allowed citizens to govern themselves through **direct democracy.**

THE CAUSES OF THE AMERICAN REVOLUTION

For almost a century before the outbreak of the American Revolution in 1775, Britain and France were involved in a rivalry for power, not only in Europe, but wherever the two nations had colonies. In 1754, Benjamin Franklin tried to get the colonies to agree to the **Albany Plan of Union** as protection against the French. The colonies rejected the plan because they feared the loss of self-government.

Events Leading to the American Revolution

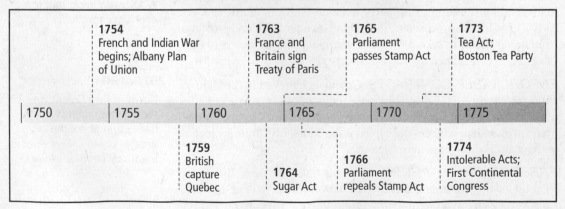

1754 French and Indian War begins; Albany Plan of Union

1763 France and Britain sign Treaty of Paris

1765 Parliament passes Stamp Act

1773 Tea Act; Boston Tea Party

1750   1755   1760   1765   1770   1775

1759 British capture Quebec

1764 Sugar Act

1766 Parliament repeals Stamp Act

1774 Intolerable Acts; First Continental Congress

Preoccupied with France, Britain governed the colonies under a policy of **salutary neglect,** or a healthy ignoring of the colonies. This policy resulted in the colonists gaining more independence in their trade practices and in local self-government. When the French wars ended in 1763, British policy toward the colonies changed.

The **Treaty of Paris of 1763** marked Britain's victory over France in the Seven Years' (or French and Indian) War. It also shifted the way power was distributed in North America. With the French defeated, Native Americans could no longer benefit from balancing the French and British against one another.

Land Claims After the French and Indian War, 1763

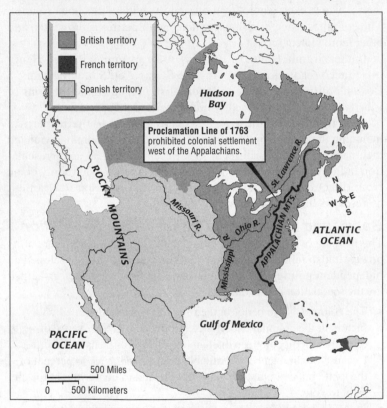

British territory

French territory

Spanish territory

Hudson Bay

Proclamation Line of 1763 prohibited colonial settlement west of the Appalachians.

ROCKY MOUNTAINS

Missouri R.

Ohio R.

Mississippi R.

St. Lawrence R.

APPALACHIAN MTS.

ATLANTIC OCEAN

Gulf of Mexico

PACIFIC OCEAN

0   500 Miles

0   500 Kilometers

With the French defeat, the colonists felt free to move west and resented the **Proclamation of 1763,** which prohibited movement into the lands gained from France.

Economic Causes of the Revolution

After winning the French and Indian War, Britain was left with a large debt. The British government believed that the colonies should pay for their own defense. Parliament began to enforce the policy of **mercantilism,** which held that colonies existed to provide raw materials and markets for the economic benefit of the home country.

Parliament passed several new tax laws, such as the Sugar Act (1764), which taxed foreign imports and the **Stamp Act** (1765), which required a tax stamp on printed materials. The colonists resented these

TURNING POINT

Why is the Treaty of Paris of 1763 considered a turning point in history?

ANALYZING DOCUMENTS

In May 1765, Patrick Henry voiced his opposition to the Stamp Act with a speech to the Virginia House of Burgesses. In that speech, he said:

"Caesar had his Brutus; Charles the First, his Cromwell; and George the Third . . . may profit by their example. If this be treason, make the most of it."

Brutus assassinated Caesar, and Cromwell defeated Charles I and had him beheaded.

- What is Patrick Henry's message?
- What might Patrick Henry have been implying but would not say?

KEY THEMES AND CONCEPTS

Economic Systems
The 16th to 18th century economic system called **mercantilism** was based on the belief that a strong nation was built by accumulating precious metals through increasing exports, protecting industries, and establishing colonies to supply raw materials and markets while limiting colonial manufacturing and trade.

READING STRATEGY

Organizing Information
The American Revolution had economic, political, and social and ideological causes. List them, then identify those you consider the most significant.

1. Economic

2. Political

3. Social and Ideological

acts and forced their repeal. Parliament then passed the Townshend Acts, which taxed imported goods. Colonists saw the Townshend Acts as a serious economic threat.

Political Causes of the Revolution

Some colonists also saw the Townshend Acts as a political threat. The money raised by the acts would be used to pay some of the English officials in the colonies. Colonial legislatures believed this undermined their power to exert control over officials by withholding their salaries. The colonists reacted to the new taxes with petitions, boycotts, and other more violent protests.

In the Virginia House of Burgesses, for example, Patrick Henry introduced resolutions opposing the Stamp Act. Samuel Adams, a Boston political organizer and journalist, helped create the Sons of Liberty and the Massachusetts Committee of Correspondence.

Colonists viewed these new taxes as a threat to their liberties, including the right to property. They charged that Britain had violated their natural rights as British citizens. Because they had no representation in Parliament, colonists reasoned that taxation could only come from the colonial legislatures. Britain insisted that Parliament represented all of its subjects.

Social and Ideological Causes of the Revolution

The British government failed to understand the colonists' fears of its power. It also failed to recognize that the colonists had developed an independent political life and thought. The following factors helped lay the foundation for revolution:

- The colonists' firm belief in their natural rights, combined with factors in the colonial experience, produced a greater sense of equality among colonists than among British citizens in general.
- Because of abundance of available land, as much as 90 percent of the white male population held enough land to qualify them for the right to vote.
- In the decades before the Revolution, the colonial population grew rapidly, while increased numbers of immigrants came from nations other than England. Appeals had to be made to all peoples.
- The Great Awakening, a religious movement, encouraged people to question authority and enjoy a sense of equality with others.

While the colonies moved toward war and demands for independence, colonists were divided. Those known as **Tories** or **Loyalists** supported the king and obedience to English laws. Opposing independence, thousands left the United States at the end of the Revolution, including large numbers from New York.

THE AMERICAN REVOLUTION AND THE DECLARATION OF INDEPENDENCE

In 1773, the issue of **taxation without representation** rose again when Parliament passed the Tea Act, which made British tea less expensive than tea imported by colonial tea merchants. Colonists protested by destroying three shiploads of British tea in the **Boston Tea Party.** The British government reacted with the **"Intolerable Acts"** of 1774. These acts punished Massachusetts by closing the port of Boston, forbidding town meetings, and reducing the powers of the legislature. More British troops were sent to occupy the colony and enforce the acts.

ANALYZING DOCUMENTS

Use the timeline to answer the following questions.

- How long did the American Revolution last?

- Was the Declaration of Independence issued before or after fighting began in the American Revolution?

The American Revolution and the Declaration of Independence, 1775–1783

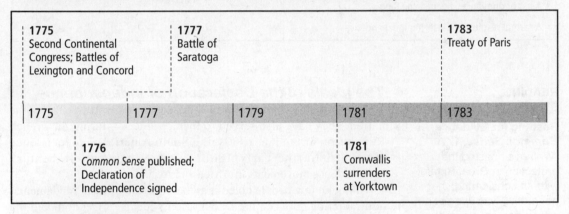

1775
Second Continental Congress; Battles of Lexington and Concord

1777
Battle of Saratoga

1783
Treaty of Paris

| 1775 | 1777 | 1779 | 1781 | 1783 |

1776
Common Sense published; Declaration of Independence signed

1781
Cornwallis surrenders at Yorktown

Colonial Efforts at Union

In the late summer of 1774, twelve of the colonies sent representatives to Philadelphia to plan a response to these British actions. This meeting became known as the **First Continental Congress.** After the start of the American Revolution in 1775, a **Second Continental Congress** met and took charge of the war effort.

Decision for Independence

In June 1776, Richard Henry Lee of Virginia presented a resolution to the Second Continental Congress calling for independence from Great Britain. The Congress appointed a committee (including Thomas Jefferson, Benjamin Franklin, and John Adams) to draft a formal declaration. The resulting **Declaration of Independence** was almost entirely the work of Thomas Jefferson. The delegates adopted the Declaration of Independence on July 4, which marks the birth of the United States of America. The key facts about this important document are listed on the next page:

JOIN, or DIE.

The Declaration of Independence

The PURPOSE of the Declaration:	The Declaration's KEY IDEAS OF GOVERNMENT:
• To announce to the world that the colonies were now a new, independent nation • To explain and justify the reasons that the united colonies had decided to become the United States of America	• People have natural rights, including the rights to "Life, Liberty, and the pursuit of Happiness." • Governments receive their power to govern "from the consent of the governed" by social contract or compact in which the government agrees to protect the people's natural rights.
The THREE PARTS of the Declaration:	• When a government fails to protect and respect those rights, it is the "Right of the People to alter or to abolish" that government.
• A theory of government • A list of grievances against the King • A formal resolution declaring independence	

READING STRATEGY

Reading for Evidence
Common Sense, 1776
"We have boasted the protection of Great Britain, without considering, that her motive was *interest* not *attachment; and that she did not protect us from *our enemies* on *our account;* but from *her enemies* on *her own account.* . . . A government of our own is our natural right: and . . . it is infinitely wiser and safer, to form a constitution of our own in a cool deliberate manner, while we have it in our power, than to trust such an interesting event to time and chance."
—Thomas Paine,
Common Sense, **1776**

• What is common sense to Paine?

The Ideals of the Declaration of Independence

The ideals of the Declaration of Independence are still goals for the nation. They have also served to inspire others—during the French Revolution of the late 1700s, the South American independence movement in the early 1800s, and even twentieth-century independence movements in Africa and Asia.

Although few people noted it at the time, there was a fundamental contradiction between the Declaration's ideals of freedom and the institution of slavery. The colonists had looked to John Locke's compact theory (which stated that no person may rule another without the consent of the other person) as justification for choosing freedom. Few, however, advocated such freedom for slaves.

Fighting the War for Independence

The American Revolution began in 1775 and ended with the British surrender at Yorktown, Virginia, in 1781. A peace treaty, the Treaty of Paris, was negotiated by John Adams, John Jay, and Benjamin Franklin and was signed in 1783.

Throughout the American Revolution, the Second Continental Congress served as the national government. The Congress had no constitutional basis but was created in a crisis and supported by popular opinion. It remained in place until 1781.

The British army was larger in number, better trained, and aided by the Creek, Cherokee, and Shawnee in the South and most Iroquois in the North. It was disadvantaged by its use of European military techniques in America and by the behavior of its troops, which alienated many colonists in the territories it occupied.

The continental army (the colonists' army) was the achievement of George Washington, the colonial commander in chief. The continental army was reinforced as it moved from region to region by an untrained militia or home guard defending their homes.

The colonists were aided by an alliance with France, negotiated by Benjamin Franklin. Motivated by its ongoing rivalry with Great Britain, France supplied the colonists with military arms, troops, and naval support and engaged Britain in war elsewhere in the world.

The American victory at Saratoga helped bring the French into the war. They saw that the colonists might possibly win the war. The victory also prevented the British from isolating New England from the rest of the colonies by taking control of the Hudson River valley and the area north of it to Canada.

Slavery, African Americans, and the Outcome of the American Revolution

Although African Americans fought on both sides during the American Revolution, more fought on the British side because of British promises of freedom from slavery. After first hesitating, Washington and the Continental Congress eventually recruited African Americans, as did state militias.

During the Revolution, some African slaves in the South successfully escaped. Others were freed in return for military service. Some left the country with the British army, while others settled in northern cities and became part of a growing free black population.

TURNING POINT

Why is the Battle of Saratoga considered a turning point in the war?

ANALYZING DOCUMENTS

Reading for Evidence

"We have in common with all other men a natural and unalienable right to that freedom which the Great Parent of the Universe hath bestowed equally on all mankind, and which they have never forfeited by any compact or agreement whatsoever."

—From a petition of a group of slaves to the Massachusetts legislature, 1777

• What evidence is there that the writers knew about Enlightenment ideas and the Declaration of Independence?

Some Effects of the American Revolution

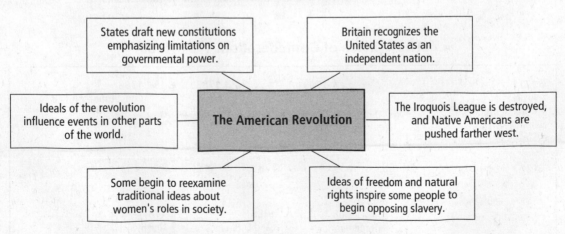

The Revolution had important consequences for many groups of people.

**READING
STRATEGY**

Reinforcing Main Ideas
Why did the Articles of
Confederation create a
weak national government?

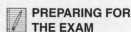 **PREPARING FOR
THE EXAM**
Why was the period
under the Articles of
Confederation called
the "critical period"?

An antislavery movement led by Quakers started in the North before the Revolution. After the war, northern states passed laws that immediately or gradually abolished slavery. Although free, African Americans in the North still faced discrimination. Many were not allowed to vote, except in New England. There was segregation in public places, housing, and transportation.

THE ARTICLES OF CONFEDERATION, 1781–1789

The first constitution of the United States was the **Articles of Confederation.** This constitution, proposed by the Second Continental Congress in 1777, went into effect in 1781 after all 13 states had ratified, or approved, it. The Articles of Confederation reflected the colonists' fear of a strong central government and the desire of the individual states to protect their powers. As a result, the Articles created a weak national government.

An Alliance of Independent States

The Articles set up a confederation among the 13 states. A confederation is an alliance of independent states in which the states give as much power as they choose to the central government, while keeping the greater part of the power and remaining sovereign. The Articles were more like a treaty among the states than a plan of centralized government.

Achievements of the Confederation Government

The government under the Articles of Confederation had the power to make treaties, declare war, and receive ambassadors. The Confederation also made some notable achievements:

The Articles of Confederation, 1781–1789

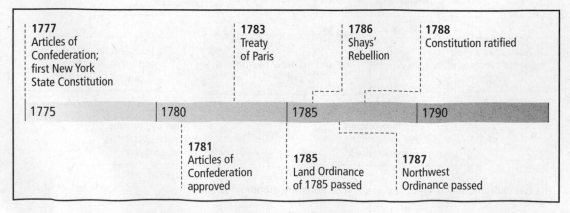

1. Successful conclusion of the American Revolution
2. Negotiation of the Treaty of Paris of 1783, ending the war and setting the United States border at the Mississippi River
3. Passage of the **Land Ordinance of 1785** and the **Northwest Ordinance of 1787,** which (a) set the pattern by which new states could join the nation, and (b) prohibited slavery in the Northwest Territory

Weaknesses of the Confederation Government

The Confederation government proved too weak to deal with the problems during the critical period of the 1780s. There was no single national currency, because the states could also coin money. The Congress could not tax the people directly but had to ask the states for funds. The government lacked a president to direct operations. The Congress did not have the money to raise an army without the consent of the states.

The new nation soon suffered severe economic problems, while its government was unable to command respect at home or abroad. However, all 13 states had to agree before the Articles could be changed, so it was nearly impossible to change this constitution.

STATE GOVERNMENTS BASED ON REPUBLICAN PRINCIPLES

Between 1776 and 1787, 11 of the 13 states adopted new constitutions. State constitutions were based on republican principles creating a government grounded in representation of the people, the consent of the governed. Special state conventions were called so that the constitutions could be written by the people. When complete, they were ratified or approved by the voters.

Fears of a strong executive led the framers of the first state constitutions to emphasize limitations on power. The New York Constitution of 1777, which even included the text of the Declaration of Independence, gave most of the power to the legislature, rather than to a single person such as a governor. In New York as in most states, the legislature remained bicameral, rather than unicameral.

Some states granted more people the right to vote by lowering property qualifications. Some states gave the right to vote to property-owning African Americans and Native Americans. State constitutions, including the New York state constitution, protected some individual rights, such as the right to religious freedom. In addition, the state government could not give money to any religion. This was part of a national movement to disestablish churches, which meant the end of government endorsement and financial support of any single religious group.

ANALYZING DOCUMENTS

Reading for Evidence

- How were the state constitutions that were adopted after the American Revolution affected by the conflict and war with Great Britain?

- What ideas and other features from New York's and other state's constitutions were eventually included in the U.S. Constitution?

 PREPARING FOR THE EXAM

What provision in the U.S. Constitution expressly supports disestablishment?

○ **KEY THEMES AND**
┃ **CONCEPTS**

Government
The Constitutional
Convention created a
government which did not
have the weaknesses of the
Articles of Confederation
while avoiding a national
government so strong that it
threatened the liberties
of its citizens.

• How did the U.S.
  Constitution create
  a stronger national
  government than that
  of the Articles of
  Confederation?

PART 2 WRITING AND RATIFYING THE CONSTITUTION, 1787–1789

By the late 1780s, it was clear that the national government created by the Articles of Confederation was too weak. The government faced increasing difficulty in regulating trade and dealing with the nation's debt.

The problems plaguing the national government led to a call for a Constitutional Convention in Philadelphia in May 1787 for "the sole and express purpose of amending the Articles of Confederation." The chart below shows how the delegates tried to correct the weaknesses of the Articles of Confederation.

THE CONSTITUTIONAL CONVENTION

Fifty-five delegates, representing all the states except Rhode Island, met in the Pennsylvania State House (now known as Independence Hall) in Philadelphia in May 1787 at the Constitutional Convention. The delegates were prominent lawyers, planters, and merchants at a time when most of the population were small farmers.

Governments of the United States: 1781 and 1789

How the Weaknesses of the Articles of Confederation Were Corrected by the Constitution	
Articles of Confederation	**Constitution of the United States**
• States have most of the power. The national government has little.	• States have some power, but most power is given to the national government.
• No executive officer to carry out the laws of Congress.	• A President heads the executive branch of the government.
• No national courts. Only state courts exist.	• Both national and state courts exist.
• Congress is responsible to the states.	• Congress is responsible to the people.
• Nine out of 13 states have to approve a law before it can go into effect.	• Laws may be passed by a majority vote of both houses of Congress.
• Congress has no power to tax.	• Congress given the power to tax.
• Congress can not regulate trade among the states.	• Congress given the power to regulate interstate and foreign trade.
• Each state coins its own money. There is no national currency.	• Only the national government has the power to coin money.

The most famous delegate was George Washington, who was elected president of the Constitutional Convention. Another well-known figure was James Madison, whom some consider to have had the most influence on the Constitution. Also attending were Benjamin Franklin and Alexander Hamilton, a strong nationalist from New York.

Some famous Americans from the Revolution were noticeably absent. Thomas Jefferson and John Adams were serving the country as diplomats in Europe. A few patriots, such as Patrick Henry, refused to attend because they suspected that the convention would try to create a strong national government, which they opposed. Still others were not selected by their states.

In addition, no women, Native Americans, African Americans, or poorer white men attended the Constitutional Convention. At that time, these groups had limited political and legal rights.

KEY COMPROMISES AT THE CONVENTION

The delegates agreed that discussions would be kept secret in order to debate freely without outside pressure. They also decided not to revise the Articles of Confederation, but to write a new constitution instead.

Most of what we know about the Convention comes to us from Madison's notes. The delegates' task was to create a government with enough authority to govern effectively while protecting individual liberties. The debates involved much conflict and much compromise. In fact, the United States Constitution has been called a "bundle of compromises." Four key compromises made the Constitution possible.

♀ KEY THEMES AND ┠ CONCEPTS

Diversity

Certain groups of people were not represented at the Constitutional Convention. How does their absence explain some sections of the Constitution? Why were these groups absent?

READING STRATEGY

Organizing Information

- Which groups stood in opposition to each other on the major issues at the Constitutional Convention?

- Why did they take their particular positions?

Major Compromises of the Constitutional Convention

Compromise	Issue	Solution
Connecticut or Great Compromise	Representation in Congress	Bicameral legislature: States have equal representation in Senate; representation in the House depends on State's population.
Three-Fifths	Counting slaves within population to determine representation	Slaves were counted as if 3/5 of one person, both for representation and taxation.
Commerce and Slave Trade	Granting Congress the power to regulate foreign and interstate trade	Congress was forbidden to tax a State's exports or take action against the slave trade for 20 years.
Presidency	Length of President's term of office and method of elections	Four-year term Electoral College system rather than popular election or selection by Congress or State governors

The Great Compromise, or Connecticut Plan

The first issue to be resolved was that of representation. The delegates from Virginia proposed the Virginia Plan, which called for a bicameral legislature. A state's representation in each house would be based on its population. Larger states supported this plan. The smaller states favored the New Jersey Plan. This plan called for a unicameral legislature in which each state had equal representation.

The Virginia Plan served as the basis for much of the new Constitution. However, the matter of representation had to be settled by what is known as the **Great Compromise** or the Connecticut Plan, which gave something to both large and small states. The compromise created the Congress, a bicameral legislature. The states had equal representation in the upper house, or the Senate. In the lower house, or the House of Representatives, representation was based on population. In addition, all bills dealing with money would have to start in the House, but would need the approval of the Senate.

The Three-Fifths Compromise

Meanwhile, a bitter debate continued over slavery and power. Southerners wanted slaves to be counted for purposes of deciding representation in the House, but not for purposes of determining taxes. The compromise reached was that three fifths of the enslaved African Americans in a state were counted for both representation and taxation purposes.

The Commerce Compromise

Northerners wanted a government that could regulate trade. Southerners, however, feared that the importing of African slaves would be prohibited and that their agricultural exports would be taxed. The delegates agreed that no export duties could be passed by Congress and that Congress could not prohibit the slave trade for 20 years.

RATIFICATION OF THE CONSTITUTION

After months of debate in Philadelphia, delegates approved the Constitution of the United States. On September 17, 1787, thirty-nine of the delegates remaining in Philadelphia signed the Constitution. The fact that three, including George Mason, author of the Virginia Declaration of Rights, refused to sign gave an indication of the coming debate. The Framers had written that 9 of the 13 states must approve the Constitution for it to go into effect. Approval would be done through special conventions called in each state rather than through the state legislatures.

The Great Debate and Ratification

Two groups formed in each state: the **Federalists,** who favored ratification, and the **Anti-Federalists,** who opposed it.

The Great Debate

The Federalist Arguments:	The Anti-Federalist Arguments:
• Wanted a strong national government to provide order and protect rights of people.	• Wanted a weak national government so that it would not threaten the rights of the people or the powers of the states.
• Claimed that a bill of rights was unnecessary because the new government's powers were limited by the Constitution.	• Wanted to add a bill of rights to protect the people against abuses of power.

The first five states ratified the Constitution within a few months. By June 1788, nine states had given their approval—enough for ratification. But these did not include the states of Virginia and New York. The success of the new government depended upon acceptance of the Constitution by these two key states.

In Virginia, James Madison led the fight for ratification against the opposition of George Mason and Patrick Henry. Virginia approved the Constitution by 10 votes but with amendments suggested. New York was the next battleground. Here, *The Federalist*—a series of pro-ratification essays by Alexander Hamilton, John Jay, and James Madison—helped turn the tide against the Anti-Federalists, led by Governor George Clinton. Ratification was by a margin of three votes. *The Federalist* remains one of the finest statements on government and the Constitution ever written.

PART 3 WHAT YOU NEED TO KNOW ABOUT THE U.S. CONSTITUTION AND GOVERNMENT

The Constitution of the United States includes a number of important basic principles, which are listed below.

Popular Sovereignty

The Constitution is based on the idea of popular sovereignty— that the source of all power or authority to govern is the people. This type of government is considered a democracy.

Limited Government

Governmental powers are defined by the Constitution. In this way, our government is limited by law. The Constitution places limits on state and national governments and government officials as well.

Separation of Powers

The Constitution establishes the **separation of powers,** meaning that power to govern is divided among the legislative, executive, and

ANALYZING DOCUMENTS

"Ambition must be made to counteract ambition . . . If men were angels, no government would be necessary. If angels were to govern men, neither external nor internal controls on government would be necessary. In framing a government which is to be administered by men over men, the great difficulty lies in this: you must first enable the government to control the governed; and in the next place oblige it to control itself."

—James Madison, *The Federalist No. 51*

• Based on this quote, what is James Madison's view of the relationship between human nature and good government?

Three Branches of U.S. Government

Legislative	Executive	Judicial
Senate **House of Representatives**	**President** **Vice President**	**Supreme Court** **Federal Courts**
Makes laws	**Enforces laws and treaties**	**Explains and interprets laws**
• Overrides presidential vetoes • Approves presidential appointments • Approves treaties • Taxes to provide services • Provides for defense, declares war • Regulates money and trade • Impeaches officials	• Can veto laws • Appoints high officials • Conducts foreign policy • Enforces laws and treaties • Commander in chief of the military • Recommends bills to Congress • Reports the state of the Union to Congress	• Settles legal disputes between states • Settles State and federal disputes • Settles disputes between States and foreign countries • Hears cases with ambassadors of foreign governments • Settles disputes between individuals and Federal Government

Source: U.S. Department of Justice

ANALYZING DOCUMENTS

"We the People of the United States . . . do ordain and establish this Constitution for the United States."
— Preamble to the U.S. Constitution

• According to the Preamble, who is creating this Constitution?

• In what other documents have we seen a concept that is restated here?

judiciary branches to ensure that no single branch can dominate the government. Each branch takes its power directly from the Constitution, not from another branch.

Checks and Balances

The system of **checks and balances** gives each branch of the national government ways to block or control the other branches in order to prevent any one branch from gaining too much power.

Flexibility

The Constitution's flexibility allows it to meet changing conditions.

THE ELASTIC CLAUSE Article I, Section 8, Clause 18, states that Congress can make all laws "necessary and proper" for carrying out the tasks listed in the Constitution.

THE AMENDMENT PROCESS The Constitution may be formally changed with approval of both Congress and the states.

JUDICIAL INTERPRETATION The Supreme Court and lower federal courts review cases which involve possible conflicts with the Constitution and federal laws. This involves interpreting local, state, and federal laws, as well as executive actions.

UNWRITTEN CONSTITUTION Congressional and Executive interpretations and actions, court decisions, customs, and traditions have developed to allow for Constitutional change and flexibility.

The Checks and Balances System

PRESIDENT
Enforces Law

Congress has power to:
- Override Presidential veto
- Reject treaties and presidential appointments
- Impeach & remove

CHECKS THE PRESIDENT
CHECKS THE CONGRESS

President has power to:
- Veto laws
- Make treaties and foreign policy
- Appoint federal officials
- Propose laws

President has power to:
- Grant pardons
- Appoint judges

Supreme Court has power to:
- Decide actions unconstitutional
- Interpret treaties

CHECKS THE PRESIDENT
CHECKS THE SUPREME COURT

Supreme Court has power to:
- Decide laws unconstitutional

CONGRESS
Makes Laws

CHECKS THE CONGRESS
CHECKS THE SUPREME COURT

SUPREME COURT
Interprets Law

Congress has power to:
- Propose amendments to overturn court decisions
- Create lower courts
- Impeach and remove
- Reject appointments

FEDERALISM IN THE CONSTITUTION

The Constitution divides the power to govern between the national and the state governments. Disputes between the national and state governments are settled by the courts, but the Supremacy Clause of Article VI of the Constitution makes the Constitution, federal laws, and treaties superior to state laws.

DELEGATED POWERS Certain powers of the national government are spelled out in the Constitution. Most of these delegated powers are listed in Article I, Section 8. One example is the power of the national government to declare war.

IMPLIED POWERS Certain powers of the national government are not stated in writing. Their existence is implied by the Elastic Clause. One example of an implied power is the regulation of child labor; this power is implied by the delegated power to regulate interstate commerce.

DENIED POWERS Certain powers are denied to the national government, for example, the power to pass an export tax. Other powers

The Supremacy Clause

U.S. Constitution
- Acts of Congress
- Treaties
- State Constitutions
- State Statutes
- City and County Charters and Ordinances

System of Federalism

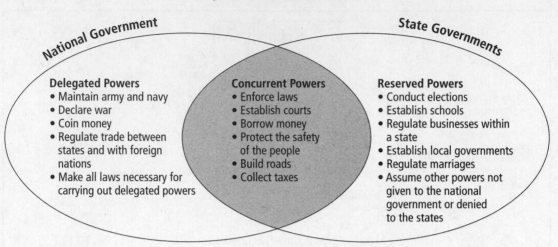

National Government

State Governments

Delegated Powers
- Maintain army and navy
- Declare war
- Coin money
- Regulate trade between states and with foreign nations
- Make all laws necessary for carrying out delegated powers

Concurrent Powers
- Enforce laws
- Establish courts
- Borrow money
- Protect the safety of the people
- Build roads
- Collect taxes

Reserved Powers
- Conduct elections
- Establish schools
- Regulate businesses within a state
- Establish local governments
- Regulate marriages
- Assume other powers not given to the national government or denied to the states

⚷ KEY THEMES AND CONCEPTS

Government

What do you call a power that is shared by both national and state governments?

Name two examples:

1.

2.

What do you call a power that is held only by the national government?

Name two examples:

1.

2.

What do you call a power that is held only by the states?

Name two examples:

1.

2.

are denied to the states, for example, the power to print money. Still other powers are denied to both national and state governments, for example, the power to deny the right to vote because of sex or race.

CONCURRENT POWER Certain powers belong to both national and state governments. One example of such a concurrent power is the power to tax.

RESERVED POWERS The reserved powers are neither delegated to the national government nor denied to the states. One example is the power to make divorce laws.

Article IV of the Constitution describes relations among the states and lists guarantees that the national government makes to the states. Article VII, which describes ratification of the Constitution, serves as a reminder that the new national government had to be approved by the individual states.

THE BASIC ORGANIZATION AND FUNCTIONS OF GOVERNMENT UNDER THE CONSTITUTION

The first three articles of the Constitution describe and define the powers of the legislative, executive, and judicial branches of the national government. These articles detail the separation of powers, while showing how each branch can check and balance the others.

Federal Officeholders

Office	Number	Term	Selection	Requirements
Representative	at least 1 per state; based on state population	2 years	Elected by voters of congressional district	• Age 25 or over • Citizen for 7 years • Resident of state in which elected
Senator	2 per state	6 years	Original Constitution-elected by state legislature Amendment 17-elected by voters	• Age 30 or over • Citizen for 9 years • Resident of state in which elected
President and Vice-President	1	4 years	Elected by electoral college	• Age 35 or over • Natural-born citizen • Resident of U.S. for 14 years
Supreme Court justice	9	Life	Appointed by President with approval of the Senate	• No requirements in Constitution

ARTICLE I: THE LEGISLATIVE BRANCH

Article I establishes the United States Congress with its two houses—
the Senate and the House of Representatives. Congress is the
legislative branch of government. Article I gives the qualifications for
election to Congress, the rights and privileges of members of
Congress, and some basic operating procedures of both houses. The
article also lists the powers delegated to Congress. Each house of
Congress also has special duties that it alone can perform.

Article I briefly outlines how a bill becomes a federal law. This
process requires the approval of each house and of the President. A
presidential veto, or rejection, of a bill can be overridden by a two-
thirds vote of each house. As the diagram on page 51 shows, the
process today is quite complex, and a bill must pass through numerous
committees before becoming a law.

 PREPARING FOR THE EXAM

Some examination ques-
tions require you to read
and interpret charts. Study
the chart above and answer
this question.

• How does the term of a
Supreme Court justice
differ from those of other
federal officeholders?

The Powers of Congress as Stated (by Clause) in Article I, Section 8 of the United States Constitution

Expressed Powers
Peace Powers

1. To lay taxes
    a. Direct (not used since the War Between the States, except income tax)
    b. Indirect (customs [tariffs], excise for internal revenue)
2. To borrow money
3. To regulate foreign and interstate commerce
4. To establish naturalization and bankruptcy laws
5. To coin money and regulate its value; to regulate weights and measures
6. To punish counterfeiters of federal money and securities
7. To establish post offices and post roads
8. To grant patents and copyrights
9. To create courts inferior to the Supreme Court
10. To define and punish piracies and felonies on the high seas; to define and punish offenses against the law of nations
17. To exercise exclusive jurisdiction over the District of Columbia; to exercise exclusive jurisdiction over forts, dockyards, national parks, federal buildings, and the like

War Powers
11. To declare war; to grant letters of marque and reprisal; to make rules concerning captures on land and water 12. To raise and support armies 13. To provide and maintain a navy 14. To make laws governing land and naval forces 15. To provide for calling forth the militia to execute federal laws, suppress insurrections, and repel invasions 16. To provide for organizing, arming, and disciplining the militia, and for its governing when in the service of the Union
Implied Powers

18. To make all laws necessary and proper for carrying into execution the foregoing powers, such as:
    To define and provide punishment for federal crimes
    To establish the Federal Reserve System
    To improve rivers, canals, harbors, and other waterways
    To fix minimum wages, maximum hours of work

Special Powers of the House and Senate

House	Senate
• To select the President if no candidate receives a majority of the electoral vote	• To select the Vice President if no candidate has a majority of the electoral vote
• To bring impeachment charges	• To act as jury in cases of impeachment
• To originate all revenue (money) bills	• To ratify treaties (by a two-thirds vote)
	• To approve presidential appointments (by a majority vote)

How Bills Become Laws

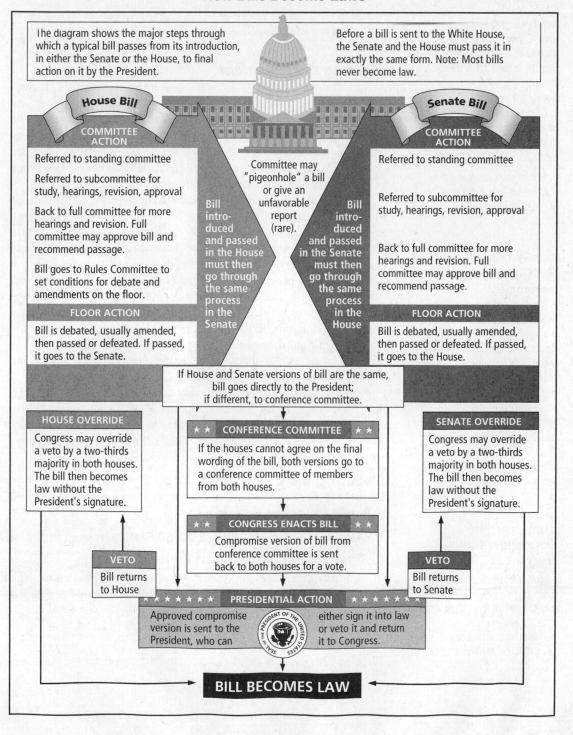

The diagram shows the major steps through which a typical bill passes from its introduction, in either the Senate or the House, to final action on it by the President.

Before a bill is sent to the White House, the Senate and the House must pass it in exactly the same form. Note: Most bills never become law.

House Bill

COMMITTEE ACTION

Referred to standing committee

Referred to subcommittee for study, hearings, revision, approval

Back to full committee for more hearings and revision. Full committee may approve bill and recommend passage.

Bill goes to Rules Committee to set conditions for debate and amendments on the floor.

FLOOR ACTION

Bill is debated, usually amended, then passed or defeated. If passed, it goes to the Senate.

Bill introduced and passed in the House must then go through the same process in the Senate

Committee may "pigeonhole" a bill or give an unfavorable report (rare).

Bill introduced and passed in the Senate must then go through the same process in the House

Senate Bill

COMMITTEE ACTION

Referred to standing committee

Referred to subcommittee for study, hearings, revision, approval

Back to full committee for more hearings and revision. Full committee may approve bill and recommend passage.

FLOOR ACTION

Bill is debated, usually amended, then passed or defeated. If passed, it goes to the House.

If House and Senate versions of bill are the same, bill goes directly to the President; if different, to conference committee.

HOUSE OVERRIDE

Congress may override a veto by a two-thirds majority in both houses. The bill then becomes law without the President's signature.

★ ★ CONFERENCE COMMITTEE ★ ★

If the houses cannot agree on the final wording of the bill, both versions go to a conference committee of members from both houses.

SENATE OVERRIDE

Congress may override a veto by a two-thirds majority in both houses. The bill then becomes law without the President's signature.

★ ★ CONGRESS ENACTS BILL ★ ★

Compromise version of bill from conference committee is sent back to both houses for a vote.

VETO

Bill returns to House

VETO

Bill returns to Senate

★ ★ ★ ★ ★ ★ PRESIDENTIAL ACTION ★ ★ ★ ★ ★ ★ ★

Approved compromise version is sent to the President, who can

either sign it into law or veto it and return it to Congress.

BILL BECOMES LAW

READING
STRATEGY

**Analyzing Cause
and Effect: Census**
The U.S. Constitution
requires that a census of
the population be taken
every 10 years. The census
is used to determine how
many representatives each
state will send to the
House.

- What impact does the
  census have on the
  electoral college?

**KEY THEMES AND
CONCEPTS**
Government
A precedent is an action
or decision which serves as
a basis for later actions or
decisions. For example,
George Washington set a
precedent when he decided
not to run for President
after completing two terms.
No President served for
more than two terms until
Franklin D. Roosevelt was
elected to a third and fourth
term in 1940 and 1944.

**ANALYZING
DOCUMENTS**

Using the chart on the next
page, which describes the
path to the presidency,
explain how the 2004 and
2008 presidential cam-
paigns and elections could
be affected by the 2000
census.

ARTICLE II: THE EXECUTIVE BRANCH

Article II outlines the workings of the executive branch, including the method of electing the President as well as the powers and duties of the office.

Electing the President

Article II describes the process by which the president is elected. Amendments 12, 20, 22, and 25 have changed this process.

A key compromise of the Constitutional Convention involved the method of electing the President. Under the resulting **electoral college** system, voters cast their ballots for electors. Those electors cast the actual votes for President and Vice President. Each state was granted as many presidential electors as it had senators plus representatives.

The Constitution requires that a **census,** or counting of the population, be taken every 10 years. Changes to reflect shifts in population are then made in the number of representatives per state, which in turn affects the electoral vote. Today, data from the census is also used to make decisions about other national needs.

Customs and precedents influenced how the President is elected. After Washington's two terms, the formation of political parties forced changes in the election process. No longer did electors exercise their own judgments. Rather, they pledged in advance to vote for the presidential candidate of their party. Today, while the names of the presidential candidates appear on the ballot, voters are actually casting their ballots for electors chosen by each candidate's party.

By 1832, national conventions had become the method of selecting party candidates. Today presidential primaries and caucuses are held in each state to select most of the delegates to the national convention. Both parties also name their officials and office holders as delegates, which make up as many as 20% of Democratic Party delegates.

Debating the Electoral College System

From the days of the Constitutional Convention, people have argued over the method of selecting the president.

REASONS TO CHANGE THE SYSTEM There are two major arguments against the electoral college system.

1. It is a "winner-take-all" system. A winning candidate gets all the electoral votes in a state, no matter how close the popular vote is. Four times—in 1824, 1876, 1888, and 2000—the winner of the popular vote has lost the presidency because he failed to win a majority of the electoral vote.

2. Generally, electors are not required by law to vote for the candidate who wins in their state.

First Step in a Presidential Campaign: Announcing Intention to Run

- Announcement made in person and/or on candidate's web site, a year or more before election.
- National and state campaign staffs organized; financial support and endorsements sought.

The Campaign for Delegates Begins

- Candidate aims to win state party delegates to national nominating convention. Most states now hold primary elections to select some or all delegates. Some states hold caucuses(meetings) to name party members to district/state conventions which in turn elect some or all of the state's delegates to the national convention.
- Trend toward more and earlier primaries has accelerated pressure for money, media attention, and campaign travel. In 1968 14 primaries were held between March and June of election year; in 2008 at least 40 states will hold primary elections or caucuses between January and March.

Raising Money for the Primaries and General Election

- Earlier primaries increase costs of presidential election. More money needed to campaign in so many closely scheduled primaries and in a longer general election campaign period.
- Presidential candidates raise money in private meetings, fundraising events to meet the candidate, and appeals through letters, phone calls, and web sites.
- Federal law provides public funding for both the primaries and general election and sets rules for raising and spending campaign money through the Federal Election Commission (FEC).
- Party committees, Political Action Committees (PACs), and 527s may, within limits, raise and spend money for voter registration, to get-out-the vote and promote issues but not candidates.
- Candidates decide whether to accept partial public funding for primaries and/or full public funding for the general election with its restrictions on spending limits and on raising other funds.
- In 2004 both nominees declined public funding for primaries but accepted it for general election.
- Each raised more than $250 million. 2008 election is predicted to cost at least a billion dollars.

The National Convention: Selecting the Party Nominee

- Party nominees are chosen at conventions held in summer before November election.
- Having won a majority of delegate votes, nominee is usually known before convention.

The Presidential Campaign

- Candidate plans strategy to win 270 of the 538 electoral votes needed to become President.
- Candidate concentrates time, and media attention on "contested" rather than "safe" states.
- Each state has as many votes as its senators plus representatives to equal 535 plus 3 electoral votes for Washington D.C. In 2000 election, Florida's electoral votes determined the presidency (271-266) even though Gore received more popular votes than G.W. Bush.
- After 2000 census 12 House seats changed from Eastern and Midwestern states to Western and Southern states in a continuing population trend that shifted electoral votes as well.

Election Day: Voters Choose the Electors Who Elect the President

- Voters cast ballots on Election Day- the Tuesday following first Monday in November.
- Voters decide which party's electors in each state will vote for President and Vice President on the Monday following the second Wednesday in December.
- The new President is sworn in (inaugurated) on January 20.

KEY THEMES AND CONCEPTS

Government

In the presidential election of 2000, George W. Bush became the fourth President to win the electoral college without winning the popular vote. The other Presidents were John Quincy Adams, elected in 1824; Rutherford B. Hayes, who ran in 1876; and Benjamin Harrison, elected in 1888.

PREPARING FOR THE EXAM

A flowchart is a diagram that shows the different steps in a process. Study the flowchart of the route to the presidency on the previous page, then answer the question below:

What are three sources of delegates to a political parties national convention?

1.

2.

3.

REASONS TO KEEP THE SYSTEM Despite such criticisms, the electoral college system remains in use for three key reasons:

1. It is very difficult to amend the Constitution.

2. Small states would lose the advantage they now have of being over-represented in the electoral college; they would, therefore, oppose any change.

3. Changes in the electoral college system might threaten the two-party political system. The fact that a presidential candidate needs a majority of the electoral college vote, critics believe, prevents many small political parties from springing up.

Presidential Roles and Powers

Article II describes the powers and duties of the President of the United States. Since power in the executive branch centers in one individual, a president can act swiftly in time of war and national crisis. In carrying out the duties of office, the president fills several different roles.

CHIEF EXECUTIVE In this role, the President has the power to
- enforce or put the laws into effect
- act as administrator of the huge federal bureaucracy
- issue executive orders that have the effect of laws
- appoint judges, diplomats, and other high government officials—some with Senate approval and others without
- remove appointed government officials within the executive branch

CHIEF DIPLOMAT In this role, the President has the power to
- make treaties
- make executive agreements with nations without Senate approval
- extend or withdraw diplomatic recognition to a nation

COMMANDER IN CHIEF In this role, the President has broad military powers that are shared with Congress. In times of war, these powers are even stronger.

CHIEF LEGISLATOR In this role of lawmaker, the President has the power to
- recommend legislation to Congress
- veto potential laws

CHIEF OF STATE In addition to being head of the government, the President is also chief of state, the ceremonial head of government, and the symbol of all the people of the nation. He fills this role in such ceremonies as the laying of a wreath on the Tomb of the Unknowns.

JUDICIAL POWERS The President can grant reprieves, pardons, and amnesties, or pardons extended to groups rather than individuals.

HEAD OF THE PARTY The President is also the leader of the political party in power. The duties of this role are not mentioned in the Constitution because the party system developed through custom.

The Federal Bureaucracy

The federal bureaucracy consists of the administrative agencies and staff that put the decisions or policies of the government into effect. Such a bureaucracy has developed through legislation, executive action, and custom.

Most of the bureaucracy is part of the executive branch and includes the White House staff, 14 executive departments, and more than 200 independent agencies. This bureaucracy is explained in more detail in the chart on the next page.

⚲ KEY THEMES AND CONCEPTS

Government
The executive branch is the largest branch of the government, as shown in the chart on the next page.

- Why is the executive branch so large?

- How were the departments and agencies shown created?

ARTICLE III: THE JUDICIAL BRANCH

Article III of the Constitution creates the Supreme Court and gives Congress the power to create lower federal courts. The role of this judicial branch is to interpret the law. In addition to this national court system, each of the 50 states has its own court system.

Jurisdiction

With two court systems—federal and state—the Constitution had to define the jurisdiction, or authority, of the federal courts in order to make clear which cases go to federal courts and which to state courts. The court that has the authority to hear a case is determined by two factors:

SUBJECT MATTER Federal courts hear cases involving federal laws, treaties, maritime law, and interpretation of the Constitution.

PARTIES Federal courts are directed to have jurisdiction if cases involve certain parties, or participants in a case. For example, cases involving representatives of foreign governments or states suing other states are tried in federal courts.

The Constitution states that in some types of cases, the Supreme Court will have original jurisdiction. This means the Supreme Court will hear the case first and make a decision. In most cases, the Supreme Court has appellate jurisdiction. This means that, in a lower court, if the losing side believes a judge made a mistake in applying the law in a case, that case may be appealed to a higher court. The Supreme Court hears only about 150 cases of the nearly 5,000 appealed to it each year.

The United States Government

Legislative	Executive	Judicial
THE CONGRESS	**THE PRESIDENT**	**SUPREME COURT OF THE UNITED STATES**
Senate House	Executive Office of the President	
• Architect of the Capitol • General Accounting Office • Government Printing Office • Library of Congress • United States Botanic Garden • Office of Technology Assessment • Congressional Budget Office • United States Tax Court	• White House Office • Office of Management and Budget • Council of Economic Advisers • National Security Council • Office of National Drug Control Policy • Office of the United States Trade Representative • Council on Environmental Quality • Office of Science and Technology Policy • Office of Administration	• Courts of Appeals • District Courts • Federal Claims Court • Court of Appeals for the Federal Circuit • Court of International Trade • Territorial Courts • Court of Appeals for the Armed Forces • Court of Veterans Appeals • Administrative Office of the United States Courts • Federal Judicial Center
	The Vice President	

Executive Departments

State	Treasury	Defense	Justice	Interior	Agriculture	Commerce
Labor	Health and Human Services	Housing and Urban Development	Transportation	Energy	Education	Veterans Affairs

Major Independent Agencies*

- Central Intelligence Agency
- Commission on Civil Rights
- Consumer Product Safety Commission
- Corporation for National and Community Service
- Defense Nuclear Facilities Safety Board
- Environmental Protection Agency
- Equal Employment Opportunity Commission
- Export-Import Bank of the U.S.
- Farm Credit Administration
- Federal Communications Commission

- Federal Deposit Insurance Corporation
- Federal Election Commission
- Federal Housing Finance Board
- Federal Maritime Commission
- Federal Mediation and Conciliation Service
- Federal Reserve System
- Federal Trade Commission
- General Services Administration
- Merit Systems Protection Board
- National Aeronautics and Space Administration

- National Labor Relations Board
- National Transportation Safety Board
- Nuclear Regulatory Commission
- Office of Government Ethics
- Securities and Exchange Commission
- Selective Service System
- Small Business Administration
- Social Security Administration
- Tennessee Valley Authority
- U.S. Arms Control and Disarmament Agency
- U.S. Postal Service

*There are more than 200 independent agencies in the executive branch.

Judicial Review

The most important power of the federal courts is the right to **judicial review.** This power enables the courts to hear cases involving the application and interpretation of law. Laws that are judged not in keeping with the Constitution's intent are declared unconstitutional and void.

The Supreme Court is the final voice in interpreting the Constitution. The right of judicial review strengthened the power of the judiciary against the other two branches of government. Chief Justice John Marshall first stated the right of judicial review in the 1803 case of *Marbury* v. *Madison.*

READING STRATEGY

Problem Solving
The process of amending the Constitution is an excellent example of federalism in practice. Why?

AMENDING THE CONSTITUTION

Article V describes methods of amending, or formally changing, the Constitution. In the most common method of amendment, Congress approves a proposed amendment by a two-thirds vote in each house. The amendment then goes to the state legislatures. If three quarters of them ratify it, the amendment becomes part of the Constitution. Twenty-six amendments have been adopted by this method. To date, only the Twenty-first Amendment has been ratified by special conventions called in the states.

The Formal Amendment Process (Four Methods)

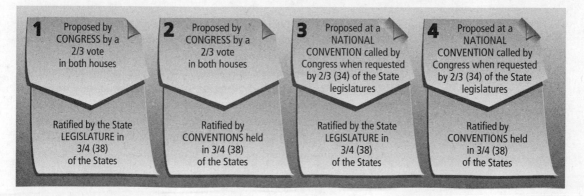

1 Proposed by CONGRESS by a 2/3 vote in both houses	2 Proposed by CONGRESS by a 2/3 vote in both houses	3 Proposed at a NATIONAL CONVENTION called by Congress when requested by 2/3 (34) of the State legislatures	4 Proposed at a NATIONAL CONVENTION called by Congress when requested by 2/3 (34) of the State legislatures
Ratified by the State LEGISLATURE in 3/4 (38) of the States	Ratified by CONVENTIONS held in 3/4 (38) of the States	Ratified by the State LEGISLATURE in 3/4 (38) of the States	Ratified by CONVENTIONS held in 3/4 (38) of the States

The Bill of Rights

The Bill of Rights is the name given to the first 10 amendments to the Constitution adopted in 1791. These amendments guarantee certain basic or fundamental rights of the people against the power of the federal government.

The Bill of Rights

Amendment	Subject
1st	Guarantees freedom of religion, of speech, and of the press; the right to assemble peacefully; and the right to petition the government.
2nd	Protects the right to possess firearms.
3rd	Declares that the government may not require people to house soldiers during peacetime.
4th	Protects people from unreasonable searches and seizures.
5th	Guarantees that no one may be deprived of life, liberty, or property without due process of law.
6th	Guarantees the right to a trial by jury in criminal cases.
7th	Guarantees the right to trial by jury in most civil cases.
8th	Prohibits excessive bail, fines, and punishments.
9th	Declares that rights not mentioned in the Constitution belong to the people.
10th	Declares that powers not given to the national government belong to the states or to the people.

Extending Constitutional Protections

In the 200 years since the Bill of Rights was added to the Constitution, the rights of the people have been expanded by court decisions and by other amendments. The Fourteenth Amendment contains the equal protection clause. Court interpretations have held that the Fourteenth Amendment extends the protections of most of the Bill of Rights against the states as well as the national government.

The courts have held that civil rights (as defined in the Bill of Rights and other amendments) are relative, not absolute. The courts have thus tried to balance an individual's rights against the rights of society and other individuals. Sometimes basic civil rights conflict with each other. For example, the Fifth Amendment right of the accused to confront witnesses might clash with a reporter's First Amendment, freedom-of-the-press right to protect news sources. In such conflicts, the courts must decide the issue.

Additional Constitutional Amendments

Between 1795 and 1992, an additional 17 amendments have been added to the Constitution. Note that the Thirteenth, Fourteenth, and Fifteenth Amendments were passed after the Civil War to make citizens of former slaves, and to give them the right to vote.

Amendments 11–27

Amendment	Year Ratified	Subject
11th	1795	Lawsuits against the states
12th	1804	Separate voting for President and Vice President
13th	1865	Abolition of slavery
14th	1868	Citizenship and civil rights
15th	1870	Voting rights for African American men
16th	1913	Income tax
17th	1913	Direct election of senators
18th	1919	Prohibition of alcoholic beverages
19th	1920	Voting rights for Women
20th	1933	Terms of the President, Vice President and Congress
21st	1933	Repeal of Eighteenth Amendment
22nd	1951	President limited to two terms
23rd	1961	Electoral votes for the District of Columbia
24th	1964	Abolition of poll taxes
25th	1967	Presidential disability and succession
26th	1971	Voting age lowered to eighteen
27th	1992	Changing congressional salaries

The Right to Vote

Year	People Allowed to Vote
1789	White men over age 21 who meet property requirements (state laws)
Early 1800s–1850s	All white men over age 21 (state laws)
1870	Black men (15th Amendment)
1920	Women (19th Amendment)
1961	People in the District of Columbia in presidential elections (23rd Amendment)
1971	People age 18 or over (26th Amendment)

ANALYZING DOCUMENTS

Based on the chart at left, what has been the most common way of extending the right to vote to more people?

NEW YORK STATE GOVERNMENT COMPARED TO THE FEDERAL GOVERNMENT

The government of New York has many similarities to the federal government. New York has a constitution and a Bill of Rights. The New York government has three branches. The executive branch is headed by the governor. The bicameral legislature has a Senate and an Assembly. The highest court in the judicial branch is the Court of Appeals.

PART 4 THE THIRTEEN BASIC CONSTITUTIONAL PRINCIPLES

Thirteen basic constitutional principles have endured since the ratification of the Constitution. These principles continue to be important to the development of American government and society.

Constitutional Principle 1
National Power—Limits and Potential

The powers of the federal government are limited. The Constitution states the powers held by each branch of government. The powers that are not delegated to the national government are reserved to the states or to the people (Tenth Amendment). The Bill of Rights also limits the government's inter-ference with basic rights.

However, the powers of all three branches of the federal government have grown.
- Has the national government become too powerful?
- Do the limits placed on the national government make it incapable of dealing with the problems of the modern age?

Examples of This Principle as a Recurring Theme in U.S. History

Need for a strong central government: debate over ratification
Loose vs. strict interpretation of the Constitution: Hamilton's financial plan, Louisiana Purchase
Conflict over slavery: 1820–1860
Civil War: establishing federal supremacy over the states
Imperialism: Spanish-American War, acquiring an overseas empire

Progressive movement: Theodore Roosevelt and Woodrow Wilson
Elastic clause: Pure Food and Drug Act, Social Security
Commerce clause: expanding powers of government
New Deal: expanding role of government
Great Society: demand for reform
New Federalism: less government involvement

Constitutional Principle 2
Federalism—Balance Between Nation and State

The Constitution created a new federal government that divided power between the states and the national government. The Constitution reserved certain powers to the states and to the people, but the Constitution and the laws and treaties of the United States are supreme to state laws.

- Is the power still balanced, or has it tilted to the federal government?
- Has the shift of power to the federal government become greater since the New Deal, or did Reagan's New Federalism reverse this trend?

Examples of This Principle as a Recurring Theme in U.S. History

Marshall Supreme Court cases: *McCulloch* v. *Maryland, Gibbons* v. *Ogden*
John C. Calhoun: nullification, states' rights
Conflict over slavery: 1820–1860
Civil War: establishing federal supremacy over the states
Reconstruction: greater federal supremacy; 13th, 14th, and 15th Amendments

Populists and Progressive reform
New Deal legislation
Rights of minorities: *Brown* v. *Board of Education*
Fourteenth Amendment: use to extend Bill of Rights protections to states
Great Society, mid-1960s
New Federalism, 1980s

Constitutional Principle 3
The Judiciary—Interpreter of the Constitution or Shaper of Public Policy

The Judiciary interprets the law (Article III) and has the power to declare laws unconstitutional. This power of judicial review dates from Marshall's decision in *Marbury* v. *Madison,* which was based on Article III, and the supremacy clause in Article VI, which states that the Constitution is the "supreme law of the land."

- By acting when Congress has not acted, or by reversing congressional actions to favor the states, have the courts become lawmakers instead of law interpreters?
- If the courts did not have the power to shape public policy, would the Bill of Rights and democracy itself be endangered?

Examples of This Principle as a Recurring Theme in U.S. History

Marbury v. *Madison:* judicial review strengthened judiciary, government, and national unity

Federal vs. state powers: *McCulloch* v. *Maryland, Gibbons* v. *Ogden*

Limiting protections and rights: *Dred Scott* v. *Sandford, Civil Rights Cases*

Reversals of decisions: *Plessy* v. *Ferguson, Brown* v. *Board of Education*

State vs. federal powers: *United States* v. *E.C. Knight Co., Lochner* v. *New York, Schechter Poultry* v. *United States*

Rights of accused: *Miranda* v. *Arizona, Gideon* v. *Wainwright*

First Amendment cases (freedom of speech, press, religion, assembly): *Engel* v. *Vitale, Schenck* v. *United States, New York Times Co.* v. *United States, Tinker* v. *Des Moines Independent Community School District*

Ninth Amendment privacy cases: *Roe* v. *Wade; Cruzan* v. *Director, Missouri Department of Health*

Checks and balances: *Watkins* v. *United States, United States* v. *Nixon*

Constitutional Principle 4
Civil Liberties—Protecting Individual Liberties from Government Abuses; the Balance Between Government and the Individual

A problem unique to a democratic government is how to balance the rights of the individual and the needs of society. The Constitution's Bill of Rights and Fourteenth Amendment guarantee certain basic rights, rights which predate any government. But these rights are not unlimited.

- What are the rights of the individual?
- Should government protect and/or extend the rights of the individual?
- Should government decide where the balance should be between individual and societal rights?

Examples of This Principle as a Recurring Theme in U.S. History

Equal protection clause: Fourteenth Amendment—*Civil Rights Cases, Heart of Atlanta Motel* v. *United States*

Freedom of speech vs. "clear and present danger": *Schenck* v. *United States*

Relocation of Japanese Americans: *Korematsu* v. *United States*

Red Scare, McCarthyism: fear of subversion, the erosion of liberties *Watkins* v. *United States*

Testing for drug use: *Vernonia School District* v. *Acton*

Rights of individuals: effects of technology

Individual's rights v. Security against terrorism: *Patriot Act, Foreign Intelligence Surveillance Act*

Constitutional Principle 5
Criminal Procedures—The Balance Between the Rights of the Accused and the Protection of the Community and Victims

This is a question of balancing the rights of individuals accused of crimes and those of citizens to be safe and secure.
- Why does an individual accused of a crime have rights?

- Are those rights easily defined?
- What are the rights of a victim of a crime?
- When do the rights of the accused interfere with society's ability to maintain law and order?

Examples of This Principle as a Recurring Theme in U.S. History

Free press vs. the rights of the accused

Death penalty: individual rights vs. rights of society

Writ of *habeas corpus:* purpose

Due process of law, search and seizure: *Mapp* v. *Ohio*

Students' rights and search and seizure: *New Jersey* v. *T.L.O.; Vernonia School District* v. *Acton*

Rights of the accused: *Miranda* v. *Arizona, Gideon* v. *Wainwright*

Constitutional Principle 6
Equality—Its Historic and Present Meaning as a Constitutional Value

This issue involves questions of who is equal and in what ways. When Jefferson wrote that "all men are created equal," he referred to the equality before the law of white, property-owning males. The equal protection clause of the Fourteenth Amendment and the due process clause of the Fifth Amendment were later interpreted to make equal justice more of a reality for all Americans.

- According to the Constitution, who is equal: men and women? All races? Rich and poor? Young and old?
- How has the Constitution expanded equality?
- Has equality been achieved?
- How are people equal: equal in opportunity? Before the law? In entitlements?

Examples of This Principle as a Recurring Theme in U.S. History

Conflict over slavery: Constitutional Convention; 1820–1860
Passage of 13th, 14th, and 15th Amendments
Equal protection clause: 14th Amendment
Jim Crow laws: legal basis for segregation
Plessy v. *Ferguson*
Brown v. *Board of Education*
Martin Luther King, Jr.: civil rights movement

19th-century women's rights movement
19th Amendment
1960s women's rights movement
Treatment of Native Americans: *Worcester* v. *Georgia*
Native American movement
New Deal: relief of human suffering
Great Society: help for less fortunate
Affirmative action: court decisions

Constitutional Principle 7
The Rights of Women Under the Constitution

Women are not mentioned in the Constitution except in the Nineteenth Amendment, which protects their right to vote.
- What is the historic and present meaning of equality for women as a constitutional value?

- How were these changes achieved?
- Are federal laws and court rulings sufficiently protective of the rights of women?
- Was there a need for the defeated Equal Rights Amendment?

Examples of This Principle as a Recurring Theme in U.S. History

Elizabeth Cady Stanton and Susan B. Anthony: Women's suffrage movement
Seneca Falls: Women's rights movement
Effects of industrialization on the role of women

1960s women's rights movement
Roe v. *Wade:* Ninth amendment, right to privacy, abortion
Affirmative action and women

Constitutional Principle 8
The Rights of Ethnic and Racial Minority Groups Under the Constitution

The Constitution has not always protected ethnic, racial, and other minority groups. When first ratified, in fact, the Constitution contained clauses that protected slavery and the rights of slaveholders.
- Has the Constitution protected the rights of ethnic and racial minority groups?

- Has the Constitution protected the rights of economically powerful groups better than those of minority groups?
- Are the gains that minorities have made secure, or do such groups need more protection of their rights?
- How do we balance minority rights and rule by a majority?

Examples of This Principle as a Recurring Theme in U.S. History

Conflict over slavery: Constitutional Convention; 1820–1860
Frederick Douglass: abolition movement
Dred Scott v. *Sandford*
Civil War: Emancipation Proclamation
Reconstruction: 13th, 14th, and 15th Amendments
Jim Crow laws, *Plessy* v. *Ferguson:* legal basis for segregation
Equal protection clause: 14th Amendment

Brown v. *Board of Education*
Martin Luther King, Jr.: civil rights movement of 1960s
Restrictions on immigration: quota system, exclusion of Chinese and Japanese
Relocation of Japanese Americans: *Korematsu* v. *United States*
Native Americans: treaty rights, *Worcester* v. *Georgia,* Dawes Act, citizenship in 1924
Native American movement

Constitutional Principle 9
Presidential Power in Wartime and in Foreign Affairs

The Constitution gives the President the power to make treaties, as well as other major foreign-policy responsibilities. The President is also the commander in chief of the armed forces. The powers of the President have grown since the early days of the United States government, and they are even greater in wartime.

- Does the President have too much power, particularly since the Civil War?
- Are broad presidential powers necessary to conduct war and foreign affairs?

Examples of This Principle as a Recurring Theme in U.S. History

George Washington: expanded governmental powers, Proclamation of Neutrality

Increase of presidential power during wartime by Lincoln, Wilson, and FDR.: *Schenck* v. *United States, Korematsu* v. *United States*

T. Roosevelt: increase of presidential power because of U.S. involvement in world affairs

T. Roosevelt: Roosevelt Corollary to Monroe Doctrine

Truman: decision to drop atomic bomb

Korean and Vietnam Wars: expanded presidential wartime powers

Kennedy: Cuban missile crisis

War Powers Act: a check on presidential power

Carter: Camp David Accords

G.H.W. Bush: Persian Gulf Crisis

Clinton: Somalia, Bosnia, Haiti, Yugoslavia

G.W. Bush: Bush Doctrine; presidential powers in wartime: *Writ of Habeas Corpus,* wiretapping

Constitutional Principle 10
The Separation of Powers and the Effectiveness of Government

The Constitution established three branches of government with separate powers, as well as a system of checks and balances among them.

- Has the system of separation of powers and of checks and balances been effective in preventing dominance by one branch?
- Is this system necessary, or has it resulted in a badly-run government that is slow to respond to the needs of the people and the nation?

Examples of This Principle as a Recurring Theme in U.S. History

Checks and balances: presidential veto

Judicial review: *Marbury* v. *Madison*

Reconstruction: period of legislative power

Checks and balances: Treaty of Versailles

Checks and balances: FDR and Supreme Court reorganization

Checks and balances: Vietnam War

Checks and balances: *Watkins* v. *United States, United States* v. *Nixon*

War Powers Act: check on presidential power

Watergate: government based on laws and not on an individual

Clinton: impeachment and acquittal

Constitutional Principle 11
Avenues of Representation

Since the Constitution was ratified, there has been a continuing expansion of the right to vote. However, while the system has become more democratic and more reflective of majority rule, the power of political parties and special interest groups has grown, as has the influence of technology.

- Has the federal government become more or less representative of "we the people"?

Examples of This Principle as a Recurring Theme in U.S. History

Great Compromise: representation in Congress

Electoral college system

Direct election of senators

Passage of 15th, 19th, 24th, and 26th Amendments

19th-century and Progressive reform movements

Populist and Grange movements

Women's suffrage movement

Third parties' effect on the political process

"One man, one vote": effect on representative government

Campaign financing: public v. private, individual rights, rights of lobbyists and other special interests

Effects of technology: electronic voting; the Internet

Constitutional Principle 12
Property Rights and Economic Policy

The Constitution gives the government responsibility for promoting the general welfare and Congress the power to regulate commerce and taxes.

- Has government balanced its two roles as the promoter of capitalism and free enterprise and as the protector of the public from the abuses of business?

Examples of This Principle as a Recurring Theme in U.S. History

Hamilton: government encouragement of business, national bank

Andrew Jackson: second national bank

Expanded interstate commerce clause: *Gibbons* v. *Ogden; Wabash, St. Louis & Pacific R.R.* v. *Illinois*

Weakened interstate commerce clause: *United States* v. *E.C. Knight Co., Lochner* v. *New York, Schechter Poultry* v. *United States*

Interstate commerce clause used against labor: *In Re Debs*

Antitrust activities: Sherman Antitrust Act, T. Roosevelt and W. Wilson, *Northern Securities Co.* v. *United States,* Clayton Antitrust Act

Federal Reserve: regulating monetary system

Government action for environmental and consumer protection

New Deal: government farm price supports

New Deal: collective bargaining, Wagner Act

Reagan: supply side economics, budget deficits

Constitutional Principle 13
Constitutional Change and Flexibility

The Constitution has adapted to changing circumstances over the years because of certain provisions built into it, such as the necessary and proper clause and the interstate commerce clause.

- Has the Constitution proven adaptable to changing times?

- Should the Constitution be easier to change?
- Has the amendment process, combined with judicial interpretation and the implied powers of the executive and legislative branches, kept the Constitution able to meet the challenges of the modern world?

Examples of This Principle as a Recurring Theme in United States History

Washington: the unwritten constitution

Hamilton's bank plan: implied powers

Commerce clause: expansion of government authority, regulation of business, Federal Reserve System

Amendments and court decisions used to expand rights

Cabinet and congressional committees: custom and precedent

Role of political parties

PART 5 PUTTING THE CONSTITUTION INTO EFFECT

From the time of our first Presidents, an **unwritten constitution** developed in response to changing times and circumstances. This unwritten constitution resulted from a combination of (1) executive interpretations and actions, (2) congressional interpretations and actions, (3) court decisions, especially judicial review, (4) customs and traditions, and (5) the actions of political parties.

EXECUTIVE INTERPRETATION, ACTION, AND CUSTOM

Starting with George Washington, presidents sought advice from the heads of the executive departments, who were called the President's **cabinet,** when developing policy. Today, the White House staff also plays a major role in this advisory process. The President appoints cabinet members with Senate approval but can dismiss a cabinet member without Senate approval.

The early Presidents also consulted with congressional leaders when developing policies. Such consultation is an informal procedure. Today, the Senate's official role often seems more "to consent" than "to advise" on presidential decisions. This method of advising the President has become custom.

Developing a Financial Plan

With Washington's support, Alexander Hamilton, the first secretary of the treasury, set out to put the government on a sound economic footing. He proposed a plan that included four key elements:

♀ **KEY THEMES AND CONCEPTS**

Government: Unwritten Constitution

In the early years of the new nation, the United States government grew from the basic framework of the Constitution to a functioning governmental system. Provide an example of how interpretation, action, and custom each contributed to this process.

Interpretation:

Action:

Custom:

First Years of the New Government, 1789–1820

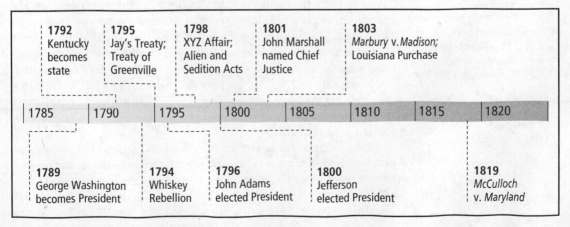

| 1792 Kentucky becomes state | 1795 Jay's Treaty; Treaty of Greenville | 1798 XYZ Affair; Alien and Sedition Acts | 1801 John Marshall named Chief Justice | 1803 *Marbury* v. *Madison;* Louisiana Purchase |

| 1785 | 1790 | 1795 | 1800 | 1805 | 1810 | 1815 | 1820 |

| 1789 George Washington becomes President | 1794 Whiskey Rebellion | 1796 John Adams elected President | 1800 Jefferson elected President | 1819 *McCulloch* v. *Maryland* |

ASSUMPTION Hamilton wanted the national government to pay off American Revolution war debts run up by the Continental Congress as well as the wartime debts of the states. Hamilton believed that this would establish the credit of the nation. Congress approved this plan.

A NATIONAL BANK Hamilton wanted Congress to create a national bank, which he believed would win the government the support of the business community. Such a bank would also help the government in all of its financial dealings. Congress chartered a national bank in 1791.

AN EXCISE TAX Hamilton proposed that the government raise operating revenues through an excise tax on whiskey.

A PROTECTIVE TARIFF Hamilton called for a protective tariff to shield products of the nation's infant industries from foreign competition. Congress rejected the protective tariff but passed other tariffs to generate income for the government.

The Hamilton plan raised some controversy, but it put the new nation on a sound financial footing. It also encouraged the wealthy to support the government and built a solid foundation for the nation's future as an industrial power.

The Whiskey Rebellion

In 1794, western Pennsylvania farmers protested and refused to pay excise tax on the whiskey they made from grain. Washington called out state militias and put down this "Whiskey Rebellion." There is debate today over how serious a threat this rebellion really was, but Washington's actions demonstrated that the new government intended to enforce federal law.

Foreign Policy in the Federalist Era

From 1789 to 1815, the French Revolution and the European wars that grew out of it put many pressures on the new nation. Washington and the other early Presidents tried to protect the nation from such pressures. Washington, for example, supported the unpopular **Jay's Treaty,** an agreement designed to resolve conflicts with Great Britain and keep the United States from going to war. With his **Proclamation of Neutrality** in 1793 and his **Farewell Address** in 1796, Washington set the tone for United States foreign policy by warning of the danger of political alliances. Instead he urged the nation to take independent action in foreign affairs.

John Adams, the first Vice President and second President, also understood the importance of keeping the new nation out of war. He settled rather than expand an undeclared naval war with France (1798–1800). His actions divided his own Federalist Party, which contributed to his failure to win a second term. But Adams, in resisting internal and external pressures for war and ending the 1778 alliance with France, made possible a peaceful and independent entry into the new century.

Reacting to Dissent: The Alien and Sedition Acts

Taking advantage of the emotions stirred up by the French Revolution, the Federalists passed the Alien and Sedition Acts (1798), which were designed to strengthen the Federalist party and weaken the Republican opposition. The Alien Acts made it more difficult to become a citizen and easier to arrest and deport any noncitizens thought to endanger national security. The Sedition Act made it easier to arrest a person for criticizing the government. Protests were made against these acts for challenging the freedom of speech and of the press. Madison and Jefferson in the Virginia and Kentucky Resolutions declared the acts dangerous to civil liberties and representative government.

The Two-Term Presidency

After serving two terms, Washington rejected a third term as president. In doing so, he established a tradition that was not broken until 1940 and 1944, when Franklin D. Roosevelt won a third and then a fourth term. Unhappiness over Roosevelt's break with tradition led to passage of the Twenty-second Amendment that limited a President to two terms in office.

CONGRESSIONAL INTERPRETATION, ACTION, AND CUSTOM

The Constitution supplied few details of how the machinery of government would operate, so early congressional actions helped set up that machinery. For example, Congress also created the first five executive departments—Treasury, State, War (Defense), Attorney General (Justice), and Postmaster General. Today, there are 14 departments and more than 200 independent agencies.

In 1789, Congress began the custom of assigning bills to committees. This developed into today's committee system, in which standing committees review all bills before sending them on to the full House or Senate. Congressional committees can also operate as investigative committees, gathering information in order to determine the need for new laws or to examine how current laws are working.

Lobbying

Custom has led to lobbying by people representing special-interest groups who act to influence legislation and elect people who support the lobby group's views. Lobbying is protected by the First Amendment's right to petition but also regulated by federal law.

⚷ KEY THEMES AND CONCEPTS
Presidential Decisions and Actions
What impact did Franklin D. Roosevelt's decision to run for a third and fourth term eventually have on the U.S. Constitution?

⚷ KEY THEMES AND CONCEPTS
Constitutional Principles
The practice of **lobbying** is protected by the First Amendment's right to petition, but it is also regulated by federal law. Lobby groups organize **Political Action Committees** or **PACs** to promote legislation and elect legislators supportive of the lobby group's views.

- Why should the government limit lobbyists' First Amendment right to petition?

- What lessons can the public learn from the Abramoff lobbying scandal?

- What major PACs are involved in election campaigns and what methods do they use to elect their candidates?

- How does federal law attempt to limit PACs?

Strict vs. Loose Construction

Hamilton's proposal for a national bank started the first national debate between "strict" and "loose" constructionists. Strict constructionists favor a narrow interpretation of the Constitution, holding that government can do only those things the document specifically spells out. Loose constructionists favor a freer reading of the Constitution that gives government more room to act.

In 1803, Jefferson had the chance to double the size of the nation through the Louisiana Purchase. However, supporting the purchase meant adopting a loose interpretation of the Constitution. Jefferson overcame his reluctance to spend public money and backed the purchase. In addition to adding new lands, the Louisiana Purchase also gave the United States control of the vital Mississippi River.

The Louisiana Purchase, 1803

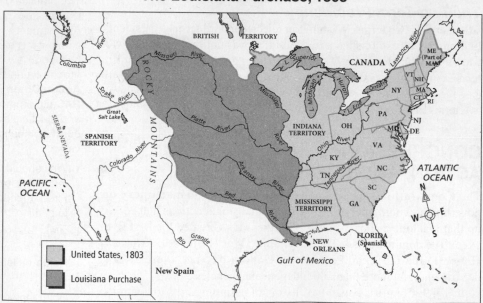

JUDICIAL INTERPRETATION OF THE CONSTITUTION

The power of the judicial branch was greatly strengthened during the period in which John Marshall served as the nation's fourth chief justice (1801–1835).

The Marshall Court

The decision of the Supreme Court in *McCulloch* v. *Maryland* (1819) upheld the congressional creation of the Second Bank of the United States. Supporting loose interpretation, this decision strengthened federal supremacy over state laws and national economic interests.

Similarly, in 1824, the verdict in *Gibbons* v. *Ogden* expanded the powers of the national government over commerce through a broad interpretation of the congressional power to regulate interstate commerce (Article I, Section 8, Clause 3).

Perhaps most critically, Marshall led the Court in the 1803 decision in *Marbury* v. *Madison*. This decision established the court's right of judicial review, its power to rule on the constitutionality of a law.

Activism versus Restraint

Those favoring judicial activism believe the Court should use this power to help make public policy, particularly when Congress has failed to act on pressing social problems. Those favoring judicial restraint believe that this power should be used only when there is an obvious violation of the Constitution. They feel that policy-making should be left to the other two branches.

ACTIONS OF POLITICAL PARTIES

Political parties developed through custom and tradition. The debate between **Federalists** and **Anti-Federalists** over ratification revealed the existence of differences of opinion on government. These differences led to the formation of the first two political parties—the Federalists and the **Democratic-Republicans.**

The formation of political parties led to constitutional changes in the method of electing the president. Party politics also gave rise to nominating conventions and the pledging of electoral votes to a candidate. Today, due to the growth of primaries and party caucuses, the presidential candidate has usually been selected before the delegates attend the nominating convention.

The First Political Parties

Federalists	Republicans
1. Led by Alexander Hamilton, John Adams	1. Led by Thomas Jefferson, James Madison
2. Wealthy and well-educated should lead nation	2. People should have political power
3. Strong central government	3. Strong state governments
4. Emphasis on manufacturing, shipping, and trade	4. Emphasis on agriculture
5. Loose interpretation of Constitution	5. Strict interpretation of Constitution
6. Pro-British	6. Pro-French
7. Favored national bank	7. Opposed national bank
8. Favored protective tariff	8. Opposed protective tariff

KEY THEMES AND CONCEPTS

Government

Supreme Court decisions have affected the separation of powers in the federal system. How did *Marbury* v. *Madison* affect the separation of powers?

KEY THEMES AND CONCEPTS

Government

The peaceful transfer of political power from one party to another is an important feature of the democratic system in the United States.

ANALYZING DOCUMENTS

Jefferson left instructions that his gravestone be inscribed:

"Author of the Declaration of Independence, the Statute of Virginia for Religious Freedom, and father of the University of Virginia."

- What does this tell you about a man who was both President and Vice President of the United States, governor of Virginia, the first secretary of state, and the second minister to France?

PREPARING FOR THE EXAM

National self-interest is the prime motivation behind a nation's foreign policy. Debates center on the issue of what actions, in a given situation, are in the best interests of a nation.

READING STRATEGY

Reading for Evidence
Is the War of 1812 best described as

- a second war for independence?

- a war of expansion?

- a war for rights on the seas?

Explain your answer.

ANALYZING DOCUMENTS

Examine the table. What effect did the War of 1812 have on U.S exports? Why?

In the first half of the 1800s, many more men had the right to vote, and the campaign techniques and organization of political parties changed to appeal to this broader electorate.

While major political parties have changed infrequently, the nation has seen many influential "third parties." Such parties have offered criticisms and suggested reforms later adopted by the major parties when in power.

FOREIGN POLICY: 1800–1823

Events in Europe from 1789 to 1815 influenced domestic and foreign policies of the United States. Presidents maintained American neutrality, staying out of European wars while insisting on the rights of the United States as a nation. The distance from Europe made it easier to keep out of European affairs. However, the right to trade with European nations remained a major concern because America's economic well-being depended on such trade.

War of 1812

Meanwhile, Britain and France remained at war, and Britain outraged Americans by seizing American merchant ships trying to reach France. Congress passed the Embargo Act of 1807—which prohibited trade with other nations—in an attempt to punish Britain. American exports fell, but Britain was largely unaffected. Protests led to the repeal of the act in 1809.

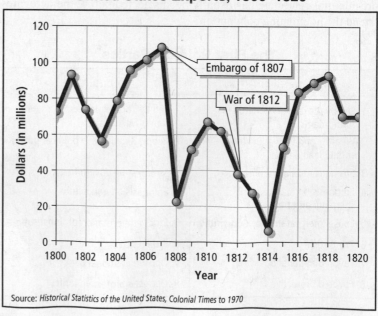

United States Exports, 1800–1820

Source: *Historical Statistics of the United States, Colonial Times to 1970*

Britain continued to violate American freedom of the seas, seizing American ships and forcing American sailors to serve in the British navy. Meanwhile, western and southern "War Hawks"—interested in expanding into British Canada and Spanish Florida—urged war. In 1812, Congress declared war on Britain. The war, however, was not supported by all Americans and provoked disputes among different sections of the nation.

Although the war ended in a draw in 1814, it produced some significant long-term results.

- The war reinforced the American belief that a policy of neutrality regarding European affairs was justified.
- Native American tribes in the West lost their ally, Britain, and were much less able to stand up to American expansion.
- American manufacturing began to grow, particularly in New England, when the United States was cut off from European imports.
- Opposing the war weakened the Federalist Party, which soon ceased to be a major factor in national politics.
- In Andrew Jackson and William Henry Harrison, the nation gained new war heroes. "The Star Spangled Banner" was inspired by the bombarding of Fort McHenry.

Foreign Policy After the War of 1812

The new national self-confidence also revealed itself in the field of diplomacy. John Quincy Adams, secretary of state for President James Monroe, settled the border between the United States and Canada. He also acquired Florida from Spain and reached agreement with that nation on the southern boundary of the Louisiana Purchase.

Monroe Doctrine

Adams was the chief adviser on the 1823 Monroe Doctrine, which became the foundation of the United States' foreign policy in the Western Hemisphere. The Monroe Doctrine called for

- an end to European colonization in the Western Hemisphere
- no intervention by Europe in existing nations in this hemisphere
- a declaration that European interference was "dangerous to our peace and safety"
- a promise of noninterference by the United States in European affairs and European colonies

In 1823, the United States lacked the military might to enforce this doctrine. However, Great Britain agreed to support the United States if this policy were challenged. By the end of the 1800s, the United States was actively enforcing the policy on its own.

KEY THEMES AND CONCEPTS
Foreign Policy
Did the motives behind American foreign policy change after the War of 1812? Why or why not?

PREPARING FOR THE EXAM

On the examination, you will need to understand the changing influences on United States foreign policy.

How was the Monroe Doctrine influenced by each of the following?

- geography
- isolationism and neutrality
- United States national interests
- concerns for the new Latin American republics

KEY THEMES AND CONCEPTS
Foreign Policy
National self-interest—sometimes mixed with a desire to extend democratic ideals to other nations—provides the basis for the foreign policies of most democratic nations, including the United States.

Questions for Regents Practice

For online Questions for Regents Practice,
visit the Prentice Hall Web site at www.phschool.com.

MULTIPLE CHOICE

Directions

Review the Test-Taking Strategies section of this book. Then answer the following questions, drawn from actual Regents examinations. Each question is followed by four choices. Read each question carefully. Decide which choice is the correct answer. Then on a separate piece of paper, mark your answer for each question.

1 "We hold these truths to be self-evident, that all men are created equal, that they are endowed by their Creator with certain unalienable rights, that among these are life, liberty, and the pursuit of happiness."

This quotation reflects beliefs mainly derived from
1 the Magna Carta
2 the divine right monarchs of Europe
3 John Locke's theory of natural rights
4 Marxist philosophy

Base your answers to questions 2 and 3 on the quotation below and on your knowledge of social studies.

"That to secure these rights, governments are instituted among men, deriving their just powers from the consent of the governed; that whenever any form of government becomes destructive of those ends, it is the right of the people to alter or abolish it, and to institute new government. . . ."

2 This quotation presents a justification for
1 anarchy
2 revolution
3 despotism
4 laissez faire

3 According to the quotation, governments get their authority from
1 the people
2 powerful leaders
3 the justice system
4 political parties

4 "The individual can be free *only* when the power of one governmental branch is balanced by the other two."

—Baron de Montesquieu, 1735 (adapted)

The idea expressed in this quotation is best illustrated by which aspect of the United States government?
1 existence of a Cabinet
2 separation of powers
3 elastic clause
4 executive privilege

5 In the colonial era, developments such as the New England town meetings and the establishment of the Virginia House of Burgesses represented
1 colonial attempts to build a strong national government
2 efforts by the British to strengthen their control over the colonies
3 steps in the growth of representative democracy
4 early social reform movements

6   "The only representatives of the people of these colonies are persons chosen therein by themselves; and that no taxes ever have been, or can be constitutionally imposed on them but by their respective legislatures."

—Statement by the Stamp Act Congress, 1765

What is a valid conclusion that can be drawn from this quotation?

1   The colonial legislatures should be appointed by the English King with the consent of Parliament.
2   Only the colonists' elected representatives should have the power to levy taxes.
3   The English King should have the right to tax the colonists.
4   The colonists should be opposed to all taxation.

7   One way in which the United States Constitution differed from the Articles of Confederation was that the Constitution

1   created a national government having three branches
2   provided for the direct election of the President by the voters
3   made the amendment process more difficult
4   increased the powers of the states

Base your answers to questions 8 and 9 on the discussion below and on your knowledge of social studies.

Speaker A: States must be represented in the national government solely on the basis of population. It is indeed the only fair situation.

Speaker B: The national legislature must be based on equal representation of the states to protect the interests of the small states.

Speaker C: States must accept the supremacy of the national government on all issues; otherwise, the system will fail.

Speaker D: The national Congress should consist of two houses: one in which representation is based on population, and one in which states are equally represented.

8   Which document was being written when this discussion most likely occurred?
1   Declaration of Independence
2   United States Constitution
3   Covenant of the League of Nations
4   Charter of the United Nations

9   Which speaker's idea about representation was actually included in the document that was written?
1   A
2   B
3   C
4   D

10   "We should consider we are providing a constitution for future generations of Americans, and not merely for the particular circumstances of the moment."

—Delegate at the Constitutional Convention of 1787

The writers of the Constitution best reflected this idea when they provided that

1   Senators should be elected directly by the people
2   Three-fifths of the slaves should be counted as part of the total population
3   Congress shall make all laws necessary and proper to carry out its constitutional powers
4   Political parties should be established to represent various viewpoints

11   During the debates over the ratification of the United States Constitution, Federalists and Anti-Federalists disagreed most strongly over the

1   division of powers between the national and state governments
2   provision for admitting new states to the Union
3   distribution of powers between the Senate and the House of Representatives
4   method of amending the Constitution

12 The main purpose of the Bill of Rights is to
 1 prevent governmental abuse of power
 2 increase the power of the Federal judiciary
 3 provide for separation of powers
 4 create a bicameral legislature

13 The fact that the United States Constitution provided for federalism and a system of checks and balances suggests that
 1 the original thirteen states sought to dominate the national government
 2 its writers desired the national government to rule over the states
 3 its writers feared a concentration of political power
 4 the American people of that time supported a military government

14 The United States Supreme Court is sometimes said to fulfill a legislative function because
 1 its members are appointed by the President
 2 its judgments may determine the effect of the law
 3 its members serve only so long as Congress approves
 4 it meets regularly with Congress to advise on the appropriateness of proposed laws

15 Which quotation taken from the United States Constitution provides for limiting the power of government?
 1 "All persons born or naturalized in the United States . . . are citizens of the United States . . ."
 2 "This Constitution . . . shall be the supreme law of the land . . ."
 3 "The President shall be commander in chief of the army and navy . . ."
 4 "Congress shall make no law respecting an establishment of religion . . . or abridging the freedom of speech, or of the press . . ."

16 Which action is an example of lobbying by a special interest group?
 1 labor union members threatening to strike if their company opens a factory in a foreign nation
 2 members of Congress introducing a bill that will provide for low-interest college loans
 3 a congressional committee investigating the activities of organized crime
 4 several lumber companies asking Senators to allow logging on Federal lands

17 If the President has vetoed a bill, the United States Constitution provides that the bill will become a law when the bill is
 1 declared constitutional by the Supreme Court
 2 passed again by two-thirds of both houses of Congress
 3 approved by three-fourths of the State legislatures
 4 approved by a joint committee of Congress

18 In the United States, the electoral college system affects the campaigns of major-party presidential candidates by influencing candidates to
 1 concentrate upon the states with large populations
 2 place more emphasis on controversial issues than on personality
 3 focus upon the states where winning by a large plurality is likely
 4 appeal to the electoral college members rather than to the general public

19 The decision of President George Washington to use the state militia to put down the Whiskey Rebellion in 1794 demonstrated that the
1 states were still the dominant power in the new nation
2 President was becoming a military dictator
3 Federal Government had no authority to impose an excise tax
4 new National Government intended to enforce Federal laws

20 In United States history, which statement best represents the political ideology of Alexander Hamilton and the Federalists?
1 Only the wealthy will survive in the economic system.
2 A strong central government is essential for the economic growth of the nation.
3 No one should have to pay taxes to the National Government.
4 Elected officials should give public jobs to those who helped them into office.

21 The major role of political parties in the United States is to
1 protect the American public from corrupt public officials
2 insure that free and honest elections are held
3 nominate candidates for public office and conduct campaigns
4 meet constitutional requirements for choosing the President

22 The term "judicial review" refers to the power of the
1 Supreme Court to determine the constitutionality of laws
2 Congress to pass laws over the veto of the President
3 states to approve amendments to the Constitution
4 President to veto bills passed by Congress

23 In deciding to purchase the Louisiana Territory, President Thomas Jefferson had to overcome the problem of
1 obtaining the support of Western settlers
2 passing the constitutional amendment necessary to authorize the purchase
3 avoiding a possible war with England over the purchase
4 contradicting his belief in a strict interpretation of the Constitution

24 "The great rule of conduct for us in regard to foreign nations is, in extending our commercial relations to have with them as little *political* connection as possible."

—George Washington, Farewell Address, 1796

This statement helped establish the United States foreign policy called
1 containment
2 internationalism
3 imperialism
4 neutrality

25 The Monroe Doctrine declared that the United States would
1 prevent the establishment of new European colonies anywhere in the world
2 help colonies in North and South America adopt a democratic form of government
3 view European interference in the Americas as a threat to the national interest of the United States
4 prevent other nations from trading with South American nations

26 "Many, if not most, of our Indian wars have had their origin in broken promises and acts of injustice on our part."

The author of this statement would most likely agree that the history of United States treatment of Native Americans was primarily the result of
1 prejudice toward Native American religions
2 the desire for territorial expansion
3 a refusal of Native Americans to negotiate treaties
4 opposing economic and political systems

27 Which was the most important reason for the social mobility that existed in the English colonies of North America during the 18th century?
1 absence of racial prejudice among the colonists
2 existence of a strong cultural heritage
3 early emphasis on rapid industrialization
4 availability of land

28 Under mercantilism, the thirteen American colonies were expected to provide Great Britain with
1 finished American-manufactured goods
2 raw materials and markets for British products
3 officials to represent colonial interests in Parliament
4 laborers to work in British factories

29 Which feature of the United States government is based upon principles found in the Magna Carta and the Petition of Right?
1 the levying of a personal income tax
2 the power of Congress to declare war
3 the power of the House of Representatives to originate all revenue bills
4 Presidential veto power

30 In the 18th century, the British colonies in North America were most similar to Great Britain in their
1 common law legal system
2 countrywide established church
3 opportunities for social mobility
4 dependence upon manufacturing as the economic base

31 Which was most influential in making the idea of separation of church and state a part of the United States political tradition?
1 the democratic heritage of ancient Athens
2 the Roman Republic's principles of religious freedom
3 practices of European colonial governments
4 the diversity of the new nation's population

32 Which idea had a major influence on the authors of the Articles of Confederation?
1 A strong central government threatens the rights of the people and the states.
2 All of the people must be granted the right to vote.
3 Three branches of government are needed to protect liberty.
4 The central government must have the power to levy taxes and to control trade.

33 At the Constitutional Convention of 1787, the Three-fifths Compromise and the Great Compromise dealt with the issue of
1 amendments to the Constitution
2 women's rights
3 representation in Congress
4 the rights of the accused

34 In the 1780s, the publication of *The Federalist* papers was intended to
1 justify the American Revolution to the colonists
2 provide a plan of operation for the delegates to the Constitutional Convention
3 encourage ratification of the United States Constitution
4 express support for the election of George Washington to the Presidency

35 Under the United States Constitution, those powers not delegated to the federal government are
1 exercised only by state governors
2 concerned only with issues of taxation
3 reserved to the states or to the people
4 divided equally between the states and the national government

36 "The accumulation of all powers, legislative, executive, and judicial, in the same hands . . . may justly be pronounced the very definition of tyranny."

The writers of the United States Constitution intended to prevent the situation described in this quotation by
1 developing a system of checks and balances
2 relying on an electoral college
3 establishing political parties
4 including the implies powers clause

37 Only a small number of amendments have been added to the United States Constitution mainly because the
1 executive branch has feared a loss of power
2 Constitution has been broadly interpreted and applied
3 public has not objected to the government's use of its power
4 Constitution is clear in its original intent and seldom needs amending

38 "The privilege of the writ of *habeas corpus* shall not be suspended, unless when in cases of rebellion or invasion the public safety may require it."

This provision is evidence that the writers of the United States Constitution
1 wanted the President to have unlimited power during wartime
2 wanted to balance individual liberty with the needs of the nation
3 did not trust the common people to obey the laws
4 expected the American people to oppose most government policies

Four statements dealing with the formation of a new government are given below. Base your answers to questions 39 and 40 on these statements and on your knowledge of social studies.

Statement A: Each person must be able to voice his or her concerns on all issues that involve this new nation and bear the responsibility for the decisions made.

Statement B: The power of this new nation must rest in a strong, stable group that makes important decisions with the approval, but not the participation, of all.

Statement C: There must be several governments within one nation to ensure adequate voice and responsibility to all.

Statement D: Individuals must not allow their freedoms to be swallowed by an all-powerful government.

39 Which statement best shows the desire for safeguards such as those in the Bill of Rights?
1 A   3 C
2 B   4 D

40 Which statement best represents the ideas of federalism?
1 A   3 C
2 B   4 D

THEMATIC ESSAY 1

In developing your answers to the essay, be sure to keep these general definitions in mind:

(a) <u>discuss</u> means "to make observations about something using facts, reasoning, and argument; to present in some detail"

(b) <u>describe</u> means "to illustrate something in words or to tell about it"

(c) <u>evaluate</u> means "to examine and judge the significance, worth, or condition of; to determine the value of"

Directions

Write a well-organized essay that includes an introduction, several paragraphs addressing the task below, and a conclusion.

Theme: Government—Separation of Powers

The Constitution of the United States provides for three branches of government— legislative, executive, and judicial—with separate powers as well as a system of checks and balances among them. Issues in United States history have sometimes led to disagreements between government branches.

Task

From your study of United States history, identify two important issues which involved disagreements between branches of the government.

For each issue identified:

- Describe the disagreement between two branches of the federal government over the issue
- Discuss the historical circumstances surrounding the disagreement
- Discuss how the disagreement was resolved
- Discuss one immediate or one long-term effect of the disagreement on United States history

Suggestions

You may use any important issue in United States history which involved disagreement between branches of the government. Some suggestions you might wish to consider include: *Marbury* v. *Madison* (1803); Andrew Jackson's Indian removal policy (1830s); extension of slavery (1850s); impeachment of President Andrew Johnson (1868); ratification of the Treaty of Versailles (1919); Franklin D. Roosevelt's New Deal legislation (1930s); War Powers Act (1973); impeachment of President Bill Clinton (1998–1999)

You are *not* limited to these suggestions.

Guidelines

In your essay be sure to:

- Address all aspects of the *Task*
- Analyze, evaluate, or compare and/or contrast issues and events whenever possible
- Fully support the theme of the essay with relevant facts, examples, and details
- Write a well-developed essay that consistently demonstrates a logical and clear plan of organization
- Introduce the theme by establishing a framework that is beyond a simple restatement of the *Task*
- Conclude your essay with a strong summation of the theme

THEMATIC ESSAY 2

In developing your answers to the essay, be sure to keep these general definitions in mind:

(a) <u>discuss</u> means "to make observations about something using facts, reasoning, and argument; to present in some detail"

(b) <u>describe</u> means "to illustrate something in words or to tell about it"

(c) <u>evaluate</u> means "to examine and judge the significance, worth, or condition of; to determine the value of"

Directions

Write a well-organized essay that includes an introduction, several paragraphs addressing the task below, and a conclusion.

Theme: Constitutional Principles and the Supreme Court

Throughout United States history, Supreme Court decisions concerning conflicts over constitutional issues have had a long-term effect on the nation.

Task

From your study of United States history, identify two Supreme Court decisions concerning conflicts over constitutional issues which have had a long-term effect on the nation.

For each Supreme Court decision identified:
* State the conflict over a constitutional issue which the Supreme Court decision addressed.
* Discuss the historical circumstances surrounding the Supreme Court decision.
* Discuss the extent to which the Supreme Court decision resolved the conflict over the constitutional issue.
* Discuss the long term impact of the Supreme Court decision.

Suggestions

You may use any Supreme Court decision concerning conflicts over constitutional issues which has had a long-term effect on the nation. Some suggestions you might wish to consider include: *McCulloch* v. *Maryland* (federalism); *Marbury* v. *Madison* (role of the judiciary); *Gibbons* v. *Ogden* (commerce); *Scott* v. *Sandford* (separation of powers); *Schenck* v. *United States* (freedom of expression); *Gideon* v. *Wainwright* (right to legal counsel); *Heart of Atlanta Motel* v. *United States* (equal protection under the law).

You are *not* limited to these suggestions.

Guidelines

In your essay be sure to:
* Address all aspects of the *Task*
* Analyze, evaluate, or compare and/or contrast issues and events whenever possible
* Fully support the theme of the essay with relevant facts, examples, and details
* Write a well-developed essay that consistently demonstrates a logical and clear plan of organization
* Introduce the theme by establishing a framework that is beyond a simple restatement of the *Task*
* Conclude your essay with a strong summation of the theme

SECTION 2 The Constitution Tested: Nationalism and Sectionalism

⭐ **THE BIG IDEA**

In the early to mid-19th century,

- the North and South developed different patterns of life and philosophies of government.

- immigration and territorial expansion produced growth and change.

- reform movements attempted to correct many of the injustices of American society.

- sectional differences increased and led to war.

🔑 **KEY TERMS**

Industrial Revolution
potato famine
spoils system
Tariff of 1828
Indian Removal
Trail of Tears
abolition
Underground Railroad
Seneca Falls Convention
manifest destiny
Compromise of 1850
popular sovereignty
secede
Confederate States of America
Battle of Antietam
Battle of Gettysburg
Emancipation Proclamation

SECTION OVERVIEW

In the first half of the 1800s, the United States grew in size and population. The North, blessed with natural resources and a growing population, began industrializing. In the agricultural South, cotton became the dominant crop, and slavery became more firmly rooted in place.

As a new age of mass politics and reform dominated the 1830s and 1840s, tensions grew among the regions, pulling North and South apart. The southern states began to see their power and influence decreasing, and soon after the election of 1860, 11 southern states seceded from the Union. The Civil War that followed tested whether the nation and its Constitution would survive.

KEY THEMES AND CONCEPTS

Places and Regions How did the sectional differences between North and South lead to civil war?

Individuals, Groups, Institutions How did territorial expansion affect the lives of Native Americans, African Americans, and white Americans?

Constitutional Principles How did the United States become more democratic from 1820 to 1865?

Reform Movements What major reform movements were organized, and how successful were they?

KEY PEOPLE

Meriwether Lewis and William Clark
Andrew Jackson
Martin Van Buren

Abraham Lincoln
Ulysses S. Grant
Robert E. Lee

KEY SUPREME COURT CASES

Worcester v. *Georgia*

Scott v. *Sandford*

PART 1 TESTING THE CONSTITUTION: STRESS AND CRISIS

In the decades before the Civil War, some forces contributed to national unity, while others began splitting the nation apart.

FACTORS UNIFYING THE UNITED STATES

The factors that unified the United States include the first and second two-party systems, the market economy and interstate commerce, and decisions of the Marshall Court.

The first two-party system consisted of the Federalists and the Democratic-Republicans, parties that offered different political philosophies and proposals for action. The second two-party system developed in 1834, when the new Whig party opposed Andrew Jackson's party, now called the Democrats. Both parties ran campaigns that attracted interest and voters.

The development of a market economy and increased interstate commerce helped to stimulate economic growth nationwide. In the 1800s, revolutions in transportation and technology led to industrialization and urbanization. Specialization was possible because people could now purchase what they did not make or grow. Banks expanded to provide the capital for investment and the funds needed for exchange of goods and services. Southern and western crops were exchanged for northern manufactured goods.

Decisions of the Marshall Court also promoted national unity. These decisions helped to encourage a national economy by expanding interstate commerce and protecting the validity of contracts.

READING STRATEGY

Organizing Information
List three factors which unified the United States between 1789 and 1861.

1.

2.

3.

Nationalism and Sectionalism, 1820–1865

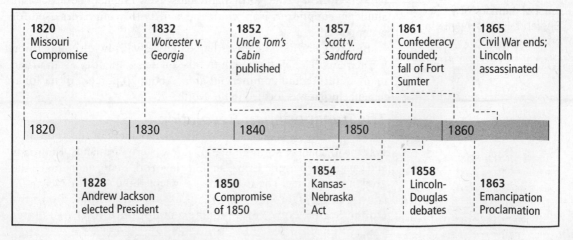

| 1820 Missouri Compromise | 1832 *Worcester* v. *Georgia* | 1852 *Uncle Tom's Cabin* published | 1857 *Scott* v. *Sandford* | 1861 Confederacy founded; fall of Fort Sumter | 1865 Civil War ends; Lincoln assassinated |

1820 — 1830 — 1840 — 1850 — 1860

| 1828 Andrew Jackson elected President | 1850 Compromise of 1850 | 1854 Kansas-Nebraska Act | 1858 Lincoln-Douglas debates | 1863 Emancipation Proclamation |

Comparing Household and Market Economies

	Household Economy	Market Economy
Producers	Household	Industries
Labor	Members of the household produce a variety of goods at home	Workers specialize in producing a certain product outside the home. They exchange their labor for cash.
Goods	Goods are made primarily to be used by the household	Goods are sold on the open market for a profit.

ANALYZING DOCUMENTS

Based on the table above and your knowledge of American history, answer the following questions.

- How were workers affected by the change to a market economy?
- How did the shift to a market economy promote nationalism?

KEY THEMES AND CONCEPTS

Factors of Production
The first successful textile mill was built in Rhode Island in 1793. By 1814, there were about 240 mills in the United States, most of them in New England, Pennsylvania, and New York.

The American System Supports a National Economy

Senator Henry Clay, supported by John Quincy Adams, designed a legislative program called the "American System." The program benefited the North, South, and West, and unified the nation by

- Establishing a better national transportation system to aid trade and national defense
- Setting the first protective tariff to encourage manufacturing and provide funds for improved transportation networks
- Creating a second national bank to promote the financial support necessary

URBAN AND INDUSTRIAL PATTERNS IN THE NORTH

The use of new technologies in manufacturing—particularly steam engines and machines to spin thread and weave cloth—gave rise to the **Industrial Revolution** in Great Britain during the 1700s. By the early 1800s, these new technologies reached the United States. Factory builders flocked to the North, particularly New England, because of its abundant supplies of iron, coal, and swiftly flowing rivers used for water power.

By 1860, northern factories had entered a worldwide competition for markets. The North began to take on a new identity as an urban manufacturing and commercial area. About 70 percent of national manufacturing was located in the North.

The Transportation Revolution

New technologies also stimulated the development of transportation systems to connect northern markets to western farmlands. Railroads and canals, such as the Erie Canal in New York State, encouraged the growth of industry. The Erie Canal connected the Atlantic Ocean (at New York City) through the Great Lakes to the vast interior of the United States. New York became a major port. Railroads later

The Transportation Revolution

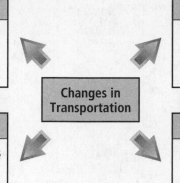

Steam Power
- In 1807, Robert Fulton's *Clermont* steams up the Hudson River.
- Steamships help farmers ship their goods to markets around the world.

Canals
- Erie Canal connects Lake Erie to New York City in 1825.
- By 1840, 3,000 miles of canals are in use.

Changes in Transportation

Roads
- By 1833, the Cumberland Road runs from Maryland to Ohio.
- New roads of stone and gravel help Americans move west.

Railroads
- In 1828, the B & O railroad line becomes nation's first railroad.
- By 1840, U.S. has more miles of railroad track than any other country in the world.

connected New York to other major cities and to the West. In the 19th century New York became the financial and industrial center of the nation.

The Factory System

By 1850, most American manufacturing was no longer done in homes and small shops, but instead in factories by workers using machines. This was called the factory system. The first mills were in New England, with the "model" Lowell mill the most well known. It employed white, teenage farm girls as its labor force, offering them an opportunity for financial independence. The girls lived at the mill in a highly regulated environment. Most planned to stay only a few years. Here the first work protests and strikes were organized against wage cuts.

By the 1840s and 1850s, the mills acquired a more permanent work force—Irish immigrant women who needed to work to help support their families. Working conditions were dictated by a strict routine. Twelve-hour days and six-day weeks were the routine. Gains made by the first union movements often were lost when demand for goods dropped in the fluctuating business cycle.

Urban Problems

By 1860, nine of the ten largest cities in the nation were in the North. After 1840, immigrants made up the majority of the population in some cities. The gap between rich and poor widened, as a distinctive rich upper class and poor working class developed in the cities. Private companies provided sanitation and water only to those who could afford to pay for these services. Cities were unsafe, and police forces did not begin to appear until the mid-1830s.

GEOGRAPHY IN HISTORY

Between 1800 and 1850, a substantial migration of people from the South to northern cities began.

- What caused this shift in population?
- What were the benefits of this migration? What problems were created?
- What was the impact on sectionalism?

♀ KEY THEMES AND ⊦ CONCEPTS

Change

Cities grew tremendously during the first half of the 19th century. The population of New York City (Manhattan only), for example, soared from about 33,000 in 1790 to 124,000 in 1820, and about 516,000 by 1850.

Urban and Rural Populations, 1800–1850

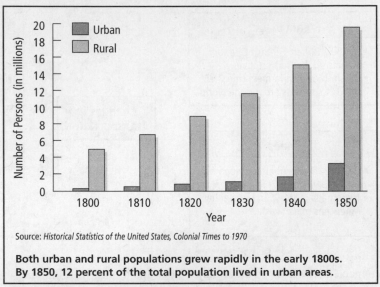

Source: *Historical Statistics of the United States, Colonial Times to 1970*

Both urban and rural populations grew rapidly in the early 1800s. By 1850, 12 percent of the total population lived in urban areas.

⚲ **KEY THEMES AND CONCEPTS**

Diversity

During the Industrial Revolution, as more work began to be done outside of the home or farm, gender-based work roles became even more sharply defined than before.

- How did the roles of working-class men and women differ?

- How did the roles of middle-class women and men differ?

Middle-Class and Working-Class Life in the North

Industrialization changed family life and gender roles. Previously, families worked together at home and on the farm, taking on different tasks according to gender. After industrialization, both working-class men and women worked, and their jobs also differed depending on their gender. More women worked as servants, more men in factories. The lives of middle-class men were often centered in the new business world, while middle-class women found their lives defined by the home. One of the few jobs considered proper for a single middle-class woman was teaching.

Working-class children usually had to make economic contributions to the family, but middle-class children did not. Childhood, as a specific stage in one's life, received new attention. Middle-class parents supported the growing movement for public schools.

Free African Americans in the North continued to face racism and legal restrictions. Public places remained segregated. African Americans also faced discrimination in hiring. Women were more likely than men to find permanent work, most often as household helpers.

Immigration

Until about 1850, most immigrants came from northern and western Europe, particularly Ireland and Germany. The Germans included many who were Jewish. Scandinavians, Dutch, Swiss, and English also immigrated. They generally settled in the North and West because of greater economic opportunities there.

REASONS FOR IMMIGRATION Between 1845 and 1850, millions of Irish people came to the United States because of the **potato famine,** a period of mass starvation caused by failure of the potato crop. Many Germans came seeking peace and stability after the failed 1848 Revolution in Germany. Most immigrants arrived in search of better economic opportunity.

AREAS OF SETTLEMENT The Irish tended to settle in northeastern cities. Some Germans also stayed in cities, but many moved west to start farms, as did many Scandinavian immigrants.

DIFFICULTIES THEY FACED Irish and German Catholic immigrants often faced hostility from native-born Americans, some of whom feared economic competition from the newcomers. Others resented the Catholic or Jewish immigrants at a time when the nation was mostly Protestant. Anti-immigrant feelings were so strong that a political party called the Know-Nothings was formed to ensure that native-born Americans received better treatment than immigrants. The party did very well in local elections in northern states.

CONTRIBUTIONS Immigrants made significant contributions to the growth of this nation. Irish workers helped build railroads and labored in factories. Germans and Scandinavians brought advanced farming techniques and new ideas on education, such as kindergarten.

KEY THEMES AND CONCEPTS

Immigration and Migration

- Where did the immigrants of the first half of the 19th century come from?
- Why did they come to the United States?
- How did their reasons for coming differ from those of earlier immigrants? How were they the same?
- What reaction did these new immigrants face from native-born Americans?

PATTERNS OF SOUTHERN DEVELOPMENT

In contrast to the North, the South remained agricultural. Its wealth remained invested in land and slaves, and its economy was dependent chiefly on its cotton crop grown with slave labor. The southern population grew slowly because it failed to attract immigrants.

Growth of a Cotton Economy

Most southern farms were small and were worked without slaves. Eli Whitney's 1793 invention of the cotton gin, which removed the seeds from cotton, transformed cotton into a successful commercial crop.

The profitability of cotton growing stimulated the growth of slavery. It also spurred westward migration of planters with their slaves, looking for new land on which to grow cotton. Planters moved first into the Old Southwest (Alabama and Mississippi), and later into Louisiana, Arkansas, and Texas.

In time, cotton made up half of all exports from the United States. However, the South's agricultural base kept it economically dependent on the North, both as a market for cotton and as a source of manufactured goods.

The Growth of "King Cotton"

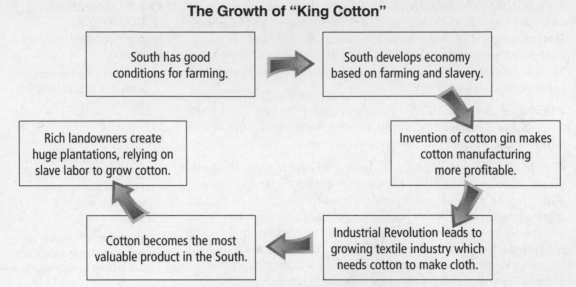

In the early 1800s, cotton became the South's most important crop.

ANALYZING DOCUMENTS

Examine the graphic organizer above. What caused the increased dependence on slavery in the first half of the 19th century?

READING STRATEGY

Reinforcing Main Ideas
What were some results of the expansion of slavery?

Men and Women on Plantations

Slaveholding men dominated political, economic, and social life in the South. Planters' wives and daughters were responsible for the domestic sphere. They managed the care, feeding, and clothing of their families and the slave families as well.

Life Under Slavery

Daily life for most slaves was very difficult. They had no control over their own lives or their children's lives, and they were at the mercy of the slaveholders or overseers. Slaves who worked as field hands often worked from dawn to sunset, while those who were house servants often worked long past sunset.

Slaves generally ate inexpensive food and wore rough clothing. Cabins housed one or two families. However, slaves were also a financial investment, and this affected their treatment. After the importing of slaves ended, the economic value of slaves increased, and their health care improved.

Slaves could not legally marry, but families remained central to the African American community. Parents instilled the importance of family in their children, while preparing them to cope with a life of slavery. Children were not educated and began work as young as eight years old. As planters moved westward in search of new lands for growing cotton, slave families were often tragically broken up.

The religious practices of slaves were a mixture of Protestant Christian and African elements. Music was an important part of worship services. Religion provided slaves with comfort and hope for salvation.

Resistance

Resistance against slavery took many forms. Most protests took the forms of escape, self-mutilation, sabotage, or work slowdowns. Although open rebellions were rare, they instilled fear within the white slaveholding society. There were several notable slave revolts.

- 1800: Gabriel Prosser's Conspiracy in Virginia led by urban skilled workers is discovered.
- 1822: Denmark Vesey's plans to lead a South Carolina revolt are uncovered.
- 1831: Nat Turner leads a revolt in Virginia.

Rebellions led southern lawmakers to pass increasingly strict laws to maintain slavery. Freeing slaves became more difficult, and teaching a slave to read became illegal.

THE AGE OF JACKSON

The rise of Andrew Jackson to the presidency in 1829 signaled a change in American politics. Born in Tennessee, Jackson was the first President from the West. He was also the first President elected on a wave of popular support, rather than through party politics.

The Rise of Mass Politics

By the mid-1820s, most states had dropped their property qualifications for voting. In 1828, the number of voters was three times larger than it had been in 1824. Andrew Jackson, a popular hero of the War of 1812, appealed to these new voters and won the popular vote.

Selecting a presidential candidate became more democratic in 1832. Candidates were chosen for the first time by a national nominating convention, rather than a few party leaders.

Rallies, slogans, and often vicious written attacks marked the advent of mass politics. "Secret" ballots became popular, but parties printed them in colors so it was easy to tell for whom a person voted. Only after the Civil War did the truly secret ballot come into general use.

The Spoils System and Civil Service Reform

During Jackson's presidency, a system developed in which government jobs were given to loyal supporters of the political party that won the election. This was called the **spoils system.**

By the 1880s, people began to demand that people should be given government jobs based on merit, rather than on party loyalty. During Chester Arthur's presidency, the **Pendleton Act of 1883** was passed, marking the beginning of civil service reform. The act required that competitive exams be used to hire certain government workers, and it set up a commission to administer the tests. It also banned the common practice of forcing government employees to give money to political parties.

ANALYZING DOCUMENTS

"This Fourth of July is yours, not mine. You may rejoice, I must mourn. . . . What, to the American slave, is your 4th of July? I answer; a day that reveals to him, more than any other days in the year, the gross injustice and cruelty to which he is the constant victim."

—Frederick Douglass, Rochester, New York, 1852

- Why does Douglass find it impossible to celebrate the Fourth of July?
- How did slavery contradict the civic values expressed in the Declaration of Independence?

PREPARING FOR THE EXAM

On the exam, you will need to understand how national elections work. Be sure you know the answers to the following questions.

- What is the difference between a popular and electoral vote?
- What happens when a candidate fails to win a majority of the electoral college?

The Presidency of Andrew Jackson

President Andrew Jackson

Fires over 2,000 government workers and replaces them with his own supporters

Vetoes more acts of Congress than all six previous Presidents combined

Closes Bank of the United States

Threatens to send huge army to South Carolina to force the state to obey tariff laws

Uses Indian Removal Act to force 100,000 Native Americans from their homelands

Jackson's forceful actions earned him both strong support and angry opposition throughout the country.

 KEY THEMES AND CONCEPTS

Economic Systems

- Why did the South believe that the North benefited from a protective tariff?

- How did this debate increase sectional conflict?

PREPARING FOR THE EXAM

After John C. Calhoun resigned the vice presidency, he was replaced by a New Yorker, Martin Van Buren, who later succeeded Jackson to the presidency.

- How is a President or Vice President replaced when one resigns? Review the case of Richard Nixon and Spiro Agnew.

GROWING SECTIONALISM

In the first half of the 1800s, growing feelings of sectionalism developed, pulling the sections of the nation apart.

States' Rights versus Federal Supremacy

Debate raged over how the balance of power between the states and the federal government should be achieved. From 1820 to 1865 this debate focused on nullification, protective tariffs and the spread of slavery.

THE TARIFF ISSUE Southern states opposed protective tariffs, which resulted in higher prices paid for imported manufactured goods. The agricultural South saw northern industries as the chief beneficiaries of such tariffs.

John C. Calhoun of South Carolina, Jackson's first Vice President, protested the **Tariff of 1828.** Calhoun argued that a state had the right to nullify, or declare void, any federal law that the state considered unconstitutional. This argument had first been advanced by Madison and Jefferson in the Virginia and Kentucky Resolutions.

In 1832 a new, lower tariff was passed, but South Carolina and Calhoun still protested. Calhoun resigned the vice presidency and led his state in nullifying the new tariff. President Andrew Jackson declared South Carolina's action treasonous.

The crisis resolved after Congress agreed to a gradual lowering of the tariff and passed a Force Bill authorizing the use of federal troops in South Carolina to collect the tariff. South Carolina withdrew its nullification of the tariff. However, South Carolina then nullified the Force Bill, indicating that the issue was not permanently settled.

The National Bank Issue—The Bank War

The Second Bank of the United States also provoked sectional differences. Most opposition to the bank came from southerners and westerners, who wanted a greater supply of money in circulation. They also resented the national bank's control over state banking.

In 1832, President Jackson vetoed a bill to recharter the bank. He then withdrew federal money from the bank, effectively killing it. To Jackson and many of his followers, the Second Bank of the United States had symbolized privilege and the power of special northern interests.

RELATIONS WITH NATIVE AMERICANS

As American settlers moved ever westward in the 1800s, conflict continued with the Native Americans who lived in these territories.

Native American Cultural Survival Strategies

Native Americans tried a variety of strategies to cope and retain their land and culture. In the early 1800s, two Shawnee brothers, Prophet and Tecumseh, tried to build a Pan-Indian Movement in the Old Northwest, but this movement died with Tecumseh in the War of 1812. Meanwhile, a Seneca named Handsome Lake urged the Iroquois to adopt a lifestyle based on temperance, education, farming, and peace. This lifestyle became known as cultural revitalization.

In 1813, Creeks attacked settlers in Georgia and Alabama in a series of raids, but in 1814, they were defeated at Horseshoe Bend, Alabama. The Southwest was now open to settlement.

The Cherokee attempted to survive and retain their culture through cultural adaptation, combining elements of Native American and European culture including a written constitution. This strategy, however, did not save them.

The Removal Policy

The federal government used a combination of treaties and force to move Indians westward. The treaties were worthless, because Native Americans were forced repeatedly to give up their land that had been guaranteed by treaty.

In the 1830s, President Andrew Jackson began his policy of **Indian removal**—forcing all Native Americans to move west of the Mississippi. In 1832, the Cherokee went to court to prevent Georgia from taking their land. In *Worcester* v. *Georgia*, Chief Justice John Marshall ruled that Georgia had no authority over Cherokee territory, but Georgia simply ignored the ruling. In 1838, the U.S. Army forced the Cherokee to leave in a forced march known as the **Trail of Tears.**

The Seminole of Florida were also faced with removal. A group fought the effort in the Second Seminole War. Many remained in Florida. By the 1840s, however, only scattered groups of Native Americans still lived in the East.

ANALYZING DOCUMENTS

"Tho oonocquences of a speedy removal will be important. . . . It will separate the Indians from immediate contact with settlements of whites; . . . and perhaps cause them . . . to cast off their savage habits and become an interesting, civilized, and Christian community."

—President Andrew Jackson, 1830

• What does this quote reveal about Jackson's attitude toward Native Americans?

ANALYZING DOCUMENTS

"We wish to remain on the land of our fathers. We have a perfect and original right to remain without interruption."

—Cherokee public appeal, July 17, 1830

• What does this quote reveal about how the Cherokee viewed their possession of the land?

Native American Land Transfer Before 1850

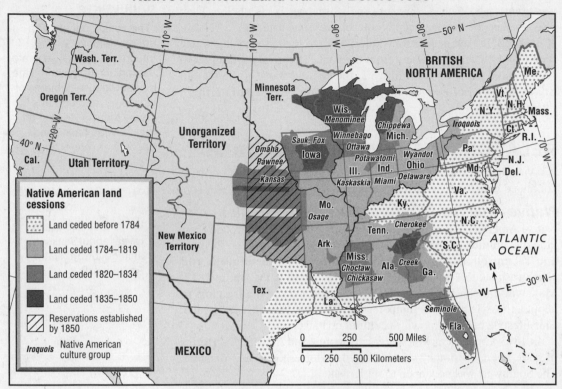

ANALYZING DOCUMENTS

Compare the map above with the map on page 92.

• How does the map above relate to the territorial expansion of the United States?

THE AMERICAN REFORM TRADITION

In the early 1800s, great changes affected the way people lived and interacted with each other. The Industrial Revolution, urbanization, growth in immigration, westward expansion, and the cotton-based southern economy created opportunities as well as serious problems.

The Second Great Awakening, a religious revival movement, motivated reform with its emphasis on self-reliance, on one's ability to affect one's future and to improve the world. The movement called for self-improvement and for joining to fight forces of evil. The religious feelings that drove reform were reinforced by the republican political belief in civic virtue—that a good citizen acts for the common good.

Reform Movements

Many areas of American life inspired reform movements, including education and care of the mentally ill.

PUBLIC SCHOOLS Reformers recognized that if the people were to govern, they needed to be educated. Under the leadership of Horace Mann, Massachusetts led the 19th-century drive for public education. Mann believed that every human being had the right to an education, and he developed an educational system with grade levels and teacher training. His ideas spread rapidly. By 1860, most people had at least an elementary education in all regions but the South. Educational opportunities for girls and young women also expanded.

CARE OF THE MENTALLY ILL In the early 1800s, most mentally ill people were kept locked up in prisons. In the 1840s, a Massachusetts reformer named Dorothea Dix studied the poor treatment of the mentally ill and reported her findings to the state legislature, which authorized funds for state mental hospitals. Dix later worked with several other states that followed the example of Massachusetts.

OTHER REFORMS Reformers also pushed for the creation of prisons, hospitals, orphanages, and institutions to care for physically disabled people. In addition, a strong temperance movement organized to eliminate alcohol consumption.

Abolition

In the 1820s, the **abolition** (or antislavery) movement grew as cotton production became more profitable and slavery spread. The abolition movement attracted a wide variety of activists, including African Americans such as Frederick Douglass, Harriet Tubman, and Sojourner Truth, and white activists such as Angelina and Sarah Grimké and William Lloyd Garrison.

Abolitionists organized the **Underground Railroad,** a series of safe houses where escaping slaves could rest safely as they made their way north and into Canada. Harriet Tubman, who made 19 trips to escort runaways, was a famous leader of the Underground Railroad.

Although the abolition movement was stronger in the North than in the South, not all northerners supported it. Some northern merchants feared that the abolition movement would further sour relations between North and South and harm trade. White workers feared the competition from escaped or freed slaves willing to work for lower wages.

Women's Rights

By the 1830s, reform-minded women recognized that they faced discrimination, even within their own organizations. For example, the women delegates attending the 1840 World Anti-Slavery Convention were not allowed, after much debate, to participate in the convention.

The women's rights movement began officially in 1848, when Elizabeth Cady Stanton and Lucretia Mott organized the **Women's Rights Convention** in **Seneca Falls,** New York. There, the **Declaration of Sentiments** was issued. The first goal of this chiefly middle class movement was to end legal inequalities faced by married women. At this time, a husband had the legal right to control his wife's property, earnings, and children.

In 1853, Susan B. Anthony joined Stanton in the drive for women's rights. By the 1850s, the women's rights movement began focusing on winning the vote for women. Women's right to vote in national elections was not won until 1920.

ANALYZING DOCUMENTS

"On this subject, I do not wish to think, or speak, or write, with moderation. No!, no! Tell a man whose house is on fire, to give a moderate alarm; . . . tell the mother to gradually extricate [pull out] her babe from the fire into which it has fallen;—but urge me not to use moderation in a cause like the present. I am in earnest . . .—I will not retreat a single inch—AND I WILL BE HEARD."

　　—William Lloyd Garrison, *The Liberator,* 1831

- Based on this quote, how would you characterize Garrison's view of how slavery should be abolished?

ANALYZING DOCUMENTS

"We hold these truths to be self-evident: that all men and women are created equal. . . . The history of mankind is a history of repeated injuries and usurpations [seizure of power] on the part of man toward woman, . . . [to establish] absolute tyranny over her. . . ."

　　— Declaration of Sentiments, 1848

This document was written by Elizabeth Cady Stanton and adopted at the Seneca Falls Woman's Rights Convention.

- Which phrase did Stanton borrow from the Declaration of Independence? Why?

Study the map below and review the physical geography of the United States from Unit 1. Then answer the following questions.

- What was the effect of the Appalachian and the Rocky Mountains on settlement?

- Why were the Great Plains the last region to be settled?

- How did the arid conditions affect settlement of parts of the Mexican Cession?

TERRITORIAL EXPANSION

From 1803 to 1853, the United States expanded to its present continental boundaries.

Manifest Destiny

Many Americans believed in **Manifest Destiny,** the conviction that the United States had a divine mission to expand in order to spread the ideals of freedom and democracy. What Americans saw as manifest destiny was viewed quite differently by the Native American and Mexican peoples, who were in possession of these western lands. Expansion increased national pride, but by raising serious questions about slavery, also contributed to growing sectional tensions.

People Moving Westward

The first Americans to move westward were explorers, naturalists, trappers, traders, and missionaries. These were followed by trailblazers and settlers who traveled westward along routes such as the Santa Fe and the Oregon Trails. Mormons, led by Brigham Young, settled at the Great Salt Lake in 1846. In order to escape religious persecution, they selected a spot which placed them far from others. Most settlers chose

Territorial Expansion of the United States and Other Acquisitions

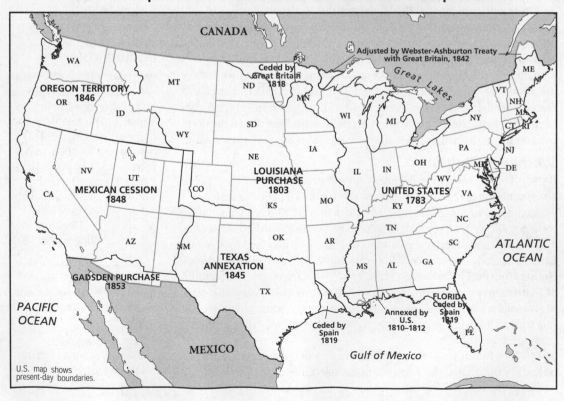

U.S. map shows present-day boundaries.

more prosperous lands in the far West, leaving the flat but dry and treeless Great Plains to be settled only after the 1860s.

Lands Acquired Between 1783–1853

By 1853, the continental United States had expanded to its present boundaries. This expansion took place in several stages.

LOUISIANA PURCHASE (1803) This huge territory was acquired from France for $15 million. President Jefferson sent Meriwether Lewis and William Clark to explore this land in 1803. The information and maps they brought back contributed to expansion into this territory.

FLORIDA (1819) This territory was acquired by treaty from Spain, satisfying southern expansionists. In the Adams-Onís Treaty, Spain also gave up its claims to the Pacific Northwest in return for the United States giving up its claims to Texas.

TEXAS (1845) The United States acquired Texas and what is now parts of New Mexico, Oklahoma, Colorado, Wyoming, and Kansas from Mexico by annexation. The Spanish had long established missions and settlements in Texas. After Mexico declared its independence from Spain in 1821, southern slaveholders and other American settlers moved into Texas. In 1836, the settlers declared independence from Mexico and created the Republic of Texas. Soon, Texas requested admission to the Union, and in 1845, Texas joined as a slave state.

OREGON COUNTRY (1846) What is now Oregon, Washington, Idaho, and parts of Montana and Wyoming, was gained from Great Britain in a compromise that continued the northern border set at the 49th parallel all the way to the coast.

MEXICAN CESSION (1848) What is now California, Nevada, Utah, Arizona, and parts of New Mexico, Colorado, and Wyoming became part of the United States by the Treaty of Guadalupe Hidalgo, which ended the Mexican War (1846–1848). The Mexican War erupted in part because of Mexican objections to the Texas annexation and a dispute over the border between Texas and Mexico. President James Polk's outspoken desires to acquire California and the Southwest made it difficult to ease tensions with Mexico. After war broke out, national opinion was divided. Expansionists welcomed an opportunity to acquire more land. Northerners feared the future addition of more slave states. Some, such as Abraham Lincoln, saw it as a "war of conquest," others saw it as fulfilling "*Manifest Destiny*."

GADSDEN PURCHASE (1853) This piece of land in southern Arizona and New Mexico was purchased from Mexico as a possible railroad route.

ANALYZING DOCUMENTS

In the 1840s, songs, writings, and slogans expressed responses to **Manifest Destiny.** Connect each example below to Manifest Destiny.

- James Polk: Fifty-four forty or fight!
- California: The Bear Republic
- Henry D. Thoreau: *Civil Disobedience*
- U.S. Marines: From the halls of Montezuma. . .

READING STRATEGY

Organizing Information
Below are eight events that led to the Civil War. Place them in order of occurrence.

- Compromise of 1850
- Confederacy formed
- *Dred Scott* decision
- John Brown's raid
- Kansas-Nebraska Act
- Lincoln elected President
- Missouri Compromise
- South Carolina secedes

⚷ KEY THEMES AND CONCEPTS

Government
Compromise is essential to democratic government.

- How did the Missouri Compromise postpone the clash between North and South?

⚷ KEY THEMES AND CONCEPTS

Constitutional Principles
In 1836, southern members of Congress succeeded in passing the so-called gag rule, which prohibited the reading of any antislavery petitions in the House. The gag rule stayed in place for eight years.

- Why might abolitionists point to the gag rule as an example of how slavery threatened the rights of all Americans?

PART 2   THE CONSTITUTION IN JEOPARDY: THE AMERICAN CIVIL WAR

Differences between the North and the South finally threatened the existence of the nation. The debate that followed on how slavery should be treated in new lands centered on constitutional issues.

GREAT CONSTITUTIONAL DEBATES: THE SLAVERY ISSUE

Until the Civil War, the Constitution had recognized and protected slavery in three ways: the Three-Fifths Compromise, the provision that Congress could not end the importing of slaves before 1808, and the fugitive slave clause. These compromises had been made in order to encourage southern states to ratify the Constitution. With the expansion of American territory in the West, controversy brewed over whether these new territories should allow slavery or not.

Northern Views

Northerners who sought to stop the spread of slavery argued that the Congress had power over the territories. The Northwest Ordinance had banned slavery in the territory north of the Ohio River, while the **Missouri Compromise** of 1820 had banned slavery in the part of the Louisiana Purchase north of 36°30' N latitude. These precedents (or previous acts), they argued, showed that Congress had the power to ban slavery in new territories.

Southern Views

Southerners argued that the Constitutional recognition and protection of slavery meant that Congress did not have the authority to prevent the extension of slavery into the territories. They also argued that Congress had a constitutional duty to protect slavery where it already existed in the South.

Differences between North and South

	Northern States	Southern States
Population	21.5 million	9 million
Number of Factories	110,100	20,600
Miles of Railroad	21,700	9,000
Bank Deposits	$207 million	$47 million
Cotton Production	4 thousand bales	5 million bales

During the 1850s, differences between the North and South continued to grow.

The Compromise of 1850

Until 1850, there were an equal number of slave and free states in the Union. The South thus maintained a balance of power in the Senate. The admission of California as a free state in 1850 threatened to upset this balance.

The issue of slavery in the new territories was settled for a brief time by the **Compromise of 1850,** which included three key provisions:

1. California entered the Union as a free state.
2. The **Fugitive Slave Law** required that escaped slaves be returned to their owners.
3. **Popular sovereignty,** or a vote of the people living in the territory, would determine whether a territory in the Mexican Cession was to be slave or free.

The Compromise of 1850 pleased almost no one. Northerners ignored the Fugitive Slave Law. The popular sovereignty provision was unclear. Would the vote to make a territory slave or free be held at the time the territory was settled or when it applied to become a state? This uncertainty almost certainly ensured future conflict.

The Kansas-Nebraska Act

In 1820, the **Missouri Compromise** had prohibited slavery in the lands that made up Kansas and Nebraska. The Kansas-Nebraska Act of 1854 overturned the Missouri Compromise by allowing those territories to decide the question of slavery by popular sovereignty.

When pro- and antislavery people rushed into Kansas to vote on the issue, violence erupted, known as **Bleeding Kansas**. A pro-slavery mob destroyed homes, stores, and an antislavery newspaper office in Lawrence, Kansas. John Brown and an antislavery group killed pro-slavery settlers at Pottawatomie Creek. Violence even erupted in the U.S. Senate, where the southern congressman Preston Brooks beat abolitionist Senator Charles Sumner because of remarks made in a Sumner speech.

Rise of the Republican Party

Reactions to the Kansas-Nebraska Act led to changes in the political party system. One major party, the Whigs, split into Northern and Southern wings and soon died out. The Democrats were seriously weakened in the North. A new party, the Republicans, was founded to oppose the spread of slavery. It was a sectional rather than a national party and proclaimed a platform of "Free Soil, Free Labor, Free Men."

The Dred Scott Case

In 1857 the Supreme Court gave its ruling on the question of slavery in the territories in *Dred Scott* v. *Sandford*. The ruling held that no African Americans, slave or free, were citizens, and therefore, they were not entitled to constitutional protection. The ruling also held that the

READING STRATEGY

Reinforcing Main Ideas
Why did the Compromise of 1850 satisfy neither side?

KEY THEMES AND CONCEPTS

Cultural and Intellectual Life
Harriet Beecher Stowe is said to have been motivated to write *Uncle Tom's Cabin* by the passage of the Fugitive Slave Law. A bestseller, the book influenced views about slavery.

ANALYZING DOCUMENTS

"It is the opinion of the Court that the Act of Congress which prohibited a citizen from holding and owning property of this kind in the territory of the United States north of the line . . ., is not warranted by the Constitution, and is therefore void. . . ."
—*Dred Scott* v. *Sanford,*
1857

- What is meant by "property of this kind"?
- What act of Congress did this decision declare unconstitutional?
- Did the decision accelerate the march toward Civil War? Did it make the war inevitable? Why or why not?

Missouri Compromise was unconstitutional because Congress could not deprive people of their right to property—slaves—by banning slavery in any territory.

The Lincoln-Douglas Debates

In Illinois in 1858, Abraham Lincoln, a Republican, challenged the well-known senator Stephen A. Douglas, author of the Kansas-Nebraska Act, in the campaign for U.S. Senate. A series of debates were held, then the Illinois legislature reelected Douglas to the Senate. The Lincoln-Douglas debates weakened Douglas in the South while making Lincoln a national political figure unacceptable to the South because of his position against the extension of slavery.

John Brown's Raid at Harper's Ferry

In 1859, John Brown led a small group in a raid against a federal arsenal in what is now West Virginia. His plan was to seize weapons and lead a slave uprising. Although he was unsuccessful and was later executed for treason, he became a Northern hero. The incident increased Southern distrust of the North.

The Election of 1860

The election of 1860 showed clearly how divided the United States had become. The only remaining national party, the Democratic party, split between North and South with each wing running a candidate. Abraham Lincoln, the first Republican to be elected President, received only 39 percent of the popular vote.

The election of a Northerner who opposed the extension of slavery drove some Southerners to threaten secession. To prevent secession, Senator John Crittenden of Kentucky proposed the Crittenden Compromise, which would have divided the nation, slave versus free territory, all the way to California, along the Missouri Compromise line. The compromise was defeated because congressional Republicans would not support it. Some did not believe that the South would go through with their threats to leave the Union.

The Secession Crisis

In December 1860, South Carolina decided to **secede** from, or leave, the Union. By February 1861, six more southern states seceded and with South Carolina formed the **Confederate States of America.**

President James Buchanan took no action to stop them. He stated that neither he nor Congress had the power to preserve the Union because it "rests upon public opinion and can never be cemented by the blood of its citizens shed in war." Lincoln disagreed and denied that states could secede. In his First Inaugural Address in March 1861, Lincoln stated that "in view of the Constitution and the law, the Union is unbroken."

PREPARING FOR THE EXAM

On the exam, you will need to understand how legislators are elected and how that has changed over time. Why did the Illinois legislature, not the people of Illinois, vote in this Senate election? Check your constitutional amendments!

TURNING POINT

The Election of 1860 can be considered a turning point in United States history. Examine the chart below and answer the question that follows.

Election of 1860

Popular Vote

Candidate	Popular Vote	% of Popular Vote
Lincoln	1,865,593	39.5
Douglas	1,382,713	29.5
Breckinridge	848,356	18
Bell	592,906	13

Electoral Vote

Candidate	Electoral Vote	% of Electoral Vote
Lincoln	180	59
Douglas	12	4
Breckinridge	72	24
Bell	39	13

Why did southern states respond to the election of 1860 by seceding from the Union?

The Union and the Confederacy, 1861

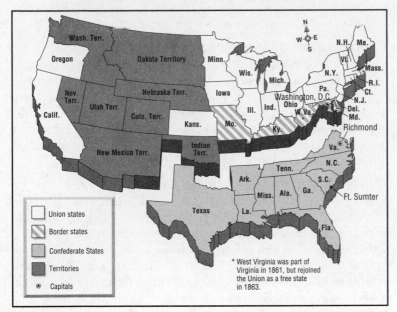

Legend:
- Union states
- Border states
- Confederate States
- Territories
- ⊛ Capitals

* West Virginia was part of Virginia in 1861, but rejoined the Union as a free state in 1863.

ANALYZING DOCUMENTS

Review the chart on page 94 and the map on this page to analyze the relative positions of the North and South at the start of the Civil War.

- What advantages did the South have at the beginning of the Civil War? What advantages did the North have?

- From your review and this data, how can the differences in the two areas best be explained?

- What advantages did each side have that are not seen on either the chart or the map?

- Why does the map show the border states differently? With which side did these states align?

THE CIVIL WAR

Lincoln's policy was to oppose secession but to take no military action until the South started fighting. In April 1861, the South seized Fort Sumter in Charleston Harbor, South Carolina. Lincoln called for troops to put down the rebellion. Four more southern states, including Virginia, seceded. The Civil War had begun.

Great Constitutional Debates: Preservation of the Union

Once a state had entered the United States, did it have the right to leave? From the Southern view, the South had the right to secede because the United States had not protected Southern rights. (In this case, only the rights of the white population were being considered.) Lincoln took the position that states could not leave the Union. No minority could act to destroy the nation and its government.

Lincoln's Aims and Actions

From the beginning of the secession crisis, Lincoln's goal was to preserve the Union. He took bold executive action to achieve this aim. He called out state militias, increased the size of the Navy, ordered a naval blockade of the South, and approved funds for military expenses while Congress was not in session. Congress later gave its approval of these actions.

Lincoln also ordered the arrest of Southern sympathizers in Maryland and Delaware to prevent secession of those states. Lincoln suspended the **writ of *habeas corpus*** in areas not in rebellion. He later won congressional approval for this step. He also declared martial law, which led to the arrests of thousands for suspected disloyalty.

Constitutional Questions

Lincoln's actions broadened the power of the executive. They also raised troubling questions: Were such actions constitutional? Did they fall within the scope of the President's war powers, or were they dictatorial? Did the fact that some Northerners sympathized with the rebelling South justify the limiting of their civil rights? Did Lincoln set precedents for expanded executive action that later Presidents might use in more questionable circumstances?

Other Government Policies During the War

In order to help to finance the Civil War, a new federal banking system was created, establishing a national currency. The currency was backed by government bonds and issued by the new federal banks.

In 1862, the Congress passed three major acts to facilitate economic growth after the war ended. The Homestead Act provided for the settlement of western lands. The Morrill Land Grant Act gave public lands to states and territories to found agriculture, mechanical arts, and military science colleges. Congress also authorized the building of the transcontinental railroad, financed with public land grants and cash loans. Government commitment to western settlement was strong.

Military Strategy

The Confederate war strategy was to attack the Union army repeatedly, inflicting casualties and wearing it down until it lost the will to fight. The Confederacy hoped to gain aid and diplomatic recognition from Great Britain and France, two nations that relied on southern cotton. Neither strategy was successful.

The Union relied on its superior resources and technology. Union ships blockaded southern ports, preventing the Confederacy from importing food and military supplies. In 1863, General Ulysses S. Grant led the victorious Union forces at Vicksburg, Mississippi, giving the North control of the Mississippi and dividing the South. In 1864, Lincoln appointed Grant to head the Union forces. As the new commander, Grant's strategy was to destroy not only the Confederate army but also all southern resources that supported the war effort.

The Human Cost

The Civil War was the bloodiest war the United States has ever known. Some 600,000 Americans lost their lives as new military technologies and old diseases struck down soldiers and civilians. Families along the border between the Union and the Confederacy were particularly devastated, as family members fought on opposite sides.

The worst single day of the war occurred in 1862 at the **Battle of Antietam** in Maryland, where the Southern commander

General Robert E. Lee attempted to invade Maryland. Some 5,000 people died and more than 17,000 were wounded. In 1863, the three-day **Battle of Gettysburg** in Pennsylvania was the most costly battle of the war, leaving more than 50,000 dead and wounded on both sides.

The Emancipation Proclamation

In 1863, Lincoln's **Emancipation Proclamation** freed all slaves in those areas still in rebellion against the Union. The Proclamation had largely a symbolic value. The Union could not enforce it, because it freed slaves only in areas under Confederate control.

Although African Americans had fought for the Union since the start of the war, after the Proclamation, their numbers in the Union military swelled. In all, more than 185,000 enlisted.

The Proclamation drew both criticism and praise. Some attacked it for freeing slaves only where the government could not enforce the decree, while permitting slavery where it could act. On the other hand, the Proclamation lessened the chances of European aid to the South. Most of all, it added a new humanitarian objective to the war.

The Gettysburg Address

In November 1863, Lincoln dedicated the Union military cemetery at Gettsyburg, just a few months after the battle there. His short speech summarized the meaning of the Civil War.

The End of the War

The Battle of Gettysburg was the last time that the South attempted to invade the North. From then on, Lee fought a defensive war. The war ended in 1865 with Lee's surrender at Appomattox Court House.

The Civil War on the Home Front

In the North, production in factories and on farms increased during the Civil War. Women and African Americans took more factory jobs to replace the white men who had gone to war. Women also ran the farms and raised money to help the wounded soldiers.

On both sides, women served as nurses, even in field hospitals. However, medicine was seen as a male profession, and even Clara Barton, founder of the American Red Cross, met with resistance.

The South lacked industrial support and a good transportation network. Furthermore, the Confederate government, led by Jefferson Davis, met opposition when calling for a military draft or attempting to collect food for the army.

In the South, the Northern blockade of southern ports led to food shortages. Inflation soared. As in the North, women took over the work on the farms. On the plantations, they supervised the slaves. They also worked as government clerks and as teachers.

By the end of the Civil War, the South was devastated. The war left a legacy of bitterness and new problems. The dead on both sides included Lincoln himself, assassinated within days of the war's end.

ANALYZING DOCUMENTS

"Four score and seven years ago our fathers brought forth on this continent, a new nation, conceived in Liberty, and dedicated to the proposition that all men are created equal.

"Now we are engaged in a great civil war, testing whether that nation, or any nation so conceived and so dedicated, can long endure. We are met on a great bat-tle-field of that war. We have come to dedicate a portion of that field, as a final resting place for those who here gave their lives that the nation might live. . . .

"It is . . . for us to be here dedicated to the great task remaining before us— . . . that we here highly resolve that these dead shall not have died in vain—that this nation, under God, shall have a new birth of free-dom—and that government of the people, by the people, for the people, shall not per-ish from the earth."

—Abraham Lincoln, The Gettysburg Address

- For what event did Lincoln make the Gettysburg Address?

- Why did Lincoln refer back to the founding of the United States?

- In Lincoln's view, what was the purpose of the Civil War?

Questions for Regents Practice

For online Questions for Regents Practice,
visit the Prentice Hall Web site at www.phschool.com.

MULTIPLE CHOICE

Directions

Review the Test-Taking Strategies section of this book. Then answer the following questions, drawn from actual Regents examinations. Each question is followed by four choices. Read each question carefully. Decide which choice is the correct answer. Then on a separate piece of paper, mark your answer for each question.

1   Base your answer to question 1 on the cartoon below and on your knowledge of social studies.

"King Andrew the First"

The cartoonist is most clearly accusing President Jackson of which behavior?

1   involving the United States in European wars

2   exceeding the constitutional limits of his authority

3   using government funds to support an extravagant lifestyle

4   violating the Federal Constitution by granting titles of nobility

2   Which was most characteristic of the early factory systems in the United States?

1   Factories provided workers with a voice in management and employment conditions.

2   Women and children were not allowed to work in factories.

3   Unsafe working conditions were common.

4   Many workers had the opportunity to move up in social class.

Base your answers to questions 3 and 4 on the quotation below and on your knowledge of social studies.

"How can an industrialized Northeast, a plantation South, and a small farms West peacefully share the same nation?"

3 This quotation best describes the United States during which time period?
   1 Federal Era (1789–1800)
   2 Pre-Civil War (1820–1860)
   3 Era of Overseas Expansion (1898–1914)
   4 Great Depression of the 1930s

4 Which term can be most accurately applied to the situation in the quotation?
   1 sectionalism
   2 protectionism
   3 liberalism
   4 militarism

5 Which was most responsible for the rapid economic growth of New York City during the 19th century?
   1 presence of the New York Stock Exchange
   2 rise of domestic and foreign commerce
   3 rise of urban mass transportation
   4 migration of blacks from the rural South

6 In the United States, the belief in manifest destiny was most similar to later demands for
   1 restrictions on immigration
   2 a laissez-faire economic policy
   3 regulation of interstate commerce
   4 imperialistic expansion

7 In United States history, which characteristic was common to the War of 1812, the Mexican War, and the Spanish-American War?
   1 They were fought to promote democratic principles.
   2 Their aim was expansion of United States self-interest.
   3 They reflected conditions in Western Europe.
   4 They were necessary to protect national security.

Base your answers to questions 8 and 9 on your knowledge of social studies and on the quotation below, from a speech made by a United States Senator in 1847.

"What is the territory, Mr. President, which you propose to wrest from Mexico? It is consecrated to the heart of the Mexican by many a well-fought battle with his old Castilian master. His Bunker Hills, and Saratogas, and Yorktowns are there and shall he surrender that consecrated home of his affection to the Anglo-Saxon invaders? What do we want with it? The Senator from Michigan says he must have this. Why, my Christian brother, on what principle of justice?"

8 The parallel between the United States and Mexico which the Senator indicated in his speech was that both
   1 claimed Oregon
   2 disliked England
   3 had a revolutionary heritage
   4 were overcrowded

9 With which position would the speaker most likely have agreed?
   1 The United States should pressure Britain out of Oregon.
   2 The pursuit of a policy of manifest destiny is unfair.
   3 The annexation of Texas is justified because most of its population are settlers from the United States.
   4 The extension of United States democracy to parts of Mexico is divinely intended.

10 Laws requiring individuals to pass civil service examinations to obtain government jobs were enacted to
   1 eliminate patronage and corruption in government hiring
   2 allow the government to compete with private industry for employees
   3 support the development of public employee labor unions
   4 encourage the growth of local political parties

11 During the 19th century, the expansion of the population of the United States affected the lives of the Native Americans in that most Indians
  1 moved to urban areas in large numbers
  2 sought to form alliances with other minority groups
  3 were forced to move westward
  4 chose to adopt the culture of the settlers

12 The reason for ending the importation of enslaved persons in the United States after 1807 was the
  1 success of the American colonial revolution against Britain
  2 rapid industrialization of the South
  3 replacement of slave labor by immigrant workers from eastern Europe
  4 passage of legislation that forbid the practice

13 The activities of Nat Turner and Denmark Vesey in the United States indicated that
  1 slave revolts occurred in the South
  2 cotton was a profitable crop
  3 political rivalries existed in the North
  4 slavery could be extended into the territories

14 A similarity between the pre-Civil War abolitionist movement and the Progressive movement is that both
  1 were mainly concerned with improving the status of African Americans
  2 worked to reduce income taxes
  3 contributed directly to the start of a major war
  4 sought to improve the conditions of poor or oppressed peoples

15 The main goal of the Seneca Falls Convention (1848) was to
  1 obtain equal rights for women
  2 make the public aware of environmental problems
  3 correct the abuses of big business
  4 organize the first labor union in the United States

16 "To the Honorable Senate and House of Representatives in Congress Assembled: We the undersigned, citizens of the United States, but deprived of some of the privileges and immunities of citizens, among which is the right to vote, beg leave to submit the following Resolution: . . ."

  —Susan B. Anthony, Elizabeth Cady Stanton (1873)

  This statement is an example of a citizen's constitutional right to
  1 petition for a redress of grievances
  2 seek election to public office
  3 receive a speedy, public trial
  4 assemble peacefully

Base your answers to questions 17 and 18 on this excerpt from a resolution adopted at the Seneca Falls Convention in 1848 and on your knowledge of social studies.

  "We hold these truths to be self-evident: that all men and women are created equal; that they are endowed by their Creator with certain inalienable rights; that among these are life, liberty, and the pursuit of happiness. . . ."

17 Which document served as the most direct model for this resolution?
  1 Articles of Confederation
  2 Emancipation Proclamation
  3 United States Constitution
  4 Declaration of Independence

18 The philosophy stated in this resolution was based on the
  1 idea of rugged individualism
  2 natural rights theory
  3 theory of separation of powers
  4 "necessary and proper" clause of the United States Constitution

19 **"Compromise Enables Maine and Missouri to Enter Union" (1820)**

"California Admitted to Union as Free State" (1850)

"Kansas-Nebraska Act Sets Up Popular Sovereignty" (1854)

Which issue is reflected in these headlines?
1 enactment of protective tariffs
2 extension of slavery
3 voting rights for minorities
4 universal public education

20 "By the 1850s, the Constitution, originally framed as an instrument of national unity, had become a source of national discord."

This quotation suggests that
1 vast differences of opinion existed over the issue of States rights
2 the federal government had become more interested in foreign affairs than in domestic problems
3 the Constitution had no provisions for governing new territories
4 the southern States continued to import slaves

21 Which event was the immediate cause of the secession of several southern states from the Union in 1860?
1 the Dred Scott decision, which declared that all prior compromises on the extension of slavery into territories were unconstitutional
2 the Missouri Compromise, which kept an even balance between the number of free and slave states
3 the raid on the federal arsenal at Harper's Ferry, which was led by the militant abolitionist John Brown
4 the election of President Abraham Lincoln, who opposed the spread of slavery into the territories

22 "You have no oath registered in heaven to destroy the government, while I shall have the most solemn one to 'preserve, protect, and defend' it."

—Abraham Lincoln, Inaugural Address, 1861

When President Abraham Lincoln made this statement, he indicated his commitment to
1 allow the southern states to leave the Union
2 defend the institution of slavery throughout the United States
3 take strong action to maintain the Union
4 make fundamental changes in the United States government

23 "Restriction of free thought and free speech is the most dangerous of all subversions. It is the one un-American act that could easily defeat us."

In the United States, the danger identified in this statement was the greatest during the
1 Age of Jackson
2 Civil War
3 Spanish-American War
4 New Deal Era in the 1930s

24 A major result of the Civil War was that the
1 economic system of the South came to dominate the United States economy
2 federal government's power over the states was strengthened
3 members of Congress from southern states gained control of the legislative branch
4 nation's industrial development came to a standstill

25 In the United States during the 1800s, the growth of industrialization resulted in
1 the end of rural life and values
2 a decline in the influence of big business
3 a decrease in child labor
4 the rising influence of the middle class

26 Which statement best explains why candidates for President of the United States are nominated during national nominating conventions?
1 It is mandated by the U.S. Constitution.
2 It is mandated by state constitutions.
3 It is part of the United States political tradition.
4 It was instituted by an act of Congress.

27 During the period from 1800 to 1865, the issues of states rights, tariffs, and slavery led most directly to the growth of
1 imperialism
2 sectionalism
3 national unity
4 industrialization

28 The United States Supreme Court decision in *Scott* v. *Sandford* (1857) was important because it
1 strengthened the determination of abolitionists to achieve their goals
2 caused the immediate outbreak of the Civil War
3 ended the importation of slaves into the United States
4 increased the power of Congress to exclude slavery from the territories

29 Which argument did President Abraham Lincoln use against the secession of the southern states?
1 Slavery was not profitable.
2 The government was a union of people and not of states.
3 The southern states did not permit their people to vote on secessions.
4 As the Commander in Chief, he had the duty to defend the United States against foreign invasion.

30 Which situation was an immediate result of the United States Civil War?
1 Women gained the right to vote as an acknowledgment of their role in the conflict.
2 Secession was no longer regarded as an option to be exercised by states.
3 Sectionalism disappeared as a force in American economic and political life.
4 The South retained its pre-Civil War economic and social structure.

Base your answer to questions 31 and 32 on the speakers' statements below and on your knowledge of social studies.

Speaker A: "Secession from the Union caused this war, and all those who supported it must now be punished."

Speaker B: "The nation's wounds will heal most quickly if we forgive the southerners and welcome them back into the Union."

Speaker C: "The freedmen must be given economic assistance and guaranteed the constitutional right to protect themselves."

Speaker D: "The war may have ended, but the fight must continue to preserve the system of white supremacy in the South."

31 Which speakers best represent the attitudes of the Radical Republicans who controlled Congress during Reconstruction?
1 A and D
2 A and C
3 B and C
4 B and D

32 The position taken by *Speaker B* is closest to the beliefs expressed by
1 Abraham Lincoln
2 Thaddeus Stevens
3 the carpetbaggers
4 the Ku Klux Klan

THEMATIC ESSAY

In developing your answers to the essay, be sure to keep these general definitions in mind:

(a) <u>discuss</u> means "to make observations about something using facts, reasoning, and argument; to present in some detail"

(b) <u>describe</u> means "to illustrate something in words or to tell about it"

(c) <u>evaluate</u> means "to examine and judge the significance, worth, or condition of; to determine the value of"

Directions

Write a well-organized essay that includes an introduction, several paragraphs addressing the task below, and a conclusion.

Theme: Government: Federalism

The United States Constitution created a new type of government—federalism—which divided power between the states and the national government. The proper balance of power under federalism has been debated throughout the history of the United States.

Task

From your study of United States history, identify two time periods in which there was an important debate about federalism.

For each era or time period identified:

- Identify a specific disagreement that occurred concerning the principle of federalism.
- Discuss the historical circumstances surrounding the disagreement over federalism.
- Describe the actions taken by each side during the disagreement over federalism.
- Discuss the extent to which these actions were successful in resolving the disagreement.

Suggestions

You may use any time period in United States history in which there was an important debate about federalism. Some suggestions you might wish to consider include: the Supreme Court under John Marshall (1801–1835); the extension of slavery (1820–1860); Civil War (1861–1865); Reconstruction (1865–1876); Populist and Progressive reform movements (1890–1920); Franklin D. Roosevelt's New Deal (1933–1945); civil rights movement (1950–1970); Ronald Reagan's New Federalism (1981–1989).

You are *not* limited to these suggestions.

Guidelines

In your essay be sure to:

- Address all aspects of the *Task*
- Analyze, evaluate, or compare and/or contrast issues and events whenever possible
- Fully support the theme of the essay with relevant facts, examples, and details
- Write a well-developed essay that consistently demonstrates a logical and clear plan of organization
- Introduce the theme by establishing a framework that is beyond a simple restatement of the *Task*
- Conclude your essay with a strong summation of the theme

DOCUMENT-BASED ESSAY

This task is designed to test your ability to work with historical documents and is based on the accompanying documents (1–6). Some of the documents have been edited for the purposes of this question. As you analyze the documents, take into account both the source of each document and any point of view that may be presented in the document.

Directions

This document-based question consists of two parts: Part A and Part B. In Part A, you are to read each document and answer the question or questions that follow the document. In Part B, you are to write an essay based on the information in the documents and your knowledge of United States history.

Historical Context

In May 1787, 55 delegates came together in Philadelphia to amend the Articles of Confederation. What they did was create a new Constitution, a plan of government designed to solve the governmental problems experienced under the Articles of Confederation. The Constitution they created has remained a flexible, living document that continues to guide this nation today.

Task

Using information from the documents and your knowledge of United States history and government, answer the questions that follow each document in Part A. Your answers to the questions will help you write the Part B essay in which you be asked to:

Discuss how the Constitution was both (a) a product of its time, and (b) a document that has had enough flexibility to meet the challenges of the future.

PART A: SHORT ANSWER

DOCUMENT #1

"The United States in Congress assembled shall never engage in a war, . . . nor enter into any treaties or alliances, nor coin money, nor regulate the value thereof, . . . nor borrow money on the credit of the United States, nor appropriate money, . . . nor appoint a commander in chief of the army or navy, unless nine States assent [agree]."

—The Articles of Confederation

1 Why might it be difficult for the government under the Articles of Confederation to be effective?

_____

_____

_____

_____

_____

_____

_____

_____

_____

DOCUMENT #2

Year Ratified	Amendment Number	Excerpt from the Amendment
1870	15	"The right of the citizens of the United States to vote shall not be denied or abridged . . . on account of race, color, or previous condition of servitude."
1920	19	"The right of citizens of the United States to vote shall not be denied or abridged . . . on account of sex"
1971	26	"The right of citizens of the United States, who are eighteen years of age or older, to vote, shall not be denied or abridged . . ."

2 How do these amendments demonstrate the ability of the Constitution to adapt to a change in attitude about who should have the right vote?

_____

_____

_____

_____

_____

_____

_____

_____

_____

DOCUMENT #3

"Representatives . . . shall be determined by adding to the . . . number of free persons . . . three fifths of all other persons [slaves]."

—**U.S. Constitution, Article I, Section 2**

3 How was the debate over the counting of slaves for representation resolved in the Constitution?

_____

_____

_____

_____

_____

_____

_____

_____

_____

_____

DOCUMENT #4

> *"The accumulation of all powers, legislative, executive, and judiciary, in the same hands, whether one, a few, or many . . . may justly be pronounced the very definition of tyranny [cruel or unjust use of power]."*
>
> —**James Madison,** *The Federalist,* **No. 47**

4 How might the system of checks and balances address the fears expressed in the quote by James Madison?

_____

_____

_____

_____

_____

_____

_____

_____

_____

_____

DOCUMENT #5

"*So if a law be in opposition to the Constitution, if both the law and the Constitution apply to a particular case . . . the court must decide that case conformably [in agreement] to the law, disregarding the Constitution or conformably to the Constitution, disregarding the law, the court must determine which of these conflicting rules governs the case. This is the very essence of judicial duty. If, then, the courts are to regard the Constitution, and the Constitution is superior to any ordinary act, the Constitution and not such ordinary act, must govern the case to which both apply.*"

—*Marbury* **v.** *Madison* **(1803)**

5 How did the ruling in *Marbury* v. *Madison* expand the power of the Supreme Court?

_____

_____

_____

_____

_____

_____

_____

_____

_____

_____

DOCUMENT #6

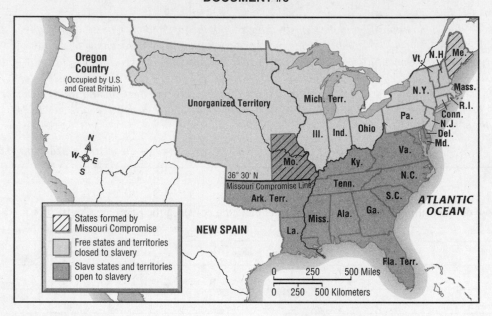

6   How does the map above demonstrate the ability of Congress to make laws to deal with the extension of slavery?

_____

_____

_____

_____

_____

_____

_____

_____

_____

_____

PART B: ESSAY

Directions
Using information from the documents provided, and your knowledge of United States history, write a well-organized essay that includes an introduction, several paragraphs, and a conclusion.

Historical Context
In May 1787, 55 delegates came together in Philadelphia to amend the Articles of Confederation. What they did was create a new Constitution, a plan of government designed to solve the governmental problems experienced under the Articles of Confederation. The Constitution they created has remained a flexible, living document that continues to guide this nation today.

Task
Using information from the documents and your knowledge of United States history and government, write an essay in which you

Discuss how the Constitution was both (a) a product of its time, and (b) a document that has had enough flexibility to meet the challenges of the future.

Guidelines
When writing your essay, be sure to
- Address all aspects of the *Task* by accurately analyzing and interpreting at least four documents
- Incorporate information from the documents in the body of the essay
- Incorporate relevant outside information throughout the essay
- Richly support the theme with relevant facts, examples, and details
- Write a well-developed essay that consistently demonstrates a logical and clean plan of organization
- Introduce the theme by establishing a framework that is beyond a simple restatement of the *Task* or *Historical Context* and conclude the essay with a summation of the theme.

UNIT OVERVIEW

The Civil War had torn the United States apart. With Union victory came the task of putting the nation back together. Yet the rebuilt nation would be a very different one. This unit reviews those changes that the Civil War brought to the United States. It also highlights how the shift from an agrarian to an industrial economy changed the United States and its people.

Some key questions to help you focus on the industrialization of the United States include

- What social, political, and economic changes occurred as the nation sought to rebuild after the Civil War?
- What factors in the United States led to the shift from an agrarian to an industrial society, and what were the results of this shift?
- How did patterns of immigration to the United States change in the 19th and early 20th centuries, and what did those changes mean for American society?

SECTION OVERVIEW

After the Civil War, the nation faced the immense task of restoring the Union. Conflicting plans for Reconstruction produced bitter political battles that led to the impeachment of a President. Enormous resources were poured into rebuilding the shattered Southern economy. Meanwhile, new political gains for African Americans were gradually rolled back in the South as whites regained power.

KEY THEMES AND CONCEPTS

As you review this section, take special note of the following key themes and concepts:

Change How did the nation rebuild and reunify after the Civil War?

Citizenship How did African Americans win political rights in the South?

Places and Regions How did white southerners react to the terms of Reconstruction?

KEY PEOPLE

As you review this section, be sure you understand the significance of these key people:

Andrew Johnson	Samuel Tilden	Thomas Nast
Ulysses S. Grant	Rutherford B. Hayes	W.E.B. Du Bois
William "Boss" Tweed	Booker T. Washington	

KEY SUPREME COURT CASES

As you review this section, be sure you understand the significance of these key Supreme Court cases:

The *Civil Rights Cases* (1883)
Plessy v. *Ferguson* (1896)
Brown v. *Board of Education of Topeka, Kansas* (1954)

★ **THE BIG IDEA**
Reconstruction followed the Civil War in the South. During this period

- President Abraham Lincoln was assassinated.
- President Andrew Johnson was impeached.
- African Americans won voting and political rights.
- Southern whites regained political control.

⚲ **KEY TERMS**
Reconstruction
Radical Republicans
Radical Reconstruction
scalawags
carpetbaggers
Thirteenth Amendment
Fourteenth Amendment
Fifteenth Amendment
solid South
Compromise of 1877
black codes
Ku Klux Klan
poll taxes
literacy tests
Freedmen's Bureau
grandfather clauses
segregation
Jim Crow laws

115

The effort to rebuild the southern states and restore the Union was known as **Reconstruction,** a period that lasted from 1865 to 1877. Reconstruction required the rebuilding of the nation's economy as well as its government. With so much at stake, rival political factions—with competing plans for the future—waged bitter battles in Washington.

The Reconstructed Nation, 1865–1876

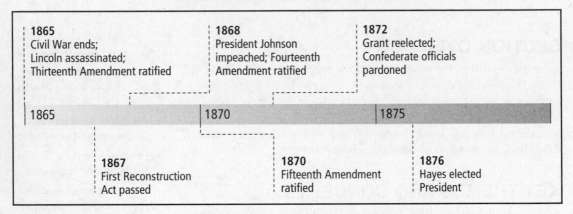

1865	1868	1872
Civil War ends; Lincoln assassinated; Thirteenth Amendment ratified	President Johnson impeached; Fourteenth Amendment ratified	Grant reelected; Confederate officials pardoned

1865   1870   1875

1867	1870	1876
First Reconstruction Act passed	Fifteenth Amendment ratified	Hayes elected President

ANALYZING DOCUMENTS

Examine the timeline above, then answer these questions.

- How many years passed between the end of the Civil War and the states' ratification of the Fifteenth Amendment?

- Which event occurred first: the impeachment of President Johnson or the election of President Hayes?

TURNING POINT

Why is President Lincoln's assassination considered a turning point in history?

PLANS OF RECONSTRUCTION

Several different plans for Reconstruction emerged during and after the war. Much debate about differing plans centered on who would control Reconstruction—the President or Congress.

Lincoln's Plan

President Lincoln had begun planning for the restoration of the South long before the end of the war. His plan of Reconstruction was based on the idea that the southern states had never left the Union. It featured the following elements:

- Pardons to southerners who swore oaths of loyalty to the United States
- Recognition of new southern state governments when 10 percent of those who had voted in the 1860 election took these oaths and when the states adopted new constitutions abolishing slavery.

Lincoln was open to suggestions from Congress for changes in his plan, but his assassination in April 1865 meant he would never carry out his program.

Johnson's Plan

Vice President Andrew Johnson became President after Lincoln's death. He intended to follow the broad outlines of Lincoln's plan. Johnson recognized four southern state governments and prepared to readmit the others. These states would participate fully in Congress.

Radical Republicans, however, controlled Congress, and they wanted harsher terms for Reconstruction. Johnson's failure to consider congressional views on Reconstruction and his efforts to block radical plans finally led Republicans in Congress to attempt to impeach him. In 1868, the House charged the President with "high crimes and misdemeanors"—specifically, for violating the Tenure of Office Act. The Senate fell one vote short of the two-thirds vote required by the Constitution to remove a President from office. Although Johnson was acquitted, his political power was gone.

Radical Reconstruction

Now the Republican-controlled Congress dictated the terms of Reconstruction. The chief features of this so-called **Radical Reconstruction** included

- The division of the South into five military districts controlled by the U.S. Army, while new state constitutions and governments were being set up
- The requirement of the new state governments to grant African American males the right to vote
- The requirement of southern states to ratify the Fourteenth Amendment. In addition to addressing several fundamental civil rights issues, the amendment prohibited many former Confederate government officials from holding office.

State Governments During Reconstruction

Immediately after the Civil War ended, white southerners who had served in leadership positions before and during the Civil War tried to reassert their control of state and local governments. They were especially concerned with limiting the freedom and movement of the former slaves.

When the radical plan of Reconstruction took effect, most of the former Confederate leaders—largely Democrats—were barred from holding office and voting. Republicans headed the new state governments that emerged and they were overwhelmingly supported by African Americans, who had recently won the right to vote. In many cases, African Americans themselves won election to office.

Many white southerners deeply resented the federal government's imposition of Radical Reconstruction. They also resented the new Reconstruction governments and the role of African Americans in them. They branded the few white southerners active in those governments as **scalawags** and the Republican northerners who came South to take part in Reconstruction as **carpetbaggers.** White southerners sometimes used terror and violence in efforts to keep African Americans from taking part in government.

READING STRATEGY

Reinforcing Main Ideas
Why did Congress impeach President Johnson?

READING STRATEGY

Organizing Information
During Radical Reconstruction, some groups of people exerted great power over the terms of Reconstruction, while others had very little power.

- Which groups had the largest roles in the Radical Reconstruction?

- Which had the smallest roles?

KEY THEMES AND CONCEPTS

Government
Which amendment to the Constitution limited the voting rights of former Confederate officers?

KEY THEMES AND CONCEPTS

Government

During Reconstruction, three new amendments to the Constitution were ratified. In the space below, name these three amendments and provide the major provisions of each.

1.

2.

3.

READING STRATEGY

Analyzing Cause and Effect

Why were scandals common during President Grant's administration?

New Constitutional Amendments

During the Reconstruction period, the states ratified three amendments to the Constitution:

- **Thirteenth Amendment** (1865)—abolished slavery in the United States
- **Fourteenth Amendment** (1868)—(1) declared that all native-born or naturalized people, including African Americans, were citizens; (2) forbade states to make laws that "abridge the privileges . . . of citizens" or that "deprive any person of life, liberty, or property, without due process of law" or that "deny to any person . . . the equal protection of the laws"; (3) limited the rights of former Confederate officers and government officials; and (4) promised to pay Civil War debts owed by the federal government, but declared Confederate debts to be void
- **Fifteenth Amendment** (1870)—declared that states could not keep citizens from voting because of "race, color, or previous condition of servitude" (slavery)

President Grant

The first presidential election after the end of the Civil War took place in 1868. Union war hero General Ulysses S. Grant ran as a Republican and won. Grant's strengths, however, were those of a military leader, not those of a politician or government leader. Scandals and corruption damaged Grant's administration, as business owners in the booming postwar economy offered bribes to politicians who would do favors for them. Among the most notorious scandals were:

- *Crédit Mobilier Scandal:* Railroad officials impoverished the railroad, then bribed members of Congress to block any investigation.
- *"Salary Grab":* Congress voted itself a 50 percent pay raise and added two years of "back pay." Public outcry forced repeal of this act.
- *"Whiskey Ring":* Whiskey distillers paid graft to federal tax collectors rather than pay tax on their liquor.

Political corruption was also common at state and local levels. Perhaps the most notorious figure was William "Boss" Tweed, who ran the Tammany Hall political machine in New York City in the 1860s and 1870s. The artist Thomas Nast attacked Tweed's behavior in a series of stinging cartoons that helped turn public opinion against Tweed.

THE END OF RECONSTRUCTION

Corruption in the Grant administration weakened the political strength of the Republican party. In addition, by the early 1870s, all but a handful of former Confederates could vote again. Most of these white southern males now voted Democratic in reaction to Radical Republican Reconstruction. For most of the next century, the Democratic party would dominate voting in the South, giving rise to the term **solid South**.

While nearly dying out in the South, the Republican party remained strong in the North and Midwest. It focused on issues of interest to businessmen and farmers, such as keeping the money supply tight and tariffs on imports high.

The Election of 1876

The emergence of the solid South gave the Democrats greater power in politics at the national level. In 1876, Democrats nominated Samuel Tilden, the governor of New York, to run for President against Republican Rutherford B. Hayes, the governor of Ohio.

Tilden clearly won the popular vote, but the electoral vote was contested. Four states sent in disputed election returns. Which votes were counted would determine the outcome of the election.

A special electoral commission was named to count the votes. The Republican majority on the commission gave all the electoral votes in question to Hayes, thus guaranteeing his victory.

In the **Compromise of 1877,** Democrats agreed to go along with the commission's decision in return for promises by Hayes to

- Withdraw remaining federal troops from the South, thus ending Reconstruction
- Name a southerner to his cabinet
- Support federal spending on internal improvements in the South

The Compromise of 1877 effectively weakened the North's political victory in the Civil War, restoring to power many of the southern families who, 16 years before, had formed the Confederacy and led it into war.

White Control in the South

The withdrawal of federal troops enabled white southerners to eliminate any political advances African Americans had made during Reconstruction. Various methods were used to curb the rights of African Americans, and by 1900, their civil rights had been sharply limited.

BLACK CODES These measures, passed in most southern states immediately after the Civil War, were based on old slave codes and aimed at keeping blacks in conditions close to slavery. The **black codes** produced an angry reaction in the North that helped passage of

GEOGRAPHY IN HISTORY

How did voting patterns in the South affect the presidential election of 1876?

 PREPARING FOR THE EXAM

On the examination, you will need to understand the influences that brought Reconstruction to an end.

- Why do you think the Democrats agreed to support the Compromise of 1877?

the Radical Reconstruction program. Reconstruction governments in the South overturned these codes.

KEY THEMES AND CONCEPTS

Individuals, Groups, Institutions

Why did some white southerners form secret societies such as the Ku Klux Klan?

SECRET SOCIETIES White southerners originally formed groups like the **Ku Klux Klan** to try to frighten African Americans and their supporters out of taking part in Reconstruction governments. The lawlessness and brutality demonstrated by these groups led the federal government to use the army against the societies. With the end of Reconstruction and the growth of white political power, the Klan and other similar groups played a less active role in the South. Such organizations, however, remain in existence to this day.

POLL TAXES Southern states imposed a tax on every voter. Those who were too poor to pay **poll taxes**—including many African Americans—could not vote.

LITERACY TESTS Some states required citizens to demonstrate that they could read and write before they voted. Often **literacy tests** involved interpreting a difficult part of the Constitution. Few African Americans could pass these tests because they had received little schooling. While the **Freedmen's Bureau,** created by Congress in 1865 to aid former slaves, established many schools for young African Americans, the bureau lasted only a few years. Thereafter, state laws forced African American children to attend separate schools that were poorly equipped and funded.

READING STRATEGY

Reading for Evidence
Reread the section entitled "White Control in the South." What were five major ways in which white southerners reasserted their control in the South after Reconstruction?

GRANDFATHER CLAUSES Poll taxes and literacy tests might have also kept poor and uneducated whites from voting. To prevent this, southern states added **grandfather clauses** to their constitutions. These clauses allowed the son or grandson of a man eligible to vote in 1866 or 1867 to vote himself even if he could neither pay the tax nor pass the test. Since few African Americans could vote in 1867, the clause benefited whites almost exclusively.

Jim Crow Laws

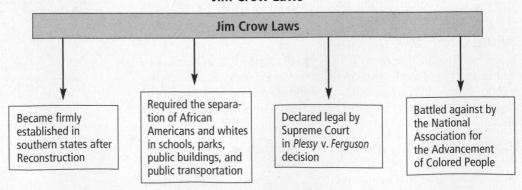

Jim Crow laws were a part of everyday life in the South after Reconstruction.

JIM CROW LAWS Southern states also passed laws establishing social **segregation,** or the separation of people on the basis of race. Such **Jim Crow laws** forbade African Americans from sharing facilities with whites, such as railroad cars or water fountains.

The Supreme Court's Response

The Supreme Court did not interfere with efforts to restore white control in the South. In the 1883 *Civil Rights Cases,* the Court ruled that the Thirteenth Amendment abolished slavery but did not prohibit discrimination and that the Fourteenth Amendment prohibited discrimination by government but not by individuals. Later, in the landmark case of *Plessy* v. *Ferguson* (1896), the Court ruled that segregation was legal as long as African Americans had access to "equal but separate" facilities.

The Court's ruling in the *Plessy* case set a precedent that justified segregation in all public facilities—schools, hospitals, passenger terminals, and more—until the 1950s. It was not until the pivotal case of *Brown* v. *Board of Education of Topeka, Kansas* (1954) that the Supreme Court reversed the finding in *Plessy* v. *Ferguson.* The *Brown* decision stated that educational facilities separated solely on the basis of race were by their nature unequal.

African Americans Debate Their Future

Two prominent leaders offered contrasting strategies to improve the lives of African Americans. Booker T. Washington argued that African Americans should temporarily put aside their desire for political equality and instead focus on building economic security by gaining useful vocational skills. W.E.B. Du Bois called for the brightest African Americans to gain an advanced liberal arts education (rather than a vocational education) and then demand social and political equality. However, widespread discrimination against African Americans made either strategy difficult to follow.

⚷ KEY THEMES AND CONCEPTS

Constitutional Principles

The following three cases deal with segregation and Jim Crow laws:

- *Civil Rights Cases* (1883) ruled that slavery was abolished but that discrimination by individuals was not prohibited by the Constitution.

- *Plessy* v. *Ferguson* (1896) established segregation to be legal as long as "equal but separate" facilities were available to African Americans.

- *Brown* v. *Board of Education of Topeka, Kansas* (1954) established that facilities separated by race were unequal.

How did these three cases influence laws concerning segregation?

2

The Rise of American Business, Industry, and Labor—1865–1920

⭐ THE BIG IDEA

The United States developed a prosperous new economy based on the mass production of goods. During this period

- economic development expanded in the North, but weakened in the South.
- entrepreneurs became wealthy and powerful.
- government began to regulate business.
- labor unions formed to improve working conditions.

🔑 KEY TERMS

transcontinental railroad
New South
sharecroppers
tenant farmers
capital
corporations
monopoly
merger
trust
entrepreneurs
assembly line
laissez-faire
free enterprise system
robber barons
Sherman Antitrust Act
collective bargaining
Haymarket Riot

SECTION OVERVIEW

From Reconstruction through World War I, the United States developed a prosperous industrial economy that revolutionized American society. New machines made possible the mass production of goods. Industrial growth led to a new type of business, the corporation, headed by a rising class of enterprising industrialists such as Henry Ford. With little government interference, these corporate giants created new business structures, some legal and some not, that brought them fabulous wealth. They used their riches both to benefit society and to increase their power. Industries attracted a new type of laborer, the factory worker, who often worked long hours in hazardous conditions. These conditions spurred the growth of labor unions, which gradually gained the right to bargain with employers.

KEY THEMES AND CONCEPTS

As you review this section, take special note of the following key themes and concepts:

Science and Technology How did technological developments lead to the growth of industrialization?

Government How did the government respond to the growth of powerful industries and to complaints about business practices?

Factors of Production What factors led to the growth of the labor movement, and what strategies did unions pursue?

KEY PEOPLE

As you review this section, be sure you understand the significance of these key people:

Andrew Carnegie	Henry Ford	Charles Darwin
John D. Rockefeller	Horatio Alger	Terence Powderly
J. Pierpont Morgan	Adam Smith	Samuel Gompers

KEY SUPREME COURT CASES

As you review this section, be sure you understand the significance of these key Supreme Court cases.

Munn v. *Illinois* (1877)
Wabash, St. Louis & Pacific Railway v. *Illinois* (1886)
United States v. *E. C. Knight Company* (1895)
In re Debs (1895)

The Civil War changed the economies of the northern and southern regions of the United States. The Civil War stimulated economic growth in the North. Meanwhile, the South struggled to recover from the devastation of the war.

Economic Developments in the North

The industrialization that had started before the war accelerated as northern factories rushed to keep up with the Union's demand for guns, ammunition, uniforms, and other necessary products. Improvements in railroad systems helped speed troop movements. Since so many northern farm workers entered the army, farms became more heavily mechanized, using fewer workers to produce more crops. Little of the fighting took place in the North, and the region was spared much physical destruction from the war.

After the war, the growing northern factories looked to overseas markets for their goods. Meanwhile, completion of the **transcontinental railroad** opened new markets in the West and brought products of western farms and mines east.

Economic growth attracted new waves of immigrants to the United States. Some sought farms in the West, but many found employment in the booming industries of the North.

Economic Developments in the South

The Civil War ruined the South's economy. It ended slavery, thus killing the plantation system on which southern wealth was based. During the fighting, plantations had been burned, railroads ripped up, and the region's few factories destroyed.

After the war, many farmers and planters had to sell off parts of their land to pay off debts or to start over. These land owners often found themselves in debt to banks or merchants. Yet despite such hardships, southern farmers again began to produce cotton and tobacco.

Some southern leaders, however, believed that the South's economy should not rest simply on agriculture. They began to create a **New South,** with rebuilt railroads, new textile and steel mills, and, later, new industries, such as oil and coal production.

Despite these changes, the South lagged behind the North in economic growth. Agriculture still offered the most jobs, and many southerners, including large numbers of former slaves, had to farm land owned by

GEOGRAPHY IN HISTORY

What factors contributed to the development of factories in the North?

 PREPARING FOR THE EXAM

On the examination, you will need to have a thorough understanding of important United States economic developments.

- What is the transcontinental railroad?

- How did it contribute to economic growth?

KEY THEMES AND CONCEPTS

Places and Regions
New manufacturing technologies were less commonly used in the South than in the North. Why?

Individuals, Groups, Institutions
As the southern economy began to grow in the decades after the Civil War, some groups still lagged behind others.

- Who were the sharecroppers?

- How did they differ from tenant farmers?

Economic Systems
What do you call a business in which many investors own shares?

Name two kinds of businesses that speeded the growth of American industry:

1.

2.

What do you call a company that has complete control over a particular kind of business?

Name two examples:

1.

2.

What do you call the merger of a group of unrelated companies?

Name an example:

1.

others. These landless farmers included **sharecroppers,** who gave part of each year's crop to the landowner and received the rest as payment, and **tenant farmers,** who paid cash to rent land.

Beginning in the 1880s, African Americans began a migration to the North in search of better jobs. This migration accelerated during and after World War I.

BUSINESS DEVELOPMENTS

Before the Civil War, sole proprietors, or single owners, and partnerships had controlled most American businesses. The mills and factories that came with industrialization, however, usually required greater **capital,** or money for investment, than one person or a few partners could raise.

The Growth of Corporations

To raise capital for expansion, many businesses became **corporations.** A corporation is a business in which many investors own shares, usually called stocks. In exchange for their investment, each stockholder receives a dividend, or part of the corporation's profits.

Besides paying dividends, the corporations also limited investor losses. If a corporation failed, an investor lost only his or her investment and was not responsible for the corporation's debts.

The money raised by corporations speeded the growth of American industry. Among the fastest growing industries were transportation (railroads, urban transportation, and, later, automobiles), building materials (steel), energy (coal, oil, and electricity), and communications (telegraph and telephone).

Other Forms of Business Organization

As the nation's economy boomed and industries grew larger in the late 1800s, other ways of organizing business appeared. Often the aim of such business organizations was to eliminate competition and dominate a particular area of the economy.

MONOPOLY A company or small group of companies that has complete control over a particular field of business is a **monopoly.** One example of a monopoly in the late 1800s was the E. C. Knight Sugar Company. Having a monopoly in a field often allowed a company to raise prices to almost any level it desired. Such abuses led to federal legislation aimed at curbing monopolies.

Some monopolies are permitted today. Public utility companies that provide gas, water, and electricity are examples of private companies that often have monopolies in their fields. Government agencies closely monitor the operations of such utilities.

CONGLOMERATE A corporation that owns a group of unrelated companies is a conglomerate. Such conglomerates are usually formed by **merger,** the process by which one company acquires legal control over another. Mergers and conglomerates are both legal and common today. General Electric, for example, is a conglomerate that has acquired many different divisions through mergers.

POOL Sometimes competing companies in one field entered into agreements to fix prices and divide business. Such an agreement was a pool. Railroad companies in the late 1800s formed such pools, which were later outlawed.

TRUST A group of corporations in the same or related fields sometimes agreed to combine under a single board of trustees that controlled the actions of all the member corporations. This was a **trust.** Shareholders in the corporations received dividends from the trust but lost any say in its operation. The Standard Oil Trust was one example of such a combination. Trusts were later made illegal.

HOLDING COMPANY To get around the outlawing of trusts, corporations formed holding companies. The holding company bought controlling amounts of stock in different corporations rather than take operations over directly as a trust did.

Innovation

While these new forms of business organization helped young industries to get started and to maximize profits, other innovations enabled businesses to market their products more effectively. In urban areas, new department stores offered customers a wide variety of goods under one roof. For rural areas, retailers developed mail-order catalogs that saved customers a trip to faraway stores. The items offered in these stores and catalogs expanded as well, thanks to new inventions such as the vacuum cleaner, the telephone, the electric light bulb, the electric iron, and the safety razor.

ANALYZING DOCUMENTS

Examine the timeline below, then answer these questions.

- How many years passed between the formation of Standard Oil Trust and the formation of Carnegie Steel?

- Which event occurred first: the invention of the telephone or the introduction of the assembly line?

Innovations and Business Developments, 1868–1913

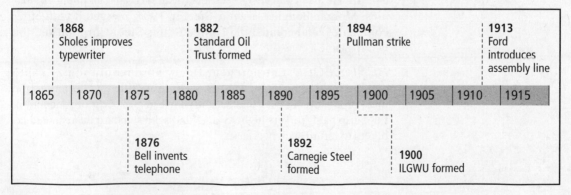

| 1868 Sholes improves typewriter | 1882 Standard Oil Trust formed | 1894 Pullman strike | 1913 Ford introduces assembly line |

| 1865 | 1870 | 1875 | 1880 | 1885 | 1890 | 1895 | 1900 | 1905 | 1910 | 1915 |

| 1876 Bell invents telephone | 1892 Carnegie Steel formed | 1900 ILGWU formed |

Entrepreneurs

These new forms of business organization and innovative ideas from inventors helped American industry grow in the late 1800s and early 1900s. Yet without the business knowledge and daring of certain individuals, that growth would have been much slower.

These individuals were **entrepreneurs,** people who take responsibility for the organization and operation of a new business venture. Entrepreneurs often risk large sums of venture capital in hopes of making enormous profits. The business decisions made by turn-of-the-century entrepreneurs had great impact on the lives of most Americans. Some of the key entrepreneurs of the late 1800s and early 1900s are listed below.

READING STRATEGY

Organizing Information
In the space below, name four key entrepreneurs of the late 1800s and early 1900s and the industries each operated.

1.

2

3.

4.

ANDREW CARNEGIE An immigrant from Scotland, Andrew Carnegie started work in a textile factory at age 12. He worked his way up through a variety of jobs and invested his money shrewdly. At age 38, Carnegie entered the steel industry, which was booming because of the growth of railroads. Carnegie sought to control all aspects of steelmaking and built his company into the world's largest steelmaker.

Carnegie sold his company in 1901 for a quarter billion dollars. He believed the wealthy had a duty to society and gave hundreds of millions to charities. He also underwrote the founding of free public libraries all across the country.

JOHN D. ROCKEFELLER Industrialist John D. Rockefeller entered the oil-refining business during the Civil War. He believed competition was wasteful and used ruthless methods to eliminate competitors. By 1882, his Standard Oil Company controlled over 90 percent of American oil refining. In 1882, he formed the Standard Oil Trust to control more aspects of oil production. Rockefeller also gave away hundreds of millions to charity.

J. PIERPONT MORGAN Trained as a banker, J. Pierpont Morgan profited by making loans to growing businesses. He took control of many bankrupt railroads in the late 1800s, reorganized them, and made a profit. He also controlled electrical, insurance, and shipping companies. Morgan bought Carnegie Steel in 1901, merged it with other companies, and created the United States Steel Corporation, the world's largest.

HENRY FORD Entrepreneur Henry Ford revolutionized auto making in 1913 by using a moving **assembly line** that permitted the mass production of cars, significantly lowering the cost of production. Ford also paid workers higher wages and set a standard that enabled laborers to afford such purchases.

Attitudes Toward Business

Industrialization and the changes associated with it caused American attitudes toward business to alter in the late 1800s. Traditional attitudes, of course, still existed. They could be found in books by the popular writer Horatio Alger. Alger's novels describe poor boys who become rich through hard work and luck.

Alger's novels illustrate what is known as the Puritan work ethic. This is the belief, brought with the Puritans to colonial New England and embodied in the preaching of Puritan minister Cotton Mather, that hard work builds character and is its own reward.

The tremendous wealth some entrepreneurs gained during the late 1800s, as well as the cut-throat business methods they used, led some Americans to rethink their ideas on the meaning of business success. New philosophies tried to explain and justify both the accumulation of wealth and the practices used to achieve it.

LAISSEZ-FAIRE Many supporters of late 1800s business growth restated the older principle of **laissez-faire,** or noninterference. Economist Adam Smith, in his 1776 book, *The Wealth of Nations,* and many other writers had supported this principle, which holds that government should not interfere in the economic workings of a nation. They believed that a **free enterprise system,** in which private individuals make the economic decisions, is most efficient.

During the late 1800s, economists restated the importance of laissez-faire policies to economic growth. Government interference with business was minimal for much of this period, and entrepreneurs expanded their businesses and earned great wealth.

SOCIAL DARWINISM Laissez-faire capitalists found justification for their beliefs in new scientific theories being developed at that time. Naturalist Charles Darwin had developed a theory of evolution that described how animal species live or die by a process of natural selection. Other writers simplified Darwin's theories and created a philosophy called Social Darwinism.

Social Darwinists held that life was a struggle for the "survival of the fittest." Unregulated business competition would see weak businesses fail and healthy businesses thrive. Government action regulating business practices would interfere with the process of natural selection. Likewise, any government programs to aid the poor or workers would also violate natural "laws."

ROBBER BARONS OR PHILANTHROPISTS? The philosophies described above and the growing gulf between rich and poor led some Americans to criticize laissez-faire policies and those who profited from them. Critics condemned the wealthy entrepreneurs as **robber barons,** those who gained their wealth by ruthless methods in their dealings with competitors at the expense of the poor and the working class. The

 PREPARING FOR THE EXAM

What system was based on the principle that private individuals should make economic decisions?

KEY THEMES AND CONCEPTS

Human Systems

Charles Darwin's theory of natural selection was simplified by philosophers and turned into a philosophy called Social Darwinism.

• How was Social Darwinism applied to business competition?

lavish lifestyles of the wealthy at this time fed such criticism. During this so-called Gilded Age, the rich spent freely to show off their wealth, a practice known as conspicuous consumption.

Public criticism and a sense of social responsibility led entrepreneurs to use a part of their wealth to aid society. People like Carnegie and Rockefeller became philanthropists, donating vast sums of money to charities and institutions such as schools, museums, libraries, and orchestras.

GOVERNMENT POLICIES TOWARD BUSINESS

The federal government generally held a laissez-faire attitude toward business for much of this period. Expanding industries and growing foreign trade seemed to justify such an attitude. In addition, many business leaders made financial contributions, legal and illegal, to the politicians who set federal policies.

A number of government policies were designed to aid the growth of business. These included loans and land grants to large railroad companies, high tariffs that discouraged competition from foreign manufacturers, tight limits on the amount of money in circulation, and few limits on immigration.

Steps Toward Government Regulation

Several factors led the government to take the first steps in the late 1800s toward regulating business:

- Periodic downturns in the national economy
- Growing criticism of practices that saw big business profit at the expense of the poor and working class
- Increasing grassroots political pressure for change

Although government intervention at this time had limited impact, it did set the course for more federal actions in years to come.

SUPREME COURT DECISIONS During the late 1800s, railroads developed a number of policies that discriminated against farmers and small shippers. These groups pressured some states to pass laws regulating railroad practices. The railroads sued to have such laws overturned.

In the 1877 case *Munn* v. *Illinois,* the Supreme Court upheld an Illinois law controlling grain elevator rates. The Court ruled that the Constitution recognized a state's right to a "police power" that permitted regulation of private property "affected with a public interest."

In the 1886 case *Wabash, St. Louis & Pacific Railway Co.* v. *Illinois,* however, the Court ruled that states could not regulate railroad rates on portions of interstate routes that lay within their borders. Under the Constitution, only the federal government can regulate interstate trade. This decision meant that states could do little to regulate the railroads.

READING STRATEGY

Reinforcing Main Ideas
What factors led the government toward regulating business in the late 1800s?

KEY THEMES AND CONCEPTS

Constitutional Principles
Two landmark Supreme Court cases dealt with railroad regulation: *Munn* v. *Illinois* (1877) and *Wabash, St. Louis and Pacific Railway* v. *Illinois* (1886).

- How did these two cases influence railroad regulation?

INTERSTATE COMMERCE COMMISSION In 1887, public pressure for reform of railroad policies led Congress to pass the Interstate Commerce Act. The act set up the Interstate Commerce Commission, an agency charged with ending such railroad abuses as pools and rebates, discounts only available to special customers. Although court decisions kept the commission ineffective for several years, its establishment set a precedent for federal regulation of interstate commerce.

SHERMAN ANTITRUST ACT By the late 1800s, some large corporations and trusts had eliminated most competition and won almost total monopolies in their fields. Politicians heeded the public protests over the ensuing abuses. One result was the **Sherman Antitrust Act** of 1890. The act prohibited monopolies by declaring illegal any business combination or trust "in restraint of trade or commerce."

Yet when the federal government tried to enforce the act, the Supreme Court, in *United States* v. *E.C. Knight Company,* 1895, ruled that many businesses were exempt from the new law. In addition, some other corporations circumvented the act by forming holding companies rather than trusts. Once again, the precedent set by the act proved more important than the act itself.

LABOR ORGANIZATIONS

Business growth in the late 1800s brought generally higher wages to American workers. Yet periodic unemployment and poor working conditions remained a fact of life for workers. In addition, employers held enormous power over the lives of their workers and could lower wages and fire employees at will.

The Growth of Unions

To improve conditions, increasing numbers of American workers formed labor unions beginning in the 1820s. As working conditions changed with industrialization, many more workers became interested in unions.

Americans had long understood the values of cooperation and association, and labor unions provided a means to put these values into action. In **collective bargaining,** union members representing workers negotiated labor issues with management. Instead of each worker trying to achieve individual aims, a united group would put pressure on management. Several early unions helped advance the cause of labor.

KNIGHTS OF LABOR Under the direction of Terence Powderly, the Knights of Labor, formed in 1869, welcomed skilled and unskilled workers as well as women and African Americans. The Knights fought for broad social reforms such as an eight-hour day for workers, an end to child labor, and equal opportunities and wages for women. As a rule, the union opposed strikes, but a successful strike against railroads in 1885 brought many new members. However, antilabor feeling swept

READING STRATEGY

Organizing Information
American workers began to form a number of labor unions in the 1800s. In the space below, name three different labor unions and describe the workers who joined each of them.

1.

2.

3.

⚲ KEY THEMES AND CONCEPTS

Interdependence
What do you call the process through which union members represent workers in labor negotiations with management?

the nation after the **Haymarket Riot** in late 1886. The Knights declined in influence due to a series of unsuccessful strikes and competition from the American Federation of Labor.

AMERICAN FEDERATION OF LABOR In 1886, Samuel Gompers formed the American Federation of Labor (AFL). The AFL was a collection of many different craft unions, unions of skilled workers in similar trades. In contrast to the Knights of Labor, the AFL fought for immediate goals such as better wages, hours, and working conditions. The policy that the AFL followed is known as *bread-and-butter unionism*. It so appealed to workers that AFL membership reached about a million by 1900, making the AFL the most powerful union in the nation. Nevertheless, groups such as women, immigrants, and African Americans generally were not welcome in the AFL.

INTERNATIONAL LADIES' GARMENT WORKERS UNION Women made up the majority of workers in the garment industries. In 1900, the International Ladies' Garment Workers Union (ILGWU) was formed to represent the laborers who toiled in sweatshops. After a successful strike in 1910, the ILGWU soon became an important part of the AFL. In March 1911 a horrific fire at the Triangle Shirtwaist Company in New York City caused the deaths of almost 150 people, mostly young immigrant women. Dozens leapt to their deaths from upper stories to escape the burning building due to locked exits and inadequate fire escapes. This event gave further impetus to the work of the ILGWU.

Labor Conflict

If collective bargaining failed, labor unions often used strikes, or work stoppages, to achieve their aims. Strikes sometimes ended in union victories; often, however, they led to violence as business owners sought state and even federal support to end walkouts. The strikes and labor-associated violence described below sometimes advanced the cause of labor and sometimes set it back.

GREAT RAILWAY STRIKE In 1877, a series of pay cuts for railroad workers led to a strike that spread across several states. At the request of state governors, President Rutherford B. Hayes sent federal troops to help end the strike. The workers gained little benefit from the strike, and owners took a harder position against unions.

HAYMARKET RIOT A labor rally called by Chicago anarchists in 1886 ended with a bomb blast and riot that left many people dead, including 7 police officers. Although the Knights of Labor had no responsibility for the violence, some public opinion blamed them.

⬛ **PREPARING FOR THE EXAM**

For the examination, you will need to understand the history of labor conflict in the United States.

Identify the outcome of each of the following strikes:

1. Great Railway Strike (1877)

2. Haymarket Riot (1886)

3. Homestead Strike (1892)

4. Pullman Strike (1894)

5. Lawrence Textile Strike (1912)

An Era of Strikes, Late 1800s

Gap between rich and poor grows larger.	→	Tensions increase between workers and business owners.	→	Workers organize into unions.	↘

Business leaders oppose unions.

Government sides with business leaders, sometimes using army troops to put down strikes.	←	Major strikes include the Great Railway Strike, Homestead Strike, and Pullman Strike.	←	The era of large, violent strikes begins in 1877 with a nationwide railroad strike.	↙

Increasing tensions between workers and employers led to large, often violent strikes.

HOMESTEAD STRIKE In 1892, union members at the Carnegie steel plant in Homestead, Pennsylvania, went on strike to protest a wage cut. Management brought in security guards to protect the plant. In the violence that followed, 16 people were killed. The National Guard finally ended the fighting and the strike. Fewer than 25 percent of the striking workers got their jobs back. The strike halted the union movement in the steel industry for 20 years.

PULLMAN STRIKE In 1894, a strike by railway-car makers in Illinois spread and tied up other rail lines. President Grover Cleveland sent in federal troops to end the strike. (The Supreme Court, in the 1895 case *In re Debs,* ruled that the President had the right to deploy the troops, even over the objection of the governor of Illinois.) Cleveland's action confirmed the belief of many that government favored the interests of business over those of labor.

LAWRENCE TEXTILE STRIKE The Industrial Workers of the World (IWW), a radical union of skilled and unskilled laborers, led a huge strike against the textile mills in Lawrence, Massachusetts, in 1912. The strike proved one of the greatest successes of that era, and workers won most of their demands.

 PREPARING FOR THE EXAM

A flow chart is a diagram that shows the different steps in a process. Based on the text and the flow chart above, answer the question.

What were three reasons that tensions increased between workers and business owners?

1.

2.

3.

SECTION 3 — American Society Adjusts to Industrialization

THE BIG IDEA
Immigration and urbanization changed the United States dramatically. During the late 1800s

- a prosperous middle class developed.
- cities became crowded and workers lived in unhealthful conditions.
- immigrants arrived from eastern Europe and Asia.
- women and other workers became a larger part of the workforce.
- settlers continued to move westward.

KEY TERMS

tenements
political machines
settlement house movement
company towns
suffrage
ghettos
nativism
reservations
Dawes Act
Grange
Populist party
free silver

SECTION OVERVIEW

Industrialization and new building technologies triggered an explosion of urban growth that brought social changes, both good and bad. A prosperous middle class emerged, while urban crowding and disease took a heavy toll on the working poor, many of whom were immigrants. New arrivals came in waves, first from western Europe and Africa, then from eastern Europe and Asia. Despite widespread discrimination, many immigrants prospered. A growing United States population and a demand for new lands and resources lured Americans westward, reducing the Native American population and forcing them into ever-shrinking parcels of land. Western land was gobbled up by miners, ranchers, and a growing political force: farmers.

KEY THEMES AND CONCEPTS

As you review this section, take special note of the following key themes and concepts:

Change What effects did industrialization and urbanization have on American culture, work life, and family life?

Immigration and Migration How did patterns of immigration change from colonial times through the early 1900s?

Places and Regions What types of land, resources, and economic opportunities caused Americans to move farther and farther westward?

KEY PEOPLE

As you review this section, be sure you understand the significance of these key people:

John Dewey
Jane Addams
Frederick Jackson Turner

William Jennings Bryan
William McKinley

Cities offered the best and the worst of life for newcomers from the countryside and from abroad. The dazzling skyscrapers and bustling streets were symbols of the new opportunities for prosperity in America. Yet behind the dazzle grew a darker side of city life.

INDUSTRIALIZATION AND URBANIZATION

Industrialization and the growth of cities went hand in hand. Cities offered large numbers of workers for new factories. Cities provided transportation for raw materials and finished goods. As more plants were built, more workers moved to cities seeking jobs. In 1880, about a quarter of Americans lived in cities. By 1900, roughly 40 percent did. By 1920, more than half of all Americans lived in cities. This shift from rural to urban life had both positive and negative effects.

Negative Effects of City Growth

Some of the negative effects of urbanization included crowded, unsanitary living conditions for workers, as well as corrupt city politics.

HOUSING Construction of decent housing often lagged behind the growth of city populations. Much city housing consisted of multifamily buildings called **tenements.** Immigrant and working-class families, who could pay little for rent, crowded into such buildings. These poorly maintained tenements deteriorated, and whole neighborhoods became slums. Crime flourished in such poor, congested neighborhoods.

HEALTH Urban crowding helped spread disease. Water and sanitation facilities were often inadequate. Poor families could not afford proper diets and lacked knowledge of basic health procedures.

POLITICS **Political machines** took control of many city governments, partly by providing help to the growing number of poor immigrant voters and thereby gaining their support. Corruption increased, and money that could have been spent on public works often ended up in private pockets.

Positive Effects of City Growth

Urbanization was aided and improved by new technologies in transportation, architecture, utilities, and sanitation. In addition, cities offered new cultural opportunities.

NEW TECHNOLOGIES Builders turned to new technologies to meet the challenge posed by huge numbers of people living together. Subways, elevated trains, and streetcars provided mass transportation. Steel girders and elevators made possible high-rise skyscrapers. Gas and electric lights brightened city streets and made them safer.

READING STRATEGY

Analyzing Cause And Effect

• How was industrialization related to urbanization?

• Did one process lead to the other, or were these processes interdependent?

READING STRATEGY

Predicting Content
The growth of cities had both positive and negative effects. Some of the negative effects included crowded and unsanitary living conditions for workers.

• How might these conditions change over time?

• How might they stay the same?

Growing health problems forced officials to design and build new water and sewage systems.

CULTURAL ADVANCES Public and private money funded new museums, concert halls, theaters, and parks. New printing presses turned out mass-circulation newspapers, magazines, and popular novels by authors such as Mark Twain and Horatio Alger. Public schools educated more students than ever before. Reformers, including the philosopher and educator John Dewey, improved the quality of teaching.

COMMUNITY IMPROVEMENT Other reformers founded groups intended to correct the problems of society. In Chicago, Jane Addams started Hull House, a model project that led a **settlement house movement** to provide education and services to the poor. Political reformers sought to unseat corrupt political machines and see that public money was spent on improved services such as police and fire departments and new hospitals, rather than on graft.

PREPARING FOR THE EXAM

Some examination questions require you to read and interpret charts. Study the chart and answer these questions.

- Approximately how much did the urban (city) population in the United States grow between 1860 and 1900?

- Did the rural population increase or decrease between 1870 and 1890?

READING STRATEGY

Organizing Information

- Into which three groups can the urban population of the late 1800s be divided into?

- Which group was the largest?

- Which group was the smallest?

Urban and Rural Population, 1850–1900

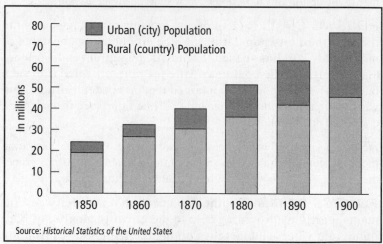

Source: *Historical Statistics of the United States*

The Urban Mixture

The people of these growing cities generally could be divided into three broad groups.

WORKERS AND THE POOR The largest group contained the workers and the poor. Most immigrants belonged to this group, whose members lived in slums and poorer neighborhoods. (Living conditions generally were better in the **company towns,** which were built and owned by a single employer, but workers in these towns were dependent on their employer for everything from housing to food to police protection.) Often workers lacked the time and money to go to theaters or museums or use other resources that cities provided.

THE MIDDLE CLASS Doctors, lawyers, office workers, and skilled laborers made up a growing middle class. Middle-class neighborhoods offered more spacious, better maintained housing. The middle-class people had both money and leisure time. Their homes contained the new consumer goods becoming available, such as sewing machines and phonographs. They could afford to go to concerts, attend increasingly popular football, basketball, or baseball games, and save money for their children's higher education.

THE WEALTHY Entrepreneurs and wealthy business people usually made the city their chief residence, although they often had summer estates outside it. The rich made up the smallest segment of urban society. They lived in large mansions or elegant apartment buildings. They often contributed to charities and cultural institutions such as opera companies and libraries. They could enjoy the broadest range of benefits of city life.

Changes for Women, Families, and Work

Industrialization and urbanization brought changes to the lives of women in all the classes. Many Americans had long held the view that the ideal woman devoted herself to home and family, instilling in her husband and children high moral values. In fact, usually only wealthy women could dedicate themselves full-time to such tasks.

In the late 1800s, more women began taking jobs outside the home, some out of economic necessity and others out of a desire for a larger role in society. These jobs provided added income and personal fulfillment but sometimes produced added stress for family members. For example, women who worked outside the home also were expected to continue performing most of the jobs in the home, and children often had to be cared for by relatives or neighbors during the day.

NEW EMPLOYMENT OPPORTUNITIES FOR WOMEN Working-class women often had to hold jobs outside the home. In addition to jobs women had traditionally filled, such as household service, sewing, or laundering, women took some new jobs created by recent inventions such as the typewriter and telephone.

Middle- and upper-class women also sought jobs. Many of these women had long been active in reform movements, including abolition and temperance, and had attended college in increasing numbers through the 1800s. They sought to apply their educations and social concerns in the job market. Women took jobs as teachers, social workers, doctors, and lawyers, often struggling against public disapproval.

Women thus became an ever-larger part of the workforce. Between 1880 and 1910, the number of working women grew from 2.6 million to more than 7 million. Conditions they met in the workplace—hostility, laws that barred women from certain jobs, unequal pay—led more women to seek legal remedies. To gain the political power to force change, however,

KEY THEMES AND CONCEPTS

Change
In the late 1800s, more women began to seek paid employment outside the home.

- What reasons led to this change?

- What kinds of new jobs did women seek outside the home?

READING STRATEGY

Problem Solving

- How much did the number of working women grow between 1880 and 1910?

- What challenges did women face in the workplace?

- How did some women address those challenges?

women first needed to win the right to vote, called **suffrage.** The women's suffrage movement grew more active.

⚲ **KEY THEMES AND CONCEPTS**

Individuals, Groups, Institutions
What other groups of workers also began working in the late 1800s? What kinds of conditions did they face?

OTHER GROUPS OF WORKERS Groups besides women faced problems in the workplace. Employers regularly discriminated against African American workers and workers who were older or disabled, refusing to hire them or keeping them in low-paying jobs.

Nor did laws protect children from dangerous and unhealthful work, such as in mines and factories. Nevertheless, many families were forced to send their children to work rather than school in order to help make ends meet.

IMMIGRATION

The United States has always been a nation of immigrants. After the Civil War, however, industrialization drew an even greater flood of immigrants. From 1865 to 1900, some 13.5 million people arrived from abroad. Not until the 1920s would the numbers begin to dwindle. Immigration to the United States can be divided into three stages.

⚲ **KEY THEMES AND CONCEPTS**

Immigration and Migration
During the colonial period, a huge number of immigrants arrived in the United States. People from England, Germany, and Sweden, for example, made up a large number of these immigrants, but people from other countries came as well.

• What motivated immigrants in the colonial period to come to the United States?

Colonial Immigration

This period lasted from the arrival of the first people from England through the Declaration of Independence. The following features characterize this period of immigration.

COLONIAL IMMIGRANTS People from England made up the largest part of these immigrants. However, Scotch-Irish, German, Swedish, and Dutch also came in significant numbers. Large numbers of Africans were also part of the colonial immigration.

REASONS FOR IMMIGRATION Some came seeking political and religious freedom. Others sought to improve their economic standing and their way of life. The Africans came unwillingly, as slaves.

GEOGRAPHY IN HISTORY

Organizing Information
During the colonial period, in what areas did most English immigrants settle? List two other examples of immigrant groups and the areas in which they settled.

1.

2.

AREAS OF SETTLEMENT English settlement spread along the Atlantic Coast from Maine to Georgia and inland to the Appalachians. Within this area, other ethnic groups became concentrated in certain regions. For example, many Dutch settled in New York and New Jersey, many Germans in Pennsylvania, and many Scotch-Irish in the backcountry areas of the Carolinas. Most Africans came at first to the Chesapeake region, then spread through the South.

DIFFICULTIES THEY FACED Immigrants came into conflict with the Native Americans. They also had to overcome the challenge of building homes, farms, and a new way of life in an unfamiliar region.

CONTRIBUTIONS The immigrants succeeded in establishing a culture much like the one they had left in Europe, yet heavily influenced by the geographic factors encountered in North America.

In addition to their language, people coming from England brought forms of government, religions, family and cultural traditions, and economic patterns from their home country. Other groups contributed customs from their home countries. All worked to build a successful economy in North America.

Old Immigration

The old immigration covered the years from the establishment of the United States until around 1850. Most immigrants came from northern and western Europe, especially Ireland, Germany, and Scandinavia.

REASONS FOR IMMIGRATION Massive famine caused by failure of the potato crop drove millions of Irish immigrants to seek opportunity in the United States. Revolution in Germany caused many immigrants to seek peace and stability in America. Many people continued to arrive in search of better economic opportunity.

AREAS OF SETTLEMENT The Irish largely settled in cities in the Northeast. Some Germans also stayed in cities, but many moved west to start farms, as did a large number of Scandinavian immigrants.

DIFFICULTIES THEY FACED Irish and German Catholic immigrants often faced hostility on their arrival in the United States. Some Americans feared economic competition from the newcomers. Since at this time the nation was predominantly Protestant, resentment toward Catholics and Jews was also strong.

CONTRIBUTIONS Irish workers helped build railroads and canals and labored in factories. Germans and Scandinavians brought, among other things, advanced farming techniques and new ideas on education such as kindergarten.

New Immigration

The new immigration covered the time from roughly 1850 to 1924. This period was marked by a shift in sources of immigration to southern and eastern Europe, especially the nations of Italy, Poland, and Russia. In addition, substantial numbers of Japanese and Chinese arrived.

REASONS FOR IMMIGRATION Hope of greater economic opportunity prompted many of these immigrants to come to America. Some also came seeking political freedom. Other groups, such as Russian Jews, sought religious freedom.

AREAS OF SETTLEMENT Most of the new immigrants settled in cities, especially industrial centers and ports, and often were concentrated in **ghettos,** or urban areas (usually poor) that are dominated by a single ethnic group. Asian immigrants tended to settle on the west coast, usually in California.

KEY THEMES AND CONCEPTS

Immigration and Migration

"Old immigration" took place during the first half of the 19th century. People from northern and western Europe, Ireland, and Scandinavia for example, made up a large number of these immigrants, but people came from other countries as well.

- What motivated immigrants in the period before 1850 to come to the United States?

GEOGRAPHY IN HISTORY

Organizing Information

- Where did most Irish and German immigrants settle?

- What difficulties did these immigrant groups face?

Immigrants

**Where they came
from 1840–1860**

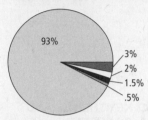

93%

3%
2%
1.5%
.5%

**Where they came
from 1880–1900**

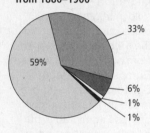

33%

59%

6%
1%
1%

☐ Northern and
   Western Europe

◼ Eastern and
   Southern Europe

◼ Americas

☐ Asia

◼ All others

Source: *Historical Statistics of
the United States*

ANALYZING
DOCUMENTS

Examine the pie charts
above, then answer the
following questions.

- What percentage of
  immigrants between
  1840 and 1860 came
  from northern and
  western Europe?

- How much did the
  percentage of immigrants
  from eastern and south-
  ern Europe increase from
  the period 1840–1860 to
  the period 1880–1900?

DIFFICULTIES THEY FACED Adjusting to life in the United States could cause strains in immigrant families. At school, immigrant children learned not only English but American tastes and customs. Immigrant parents often feared that their children were losing their religious and cultural heritage.

In addition, the growing numbers of new immigrants produced reactions of fear and hostility among many native-born Americans whose ancestors had come from very different backgrounds. Newcomers faced discrimination in jobs and housing. (As low-wage workers, they also competed against other minority groups, such as African Americans.) Popular pressure to limit immigration increased.

CONTRIBUTIONS The new immigrants found an abundance of jobs in the nation's expanding industries. Yet the steady stream of incoming workers to fill such jobs kept wages low. Young Italian and Jewish girls worked in the sweatshops of the garment industry. Poles and Slavs labored in the coal mines and steel mills of Pennsylvania and the Midwest. Chinese workers helped build the transcontinental railroad. These immigrants aided America's economic expansion and contributed to the nation's rich cultural diversity.

Reaction Against Immigration

The flood of immigration in the late 1800s brought with it a new wave of **nativism.** This was the belief that native-born Americans and their ways of life were superior to immigrants and their ways of life. In the late 1800s, descendants of the old immigrants were often among the nativists protesting the arrival of new immigrants.

Nativists believed that immigrant languages, religions, and traditions would have a negative impact on American society. Nativist workers believed that the many new immigrants competing for jobs kept wages low. A series of downturns in the economy added to fears that immigrants would take jobs from native-born Americans.

Immigrants thus often met with prejudice and discrimination. Jokes and stereotypes about the newcomers were common. Nativists also tried to influence legislation against immigrants. Key developments in this area are included in the chart on the following page.

Immigrants and American Society

Over the years, sociologists and others who studied immigration developed different theories on how immigrants were absorbed into the larger society.

"MELTING POT" THEORY According to this theory, people from various cultures have met in the United States to form a new American. The contributions of individual groups are not easily distinguished. The resulting culture is more important than its parts.

Reaction Against Immigration

- **Know-Nothing Party:** The party's members worked during the 1850s to limit the voting strength of immigrants, keep Catholics out of public office, and require a lengthy residence before citizenship. Also known as the American party, the Know-Nothing party achieved none of these goals and died out by the late 1850s.

- **Chinese Exclusion Act of 1882:** Some native-born Americans labelled immigration from Asia a "yellow peril." Under pressure from California, which had already barred Chinese from owning property or working at certain jobs, Congress passed this law sharply limiting Chinese immigration.

- **"Gentlemen's Agreement":** In 1907 President Roosevelt reached an informal agreement with Japan under which that nation nearly halted the emigration of its people to the United States.

- **Literacy Tests:** In 1917 Congress enacted a law barring any immigrant who could not read or write.

- **Emergency Quota Act of 1921:** This law sharply limited the number of immigrants to the United States each year to about 350,000.

- **National Origins Act of 1924:** This law further reduced immigration and biased it in favor of those from northern and western Europe.

ASSIMILATION According to this theory, immigrants disappeared into an already established American culture. They gave up older languages and customs and became Americanized, adopting the appearances and attitudes of the larger society in order to be accepted. Immigrants from Africa and Asia, who looked least like nativist Americans, had the hardest time becoming assimilated.

PLURALISM This theory recognizes that groups do not always lose their distinctive characters. They can live side by side, with each group contributing in different ways to society. This approach is sometimes called the salad bowl theory, since groups, like different vegetables in a salad, remain identifiable but create a new, larger whole.

THE AMERICAN WEST IN THE LATE 1800s

In 1893, Frederick Jackson Turner wrote in his paper "The Significance of the Frontier in American History" that the frontier "and the advance of American settlement westward, explain American development." Turner claimed life in the West had given rise to inventiveness, independence, and unique American customs. (While other historians would argue instead that other factors, such as the nation's European heritage or economic abundance, were the key influences, Turner's thesis has had lasting influence.) In 1890, the government had announced that the West was closed. Industrialization had aided the settling of the West.

ANALYZING DOCUMENTS

Examine the chart above, then answering the following questions.

- How influential was the Know-Nothing party?

- What prompted Congress to pass the Chinese Exclusion Act of 1882?

- Which laws restricted the number of immigrants to the United States each year?

 **PREPARING FOR THE EXAM**

Which sociological theory argues that different immigrant groups can live side-by-side without losing their distinctive characters?

The American West, 1862–1896

1862 Homestead Act	**1887** Dawes Act	**1896** McKinley defeats Bryan

1860   1865   1870   1875   1880   1885   1890   1895   1900

1876 Sioux War; Battle of the Little Bighorn

1890 Battle of Wounded Knee

ANALYZING DOCUMENTS

Examine the timeline above, then answer the following questions.

• How many years passed between the Homestead Act and the Battle of Wounded Knee?

• Which event occurred first: the Battle of Little Bighorn or passage of the Dawes Act?

⚷ KEY THEMES AND CONCEPTS

Government
The Dawes Act was aimed at breaking up Native American tribes and reservations. It offered Native Americans who gave up tribal ways the deeds to their land and United States citizenship after 25 years.

• Was the Dawes Act fair to Native Americans?

• Did Native Americans support it?

Native Americans and Westward Expansion

The westward expansion of the late 1800s continued to create problems for the Native Americans who stood in its path. By the 1840s, only scattered groups of Native Americans still lived in the East. Most lived west of the Mississippi on lands that few whites wanted. The California gold rush, the building of the transcontinental railroad, and the discovery of rich farmland in the Great Plains changed this situation. Now white people began to move onto Native American lands in the West.

INDIAN WARS The Native Americans fought back. From the 1850s to 1890, a series of wars raged in the West. Gradually the Native Americans were forced to accept treaties that crowded them into smaller and smaller areas of land called **reservations.** Native American resistance was weakened by the greater numbers of whites with superior technology, and divisions among Native American peoples that did not permit a unified resistance. The defeat of the Sioux at Wounded Knee, South Dakota, in 1890 is usually considered the end of the Indian wars.

CHANGING GOVERNMENT POLICIES In victory, the federal government continued to display little understanding or respect for Native American cultures and values. Native Americans were given reservation land that rarely could produce adequate crops or support game for the people living on it. Further, in 1887, Congress passed the **Dawes Act,** aimed at Americanizing the Native Americans. It proposed to break up tribes and reservations and to grant land directly to Native Americans as individuals and families. Native Americans who abandoned tribal ways would be granted deeds to their land and United States citizenship. Relatively few Native Americans accepted the terms

The Sioux Wars

1865	Federal government decides to build a road through Sioux territory. Sioux warriors resist violently, sparking Red Cloud's War.
1867	Red Cloud's War ends. Sioux agree to live on reservation in Dakota Territory.
1875	Federal government allows miners to search for gold on Sioux reservation. Second Sioux War begins. Chief Sitting Bull leads many Sioux off the reservation.
1876	At the Battle of the Little Bighorn, Sitting Bull's warriors destroy General Custer's army. In response, federal government sends more troops to the region. Most Sioux agree to move to reservations.
1890	At the Massacre of Wounded Knee, American soldiers open fire on unarmed Sioux, killing 200.

of the Dawes Act. By the turn of the twentieth century, the effect of the government policies had greatly reduced the size of the Native American population and had made them among the poorest Americans.

The Economy of the West

New technologies helped people who moved onto Native American lands exploit the wealth of the West. Railroads brought people and carried western crops and products to eastern markets. Barbed wire aided the growth of both farming and ranching. Steel plows cut tough prairie soil. Windmills pulled water to the surface of dry western lands. Mechanical reapers and farm tools allowed a smaller number of workers to plant and harvest larger crops.

The riches of the West, like the land itself, took many forms. In the Rocky Mountains, miners dug millions of dollars in gold, silver, copper, lead, and zinc ore. In the Great Plains, ranchers turned cattle raising into big business, as cowhands moved huge herds across the open ranges to rail lines. Farmers, too, were attracted to the Great Plains because of its rich topsoil and overcame heat, blizzards, droughts, insects, and occasional conflicts with ranchers to raise crops. Many settled lands claimed under the Homestead Act and later built huge farms. (Through the Homestead Act, as well as government land grants and other aid to large railroad companies, the federal government played a significant role in encouraging development of the resources of the West.) By the late 1800s, American farmers were raising enough to feed the nation and still export wheat and other crops.

Spurred by the expansion of mining, ranching, and farming, cities like Omaha, Denver, and San Francisco became some of the fastest-growing in the nation.

ANALYZING DOCUMENTS

American expansion onto Native American lands led to many wars and the near destruction of western Native American nations. The table at left outlines the struggle experienced by one tribe, the Sioux. Examine the chart, then answer the following questions.

- What caused the first Sioux War in 1865?

- How did the federal government respond to Sitting Bull's defeat of General Custer?

- How many Sioux were killed by American soldiers at the Massacre of Wounded Knee?

♀ KEY THEMES AND ↑ CONCEPTS

Economic Systems
Did the economy of the West rely on the same kinds of businesses as the economy of the North? Why or why not?

GEOGRAPHY IN HISTORY

How was the economy of the West influenced by each of the following?

- Rocky Mountains

- Great Plains

- Railroads

- Homestead Act

⚲ KEY THEMES AND
⌐ CONCEPTS

Civic Values

Many farmers joined the Populist party, which had strong support from people rather than powerful politicians. List three goals of the Populist party.

1.

2.

3.

Farmers, Populists, and Politics

Farmers gained more influence and power through two organizations: the Grange and the Populist party.

THE GRANGE Many farmers facing the hardships and isolation of rural life joined the **Grange.** This organization, founded in 1867, was originally meant to develop social ties. However, poor economic conditions made farmers aware that railroad companies, which often stored farmers' crops and carried them to market, had great control over their livelihoods. To win back some of this control, the Grange began to press for political changes to limit the power of the railroads. Pressure from the Grange and other groups led to the state laws regulating railroads that were upheld in *Munn* v. *Illinois* and to the federal law creating the Interstate Commerce Commission.

THE POPULIST PARTY Farmers realized that the best hope of winning more reforms was the formation of a new political party. In 1891, they founded the **Populist party,** which had among its goals a graduated income tax, direct election of United States senators, and government ownership of railroads, telegraphs, and telephones. The new party had strong grassroots support—support directly from the people rather than established political figures. Populist candidates soon made strong showings in elections for state legislatures and for the United States Congress.

▨ PREPARING FOR
▨ THE EXAM

During the election of 1896, the chief Populist party issue was free silver. Populist candidate William Jennings Bryan believed that the free coinage of silver would make it easier for farmers to pay off debts.

• Why do you think Republican candidate William McKinley opposed the idea of free silver?

READING STRATEGY

Reinforcing Main Ideas

What changes did the outcome of the election of 1896 symbolize in the United States?

THE ELECTION OF 1896 The Populists made their strongest showing in the election of 1896, the first election to follow an economic depression that had begun in 1893. The chief Populist issue in the campaign was **free silver.** The free coinage of silver would produce cheap money, or currency inflated in value that would make it easier for farmers to pay off debts. William Jennings Bryan, who ran on both the Populist and Democratic tickets, argued tirelessly for this idea. Republican candidate William McKinley had the support of big business, which contributed heavily to his campaign. McKinley claimed the nation's economy was sound and opposed free silver.

McKinley won the election by a fair margin. The nation's economy meanwhile improved, and the Populists disappeared as a political party. Yet, as has happened with other minor parties in American history, some of the Populists' ideas were later adopted by the other political parties.

The defeat of the Populists symbolized the great changes that had swept the nation since the Civil War. The economy had changed from agrarian to industrial. The United States was becoming a nation of cities rather than farms and villages. The West was closing and its influence coming to end. New immigrants were creating a new, complex, pluralistic culture in America. By 1900, the United States was entering both a new century and a modern age.

Questions for Regents Practice

For online Questions for Regents Practice,
visit the Prentice Hall Web site at www.phschool.com.

MULTIPLE CHOICE

Directions

Review the Test-Taking Strategies section of this book. Then answer the following questions, drawn from actual Regents examinations. Each question is followed by four choices. Read each question carefully. Decide which choice is the correct answer. Then on a separate piece of paper, mark your answer for each question.

1 Which problem in American society is dealt with in this poem?

Merry-Go-Round
Where is the Jim Crow section
On this merry-go-round,
Mister, 'cause I want to ride?
Down South where I come from
White and colored
Can't sit side by side,
Down South on the train
There's a Jim Crow car
On the bus we're put in the back-
But there ain't no back
To a merry-go-round!
Where's the horse
For a kid that's black?

—Langston Hughes

1 nationalism
2 migration
3 sectionalism
4 discrimination

2 The literacy tests and poll taxes used in the southern states after 1870 were designed to
1 ensure that only well-informed people voted
2 prevent African Americans from voting
3 provide an alternative to citizenship tests
4 promote advances in public education

3 President Abraham Lincoln's post-Civil War plan for reconstruction of the South was based on the theory that the former Confederate States
1 should be treated as conquered territories
2 could be readmitted to the Union only by Congress
3 had never actually left the Union
4 must grant full equality to all people

4 During Reconstruction, what was a belief of the Radical Republicans?
1 The former Confederate States should be brought back into the Union as quickly as possible.
2 Reconstruction should be used to force political and social reform in the southern states.
3 The North and South should take equal responsibility for causing the Civil War.
4 The freedmen should be denied equal civil rights.

5   One similarity between the Know-Nothings and the Ku Klux Klan is that both
  1   opposed the spread of communism
  2   exposed abuses in big business and government
  3   believed the problems of society were caused by the growth of labor unions
  4   fostered resentment against minority groups in American society

6   The most long-lasting victory for civil rights achieved during Reconstruction was the
  1   ratification of the 13th, 14th, and 15th amendments to the United States Constitution
  2   establishment of a strong two-party political system in the South
  3   increased prominence given to the Office of the President
  4   passage of Black Codes throughout the South

7   The Solid South refers to the political situation in the post-Reconstruction South where
  1   most eligible voters supported the Prohibition party
  2   freedmen held most government posts
  3   the Democratic party was dominant
  4   civil rights issues were strongly supported

8   Which statement best describes a major economic trend in the United States during the period from 1865 to 1900?
  1   Many business practices were developed to eliminate competition.
  2   Workers determined working conditions and factory output.
  3   The gross national product decreased steadily.
  4   Basic industries were taken over by the government.

9   An important result of industrialization in the United States was a growth in the
  1   influence of small family-owned businesses
  2   idea of socialism as the main political philosophy
  3   power of large corporations
  4   political power of small farmers

10   The Interstate Commerce Act, Sherman Antitrust Act, and Clayton Antitrust Act were attempts to limit
  1   business competition
  2   labor unions
  3   monopolies
  4   tariffs

11   Which factor that contributed to the economic growth of the United States in the period from 1865 to 1920 aroused the most opposition?
  1   growth of rapid transportation
  2   existence of democratic government
  3   mechanization of agriculture
  4   liberal immigration policies

12   Between 1865 and 1900, an issue that dominated national politics in the United States was
  1   slavery
  2   the rise of big business
  3   sectionalism
  4   environmental protection

13   During the second half of the 19th century, a major goal of new types of business organizations was to
  1   introduce safer and less expensive products to consumers
  2   consolidate the manufacture and distribution of products
  3   support the large number of government regulations
  4   compete successfully with Japanese imports.

Base your answers to questions 14 and 15 on the chart below and on your knowledge of social studies.

American Territorial Growth
(As a percentage of present United States territory)

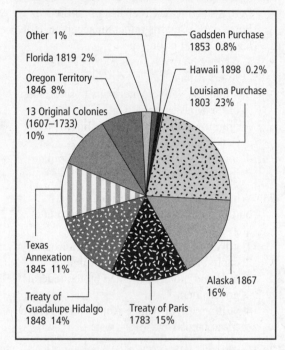

14 Which territorial gain accounted for the largest increase in United States land growth?
1 Treaty of Guadalupe Hidalgo
2 Texas Annexation
3 Louisiana Purchase
4 purchase of Alaska

15 Which policy is best illustrated by the chart?
1 isolationism
2 manifest destiny
3 containment
4 globalization

16 "[Buffalo hunters] have done more in the last two years, and will do more in the next year, to settle the . . . Indian question than the entire regular army has done in the last thirty years. . . . For the sake of peace let them kill, skin, and sell until the buffalo are destroyed."

—General Philip Sheridan

What was the result of the process described in this quotation?
1 Native Americans were granted farmland under the Homestead Act.
2 The disappearance of their economic base helped drive Native Americans onto reservations.
3 Many Native Americans moved to eastern cities to work in factories.
4 Most Native Americans migrated to Canada to find new ways to earn a living.

Base your answer to question 17 on the graph below and on your knowledge of social studies.

Farm and Nonfarm Workers
1860–1900

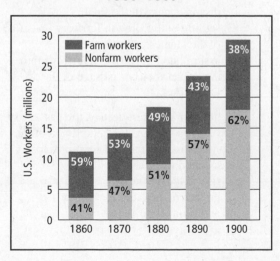

17 Which development contributed most to the trends shown in this graph?
1 industrialization
2 westward migration
3 commercial revolution
4 trade restrictions

18 A pioneer wanting to settle in the West in the 1870s would have benefited most from the
1 Homestead Act
2 Sherman Antitrust Act
3 Interstate Commerce Act
4 Agricultural Adjustment Act

19 Unlike other minorities in the United States, Native Americans have some of their rights guaranteed by
1 the Emancipation Proclamation
2 treaties with the federal government
3 the Declaration of Independence
4 black codes

20 In which pair of events did the first event most directly influence the second?
1 discovery of gold in California / Louisiana Purchase
2 building of the transcontinental railroad / disappearance of the frontier
3 settling of the Oregon Territory / passage of the Homestead Act
4 assimilation of Native Americans into American society / passage of the Dawes Act

21 A belief in manifest destiny, the passage of the Dawes Act, and the completion of the transcontinental railroad are most closely associated with the
1 rise of big business
2 growth of the labor movement
3 abolitionist movement
4 expansion and settlement of the West

22 "I am tired of fighting. . . . Hear me, my chiefs. I am tired. My heart is sick and sad. From where the sun now stands, I shall fight no more forever!"

—Chief Joseph, 1877

In this statement, Chief Joseph of the Nez Percé expressed his reluctant acceptance of a government policy of
1 placing Native American tribes on reservations
2 requiring Native Americans to settle west of the Mississippi River
3 granting immediate citizenship to Native Americans
4 forcing Native Americans to assimilate into American culture

23 Which factor was most critical to the building of the transcontinental railroads after the Civil War?
1 government ownership of the railroads
2 capital investments by labor unions
3 land and money provided by the federal government
4 willingness of Native Americans to leave tribal lands

24 During the late 1800s, the growing of cash crops by an increasingly large number of farmers resulted in
1 greater isolation of farmers from American economic life
2 a shift from self-sufficiency to commercial farming
3 less food available for export
4 general economic prosperity for all farmers

25 In the late 1800s, the desire for new markets for manufactured goods and coaling stations led the United States to pursue a policy of
1 isolationism
2 containment
3 collective security
4 imperialism

26 A primary source for information on the Spanish-American War would be
1 a historical novel about the war
2 a movie called *Theodore Roosevelt: The Rough Rider*
3 the diary of a soldier who fought in the war
4 a chapter on wars in an American history textbook

27 As the United States became industrialized, an important effect of mechanization and the division of labor was that
1 smaller industries had difficulty maintaining their competitiveness
2 the price of most manufactured goods increased
3 the demand to improve transportation systems decreased
4 pools and trusts became less efficient forms of business organization

28 In the late 1800s, most strikes by unions were unsuccessful mainly because
1 unions were generally considered to be unconstitutional
2 government usually supported business instead of workers
3 strikes had never been used before in labor disputes
4 strikers failed to use militant tactics

29 The poll tax, the literacy test, and the actions of the Ku Klux Klan were all attempts to limit the effectiveness of
1 the 14th and 15th amendments
2 the Supreme Court's decision in *Brown* v. *Board of Education*
3 civil rights legislation passed in all states after the Civil War
4 immigration laws such as the Gentleman's Agreement and the Chinese Exclusion Act

30 The Rockefeller Foundation, Carnegie Hall, and the Morgan Library illustrate various ways that entrepreneurs and their descendants have
1 suppressed the growth of labor unions
2 supported philanthropic activities to benefit society
3 applied scientific discoveries to industry
4 attempted to undermine the United States economic system

31 The major reason the United States placed few restrictions on immigration during the 1800s was that
1 few Europeans wished to give up their economic security
2 little opposition to immigration existed
3 the growing economy needed a steady supply of cheap labor
4 most immigrants spoke English and thus needed little or no education

32 From 1865 to 1900, how did the growth of industry affect American society?
1 The United States experienced the disappearance of the traditional "family farm."
2 Population centers shifted from the Northeast to the South.
3 Restrictions on immigration created a more homogenous culture.
4 The percentage of Americans living in urban areas increased.

33 Many wealthy American industrialists of the late 19th century used the theory of social Darwinism to
1 support the labor union movement
2 justify monopolistic actions
3 promote legislation establishing a minimum wage
4 encourage charitable organizations to help the poor

34 A main goal of the Grange movement of the 1870s and 1880s was to
1 force the railroads to lower freight rates
2 reduce the rate of inflation
3 strengthen labor unions
4 improve living conditions in urban slums

THEMATIC ESSAY

In developing your answers to the essay, be sure to keep these general definitions in mind:
(a) <u>discuss</u> means "to make observations about something using facts, reasoning, and argument; to present in some detail"
(b) <u>describe</u> means "to illustrate something in words or to tell about it"
(c) <u>evaluate</u> means "to examine and judge the significance, worth, or condition of; to determine the value of"

Directions
Write a well-organized essay that includes an introduction, several paragraphs addressing the task below, and a conclusion.

Theme: Industrialization
The growth of industry in the 19th century had a major impact on many aspects of American society.

Task
Identify any three aspects of American society. Using specific examples, discuss how the growth of industry had an impact on that aspect of society. Evaluate whether the role of industrialization had a positive or a negative effect and explain your reasoning using specific historic examples.

Suggestions
You may use any examples from your study of industrialization in the United States. Some suggestions you might wish to consider include: rise of organized labor, government involvement in the economy, status of the farmer, urbanization, or the role of women.

You are *not* limited to these suggestions.

Guidelines
In your essay be sure to:
- Address all aspects of the *Task*
- Analyze, evaluate, or compare and/or contrast issues and events whenever possible
- Fully support the theme of the essay with relevant facts, examples, and details
- Write a well-developed essay that consistently demonstrates a logical and clear plan of organization
- Introduce the theme by establishing a framework that is beyond a simple restatement of the *Task*
- Conclude your essay with a strong summation of the theme

DOCUMENT-BASED ESSAY

> For online Document-Based Essays,
> visit the Prentice Hall Web site at www.phschool.com.

This task is designed to test your ability to work with historical documents and is based on the accompanying documents (1–8). Some of the documents have been edited for the purposes of this question. As you analyze the documents, take into account both the source of each document and any point of view that may be presented in the document.

Directions

This document-based question consists of two parts: Part A and Part B. In Part A, you are to read each document and answer the question or questions that follow the document. In Part B, you are to write an essay based on the information in the documents and your knowledge of United States history.

Historical Context

After the Civil War, America faced new challenges including the rebuilding of the South and the rise of big business. These events changed American society.

Task

Using information from the documents and your knowledge of United States history and government, answer the questions that follow each document in Part A. Your answers to the questions will help you write the Part B essay in which you be asked to:

Discuss whether or not the changes that occurred after the Civil War created a more democratic America with greater opportunities for all.

PART A: SHORT ANSWER

DOCUMENT #1

"This case turns upon the constitutionality of an act of the General Assembly of the State of Louisiana, passed in 1890, providing for separate railway carriages for the white and colored races. . . .

"We consider the underlying fallacy [error in reasoning] of the plaintiff's argument to consist in the assumption that the enforced separation of the two races stamps the colored race with a badge of inferiority. If this be so, it is . . . solely because the colored race chooses to put that construction upon it. . . . The argument also assumes that social prejudices may be overcome by legislation, and that equal rights cannot be secured . . . except by an enforced commingling [mixing] of the two races. We cannot accept this proposition. . . . If the civil and political rights of both races be equal, one cannot be inferior to the other civilly or politically. If one race be inferior to the other socially, the Constitution of the United States cannot put them upon the same plane. . . ."

—*Plessy* v. *Ferguson* (1896)

1 State one reason why the Supreme Court ruled in 1896 that separate railroad cars for African Americans and white Americans were constitutional.

_____

_____

_____

_____

_____

_____

DOCUMENT #2

"In piecework they would reduce the time, requiring the same work in a shorter time, and paying the same wages. . . . They would start work every morning at seven, and eat their dinners at noon, and then work until ten or eleven at night without another mouthful of food."

—**Upton Sinclair,** *The Jungle*

2   What conditions would a labor union leader want to change in the factory described?

_____

_____

_____

DOCUMENT #3

THE VULTURES' ROOST

3   How does this cartoon portray the relationship between the trusts and the United States Senate?

_____

_____

_____

DOCUMENT #4

> *"Every contract, combination in the form of trust or otherwise, or conspiracy, in restraint of trade or commerce among the several States, or with foreign nations, is declared to be illegal. Every person who shall make any contract or engage in any combination or conspiracy hereby declared to be illegal shall be deemed guilty of a felony, and, on conviction thereof, shall be punished by fine not exceeding $10,000,000 if a corporation, or, if any other person, $350,000, or by imprisonment not exceeding three years . . ."*
>
> **—Sherman Antitrust Act (1890)**

4 How did the Sherman Antitrust Act restrict monopolies?

_____

_____

_____

_____

DOCUMENT #5

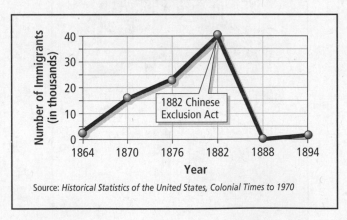

Source: *Historical Statistics of the United States, Colonial Times to 1970*

5 What effect did the Chinese Exclusion Act (1882) have on immigration?

_____

_____

_____

_____

DOCUMENT #6
Major Reconstruction Legislation

Date	Legislation	Purpose
1865	13th Amendment	• Abolished slavery
1865, 1866	Freedmen's Bureau	• Provided services for newly freed people
1867	Reconstruction Acts	• Established Republican Reconstruction program
1868	14th Amendment	• Defined citizenship to include African Americans • Guaranteed equal protection under the law
1870	15th Amendment	• Guaranteed voting rights
1875	Civil Rights Act	• Protected the rights of African Americans in public places

6 Based on the chart, what are two rights that were given to African Americans during Reconstruction?

_____

_____

_____

_____

_____

_____

_____

DOCUMENT #7

> *"American social development has been continually beginning over again on the frontier. This perennial [lasting for a long time] rebirth, this fluidity of American life, this expansion westward with its new opportunities, . . . furnished the forces dominating American character. The true point of view in the history of this nation is not the Atlantic Coast, it is the Great West. The frontier is the line of most rapid and effective Americanization. The wilderness masters the colonists."*
>
> **—Frederick Jackson Turner,**
> **"The Significance of the Frontier in American History" (1893)**

7 According to Frederick Jackson Turner, why was the frontier significant in the development of America?

_____

_____

_____

DOCUMENT #8
A Squelcher for Woman Suffrage

A SQUELCHER FOR WOMAN SUFFRAGE.

How Can She Vote, when the Fashions Are so Wide, and the Voting Booths Are so Narrow?

8 According to the cartoonist, what is one problem associated with granting women the vote?

_____

_____

9 What does this cartoon suggest about the cartoonist's opinion of woman suffrage?

_____

_____

PART B: ESSAY

Directions
Using information from the documents provided, and your knowledge of United States history, write a well-organized essay that includes an introduction, several paragraphs, and a conclusion.

Historical Context
After the Civil War, America faced new challenges including the rebuilding of the South and the rise of big business. These events changed American society.

Task
Using information from the documents and your knowledge of United States history and government, write an essay in which you

Discuss whether or not the changes that occurred after the Civil War created a more democratic America with greater opportunities for all.

Guidelines
When writing your essay, be sure to
- Address all aspects of the *Task* by accurately analyzing and interpreting at least four documents
- Incorporate information from the documents in the body of the essay
- Incorporate relevant outside information throughout the essay
- Richly support the theme with relevant facts, examples, and details
- Write a well-developed essay that consistently demonstrates a logical and clean plan of organization
- Introduce the theme by establishing a framework that is beyond a simple restatement of the *Task* or *Historical Context* and conclude the essay with a summation of the theme.

4

The Progressive Movement: Responses to the Challenges Brought About by Industrialization and Urbanization

Section 1   Reform in America

Section 2   The Rise of American Power

UNIT OVERVIEW

Between the end of the Civil War and the turn of the twentieth century, the United States became a more industrialized and urbanized nation. These changes brought many benefits to society, but they created problems as well. In this unit, you will review how Americans responded to change, both at home and overseas, in the years from 1900 to 1920. This period is called the Progressive Era. The term comes from the word "progress" and indicates that Americans were reacting to problems by working for reform.

Some key questions to help you focus on the Progressive Era include:

- What were the pressures for reform that led to the Progressive movement?
- Who were the Progressives?
- How successful were the Progressives in meeting their goals?
- What were the causes of increased international involvement of the United States from 1890 to 1920?
- What were the effects of this involvement on the United States and other peoples around the world?

SECTION OVERVIEW

The process of industrialization and urbanization in the United States had both positive and negative effects. From the 1890s to 1920, a reform movement swept the nation as many people began focusing their energies on correcting those negative effects. These reformers were known as Progressives, and their movement was so strong that this period has become known as the **Progressive Era.** Progressive reformers had a variety of motivations, used different methods, and had different degrees of success in achieving reform. Progressives supported the use of government power to bring about reform. Two strong Progressive Presidents—Theodore Roosevelt and Woodrow Wilson—implemented bold domestic programs to take Progressive reform to the national level.

KEY THEMES AND CONCEPTS

As you review this section, take special note of the following key themes and concepts:

Reform Movements What conditions stirred Progressive reformers to action?

Diversity How did women and African Americans work for their own rights during the Progressive era, and how successful were they?

Environment How did Progressive reform result in certain environmental protections?

Government What role did the government play in Progressive reform?

⭐ THE BIG IDEA

The Progressive Era was a period of great reform movements, including

- political reforms at the city, state, and federal levels.
- social welfare reforms.
- economic reforms.

These reforms affected some groups differently and had varying degrees of success.

⚷ KEY TERMS

Progressive Era
muckrakers
secret ballot
initiative
referendum
recall
direct primary
New Nationalism
New Freedom
Federal Reserve system
Clayton Antitrust Act

KEY PEOPLE

As you review this section, be sure you understand the significance of these key people:

Upton Sinclair	Marcus Garvey
Jane Addams	Ida B. Wells-Barnett
Jeannette Rankin	Robert M. La Follette
Carrie Chapman Catt	Theodore Roosevelt
Alice Paul	Gifford Pinchot
Margaret Sanger	John Muir
Booker T. Washington	William Howard Taft
W.E.B. Du Bois	Woodrow Wilson

ANALYZING DOCUMENTS

Using the information in this section and the timeline below, answer the following questions.

- During whose presidency was the Supreme Court case *Lochner* v. *New York* decided?

- Which event on the time-line involved the creation of an organization that worked for the rights of African Americans?

- How did Sinclair's *The Jungle* lead to reform?

KEY SUPREME COURT CASES

As you review this section, be sure you understand the significance of these key Supreme Court cases:

Lochner v. *New York* (1905)

Muller v. *Oregon* (1908)

Northern Securities Co. v. *United States* (1904)

Reform During the Progressive Era, 1901–1916

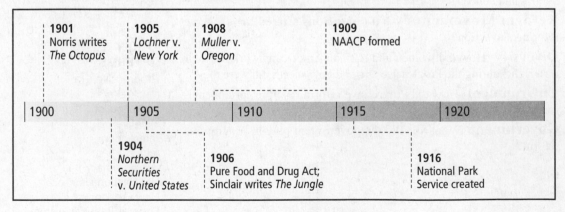

1901 Norris writes *The Octopus*

1905 *Lochner* v. *New York*

1908 *Muller* v. *Oregon*

1909 NAACP formed

1900 | 1905 | 1910 | 1915 | 1920

1904 *Northern Securities* v. *United States*

1906 Pure Food and Drug Act; Sinclair writes *The Jungle*

1916 National Park Service created

PRESSURES FOR PROGRESSIVE REFORM

By 1900, the United States was a rich and powerful nation. Industrialization, urbanization, and immigration had transformed the United States into a major world economy. The changes in American life, however, also brought problems. The negative effects of these changes led many Americans to call for reform.

Effects of Business Practices

In technology-driven fields such as railroads, steel production, and electric utilities, powerful monopolies restricted competition, often by using unfair methods. Without competition, monopolies could raise prices as much as they wished. Abuse of the nation's natural resources was accepted practice.

The corporate world grew increasingly wealthy and more powerful. Industrial leaders justified their actions by using the philosophy of **social Darwinism**—the concept that in society as in nature, the strong would survive and the weak would not. Those who succeeded earned their position, and those who failed deserved their failure. Social Darwinists believed that the government should not intervene in this process, a belief consistent with the ideas of laissez-faire economics.

Conditions for Industrial Workers

Working conditions for factory workers continued to be harsh. Many laborers worked 60-hour weeks on machinery, often in unsafe, unhealthy conditions. Getting hurt on the job often resulted in the worker being fired. Workers earned low wages, and women and children were paid even less than male workers. Workers had little security, because their employers could fire them at any time.

Soon, workers grew less tolerant of these terrible working conditions. Some tried to organize labor unions, but employers often fired those who did. Strikes were met with armed attacks from factory security guards and sometimes even federal troops.

Life for the Urban Poor

The gap between living standards of the rich and the poor increased widely during this period. This gap was most apparent in the cities. As the rich grew richer, building lavish townhouses in relatively safe and clean neighborhoods, the poor grew even poorer. They lived in urban slums characterized by poverty, crime, congestion, and poor sanitation. Housing in the cities was segregated by social and economic status, by race, and often by ethnic background.

Mixed Response of Government at All Levels

Government at all levels remained relatively unresponsive to the impact of industrialization and urbanization. Industries were unrestrained by federal and many state governments; the courts most

 PREPARING FOR THE EXAM

Movements can be traced through history. In Unit Two you reviewed the birth of the American reform tradition. For the exam, you may need to be able to identify and understand the different periods of reform in United States history.

- The Populists preceded the Progressives in the 19th and early 20th century reform movements.

- Reform continued under the New Deal of the 1930s and the period of reform in the 1960s.

KEY THEMES AND CONCEPTS

Government

Two landmark Supreme Court cases dealt with state laws limiting the number of working hours.

"There is no reasonable ground for interfering with the liberty of a person or the right of free contract by determining the hours of labor . . . Clean and wholesome bread does not depend upon whether the baker works but ten hours per day or only sixty hours per week. . . ."

—*Lochner* v. *New York* (1905)

- What seems to be the position of the Court on Progressive reform?

- How does the Court's action compare with the Supreme Court's decisions during the New Deal?

often failed to support fair standards of business. The laissez-faire philosophy prevailed, and so did political corruption at all levels of government. The public received little help from its elected representatives.

Several United States Supreme Court rulings provide examples of the mixed response of the federal government in the struggle for improved working conditions:

- In *Lochner* v. *New York* (1905), the Supreme Court ruled that a New York law limiting bakers' hours was unconstitutional because it interfered with the contract between employer and employee.
- In *Muller* v. *Oregon* (1908), the Court let stand an Oregon law limiting women to a ten-hour work day, ruling that the law was justified because it protected women's health. The effect of laws like this, however, was to keep women out of better paying jobs.

WHO WERE THE PROGRESSIVES?

The Progressives set out to tackle the problems of their era. They did not form one single group. The Progressive movement was made up of many different movements, and the Progressives were many different kinds of Americans. Their commitment and their success varied from person to person and from cause to cause. They did have some things in common, however.

Characteristics

The Progressives were influenced by the Populists but differed from them. While the Populists lived in the country or in small towns, the Progressives were largely city dwellers. Most of the Populists were farmers, who focused on farm problems. The Progressives tended to be educated professionals—doctors, lawyers, social workers, clergy, and teachers—with a wide range of concerns. The Progressive movement demonstrated the rising power and influence of America's middle class.

Beliefs and Goals

Like all reformers, the Progressives were optimists. They believed that abuses of power by government and business could be ended. They believed that new developments in technology and science could be used to improve the basic institutions of American society—business, government, education, and family life. Progressives believed in capitalism and were concerned about the growth of socialism as a more radical reaction to the effects of industrialization. Progressives wanted to bypass party politics, which they saw as corrupt, but they had faith that a strong government could and should correct abuses and protect rights.

Not all Americans were Progressives or agreed with Progressive goals. Many business and political leaders opposed business regulation. They accepted the social Darwinists' view that the vast differences in wealth and power in American society were the result of scientific forces that could not be changed. Many workers and farmers did not benefit from Progressive reform, nor did most African Americans, Asian immigrants, and Native Americans.

Factors Aiding the Movement

Many Progressives worked with national voluntary organizations, which grew rapidly in the 1890s. The movement was centered in cities at a time when more of the population was living in cities. This helped communication among Progressives, as did the expanding telephone and telegraph systems. The availability of inexpensive mass-circulation magazines and newspapers also helped spread Progressive ideas. Finally, the Progressives were aided by an improved economy. The first decade of the twentieth century brought prosperity. Industrial profits, wages, and employment all rose; farmers thrived. The result was an optimistic climate and the financial resources to support reform.

PROGRESS TOWARD SOCIAL AND ECONOMIC REFORM AND CONSUMER PROTECTION

A wide variety of reform movements developed from the 1890s to the 1920s.

The Muckrakers and Reform

Muckrakers helped bring reform issues to the attention of the public. Most were journalists and writers, but others were artists and photographers. Muckrakers investigated and exposed corruption and injustice through articles in mass-circulation magazines. They also wrote novels dramatizing situations that demanded reform.

In 1906, the work of the muckrakers resulted in the passage of the **Pure Food and Drug Act** and the **Meat Inspection Act**—the first two acts of consumer protection legislation. The federal government passed these laws after it became clear that the unsanitary conditions exposed by Upton Sinclair's novel *The Jungle* were based on fact.

As time passed, the muckrakers' influence declined, partly because readers tired of their sensationalism. Nevertheless, their tradition has continued to the present day.

Other Areas of Concern

Other people and groups also worked to bring Progressive reforms to American society.

PROBLEMS OF POVERTY Attempts to end the poverty, crowding, and disease in American cities began before 1900. Once the germ theory of disease was accepted, cities put more effort into improving water and sewage systems. A well-known urban reformer was Jacob Riis,

---

⚷ KEY THEMES AND CONCEPTS

Culture and Intellectual Life

Media has played an investigative role at various times in United States history. Newspaper, radio, and television journalists provide a different view in order to balance that of governments, corporations, and other sources of power.

The muckraking tradition continued long after the Progressive Era. The publication by *The New York Times* of the Pentagon Papers and the reporting of the Watergate scandal by Bob Woodward and Carl Bernstein in *The Washington Post* are two later examples of the muckraking tradition.

• What are some current examples of investigative media using television and other new media forms?

• What is the difference between investigative reporting and sensationalism in the media?

Progressive Era Muckrakers

Muckraker	Book/Article	Subject of Exposé
Frank Norris	*The Octopus* (1901)	monopolistic railroad practices in California
Ida Tarbell	*History of the Standard Oil Company* (1904)	ruthless practices of Standard Oil
Lincoln Steffens	*The Shame of the Cities* (1906)	urban political corruption
Jacob Riis	*How the Other Half Lives* (1890)	life in New York's tenements
Upton Sinclair	*The Jungle* (1906)	dangerous conditions in meatpacking industry

READING STRATEGY

Analyzing Cause and Effect

Examine the chart above. What effect did the work of each muckraker have on Progressive reform? Use the text and the chart on page 169 to answer this question.

GEOGRAPHY IN HISTORY

Some urban problems persist over time, while others change. When answering the following questions, consider issues of concern in urban areas, such as waste disposal, water and air pollution, energy usage, and congestion.

- Which urban problems at the beginning of the 20th century continue to be urban problems today?
- What new problems exist today?

who used writings and photographs to show the need for better housing for the poor. Some Protestant church leaders became part of the Social Gospel movement, which worked to help poor city dwellers. One goal of urban reformers was building codes that would require safer, better-lighted, better-ventilated, and more sanitary tenements.

SOCIAL SETTLEMENT MOVEMENT One early group of Progressive urban reformers was the settlement-house workers. Settlement houses, located in working-class slums, offered people—especially immigrants—education, child care, social activities, and help in finding jobs. Well-known settlement houses included Hull House in Chicago, founded by Jane Addams, and the Henry Street Settlement in New York City, founded by Lillian Wald.

THE PEACE MOVEMENT Addams and Wald were among the Americans who led peace groups, such as the Woman's Peace Party, in the period before and during World War I. Support of pacifism—the policy of opposition to war and fighting—weakened with America's entry into World War I in 1917 but was later revived. Pacifist Jeannette Rankin, the first woman elected to Congress (1916), voted against the United States entry into World War I (and World War II as well). For her pacifist efforts, Jane Addams won the Nobel Peace Prize in 1931.

TEMPERANCE AND PROHIBITION The temperance movement, which opposed the use of alcoholic beverages, began in the 1820s. Over the years, its chief goal became prohibition—outlawing the manufacture and sale of alcoholic beverages. Under the leadership of Frances Willard, the Woman's Christian Temperance Union (WCTU), founded in 1874, was a strong advocate of prohibition. Its members included many Populists and Progressives. It joined with the Anti-Saloon League, and the two groups sought moral reform through prohibition. They believed that through prohibition, problems of poverty and disease could be eased, family life improved, and the national economy made more productive. The temperance crusade led to national prohibition with the adoption of the **Eighteenth Amendment,** which banned the manufacture, sale, and transportation of alcoholic beverages in the United States as of 1920.

Women's Rights

Women were involved in all aspects of social reform, but suffrage for women continued to be the main goal of the women's rights movement in the Progressive Era. Women who had experienced success in other reform activities wanted to be able to vote. Furthermore, many suffragists thought that the women's vote would serve to correct various social problems.

WOMEN'S SUFFRAGE MOVEMENT The women's suffrage movement began as part of a larger drive for women's rights in 1848 at Seneca Falls, New York. The intellectual leader was Elizabeth Cady Stanton, author of the Declaration of Sentiments. She was joined in the 1850s by Susan B. Anthony, who provided the driving leadership of the movement. In the 1860s, the women's suffrage movement split over the best way to achieve its goals. The more radical organization was led by Stanton and Anthony; the more moderate organization was headed by Lucy Stone and her husband Henry Blackwell. In 1890, the groups merged to form the National American Woman Suffrage Association (NAWSA).

Stanton died in 1902, and Anthony died in 1906, without achieving the objective of their life work. However, the Progressive spirit gave the movement a new surge. In the early 1900s, leadership of NAWSA and the campaign passed to Carrie Chapman Catt, who devised the strategy that was to win women the vote. She abandoned the state-by-state efforts for women's suffrage, which had given women the vote in only nine states by 1912. Now, the movement would concentrate on achieving women's suffrage through a constitutional amendment. NAWSA swelled to two million members.

Alice Paul led the more militant Congressional Union until she was expelled from NAWSA. She then formed the National Woman's Party. Paul alienated many women by her use of militant tactics and her campaigning against Woodrow Wilson for reelection in 1916. In the end, it was the highly visible activity of women during World War I that brought them the final public support needed. In 1920, the Nineteenth Amendment was ratified, giving women the right to vote.

EDUCATION FOR WOMEN Another sign of women's progress was the growth of educational opportunities. Among women's colleges founded in the late 1800s were Vassar (1861), Wellesley (1870), and Smith (1871). State universities set up under the Morrill Act of 1862 were coeducational. By the early 1900s, more than 100,000 women were attending college.

THE FIGHT FOR BIRTH CONTROL The women's movement also included a campaign for family planning through birth control. This

---

READING STRATEGY

Reading for Evidence
Reread the section entitled "Women's Suffrage Movement." Based on the information in that section, answer the following questions.

- How many years passed between the beginning of the women's rights movement and the passage of the Nineteenth Amendment?

- How did suffragists change their tactics over time?

- What finally resulted in women winning the right to vote?

♀ KEY THEMES AND CONCEPTS

Civic Values
"The right of citizens of the United States to vote shall not be denied or abridged by the United States or by any state on account of sex."
　　　—Section 1, Nineteenth Amendment

- Whose rights does this amendment protect?

- What are the other important steps in U.S. history in the extension of the right to vote?

Women's Suffrage Before 1920

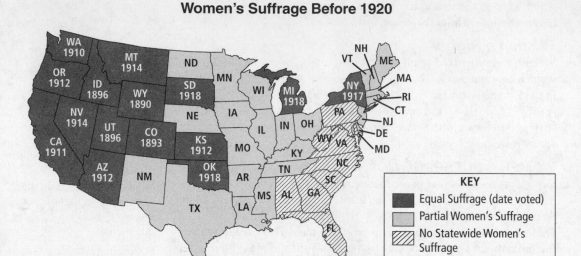

By the time the Nineteenth Amendment became law, many western states had already given women the right to vote.

campaign was led by Margaret Sanger, who began her work as a nurse caring for poor immigrant women in New York City. The American Birth Control League founded by Sanger later became the Planned Parenthood Federation. Sanger's movement was very controversial. She was arrested several times for sending information about contraception through the mail.

The Rights of African Americans

The decades after the Civil War were a difficult time for African Americans. Laws prevented them from exercising their right to vote. In *Plessy* v. *Ferguson* (1896), the Supreme Court upheld the Jim Crow laws, which required segregated—"separate but equal"—public facilities for African Americans and whites.

Lynchings by white mobs took the lives of hundreds of African Americans. Key African American leaders who worked to secure their people's rights are described below.

- Booker T. Washington, a former slave and founder of Tuskegee Institute, urged African Americans to get vocational training in order to establish themselves economically. This strategy, he believed, would increase their own self-esteem and earn them respect from white society. Washington's policy, called accommodation, was expressed in an 1895 speech known as the Atlanta Compromise.

- W.E.B. Du Bois, a Harvard-educated professor, shared Washington's view of the importance of education but rejected accommodation. He felt that African Americans should protest unfair treatment and receive a broad, liberal education, rather than a vocational one. In 1905, Du Bois founded the Niagara Movement to work for equal rights. More successful was the National Association for the Advancement of Colored People (NAACP), started in 1909 by a group of reformers that included Du Bois and Jane Addams. The NAACP successfully used lawsuits as a weapon on behalf of civil rights.

- In 1914, Marcus Garvey founded the Universal Negro Improvement Association, an African American nationalist and separatist group. The group wanted a separate black economy and urged African Americans to emigrate to Africa. Many of Garvey's ideas influenced the Black Power movement of the 1960s.
- Ida B. Wells-Barnett was a journalist who launched a national crusade against lynching in the 1890s. She was also a suffragist and one of the founders of the NAACP.

Rights of Jewish Americans

In 1913, a group of American Jews established the Anti-Defamation League, an agency of the Jewish service organization B'nai B'rith ("Sons of the Covenant") which had been founded in 1843. The Anti-Defamation League worked mainly to combat defamation, or libel and slander, directed against Jews. Later, its program was broadened to aim at securing the civil liberties of all Americans.

PROGRESSIVISM AND GOVERNMENT ACTION

During the Progressive Era, political reform took place at all levels of government—city, state, and national.

Reform of City Government

Given the Progressives' urban, middle-class roots, it is not surprising that they first concentrated their efforts on the governments of the cities in which they lived and in which they were influential citizens. In the 1890s, Americans interested in good government worked to elect reformist mayors. Success in doing so, however, did not always insure permanent improvement. Progressives had to change not only the leader, but also the way city government worked.

Two new types of city government are associated with the Progressive movement. They were popular in small and medium-sized cities. In the city commissioner plan, the city is run by a group of commissioners, rather than by a mayor and city council. In the city manager plan, the city council hires a professional city manager to run the various municipal departments.

Cities Respond to Urban Problems

Some Progressives concentrated not only on making city governments more efficient and less corrupt, but on improving city services. They worked to regulate services such as transportation systems, water, sanitation, and other utilities. They also tried to improve the appearance of cities by constructing large, elaborate libraries, museums, and other public buildings.

Reform of State Government

Progressives also acted to limit the power of boss-controlled political machines and powerful business interests at the state level. Progressives recognized that states exercised control over many of their cities. Extension of reform to the state, even the national level, was necessary to protect any gains made at the municipal level.

Progressive reforms often proved difficult to enforce, meeting opposition from business interests and the courts. Thus, changes in the way state governments worked were also part of the Progressive program. These changes, aimed at increasing citizen participation in government, included the following:

- The **secret ballot** prevents party bosses (and anyone else) from knowing how people vote.
- The **initiative** is a system that allows voters to petition the legislature to consider a proposed law.
- In a **referendum,** voters decide whether a given bill or constitutional amendment should be passed.
- **Recall** is the method used to force elected officials from office.
- A **direct primary** allows voters, rather than party leaders, to select candidates to run for office.

In 1913, Progressive reform resulted in ratification of the **Seventeenth Amendment,** which provided for the direct election—election by the people—of United States senators. Up to this time senators had been elected by state legislatures, which were often controlled by corporations or political bosses.

Remember that the secret ballot, initiative, referendum, and direct election of senators were all parts of the Populist party program. Adoption of these reforms offers an example of how third parties can influence major parties.

State Social, Economic, and Environmental Reforms

Wisconsin, under Governor Robert M. La Follette, was the model for Progressive reform. The state passed laws to regulate railroads, lobbying, and banking. It also started civil service reforms, shifted more of the tax burden to the wealthy and to corporations, required employers to compensate workers injured on the job, and provided for factory inspections.

Several other states passed laws like those of Wisconsin. Leading Progressive governors included Hiram Johnson of California, who reformed the railroad industry, and Theodore Roosevelt of New York. As governor of New York (1899–1900), Roosevelt, a friend of Jacob Riis and other Progressives, was concerned about social and economic reform. He supported the creation of the New York State Tenement Commission to investigate New York City tenements. He also worked to eliminate sweatshop factory conditions which forced women and children to work long hours for very low pay in dangerous conditions.

THEODORE ROOSEVELT AND THE SQUARE DEAL

The first three Presidents of this century—Theodore Roosevelt, William Howard Taft, and Woodrow Wilson—are known as the Progressive Presidents. Roosevelt, elected Vice President in 1900, became President when President William McKinley was assassinated in 1901. He was elected in his own right in 1904.

Roosevelt saw his job as one of stewardship—leading the nation in the public interest, like a manager or supervisor. He believed that the President had any powers not specifically denied to the executive in the Constitution. Roosevelt's administration is often known as the Square Deal because of the many reforms made during his presidency.

Consumer Protection

Although basically conservative, Roosevelt did not hesitate to use the power of the presidency to deal directly with social and economic problems. On the national level, he recognized the need for consumer protection, influencing passage in 1906 of the Pure Food and Drug Act and the Meat Inspection Act.

◳ PREPARING FOR THE EXAM

- What did Theodore Roosevelt mean by the Square Deal?

- What was meant by the stewardship theory of government?

- What did Wilson mean by the New Freedom?

- How did Theodore Roosevelt use the Presidency?

- What was the effect on the powers of that office?

○ KEY THEMES AND ⌁ CONCEPTS

Government
The three Progressive Presidents were Theodore Roosevelt, Taft, and Wilson. Based on the information in the text, what would you consider the most significant reform made during each President's administration? Why?

The Presidents of the Progressive Era

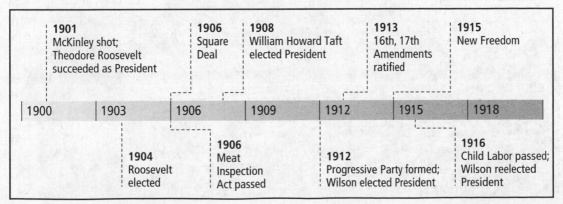

| 1901 McKinley shot; Theodore Roosevelt succeeded as President | 1906 Square Deal | 1908 William Howard Taft elected President | 1913 16th, 17th Amendments ratified | 1915 New Freedom |

1900 — 1903 — 1906 — 1909 — 1912 — 1915 — 1918

| 1904 Roosevelt elected | 1906 Meat Inspection Act passed | 1912 Progressive Party formed; Wilson elected President | 1916 Child Labor passed; Wilson reelected President |

Regulating Business

Roosevelt's reforms in business focused on strengthening regulations and breaking up trusts.

STRENGTHENING RAILROAD REGULATION In 1906, Congress passed the Hepburn Act, strengthening the Interstate Commerce Commission (ICC) and allowing it to regulate railroad shipping rates. Also, the ICC's powers were expanded to include regulation of pipelines, ferries, bridges, and terminals. Some complained because the act allowed railroads to appeal to the courts. However, Roosevelt was often willing to compromise on details to make a larger point—in this case the right of government to regulate business.

TRUST-BUSTING Roosevelt saw a difference between "good trusts," which were to be subject only to regulation, and "bad trusts," which were to be dissolved. The actions he took against big business earned him a reputation as a trust buster.

In 1903, Roosevelt convinced Congress to form the Bureau of Corporations within the Department of Commerce and Labor. He used the bureau to pressure corporations through investigations and publicity about their activities.

THE NORTHERN SECURITIES CASE By the end of the 1800s, the Northern Securities Company controlled the railroad system in the Pacific Northwest. In 1901, the Justice Department began prosecution of Northern Securities under the Sherman Antitrust Act. The case was eventually appealed to the Supreme Court. In its 1904 ruling

ANALYZING DOCUMENTS

Examine the cartoon, then answer the following questions.

- Who are the men at the desks?

- What place is pictured?

- Who do the large figures represent?

- Which constitutional amendment was the result of concern over the problem that is the subject of this cartoon?

in *Northern Securities Co.* v. *United States,* the Supreme Court upheld the judgment against the company and ordered the company to be dissolved.

THE "BEEF TRUST" Another government antitrust action was directed against a group of meatpackers known as the "beef trust." This prosecution, too, was upheld by the Supreme Court in its 1905 ruling in *Swift & Co.* v. *United States.* This decision reversed one the Court had made in 1895.

Labor Conditions

Roosevelt also achieved important reforms in working conditions.

THE ANTHRACITE COAL STRIKE In 1902, when Pennsylvania coal mine owners refused to negotiate with striking workers, Roosevelt threatened to send the army to take over the mines. The mine owners then agreed to arbitration, and the United Mine Workers, under John Mitchell, won shorter hours and higher wages.

Progressive Era Legislation

Date	Legislation	Purpose
1890	Sherman Antitrust Act	Outlawed monopolies and practices that result in restraint of trade, such as price fixing
1902	National Reclamation Act	Created to plan and develop irrigation projects
1905	United States Forest Service	Created to manage the nation's water and timber resources
1906	Hepburn Act	Required railroads to obtain permission from the Interstate Commerce Commission before raising rates
1906	Pure Food and Drug Act	Outlawed interstate transportation of impure or diluted foods and the deliberate mislabeling of foods and drugs
1906	Meat Inspection Act	Required federal inspection of meat processing to ensure sanitary conditions
1913	Department of Labor	Cabinet department created to protect and promote the welfare and employment of working people. Began with four existing bureaus, including the Children's Bureau
1913	16th Amendment	Gave Congress the power to levy an income tax
1913	17th Amendment	Provided for the direct election of senators
1916	National Park Service	Created to take over the administration of the nation's parks
1919	18th Amendment	Prohibited the manufacture and sale of liquor (repealed in 1933)
1920	Women's Bureau	Created within the Department of Labor to promote the status of working women

EMPLOYERS' LIABILITY One Progressive goal was to make employers assume more liability, or responsibility, for their workers. The Employers Liability Act of 1906 provided accident insurance for workers on interstate railroads and in Washington, D.C.

WORKING HOURS Another Progressive goal was to limit workers' hours on the job. As you read above, in *Lochner* v. *New York* (1905) and *Muller* v. *Oregon* (1908), there were inconsistent results in conflicts between the rights of individuals and the rights of businesses.

Conservation

As a naturalist, Theodore Roosevelt was interested in protecting the nation's environment and its wilderness lands. His policies were influenced by the conservationists Gifford Pinchot and John Muir.

Before Roosevelt, the government's land policy put land in the private hands of homesteaders, railroads, and colleges. Roosevelt shifted this policy and kept some land under federal government protection. This was the philosophy of John Muir, a founder of the Sierra Club, who was also instrumental in the creation of Yosemite National Park.

- Roosevelt used the Forest Reserve Act of 1891 to place national forests under the control of the U.S. Forest Service, headed by conservationist Gifford Pinchot. A total of about 150 million acres of public lands were placed under the protection of the federal government. When Roosevelt left office, he had tripled the amount of land set aside for the public as national forests, national parks, wildlife refuges, and national monuments.
- The National (Newlands) Reclamation Act of 1902 set aside money from the sale of public lands to build dams and irrigation systems in the West.
- In 1908, Roosevelt called a national Conservation Congress, attended by hundreds of naturalists and conservationists as well as by 44 governors.

PROGRESSIVISM UNDER TAFT

After Roosevelt declined to run for a third term, William Howard Taft succeeded him in 1909. Taft began his presidency with the support of Roosevelt and the Progressive wing of the Republican party.

Reforms Under Taft

Under Taft, the Justice Department brought twice as many suits against big business as it had under Roosevelt. One of the most important cases involved the Standard Oil Company. The Supreme Court's ruling in *Standard Oil Co. of New Jersey* v. *United States* (1911) held that the monopoly should be dissolved. But it also applied the so-called "rule of reason" to the Sherman Antitrust Act. There was a difference, said the Court, between "reasonable" and "unreasonable" business combinations. Size alone did not mean that a company was "unreasonable."

The Taft era witnessed other reforms, too. The Mann-Elkins Act of 1910 gave the ICC the power to regulate communication by telephone and telegraph. In 1913, the Sixteenth Amendment was ratified, authorizing Congress to impose an income tax.

Problems for Taft

Taft, who not as politically able as Roosevelt, soon ran into problems that split the Republican Party into a Taft faction and a Progressive faction. Like other Progressives, Taft wanted to lower tariffs, but he was unable to stand up to the Republican Congress that raised them with the Payne-Aldrich Act of 1909. Taft angered Progressives by calling the law "the best bill that the Republican party ever passed."

Taft ran into more trouble the following year when he dismissed Forest Service head Gifford Pinchot—a favorite of Progressive conservationists. Taft's secretary of the interior, Richard A. Ballinger, had allowed a group of business people to obtain several million acres of Alaskan public lands. Pinchot protested the action, and Taft fired him. Ballinger was identified with mining, lumbering, and ranching interests who wanted to develop the land for personal profit. They were supported by many senators from western states.

WOODROW WILSON AND THE NEW FREEDOM

In 1912, Theodore Roosevelt challenged Taft for the Republican presidential nomination. When the nomination went to Taft, Roosevelt ran as the candidate of a third party, the Progressive Party. Woodrow Wilson was the Democratic candidate, and Eugene Debs ran on the Socialist ticket.

Roosevelt offered what he called the **New Nationalism,** while Wilson called his program the **New Freedom.** Both were Progressive philosophies. Roosevelt, however, accepted social legislation and business regulation. The more traditional Wilson aimed for a return to competition in the marketplace with enforcement of antitrust laws. Wilson won the election of 1912 by a landslide of electoral votes, although he received only 41 percent of the popular vote. In 1916, he was reelected into office in an even closer race.

Financial Reforms

Wilson accomplished two major financial reforms while in office. In 1913, he pressured Congress to pass the Underwood Tariff Act, which lowered tariffs for the first time since the Civil War. The law also provided for a graduated income tax—one that taxed larger

READING STRATEGY

Formulating Questions
Taft, a Progressive President, wanted to keep tariffs low, but when Congress raised tariffs with the Payne-Aldrich Act of 1909, he praised the bill. What might have prompted him to do this?

KEY THEMES AND CONCEPTS

Government
What was the central theme of Wilson's New Freedom philosophy?

incomes at a higher rate (6 percent) than it did lower ones (1 percent). This kind of tax, which takes a bigger share of higher incomes, is known as a progressive tax.

Also in 1913, the **Federal Reserve system** was created. This national banking system is divided into 12 districts, each with a Federal Reserve bank. The federal government could now (1) issue a new, sound currency—Federal Reserve notes; (2) control the amount of money in circulation and interest rates; and (3) shift money from one bank to another as needed. The Federal Reserve Board lowers interest rates to stimulate consumer spending in times of recession or raises interest rates to control inflation.

Business Regulation

Wilson also achieved two important business regulations. The Federal Trade Commission Act of 1914 aimed to prevent unfair competition. It created a commission to investigate such practices as false advertising and mislabeling.

The **Clayton Antitrust Act** of 1914 strengthened the government's power to control business practices that threatened competition. Among other things, the act prohibited companies from price fixing and from buying stocks in competing firms. The Clayton Act tried to end the practice of using antitrust laws against unions, but later Supreme Court decisions undercut this provision. Later in the 20th century, federal prosecutions of alleged violations of antitrust laws continued against corporations such as AT&T and Microsoft.

Other Reforms Under Wilson

- The Adamson Act (1916) set an eight-hour day for workers on railroads in interstate commerce.
- The Federal Farm Loan Act (1916) made low-interest loans available to farmers.
- The Keating-Owen Child Labor Act (1916) tried to outlaw child labor, but the Supreme Court ruled the law unconstitutional in the case of *Hammer* v. *Dagenhart* (1918).
- Ratification of the Nineteenth Amendment in 1920 gave women the right to vote.

END OF THE PROGRESSIVE ERA

The Progressive Era came to an end when the United States entered World War I. During the war, American priorities shifted to the war effort, and in the 1920s, the trend shifted away from reform and toward acceptance of society as it was.

 PREPARING FOR THE EXAM

Established in 1913, the Federal Reserve system created the first central banking system since the Second Bank of the United States. Twelve banks, rather than just one, exercised monetary controls.

- Who proposed the first national bank of the United States?
- Why was the Second Bank of the United States terminated?
- What is the primary role of the Federal Reserve system?

2 The Rise of American Power

SECTION OVERVIEW

This section deals with American foreign policy during the Progressive Era, after reviewing the background of American expansion since 1865. From 1865 until 1920, the United States moved beyond the borders of North America to become an imperialist power on a global scale. Presidential power is the central issue. You will review the reasons for these actions and the national debate caused by them. Again, Theodore Roosevelt and Woodrow Wilson dominate foreign policy in the first two decades of the twentieth century. Their motivations, their policies, and the effects on people at home and abroad are all important understandings.

KEY THEMES AND CONCEPTS

As you review this section, take special note of the following key themes and concepts:

Places and Regions How did America's industrialization increase pressures for overseas expansion?

Constitutional Principles How did reactions to the Russian Revolution and World War I result in the restriction of some people's civil rights in the United States?

Change How did World War I change the role of the United States in the world?

KEY PEOPLE

As you review this section, be sure you understand the significance of these key people:

Frederick Jackson Turner
Henry Cabot Lodge
Matthew Perry

Theodore Roosevelt
William Howard Taft
Woodrow Wilson

⭐ **THE BIG IDEA**
From 1865 until 1920, the United States emerged from isolation to become an imperial power. The United States gained power and territory through

- victory in war.
- annexation.
- purchase.
- economic influence.

🔑 **KEY TERMS**

Open Door Policy
jingoism
imperialism
Roosevelt Corollary
dollar diplomacy
Central Powers
Allies
U-boats
Zimmermann note
Russian Revolution
Selective Service Act
Fourteen Points
self-determination
Treaty of Versailles
League of Nations
reparations

KEY SUPREME COURT CASES

As you review this section, be sure you understand the significance of this key Supreme Court case:

Schenck v. *United States* (1919)

EMERGING GLOBAL INVOLVEMENT

In the late 1800s and early 1900s, American expansion was in many ways a resumption of the expansionist drive that had been halted by the Civil War. A number of factors led the United States into greater global involvement in the late 1800s.

New Technology

Improvements in transportation and communication technology shortened distances around the world. At the same time, other inventions accelerated industrial growth. Railroads connected factories and farms to Atlantic and Pacific ports, from which steamships carried goods to Europe, Latin America, and Asia. Communication was faster and easier thanks to the telegraph, telephone, and transatlantic cable. Communications technology quickly provided information on international markets and on events in other nations that might affect the United States. The world was becoming more interdependent.

Drive for Markets and Raw Materials

Economics linked the domestic and foreign policy goals of the United States. Business leaders wanted raw materials from abroad. Both business leaders and farmers also wanted overseas markets. Overseas markets could provide economic stability, especially when, as in the 1890s, domestic consumption could not absorb the nation's output. At the same time, international competition increased as European nations, Japan, and the United States sought raw materials and

◌ KEY THEMES AND CONCEPTS

Change

Using the chart below and the text, answer the following questions.

- How did U.S. foreign policy between 1890 and 1919 change from previous policy directions?

- In what ways was it a continuation of existing foreign policy directions?

- How did the motives for expansion differ between the period 1803–1867 and 1890–1914?

United States Expansion, 1803–1867

Date	Territory	How Acquired
1803	Louisiana Purchase	purchased from France
1819	Florida	occupation, followed by treaty with Spain
1845	Texas	annexation
1846	Oregon Country	agreement with Great Britain
1848	Mexican Cession	Mexican War/treaty with Mexico
1853	Gadsden Purchase	purchase from Mexico
1867	Alaska	purchase from Russia
1867	Midway	annexation

Value of United States Exports, 1870–1920

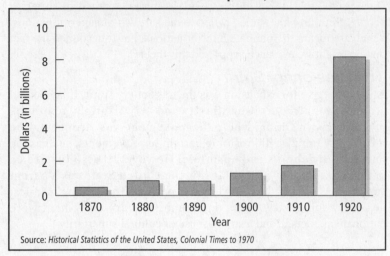

Source: *Historical Statistics of the United States, Colonial Times to 1970*

ANALYZING DOCUMENTS

Bar graphs help you to compare quantities over a period of time. Based on the graph at left, answer the following question.

What was the value of United States foreign trade

- in 1865?
- in 1900?
- in 1915?

markets. Foreign trade increased dramatically. High U.S. tariffs played a role in revolutions in Hawaii and in Cuba.

Growth of Naval Power

The U.S. Navy began to expand in the 1880s, building steel-hulled warships with steam engines and the latest in weapons. Behind this growth was the urging of expansionists like Alfred T. Mahan, who argued that as foreign trade grew, a nation needed a strong navy to protect shipping routes. The navy, in turn, needed bases at which to refuel and restock supplies.

Manifest Destiny and the Closing of the Frontier

As you will recall, the idea of Manifest Destiny took hold in the United States in the mid-1800s. Manifest Destiny is the idea that the United States had a divine mission to expand in order to spread the ideals of freedom and democracy.

This belief was fueled by historian Frederick Jackson Turner's frontier thesis. In a famous 1893 essay, Turner argued that the existence of a frontier throughout our history had been vital in shaping the American character. By 1893, Turner noted, that frontier no longer existed, an argument supported by the 1890 census. Some people interpreted this development to mean that Americans needed new frontiers beyond the current borders.

Social Darwinism

Closely tied to manifest destiny was the idea that the American way of life was so superior that the United States was obliged to carry its benefits to other peoples. Few wondered whether these peoples wanted American "benefits," or recognized that this notion implied that other peoples and their ways of life were inferior. The belief in American

PREPARING FOR THE EXAM

The history of United States foreign policy can be viewed as a sequence of stages listed below.

1776–1823
Protecting national independence

1824–1897
Fulfilling Manifest Destiny

1898–1918
Emerging global involvement

1919–1940
Limiting international involvement

1941 to the present
Accepting world leadership

READING STRATEGY

Formulating Questions
The drive for expansion into new territories was fueled by a belief in manifest destiny, social Darwinism, and the missionary spirit. How might the residents of those territories have reacted to these American attitudes?

ANALYZING DOCUMENTS

Examine the timeline below, then answer the following questions.

• Which event occurred first—Roosevelt's use of "big stick diplomacy" or the Spanish-American War?

• Based on the timeline and the text, what relationship was there between "big stick diplomacy" and the outcome of the Spanish-American War?

superiority was a form of social Darwinism. According to social Darwinists, the law of nature resulted in the survival of superior people. Similarly, the same law led to the survival of superior nations, which are meant to dominate inferior nations. Few questioned the fact that no scientific evidence supported this theory.

The Missionary Spirit

Another motive for expansion was the missionary spirit. It lay behind attempts to introduce Christianity and "civilization" to others, particularly in China, where the movement was strongest. The missionary impulse did result in certain improvements, such as the building of schools and hospitals. However, it also fostered a paternalistic view—one that saw the United States as a parent supervising weaker, less "developed" peoples. Underlying manifest destiny, social Darwinism, and the missionary movement were nationalism, racism, and a strong sense of cultural superiority.

THE UNITED STATES AS A WORLD POWER: ASIA AND THE PACIFIC

The United States role in Asia expanded because of the establishment of trade with China and Japan and the acquisition of Hawaii, Pacific bases, and the Philippines.

China

American trade with China began in the 1780s through the port of Canton. By the late 1800s, however, Americans were afraid that their economic opportunities in China might be limited. Throughout the nineteenth century, China had been subjected to imperialistic demands by Japan, Germany, Russia, Britain, and France. Each nation gained a sphere of influence—a region in which it had exclusive trade, mining, or other economic rights.

American Imperialism, 1867–1914

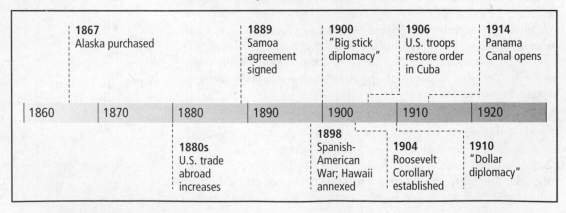

Open Door Policy

In 1899, Secretary of State John Hay tried to assure economic opportunity for the United States. He asked the European powers to keep an "open door" to China. He wanted to ensure through his **Open Door Policy** that the United States would have fair access to the Chinese market. The European powers, however, met his request with a cool response.

The Boxer Rebellion

In 1900, a secret patriotic Chinese society called the Boxers attacked missionaries, diplomats, and other foreigners in China in what is known as the Boxer Rebellion. The Boxers were revolting against the Manchu Dynasty and against the intervention of Western powers in China. The Western powers, including the United States, sent troops to restore order. Fearing that rival nations would take even more Chinese land, Hay expanded the Open Door Policy to mean that the current boundaries of China should be preserved.

Japan

Japan had developed into a major economic power after 1854, the year Commodore Matthew Perry ended Japan's isolation by negotiating a treaty opening two Japanese ports to ships from the United States. Unlike China, Japan carried out a far-reaching modernization program making it a major economic power by 1900.

From 1900 to 1941, a key aim of American foreign policy in Asia became providing the balance of power to restrict Japanese expansion. Japan displayed its growing strength by defeating Russia in the Russo-Japanese War of 1904–1905. In an effort to protect American interests in Asia, President Theodore Roosevelt mediated the peace treaty that ended the war. It was understood that Japan could remain in Manchuria and annex Korea. The agreement of the United States to the Japanese takeover of Korea was formalized in the 1905 Taft-Katsura Agreement. In return, Japan would not threaten the Philippines.

Relations between Japan and the United States experienced a setback when the San Francisco schools placed Japanese children in separate classes in the early 1900s. The Japanese government condemned this segregation. President Theodore Roosevelt achieved a compromise with Japanese officials called the **Gentlemen's Agreement of 1907.** This agreement ended school segregation in San Francisco but also restricted Japanese immigration to the United States.

In 1908, the two nations also entered into the Root-Takahira Agreement, in which both countries agreed to uphold the Open Door Policy and support China's independence and integrity. It also meant each nation would not attempt to seize the other's possessions.

ANALYZING DOCUMENTS

"The policy of the United States is to seek a solution which may bring about permanent safety and peace to China, preserve Chinese territorial and administrative entity, protect all rights guaranteed to friendly powers by treaty and international law, and safeguard for the world the principle of equal and impartial trade with all parts of the Chinese Empire."

—Open Door Policy, 1899

- Is this policy different from the principles of the Monroe Doctrine? If so, how?

- Why was it in American self-interest to call for the preservation of Chinese territorial and administrative integrity?

ANALYZING DOCUMENTS

The power that rules the Pacific . . . is the power that rules the world. And, with the Philippines, that power is and will forever be the American Republic."

—Congressional Record, 1900

Which policy is supported by this quotation?

1. Imperialism

2. Self-determination

3. Isolationism

4. Humanitarianism

**GEOGRAPHY
IN HISTORY**
Locate China, Japan,
Korea, and the Philippines
on a world map.

- How did geography affect
United States policies in
this part of Asia?

- Why were the strategic
locations of Hawaii, the
Philippines, Panama, and
Samoa important to the
United States?

**KEY THEMES AND
CONCEPTS**
Economic Systems
The acquisition of Hawaii
was motivated in part by
Americans living there
wanting to avoid U.S.
protective tariffs.

Backers of free trade
oppose protective tariffs.
When tariffs rise, nations
that are hurt economically
raise their own tariffs in
retaliation. Free trade, its
supporters say, increases
world trade in an era of
economic interdependence.
It also forces a nation's less
competitive industries to
improve.

Hawaii

Until the 1890s, Hawaii was an independent country ruled by a monarch. The United States had important business interests there, namely, sugar plantations. In 1890, the United States placed a protective tariff on imported sugar, including that from Hawaii, in order to protect sugar producers in the United States. This meant that Americans would be more likely to buy domestic sugar rather than Hawaiian sugar, and American planters in Hawaii would lose money.

In addition to being hurt economically by this protective tariff, American planters in Hawaii also feared the growth of Hawaiian nationalism and resentment toward the power of American interests.

In 1893, American planters, aided by the chief U.S. diplomat to Hawaii and by marines, carried out a successful revolution against the Hawaiian ruler. Against the wishes of the Hawaiian people, the American sugar growers asked that the United States annex Hawaii, but President Grover Cleveland opposed expansion by force. Hawaii remained in the hands of the American sugar interests as the independent Republic of Hawaii. Now American planters in Hawaii could get as much for their sugar as growers on the mainland.

Not until 1898 during the Spanish-American War did Hawaii become a United States possession. Then it became important as a military and commercial link to the Philippines and the rest of East Asia. Annexation was accomplished by a joint resolution of Congress rather than a treaty.

Samoa

In 1878, the United States gained the rights to a naval station at Pago Pago in the Samoan Islands. The port was also used by Germany and Great Britain. Samoa was situated in the Pacific on the trade route to Australia. Conflicts arose among the three nations. In 1899, Germany and the United States divided Samoa.

IMPERIALISM:
THE SPANISH-AMERICAN WAR

In 1898, the United States began to acquire new territories, making it an imperial power. Most of these territorial gains resulted from the Spanish-American War.

Underlying Causes of the Spanish-American War

There were several underlying causes of the war between Spain and the United States.

ECONOMIC In Spanish-controlled Cuba, economic chaos led to revolution and a demand for U.S. intervention. In the 1890s, Spain had imposed increased taxes on Cuba. In addition, the United States placed a protective tariff on Cuban sugar, which had previously entered the nation duty-free. The effect of these taxes was economic collapse. Resentment toward Spain fueled Cuban anger, and soon revolution erupted. Cubans provoked U.S. involvement by destroying American sugar plantations and mills in Cuba.

HUMANITARIAN Many Americans sympathized with the Cuban revolution and were appalled by the tactics of the Spanish military commander, Valeriano Weyler. He imprisoned hundreds of thousands of Cuban civilians in camps, where about 30 percent of them died from disease and starvation.

EXPANSIONIST American expansionists—including Theodore Roosevelt, Senator Henry Cabot Lodge, and Secretary of State John Hay—recognized that war offered an opportunity to seize territory from Spain, a weak nation.

Immediate Causes of the Spanish-American War

In addition to the underlying causes of the Spanish-American War, several immediate events aroused Americans' emotions. These fed a growing **jingoism**—a super patriotism and demand for aggressive actions—that created a warlike mood.

YELLOW JOURNALISM In the late 1890s, two of the most famous American publishers, William Randolph Hearst of the *New York Morning Journal* and Joseph Pulitzer of the *New York World,* were battling for readers in a circulation war. Both newspapers printed the most sensational stories and pictures they could find about the horrors of the Cuban revolution. The stories often exaggerated and distorted events for emotional effect. This kind of sensationalism is called "yellow journalism."

THE DE LÔME LETTER A personal letter written by the Spanish minister to the United States, Enrique Dupuy de Lôme, was printed in the *New York Journal* in February 1898. De Lôme's unfavorable comments—he called McKinley "weak and catering to the rabble"—made it hard for the President and other political leaders to withstand demands for war.

SINKING OF THE MAINE Less than a week after publication of the de Lôme letter, the United States battleship *Maine* exploded and sank in the harbor of Havana, Cuba, killing 266 Americans. The public blamed Spain, although a later investigation was never able to determine the cause of the explosion nor assign responsibility.

Fighting the Spanish-American War

In April 1898, despite Spain's agreement to an armistice with Cuba, McKinley asked Congress to declare war. Congress complied. It also approved the Teller Amendment, which promised that the United States would not annex Cuba.

ANALYZING DOCUMENTS

The term *jingoism* comes from a British song of the 1870s:

"We don't want to fight
But by Jingo, if we do,
We've got the men, we've got the ships,
We've got the money too."

- Based on the attitudes expressed in this song, how can you explain the meaning of the term *jingoism*?

 PREPARING FOR THE EXAM

Another vocabulary word associated with this time period is *yellow journalism.* The term has two possible origins. It comes either from a comic strip called "The Yellow Kid," or from the yellow paper on which newspaper comics were printed.

The Spanish-American War

Causes
- United States wants to expand in Latin America and Pacific.
- In Cuba and Philippines, people rebel against Spanish rule.
- Demands for involvement from American expansionists and newspapers.
- Explosion sinks American battleship U.S.S. *Maine* in Cuban harbor. Cause of the explosion is unknown, but angry Americans blame Spain.

The Spanish-American War

Effects
- United States defeats Spain in less than four months.
- Spain recognizes Cuba's independence. United States begins to control Cuban politics and economy.
- Puerto Rico, Philippines, and Guam become United States territories.
- United States is recognized as a world power.

With a quick victory in the Spanish-American War, the United States established itself as a new world power.

ANALYZING DOCUMENTS

Examine the graphic organizer above, then answer the following questions.

- Which are the *basic* causes of the war?
- Which are the *immediate* causes of the war?
- Which effects were long term?

ANALYZING DOCUMENTS

"It has been a splendid little war; begun with the highest motives, carried out with magnificent intelligence and spirit."

—Secretary of State John Hay, 1898

- How is this description of a war unusual?
- Why would anti-imperialists and pacifists object to this description?

The war lasted four months, with fighting in both the Caribbean Sea and the Pacific Ocean. Of the 2,446 Americans who lost their lives, fewer than 400 were killed in combat; the rest died from infection and disease.

The Results of the Spanish-American War

In December 1898, the Treaty of Paris, negotiated with Spain granted Cuba its independence, gave the United States the Philippines, in return for $20 million, and ceded Puerto Rico and Guam to the United States.

The Treaty of Paris of 1898 led to the acquisition of many former Spanish territories that formed the basis of an American empire. This set off a national debate among imperialists and anti-imperialists. It also led to increased American involvement in Latin America and Asia as the nation sought to protect its new lands.

IMPERIALISM: THE GREAT DEBATE

Ratification of the Treaty of Paris set off a great debate in the United States. As with all treaties, it had to be approved by a two-thirds vote of the Senate. The fundamental question was whether the United States should pursue **imperialism**—the policy of expanding a nation's power by foreign acquisitions.

Debating Imperialism

Americans in both political parties, in all regions, and from all social classes could be found on either side of the debate. Progressives were also divided. Imperialists included Theodore Roosevelt, Senator Henry

The American Empire During the Progressive Era, 1898–1917

Date	Territory	How Acquired
1898	Hawaii	annexation after 1893 revolution
1898	Puerto Rico	gained from Spain after war
1898	Guam	gained from Spain after war
1898	Philippines	gained from Spain after war
1899	Samoa	treaty with Great Britain
1899	Wake Island	annexation
1903	Panama Canal Zone	treaty with Panama
1917	Virgin Islands	purchased from Denmark

Cabot Lodge, and Alfred T. Mahan. Among the anti-imperialists were Andrew Carnegie, Mark Twain, Jane Addams, William Jennings Bryan, Booker T. Washington, and former Presidents Grover Cleveland and Benjamin Harrison. The chart summarizes the arguments of the two groups.

Acquiring the Philippines

In February 1899, the Senate approved the Treaty of Paris by a small margin. That January, Emilio Aguinaldo, who had been fighting the Spanish for Philippine independence, declared the Philippines a republic. The bitter war ended in 1902. More 4,000 Americans and some 16,000 Filipinos were killed in the Philippine insurrection. An additional 200,000 Filipinos died from starvation and disease. Atrocities were committed by both sides. At the end of the insurrection, the Philippines were under American control.

TURNING POINT

It what ways was the Spanish-American War a turning point in United States history?

Imperialists' Point of View	Anti-Imperialists' Point of View
The United States needs colonies to compete economically.	Supporting an empire would be a financial burden.
To be a true world power, the United States needs colonies and naval bases.	The United States should concentrate its energies on solving problems at home.
It is the American destiny to expand, and its duty to care for poor, weak peoples.	Nonwhite people cannot be assimilated into American society.
To abandon territories makes the United States appear cowardly before the world.	An empire would involve the United States in more wars.
It is only honorable to keep land that Americans lost their lives to obtain.	It is a violation of democratic principles to annex land and not offer its people the same rights as those of U.S. citizens.

The Constitution and the Territories

Imperialism was supported by the Supreme Court from 1901 to 1904, with decisions in the Insular Cases. The Court ruled that the Constitution only applied in those territories that Congress decided would be incorporated into the United States. The Court also held that people in annexed territories did not automatically have the rights of United States citizens. Congress would make that decision, based on the status given to a territorial possession.

Governing the Territories

The United States set up different means of governing its new territories.

- Hawaii was made a territory in 1900, its first step on the way to statehood.
- In 1916, the Jones Act promised the Philippines independence, but the law did not name a date. In 1934, the Philippines was promised independence in 10 years. This promise was delayed because of World War II but was honored in 1946.
- The Foraker Act of 1900 provided for a Puerto Rican legislature elected by the people with a governor and council appointed by the American President. Puerto Ricans received United States citizenship in 1917. In 1952, the island became a commonwealth. This status gives Puerto Rico many rights of a state excluding sending representatives to Congress.

GEOGRAPHY IN HISTORY

Based on the map below and the text, answer the following questions.

- Which United States acquisition was closest to Japan?
- Under what circumstances did the United States acquire the Philippines?
- What was particularly controversial about these circumstances?

United States Expansion, 1857–1903

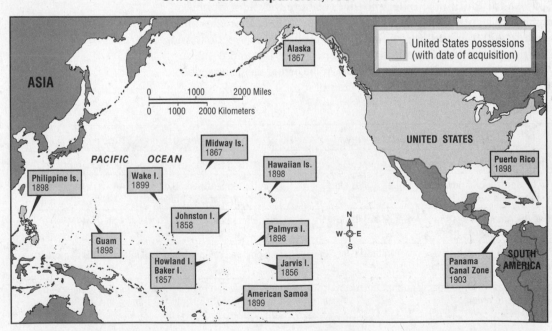

- U.S. troops remained in Cuba until 1902. American troops were sent to Cuba twice between 1902 and 1922. Cuban independence was limited by the Platt Amendment (1901), which remained part of the Cuban constitution until 1934. The amendment (1) required that the United States approve treaties between Cuba and other nations, (2) gave the United States the right to lease naval bases in Cuba, and (3) allowed the United States to intervene in Cuba to preserve order or peace.

AMERICA AS A WORLD POWER: LATIN AMERICA

Having acquired an empire, the United States found itself increasingly involved around the globe as it protected its new territories and interests. Of particular interest to the United States was Latin America.

Expanding the Monroe Doctrine

The Monroe Doctrine of 1823 warned foreign powers to stay out of the Western Hemisphere. For several decades, the relatively weak United States seldom referred to the doctrine. It was used, however, to support the American annexation of Texas as well as the Mexican War. It was used again, at the end of the Civil War, against France, which had set up a puppet government in Mexico and refused to give in to American demands to withdraw. France withdrew only after the United States massed troops along the Mexican border.

THE VENEZUELAN BORDER DISPUTE
In 1895, the United States had an opportunity to restate and expand the Monroe Doctrine. Great Britain and Venezuela were involved in a quarrel over the boundary between Venezuela and British Guiana (now Guyana). The United States offered to arbitrate, or help settle the dispute. When Britain refused arbitration, the United States claimed that the British were violating the Monroe Doctrine and forced them to negotiate by threatening war. Secretary of State Richard Olney, in the Olney Interpretation of the Monroe Doctrine, claimed, "Today, the United States is practically sovereign of this continent."

THE ROOSEVELT COROLLARY
President Theodore Roosevelt, further reinforced, even reinterpreted, the Monroe Doctrine. Economic problems in Venezuela and the Dominican Republic led to threats of European intervention. In both cases, the United States stepped in to restore order. Roosevelt explained American policy in a 1904 message to Congress. If a nation in the Western Hemisphere is guilty of consistently behaving wrongly, he said, the Monroe Doctrine requires that the United States step in and act "as an international police power." This policy is known as the **Roosevelt Corollary** to the Monroe Doctrine.

READING STRATEGY

Organizing Information

- For each of the following Presidents, summarize U.S. foreign policy in Latin America in the first half of the 20th century.

Theodore Roosevelt:

William Howard Taft:

Woodrow Wilson:

Franklin D. Roosevelt:

- Which presidents in the second half of the 20th century should be added to this list because they made important Latin American foreign policy decisions?

ANALYZING DOCUMENTS

Theodore Roosevelt was famous for the statement, "Speak softly and carry a big stick." Examine the cartoon, then answer the questions that follow.

- What does the big stick in the cartoon represent?

- What evidence is there that in recent decades the Roosevelt Corollary was used in Latin America?

- The Roosevelt Corollary to the Monroe Doctrine stated that "Chronic wrongdoing . . . may force the United States, however, reluctantly . . . to the exercise of an international police power. "How is his attitude expressed in the cartoon?

THE "BIG STICK" POLICY With the Monroe Doctrine as its justification, the United States intervened often in Latin American affairs, usually to protect American economic interests. President Theodore Roosevelt was famous for the motto "Speak softly and carry a big stick." This meant that the United States would use peaceful methods to protect its interests whenever possible, but that it would use military force if necessary.

The United States occupied Nicaragua with troops from 1912 until 1933. It also maintained a military occupation of Haiti (1915–1934) and the Dominican Republic (1916–1924).

The Dominican Republic had trouble paying its debts to European nations. When the Europeans threatened force, the United States took over Dominican finances, supervising them between 1905 and 1941. Haiti was supervised between 1916 and 1941 as was Nicaragua from 1911 until 1924.

DOLLAR DIPLOMACY President Taft's foreign policy approach was known as **dollar diplomacy.** This meant that the United States could help maintain orderly societies in other countries by increasing American investment in foreign economies. These investments tended to increase American intervention in foreign affairs.

INTERVENTION IN MEXICO During the Mexican Revolution, President Wilson intervened in Mexico's affairs in order to protect huge U.S. investments there. He also believed in moral diplomacy—conducting foreign affairs in terms of judgments about right and wrong. In 1913, after Victoriano Huerta overthrew the Mexican president and had him murdered, Wilson refused to recognize Huerta's government. The next year, the U.S. Navy seized the port of Vera Cruz to prevent a German shis from landing its cargo of arms for Huerta. Wilson also sent a force into northern Mexico in 1916 in an attempt to capture Pancho Villa, a Mexican rebel whose border raid into New Mexico in 1916 led to American deaths.

THE GOOD NEIGHBOR POLICY Only under Presidents Herbert Hoover (1929–1933) and Franklin D. Roosevelt (1933–1945) did the United States try to improve its relations with Latin America. Roosevelt backed what came to be called the "good neighbor policy." This meant less emphasis on intervention and more on cooperation. However, American economic dominance of the region continued.

THE PANAMA CANAL Since the mid-1850s, the advantages of a canal linking the Atlantic and Pacific Oceans were well recognized. With a canal, navy and merchant ships could move more quickly between the two oceans. Interest in a canal increased when the United States aquired colonies in the Pacific. In 1901 the United States, through negotiations, gained the sole right to build and control such a canal as long as it would be open to all nations.

Under Theodore Roosevelt, the United States settled on a route across Panama, which was part of Colombia. When Colombia seemed reluctant to agree to financial terms, Roosevelt encouraged Panamanians to revolt and declare their independence. The United States quickly negotiated a treaty with the new nation of Panama, which gave the United States a 99-year renewable lease on a 10-mile-wide strip of land across Panama. Panama remained a United States protectorate from 1903 to 1939.

Building the canal was a mammoth task, begun in 1904. Yellow fever and malaria caused delays as did the difficulty of moving more than 250 million cubic yards of soil. However, workers made the remarkable achievement of completing the canal ahead of schedule and under budget. The canal opened to traffic in 1914.

Responding to Panamanian demonstrations, the United States agreed in a 1977 treaty to return the canal to Panamanian control. Panama took over the canal on December 31, 1999.

THE UNITED STATES AND WORLD WAR I

World War I began in Europe in 1914 and lasted until 1918. The United States did not enter the war until 1917. The financial and human costs of this devastating conflict were enormous.

Causes of World War I

There were several factors that led to the outbreak of war in Europe.

NATIONALISM Strong nationalistic competition had developed among France, Britain, Russia, Austria-Hungary, and Germany, espe-

 PREPARING FOR THE EXAM

Before understanding how the United States became involved in World War I, it is important to review the basic causes of that war which began in 1914.

For each cause listed, give an example.

Nationalism:

Industrialism:

Imperialism:

Alliances:

Militarism:

READING STRATEGY

Analyzing Cause and Effect
Use the text and these three quotes to summarize the steps by which the United States entered World War I. Note the dates on each quote.

" . . . impartial in thought as well as in action."
—Woodrow Wilson, 1914

"He kept us out of war."
—Wilson campaign slogan, 1916

"The world must be made safe for democracy."
—Wilson request for declaration of war, April 2, 1917

• Did United States policy contradict Wilson's earlier statements and therefore involve the U.S. in the war, OR

• Did circumstances beyond the United States' control lead the nation to break its policy of neutrality?

cially after the unification of Germany in 1871. There was also national unrest within nations. For instance, the Czechs and Slovaks wanted to free themselves from Austro-Hungarian control.

IMPERIALISM Several nations were involved in keen competition for markets and colonies throughout the world.

THE ALLIANCE SYSTEM As national and imperial goals conflicted, two groups of nations organized against each other in an effort to maintain a balance of power. The Triple Alliance consisted of Germany, Austria-Hungary, and Italy. The Triple Entente was made up of France, Russia, and Great Britain. If fighting were to break out, members of either alliance were pledged to help each other.

MILITARISM The early 1900s witnessed a continual buildup of armies and navies. Germany, for instance, tripled naval construction in order to challenge Britain's control of the seas.

Causes of United States Entry into World War I

War broke out in Europe in July 1914, after the heir to the Austro-Hungarian throne was assassinated. Because of the alliance system, most major European nations soon joined the conflict. The United States was officially neutral. In 1917, however, the United States was drawn into the war. There were several reasons for this.

CULTURAL LINKS Few Americans were truly neutral. Some sympathized with the **Central Powers,** dominated by Germany and Austria-Hungary. These included German-Americans because of ties to Germany and Irish-Americans because of anti-British feeling. The majority of Americans, however, favored the **Allies,** or the Triple Entente nations. Americans had long-standing cultural ties with Britain. Many also felt loyalty to their first ally, France.

ECONOMIC TIES United States links to the Allies were economic as well as cultural. A British blockade of the North Sea effectively

The United States and World War I

Europe During the War

Map legend:
- Allied Powers
- Central Powers
- Neutral nations

Map labels: FINLAND, NORWAY, SWEDEN, ATLANTIC OCEAN, North Sea, DENMARK, Baltic Sea, RUSSIA, GREAT BRITAIN, NETH., BELG., GERMANY, LUX., AUSTRIA-HUNGARY, FRANCE, SWITZ., ITALY, ROMANIA, Black Sea, SERBIA, BULGARIA, MONTENEGRO, ALBANIA, OTTOMAN EMPIRE (TURKEY), GREECE, Corsica (Fr.), Sardinia (It.), Sicily (It.), Crete (Gr.), Cyprus (Br.), Mediterranean Sea, PORTUGAL, SPAIN, SP. MOROCCO, MOROCCO (Fr.), ALGERIA (Fr.), TUNISIA (Fr.), LIBYA (It.), EGYPT (Br.)

Scale: 0 200 400 Miles / 0 200 400 Kilometers

ANALYZING DOCUMENTS

Examine the map at left, then answer the following questions.

- Which nations were the Allied Powers?
- Which were the Central Powers?
- Which nations remained neutral?

ended American exports to Germany, which dropped in value from about $345 million in 1914 to $29 million in 1916. Meanwhile, the value of trade with the Allies increased fourfold. American business and agriculture benefited from this trade, much of it financed by U.S. government loans to the Allies, totaling more than $2 billion by 1917.

Most Americans did not believe that trade with or loans to the Allies violated the nation's neutrality. In fact, President Wilson and his closest advisers were in favor of the Allies. However, even in the 1916 election for President, Wilson continued to proclaim American neutrality, campaigning on the slogan "He kept us out of war."

PROPAGANDA Aided by their control of the transatlantic cable, the Allies conducted an effective propaganda campaign in the United States. They pictured the war as one of civilized, democratic nations against the barbaric monarchy of Germany.

GERMAN SUBMARINE WARFARE The Germans made frequent use of submarines in World War I. Because a submarine was very vulnerable when surfaced, Germany announced a policy of unrestricted submarine warfare, ignoring international law that required a warship to stop and identify itself before its crew boarded the enemy vessel and to remove the ship's crew before sinking it. Germany's attempt to destroy the British blockade by attacking Allied ships was the single most important reason for American entrance into the war. Wilson still insisted that America as a neutral nation had the right to trade with the nations at war and to send its civilians on ships into war zones.

READING STRATEGY

Organizing Information
Suppose you were a member of Congress in 1917. You must decide whether the United States should go to war against Germany and the other Central Powers.

- Based on the information from this section, which events would influence your decision?
- How important to your decision is the policy of *Freedom of the Seas?*

ANALYZING DOCUMENTS

American public opinion was extremely critical of Germany and its use of U-boats. Germany, however, did warn travelers—including passengers of the *Lusitania*—to stay out of the war zone.

NOTICE!

TRAVELLERS intending to embark on the Atlantic voyage are reminded that a state of war exists between Germany and her allies and GreatBritian and her allies; that the zone of war includes the waters adjacent to the British Isles; that, in accordance with formal notice given by the Imperial German Government, vessels flying the flag of Great Britian, or of any of her allies, are liable to destruction in those waters and that travellers sailing in the war zone on ships of Great Britian or her allies do so at their own risk.

IMPERIAL GERMAN EMBASSY,

WASHINGTON, D. C., APRIL 22, 1915.

CUNARD

EUROPE VIA LIVERPOOL

LUSITANIA

Fastest and Largest Steamer now in Atlantic Service Sails

SATURDAY, MAY 1, 10 A. M.

Transylvania - Fri, May 7, 5 P.M.
Orduna, - - - Tues., May 18, 10 A.M.
Tuscania, - - - Fri., May 21, 5 P.M.
LUSITANIA, - Sat., May 29, 10 A.M.
Transylvania, - - - 5 P.M.

ANALYZING DOCUMENTS

"We shall endeavor to keep the United States neutral. In the event of this not succeeding, we make Mexico a proposal of alliance. . . : Make war together, make peace together, . . . and . . . Mexico is to reconquer the lost territory in Texas, New Mexico, and Arizona."
—German foreign secretary Arthur Zimmermann

• What was Germany's first plan concerning the United States?

• If that plan failed, what did Germany propose to do in alliance with Mexico?

• What reaction would this note have had in the United States?

When a German submarine sank the British passenger liner *Lusitania* in 1915, almost 1,200 persons lost their lives, including 128 Americans. Even though the ship was carrying ammunition and Germany had posted warnings, the United States was outraged by the attack on civilians. In 1916, the Germans torpedoed a French steamer, the *Sussex,* with injury to Americans. Wilson threatened to break diplomatic relations with Germany, which then agreed to the Sussex Pledge. This stated that Germany would no longer sink passenger or merchant ships without warning and that the Allies would no longer violate international law with their blockade. Wilson accepted the first part of the pledge but ignored the second.

EVENTS OF 1917 A series of events early in 1917 finally led to America's entry into World War 1.

• On February 1, Germany announced a policy of unrestricted submarine warfare. It warned it would attack without warning all vessels headed for Allied ports. The main reason for Germany's decision was that the war was at a stalemate. Germany knew that its move would probably bring the United States into the war. However, Germany believed its **U-boats,** or submarines, could break the blockade and defeat the Allies before the United States could get troops to the battlefields.

• Two days later, the United States broke diplomatic relations with Germany. Tension and suspicion increased with the **Zimmermann note** of March 1. This was a message from the German foreign secretary, Arthur Zimmermann, to the German minister in Mexico. It urged a German military alliance with the Mexicans, promising them support in regaining their "lost territories" in the southwestern United States. When the message was made public, Americans reacted angrily.

- Four U.S. merchant ships were sunk by the Germans in March.
- Also in March, the **Russian Revolution** overthrew the czar. It appeared that more democratic forces would take control in Russia, so that if the United States went to war, it would be joining an alliance of democratic nations.

Role of the United States in the War

The United States entered World War I on the side of the Allies in April 1917. But earlier, in 1916, passage of the National Defense Act and the Navy Act, began the expansion of the armed forces. The 1916 Revenue Act was also passed to pay for military expansion.

THE DRAFT ISSUE Even before the entrance of the United States into World War I, the question of how to raise an army was being debated. Those favoring the draft saw it as being fair and democratic, with all Americans serving together. Those opposed to the draft—who preferred that military service be voluntary—viewed the draft as an example of the rich and educated exercising power over the poor, the working class, and immigrants. In May 1917, Congress passed the **Selective Service Act,** which established a draft. Eventually all males between the ages of 18 and 45 had to register. The constitutionality of the draft was challenged but upheld by the Supreme Court.

AMERICAN EXPEDITIONARY FORCE By the end of the war, 4.8 million Americans had served in the armed forces, 2.8 million of them draftees. Eventually, over 2 million Americans served in France in a separate command, the American Expeditionary Force, led by General John J. Pershing.

The United States supplied fresh troops to a war in which both sides were exhausted by years of trench warfare. Neither side had moved more than a few miles, but casualties were in the millions. The entry of the United States tipped the scale in favor of the Allies. The United States lost about 51,000 men, far fewer than the millions lost by other nations.

MOBILIZING THE ECONOMY To get the nation's economy geared up for war, certain economic operations were centralized and concentrated through a series of government agencies. Relying on the broad wartime powers of the President, Wilson used the Council of National Defense to oversee these agencies. Government control over the American economy increased vastly during World War I. For the first time, the government entered fields such as housing and labor relations. It also supervised various public utilities, including the telephone and

KEY THEMES AND CONCEPTS

Diversity

Discrimination in the armed forces denied African Americans the opportunity to serve in combat. Many volunteered to fight with the French as the 369th Infantry Regiment. Though facing combat for the first time, they performed with such skill and bravery that they were awarded the French Croix de Guerre.

ANALYZING DOCUMENTS

Examine the graphs, then answer the questions that follow.

- Approximately how many casualties did Russia suffer in the war?

- Approximately, how much money did the United States spend on the war?

Costs of the War for the Allies

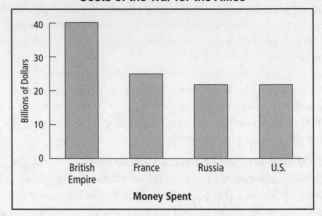

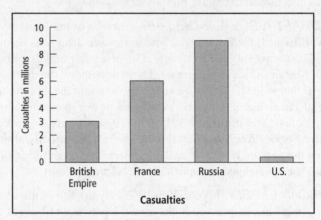

Source: V.J. Esposito, *A Concise History of World War I*

KEY THEMES AND CONCEPTS

Diversity
The entry of the United States into World War I led to a general hostility toward Germans and German Americans. German composers and musicians were banned from symphony concerts. German measles became "liberty measles," and a hamburger (named after the German city of Hamburg) became a "liberty sandwich."

telegraph. About 16 percent of male workers went into the military, and their jobs were filled by women, African Americans, and retirees.

PATRIOTISM To Wilson, World War I was a crusade. He believed that the Allies were fighting the war to end all wars, a war to make the world "safe for democracy." These idealistic goals helped make Wilson the Allies' moral leader. They also helped mobilize the American people to support the first conflict the United States had ever fought outside the Western Hemisphere. The nation geared up for the war with patriotic enthusiasm.

A propaganda campaign organized by the Committee on Public Information encouraged patriotism. Songs, posters, and pamphlets attacked Germany, urged the purchase of Liberty Bonds, and encouraged the conservation of resources. Patriotism was accompanied by an outbreak of anti-German and anti-immigrant hysteria. Americans burned German books, banned the teaching of German in some schools, and renamed sauerkraut "liberty cabbage." Nativism was expressed in a 1917 law, passed over Wilson's veto, that required a literacy test for immigrants.

Wartime Constitutional Issues

This social climate of patriotism and nativism led to actions that restricted some people's civil rights, usually in the name of national security. Not only were German Americans and other immigrants suspected of being possible traitors, but so were socialists, pacifists, and others who questioned the war.

THE ESPIONAGE AND SEDITION ACTS Two broadly worded acts served to control and punish those who opposed the war effort. The Espionage Act of 1917 made it a crime to interfere with the draft and allowed the postmaster general to bar "treasonous" materials from the mail. The Sedition Act of 1918 made it a crime to speak or publish anything "disloyal, profane . . . or abusive" about the government, Constitution, flag, or military services of the United States.

Under these acts, the government prosecuted more than 2,000 Americans and sent 1,500 of them to jail. Pacifists, socialists, and others seen as extremists suffered the most. A special target was the Industrial Workers of the World (IWW), a radical union active in the West. Its leaders were arrested, its strikes broken up, and many of its members interned.

SCHENCK V. UNITED STATES In 1919, the Supreme Court ruled that free speech could be restricted during wartime in the landmark case *Schenck* v. *United States*. In a unanimous decision, Justice Oliver Wendell Holmes wrote, "Free speech would not protect a man falsely shouting *fire* in a theater and causing a panic." Holmes went on to say that Congress has the right to prevent words that would cause "a clear and present danger." That same year, the Court upheld the Sedition Act, but in that decision the minority expressed concern that freedom of expression was endangered.

THE RED SCARE 1918–1919 In 1917, the Russian Revolution resulted in the communist overthrow of the czar. The communist system was openly hostile to American values and beliefs, such as capitalism, private ownership of property, and certain freedoms. By 1918, an intense fear of communism swept the United States, and many Americans began to call for the imprisonment or exile of communists in the United States, even though the number of American

ANALYZING DOCUMENTS

In wartime (particularly during the Civil War, World War I, and World War II), civil liberties were restricted. The Red Scare and McCarthyism that followed each of the world wars also led to violations of certain civil liberties.

"Words can be weapons. . . . The question . . . is whether the words used are used in such circumstances and are of such nature as to create a clear and present danger that will bring about the substantial evils that Congress has a right to prevent."
—*Schenck* v. *United States* (1919)

• According to this Supreme Court ruling, under what circumstances was it constitutional to restrict freedom of speech?

communistswas very small. This fear led some Americans to target others as well, including socialists, anarchists, labor leaders, and immigrants.

THE SEARCH FOR PEACE AND ARMS CONTROL

World War I ended in November 1918 with an Allied victory. The United States, particularly President Wilson, played a major role in the peacemaking process.

⚲ **KEY THEMES AND CONCEPTS**

Government

- Were Wilson's Fourteen Points a realistic basis for the peace treaty written at Versailles?

- Why did the Senate refuse to ratify the Treaty of Versailles?

- Was the failure to approve the Treaty of Versailles a turning back or a temporary halt in United States foreign policy?

The Fourteen Points

Wilson had first suggested his own peace proposals in January 1918. His **Fourteen Points** included the following:

- Open, not secret, diplomacy
- Freedom of the seas
- Removal of trade barriers
- Arms reduction
- **Self-determination** of peoples—that is, letting various national groups make their own political decisions
- An "association of nations" to guarantee political independence and territorial integrity

Wilson and the Treaty of Versailles

The Fourteen Points became the basis for the peace negotiations held at Versailles, France, beginning in January 1919. Wilson led the American delegation, thus becoming the first President of the United States to leave American soil while in office. Other Allied leaders included Georges Clemenceau of France, David Lloyd George of Britain, and Vittorio Orlando of Italy.

European nations, who had suffered far more than the United States, were cool to Wilson's plans. They wanted to be repaid for some of their losses, and some had made secret wartime deals involving territorial changes and money settlements that contradicted provisions of the Fourteen Points.

The most important agreement reached at Versailles was the treaty with Germany, the **Treaty of Versailles.** According to its provisions, Germany had to do the following:

- Accept complete responsibility for causing the war
- Pay huge reparations to the Allies
- Give up its military forces
- Cede lands to the new nations of Poland and Czechoslovakia
- Give up its overseas colonies

Wilson opposed many of the settlements of the Versailles Treaty and treaties with the other Central Powers. However, he was willing to

THE CHILD WHO WANTED TO PLAY BY HIMSELF.
President Wilson: "Now come along and enjoy
yourself with the other nice children. I promised
that you'd be the life and soul of the party."

compromise because the treaties provided for a new world organization, the League of Nations. The League, Wilson believed, would correct any problems caused by the peace treaties.

The League of Nations

The United States Senate had to approve the Versailles Treaty, and there Wilson ran into a great deal of opposition. Wilson had angered Republicans by excluding them from the American delegation to the Versailles Conference. Yet Republicans had a majority of seats in the Senate. The chairman of its foreign relations committee, Henry Cabot Lodge, distrusted and disliked Wilson. The feeling was mutual.

Some features of the League of Nations worried Americans. They feared, for instance, that the United States might be obligated to furnish troops to defend member nations.

Wilson stubbornly refused to allow any but the most minor changes in the Treaty of Versailles. He became increasingly moralistic and uncompromising.

When Wilson went on a speaking tour to gain popular support for the treaty, he collapsed and then suffered a stroke. His illness thereafter prevented him from playing an active role in the treaty debate.

The Senate voted several times on the Treaty of Versailles, but always defeated it. The United States made a separate peace with Germany, and never did join the League. Fundamentally, the nation had voted to retain its traditional foreign policy of preferring nonintervention and of acting alone when it did choose to play a role.

The Peace Movement: Women's International League for Peace and Freedom

Although the United States failed to join the League of Nations, there was still great concern in the United States about keeping the peace. During the Paris Peace Conference, for example, many American women met with others from around the world to form the Women's International League for Peace and Freedom. Jeannette Rankin, a prominent American pacifist, and reformer Jane Addams were among this group, and Addams was voted the first president of the league.

The Women's International League opposed peace terms that would create additional anger and hostility among nations. The organization opposed the Treaty of Versailles for that reason, suggesting that its legacy would only be more war. Peace organizations wanted disarmament, arms control, and neutrality.

Postwar Loans and Debts

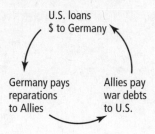

U.S. loans $ to Germany

Germany pays reparations to Allies

Allies pay war debts to U.S.

Reparations and War Debts

In 1914, the United States had been a debtor nation, meaning that it owed more money to foreign nations than they owed to the United States. After World War I, the United States became the world's leading creditor nation, meaning that other countries owed more to the United States than it owed them. The nation was also the world's leading industrial producer, exporter, and financier. These changes were due in large part to money from the payment of war debts owed this nation by the former Allies.

During World War I, the European Allies borrowed a great deal of money from the United States in order to buy war supplies from American manufacturers. After the war, these debts became a source of conflict. European nations argued that their debts should be canceled because, while the United States had contributed money, Europe had paid a heavy price in lives. Nevertheless, the United States insisted on repayment.

A factor that made repayment difficult was U.S. protectionist policy. High American tariffs limited European trade with the United States and thus reduced earnings that might have been used to pay off war debts. These tariffs also led to retaliation by 26 nations, which raised their own tariff rates.

One step aimed at making repayment easier was the Dawes Plan, adopted in 1924. Under this plan, the United States lent funds to Germany so that it could make war **reparations**—money it owed to the European Allies as payment for economic losses during the war. The Allies would, in turn, use the funds to make payments on the war debts they owed the United States.

Steps Toward Peace and Arms Control

In 1921, President Warren G. Harding hosted the Washington Naval Conference. The United States, Britain, France, Italy, and Japan agreed to set limits on the number of warships each nation could build. They also pledged to keep the peace in Asia and to protect the independence of China. The conference, however, failed to establish any means of enforcement.

In 1928, 15 nations met in Paris to sign the Kellogg-Briand Pact, which outlawed war except in self-defense. Enforcement provisions were missing from the pact, which 60 nations eventually signed.

Although the United States never joined the League of Nations or the World Court, it did send observers to League meetings. American judges also served on the World Court, which was based in Geneva, Switzerland.

Questions for Regents Practice

For online Questions for Regents Practice,
visit the Prentice Hall Web site at www.phschool.com.

MULTIPLE CHOICE

Directions

Review the Test-Taking Strategies section of this book. Then answer the following questions, drawn from actual Regents examinations. Each question is followed by four choices. Read each question carefully. Decide which choice is the correct answer. Then on a separate piece of paper, mark your answer for each question.

1 In the late 1800s, which reason led the United States to give greater attention to the world beyond its borders?
  1 fear of revolution in Latin America
  2 fear of Russian expansion in Alaska
  3 interest in finding places to settle surplus population
  4 interest in obtaining markets for surplus goods

2 The United States government economic policy shifted away from laissez-faire in the early 1900s. The main reason for this shift was the desire to
  1 increase government ownership of major industries
  2 make the United States more competitive with foreign economies
  3 coordinate the economy for a war effort
  4 reduce the abuses of big business

3 "Third parties in the United States are not . . . especially important in their own right, but only in terms of their influence on the major parties." Which is the most valid conclusion to be drawn from this quotation?
  1 The contribution of third parties has been insignificant in American history.
  2 The ideas of third parties have often been adopted by the two major parties.
  3 Third-party leaders have often become the candidates of the major parties.
  4 Third parties have failed to become important because they have been unable to develop new ideas.

4 Which is the most valid conclusion to be drawn from a study of the role of the Populist, Progressive, and Prohibition parties in United States history?
  1 Coalition government is a practical idea for United States society.
  2 Improvements for racial minorities are often initiated by third parties.
  3 Third-party platforms are often important in helping to bring about change.
  4 Voters are most greatly influenced by the religious beliefs they hold.

5 In the United States, the term "muckraker" has been used to describe authors whose writings deal mainly with
   1 criticizing the government's social welfare policies
   2 publicizing constitutional issues relating to minorities' rights
   3 advancing the cause of socialism
   4 exposing social conditions in need of reform

6 Which event of the early 1900s is evidence that Upton Sinclair's novel *The Jungle* had an important impact on the United States?
   1 adoption of reform in public education
   2 passage of legislation limiting immigration
   3 adoption of the 18th amendment establishing Prohibition
   4 passage of legislation requiring federal inspection of meat

7 "All forms of life developed from earlier forms. In every case the fittest survived and the weak died out. It is the same for people and nations." This passage expresses a view most often found in
   1 fundamentalism
   2 social Darwinism
   3 liberalism
   4 utopian socialism

8 Jacob Riis's photographs and the settlement house movement led by Jane Addams drew attention to the needs of the
   1 former slaves immediately after the Civil War
   2 farmers in the 1880s and 1890s
   3 urban poor in the late 19th and early 20th centuries
   4 Japanese and Chinese laborers in the late 1800s

9 "In the period between the Civil War and World War I, often the first American to greet the sea-weary immigrants when they walked down the gangplank into the United States was a member of the local political machine. This considerate politician helped the immigrant through customs, got him a job, and lent him a few dollars until payday."

   The process described in the quotation was a major benefit to the immigrant and to the nation because political machines
   1 encouraged new citizens to vote according to issues, not party labels
   2 helped provide a supply of cheap and willing labor for industry
   3 assisted the social, economic, and political assimilation of immigrants into the community
   4 helped to assure honest government

10 Western territories were among the first to adopt laws granting political rights to women because the
   1 Native American heritage of matriarchy served as an example to territorial governors
   2 strongest women's rights movements began in the West
   3 settlers brought a tradition of women's suffrage to American homesteads
   4 hardships of pioneer life encouraged men and women to share responsibilities

11 A major purpose of the Federal Reserve System is to
   1 deal with the trade deficit through tariffs and quotas
   2 control the minimum wage
   3 establish the federal budget
   4 regulate interest rates and the money supply

12 The views of W.E.B. Du Bois clashed with those of Booker T. Washington, because Du Bois insisted that African Americans should
   1 seek immediate equality of all types and resist any form of second-class citizenship
   2 pursue a policy of gradual integration
   3 accept racial segregation laws because they were constitutional
   4 learn a trade before pursuing political equality

13 Theodore Roosevelt's New Nationalism and Woodrow Wilson's New Freedom were designed primarily to
   1 increase the power and influence of the United States in foreign affairs
   2 reduce the role of government in the economy
   3 help the United States solve problems caused by industrialization
   4 protect the constitutional rights of religious and racial minorities

14 Which statement reflects a foreign policy view held by both President James Monroe and President Theodore Roosevelt?
   1 Revolutionary movements in western Europe must be stopped.
   2 Close economic ties with Asia must be maintained.
   3 Noninvolvement in world affairs is the wisest policy for the United States.
   4 United States influence in Latin America must by accepted by other countries.

Base your answers to questions 15 and 16 on the excerpt from the Progressive party platform of 1912 below and on your knowledge of United States history.

"We of the Progressive party here dedicate ourselves to the fulfillment of the duty laid upon us by our fathers to maintain the government of the people, by the people, and for the people whose foundations they laid. . . .

"To destroy this invisible government, to dissolve the unholy alliance between corrupt business and corrupt politics is the first task of statesmanship of the day."

15 The phrase "invisible government" refers to the power exerted by
   1 the President's cabinet
   2 the Supreme Court
   3 pressure groups
   4 minority parties in Congress

16 The phrase "government of the people, by the people, and for the people" has been previously stated in the
   1 Declaration of Independence
   2 Bill of Rights
   3 Preamble to the Constitution
   4 Gettysburg Address

17 Which pair of terms represent two major causes of imperialism in the 19th century?
   1 industrialism and communism
   2 communism and fascism
   3 nationalism and industrialism
   4 collectivism and missionary zeal

18 "The Constitution rides behind
   And the Big Stick rides before
   (Which is the rule of precedent
   In the reign of Theodore)."

This rhyme from the early 1900s suggests that President Theodore Roosevelt
   1 relied heavily on the advice of his cabinet and Congress
   2 failed to make adequate use of executive power
   3 developed strong foreign policies but neglected domestic needs
   4 ignored democratic principles in carrying our foreign policy

19 During the late 19th century, some United States newspapers printed exaggerated accounts of Spanish cruelty in Cuba. These reports helped to bring about the Spanish-American War primarily by
  1 arousing public anger against Spain
  2 provoking the anger of the business community
  3 alienating the Spanish government
  4 encouraging the formation of Spanish revolutionary groups

20 In the late 19th and early 20th centuries, United States intervention in Latin America was motivated mainly by the United States desire to
  1 suppress Latin American movements for national independence
  2 reduce the influence of communism
  3 ensure the safety of its growing investments in the area
  4 counteract Spain's economic dominance of the area

21 The main reason the United States developed the Open Door Policy was to
  1 allow the United States to expand its trade with China
  2 demonstrate the positive features of democracy to Chinese leaders
  3 aid the Chinese Nationalists in their struggle with the Chinese Communists
  4 encourage Chinese workers to come to the United States

22 The "clear and present danger" ruling in the Supreme Court case *Schenck* v. *United States* (1919) confirmed the idea that
  1 prayer in public schools is unconstitutional
  2 racism in the United States is illegal
  3 interstate commerce can be regulated by state governments
  4 constitutional rights are not absolute

23 The main objective of President Woodrow Wilson's Fourteen Points was to
  1 establish a military alliance with European nations
  2 punish Germany for causing World War I
  3 provide for a just and lasting peace
  4 encourage open immigration in industrial nations

24 "Why, by interweaving our destiny with that of any part of Europe, entangle our peace and prosperity in the toils of European ambition, rivalship, interest, humor, or caprice?"

  Which action by the United States best reflects the philosophy expressed in this quotation?
  1 passage of legislation restricting immigration
  2 rejection of the Treaty of Versailles
  3 enactment of the Lend-Lease Act
  4 approval of the United Nations Charter

25 "The chief opponents of the Versailles Treaty were dead men: Washington, Jefferson, and Madison."

  This statement suggests that opposition in the United States to the Versailles Treaty was based on the
  1 rejection of Woodrow Wilson's Fourteen Points
  2 fear that the treaty would violate the tradition of noninvolvement
  3 belief that the treaty was too harsh on the Central Powers
  4 unhappiness of citizens with United States participation in World War I

26 The greatest contribution of the United States to world peace during the period between World War I and World War II was
  1 support of the League of Nations
  2 support of the disarmament movement
  3 membership in the World Court
  4 adoption of free trade

THEMATIC ESSAY

In developing your answers to the essay, be sure to keep these general definitions in mind:

(a) <u>discuss</u> means "to make observations about something using facts, reasoning, and argument; to present in some detail"

(b) <u>describe</u> means "to illustrate something in words or to tell about it"

(c) <u>evaluate</u> means "to examine and judge the significance, worth, or condition of; to determine the value of"

Directions

Write a well-organized essay that includes an introduction, several paragraphs addressing the task below, and a conclusion.

Theme: Foreign Policy

The primary aim of a nation's foreign policy is the self-interest of that nation. Throughout United States history, certain foreign policy actions have led to debate over whether they were in the national interest.

Task

From your study of United States history, identify two foreign policy actions that have led to debate over whether they were in the national interest.

For each foreign policy action identified:

- Discuss the historical circumstances that led the United States to take a specific foreign policy action.
- Describe the foreign policy action that was taken.
- Describe the opposing viewpoints about the role of national self-interest in that action.
- Evaluate whether the action taken succeeded in promoting the national self-interest.

Suggestions

You may use any major controversial foreign policy action from your study of United States history. Some suggestions you might wish to consider include: War of 1812; Mexican War (1846–1848); acquisition of the Philippines(1898–1902); Roosevelt Corollary to the Monroe Doctrine (1904); Treaty of Versailles (1919); Lend Lease Act (1941); Vietnam War; Persian Gulf Crisis (1990–1991).

You are *not* limited to these suggestions.

Guidelines

In your essay be sure to:

- Address all aspects of the *Task*
- Analyze, evaluate, or compare and/or contrast issues and events whenever possible
- Fully support the theme of the essay with relevant facts, examples, and details
- Write a well-developed essay that consistently demonstrates a logical and clear plan of organization
- Introduce the theme by establishing a framework that is beyond a simple restatement of the *Task*
- Conclude your essay with a strong summation of the theme

DOCUMENT-BASED ESSAY

> For online Document-Based Essays,
> visit the Prentice Hall Web site at www.phschool.com.

This task is designed to test your ability to work with historical documents and is based on the accompanying documents (1–5). Some of the documents have been edited for the purposes of this question. As you analyze the documents, take into account both the source of each document and any point of view that may be presented in the document.

Directions

This document-based question consists of two parts: Part A and Part B. In Part A, you are to read each document and answer the question or questions that follow the document. In Part B, you are to write an essay based on the information in the documents and your knowledge of United States history.

Historical Context

As the United States transformed into an industrialized nation, the effects of this massive change were felt at all levels of society. Industrialization had long-term social, economic, and political effects on American society.

Task

Using information from the documents and your knowledge of United States history and government, answer the questions that follow each document in Part A. Your answers to the questions will help you write the Part B essay in which you be asked to:

Discuss the social, economic, and political reactions to industrialization and urbanization in the United States from 1890 to 1920.

PART A: SHORT ANSWER

DOCUMENT #1

> *"Today three-fourths of [New York's] people live in tenements. . . . The gang is the ripe fruit of tenement-house growth. It was born there, endowed with a heritage of instinctive hostility to restraint by a generation that sacrificed home to freedom, or left its country for its country's good. . . . New York's tough represents the essence of reaction against the old and the new oppression, nursed in the rank soil of its slums."*
>
> **—Jacob Riis, *How the Other Half Lives*, 1890**

1   According to Jacob Riis, what problems developed as a result of urbanization?

_____

_____

_____

DOCUMENT #2

> *"I insist that the true object of all true education is not to make men carpenters, it is to make carpenters men. . . . The Talented Tenth of the Negro race must be made leaders of thought and missionaries of culture among their people. No others can do this work and Negro colleges must train men for it."*
>
> **—W.E.B. Du Bois**

2   According to Du Bois, what should be the role of well-educated African Americans in society?

_____

_____

_____

DOCUMENT #3

Reform	Before the Reform	After the Reform
Primary	Party leaders pick candidates for state and local offices	Voters select party's candidates
Initiative	Only members of state legislatures can introduce bills	Votes can put bills before state legislatures
Referendum	Only legislators pass laws	Voters can vote on bills directly
Recall	Only courts or legislatures can remove corrupt officials	Voters can remove elected officials from office

3 State one way in which Progressive legislation granted citizens greater participation in state governments.

_____

_____

_____

DOCUMENT #4

"It shall be unlawful for any person engaged in commerce . . . to discriminate in price between different purchasers of commodities of like grade and quality . . . where the effect of such discrimination may be substantially to lessen competition or tend to create a monopoly. . . .

"No person engaged in commerce . . . shall acquire . . . the whole or any part of the stock . . . where in any line of commerce or in any activity affecting commerce in any section of the country, the effect of such acquisition may be substantially to lessen competition, or to tend to create a monopoly."

—Clayton Antitrust Act

4 What effect did the Clayton Antitrust Act have on monopolies such as Standard Oil?

_____

_____

DOCUMENT #5
Value of United States Exports, 1870–1920

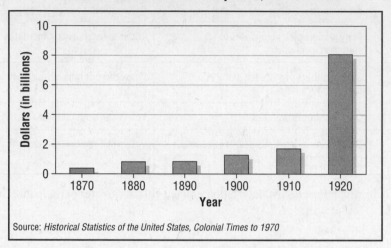

Source: *Historical Statistics of the United States, Colonial Times to 1970*

5 Based on this graph and your knowledge of United States history, how did industrialization affect the activity of American businesses in international markets?

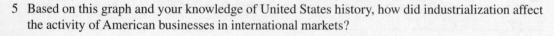

PART B: ESSAY

Directions
Using information from the documents provided, and your knowledge of United States history, write a well-organized essay that includes an introduction, several paragraphs, and a conclusion.

Historical Context
As the United States transformed into an industrialized nation, the effects of this massive change were felt at all levels of society. Industrialization had long-term social, economic, and political effects on American society.

Task
Using information from the documents and your knowledge of United States history and government, write an essay in which you

Discuss the social, economic, and political reactions to industrialization and urbanization in the United States from 1890 to 1920.

Guidelines
When writing your essay, be sure to
- Address all aspects of the *Task* by accurately analyzing and interpreting at least <u>four</u> documents
- Incorporate information from the documents in the body of the essay
- Incorporate relevant outside information throughout the essay
- Richly support the theme with relevant facts, examples, and details
- Write a well-developed essay that consistently demonstrates a logical and clean plan of organization
- Introduce the theme by establishing a framework that is beyond a simple restatement of the *Task* or *Historical Context* and conclude the essay with a summation of the theme.

5 At Home and Abroad: Prosperity and Depression, 1917–1940

UNIT OVERVIEW

During the decades of the 1920s and 1930s, the United States completed the transition to a modern, urban, industrial nation. In the 1920s, the United States experienced sharp differences in income levels and shifts in cultural values, which created tensions in society and raised issues of civil liberties. At the end of that decade, the nation and the world plunged into a severe economic depression. President Franklin D. Roosevelt's New Deal programs in the 1930s attempted to overcome the effects of the Great Depression in the United States.

Some key questions to help you focus on America between the wars include:

- What tensions developed between the people who were a part of the traditional rural culture and those who were members of the new, urban-based society in the 1920s?
- What were the causes of the Great Depression, and how did that event affect the American people and their institutions?

SECTION 1
War and Prosperity: 1917–1929

SECTION OVERVIEW

The 1920s were a time of many changes in the economic and social aspects of life in the United States. Following World War I, the United States struggled to return to what President Harding called "normalcy." However, the impact of the war, the new age of consumerism, the automobile, and the growth of the suburbs contributed to the creation of a different and new national lifestyle.

While transportation and communications technology served to unite the nation, a clash of values between the new urban-centered life and the legacy of the traditional rural life caused uneasiness and conflict. In addition, all Americans did not share in the good times. Beneath the surface was an economy with structural flaws that brought the Roaring Twenties to an abrupt end with the stock market crash in October 1929.

KEY THEMES AND CONCEPTS

As you review this section, take special note of the following key themes and concepts:

Diversity What effects did World War I have on women and minorities?

Economic Systems Who benefited, and who was left out of economic growth in the 1920s?

Factors of Production What caused the increase in mass consumption in the 1920s?

Culture and Intellectual Life What social changes caused a clash of values during the twenties?

Government What major constitutional and legal issues emerged during the twenties, and how were these issues resolved?

☆ THE BIG IDEA
In the 1920s and 1930s:

- American society was unsettled by social and cultural change.

- The boom economy of the 1920s was not shared by all, and it came to an end with the 1929 stock market crash.

- The Great Depression dominated American life in the 1930s.

- FDR's New Deal helped relieve some of the suffering, but did not end the Great Depression.

⚷ KEY TERMS

Coolidge prosperity
on margin
flapper
Harlem Renaissance
Jazz Age
Red Scare
quotas
Scopes Trial

KEY PEOPLE

As you review this section, take special note of the following key people:

Warren G. Harding	Zora Neale Hurston
Calvin Coolidge	Alain Locke
Charles Evans Hughes	Duke Ellington
Albert Fall	Bessie Smith
Andrew Mellon	A. Mitchell Palmer
Sigmund Freud	Nicola Sacco
Charlie Chaplin	Bartolomeo Vanzetti
F. Scott Fitzgerald	Clarence Darrow
Ernest Hemingway	William Jennings Bryan
Langston Hughes	

THE IMPACT AND AFTERMATH OF WAR

World War I triggered a number of important changes in American society, most notably for some women and for many immigrants and African Americans. Some changes were subtle and gradual, while others were immediate and dramatic.

The Twenties

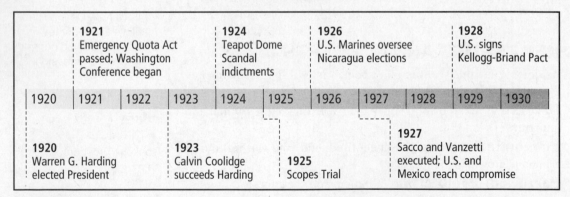

1921 Emergency Quota Act passed; Washington Conference began

1924 Teapot Dome Scandal indictments

1926 U.S. Marines oversee Nicaragua elections

1928 U.S. signs Kellogg-Briand Pact

1920 | 1921 | 1922 | 1923 | 1924 | 1925 | 1926 | 1927 | 1928 | 1929 | 1930

1920 Warren G. Harding elected President

1923 Calvin Coolidge succeeds Harding

1925 Scopes Trial

1927 Sacco and Vanzetti executed; U.S. and Mexico reach compromise

ANALYZING DOCUMENTS

Based on the timeline above, how many years did Warren G. Harding serve as President?

Effects on Women and Minorities

As many men went off to fight in Europe, the roles and responsibilities of women were affected in limited ways. Some women went to work in male-dominated fields, such as weapons factories. Many women served overseas with the Red Cross and the Salvation Army. Most, however, worked in traditionally female jobs, for which there was an increased demand. Only about five percent of the women entering the wartime workforce were new to work outside the home. At war's end, with the return of male workers, women were expected to quit their jobs. Between 1910 and 1920, only 500,000 more women were added to the workforce.

The war had harsh consequences for immigrant families. Further immigration to the United States was halted. Many immigrant families already in the country faced fierce social and job discrimination in an antiforeign climate whipped up by the war.

Most African American civil rights leaders supported World War I, and some 400,000 African American troops served in it. Black soldiers were assigned to segregated units and often worked as laborers. Discrimination was common.

Where they saw combat, African American soldiers served with distinction. Several black regiments fighting alongside of French troops were honored by that nation. Many returning black soldiers questioned why the liberties and freedoms they had fought to preserve in Europe were denied them in their own country. Civil rights leader W.E.B. Du Bois expressed resentment at the continuing racism.

> We return.
>
> We return from fighting.
>
> We return fighting.
>
> —*W.E.B. Du Bois*

PREPARING FOR THE EXAM

Examine the graphic below and use your knowledge of social studies to answer the following questions.

- What is the cause of the effects of World War I shown in the graphic?

- Did any of these conditions exist after World War II? If so, what actions were taken in the late 1940s and 1950s?

READING STRATEGY

Formulating Questions
Read the quote in the text by W.E.B. Du Bois again.

- What question does it raise?

- What message is Du Bois sending?

- To whom is he speaking?

After World War I

United States after the war

- American economy slows as war-time production ends.

- Returning troops face difficult adjustment to civilian society.

- Many women and minority workers faced with loss of jobs as men return to workforce.

- Despite contribution to war effort, returning African American troops continue to face discrimination and segregation.

- Death and destruction of war leads to feelings of gloom among many Americans.

After World War I, many Americans faced a difficult adjustment to peacetime life.

GEOGRAPHY IN HISTORY

- Who participated in the Great Migration to the North from 1910 until the 1940s?

- What was the reason for this Great Migration?

Election of 1920

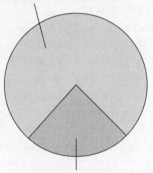

Republican Warren G. Harding 76% of electoral vote

Democrat James M. Cox 24% of electoral vote

ANALYZING DOCUMENTS

"America's present need is not heroics, but healing, not nostrums [remedies] but normalcy, not revolution but restoration, not surgery but serenity."

— Warren G. Harding

Examine the pie graph and the quotation.

- How does the pie graph support the statement that the 1920 election was a landslide in favor of "normalcy"?

Migration to the North

World War I accelerated the migration of African Americans to northern cities. This migration began after the Civil War. From about 1910 to 1920, southern agricultural jobs were lost to floods and to crop damage. About 500,000 African Americans moved from the South to jobs in the industrial North. Meanwhile in the North, workers were needed to meet war production goals. The wartime immigration ban produced an additional need for workers to replace those in uniform.

After the war, this northward migration continued. Between 1910 and the 1940s, almost 2 million African Americans left the South. Although they were usually able to improve their economic situation, they still faced discrimination, segregation, and sometimes even race riots.

The "Return to Normalcy," 1918–1921

After World War I, disillusioned Americans wanted to return to the traditional foreign policy of isolationism. The 1920 landslide election of Republican President Warren G. Harding and Vice President Calvin Coolidge represented the desire of many Americans to remove themselves from the pressures of world politics. Progressivism continued, but at a slower pace, and reforms took place largely at the state and local levels.

THE 1920s: BUSINESS BOOM OR FALSE PROSPERITY?

For many Americans, postwar life did return to "normalcy." Yet beneath the surface, troubling political and economic problems had begun to develop.

Greed and Scandal Under Harding

Harding was an Ohio newspaper publisher with little experience in politics. Historians credit him for pardoning socialist Eugene V. Debs (who had been jailed for opposing the war) and for supporting antilynching legislation. Harding appointed some dedicated people to office, including Charles Evans Hughes as secretary of state.

However, the President also gave political jobs to members of the so-called Ohio Gang, corrupt associates who took advantage of him. After Harding's death in 1923, the public learned of several scandals during his administration.

- *Theft:* The head of the Veterans Bureau was convicted of selling hospital supplies for his own profit. He was imprisoned and fined.
- *Fraud:* The Alien Property Custodian was imprisoned for selling former German property for private profit.
- *The Teapot Dome Scandal:* Secretary of the Interior Albert Fall was convicted of accepting bribes from two oil executives in exchange for allowing them to lease government-owned petroleum reserves. One of the oil fields was at Teapot Dome, Wyoming.

Under Coolidge, Prosperity for Some

Calvin Coolidge became President when Harding died in office in 1923. In the 1924 election, Coolidge was returned to office. Coolidge is best known for his laissez-faire approach to the economy and his strong commitment to business interests. Coolidge retained financier Andrew Mellon as secretary of the treasury. Mellon acted on the philosophy that government's role was to serve business.

RECESSION The end of World War I was followed by a recession caused by the shift from a wartime to a peacetime economy. Production, farm income, and exports fell. Unemployment rose, reaching 12 percent in 1921. For farmers, in particular, hardship continued throughout the decade.

RECOVERY In other sectors of the economy, however, a period of economic recovery had begun by 1923, when Coolidge became President. The years between 1923 and 1929 were seen as a time of booming business. The Gross National Product (GNP) rose 40 percent. Per capita income went up 30 percent. With little inflation, actual purchasing power—and therefore the standard of living—increased. At the time, few people questioned this **Coolidge prosperity.**

PRO-BUSINESS POLICIES Some groups, especially big corporations and the wealthy, benefited greatly from Coolidge prosperity. For example:

- Businesses and the most wealthy were helped by tax laws that reduced personal income tax rates, particularly for upper income groups, removed most excise taxes, and lowered corporate income taxes.
- The government reduced the national debt and balanced the budget by raising tariffs and demanding repayment of war debts.
- Tariff rates were raised in a return to protectionism. Republicans argued that higher tariffs would limit foreign imports, thus helping both industry and agriculture. However, the actual effect was to weaken the world economy.
- Regulatory agencies such as the Federal Reserve Board, the Federal Trade Commission, and the Interstate Commerce Commission saw their role as assisting business rather than regulating it.
- A relaxed attitude toward corporate mergers was supported by the executive branch and by the Supreme Court. By 1929, about 1,300 corporations produced three fourths of all American manufactured goods, and 200 companies owned half the nation's wealth.

Economic Boom Bypasses Others

Coolidge prosperity was not for everyone. Key segments of the population failed to share in the general rise in living standards.

Election of 1924

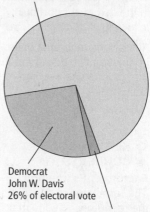

Republican Calvin Coolidge
72% of electoral vote

Democrat
John W. Davis
26% of electoral vote

Progressive Party
Robert M. La Follette
2% of electoral vote

 PREPARING FOR THE EXAM

You will need to understand certain important economic terms on the exam.

The **Gross National Product** (GNP) is the total value of all goods and services produced in one year.

Per Capita Income means income per individual; it is based on the national income divided by the population.

READING STRATEGY

Reading for Evidence

What evidence is presented in the text to support the following statement?

"Important segments of the population failed to share in the general rise in living standards."

⚷ KEY THEMES AND CONCEPTS

Factors of Production

The term used to describe the resources used to make all goods and services is the *factors of production.* The three factors of production are land, labor, and capital.

- *Land* refers to all natural resources needed to produce goods and services. Land includes coal, water, or farmland.

- *Labor* is the paid effort that a person devotes to a task. Labor can include the medical aid provided by a doctor as well as the tasks performed by an assembly-line worker.

- *Capital* is any human-made resource used to produce other goods and services. Physical capital includes factory buildings and tools, while human capital includes workers' knowledge and experience.

LABOR Strikes had dropped sharply during World War I, mainly because the Wilson government supported collective bargaining in return for a no-strike pledge. Membership in the American Federation of Labor grew, and wages for war industry employees rose sharply. However, inflation wiped out any real gains in buying power.

The 1920s saw a reversal of any union gains. Strikes in the steel, mining, and railroad industries failed, in part because the government used not only troops to end the strikes but also injunctions, which are court orders that prohibit specified actions. The Supreme Court also ruled against child labor laws and against minimum wages for women and children. In addition, some companies began to offer health and life insurance in hopes of lessening workers' interest in unions. The strategy often worked. Membership in labor unions fell from a high of about 5 million in 1921 to under 3.5 million in 1929.

Unemployment remained between 1 and 11 percent throughout the 1920s. In general, however, real wages for workers increased only slightly during this period, boosted primarily by wages of workers in the new industries, such as communications and automobile manufacturing. Therefore, even though workers' wages increased 26 percent and their productivity increased 40 percent, they could not afford to buy many of the new consumer goods.

FARMERS The only farmers to benefit from Coolidge prosperity were those involved in large commercial operations. Small farmers were hurt by a combination of factors.

- Farmers expanded production during World War I in response to rising prices and the demand for food. They added to their acreage and bought more farm machinery.
- New machinery and new farm techniques increased farmers' crop yield per acre.
- After the war, when European farms began producing again, American farmers were growing too much. The prices of both farm products and farmland decreased dramatically.
- Net farm income fell 50 percent during the 1920s. As a result, the number of farmers declined, too. By 1930, only about 20 percent of the labor force made a living by farming.

NATIVE AMERICANS During the 1920s, Native Americans had the highest unemployment rate of any group and the shortest average life span. Most lived on reservations, without the basics of heat and running water.

AFRICAN AMERICANS African Americans who migrated to the North enjoyed a higher standard of living than in the South. However, they still earned less than white workers and experienced a higher rate of unemployment.

Stock Market Speculation

The economic recovery helped produce a surge of investment in the stock market. Optimistic business and government leaders saw no end to the boom. They encouraged everyone to play the bull market—that is, the rising stock market. Some families invested their life savings. The profits rolled in—for a while.

Yet the new wealth flowed from a stock market with a deeply flawed structure. Many stocks were traded **on margin.** This meant that buyers could purchase stocks by making only small down payments in cash—sometimes as low as 5 percent of the value of the stocks. They borrowed the rest from brokers and counted on their profits to repay the loans. The system worked as long as the profits continued.

MASS CONSUMPTION

The 1920s were a time of mass consumption—huge quantities of manufactured goods were available, and many people had more money to spend on them.

The Effects of New Industries on American Life

Automobile Industry:
1. stimulated steel, rubber, paint, glass, and oil industries
2. set off a real-estate boom in suburbs
3. led to an increase in highways and a decline in railroad construction and use
4. caused tractors to replace horses on farms
5. increased social equality as low prices made cars available to Americans at almost all income levels
6. stimulate installment buying
7. contributed to growing sophistication of advertising techniques

The Electrical Industry:
1. changed homes, businesses, and cities through electric lights
2. helped double business productivity through electric power
3. transformed life and leisure with electric-powered durable goods such as washing machines, stoves, vacuum cleaners, refrigerators, and irons
4. stimulated installment buying

Radio and Motion Pictures:
1. helped erase regional differences and homogenize American culture
2. increased people's expectations, often unrealistically
3. helped end rural isolation
4. helped popularize ragtime and jazz
5. provided an outlet for advertising
6. increased interest in politics and spectator sports

KEY THEMES AND CONCEPTS

Science and Technology
Homogenization is a process used to keep the cream in milk distributed throughout the container rather than rising to the top. The term can also be applied to cultures. Radio, movies, and telephones helped produce a more homogenized national culture in which regional differences became less distinct.

- What technology since the 1920s has resulted in further national and even international homogenization?

- According to the chart, in what ways did the automobile, electrical industry, radio, and motion pictures influence the lifestyle of the 1920s?

READING STRATEGY

Formulating Questions
Consider that in the 1920s:

- 15 million cars were sold.
- 80 percent were bought on credit.
- A Model T Ford cost $290 in 1920.
- 20% of U.S. homes had electricity by the end of the decade.
- 10 million families owned radios by 1929.

In addition to these facts, what information do you need in order to have a more complete picture of the effect of new technologies in the 1920s?

Role of Technology

Technology, combined with new marketing strategies, best explains the transformation of American society in the 1920s. Led by Henry Ford and the automobile industry, mass production and the moving assembly line resulted in uniform products produced at lower costs. It made possible a consumer-oriented economy, one in which more goods were available to more Americans. Often these goods were purchased over time through installment buying.

Growing Cultural Homogenization

The new technology also made American culture more homogeneous, or uniform. Americans from one coast to the other tended to use the same products, wear the same styles, see the same movies, and listen to the same music. Regional and class differences were blurred, and individualism became less important than conformity.

Suburban Growth

With over half the population living in places with populations of more than 2,500 people, the United States in the 1920s was an urban rather than a rural nation for the first time in its history. Only the Great Depression ended the building boom that was part of this growth. Suburbs grew even faster than cities. These new suburbs drew people from the cities. The ultimate result was the present-day conflict between urban and suburban needs, priorities, and values.

SHIFTING CULTURAL VALUES

During the 1920s, American society experienced a struggle with social change as it became an urban, industrial nation. Changes in lifestyle, values, morals, and manners increased tension and conflict. Wealth, possessions, having fun, and sexual freedom—ideas influenced by the psychology of Sigmund Freud—were the new values.

LEISURE With a shorter work week and with more paid vacation, Americans had more leisure time. Movies such as *The Ten Commandments* and the first movie with sound, *The Jazz Singer,* drew millions of people a week to theaters during the 1920s. Americans idolized Charlie Chaplin and other movie stars. They also admired sports figures, such as Babe Ruth. Games such as bridge, crossword puzzles, and the board game of mah-jongg swept the country.

The popular image of young women of the 1920s was the **flapper,** a young, pretty woman with bobbed hair and raised hemlines. She drank alcohol, she smoked, she thought for herself, and she took advantage of women's new freedoms. However, the flapper lived more in the media than in reality. The flapper figured in movies, magazines, advertising, and novels, such as those of F. Scott Fitzgerald.

LITERATURE The conflict and concern created by changing American values also saw expression in literature. American writers of the 1920s protested the effects of technology and mass consumption. They criti-

Passenger Car Sales, 1920–1929

Source: *Historical Statistics of the United States, Colonial Times to 1970*

ANALYZING DOCUMENTS

What information from the graph at left helps you to gain a more complete picture of the effect of the automobile industry in the 1920s?

cized the business mentality, the conformity of the times, and the preoccupation with material things. Some writers, such as Ernest Hemingway, became expatriates, leaving the United States to settle in Europe.

HARLEM RENAISSANCE One of the most important cultural movements of the 1920s was the **Harlem Renaissance,** led by a group of African American writers in the New York City neighborhood of Harlem. These creative intellectual figures—mainly well-educated members of the middle class—felt alienated from the society of the 1920s. In their works they called for action against bigotry and expressed pride in African American culture and identity. Outstanding literary figures of the Harlem Renaissance include W.E.B. Du Bois, Langston Hughes, Zora Neale Hurston, and Alain Locke.

The Great Depression of the 1930s ended the Harlem Renaissance, cutting the sales of books and literary magazines. However, during the civil rights movement of the 1960s, the writers of the Harlem Renaissance and their works attracted renewed interest.

African American artists, musicians, and dancers also participated in the Harlem Renaissance. Black musicians in the South blended elements of African, European, and American music to create the distinctive sounds of jazz and the blues. This music was carried all over the country and abroad.

ANALYZING DOCUMENTS

"We build our temples for tomorrow, strong as we know how, and we stand on the top of the mountain, free within ourselves."
—Langston Hughes, on the Harlem Renaissance in *The Big Sea*

• What ideas of the Harlem Renaissance are expressed in this quote?

⚷ KEY THEMES AND
⚷ CONCEPTS

Culture and Intellectual Life

The culture and intellectual life of a time period reflects the era's social, economic and political mood. The writers of the period between World War I and World War II were sometimes called the "Lost Generation." They were called this because they often found little in life that they considered worth believing in, and this attitude was reflected in their work.

- How did the work of each writer in the chart at right reflect the 1920s?

- How did the Harlem Renaissance express the feelings of its participants?

- How did it have an influence beyond its time?

Leading Writers of the Twenties

Willa Cather	novelist	*My Antonia*
F. Scott Fitzgerald	novelist	*The Great Gatsby*
Ernest Hemingway	novelist	*A Farewell to Arms*
Langston Hughes	poet, novelist	*The Weary Blues*
Sinclair Lewis	novelist	*Main Street, Babbitt*
Eugene O'Neill	playwright	*Desire Under the Elms*
Edith Wharton	novelist	*The Age of Innocence*

Edward K. "Duke" Ellington is one of the towering figures in jazz. Ellington recorded and composed music, performed on the piano, and conducted his own orchestra until his death in 1974. Bessie Smith, known as the "Empress of the Blues," was one of the most popular singers of the 1920s. This new music, to which people danced such daring new steps as the Charleston, became so popular that the period of the 1920s is often called the **Jazz Age.**

Women's Changing Roles

The conflict between modern and traditional values in the 1920s also found expression in the contradictory roles of women.

WOMEN IN THE WORKFORCE Throughout the 1920s, the number of women in the workforce increased. By 1930, 10.5 million women were working outside the home, making up 22 percent of the workforce. This figure, however, represented an increase of only 1.4 percent of the total workforce. Most working women were single, widowed, or divorced. Most Americans still believed that married women belonged at home, where 90 percent of them were to be found. When working women married, they usually quit or were fired from their jobs.

Most women who worked outside the home continued to hold jobs in traditionally female—and traditionally low-paying and low-status—occupations, such as teaching, clerical work, and retail sales. Fewer than 20 percent worked in better-paying factory jobs. The number of female doctors and scientists actually decreased.

One important gain for working women was the creation in 1920 of the Women's Bureau, part of the federal Department of Labor. It tried to improve working conditions for women from inside the government and provided data about working women.

INVOLVEMENT IN POLITICS In 1920, women voted in a national election for the first time. However, their vote did not have a distinctive effect on the outcome. Women did not vote in large numbers, nor did they vote as a bloc. To encourage women to play a greater part in politics, the National American Woman Suffrage Association reorganized itself as the nonpartisan League of Women Voters.

HEALTH, RIGHTS, AND WORKING CONDITIONS The divisions of the 1920s were reflected in the fate of two pieces of legislation. Encouraged by women reformers, Congress passed the Sheppard-Towner Act in 1921. With the aim of reducing infant mortality, the law provided for public health centers where women could learn about nutrition and health care. The program came to an end in 1929, largely because of opposition from physicians.

An equal rights amendment to the Constitution, proposed by Alice Paul in 1923, led to bitter disagreement among women. Many feminists supported it, but others opposed it because they believed it would do away with special laws protecting women workers.

DAILY LIFE Contrary to the image of the flapper, women were still restricted by economic, political, and social limits. The image of the flapper meant little to most women.

In some ways, technology made life easier in the 1920s. With electric washing machines, vacuum cleaners, stoves, and refrigerators, household chores did not require so much time, and there was less need for servants. On the other hand, the typical homemaker now was expected to handle almost all the household tasks herself and to meet higher standards of cleanliness.

EMPHASIS ON WIFE RATHER THAN MOTHER The role of the woman as wife received increased importance. Women did have more choices in life. Families changed during this period, and divorce and family planning became more acceptable. However, divorce laws continued to favor men, and wives were expected to stay at home rather than work outside the home. Family size decreased; only 20 percent of women who married during the 1920s had five or more children. The family, which in earlier times had been a producing unit, growing and processing much of its food, was now a consuming unit. Marketing and advertising appeals flooded the media, encouraging consumers to buy more goods.

CONSTITUTIONAL AND LEGAL ISSUES

Major constitutional and legal issues divided Americans in the 1920s. Many issues reflected the struggle between modern and traditional values and showed how international affairs affected domestic policies and attitudes.

Threats to Civil Liberties
In the 1920s, the Red Scare and the Ku Klux Klan threatened the civil liberties of some Americans.

THE RED SCARE 1918–1919 The imposition of stern measures to suppress dissent after World War I in a crusade against internal enemies was known as the **Red Scare.** It was fueled by the October 1917

⚲ **KEY THEMES AND CONCEPTS**

Diversity
In the 1920s women were workers, flappers, wives, mothers, voters, students, and housewives. In what ways were their lives different from the lives of women during the following periods in history?

- the first half of the 19th century
- the second half of the 19th century
- the Progressive Era
- World War I
- the Great Depression
- World War II
- the 1950s
- the 1960s and 1970s
- today

PREPARING FOR THE EXAM

Remember that fear of foreigners and of foreign ideas has been an issue that has arisen many times throughout United States history.

- 1790s: Alien and Sedition Acts

- 1840s: nativism and Know-Nothings

- 1917–1918: suppression of dissent during World War I

- 1920s: Ku Klux Klan, Sacco and Vanzetti case, National Origins Quota Acts

- 1940s: internment of Japanese Americans during World War II

- 1950s: McCarthyism

Bolshevik Revolution, an uprising of Communists in Russia. In the United States, Communists made up only one half of 1 percent of the population, but many of them were targeted by the crackdown, as were various other groups viewed as un-American. Among them were socialists, anarchists, labor leaders, and foreigners.

The **Red Scare** was led by Attorney General A. Mitchell Palmer. It was sparked by several events that took place after the war ended. Frustration over discrimination led to race riots in more than 25 cities. In Boston, a series of labor strikes climaxed with a walkout by the police. Several unexplained bombings added to the hysteria. All these events were seen as part of a Communist conspiracy.

The attorney general ordered the first so-called **Palmer Raids** late in 1919. In 33 cities, police without warrants raided the headquarters of Communists and other organizations. Eventually they arrested 4,000 people, holding them without charges and denying them legal counsel. Some 560 aliens were deported. Palmer's extreme actions and statements soon turned the public against him. However, the Red Scare had lingering effects, discouraging many Americans from speaking their minds freely in open debate, thus squelching their constitutional right to freedom of speech.

SACCO AND VANZETTI Closely linked to the Red Scare was the case of Nicola Sacco and Bartolomeo Vanzetti. These two Italian immigrants—admitted anarchists—were convicted of murder in 1921 in connection with a Massachusetts robbery. Many people questioned the evidence against Sacco and Vanzetti, concluding that the two men were convicted more for their beliefs and their Italian origin than for a crime. In spite of mass demonstrations and appeals, the two men were executed in 1927. The governor of Massachusetts eventually cleared the two men in 1977, some 50 years later.

THE KU KLUX KLAN Antiforeign attitudes encouraged a revival of the Ku Klux Klan. The first organization, active during Reconstruction, had died out in the late 1800s. A reorganized Klan, formed in 1915, grew slowly until 1920. In that year, it added 100,000 members. The Klan of the 1920s targeted not only African American but also Catholics, Jews, and immigrants. To the Klan, the only true Americans were white, Protestant, and American-born.

Restrictions on Immigration

The nativism expressed in the Red Scare, the Sacco-Vanzetti case, and the new Klan was also evident in 1920s immigration legislation. Immigrants were seen by many as somehow threatening to American values. The nativist climate led to the Immigration Act of 1924. This act established a system of national **quotas,** which limited the number of immigrants from each country. These quotas deliberately kept the totals for eastern and southern Europe low and excluded all immigration from Asia.

Immigration to the United States, 1921 and 1926

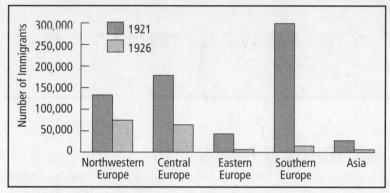

Prohibition

Both the rebirth of the Klan and the movement to restrict immigration reflected the struggle in the 1920s between what some saw as old, rural American values and the new values of a changing urban, industrialized culture. However, the clash between these two sets of values did not divide on the basis of where one lived.

For example, the movement for Prohibition, a ban on the sale and consumption of alcoholic beverages, was not confined to rural America, though it received much support there. The **Eighteenth Amendment,** allowing Prohibition, became part of the Constitution in 1919. Congress passed the **Volstead Act** to implement Prohibition, but the law turned out to be unenforceable. Most Americans were simply unwilling to accept a total ban on alcohol. Furthermore, it stimulated crime, encouraging smuggling and **bootlegging,** the illegal manufacture and sale of alcoholic beverages. In 1933, the Twenty-first Amendment ending Prohibition was ratified.

The Scopes Trial

The 1925 **Scopes Trial,** held in Dayton, Tennessee, received nationwide attention because it pitted the scientific ideas of Darwinian evolution against the Protestant fundamentalist view of biblical creationism. John Scopes, a biology teacher, had deliberately violated a state law forbidding anyone to teach the theory of evolution. Scopes was represented by a famous trial lawyer, Clarence Darrow. The prosecution relied on the assistance of William Jennings Bryan, three-time presidential candidate and a firm believer in fundamentalist Christianity. Although Scopes was convicted and fined $100, Bryan's confused testimony weakened fundamentalist arguments.

KEY THEMES AND CONCEPTS

Immigration and Migration

During the 1920s, immigration from the western hemisphere was not limited. Large numbers of Mexicans moved into southwestern cities and Puerto Ricans into New York City, most in search of economic opportunities.

- What are the most dramatic changes pictured on the chart at left?

- What changes were made in immigration laws in the 1920s? Why?

PREPARING FOR THE EXAM

Prohibition turned out to be unenforceable because too many Americans were unwilling to accept it. The massive evasion of this law is often compared to the reaction to the 1850 Fugitive Slave Law. In 1933, the 21st Amendment repealed the 18th Amendment.

SECTION 2 | The Great Depression

⭐ **THE BIG IDEA**
In the 1930s:

- The world economy collapsed after the 1929 crash of the stock market started the Great Depression.

- President Hoover's efforts toward economic recovery did not succeed.

- President Franklin Roosevelt's New Deal provided relief, but did not end the Great Depression.

🔑 **KEY TERMS**

Great Crash
Great Depression
Bonus Army
Hoovervilles
Dust Bowl
New Deal

SECTION OVERVIEW

The 1930s were dominated by the Great Depression, which affected virtually every aspect of American life and caused ripple effects throughout the worldwide economy. With roots in unregulated stock market speculation, a flawed banking system, and the overproduction of goods, the Great Depression was triggered by the stock market crash in 1929. Banks failed, and many people lost their life savings. The losses shut down businesses, producing widespread unemployment, homelessness, and hunger.

President Franklin D. Roosevelt's New Deal launched ambitious programs to speed economic recovery. The New Deal dramatically increased the role of government in American life and strengthened the power of the presidency. The entry of the United States into World War II in 1941 finally put an end to the nation's worst economic collapse.

KEY THEMES AND CONCEPTS

As you review this section, take special note of the following key themes and concepts:

Economic Systems What were the main causes of the Great Depression?

Government How did Hoover respond to the depression, and why did people disapprove of his actions?

Culture and Intellectual Life How did the depression affect daily life and culture in America?

Government What were some of the key programs of the New Deal?

Diversity How did the New Deal affect organized labor, minorities, and women?

KEY PEOPLE

As you review this section, take special note of the following key people:

Herbert Hoover	Eleanor Roosevelt
John Steinbeck	John L. Lewis
Walker Evans	Mary McLeod Bethune
Margaret Bourke-White	John Maynard Keynes
William Faulkner	Al Smith
Louis Armstrong	Norman Thomas
Franklin Delano Roosevelt	Francis E. Townsend
Frances Perkins	Father Charles E. Coughlin
Harry Hopkins	Huey Long

KEY SUPREME COURT CASES

As you review this section, take special note of the following key Supreme Court case:

Schechter Poultry Corporation v. *United States* (1935)

The Great Depression

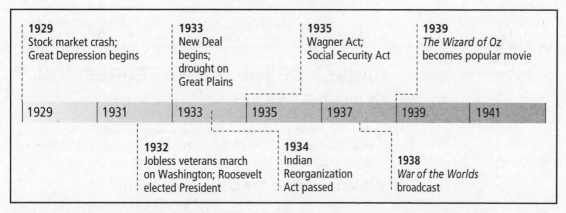

1929
Stock market crash; Great Depression begins

1933
New Deal begins; drought on Great Plains

1935
Wagner Act; Social Security Act

1939
The Wizard of Oz becomes popular movie

1929   1931   1933   1935   1937   1939   1941

1932
Jobless veterans march on Washington; Roosevelt elected President

1934
Indian Reorganization Act passed

1938
War of the Worlds broadcast

In the 1920s, the science of economics was still fairly young. Few scholars—and even fewer business leaders or politicians—recognized the many warning signs of a looming crisis in the economy. In 1929 and the years to follow, the nation would wake up to the terrible reality that the economic freewheeling of the 1920s came at a price.

ANALYZING DOCUMENTS

According to the timeline above, who was President when the New Deal began?

THE GREAT CRASH

The end of the prosperity of the 1920s was marked by a series of plunges in the U.S. stock market in 1929 known as the **Great Crash.**

Throughout the 1920s, the stock market had grown on speculation by people who bought on margin and, in fact, owned only a small portion of their stocks. Many could not meet margin calls, demands to put up the money to cover their loans. The result was panic selling. On October 29 (Black Tuesday) alone, stock values fell $14 billion. They dropped lower and lower in the weeks that followed.

The Great Crash triggered the start of the **Great Depression.** It broke the national sense of optimism and confidence of the 1920s. The Great Crash dramatically exposed the fact that the national economy had serious weaknesses.

ANALYZING DOCUMENTS

Based on the graph at right and your knowledge of social studies, answer the following questions.

- When did the stock market crash occur?

- In what year did stock prices reach their lowest point?

- What role did speculation play in the crash?

- What is the relationship of the stock market crash to the Great Depression?

The Stock Market Crash

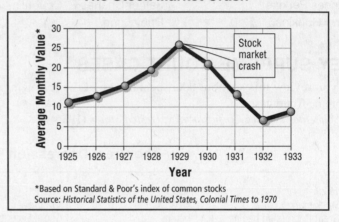

*Based on Standard & Poor's index of common stocks
Source: *Historical Statistics of the United States, Colonial Times to 1970*

CAUSES OF THE GREAT DEPRESSION

The Great Depression was caused by weaknesses in the economy—overproduction and underconsumption, overexpansion of credit, and fragile corporate structures—combined with ineffective government action. The growing interdependence of international trade and banking made the effects even more damaging.

Weaknesses in the Overall Economy

Weaknesses in the economy had existed before 1929 and were expanding.

- The agricultural sector had been depressed throughout the 1920s, with a worldwide drop in prices.
- Unemployment plagued the railroad, coal, and textile industries well before 1929.
- Speculation in real estate and the resulting building boom had declined.
- Automobile sales had slowed.
- As early as the summer of 1929, the economy showed signs of underconsumption. Inventories of unsold goods began to accumulate in warehouses as consumer demand slowed.

 PREPARING FOR THE EXAM

Underconsumption or overproduction means that people buy fewer goods than are produced. In other words, supply is greater than demand.

Some Economic Changes Between 1928 and 1932
(Figures in millions unless otherwise noted)

	1928	1929	1930	1931	1932
A. United States exports (merchandise)	$5,030	$5,157	$3,781	$2,378	$1,576
B. Spending for new housing	$4,195	$3,040	$1,570	$1,320	$485
C. Farm spending for lime and fertilizer	$318	$300	$297	$202	$118
D. Federal spending	$2,933	$3,127	$3,320	$3,578	$4,659
E. Cash receipts from farming	$10,991	$11,312	$9,055	$6,331	$4,748
F. Lumber production (billions of board ft.)	36.8	38.7	29.4	20	13.5
G. Unemployment (in thousands)	2,080	1,550	4,340	8,020	12,060
H. Average weekly earnings of production works in manufacturing (actual dollars)	$24.97	$25.03	$23.25	$20.87	$17.05

Unequal Distribution of Income

Contributing to underconsumption and to the weakness of the economy was an unequal distribution of wealth.

- In the 1920s, some 40 percent of all families had an income of less than $1,500, which put them below the poverty line. At the same time, the 24,000 richest families in the nation had a total income *three times as large* as the total income of the 6 million poorest families. In short, while 1 percent of the population owned 59 percent of the nation's wealth, 87 percent of the population owned only 10 percent of the wealth.
- As a result, the economy was dependent on the spending of a very small portion of the population. These wealthy people spent their money on luxury goods and on investments. This type of spending was greatly affected by the stock market crash.
- The wealthy, not the great mass of the population, had benefited from increased output per worker in the face of stable salaries. With the increased output, production costs had dropped and profits had risen, but the workers could not buy what they produced. As a result, demand dropped. As the economy weakened, this non-purchasing group grew in size and became less and less able to buy even the necessities of life.

Excessive Buying on Credit

Excessive buying on credit resulted from these low and unequally distributed wages. Under consumption grew as workers could no longer make installment payments.

Weak Corporate Structure

The Great Crash set off the collapse of the nation's business structure. Business consolidations of the 1920s resulted in a few large companies

Income Distribution, 1929

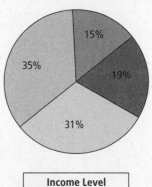

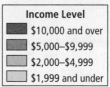

Income Level	
■	$10,000 and over
■	$5,000–$9,999
□	$2,000–$4,999
□	$1,999 and under

The prosperity of the 1920s did not bring great wealth to most Americans.

in each industry. Holding companies controlled the stock of many different corporations and depended on the earnings of the various companies they held. This was a very fragile system, because when one company collapsed, it affected—in a domino fashion—the rest of the holding company.

Weak Banking Structure

Some 6,000 banks failed in the 1920s. This showed clearly that there were serious weaknesses in the banking industry.

Inadequate Government Policies

Actions by the federal government contributed to the depression.

- Stock market speculation was unregulated by the government.
- Tax policies that favored the wealthy resulted in further uneven distribution of income.
- The consolidation of corporations was not challenged under antitrust laws.
- The Federal Reserve Board allowed a low discount rate—the interest charged to member banks. This policy led to stock speculation. The board then raised interest rates in 1931, discouraging spending at just the time when spending would have helped the economy.

Weak International Economy

The world's economies were affected by the collapse triggered by the crash of the U.S. stock market. Many European economies had never fully recovered from World War I, and the international economy depended heavily on the economy of the United States.

Foreign nations owed the United States money that they could repay only after the United States bought their goods and made foreign investments and loans. However, high American tariffs kept out goods from overseas and led to high foreign tariffs. Meanwhile, Americans invested at home in businesses or in the stock market rather than abroad.

When the U.S. economy slowed, the United States made fewer foreign investments and had less money to lend. This meant that foreign nations had less money to buy American goods and often defaulted on loans. The international nature of the banking system can be seen by the fact that banks in both Europe and the United States failed as a result of defaults on loans.

HOOVER'S RESPONSE TO THE GREAT DEPRESSION, 1929–1933

Herbert Hoover was the President who first had to deal with the deepening depression. Hoover had taken office in 1929, after having served as Coolidge's secretary of commerce. An engineer by training, Hoover was a good businessman, a self-made millionaire, and a humanitarian. During and after World War I, he had an international

ANALYZING DOCUMENTS

Examine the chart on the previous page entitled "Some Economic Changes Between 1928 and 1932," then answer the following questions.

- How much did spending for new housing change between 1928 and 1932?

- What does the drop in U.S. exports indicate about the nature of the depression?

- How much did unemployment increase between 1928 and 1932?

- Based on this chart, which year was the economy in its most serious state?

reputation as leader of a successful relief effort to aid starving Europeans and to help Europe recover economically.

Hoover's Economic Plan

In order to improve economic conditions, Hoover took the following actions:

- Tried to restore confidence in the American economy with such statements as "Prosperity is just around the corner."
- Altered his view that government should not become directly involved in the economy. He promoted programs that aided businesses, on the theory that as businesses recovered, economic benefits would trickle down to the workers and consumers.
- Allowed the organization of the Reconstruction Finance Corporation (1932) to lend money to railroads, mortgage and insurance companies, and banks on the verge of bankruptcy.
- Set a precedent for Franklin Roosevelt's New Deal with his use of federal works projects to create jobs and stimulate the economy.
- Obtained voluntary agreements from businesses not to lower wages or prices. However, as companies increasingly faced collapse, they often could not honor these promises.
- Halted the payment of war debts by European nations.

Failure of Hoover's Program

Despite these efforts, Hoover's refusal to provide direct relief damaged his image as the nation's leader. Also damaging was his insistence, in the face of worsening conditions, that the economy was actually improving.

In the summer of 1932, thousands of unemployed World War I veterans and their families set up camps in Washington, D.C., to demand early payment of the bonus due to them for their war service. When the bill was defeated by Congress, most of **Bonus Army,** as they were called, refused to leave town. Hoover insisted that the veterans were influenced by Communists and other agitators. He called out the army to break up the Bonus Army's camps and disperse the veterans. The news photographs showing tanks and tear gas being used against war veterans destroyed what little popularity Hoover had left.

Herbert Hoover took many steps to use the power of the federal government to stop the growing depression. In the end, his efforts were too little. Historians still debate whether he should be praised for the efforts he did make or condemned for not going far enough. Hoover's ability to act was limited by his beliefs. For example:

- He had great faith in the American economic system, insisting that the forces of the market would eventually set the economy right again.
- He stood for the Puritan work ethic—the idea that hard work earns its own rewards.
- He believed in voluntary rather than governmental action to solve problems of society.

Election of 1928

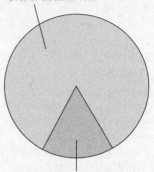

Republican Herbert C. Hoover 84% of electoral vote

Democrat Alfred E. Smith 16% of electoral vote

ANALYZING DOCUMENTS

"Our Republican leaders tell us economic laws . . . cause panics which no one could prevent. But while they prate of [chatter about] economic laws, men and women are starving . . . I pledge you, I pledge myself, to a new deal for the American people.
—F. D. Roosevelt, 1932

"The urgent question today is the prompt balancing of the budget. When that is accomplished, I propose to support adequate measures for relief of distress and unemployment."
—Herbert Hoover, 1932

Both of these quotes were made during the 1932 presidential campaign.

- What is the clearest difference between Roosevelt's and Hoover's approaches to the Great Depression?

- He believed in self-help and opposed direct relief on the grounds that it would destroy people's "rugged individualism."

THE HUMAN IMPACT OF THE GREAT DEPRESSION

The Great Depression had a profound effect on all Americans.

Unemployment

By 1932, some 12 million people—25 percent of the American labor force—were unemployed. The human toll was seen in long "bread lines" at soup kitchens. Relief efforts by organizations such as the Red Cross were limited, because voluntary contributions slowed down. As banks failed, people lost their savings; as companies failed, people lost their jobs as well.

African Americans and unskilled workers were the first to experience unemployment. In 1931, African American unemployment was estimated as 30 to 60 percent greater than white unemployment. Women were criticized for working while men could not find jobs. In truth, female occupations, usually in service sectors such as nursing and clerical work, were less affected than positions in manufacturing that were usually given to men. Family life was disrupted as parents looked for ways to stretch what money the family had. Families moved in with relatives. Marriages were postponed. The birth rate dropped, as did college enrollment.

READING STRATEGY

Reading for Evidence
Unemployment affected more than just those people who lost their jobs. After individuals became unemployed, what other people or organizations were affected?

ANALYZING DOCUMENTS

Based on the graph below, what relationship was there between the unemployment rate and Hoover's defeat in the election of 1932?

Unemployment, 1929–1940 (in millions)

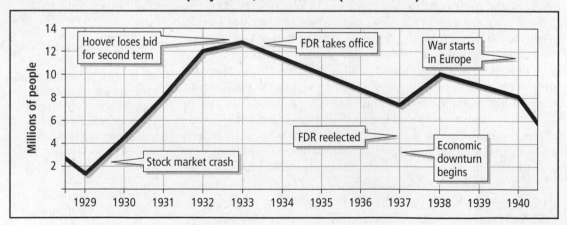

Urban Life

In many cities, families who had lost their homes lived in unheated shacks they had built of cardboard, tin, or crates. These communities became known as **Hoovervilles.** Some people slept under old newspapers called "Hoover blankets." Others slept in city parks.

People selling apples and shoelaces on the street became a common sight. Cases of malnutrition, tuberculosis, and typhoid increased, as did deaths from starvation and suicide. Parents often went hungry to give what food they had to their children.

Rural Life

With more people unable even to buy food, farmers found that their already depressed income dropped by one half. Farm foreclosure sales grew in number. The farmers' desperate situation only worsened in the 1930s with a prolonged drought in parts of Texas, Oklahoma, Kansas, Colorado, and New Mexico, a region that became known as the **Dust Bowl.** The drought, combined with poor farming methods, resulted in the loss of the topsoil, which was whipped into giant dust storms that swept across the Great Plains. Devastation in the Dust Bowl created a group of migrant farmers called "Okies" who moved to California in search of work. Their sufferings were made famous in John Steinbeck's novel *The Grapes of Wrath.*

The Culture of the Great Depression

The sufferings of people during the Great Depression changed the popular culture of the 1930s, as people sought inexpensive and escapist leisure activities.

Spectator sports, especially baseball, remained popular, but fewer people could afford to attend. Instead, they played miniature golf, softball, pinball machines, the new board game Monopoly, or they read comic books. Dick Tracy was one of the most popular comic strips of the decade.

About one third of the nation's movie theaters closed during the depression, but each week as many as 90 million people turned out to see Hollywood films. Movies of the 1930s often dealt with issues other than the grim realities of depression life. Depression-era movies included *King Kong, Gone With the Wind,* and *The Wizard of Oz,* as well as cowboy adventures, serials, musicals, comedies, and Walt Disney cartoons starring characters such as Mickey Mouse.

Radio, which was free, offered the comedy of George Burns and Gracie Allen or Jack Benny, as well as soap operas, news, sports, serials, and music. Radio was to the 1930s what television is today—an influential, unifying means of communication.

Literature, photography, and paintings of the 1930s reflected the concerns of the times. The photographs of Walker Evans and Margaret Bourke-White revealed the suffering of the people. Bourke-White's work appeared in *Life* magazine, which for decades depicted American life in pictures. Government programs provided work for artists, writers, and actors through theater and art projects. Artists painted murals on public buildings. Writers wrote histories and guide books about various regions. Actors appeared in plays funded by the Federal Theater Project. Dancers performed, and orchestras played.

GEOGRAPHY IN HISTORY

Starting in the late 1800s, farmers using steel plows cut through the thick grasses that covered the Great Plains. They grew wheat in areas too dry to grow corn. After World War I, when farm prices dropped, farmers responded by clearing more land and growing more wheat. The 1930s were a decade of drought. For seven years, winds blew the top soil, no longer protected by the grass cover, east from New Mexico, Texas, Oklahoma, Colorado, and Kansas to the Atlantic and beyond. Sixty percent lost their farms.

READING STRATEGY

Formulating Questions
Reread the section about the culture of the Great Depression, then answer the following questions.

- What forms of entertainment were most popular during the Great Depression?

- Why were these forms of entertainment so popular?

- How did the tone of popular entertainment (such as movies and radio) differ from that of art and literature?

Some novels, such as those of John Dos Passos or John Steinbeck, protested the life of the 1930s. Other works, such as those of William Faulkner, were less political. Langston Hughes continued to write about African Americans, especially the poor and working class. He also wrote a novel about life in Chicago, which succeeded Harlem in the 1930s and 1940s as the center of African American culture.

Music of the 1930s continued to be dominated by jazz created by Louis Armstrong, Duke Ellington, and other musicians. It was also the age of big swing bands, such as those of Glenn Miller and Benny Goodman. The musical became a popular form of theater, with music by greats such as George Gershwin, Irving Berlin, Cole Porter, and Jerome Kern.

FRANKLIN DELANO ROOSEVELT

"I pledge you, I pledge myself, to a new deal

for the American people."

—*Franklin Delano Roosevelt*

In 1932, Franklin Delano Roosevelt was elected the thirty-second President. He was educated at Harvard University and the School of Law at Columbia University. He served as a Democrat in the New York State legislature, as assistant secretary of the navy under Woodrow Wilson, and as governor of New York before being elected President. He served as President throughout the rest of the depression and most of World War II, until his death in 1945.

Restoring Public Confidence

Franklin Roosevelt is ranked by historians as one of the greatest Presidents in American history. He inspired support and confidence in people. He was a master politician—intelligent, energetic, self-confident, charming, and optimistic. He had been tested by polio, which had left him in a wheelchair but made him tougher, more patient, and more compassionate.

Roosevelt, popularly called FDR, was also a master communicator. He held press conferences and effectively used the radio for "fireside chats" with the American public. He involved the public emotionally in his explanations of what he was doing to solve the nation's economic problems. He was able to convince people that he had confidence in himself and in our nation as well as genuine concern for the people.

FDR was controversial. While many respected and even loved him, others saw him as taking on almost dictatorial powers for himself and for the government. His attempt to make major changes in the Supreme Court is one example of controversy in his administration.

Election of 1932

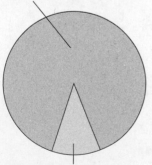

Democrat Franklin D. Roosevelt
89% of electoral vote

Republican Herbert C. Hoover
11% of electoral vote

Another is his decision to break the so-called unwritten Constitution and run for a third term in 1940. Roosevelt ran for and was elected to a fourth term in 1944. He died in office in 1945. In 1951, the Twenty-second Amendment was added to the Constitution, limiting a President to two terms in office. Some saw it as a reaction against Roosevelt.

Preparing to Lead the Nation

In the months between his election and his inauguration, Roosevelt surrounded himself with a group of formal and informal advisers. His cabinet members included Postmaster James Farley, Secretary of State Cordell Hull, and the first woman to hold a Cabinet post, Frances Perkins, as secretary of labor. FDR's informal advisers, known as the "brain trust," were a group of intellectuals and lawyers, several of whom were Columbia University professors. They favored reform and strongly influenced Roosevelt's New Deal administration. The most well-known brain trust member was social worker Harry Hopkins.

FDR's Eyes and Ears: Eleanor Roosevelt

Another major influence on Roosevelt and his New Deal was his wife, Eleanor Roosevelt. She was a humanitarian, active on behalf of women and minorities, especially African Americans. As First Lady, she became an important political figure in the nation. Through her travels, she served as the President's eyes and ears, but what he heard and saw was filtered through her progressive views and sensitivity to the plight of others. She helped to mold New Deal policy in several ways: through intervention with her husband on behalf of social reform; through her syndicated newspaper column; and through her travels and speeches around the nation. After Franklin Roosevelt's death in 1945, Eleanor Roosevelt became a leader in the issue of human rights, playing a key role in the creation of the 1948 Universal Declaration of Human Rights.

Old Reliable

Source: Berryman, Graff Collection Apr 12, 1938

ANALYZING DOCUMENTS

Note that cartoons can convey a great amount of information quickly. Examine the cartoon above. Does the cartoonist support or oppose FDR's policies?

THE NEW DEAL IN ACTION: RELIEF, RECOVERY, REFORM

Roosevelt's program to combat the problems caused by the depression was called the New Deal. The programs of the New Deal had the following goals:

- Relief for those people who were suffering
- Recovery for the economy, so it could grow again
- Reform measures to avoid future depressions

Relief Legislation of the New Deal

Congress passed a wide range of relief legislation as part of the New Deal.

READING STRATEGY

Organizing Information
Organize the information on the chart to categorize those programs that provided for:

1. Relief
2. Recovery
3. Reform

EMERGENCY BANKING ACT, 1933 Roosevelt's first act as President was to close the nation's banks by declaring a bank holiday in order to stop the collapse of the national banking system. The time was used to assure the public that it could have confidence in the banks once they reopened. The law required the examination of banks to ensure that only financially sound banks were operating.

FEDERAL EMERGENCY RELIEF ACT (FERA), 1933 Between 1933 and 1935, some $500,000 was provided for distribution by states and cities for direct relief and work projects for hungry, homeless, and unemployed people.

PUBLIC WORKS ADMINISTRATION (PWA), 1933 Operating from 1933 until 1939, the PWA provided jobs through construction projects, such as bridges, housing, hospitals, schools, and aircraft

New Deal Programs

Program	Initials	Begun	Purpose
Civilian Conservation Corps	CCC	1933	Provided jobs to young men to plant trees, build bridges and parks, and set up flood control projects
Tennessee Valley Authority	TVA	1933	Built dams to provide cheap electric power to seven southern states; set up schools and health centers
Federal Emergency Relief Administration	FERA	1933	Gave relief to unemployed and needy
Agricultural Adjustment Administration	AAA	1933	Paid farmers not to grow certain crops
National Recovery Administration	NRA	1933	Enforced codes that regulated wages, prices, and working conditions
Public Works Administration	PWA	1933	Built ports, schools, and aircraft carriers
Federal Deposit Insurance Corporation	FDIC	1933	Insured savings accounts in banks approved by government
Rural Electrification Administration	REA	1935	Loaned money to extend electricity to rural farmers
Works Progress Administration	WPA	1935	Employed men and women to build hospitals, schools, parks, and airports; employed artists, writers, and musicians
Social Security Act	SSA	1935	Set up a system of insurance for elderly, unemployed, and disabled. Later added benefits for surviving spouses and children

carriers. The PWA also moved government money into the economy. It was hoped that this "pump priming" would create jobs, revive production, and lead to more consumer spending.

CIVILIAN CONSERVATION CORPS (CCC), 1933 Between 1933 and 1941, the CCC provided work for 2.5 million young men ages 18 to 25 conserving natural resources. Only 8,000 young women joined the CCC.

WORKS PROGRESS ADMINISTRATION (WPA), 1935 From 1935 until 1943, the WPA provided temporary jobs for 25 percent of adult Americans. The agency was created to replace direct relief with public works projects. The WPA spent more government money than any other program. While WPA workers built roads, bridges, airports, public buildings, playgrounds, and golf courses, the program also offered work to writers, artists, musicians, scholars, and actors. Critics attacked the cultural work projects in particular. Others criticized the WPA for being inequitable. With WPA employment limited to one member of a family, only women who were heads of households were eligible for WPA jobs.

TENNESSEE VALLEY AUTHORITY (TVA), 1933 The federally funded TVA provided jobs, cheap electricity, and flood control to poor rural areas of seven states through dam construction on the Tennessee River and its tributaries. The TVA was made possible through the efforts of Republican Senator George Norris of Nebraska. The TVA was praised as a bold experiment in government intervention to meet regional needs. It was attacked as "creeping socialism."

Recovery Legislation of the New Deal
Congress also passed a wide range of recovery legislation as part of the New Deal.

NATIONAL INDUSTRIAL RECOVERY ACT, 1933 The National Recovery Administration (NRA) had the authority to work with businesses to help them recover. The NRA set "codes of fair competition" within industries to maintain prices, minimum wages, and maximum hours. The public was encouraged to buy from companies that followed the NRA codes. The NRA was not popular, however. Some consumers complained that the NRA plan raised prices. Companies opposed the provisions giving unions the right to organize. Small companies felt at a disadvantage compared to larger companies. The NIRA was declared unconstitutional in 1935.

HOME OWNERS LOAN CORPORATION (HOLC), 1933 This agency was created to help homeowners save their houses from foreclosure. It provided funds to pay off mortgages and provided new long-term mortgages at lower, fixed-interest rates.

READING STRATEGY

Organizing Information
A timeline can help you understand how the New Deal progressed. Create a timeline of the most significant legislation of the New Deal. Be sure to include all three categories of New Deal legislation (relief, recovery, and reform).

PREPARING FOR THE EXAM

The purpose of agricultural price supports is to keep the prices of farm products at a reasonable and stable level. By paying farmers to reduce the number of acres they plant, the government helps reduce the supply of farm products. When demand stays the same for the reduced supply, prices will rise.

- Does this type of a program still exist today?
- If so, in what form?

FEDERAL HOUSING ADMINISTRATION (FHA), 1934 The FHA was created by the National Housing Act to insure bank mortgages. These mortgages were often for 20 to 30 years and at down payments of only 10 percent.

FIRST AGRICULTURAL ADJUSTMENT ACT (AAA), 1933 The aim of the AAA was to raise farmers' income by cutting the amount of surplus crops and livestock. In that way, farmers would be able to sell their crops at the same prices of the years 1909–1914, a time when farm prices were high. The government paid farmers for reducing the number of acres they planted. The plan was financed through a processing tax on companies that made the wheat, corn, cotton, hogs, milk, and tobacco into consumer products. Large farmers, rather than small farmers and tenant farmers, benefited from the AAA. The public was outraged at the destruction of crops and animals in order to keep production down. However, farm prices did increase. Although the AAA was declared unconstitutional in 1936, the principle of farm price supports had been established. The AAA was replaced with a law that encouraged using soil conservation methods.

SECOND AGRICULTURAL ADJUSTMENT ACT (AAA), 1938 The second AAA was passed in response to a drop in farm prices in 1938. The government paid farmers to store portions of overproduced crops until the price reached the level of 1909–1914 prices. In spite of New Deal efforts, America's farmers did not regain prosperity until the 1940s, when World War II brought increased demand for food.

Reform Legislation of the New Deal

Congress also passed a wide range of reform legislation as part of the New Deal.

GLASS-STEAGALL ACT, 1933 This law created the Federal Deposit Insurance Corporation (FDIC), which guaranteed individual bank deposits up to $5,000. The law also increased the powers of the Federal Reserve Board so that it had more control over speculation on credit.

KEY THEMES AND CONCEPTS

Government

"Every qualified person shall be entitled to receive, with respect to the period beginning on the date he attains the age of sixty-five . . . an old-age benefit. . . ."
—Social Security Act, 1935

- What was the reason for the Social Security Act?
- How was it funded?
- What are current concerns and proposals regarding social security?

SECURITIES EXCHANGE ACT, 1934 This act created the Securities and Exchange Commission (SEC), which had the authority to regulate stock exchanges and investment advisers. SEC powers included the right to bring action against those found practicing fraud. The SEC could require financial information about stocks and bonds before they were sold.

SOCIAL SECURITY ACT, 1935 The 1935 Social Security Act was a combination of public assistance and insurance. The law had three main parts: (1) It provided old-age insurance, paid by a tax on both the employer and employee while the employee was working. The worker and employer, not the government funded this part of social security.

(2) It provided unemployment insurance for workers, paid by employers. (3) It gave assistance to dependent children and to the elderly, ill, and handicapped.

NATIONAL LABOR RELATIONS ACT (WAGNER ACT), 1935
The Wagner Act, named for its author, New York Senator Robert Wagner, guaranteed labor the right to form unions and to practice collective bargaining. It created the National Labor Relations Board (NLRB) to ensure that elections to select unions were conducted fairly.

FAIR LABOR STANDARDS ACT, 1938 This law set a minimum wage (originally 25 cents per hour) and a maximum work week (originally 44 hours) for workers in industries involved in interstate commerce. The law also banned child labor in interstate commerce. It is one of many examples of New Deal legislation passed using the power given to Congress to regulate interstate commerce.

THE NEW DEAL AND ORGANIZED LABOR

Roosevelt was interested in helping workers primarily through social legislation, such as social security. He also wanted to work cooperatively with business, as seen in the NRA legislation. When the NRA was ruled unconstitutional and with it the part that ensured labor the right to form unions, Roosevelt turned to the Wagner Act as a means of aiding labor. By 1935, he had turned away from business and saw organized labor unions as a force in society that would balance the power of big business.

This pro-labor attitude of the New Deal resulted in an increase in union membership of more than 1.5 million members between 1933 and 1935. After the Wagner Act became law in 1935, membership grew another 3 million. By 1938, it had reached 7 million organized workers. These gains took place during a split within organized labor over how to unionize workers.

The American Federation of Labor (AFL), whose craft unions of skilled workers had dominated the labor movement since 1886, was challenged for control by a new union organized by industry. These new unions organized all workers, skilled and unskilled, in a given industry, such as textiles, coal, steel, and automobiles, much like the old Knights of Labor. But unlike the Knights, the industrial unions concentrated on "bread and butter" issues of wages, hours, and working conditions. Led by John L. Lewis, head of the United Mine Workers, the new industrial unions formed the Committee for Industrial Organization (CIO) within the AFL. In 1937 the CIO became a separate union, the Congress of Industrial Organizations (CIO).

In addition to the way it organized workers, the CIO differed from the AFL because its members included women, African Americans, and immigrants from southern and eastern Europe. These groups made

ANALYZING DOCUMENTS

"Employees shall have the right of self-organization, to form, join, or assist labor organizations, to bargain collectively through representatives of their own choosing. . . ."
—National Labor Relations Act (Wagner Act) July 5, 1935

• Why can this act be called the "Magna Carta of Labor"?

up a large percentage of the unskilled work force that comprised the CIO unions. Despite their differences, the two organizations merged in 1955 to form the powerful AFL-CIO.

The 1930s were marked by a series of bitter strikes as the CIO attempted to unionize large industries, including the steel and automobile industries. Union workers demanded that companies enter into collective bargaining. Often police and company-paid guards used force against strikers. The workers made effective use of the **sit down strike,** a tactic in which they remained in the plant but refused to work until their demands were met.

THE NEW DEAL'S EFFECTS ON MINORITIES AND WOMEN

The New Deal legislation affected Native Americans, African Americans, Latinos, and women in a variety of ways.

Native Americans and the New Deal

In 1924, Native Americans were finally granted citizenship by Congress. However, Native Americans continued to suffer under the government policy of forced assimilation enacted in 1887 by the Dawes Act. It aimed at breaking up the tribal structure of Native American life and forcing Indians to become landowning farmers. The Native Americans lost an additional 90 million acres of land between 1887 and 1934.

Under Roosevelt and the New Deal, government policy changed to one of tribal restoration. The 1934 Indian Reorganization Act, also called the Wheeler-Howard Act, was passed largely through the efforts of Roosevelt's commissioner of Indian affairs, John Collier. The bill's aim was restore tribal self-government as well as Native American languages, customs, and religious freedom. Another New Deal program provided for the education of Native American children under the Bureau of Indian Affairs.

African Americans and the New Deal

African Americans were not a well-organized interest group in the 1930s. Therefore, they benefited less from the New Deal than did other groups. Roosevelt was not a strong advocate of civil rights, in part because he did not want to alienate southern Democrats in Congress, whose votes he needed to pass New Deal legislation. He did not support African American efforts to abolish the poll tax or to pass an antilynching law. Lynchings, in fact, increased during the 1930s.

However, within the New Deal programs, Eleanor Roosevelt and Harry Hopkins gave strong support to African Americans. As many as 50 African Americans were appointed to posts in various New Deal agencies. The most influential among them was Mary McLeod Bethune, who served in the National Youth Administration. While

African Americans protested discrimination within New Deal programs, some 40 percent of the nation's African Americans received help through a New Deal program. Many moved from the Republican party to the Democratic party during the New Deal.

Latinos and the New Deal

Many Latinos worked in agriculture and were particularly hard hit by the depression. "Okies" fleeing the Dust Bowl competed with Mexicans and Mexican Americans for migrant farm work in California. While the New Deal provided relief for these workers, the government's policy was to stop immigration and return to Mexico any unemployed noncitizens.

Women and the New Deal

Like African Americans, women were not an organized group during the 1930s. As you have read, women experienced less unemployment during this period, because they worked in low-paying jobs less affected by the depression. Single women and female heads of families made up a large portion of the female work force. Women earned about 50 cents for every dollar a man was paid, and they were often expected to give up jobs to male heads of families. The belief that the proper work for women was that of a wife and mother remained strong. Many New Deal programs simply would not hire women.

While women made little progress in the workplace, the New Deal did help women in government. Eleanor Roosevelt, Frances Perkins, and Mary McLeod Bethune were only a few of the women visibly active in the New Deal administration. More women also ran for and won political office although they were still far outnumbered by men.

The 1936 Election Mandate

In his first term, Roosevelt won the support of large numbers of Americans. Popular belief in him and in his New Deal program that seemed to offer something to everyone translated into votes. Roosevelt carefully built what is known as the New Deal coalition, a voting bloc that embraced the solid Democratic South, new immigrant workers, the big cities, African Americans who had previously voted Republican, organized labor, the elderly, and farmers who usually voted Republican.

This coalition emerged in the 1936 election, when Roosevelt was reelected to a second term. Roosevelt received a mandate, or a clear endorsement, from the electorate, carrying all but two states. This change in the two-party system was to dominate American politics over the next generation.

READING STRATEGY

Organizing Information
The New Deal affected various groups in different ways. To help you understand how different people were affected by the New Deal, create a chart showing the impact of the New Deal on:

- African Americans
- Latinos
- Women

ANALYZING DOCUMENTS

Examine the chart at right, then answer the following questions.

- What was the significance of the "First Hundred Days"?

- What is meant by the term *Second New Deal,* and what did it accomplish?

- Why did the economy weaken in 1937 and 1938?

- What ultimately caused the unemployment rate to improve?

PREPARING FOR THE EXAM

Compare the New Deal to other reform movements, such as Progressivism and the Great Society.

- Do they too appear to have stages?

Stages of the New Deal

1. **1933–early 1935:** New Deal legislation dealt with relief and recovery. Much of this legislation was passed in the "First Hundred Days" after FDR took office in March 1933. The 1934 Congressional elections increased the size of the Democratic majority in each house, which helped the New Deal legislative effort.

2. **1935 and early 1936:** Often called the "Second Hundred Days" or the "Second New Deal," this period's legislation focused more on social reform.

3. **1936 election:** This year is considered the high point of the New Deal.

4. **1937–1938:** A recession led to a new collapse in the weak economy that had just been starting to improve. The recession was due in part to New Deal cutbacks in spending after the 1936 election.

5. **1938:** By 1938 the New Deal had ended due to increased opposition in Congress and preoccupation with the danger of world war. Unemployment did not improve significantly until World War II created jobs in the production of war goods.

NEW DEAL GENERATES CONTROVERSY

Roosevelt and his New Deal mobilized the government and the nation to fight the effects of the Great Depression. His program for relief, recovery, and reform provoked controversy. Criticisms came from those who it felt that it was too radical or went too far as well as from those who felt its programs were too conservative or did not go far enough.

FDR's Policy Strategies

Roosevelt was a pragmatist. That means he did not come to office committed to a single theory or set of beliefs but rather was a man of action, interested in whatever worked to solve a problem. In short, he was an experimenter. The New Deal showed his willingness to make choices based on trial and error in order to solve problems.

FDR was influenced by Populist and Progressive philosophies of using the government to solve social and economic problems. He also used ideas of the Hoover administration and lessons learned in mobilizing the nation to fight World War I. The strategies used by the New Deal included:

- Passing relief measures that involved the federal government in the nation's economy to a greater degree than ever before. This direct governmental action was justified by using the commerce and elastic clauses of the Constitution.
- Taking fiscal action to stimulate the economy and lower unemployment by lowering taxes and increasing government spending.
- Assuming responsibility for the general welfare by protecting people against risks that they could not handle on their own.

- Increasing the regulatory role of the federal government over banks, businesses, and the stock exchange.
- Adopting deficit spending as an economic means of reviving the economy. This policy was based on the theories of economist John Maynard Keynes, who argued that the government must spend huge amounts of money to encourage production levels and purchasing power to increase. This policy, Keynes argued, would result in economic recovery.

Federal Income and Spending, 1928–1940

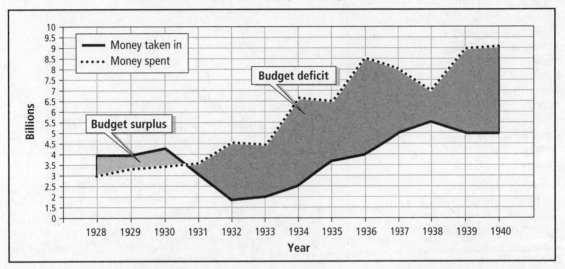

Supreme Court Reaction

Throughout the New Deal, the Supreme Court majority practiced judicial restraint, narrowly interpreting the interstate commerce clause and striking down many of FDR's programs, which were based on a broad interpretation of that part of the Constitution. In a series of decisions, the Court ruled that several key New Deal laws were unconstitutional.

SUPREME COURT AND THE NRA The National Recovery Act (NRA) was declared unconstitutional in *Schechter Poultry Corporation* v. *United States* (1935). The Court ruled that the law illegally gave Congress power to regulate intrastate commerce (or commerce within a single state) and violated the separation of powers by giving the legislative powers to the executive branch.

SUPREME COURT AND THE AAA In *United States* v. *Butler* (1936), the Supreme Court struck down the Agricultural Adjustment Act (AAA) on the grounds that agriculture was a local, not an interstate, matter under the provisions of the Tenth Amendment.

ANALYZING DOCUMENTS

Use the chart above and your knowledge of social studies to answer the following questions.

- What is the definition of a *budget deficit*?
- In what year was the budget deficit the largest?
- What caused this increase in the budget deficit?

Review the New Deal programs to determine on what these funds were spent.

FDR's Court-Packing Plan

Supreme Court opposition to FDR's programs continued with the Court consistently vetoing New Deal legislation. Franklin Roosevelt asked Congress to approve a law that would permit the President to increase the number of judges from nine to fifteen if the judges refused to retire at the age of 70.

The Judicial Reorganization Bill—or the "court-packing" plan, as its opponents called it—was intended to make the Supreme Court approve the New Deal laws. It never became law because it was a threat to the separation of powers.

THE INGENIOUS QUARTERBACK!

Political Opposition

In his first two terms, Roosevelt's strongest opposition was from big business. In 1934, a group of conservative Democratic and Republican business owners and politicians, including former presidential candidate Al Smith, formed the American Liberty League. It claimed that Roosevelt was exercising too much power as President. It attacked the New Deal because its programs were being financed through deficit spending. The group expressed fear that the American free enterprise system was being destroyed.

Radical groups such as the Communist party also offered alternatives to the New Deal but failed to gain any major public support. At its peak in 1938, the Communist party of the United States of America had only 55,000 members, and its 1936 presidential candidate won only 80,000 votes. Meanwhile, the pro-Nazi German-American Bund became active, as did the **Black Shirts,** fascists who supported the views of Italian dictator Benito Mussolini.

The Socialist party in America drew some rising support, although some members began to vote for Roosevelt. The party was led by Eugene Debs and by Norman Thomas, the party's presidential candidate. Unlike the Communist party, the Socialists believed in the use of democratic means to make changes in the American economic structure.

As frustration grew in the face of the prolonged depression, various individuals entered the political scene, each criticizing the New Deal and offering often simplistic solutions to the economic crisis. These men were called "homegrown demagogues" because their philosophies did not come from a foreign nation and because they appealed to people's emotions and prejudice. These demagogues included:

- Francis E. Townsend, who created a financially impossible plan to provide government pensions for the elderly.
- Father Charles E. Coughlin, a Catholic priest who blamed business owners, especially Jewish ones, for the economic crisis.
- Huey Long, a powerful United States senator from Louisiana, who proposed that income and inheritance taxes on the wealthy be used to give each American a $2,500 income, a car, and a college education. Long was assassinated in 1935.

ANALYZING DOCUMENTS

Using the table below and the text, answer the following questions.

- Who are some specific people who voiced the criticisms shown in the graphic summary?
- What evidence is there to support each of these positions?

Critics of the New Deal

Women and African Americans	Progressives and Socialists	Republicans and other political opponents
New Deal programs offer more opportunities to white men than to women and minorities. Women and African Americans are paid less for the same work.	New Deal programs are not doing enough to solve the nation's problems. More should be done to distribute the nation's wealth among all Americans.	Government is becoming too powerful. The Constitution is threatened. FDR is like a dictator. New Deal taxes on the wealthy are unfair. New Deal programs are too much like socialism.

EVALUATING THE NEW DEAL

Most historians agree on the following assessment of the New Deal:

- World War II was largely responsible for ending the Great Depression. The New Deal did not solve unemployment, the farm crisis, or underconsumption.
- Nevertheless, the New Deal did help people cope with the effects of the Great Depression.
- The New Deal brought more power to the presidency and to the federal government. The government now had a role and a responsibility in more aspects of the nation's economic and social life.
- The New Deal preserved the free-enterprise system.
- The deficit spending of the New Deal raised the national debt.

ANALYZING DOCUMENTS

"Roosevelt is the only President we ever had that thought the Constitution belonged to the poor man too."

—George Dobbin, mill worker, 1939

- How would a worker such as George Dobbin evaluate the New Deal?

Questions for Regents Practice

For online Questions for Regents Practice,
visit the Prentice Hall Web site at www.phschool.com.

MULTIPLE CHOICE

Directions

Review the Test-Taking Strategies section of this book. Then answer the following questions, drawn from actual Regents examinations. Each question is followed by four choices. Read each question carefully. Decide which choice is the correct answer. Then on a separate piece of paper, mark your answer for each question.

1   Which was a major problem faced by United States farmers in both the 1890s and 1920s?
  1 lagging technology
  2 lack of tariff protection
  3 overproduction of basic staples
  4 inflationary currency

2   In which respect were the decades of the 1920s and the 1960s in the United States most similar?
  1 organized militancy by ethnic minorities
  2 public concern with pollution of the environment
  3 widespread government activity dealing with social issues
  4 significant changes in manners and morals

3   What was the one similarity between the Red Scare following World War I and the Cold War following World War II?
  1 Fear of communism led to the suppression of the civil liberties of some Americans.
  2 Large numbers of Russian revolutionaries settled in the United States.
  3 Congressional investigations proved that the federal government was heavily infiltrated by Communist spies.
  4 Renewed fighting between wartime enemies was a constant threat.

4   Which is most commonly associated with the presidencies of Ulysses S. Grant and Warren G. Harding?
  1 depression in business
  2 corruption of public officials
  3 humanitarian reforms
  4 territorial expansion

5   In the United States, the widespread disregard of the fugitive slave laws and of Prohibition laws most clearly indicated that
  1 strongly held values are difficult to regulate
  2 the federal government is generally unable to enforce its own laws
  3 little respect is given to the legal system
  4 the judicial system is too lenient in its treatment of offenders

6   A major reason for the isolationist trend in the United States following World War I was
  1 a desire to continue the reforms of the Progressives
  2 the public's desire to end most trade with other nations
  3 the failure of the United States to gain new territory
  4 a disillusionment over the failure to achieve United States goals in the postwar world

7 The "boom" years of the 1920s were characterized by
1 decreases in both agricultural surpluses and farm foreclosures
2 limited investment capital and declining numbers of workers in the labor force
3 widespread use of the automobile and an increase in buying
4 increased regulation of the marketplace by both federal and state governments

8 The racial segregation and poverty experienced by African Americans in the South during the 1920s led them to
1 move to the North in great numbers to find factory jobs
2 join with whites in strong national movements to protest unjust laws
3 evolve their own strong labor movement
4 support federal programs that gave them their own farmland

9 The Harlem Renaissance of the 1920s was a period when African Americans
1 left the United States in large numbers to settle in Nigeria
2 created noteworthy works of art and literature
3 migrated to the West in search of land and jobs
4 used civil disobedience to fight segregation in the armed forces

10 In the 1920s, the Sacco and Vanzetti case, the Red Scare, and the activities of the Ku Klux Klan all represented
1 threats to civil liberties
2 victories over discrimination and persecution
3 support for the Prohibition movement
4 greater social freedom for Americans

11 The conviction of John Scopes in 1925 for teaching about evolution supported the ideas of those Americans who
1 believed in religious freedom and the separation of church and state
2 hoped to lessen the differences between rural and urban lifestyles
3 wanted to promote traditional fundamentalist values
4 favored the changes resulting from the new technology of the 1920s

12 One important cause of the Great Depression in the United States was that by the end of the 1920s
1 the government controlled almost every aspect of the economy
2 tariffs were so low that foreign products had forced many United States companies out of business
3 investors were too cautious and put their money only into government bonds
4 factories and farms were able to produce far more than buyers could afford to purchase

13 President Herbert Hoover's refusal to provide funds for the unemployed during the Depression was based on his belief that
1 the unemployment problem was not serious
2 workers would not accept government assistance
3 labor unions should provide for the unemployed
4 federal relief programs would destroy individual initiative

14 Which is a valid conclusion based on a study of the presidencies of Thomas Jefferson and Franklin D. Roosevelt?
1 Strong third parties develop when the two major parties ignore popular demands.
2 Presidential success depends mainly on a sympathetic Supreme Court.
3 Economic crisis can force a President to suspend basic civil liberties.
4 A President's political program may change in the face of current needs.

15 The rapid, worldwide spread of the Great Depression of the 1930s was evidence of
1 the failure of government job programs
2 global financial interdependence
3 a shortage of American factories making consumer goods
4 the negative effects of unrestricted immigration

16 Which New Deal reforms most directly targeted the basic problem of the victims of the Dust Bowl?
1 guaranteeing workers the right to organize and bargain collectively
2 regulating the sale of stocks and bonds
3 providing farmers low-cost loans and parity payments
4 raising individual and corporate income tax rates

17 Deficit spending by the federal government as a means of reviving the economy is based on the idea that
1 purchasing power will increase and economic growth will be stimulated
2 only the national government can operate businesses efficiently
3 the national government should turn its revenue over to the states
4 lower interest rates will encourage investment

18 The main purpose of the New Deal measures such as the Securities and Exchange Commission (SEC) and the Federal Deposit Insurance Corporation (FDIC) was to
1 provide immediate employment opportunities
2 develop rules to limit speculation and safeguard savings
3 enable the federal government to take over failing industries
4 assure a guaranteed income for American families

19 During President Franklin D. Roosevelt's administration, which situation was viewed by critics as a threat to the principle of separation of powers?
1 changing the date of the Presidential inauguration
2 congressional support of banking legislation
3 proposing the expansion of Supreme Court membership
4 passage of Social Security legislation

20 "Section 202. (a) Every qualified individual shall be entitled to receive . . . on the date he attains the age of sixty-five . . . and ending on the date of his death, an old-age benefit. . . ."

A major purpose of this section of federal legislation was to
1 guarantee an annual income to experienced employees
2 assure adequate medical care for the elderly
3 reward workers for their support of the union movement
4 provide economic assistance to retired workers

21 The popularity of escapist novels and movies during the Great Depression is evidence that
1 the Great Depression was not really a time of economic distress
2 popular culture is shaped by economic and social conditions
3 American society did not try to solve the problems of the Great Depression
4 the greatest employment opportunities for the average person in the 1930s were in the field of entertainment

22 A major effect of the National Labor Relations Act (Wagner Act, 1935) was that labor unions
1 were soon controlled by large corporations
2 experienced increasing difficulty in gaining new members
3 obtained the right to bargain collectively
4 lost the right to strike

23 The effectiveness of the New Deal in ending the Great Depression is difficult to measure because
1 President Franklin D. Roosevelt died during his fourth term
2 United States involvement in World War II rapidly accelerated economic growth
3 the Supreme Court declared most New Deal laws unconstitutional
4 later Presidents failed to support most New Deal reforms

24 Many opponents of New Deal programs claimed that these programs violated the American tradition of
1 welfare capitalism
2 governmental regulation of business
3 collective bargaining
4 individual responsibility

25 A lasting result of the New Deal in the United States has been the
1 reduction of the national debt
2 control of stock prices by the federal government
3 joint effort of business and labor to strengthen the Presidency
4 assumption by the federal government of greater responsibility for the nation's well-being

26 The process of collective bargaining is best described as
1 meetings of joint congressional committees to achieve compromise on different versions of a proposed law
2 diplomatic strategies used to make treaties between two nations
3 discussions between labor union leaders and management to agree on a contract for workers
4 negotiations between a multinational company and a nation with which the company wishes to do business

27 Which generalization most accurately describes the literary work of Langston Hughes, Sinclair Lewis, and John Steinbeck?
1 Politics and art seldom mix well.
2 The best literature concerns the lives of the wealthy.
3 Literature often reflects the times in which it is created.
4 Traditional American themes are the most popular.

28 An immediate result of the Supreme Court decision in *Schechter Poultry* v. *United States* was that
1 some aspects of the New Deal were declared unconstitutional
2 state governments took over relief agencies
3 Congress was forced to abandon efforts to improve the economy
4 the constitutional authority of the President was greatly expanded

THEMATIC ESSAY

In developing your answers to the essay, be sure to keep these general definitions in mind:

(a) <u>discuss</u> means "to make observations about something using facts, reasoning, and argument; to present in some detail"

(b) <u>describe</u> means "to illustrate something in words or to tell about it"

(c) <u>evaluate</u> means "to examine and judge the significance, worth, or condition of; to determine the value of"

Directions

Write a well-organized essay that includes an introduction, several paragraphs addressing the task below, and a conclusion.

Theme: Reform Movements

Throughout United States history, there have been times when movements or programs have developed in response to demands for political, economic, or social reform.

Task

From your study of United States history, identify two movements or programs which developed in response to demands for reform.

For each movement or program identified:

- State one problem that led to the movement or program.
- Describe a specific reform advocated by the movement or program to deal with the problem.
- Describe the tactics or means used by supporters of the movement or program to achieve the specific reform.
- Discuss the extent to which the movement or program reform was successful in achieving the specific reform.

Suggestions

You may use any major reform movement or program from your study of United States history. Some suggestions you might wish to consider include: abolitionist movement (1830–1865); temperance movement (1830–1933); women's movement (1848–1920); Progressivism (1900–1920); New Deal (1933–1945); Great Society (1960s); American Indian movement (1960–present).

You are *not* limited to these suggestions.

Guidelines

In your essay be sure to:

- Address all aspects of the *Task*
- Analyze, evaluate, or compare and/or contrast issues and events whenever possible
- Fully support the theme of the essay with relevant facts, examples, and details
- Write a well-developed essay that consistently demonstrates a logical and clear plan of organization
- Introduce the theme by establishing a framework that is beyond a simple restatement of the *Task*
- Conclude your essay with a strong summation of the theme

DOCUMENT-BASED ESSAY

> For online Document-Based Essays,
> visit the Prentice Hall Web site at www.phschool.com.

This task is designed to test your ability to work with historical documents and is based on the accompanying documents (1–5). Some of the documents have been edited for the purposes of this question. As you analyze the documents, take into account both the source of each document and any point of view that may be presented in the document.

Directions

This document-based question consists of two parts: Part A and Part B. In Part A, you are to read each document and answer the question or questions that follow the document. In Part B, you are to write an essay based on the information in the documents and your knowledge of United States history.

Historical Context:

The federal government responded quite differently to the prosperity of the 1920s and the Great Depression that followed. Roosevelt's New Deal was not only a decisive plan to combat the Depression, but it also marked a new direction in the role of government in managing the economy—a role that is still being debated today.

Task:

Using information from the documents and your knowledge of United States history and government, answer the questions that follow each document in Part A. Your answers to the questions will help you write the Part B essay in which you be asked to:

Discuss the response of the United States government to the Great Depression. In your essay, include a discussion of how this response can be considered a turning point in the role of the federal government in managing the economy.

PART A: SHORT ANSWER

DOCUMENT #1

" . . . we must have tax reform. The method of raising tax revenue ought not to impede the transaction of business; it ought to encourage it. I am opposed to extremely high taxes, . . . because they are bad for the country, and because they are wrong. We cannot finance the country through any system of injustice, even if we attempt to inflict it on the rich. . . . The wise and judicious course to follow in taxation and economic legislation is not to destroy those already who have secured success, but to create conditions under which everyone will have a better chance to be successful.

—**Calvin Coolidge,** *Inaugural Address,* **March 4, 1925**

1   According to this quote, how did Calvin Coolidge feel about the role of government in managing business?

_____

_____

DOCUMENT #2
Economic Impact of the Great Depression

Source: *Historical Statistics of the United States, Colonial Times to 1970*

2   Based on the chart above, what effect did the stock market crash of 1929 have on the overall economy of the United States?

_____

_____

_____

DOCUMENT #3

> *"I have recounted to you in other speeches, and it is a matter of general information, that for at least two years after the crash, the only efforts by the [Hoover] administration to cope with the distress of unemployment were to deny its existence."*
>
> **—Franklin D. Roosevelt, 1932**

3 Based on this quote that Roosevelt made during the 1932 presidential campaign, how did Roosevelt evaluate the efforts made by the Hoover administration to resolve the nation's economic problems?

_____

_____

_____

DOCUMENT #4

> *"So, first of all, let me assert my firm belief that the only thing we have to fear is fear itself- nameless, unreasoning, unjustified terror which paralyzes needed efforts to convert retreat into advance. In every dark hour of our national life a leadership of frankness and vigor has met with that understanding and support of the people themselves which is essential to victory. I am convinced that you will again give that support to leadership in these critical days.*
>
> *In such a spirit on my part and on yours we face our common difficulties. They concern, thank God, only material things. Values have shrunken to fantastic levels; taxes have risen; our ability to pay has fallen; government of all kinds is faced by serious curtailment of income; the means of exchange are frozen in the currents of trade; the withered leaves of industrial enterprise lie on every side; farmers find no markets for their produce; the savings of many years in thousands of families are gone.*
>
> *More important, a host of unemployed citizens face the grim problem of existence, and an equally great number toil with little return. Only a foolish optimist can deny the dark realities of the moment."*
>
> **—Franklin D. Roosevelt, *First Inaugural Address*, March 4, 1933**

4 In this excerpt from FDR's first inaugural speech, how did he attempt to win the support of the American people for his leadership during the economic crisis of the Great Depression?

_____

_____

_____

DOCUMENT #5

5 According to the above cartoon, how did some Americans view the New Deal?

_____

_____

_____

PART B: ESSAY

Directions: Using information from the documents provided, and your knowledge of United States history, write a well-organized essay that includes an introduction, several paragraphs, and a conclusion.

Historical Context

The federal government responded quite differently to the prosperity of the 1920s and the Great Depression that followed. Roosevelt's New Deal was not only a decisive plan to combat the Depression, but it also marked a new direction in the role of government in managing the economy-a role that is still being debated today.

Task

Using information from the documents and your knowledge of United States history and government, write an essay in which you

Discuss the response of the United States government to the Great Depression. In your essay, include a discussion of how this response can be considered a turning point in the role of the federal government in managing the economy.

Guidelines

When writing your essay, be sure to
- Address all aspects of the *Task* by accurately analyzing and interpreting at least four documents
- Incorporate information from the documents in the body of the essay
- Incorporate relevant outside information throughout the essay
- Richly support the theme with relevant facts, examples, and details
- Write a well-developed essay that consistently demonstrates a logical and clean plan of organization
- Introduce the theme by establishing a framework that is beyond a simple restatement of the *Task* or *Historical Context* and conclude the essay with a summation of the theme.

UNIT 6

The United States in an Age of Global Crisis

Section 1   Peace in Peril, 1933–1950

Section 2   Peace with Problems, 1945–1960

UNIT OVERVIEW

This unit covers the time period from 1933 to 1960, a period that included the Great Depression, World War II, and the Cold War. This unit focuses on American foreign policy and how it affected life in the United States during those years.

Some of the key questions about the United States history during this period include:

- What caused the United States to change its foreign policy from isolationism and neutrality to a growing commitment to global involvement?

- Why did the world go to war from 1939 until 1945? How and when did the United States become involved in the conflict? How did the Allies strategize to end the war? How did World War II affect the lives of Americans on the home front?

- Why did the United States and the Soviet Union change from being allies in World War II to enemies during the Cold War?

- How did the United States try to stop the spread of communism in Europe and Asia? How did the desire to halt the spread of communism lead the United States into war in Korea? What effects did the fear of communism have within the United States?

SECTION OVERVIEW

In the 1930s, great changes were happening in Europe and Asia. Totalitarian regimes rose to power in Germany, Italy, and Japan, threatening the freedom of nations on their borders. In 1939, the German invasion of Poland launched World War II, which quickly engulfed Europe and much of Asia. The United States, still embracing isolationism, tried to maintain neutrality, but the 1941 Japanese bombing of Pearl Harbor drew the nation into the conflict. Four more years of bloody fighting in Europe and Asia left millions of soldiers and civilians dead and hundreds of cities damaged or destroyed. The United States suffered relatively light losses in comparison to other nations, and it emerged as a world leader with a growing commitment to international involvement.

KEY THEMES AND CONCEPTS

As you review this section, take special note of the following key themes and concepts:

Presidential Decisions and Actions How did Presidents Roosevelt and Truman influence the events and outcomes of World War II?

Foreign Policy How did world events change American foreign policy from one of isolationism to a growing commitment to global involvement?

Diversity How did World War II change the lives of women, African Americans, and Japanese Americans?

KEY PEOPLE

Adolf Hitler	Franklin D. Roosevelt	Robert Oppenheimer
Benito Mussolini	Winston Churchill	Harry S Truman
Francisco Franco	Joseph Stalin	

★ THE BIG IDEA

The United States fought on the side of the Allies in World War II. The United States

- entered the war in 1941 when the Japanese bombed Pearl Harbor in Hawaii.
- fought in Europe and defeated the Germans.
- fought in Asia and defeated the Japanese.
- emerged from the war as a world leader.

⚷ KEY TERMS

totalitarian
fascism
appeasement
Lend-Lease Act
Allies
Axis Powers
Manhattan Project
Holocaust
Rosie the Riveter
Nisei
WRA camps

In the 1920s and 1930s, the United States pursued a policy of neutrality and isolationism. In order to understand the reasons for this policy, we must examine the lingering impact of World War I.

GEOGRAPHY IN HISTORY

How did the United States' location relative to Europe and Asia contribute to isolationist sentiment before and after World War I?

ISOLATIONIST SENTIMENT AFTER WORLD WAR I

The United States had been reluctant to enter World War I. Fighting had begun in Europe in 1914, and the United States stayed out of the war until 1917. Between April 1917, when the United States formally declared war, and Germany's surrender in November 1918, some 48,000 American soldiers were killed in battle, 2,900 were declared missing in action, and 56,000 soldiers died of disease. These losses were far less than those of the European nations, some of which had lost millions of soldiers and civilians. Nevertheless, the American losses were great enough to cause Americans to take a close look at the reasons for the entry of the United States into the war and at the nation's foreign policy.

 PREPARING FOR THE EXAM

Many questions on the exam will require you to distinguish between similar concepts and terms.

- What is the difference between isolationism and neutrality?

Isolation and Neutrality

Isolationism and neutrality are similar foreign policies, but an important difference exists between them. Isolationism is a national foreign policy of remaining apart from political or economic entanglements with other countries. Strict isolationists do not support any type of contact with other countries, including economic ties or trade activities.

When a country chooses a policy of neutrality, it deliberately takes no side in a dispute or controversy. Countries following this path are often referred to as being nonaligned or noninvolved. Neutral nations do not limit their trading activities with other nations, unless a trading partnership would limit that country's ability to stay politically noninvolved.

Events Preceding American Involvement in World War II

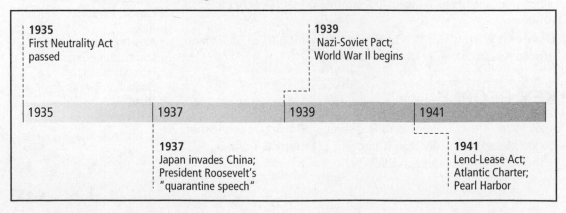

1935
First Neutrality Act passed

1937
Japan invades China; President Roosevelt's "quarantine speech"

1939
Nazi-Soviet Pact; World War II begins

1941
Lend-Lease Act; Atlantic Charter; Pearl Harbor

1935   1937   1939   1941

Historical Roots of Isolationism and Neutrality

The roots of isolationist and neutralistic sentiments in the United States can be traced to the late eighteenth and early nineteenth centuries.

PRECEDENTS SET BY GEORGE WASHINGTON In his years as President, George Washington set the important precedent of an American foreign policy of neutrality—but not isolationism. He knew that trade was necessary for the new nation to prosper, but that foreign alliances might force it into war.

In 1793, Washington issued his Proclamation of Neutrality, making it clear that the United States would not respond to requests for aid during the French Revolution. In his farewell address of 1796, Washington warned the United States to steer clear of "entangling alliances," or political commitments to other nations, although he supported economic ties to foreign countries. These basic ideas guided American foreign policy into the twentieth century.

MONROE DOCTRINE The policy that became known as the Monroe Doctrine reinforced the neutral position of the United States toward Europe. In 1823, President Monroe proclaimed that the United States would not interfere in European affairs. He also warned European powers to remain out of the affairs of nations in the Western Hemisphere. This doctrine formed the backbone of American foreign policy for many years.

Isolationism in the 1930s

In 1934, when the United States was trying to recover from the worst economic depression in its history, Senator Gerald Nye led an investigation into the reasons the United States entered World War I. The committee concluded that the United States had gone to war at the encouragement of financiers and armament makers, eager for profits. As a result of this investigation, many Americans supported a return to isolationism. They believed that the country would be secure without worrying about the actions of the rest of the world.

The refusal of the United States to join the League of Nations was reinforced by the Senate's move in 1935 to forbid the United States to join the World Court. That same year, Congress also passed the first of a series of neutrality acts, intended to prevent Americans from making loans to nations at war. Any sales of goods to such nations were to be strictly on a "cash and carry" basis. In 1937, President Roosevelt made his famous quarantine speech, in which he likened the spreading world lawlessness to a disease. He stated that the United States would attempt to quarantine the "patients" in order to protect the rest of the community of nations.

READING STRATEGY

Reinforcing Main Ideas
How did the Monroe Doctrine contribute to isolationist and neutralist sentiments in the United States prior to World War II?

KEY THEMES AND CONCEPTS

Foreign Policy
The Neutrality Acts passed in 1935, 1936, and 1937 declared that the United States would withhold weapons and loans of money from all nations at war and that U.S. citizens who traveled on ships belonging to nations at war did so at their own risk. The acts also required that nonmilitary goods sold to nations at war be paid for in cash and transported by the purchaser.

• What events in the nation's history caused the government to be wary of Americans' involvement in ocean trade and travel?

EVENTS LEADING TO WORLD WAR II

The rise of totalitarian governments in Germany and Italy in the 1930s set the stage for World War II.

The Rise of Totalitarian Governments

In **totalitarian** governments, one political party has complete control over the government and bans all other parties. Totalitarian governments rely on terror to suppress individual rights and silence opposition. In other words, totalitarian governments are the opposite of all that the United States considers its tradition of political freedom and liberty.

In Germany and Italy, totalitarian governments were established based on the philosophy of **fascism.** Fascism places the importance of the nation above all else, and individual rights and freedoms are lost as everyone works for the benefit of the nation. Nazi Germany (led by Adolf Hitler) and Fascist Italy (led by Benito Mussolini) were two fascist governments characterized by extreme nationalism, racism, and militarism (desire to go to war).

Hitler and Mussolini provided military assistance to Francisco Franco, a Fascist leader in Spain who was attempting to overthrow the republican government there and establish a totalitarian one. The devastating Spanish civil war that erupted in 1936 would become a "dress rehearsal" for World War II. The war in Spain was a testing ground for new weapons and military strategies that would later be used in World War II.

In the United States, opinions about support for the Spanish civil war were divided. Some Americans traveled to Spain to fight for the republican cause. The United States government, however, continued to pursue a policy of neutrality. Congress passed a resolution forbidding the export of arms to either side in 1937. Franco won the Spanish civil war in 1939, established a fascist government, and remained leader of Spain until his death in 1975.

Major World Events, 1919–1941

The chart on the next page summarizes the major events between the end of World War I and the entry of the United States into World War II. During this time, peace failed, and aggressors achieved their goals, even though their success did not last long. As you review the chart, look for relationships between events in order to understand how certain events caused others that occurred later.

Some events in the chart on the next page are so significant that they require further discussion.

1938 MUNICH AGREEMENT With this agreement, Great Britain and France allowed Germany to annex the Sudetenland, a region of Czechoslovakia with a large German-speaking population. Hitler convinced the British prime minister Neville Chamberlain and the French premier Édouard Daladier that Germany would make no further terri-

 PREPARING FOR THE EXAM

One way to remember the meaning of the term *totalitarianism* is from the word *total*: totalitarian governments have total control over every aspect of life. They suppress all individual rights and silence all opposition with threats. Fascism places the importance of the nation above individual rights.

• What is the relationship between totalitarianism and fascism?

ANALYZING DOCUMENTS

Examine the chart on the next page, then answer these questions.

• How might dissatisfaction with the outcome of World War I and economic depression have contributed to the rise of dictators in Italy and Germany?

• Which events described in the chart represent actions of appeasement on the part of France and Britain?

Major World Events, 1918–1941

• **1918** Germany surrenders. World War I is concluded.	• **1935** Italy Invades Ethlopia. The United States passes the first Neutrality Act.
• **1919** Germany signs the Treaty of Versailles. The United States refuses to approve the Treaty of Versailles.	• **1936** Hitler reoccupies the Rhineland. The German/Italian Axis is formed. The Spanish Civil War begins (ending in 1939). The United States passes the second Neutrality Act. The United States votes for nonintervention at the Pan-American Conference.
• **1921** Great Britain, France, and Japan attend the Washington Naval Conference on limiting arms. The conference produces the Four Power and Nine Power treaties.	
	• **1937** Japan invades China. Japan sinks an American gunboat in Chinese waters.The United States passes the third Neutrality Act, including a "cash and carry" plan.
• **1922** Benito Mussolini becomes Italy's Fascist dictator. The USSR is officially formed, following the Communist victory in the Russian Revolution.	
	• **1938** Germany annexes Austria (the *Anschluss*). Hitler demands the Sudetenland of Czechoslovakia. Great Britain, France, and Germany sign the Munich Pact, giving in to Hitler's demands.
• **1923** Adolf Hitler writes *Mein Kampf* in prison.	
• **1924** In the USSR, Lenin dies. Stalin continues his rise to power.	• **1939** A German/Soviet nonaggression pact is signed. Japanese and American relations are deadlocked. The United States Senate refuses to grant aid to Great Britain or France. Hitler invades Poland, marking the beginning of World War II.
• **1928** The Kellogg-Briand Pact outlawing war is signed by 62 nations. The pact contains no method of enforcement.	
• **1929** The most serious economic depression in history begins, continuing through the 1930s.	• **1940** Germany occupies Norway, Denmark, the Netherlands, Belgium, Luxembourg, and France. Germany attacks Great Britain. Japan joins the Axis powers. President Roosevelt arranges to supply destroyers to Great Britain. Congress passes the Selective Training and Service Act, the first peacetime draft in United States history.
• **1930** Japan occupies Manchuria.	
• **1932** Japan seizes Shanghai. The United States issues the Stimson Doctrine, condemning Japanese aggression against Manchuria.	
• **1933** Hitler assumes power in Germany. Japan announces its withdrawal from the League of Nations. President Roosevelt announces the Good Neighbor Policy in Latin America. The USSR is formally recognized by the United States. Nazi Germany begins operation of the first concentration camp at Dachau, near Munich.	• **1941** Germany invades the USSR. The United States passes the Lend-Lease Act, granting aid to countries whose defense was seen as critical to the defense of the United States. President Roosevelt and Prime Minister Churchill agree to the Atlantic Charter. Japan attacks the United States at Pearl Harbor. The United States enters World War II.

torial demands in Czechoslovakia after annexing the Sudetenland. When Chamberlain returned to Britain with this agreement, he told the world that he had achieved "peace for our time." Six months later, however, Hitler seized the rest of Czechoslovakia.

Great Britain and France had resorted to the policy of **appeasement,** which means to agree to the demands of a potential enemy in

⚲ KEY THEMES AND
CONCEPTS
Foreign Policy
President Roosevelt explained the Lend-Lease policy to the American people through the use of a simple comparison:

If your neighbor's house is on fire, you don't sell him a hose. You lend it to him and take it back after the fire is out.

- How did the Lend-Lease policy lead to greater U.S. involvement in the war?

⚲ KEY THEMES AND
CONCEPTS
Science and Technology
How did advances in aviation technology contribute to changes in American isolationist sentiments?

READING STRATEGY
Organizing Information
Who were the three major Allied powers?

1.

2.

3.

Who were the three major Axis powers?

1.

2.

3.

order to keep the peace. Hitler demonstrated by his action that he could not be permanently appeased, and the world learned a costly lesson.

LEND-LEASE ACT Although the United States was officially committed to a policy of neutrality, President Roosevelt soon found a way around the Neutrality Acts to provide aid, including warships in the Destroyer Deal, to Great Britain. In 1941, Roosevelt convinced Congress to pass the **Lend-Lease Act,** which allowed the United States to sell or lend war materials to "any country whose defense the President deems vital to the defense of the United States." Roosevelt intended to keep the United States out of the war, but he said that the nation would become the "arsenal of democracy," supplying arms to those who were fighting for freedom.

JAPAN'S ATTACK ON PEARL HARBOR The United States did not enter World War II until 1941. President Franklin D. Roosevelt had promised that the United States would not fight in a war in which the country was not directly involved. However, on December 7, 1941, Japanese war planes attacked the U.S. Navy fleet at Pearl Harbor, Hawaii. Roosevelt called the attack a day that would "live in infamy," a day that Americans would never forget. This surprise attack shattered the American belief that the Atlantic and Pacific Oceans would safely isolate the United States from fighting in Europe and Asia. The attack on Pearl Harbor fueled American nationalism and patriotism. Suddenly the war was no longer oceans away. The day after the attack, Congress agreed to President Roosevelt's request to declare war on Japan.

WORLD WAR II IN REVIEW

World War II began in 1939, when German forces invaded Poland. The United States entered the war two years later, after the Japanese attacked Pearl Harbor. War in Europe ended in May 1945, and fighting in the Pacific ended on August 14, 1945, when the Japanese surrender brought World War II to a conclusion.

Major Powers

The war pitted 26 nations united together as the **Allies** against eight **Axis Powers.** The major powers among the Allies were Great Britain, the Soviet Union, and the United States. Germany, Italy, and Japan were the major Axis nations. Leaders of the major powers are listed on the next page.

Major Events

World War II was fought primarily in two major regions: Europe and North Africa, and in the Pacific. Major military engagements and turning points in World War II are presented on the next page.

Europe During World War II

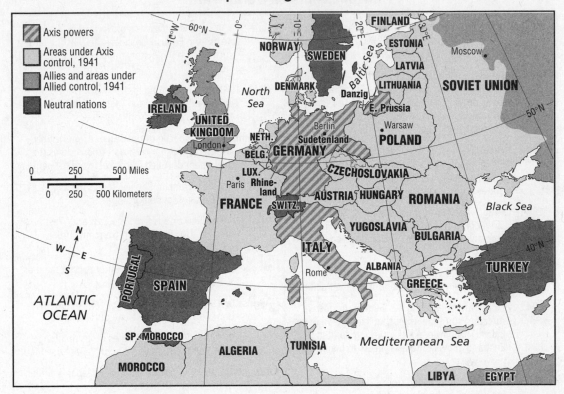

Axis powers

Areas under Axis control, 1941

Allies and areas under Allied control, 1941

Neutral nations

Leaders During World War II

Allies	
• Great Britain	Winston Churchill, Prime Minister
• USSR	Joseph Stalin, Communist dictator
• United States	Franklin D. Roosevelt, President until his death in April 1945
	Harry S Truman, President following Roosevelt's death
	Dwight D. Eisenhower, Supreme Commander of Allied troops in Europe
	Douglas MacArthur, Commander of the Allied troops in the Pacific
• France	Charles de Gaulle, leader of the Free French during the Nazi occupation

Axis Powers	
• Germany	Adolf Hitler, leader of the National Socialist German Workers' Party (Nazis), known as "Der Führer" ("The Leader")
• Italy	Benito Mussolini, Fascist dictator known as "Il Duce" ("The Leader")
• Japan	Emperor Hirohito
	Tojo Hideki, General and Prime Minister

Major Events of World War II

• 1939 Germany invades Poland with a rapid attack by armored vehicles supported by airplanes that is called **blitzkrieg**, or "lightning war."	**• June 6, 1944** Allied invasions of Normandy, France, across the English Channel. This was the largest such invasion in history, involving over 150,000 soldiers.
• 1940 Denmark, Norway, Belgium, the Netherlands, and much of northern France fall to Nazi invasion. Battle of Britain—months of terrifying air raids by Germany against Britain known as the **blitz**.	**• 1944–1945** Bitter fighting in the Pacific (for example at Leyte, Iwo Jima, and Okinawa) costs thousands of American lives.
• 1941 Germany invades the Soviet Union. The siege of Leningrad begins and lasts 17 months. Japan attacks Pearl Harbor, Hawaii. The United States enters the war.	**• December 1944** Battle of the Bulge. A surprisingly strong response by German troops slows the movement of Allied forces eastward to Germany.
	• April 12, 1945 Franklin Roosevelt dies unexpectedly from a cerebral hemorrhage.
• 1941–1942 Japan seizes the Philippines, Burma, Singapore, the Dutch East Indies, and French Indochina. Japan continues to press southward toward Australia.	**• April 1945** Allied troops from the East and West meet at the Elbe River in Germany. Hitler commits suicide.
• 1942 Battle of Midway in the Pacific. The United States regains naval superiority in the Pacific.	**• May 8, 1945** The end of war in Europe, celebrated as V-E Day (Victory in Europe).
• 1942–1943 Battle of Stalingrad. German troops are forced to surrender after thousands have been killed. This battle marks a turning point in the East and allows Russian soldiers to begin to move west.	**• August 6, 1945** The United States drops an atomic bomb on the Japanese city of Hiroshima.
	• August 9, 1945 The United States drops an atomic bomb on the Japanese city of Nagasaki.
• 1943 In North Africa, Allied troops defeat Axis armies for control of the Mediterranean Sea and the Suez Canal.	**• August 14, 1945** Hirohito announces Japan's defeat to the Japanese people.
	• September 2, 1945 Japan formally surrenders.

ANALYZING DOCUMENTS

Examine the chart above. Then answer the following questions.

- What was the significance of the Battle of Midway?

- Which ended first, the war in Europe or the war in the Pacific?

Wartime Diplomacy

During the war, leaders of the Allied nations met in a series of conferences to discuss wartime strategies and plans for the postwar world. Key meetings are described below.

ATLANTIC CHARTER MEETING, 1941   Roosevelt and Churchill met on battleships in the North Atlantic to agree on certain principles for building a lasting peace and establishing free governments in the world. The document containing these agreements was called the Atlantic Charter.

CASABLANCA, 1943   Roosevelt met with Churchill to plan "victory on all fronts." They used the term "unconditional surrender" to describe the anticipated victory.

CAIRO, 1943   Roosevelt, Churchill, and Chiang Kai-shek of China planned the Normandy invasion.

World War II in the Pacific

TEHRAN CONFERENCE, 1943 Roosevelt and Churchill met with Stalin to discuss war strategy and plans for the postwar world.

YALTA, 1945 Roosevelt, Churchill, and Stalin outlined the division of postwar Germany into spheres of influence and planned for the trials of war criminals. The Soviet Union promised to enter the war against Japan.

POTSDAM, 1945 Allied leaders (with Truman now replacing Roosevelt) warned Japan to surrender to prevent utter destruction.

The Atomic Bomb

In an effort to bring the war to a speedy conclusion and to prevent further destruction and loss of life, Allied leaders decided to embark on an atomic research project.

THE MANHATTAN PROJECT In the spring of 1943, a group of scientists from the United States, Canada, Britain, and other European

READING STRATEGY

Analyzing Cause and Effect
At Yalta, Roosevelt, Churchill, and Stalin agreed to split Germany into four zones, each under the control of one of the major Allies. Stalin promised to allow elections in the nations his army liberated from the Germans in Eastern Europe. Stalin did not fulfill this promise.

- How did the agreements at Yalta set the stage for the problems that later arose during the Cold War?

countries began work on the top-secret atomic research program known as the **Manhattan Project.** The research was done primarily at Los Alamos, New Mexico, under the direction of Dr. Robert Oppenheimer. Many of the scientists involved in the projects were refugees from Hitler's Germany. By July 1945, the first atomic bomb was tested in New Mexico. The success of this project left the United States in the position of determining the ultimate use of the new weapon.

THE BOMBINGS OF HIROSHIMA AND NAGASAKI Within days after the first atomic test, Allied leaders warned Japan to surrender or face "prompt and utter destruction." Since no surrender occurred, President Truman made the decision to drop atomic bombs on the Japanese cities of Hiroshima and Nagasaki. The bombs killed more than 100,000 Japanese instantly, and thousands more died later from radiation sickness. For a time after World War II, the United States held a monopoly on atomic weapons. The world had entered the atomic age.

JAPAN SURRENDERS Within days of the devastating bombings of Hiroshima and Nagasaki, Japan formally surrendered, and World War II came to an end. Following Japan's surrender, the United States occupied Japan under the leadership of General Douglas MacArthur. A new constitutional monarchy went into effect introducing democratic reforms to Japan. Emperor Hirohito retained his throne, but only as a figurehead.

TURNING POINT

Several alternatives were considered before dropping the atomic bombs on Hiroshima and Nagasaki, Japan. The final decision rested with President Truman who made the decision to use the bombs to end the war as quickly as possible and thereby save American lives.

- Why might the dropping of the atomic bombs be considered a turning point in American history?

ANALYZING DOCUMENTS

Study the chart at right then answer the following question.

- Which country had the greatest number of military casualties during World War II?

Casualties in World War II

	Military Dead	Military Wounded	Civilian Dead
Britain	373,000	475,000	93,000
France	213,000	400,000	108,000
Soviet Union	11,000,000	14,102,000	7,000,000
United States	292,000	671,000	*
Germany	3,500,000	5,000,000	780,000
Italy	242,000	66,000	153,000
Japan	1,300,000	4,000,000	672,000

All figures are estimates
* Very small number of civilian dead

THE HOLOCAUST

When Adolf Hitler rose to power in Germany, he did so by finding a scapegoat, someone to blame for Germany's problems after World War I. By appealing to anti-Semitism, feelings of hatred against Jewish people, Hitler encouraged the Germans to turn viciously on all Jewish citizens.

The "Final Solution"

Early in his rise to power, Hitler had seized Jewish property, homes, and businesses and barred Jews from many jobs. At the Wannsee Conference of 1942, the Nazis set as a primary goal the total extermination, or genocide, of all Jews under their domination. This effort was to be kept secret from the German people and from the rest of the world. Hitler's plan to eliminate the Jews was known to the Nazis as the **Final Solution.**

The Horror of Concentration Camps

In the 1930s, the Nazis began to build concentration camps to isolate Jews and other groups from society and provide slave labor for industry. As Hitler's conquest of Europe continued, the camps became factories of death. More than six million Jews were killed in the camps as were another four million people—dissenters, Gypsies, homosexuals, the mentally and physically handicapped, Protestant ministers, and Catholic priests. Today, concentration camp names such as Auschwitz, Treblinka, and Dachau stand as memorials to the incredible human suffering and death of this time, a period now called the **Holocaust.**

The United States and other nations failed to take strong action to rescue Jews from Nazi Germany before World War II. In 1939, the *St. Louis,* a passenger ship carrying more than 900 Jewish refugees, left Europe for Cuba, but when they arrived, most of the refugees were denied permission to land there. The refugees were also denied permission to enter the United States, and the ship was forced to return to Europe. Most of the ship's passengers eventually were killed in the Holocaust.

After war broke out, the Allies still failed to speak out forcefully against the treatment of Jews or to make direct attempts to stop the genocide. Only toward the end of the war did the United States create the War Refuge Board to provide aid for Holocaust survivors.

War Crimes Trials

A final chapter to the Holocaust occurred in Nuremberg, Germany, in 1945 and 1946. At that time an international military court tried 24 high-level Nazis for atrocities committed during World War II. By finding former Nazis guilty of "crimes against humanity," a precedent was established that soldiers, officers, and national leaders could be held responsible for such brutal actions. Escaped Nazis who were found after the end of the war—even decades later—were also brought to trial for war-related crimes.

KEY THEMES AND CONCEPTS

Individuals, Groups, Institutions

During the Holocaust, individuals were singled out for persecution because of their membership in a group. Institutions were developed and individuals were put in place within those institutions to carry out the atrocities of the Holocaust. Genocide is the deliberate murder of an entire people.

List two other examples of genocide in the twentieth century.

1.

2.

READING STRATEGY

What important legal precedent was set at the Nuremberg trials?

Among the most infamous Nazis who were tried and convicted was Adolf Eichmann. He was captured in Argentina in 1960 and tried in Israel for the torture and deaths of millions of Jews. Eichmann was convicted of crimes against humanity and was hanged in 1962. Klaus Barbie, known as the "Butcher of Lyon" (France), was also apprehended and tried in 1987 for his wartime brutality to Jews.

War crime trials also occurred in Japan. These trials led to the execution of former premier Tojo and six other war leaders. About 4,000 other Japanese war criminals were also convicted and received less severe sentences.

AMERICAN PATRIOTISM DURING WORLD WAR II

After the United States entered the war, the nation moved to full-scale wartime production and mobilization of the armed forces. Americans rallied behind the war effort.

With the exception of the attack on Pearl Harbor and battles on several Pacific islands, World War II was not fought on American soil. Nonetheless, Americans were constantly preparing for attack. America's coastal areas and large cities held blackout drills. Americans were encouraged to support the war effort by rationing food, gasoline, and other necessities and luxuries. Government campaigns encouraged Americans to have "meatless Tuesdays," and many Americans planted "victory gardens" of their own to increase the food supply. Hollywood entertainers made special presentations to encourage citizens to buy war bonds to help the government finance the war.

The Role of American Women

World War II brought dramatic changes to the lives of American women in the military and in the civilian workforce.

IN THE MILITARY By the end of the war, more than 200,000 women had joined the military services. Although women served in separate units from men, such as the Women's Army Corps (WAC), women performed a variety of vital military duties. They operated radios and repaired planes and vehicles. They also were assigned, along with men, to clerical duties.

IN THE CIVILIAN WORKFORCE As millions of men joined the military, new employment opportunities opened up to women. Women who had been employed before the war eagerly applied for better-paying jobs, and many women who had worked inside the home now entered the paid workforce. Many women took jobs that had once been open to men only. More than five million women eventually worked in factories devoted to wartime production, although their pay never came close to equaling men's pay of the time. One song about a woman named **Rosie the Riveter** became popular during the war years because it captured the sense of duty and patriotism felt by millions of women. The term "Rosie the Riveter" became a slang term for all women who worked in wartime factories.

RESULTING CHANGE Women's wartime work resulted in important changes in employment and lifestyle, even after the war. Before the war, most employed American women were young and unmarried. During the war, large numbers of married women and mothers who had never worked outside the home before took jobs. This trend continued after the war. Although many women willingly returned to their homes and the roles of wife and mother at the end of the war, thousands more enjoyed the challenge of paid employment, as well as an improved standard of living.

The entry of so many women into the paid workforce during World War II marked the beginning of a long-term trend, as women continued to enter the workforce in greater numbers throughout the rest of the century. New issues became important. For example, child care became an important issue during the war years, and it remains an important one today.

African Americans

The experiences of African Americans during the war years provided the foundation of the civil rights movement of the 1950s and 1960s.

IN THE MILITARY Nearly one million African American men and women served in the military during World War II. Military units were segregated, and initially, African American soldiers were limited to support roles. As the war went on, these soldiers soon saw combat, where many distinguished themselves.

AT HOME In the 1940s, many southern African Americans began moving to northern cities in search of economic opportunity and freedom from discrimination. However, they met discrimination in the North as well, as white workers and homeowners feared the movement of African Americans into their workplaces and neighborhoods. Race riots broke out in Detroit and New York City in the summer of 1943. Membership in civil rights organizations began to grow as African Americans struggled against discrimination.

African Americans experienced gains during the war years. Politically, their migration north had made them a significant voting bloc in urban areas. Economically, new jobs in war industries brought many African Americans the chance to earn more than they ever had before. Although these gains were made, African Americans were still experiencing widespread discrimination and inequalities in salaries in the workplace. The black press urged that the struggle for freedom be fought on two fronts—overseas and at home as well.

 PREPARING FOR THE EXAM

What trend emerged following World War II in regard to women's participation in the labor force?

READING STRATEGY

Predicting Content
How might the experiences of African Americans during World War II have contributed to the rise of the civil rights movement during the 1950s?

Japanese Americans

Thousands of Japanese Americans faced hardship and economic losses after the attack on Pearl Harbor.

IMMIGRATION TO AMERICA Immigrants from Japan began arriving in the United States shortly after the Civil War. These immigrants settled mainly on the west coast of the United States. By 1941, thousands of Americans of Japanese descent, called **Nisei,** had been born in the United States and were American citizens. Thousands of them had never been to Japan, and many had no desire to go there.

WARTIME RELOCATION AUTHORITY (WRA) After the Japanese attack on Pearl Harbor, many Americans feared that Japanese Americans presented a threat to national security. Anti-Japanese sentiment grew, and in 1942 President Roosevelt issued Executive Order 9066, establishing military zones for the imprisonment of Japanese Americans. More than 100,000 people of Japanese descent were forced to leave their homes and move to **WRA camps,** hastily constructed military-style barracks ringed with barbed wire and guarded by troops. This discrimination was focused entirely on Japanese Americans; no such action was taken against citizens or residents of German or Italian descent.

KOREMATSU V. UNITED STATES In the 1944 landmark case *Korematsu* v. *United States,* the Supreme Court upheld the forced evacuation as a reasonable wartime emergency measure. However, no acts of Japanese-American sabotage or treason were ever identified, and thousands of Nisei fought honorably in the war. Almost 50 years after World War II, the United States government admitted that the wartime relocation program had been unjust. In 1988, Congress voted to pay $20,000 to each of the approximately 60,000 surviving Americans who had been interned. The first payments were made in 1990, and the government also issued a formal apology.

NISEI SOLDIERS Despite the injustices endured by Japanese Americans, thousands proved their loyalty by serving in the U.S. armed forces, primarily in Europe. The 442nd Regimental Combat Team, made up entirely of Japanese Americans, won more medals for bravery than any other unit of its size in the war.

 PREPARING FOR THE EXAM

"It is a fact that the Japanese navy has been reconnoitering [investigating] the Pacific Coast.... It is [a] fact that communication takes place between the enemy at sea and enemy agents on land."

• Would the writer of this excerpt have supported the Supreme Court's decision in *Korematsu* v. *United States?*

DEMOBILIZATION

During the war, American factories, geared up for wartime production, had helped the nation recover from the Great Depression. Now the challenge was to convert from a wartime to a peacetime society. The United States underwent a period of demobilization, or the movement from a military to a civilian status. The United States armed forces reduced from 12 million members to 1.5 million. Factories that had made planes and tanks now began producing consumer goods. It also meant ensuring that the nation would not slip back into depression.

During President Truman's administration, legislation was passed to deal with different issues raised by demobilization.

SERVICEMEN'S READJUSTMENT ACT Also known as the GI Bill of Rights, this act authorized billions of dollars to pay for veterans' benefits, such as college education, medical treatment, unemployment insurance, and home and business loans. The GI Bill made it possible for more people to attend college and buy homes than ever before.

EMPLOYMENT ACT OF 1946 This act made full employment a national goal and set up a Council of Economic Advisors to guide the President on economic matters.

AN END TO PRICE CONTROLS Wartime legislation had put controls on the prices of most goods. In 1946, the government moved to end most such controls. However, the end of controls coupled with a tax cut caused a rapid increase in inflation. For example, food prices soared 25 percent in just two years.

THE TAFT-HARTLEY ACT Workers' wages could not keep up with inflation after the war. Major strikes were held as unions pushed for higher wages. Anti-union feelings grew and led Congress to pass the Taft-Hartley Act over Truman's veto. The act
- Provided an 80-day "cooling-off" period through which the President could delay a strike that threatened national welfare
- Barred the closed shop, under which workers had to belong to a union before being hired
- Allowed states to pass "right-to-work laws," which said workers could take jobs and not have to join a union
- Banned union contributions to political campaigns
- Required union leaders to swear they were not communists

National Security Concerns

Truman also moved to help the nation meet postwar international concerns. The National Security Act of 1947 created the National Military Establishment, which later became the Department of Defense. The act also created the Central Intelligence Agency to oversee intelligence gathering activities. As commander in chief, Truman also issued an executive order banning discrimination in the armed forces.

The Baby Boom

In addition to problems caused by converting to a peacetime economy, the nation also had to cope with the largest population explosion in its history. The economic hardships of the Great Depression that had encouraged smaller families were gone. Families grew larger once more. This "baby boom" brought with it the expansion of many public services, especially schools. You will learn more about the long-term effects of the baby boom in the next unit.

PREPARING FOR THE EXAM

Truman's legislative program aimed at promoting full employment, a higher minimum wage, greater unemployment compensation for workers without jobs, housing assistance, and other items was known as the Fair Deal, a play of words on Franklin Roosevelt's New Deal.

PREPARING FOR THE EXAM

The Taft-Hartley Act of 1947 was a setback for organized labor. It gave the President the power to delay (through court injunction) any strike that took place within an industry that the President deemed important to the nation's health or safety.

⚲ **KEY THEMES AND**
CONCEPTS

Change
How did the prosperity of the 1940s and 1950s influence the nation's population growth rate?

The Election of 1948

Many voters had become dissatisfied with Truman's presidency because of inflation, strikes, Truman's actions on civil rights, and the developing cold war. Polls predicted that the Republican candidate, Governor Thomas Dewey of New York, would defeat Truman easily in the 1948 presidential election. Yet Truman pulled off one of the greatest upsets in American political history by winning reelection. He then attempted to build on this victory by proposing a program called the Fair Deal that aimed to extend reforms started under FDR's New Deal.

2 Peace with Problems, 1945–1960

SECTION OVERVIEW

The end of World War II brought the desire to prevent such devastation from ever happening again. The United Nations was established to help nations find peaceful solutions to conflicts. Meanwhile, the uneasy wartime alliance between the United States and the Soviet Union dissolved as the Cold War took hold. As communism spread through the efforts of the Soviet Union and later China, the United States worked to strengthen its influence in Western Europe and Asia by providing economic aid and building strategic alliances. A growing anxiety about the spread of communism led the United States to become more deeply involved in global affairs, while also fearing a communist influence at home.

KEY THEMES AND CONCEPTS

As you review this section, take special note of the following key themes and concepts:

Change Why did the United States and the Soviet Union change from being allies in World War II to enemies during the Cold War?

Foreign Policy How did the United States use economic aid to build its influence in Europe and Asia?

Constitutional Principles How did the fear of communism lead to the violations of some people's civil rights in the United States?

KEY PEOPLE

Eleanor Roosevelt
George C. Marshall
Mao Zedong
Chiang Kai-shek

Douglas MacArthur
Alger Hiss
Joseph McCarthy
Ethel and Julius Rosenberg

⭐ THE BIG IDEA
The post-World War II hostilities between the United States and the Soviet Union are together known as the Cold War.

The Cold War

- lasted from about 1946 to 1991.

- was brought about by competition between the United States and the Soviet Union for power and influence in the world.

- consisted of political and economic conflict and military tensions throughout the globe.

🔑 KEY TERMS
containment
"iron curtain"
Truman Doctrine
Marshall Plan
Cold War
NATO
Warsaw Pact
38th parallel
HUAC

The United States emerged from World War II as the world's greatest military power. Compared to other nations, it had suffered relatively little physical destruction. For a short time, the United States held a monopoly on the ability to use nuclear power. After World War II, the United States was aware of its strength as a nation and its responsibility to preserve world peace.

READING STRATEGY

Organizing Information
Who are the five permanent members of the United Nations Security Council?

1.

2.

3.

4.

5.

THE UNITED NATIONS

American foreign policy changed dramatically as a result of World War II. Even before the conclusion of the war, the United States began planning for an international peacekeeping organization. Plans were made at the Yalta Conference for a United Nations Conference to be held in San Francisco in April 1945. The Soviet Union, under the leadership of Joseph Stalin, agreed to participate in planning the new organization which would be known as the United Nations. The United States Senate approved the United Nations Charter by a vote of 82 to 2.

Organization of the United Nations

The structure of the United Nations (UN) includes a General Assembly of all its members and a Security Council of 15 members. The Security Council consists of 10 rotating member nations and five permanent members. (The original permanent members were the United States, Great Britain, the Soviet Union, China, and France. After the breakup of the Soviet Union, the Russian Federation became a permanent member.)

The General Assembly serves as a forum for world leaders to speak on a variety of concerns. Although the UN has become militarily involved in a number of world crises, most of its members would agree that its greatest accomplishments have been in fighting hunger and disease and in promoting education. The headquarters of the United Nations is in New York City.

ANALYZING DOCUMENTS

Review the timeline below then answer the following questions.

• How long did the Korean War last?

• In what year was NATO formed?

The United States and the World, 1945–1954

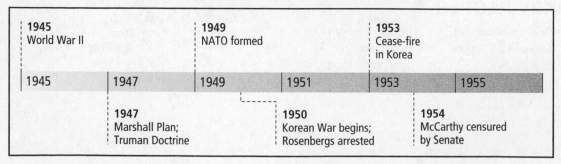

1945 World War II		1949 NATO formed		1953 Cease-fire in Korea	
1945	1947	1949	1951	1953	1955
	1947 Marshall Plan; Truman Doctrine		1950 Korean War begins; Rosenbergs arrested		1954 McCarthy censured by Senate

The United Nations

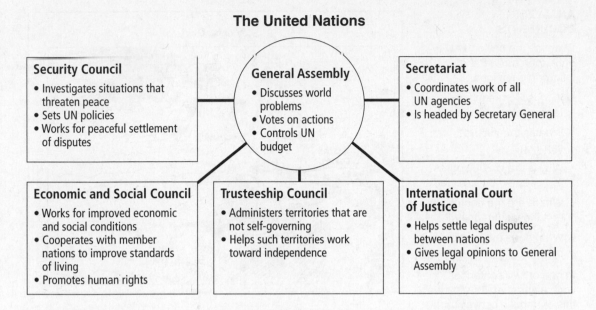

Security Council
- Investigates situations that threaten peace
- Sets UN policies
- Works for peaceful settlement of disputes

General Assembly
- Discusses world problems
- Votes on actions
- Controls UN budget

Secretariat
- Coordinates work of all UN agencies
- Is headed by Secretary General

Economic and Social Council
- Works for improved economic and social conditions
- Cooperates with member nations to improve standards of living
- Promotes human rights

Trusteeship Council
- Administers territories that are not self-governing
- Helps such territories work toward independence

International Court of Justice
- Helps settle legal disputes between nations
- Gives legal opinions to General Assembly

UNIVERSAL DECLARATION OF HUMAN RIGHTS In 1946, President Truman appointed former first lady Eleanor Roosevelt as a United Nations delegate, the only woman in the American delegation. The committee that Eleanor Roosevelt led authored the Universal Declaration of Human Rights, a proclamation that is still part of the guiding philosophy of the UN today. In the postwar years, people all over the world were especially eager to have an international organization succeed at defining human rights for all people.

ANALYZING DOCUMENTS

Study the chart above then answer the following questions.

- Which branch of the United Nations would help two countries resolve a legal dispute?

- Which branch sets UN policies?

CONTAINMENT AS A FOREIGN POLICY

American foreign policy after World War II was influenced by two factors: the willingness of the United States to become involved in international peacekeeping efforts and its determination to prevent the spread of communism.

Growing Distrust of the Soviet Union

In 1939, Germany and the Soviet Union had signed a nonaggression treaty, but after Germany violated the pact, the Soviet Union sought a new alliance to protect itself from Germany. The United States then allied with the Soviet Union throughout World War II. Although they were allies, American and Soviet leaders did not fully trust one another. After the war, it became apparent that the only common goal shared by the United States and the Soviet Union was the defeat of the Axis powers.

After World War II, the Soviet Union was viewed as a grave threat to the security of the noncommunist world. In defeating Nazi

Step on it, Doc!

Roy Justus, *The Minneapolis Star*, 1947.

Germany, the Soviets had moved troops into the nations of Eastern Europe. After the war, the Soviet Union actively supported communist governments in those nations.

The United States, which had emerged as a superpower nation, took on the task of limiting communist expansion—a policy known as **containment**. The goal of containment was to confine communism to the area in which it already existed—the Soviet Union and the Eastern European nations. American presidential power increased during this time period as the United States sought to carry out this policy.

Following are key foreign policy developments related to the containment of communism immediately after World War II.

Churchill's "Iron Curtain" Speech

In his 1946 speech at Westminster College in Fulton, Missouri, Prime Minister Winston Churchill of Great Britain cautioned the world about the threat of communist expansion. He warned that "from Stettin in the Baltic to Trieste in the Adriatic, an iron curtain has descended across the Continent." Churchill's phrase **"iron curtain"** drew a clear picture of the postwar world. There had come to be recognizable division between the free Western Europe and the communist Eastern Europe.

The Truman Doctrine

Before World War II, Britain had been a powerful force in the Mediterranean. The tremendous losses and expense of World War II, however, weakened Britain's influence there. The Soviet Union, which had long been striving for access to the Mediterranean Sea by way of the Turkish straits, sought to extend its influence in the area.

The Soviets supported communist rebels in their attempt to topple the government of Greece. This led the United States to try to contain the spread of communism in the Mediterranean region. On March 12, 1947, President Truman asked Congress for $400 million in aid to Turkey and Greece. He called on the United States to support free people in resisting control by armed minorities or outside pressures. Truman believed that the failure of the United States to act at this time would endanger both the nation and the free world.

Congress approved Truman's request. By 1950, more than $660 million had been spent in aid to Turkey and Greece. This policy of economic and military aid became known as the **Truman Doctrine.** It represents a major step in the evolution of American foreign policy further away from isolationism and neutrality.

The Marshall Plan

World War II left much of Europe in ruins. Major cities and industrial centers were destroyed. Survivors of the war struggled to find food, shelter, and clothing. Dissatisfaction with such conditions grew rapidly. In many war-torn countries, the Communist party seemed to offer solutions to such problems.

To prevent the spread of communist influence in Europe, General George C. Marshall, secretary of state under President Truman, announced a new economic-aid program called the **Marshall Plan.** In a speech delivered on June 5, 1947, Marshall announced that the United States was against "hunger, poverty, desperation, and chaos." Between 1948 and 1952, about $13 billion in economic aid was allocated by the Republican-dominated Congress for the rebuilding of Europe under the Marshall Plan. The largest amount went to Britain, France, Italy, and West Germany.

This aid enabled Western Europe to begin consumer production once more and to build prosperous economies. Both Western Europe and the United States felt that with stabilized and improving economies, communist expansion would be halted.

The Beginning of the Cold War: Germany 1948–1949

At the end of World War II, Germany was divided into four zones of occupation controlled by Great Britain, France, the Soviet Union, and the United States. Berlin, the capital of Germany, was located in the Russian sector. However, the city was divided into four sections, each controlled by one of the four Allies. Disagreements during this period of occupation marked the beginning of the **Cold War,** a period of tension between the United States and the Soviet Union from the end of World War II to 1990.

THE BERLIN BLOCKADE The United States, France, and Great Britain cooperated in governing the western sectors of Germany.

ANALYZING DOCUMENTS

"In these circumstances, it is clear that the main element of any United States policy toward the Soviet Union must be that of a long-term, patient but firm and vigilant containment of Russian expansive tendencies."
—American diplomat George Kennan, July 1947

- In what ways were the Truman Doctrine and the Marshall Plan examples of "long-term, patient but firm and vigilant" containment of communism?

READING STRATEGY

Reading for Evidence
How were the Truman Doctrine and the Marshall Plan related?

READING STRATEGY

Organizing Information
Who controlled the four zones of occupation in Germany following World War II?

1.

2.

3.

4.

• In which zone was the capital Berlin located?

• Which zones were combined to form West Germany?

• How did the Soviets attempt to take control of Berlin?

♀ **KEY THEMES AND CONCEPTS**

Foreign Policy
NATO represented the principle of mutual military assistance or collective security. By joining NATO the United States dropped its opposition to military treaties with Europe for the first time since the Monroe Doctrine. As a member of NATO the United States became actively involved in European affairs.

Unable to reach agreement with the Soviet Union over the eventual unification of Germany, the three western powers decided to unify their zones without the Soviet zone. In 1949, the Federal Republic of Germany, commonly known as West Germany was established. The Soviets opposed the establishment of this separate government. On June 24, 1948, the Soviets cut off all access to West Berlin by blockading the roads leading to the city, all of which had to go through the Soviet-controlled sector of Germany. The Soviets hoped that the blockade would force the western powers out of Berlin.

THE BERLIN AIRLIFT The United States, Great Britain, and France would not back down. Recognizing that West Berlin could not get supplies by road anymore, the western powers began an airlift of food, clothing, coal, medicine, and other necessities to the city. Almost a year later, on May 12, 1949, the Soviets recognized their defeat in the area and ended the blockade. Shortly afterward, the Soviets announced the formation of the German Democratic Republic, commonly known as East Germany. In 1955, West Germany was given full sovereignty. The West had learned once again that although World War II was over, its struggle against aggressor nations was not.

Point Four Program

The United States recognized that the Soviet Union's expansionist aims were targeted not only at Europe but at developing nations of the world as well. In 1950, Congress approved President Truman's Point Four Program, which provided nearly $400 million for technical development programs in Latin America, Asia, and Africa. The Point Four Program was designed to modernize and strengthen the economies of developing nations and thereby discourage the growth of communism.

The North Atlantic Treaty Organization

The United States and other Western European nations also fought the spread of communism by forming alliances. In April 1949, the United States and 11 other western nations signed a collective security agreement called the North Atlantic Treaty. This agreement bound the participating nations to act together for their common defense. Members pledged that an attack on any one of them would be considered an attack on all of them. Defense arrangements were coordinated through the North Atlantic Treaty Organization (**NATO**). The Soviets later formed an opposing alliance with seven Eastern European nations under the **Warsaw Pact.**

In 1949, President Truman announced that the Soviet Union had successfully exploded an atomic bomb. Fearing the power that this gave the Soviets, the United States worked to strengthen its influence in the world by committing several billion dollars in assistance to countries in Western Europe and elsewhere.

The Cold War in Europe

The Cold War in Europe

Legend:
- "Iron curtain"
- Communist nations
- Capitalist nations
- ⊛ Capital cities

European Cooperation

In order to rebuild and strengthen their economies after the war, Western European nations made ever-increasing efforts at economic cooperation. In 1951, the European Coal and Steel Community formed to enable six European nations to set prices and regulate the coal and steel industries. By 1957, the scope of economic cooperation had broadened to include efforts to improve transportation and eliminate tariff barriers within Europe. Those same six nations signed a treaty in 1957 to form the European Economic Community (EEC), also known as the Common Market. As economic cooperation continued to broaden, this organization later transformed into the European Union (EU) that exists today.

The European Union has experienced many changes in recent years. The European Parliament, the legislative branch of the EU, now has the power to approve or reject the EU's budget. In 1999, eleven member states began using a common currency called the euro. The EU continues to grapple with such key issues as increasing employment opportunities for citizens in all member nations. The EU today has 15 member states and is preparing for the admission of new members from eastern and southern Europe.

ANALYZING DOCUMENTS

After losing more than 20 million people during the war and suffering wide-spread destruction, the Soviet Union was determined to rebuild in ways that would protect its own interests. One way was to establish satellite nations, countries subject to Soviet domination, on the western borders of the Soviet Union.

- How does this map illustrate the Soviet Union's desire to protect itself from non-communist rivals?

CONTAINMENT IN ASIA

During World War II, the United States had been an ally of China and an enemy of Japan. After World War II, the United States reversed its political alliances in Asia. With its new constitutional democracy, Japan became an American ally. Meanwhile a communist takeover in China made the United States increasingly suspicious of and hostile to that nation.

READING STRATEGY

Analyzing Cause and Effect
How might the victory of the Communists in the Chinese civil war in 1949 have contributed to United States involvement in the Korean War in 1950?

Communist Victory in China

In the 1930s, China had plunged into civil war. Mao Zedong, leader of the communist forces in China, sought to defeat the nationalist regime of Chiang Kai-shek. In 1949, the communist forces defeated the nationalists and renamed the now communist-led country the People's Republic of China. Chiang Kai-shek and the nationalists fled to the island of Taiwan.

The United States was alarmed by this development, because it feared that communism would spread beyond China. Because the United States had overseen the initial rebuilding of postwar Japan and had helped put a new constitutional democracy in place, it did not want to see communism spread to Japan. Support for Japan was now seen as a way of offsetting communist China's influence in Asia.

READING STRATEGY

Organizing Information
- Who fought on the side of communist North Korea during the Korean War?
- Who fought on the side of anticommunist South Korea during the Korean War?

The Korean War

During World War II, Korea had been occupied by Japan. At the end of the war, Korea was divided along the **38th parallel,** or line of latitude. The northern zone was under the influence of the Soviet Union, and the southern zone was controlled by the United States. By 1948, the southern zone had elected an anticommunist government headed by Syngman Rhee and was now called the Republic of Korea. In the northern zone, now named the Democratic People's Republic of Korea, a communist government ruled.

FIGHTING BEGINS North Korea invaded South Korea in 1950 in an attempt to unify the country. President Truman responded to this invasion by committing American troops to major involvement in the Korean conflict.

MacARTHUR IN COMMAND General Douglas MacArthur, a World War II hero, was sent to command the United States military in Korea. Troops from the United States, along with small numbers of soldiers from other UN member nations, were soon involved in battles as fierce as those of World War II. A particularly devastating loss came at the Yalu River, when Chinese forces entered the conflict and pushed UN troops south. By the middle of 1951, the war had reached a stalemate. Fighting continued, but neither side was able to advance successfully.

Disagreement over the objectives and military strategies of the Korean War caused a major conflict between President Truman and

General MacArthur. Although Truman was a civilian, the Constitution makes the President the commander in chief of the armed forces. When General MacArthur disagreed with Truman publicly about the conduct of the war, the President recalled him to the United States and dismissed him from command.

HOSTILITIES END Although truce talks began in June 1951, no resolution was reached before the American presidential election of 1952. During that campaign the Republican candidate, World War II hero Dwight D. Eisenhower, promised that if he were elected President he would go to Korea to aid in the peace negotiations. Eisenhower won the election and did keep his campaign promise, but a truce or cease-fire was not officially signed until July 27, 1953.

The war in Korea lasted for more than three years and cost more than $15 billion. Approximately 34,000 Americans and one million Koreans and Chinese died in the conflict.

NEW DIRECTIONS The policy of containment took a different course with American involvement in the Korean conflict. Early containment efforts focused primarily on economic aid programs. With the Korean War, the United States now showed its willingness to undertake military action to contain communism if it was necessary. American experiences in Korea were a warning of future global confrontations between democratic and communist opponents.

THE COLD WAR AT HOME

Even as the United States defended democratic freedoms worldwide, sometimes those same freedoms were in danger at home. The spreading of communism to China and the apparent growing strength of the Soviet Union led some Americans to fear that communism could spread to the United States. This fear led some Americans to take actions that violated the civil rights of others.

Many Americans charged that communist agents were trying to subvert, or destroy, the American political system. Other Americans responded that the actions of anticommunists were more subversive of American values and more dangerous to the nation.

Looking for Communists

The fear of communism in the United States had its roots in the period before World War II. Anticommunist activity began in the 1930s.

HUAC In 1938, the House Un-American Activities Committee (**HUAC**) was formed as a temporary investigative unit to look into communist activity in the United States. HUAC operated for more than 30 years. Its well-publicized probe of the movie industry in the 1940s and 1950s led to the blacklisting, or cutting off from employment, of many actors, writers, and directors.

⚲ **KEY THEMES AND CONCEPTS**
Civic Values
The Korean War caused enormous frustration at home. When the truce was signed in 1953, Korea remained divided at almost exactly the same place as before the war, near the 38th parallel. Americans wondered why more than 54,000 of their soldiers had been killed and 113,000 wounded for such limited results. Some Americans wondered if their government was serious about stopping communism.

⚲ **KEY THEMES AND CONCEPTS**
Foreign Policy
In what way did the Korean War mark a change in the United States' policy of containment?

READING STRATEGY

Reinforcing Main Ideas

Americans' fears of communism resulted from the fact that Communists were openly hostile to American beliefs and values such as capitalism, private ownership of land and business, and First Amendment freedoms.

- What other foreign and domestic events contributed to Americans' fears of the spread of communism?

J. Edgar Hoover, director of the Federal Bureau of Investigation, often aided HUAC investigations. Critics argued that Hoover conducted anticommunist activities that often violated the civil rights of Americans.

THE SMITH ACT In 1940, Congress passed the Smith Act, which made it illegal for anyone to advocate "overthrowing . . . any government in the United States by force" or to "affiliate" with groups that called for such action.

In the 1951 landmark case of *Dennis* v. *United States,* the Supreme Court upheld the Smith Act. Eugene Dennis, general secretary of the Communist Party in the United States, and 10 others were convicted of advocating the violent overthrow of the government.

Two court decisions in 1957 weakened the intent of the Smith Act. In *Watkins* v. *United States,* the court ruled the HUAC could not punish witnesses who refused to cooperate with its investigations. In *Yates* v. *United States,* the court ruled that the Smith Act applied only to those who teach or advocate direct "action" to overthrow government, not to those who merely advocate it in principle.

THE LOYALTY PROGRAM In 1947, President Truman fueled anticommunist feelings by ordering a Loyalty Review Board to conduct security checks on thousands of government employees. Those whose loyalty was considered doubtful were dismissed.

In the early 1950s, Robert Oppenheimer, who had led the research to develop the atomic bomb, voiced his opposition to building the new, more destructive hydrogen bomb. This action and his past association with others whose loyalty was being questioned led to a government hearing about his own loyalty. He was determined to be a "loyal citizen," but his security clearance was removed, and he was barred from future government research.

PREPARING FOR THE EXAM

What was the outcome of the Alger Hiss case and what was its significance?

THE HISS CASE The Alger Hiss case led many Americans to believe that there was a reason to fear that there were communists in the government. In 1948, Alger Hiss, a former adviser to President Roosevelt, was charged with having been a Communist spy during the 1930s. Whittaker Chambers, a former Communist party member, made these charges, which Hiss denied. A congressional committee investigated them.

A young Republican committee member from California, Richard Nixon, believed that Hiss was guilty. Nixon's pursuit of the case and Hiss's eventual conviction on perjury charges made Nixon a national figure. The conviction also added weight to Republican charges that Roosevelt and Truman had not been alert enough to the dangers of communism.

McCarthyism

Against this political background, Senator Joseph McCarthy of Wisconsin began his own hunt for communists. In 1950, McCarthy charged he had a list of State Department employees known to be communists. Over the next four years, McCarthy went on to charge that many other people and government agencies had been corrupted by communism.

McCarthy made bold accusations without any evidence. This tactic became known as "McCarthyism." He ruined the reputations of many people he carelessly accused of being communists. Meanwhile, the Rosenberg case and congressional legislation helped win public support for McCarthy's actions.

THE ROSENBERG CASE In 1950, Ethel and Julius Rosenberg and Morton Sobell were charged with giving atomic secrets to the Soviets during World War II. After a highly controversial trial, they were convicted of espionage. The Rosenbergs were sentenced to death and Sobell to prison. The Rosenbergs were executed in 1953.

CONGRESSIONAL LEGISLATION In the same year the Rosenbergs were arrested, Congress passed the McCarran Internal Security Act. The law aimed at limiting the actions of anyone the government considered a threat to United States security. The McCarran-Walter Act of 1952 restricted the immigration of persons from communist-dominated nations in Asia and southern and central Europe. President Truman vetoed the bill, but Congress passed it over his veto.

McCARTHY'S FALL In 1954, McCarthy charged that even the army was full of communists. He held televised investigations into these charges. For the first time, millions of Americans saw McCarthy's bullying tactics for themselves. His public support quickly faded, and in December 1954 the Senate censured, or denounced, him for "conduct unbecoming a member." The fall of McCarthy ended the red scare of the 1950s, although anticommunist attitudes lingered as the Cold War continued to drag on.

KEY THEMES AND CONCEPTS
Constitutional Principles
Although many people knew that Senator McCarthy's claims were exaggerated at best, he was still able to gain power and ruin the lives of many people.

- How did McCarthy contribute to the suppression of free speech and open, honest debate?

PREPARING FOR THE EXAM
McCarthyism during the 1950s had many similarities to the Red Scare following World War I.

- How were the actions of Attorney General A. Mitchell Palmer and McCarthy similar?

Questions for Regents Practice

For online Questions for Regents Practice,
visit the Prentice Hall Web site at www.phschool.com.

MULTIPLE CHOICE

Directions

Review the Test-Taking Strategies section of this book. Then answer the following questions, drawn from actual Regents examinations. Each question is followed by four choices. Read each question carefully. Decide which choice is the correct answer. Then on a separate piece of paper, mark your answer for each question.

1   United States senators who opposed the Treaty of Versailles objected mainly to
    1   United States membership in the League of Nations
    2   payment of reparations by Germany to the Allied nations
    3   the transfer of Germany's colonial possessions to the League of Nations
    4   the creation of new and independent nations in Eastern Europe

2   A major reason for the United States neutrality in the 1930s was the nation's
    1   belief in the domino theory
    2   disillusionment resulting from World War I
    3   strong approval of political conditions in Europe
    4   military and naval superiority

3   At the outbreak of both World War I and World War II in Europe, public opinion in the United States generally favored
    1   remaining neutral
    2   entering the war on the side of the Allies
    3   invading Europe in order to acquire territory
    4   settling the conflict through an international peace organization

4   Isolationism as a foreign policy is more difficult to achieve in the 20th century than in prior times mainly because
    1   the increase in the world's population has forced people to live more closely together
    2   there are more sovereign nations today than in the past
    3   modern technology had made nations more interdependent
    4   public opinion on issues is more easily disregarded

5   The appeasement policy followed by Western European leaders in the late 1930s was based primarily on the belief that war could be avoided by
    1   satisfying Hitler's desire for territorial expansion
    2   encouraging communist expansion into Nazi Germany
    3   limiting the development of Germany's armed forces
    4   appealing to the League of Nations for international cooperation

6 Which event led directly to United States entry into World War II?
1 invasion of Poland by Germany and Russia
2 attack on France by Italy
3 sinking of the *Lusitania* by Germany
4 attack on Pearl Harbor by Japan

Base your answer to question 7 on the announcement below and on your knowledge of social studies.

WESTERN DEFENSE COMMAND AND FOURTH ARMY WARTIME CIVIL CONTROL ADMINISTRATION

Presidio of San Francisco, California
April 1, 1942

INSTRUCTIONS
TO ALL PERSONS OF

JAPANESE

ANCESTRY

Living in the Following Area:
All that portion of the City and County of San Francisco, State of California, lying generally west of the north-south line established by Junipero Serra Boulevard, Worcester Avenue, and Nineteenth Avenue and lying generally north of the east-west line established by California Street, to the intersection of Market Street, and thence on Market Street to San Francisco Bay.

All Japanese persons, both alien and non-alien, will be evacuated from the above designated area by 12:00 o'clock noon Tuesday, April 7, 1942.

---

7 During World War II, the action required by this announcement was based largely on
1 racial prejudice
2 a labor shortage
3 the needs for skilled workers in defense industries
4 a desire to protect Japanese Americans from military attack

8 The rulings of the Supreme Court in *Scott* v. *Sandford* (1857), *Plessy* v. *Ferguson* (1896), and *Korematsu* v. *United States* (1944) all demonstrate that the Supreme Court has
1 continued to extend voting rights to minorities
2 protected itself from internal dissent
3 sometimes failed to protect the rights of minorities
4 often imposed restrictions on free speech during wartime

9 An important effect of World War II on United States foreign policy was a
1 refusal to become involved in world affairs
2 smaller role for the President in foreign policy and national security issues
3 stronger commitment to collective security and world leadership
4 willingness to intervene only when the national economy is involved

10 After World War II, the United States was better able than its allies to adjust its economy from wartime to peacetime because the United States
1 possessed nuclear weapons
2 raised tariffs on imports
3 had collected its war debts from the Allies
4 had suffered no widespread wartime destruction

11 What was a major effect of World War II on women and minorities in the United States?
1 They were drafted into the military.
2 They had new opportunities in the workforce.
3 They received equal voting rights for the first time.
4 They were granted equal pay for equal work.

Base your answers to questions 12 and 13 on the speakers' conversation below and on your knowledge of social studies.

Speaker A: "We must provide arms to the legitimate governments of Greece and Turkey if they are to defeat Soviet-sponsored subversion."

Speaker B: "The first priority is to help rebuild the postwar economies of European countries so that democratic governments can survive."

Speaker C: "Our main goal is to create a system of collective security agreements to deal with any military threats."

Speaker D: "We must continue to build both our nuclear and our conventional arsenals if we are to have any hope of world peace."

12 The central concern of all the speakers is
  1 the containment of communism
  2 the defeat of the Axis Powers in World War II
  3 a ban on the proliferation of nuclear weapons
  4 the support of United Nations peace-keeping efforts

13 These speakers' statements would most likely have been made during the Presidential administration of
  1 Franklin D. Roosevelt
  2 Harry S Truman
  3 John F. Kennedy
  4 Richard M. Nixon

14 **"Wilson Order Controls on U.S. Industry to Fight War Against Germany"**

"FDR OK's Destroyer Deal with England to Fight Sub Threat"

"Truman Orders Airlift of Supplies to Berlin"

Which generalization about governmental power in the United States is supported by these headlines?
  1 Important Presidential decisions usually follow the results of public opinion polls.
  2 Presidential actions during international crises have increased executive power.
  3 Foreign policy is ultimately determined by Congress's power to allocate funds.
  4 Presidential power to act in wartime cannot be exercised without bipartisan support.

15 The Truman Doctrine and the Eisenhower Doctrine were United States foreign policies concerning
  1 the international balance of payments
  2 the containment of communism
  3 worldwide environmental pollution
  4 nuclear disarmament

16 The North Atlantic Treaty Organization (NATO) and the Truman Doctrine were attempts to carry out a United States foreign policy of
  1 brinkmanship
  2 containment
  3 appeasement
  4 neutrality

17 After World War II, relations between the Soviet Union and the United States were marked by
1 conflicts where the superpowers supported opposing sides, but did not confront each other directly
2 refusal to negotiate on any issues
3 slow by steady decreases in military forces and armaments
4 reliance on international peace organizations to resolve disputes

18 The Red Scare and McCarthyism were similar in that both
1 advocated the development of the arts and sciences
2 supported United States foreign aid programs
3 encouraged nativist ideas
4 promoted economic development

19 The NATO alliance, Truman Doctrine, and Marshall Plan were all attempts to
1 contain the spread of communism
2 give military assistance to China
3 defend United Nations peacekeeping forces
4 bring peace to the Middle East

20 During the 1950s, Senator Joseph McCarthy held congressional hearings to expose suspected
1 Nazis
2 members of organized crime
3 terrorists
4 communists

21 The Cold War developed after World War II as a result of
1 a decrease in arms production
2 the collapse of the United Nations
3 Japan's new economic growth
4 tension between the superpowers

22 The need for an international peacekeeping organization after World War II resulted in the development of the
1 Red Cross
2 League of Nations
3 United Nations
4 Alliance for Progress

23 "We Americans live in a world we can no longer dominate, but from which we cannot isolate ourselves." The author of this quotation is saying that the United States should
1 become less dependent on foreign nations
2 realize that it is no longer a world power
3 recognize important changes in international relations
4 increase its economic and military strength

24 What was a major goal of United States foreign policy in Europe after 1945?
1 development of nuclear weapons for World War II Allies of the United States
2 liberation of nations under the control of the Soviet Union
3 military support for nationalist movements within individual European nations
4 promotion of international cooperation through political and economic agreements

25 In its dependence upon members to enforce human rights declarations, the United Nations most closely resembles the
1 Soviet Union under Josef Stalin.
2 United States under the federal Constitution.
3 United States under the Articles of Confederation.
4 Japanese government before World War II.

THEMATIC ESSAY

In developing your answers to the essay, be sure to keep these general definitions in mind:

(a) <u>discuss</u> means "to make observations about something using facts, reasoning, and argument; to present in some detail"

(b) <u>describe</u> means "to illustrate something in words or to tell about it"

(c) <u>evaluate</u> means "to examine and judge the significance, worth, or condition of; to determine the value of"

Directions

Write a well-organized essay that includes an introduction, several paragraphs addressing the task below, and a conclusion.

Theme: Foreign Policy

The primary aim of a nation's foreign policy is the self-interest of that nation. Throughout United States history, certain foreign policy actions have led to debate over whether they were in the national interest.

Task

Identify three different foreign policies that have been followed by the United States. Discuss a specific application of that policy by the United States. Include in your discussion one reason the United States applied that policy and one result of the application of that policy.

Suggestions

You may use any example from your study of United States foreign policy actions during the twentieth century. Some suggestions you might wish to consider include: isolationism, containment, formation of military alliances, reliance upon international alliances, nonrecognition.

You are *not* limited to these suggestions.

Guidelines

In your essay be sure to:

- Address all aspects of the *Task*
- Analyze, evaluate, or compare and/or contrast issues and events whenever possible
- Fully support the theme of the essay with relevant facts, examples, and details
- Write a well-developed essay that consistently demonstrates a logical and clear plan of organization
- Introduce the theme by establishing a framework that is beyond a simple restatement of the *Task*
- Conclude your essay with a strong summation of the theme

DOCUMENT-BASED ESSAY

> For online Document-Based Essays,
> visit the Prentice Hall Web site at www.phschool.com.

This task is designed to test your ability to work with historical documents and is based on the accompanying documents (1–7). Some of the documents have been edited for the purposes of this question. As you analyze the documents, take into account both the source of each document and any point of view that may be presented in the document.

Directions

This document-based question consists of two parts: Part A and Part B. In Part A, you are to read each document and answer the question or questions that follow the document. In Part B, you are to write an essay based on the information in the documents and your knowledge of United States history.

Historical Context

World events after 1939 drew the United States into greater international involvement. These events forced the United States to abandon its isolationist foreign policy in favor of more active global involvement.

Task

Using information from the documents and your knowledge of United States history and government, answer the questions that follow each document in Part A. Your answers to the questions will help you write the Part B essay in which you be asked to:

Discuss how the need for military security and the protection of democratic ideals have shaped American foreign policy since 1939.

PART A: SHORT ANSWER

DOCUMENT #1

"Yesterday, December 7, 1941, a date which will live in infamy, the United States of America was suddenly and deliberately attacked by naval and air forces of the Empire of Japan.

"The attack yesterday on the Hawaiian Islands has caused severe damage to American naval and military forces. Very many American lives have been lost. In addition, American ships have been reported torpedoed on the high seas between San Francisco and Honolulu.

"As Commander in Chief of the Army and Navy I have directed that all measures be taken for our defense. . . . I believe I interpret the will of the Congress and of the people when I assert that we will not only defend ourselves to the uttermost but will make very certain that this form of treachery shall never endanger us again.

"I ask that the Congress declare that since the unprovoked and dastardly attack by Japan on Sunday, December 7, a state of war has existed between the United States and the Japanese Empire."

—Franklin D. Roosevelt, "Address to Congress," December 8, 1941

1 Why did President Roosevelt believe that the attack on Pearl Harbor justified the United States officially declaring war on Japan?

_____

_____

_____

_____

DOCUMENT #2

2 This cartoon represents Roosevelt, Stalin, and Churchill at the Yalta Conference. What does their activity in this cartoon say about their accomplishments at Yalta?

_____

_____

_____

DOCUMENT #3

> "[The Soviet Union] cannot be easily defeated or discouraged by a single victory on the part of its opponents . . . but only by intelligent long-range policies . . . no less steady in their purpose . . . than those of the Soviet Union itself. In these circumstances, it is clear that the main element of any United States policy toward the Soviet Union must be that of a long-term, patient but firm and vigilant containment of Russian expansive tendencies."
>
> **—Foreign service officer George Kennan, July 1947**

3 What foreign policy position did Kennan believe the United States should take toward the Soviet Union?

_____

_____

_____

DOCUMENT #4

"The Parties agree that an armed attack against one or more of them in Europe or North America shall be considered an attack against them all and consequently they agree that, if such an armed attack occurs, each of them, in exercise of the right of individual or collective self-defense. . . will assist the Party or Parties so attacked by taking . . . such action as it deems necessary, including the use of armed force, to restore and maintain the security of the North Atlantic area."

—The North Atlantic Treaty, April 4, 1949

4   How did joining NATO demonstrate the long-term commitment of the United States to international involvement?

_____

_____

_____

_____

DOCUMENT #5

"I believe that it must be the policy of the United States to support free peoples who are resisting attempted subjugation [takeover] by armed minorities or by outside pressures. . . . I believe that our help should be primarily through economic and financial aid which is essential to economic stability and orderly political processes. . . .

"I therefore ask the Congress to provide authority for assistance to Greece and Turkey in the amount of $400,000,000. . . .

"The free peoples of the world look to us for support in maintaining their freedoms. If we falter in our leadership, we may endanger the peace of the world-and we shall surely endanger the welfare of our own nation. Great responsibilities have been placed upon us by the swift movement of events. I am confident that the Congress will face these responsibilities squarely."

—President Harry S Truman, *Address Before a Joint Session of Congress*, March 12, 1947

5   Based on this quote, why did President Truman believe that the United States should help Greece and Turkey in their fight against a communist takeover?

_____

_____

_____

DOCUMENT #6
Berlin Airlift Statistics, 1948–1949

	Flights	Cargo (short tons)			
		Total	Food	Coal	Other
USA	189,963	1,783,573	296,319	1,421,119	66,135
UK	87,841	541,937	240,386	164,911	136,640
France	424	896	unknown	unknown	unknown
Total	278,228	2,326,406			

6 How does the chart above demonstrate the commitment that the United States made to prevent the Soviet Union from crippling West Berlin in the blockade of 1948–1949?

_____

_____

_____

_____

_____

DOCUMENT #7

"Our purpose in the Persian Gulf remains constant: to drive Iraq out of Kuwait, to restore Kuwait's legitimate government, and to ensure the stability and security of this critical region. Let me make clear what I mean by the region's stability and security. . . . We seek a Persian Gulf where conflict is no longer the rule, where the strong are neither tempted nor able to intimidate the weak.

"Most Americans know instinctively why we are in the Gulf. They know we had to stop [Iraqi leader] Saddam [Hussein] now, not later. . . .They know we must make sure that control of the world's oil resources does not fall into his hands, only to finance further aggression. They know that we need to build a new, enduring peace, based not on arms races and confrontation but on shared principles and the rule of law."

—President George Bush, State of the Union Address, January 29, 1991

7   According to this quote, why did President Bush believe that American involvement in the Persian Gulf War was necessary?

_____

_____

_____

_____

_____

_____

PART B: ESSAY

Directions
Using information from the documents provided, and your knowledge of United States history, write a well-organized essay that includes an introduction, several paragraphs, and a conclusion.

Historical Context
World events after 1939 drew the United States into greater international involvement. These events forced the United States to abandon its isolationist foreign policy in favor of more active global involvement.

Task
Using information from the documents and your knowledge of United States history and government, write an essay in which you

Discuss how the need for military security and the protection of democratic ideals have shaped American foreign policy since 1939.

Guidelines
When writing your essay, be sure to
- Address all aspects of the *Task* by accurately analyzing and interpreting at least <u>four</u> documents
- Incorporate information from the documents in the body of the essay
- Incorporate relevant outside information throughout the essay
- Richly support the theme with relevant facts, examples, and details
- Write a well-developed essay that consistently demonstrates a logical and clean plan of organization
- Introduce the theme by establishing a framework that is beyond a simple restatement of the *Task* or *Historical Context* and conclude the essay with a summation of the theme.

UNIT 7

The World in Uncertain Times, 1950–the Present

UNIT OVERVIEW

The foreign policies that began after World War II continued to shape America's response to events abroad for decades. The policy of containment, begun under President Truman, eventually led the United States into its longest war, one that caused deep splits within American society.

During the period from the 1950s to the present, life changed at home for Americans. An expanding civil rights movement, a major constitutional crisis, new technologies, and a changing economic picture are some of the highlights of these years.

Some key questions to help you focus on this time period include:

- How did the foreign policy concerns of the United States become more global in scope?
- What were the goals and the achievements of the civil rights movement?
- How did the war in Vietnam affect American society?
- How did relations of the United States with the Soviet Union change under Presidents Reagan and Bush?
- What are some of the major challenges that the nation will face in years to come?

1 Containment Abroad and Agreement at Home

SECTION OVERVIEW

During the 1950s, the Cold War intensified and spread to new locations around the world. Meanwhile, the new economic prosperity allowed many Americans to enjoy greater wealth and leisure than their parents had. At the same time, the civil rights movement intensified as African Americans demanded justice and equality.

KEY THEMES AND CONCEPTS

As you review this section, take special note of the following key themes and concepts:

Foreign Policy How did tensions between the United States and the Soviet Union increase and decrease during Eisenhower's presidency?

Citizenship How did African Americans begin to organize the civil rights movement?

Economic Systems Who benefited from the "Eisenhower prosperity," and who did not?

KEY PEOPLE

Dwight D. Eisenhower
Nikita Khrushchev
Fidel Castro
Jackie Robinson
Rosa Parks
Martin Luther King, Jr.

KEY SUPREME COURT CASE

Brown v. Board of Education of Topeka, Kansas

★ THE BIG IDEA

Foreign policy, especially the Cold War, influenced events in the 1950s. During this period

- President Eisenhower attempted to limit communism.

- policies toward Asia, the Middle East , and Latin America took shape.

- the economy of the United States improved.

- African Americans renewed their struggle for civil rights.

⚷ KEY TERMS

balance of power
brinkmanship
arms race
Sputnik
domino theory
Eisenhower doctrine
suburbanization
civil rights movement

THE COLD WAR CONTINUES

The United States emerged from World War II as the strongest nation in the world. It controlled the atomic bomb, and its economy was undamaged by the destruction of war. The Soviet Union, however, quickly became America's chief rival. By 1949, it too had the atomic bomb. It had also taken control of most of the nations of Eastern Europe and was seeking to extend its influence elsewhere.

The Cold War, 1950–1960

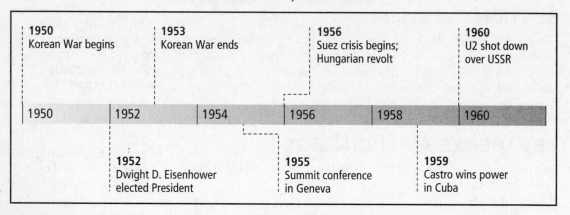

1950
Korean War begins

1953
Korean War ends

1956
Suez crisis begins; Hungarian revolt

1960
U2 shot down over USSR

| 1950 | 1952 | 1954 | 1956 | 1958 | 1960 |

1952
Dwight D. Eisenhower elected President

1955
Summit conference in Geneva

1959
Castro wins power in Cuba

ANALYZING DOCUMENTS

Examine the timeline, then answer the following questions.

- Did the Korean War begin before or after Eisenhower became President?

- Which events on the timeline took place in Europe?

President Harry S Truman began the policy of containment after the war in an attempt to limit the spread of communism. As the United States and the Soviet Union—the two world superpowers—attempted to maintain a **balance of power,** a cold war developed.

Eisenhower's Foreign Policy

As President, Dwight D. Eisenhower continued Truman's basic policy of containment. However, he and his secretary of state John Foster Dulles introduced some new ideas.

MASSIVE RETALIATION Eisenhower worried that defense spending would bankrupt the nation. Yet he feared that the Soviets might see cutbacks in military spending as a sign of weakness.

Eisenhower and Dulles instead devised a "new look" for the nation's defense. The United States would rely more heavily on air power and nuclear weapons than on ground troops. Dulles announced a policy of massive retaliation. This meant that the United States would consider the use of nuclear weapons to halt aggression if it believed the nation's interests were threatened.

Dulles further stated that the nation must be ready to go "to the brink of war" in order to preserve world peace. This policy of **brinkmanship** greatly increased world tensions during the 1950s.

THE ARMS RACE The United States and the Soviet Union began an **arms race,** stockpiling nuclear and nonnuclear weapons. The United States exploded a hydrogen bomb in 1952, and the Soviets tested one a year later. Both nations rushed to develop missiles capable of carrying nuclear weapons. The balance of power became a balance of terror.

In 1953, Eisenhower announced the Atoms for Peace Plan at the United Nations. The plan called for United Nations supervision of a world search to find peaceful uses for nuclear technology. The Soviet Union refused to participate.

In 1957, the Soviets launched a satellite, **Sputnik,** into orbit around the earth. The arms race then became a space race as the United States rushed to launch its own satellites, some for military purposes.

Foreign Policy in Asia

Asia became a major area of concern for United States foreign policy. The communist victory in China in 1949 raised fears of further communist expansion. The war in Korea, even though it ended in what was basically a draw in 1953, added to these fears.

THE DOMINO THEORY As communists took control of the governments of China and, later, some nations of Southeast Asia, American worries about Communist expansion increased. Eisenhower stated that the United States must resist further aggression in the region and explained what came to be known as the **domino theory.** The nations of Asia, he said, were like a row of dominoes standing on end. If one fell to communism, the rest were sure to follow.

SEATO One way to resist aggression, Dulles claimed, was through alliances. To mirror the formation of NATO in Europe, Dulles in 1954 pushed for the creation of the Southeast Asia Treaty Organization (SEATO). Its original members—Pakistan, Thailand, the Philippines, Australia, New Zealand, Great Britain, and the United States— pledged to meet any "common danger" from communist aggression.

Foreign Policy in the Middle East

The Middle East was the scene of several outbreaks of trouble during the Eisenhower administration.

IRAN In 1954, the prime minister of Iran tried to nationalize that country's foreign-owned oil industry. The United States, through the Central Intelligence Agency, secretly arranged the overthrow of the prime minister's government and the restoration of the shah to the throne of Iran. This action helped secure America's supply of oil at the time but caused problems for the nation in years to come.

EGYPT Gamal Abdel Nasser, president of Egypt, had counted on economic support from the Soviet Union and the United States to build a huge dam at Aswan on the Nile River. Nasser's friendliness to the Soviet Union led the United States to withdraw its support. Nasser

⚲ KEY THEMES AND CONCEPTS

Interdependence

In 1954, the Central Intelligence Agency tried to overthrow the government of Iran and restore the country's former ruler, the shah. Why?

GEOGRAPHY IN HISTORY

Nasser's seizure of the Suez Canal sparked a crisis that involved Great Britain, France, and Israel. Why was the Suez Canal so important to these nations?

PREPARING FOR THE EXAM

On the examination, you will need to understand United States foreign policy during the 1950s in the Middle East.

What is the Eisenhower Doctrine? List two countries to which it is applied.

1.

2.

READING STRATEGY

Analyzing Cause and Effect

Why did the policies of Fidel Castro anger the Eisenhower administration?

then nationalized the Suez Canal, which was run by a British and French company. He planned to use revenues from the canal to pay for the dam.

Great Britain and France, joined by Israel, sent troops to seize the canal. Fearing that fighting would spread through the region, both the United States and the Soviet Union supported a United Nations resolution condemning the attack. Britain, France, and Israel withdrew, and the canal remained under Egyptian control.

THE EISENHOWER DOCTRINE Troubles in the Middle East led Congress to adopt what became known as the **Eisenhower Doctrine** in 1957. The United States pledged to help any Middle Eastern nation resist communist aggression.

LEBANON In 1958, the Eisenhower Doctrine was tested when the governments of Lebanon and Jordan asked for help. The United States sent marines to Lebanon, and Great Britain sent troops to Jordan to help restore political calm in those nations.

Foreign Policy in Latin America

Troubles also flared up closer to home during Eisenhower's time in office. Three instances are especially notable.

GUATEMALA The CIA staged a successful covert operation in Guatemala in 1954. It arranged a revolt that toppled a government considered to be too friendly to communists.

NIXON'S TOUR In 1958, Vice President Richard Nixon went on a goodwill tour of Latin America. In Peru and Venezuela, however, angry mobs surrounded his limousine, throwing rocks and eggs at it. This event revealed the strong anti-American feelings that had built up in Latin America in response to repeated interventions in the region by the United States.

CUBA In 1956, Fidel Castro began a revolt against the government of Cuban dictator Fulgencio Batista. When the revolt ended with Castro's victory in 1959, the United States quickly recognized the new government.

Castro, however, soon adopted policies that angered the Eisenhower administration. He limited civil liberties and imprisoned political opponents. He also nationalized key industries and turned to the Soviet Union for aid.

Large numbers of Cubans fled Castro's rule, with many settling in southern Florida. Some worked actively to end Castro's rule. Meanwhile, they became one more immigrant group that contributed to the richness of the American multicultural experience.

Changing Relations with the Soviet Union

Tensions between the United States and the Soviet Union rose and fell during Eisenhower's time in office.

NEW SOVIET LEADERSHIP Josef Stalin, leader of the Soviet Union since the 1920s, died in 1953. In time, Nikita Khrushchev took over as the head of the Soviet government. This change marked a temporary easing of Cold War tensions as the Soviets began to focus more on improving conditions within their nation.

PEACEFUL COEXISTENCE Relations between the superpowers gradually improved. In 1955, the leaders of the United States, the Soviet Union, Great Britain, and France held the first summit meeting since World War II in Geneva, Switzerland. The superpower leaders began talks on disarmament that, in time, led to a suspension of nuclear testing.

POLAND AND HUNGARY In 1956, riots by Polish workers won concessions from the Communist Polish government. Inspired by this, students and workers in Hungary began demonstrations that fall that ended with the Soviet Union sending tanks and troops to bring that nation firmly back under Communist control. The suppression of the Hungarian revolt cooled relations between the United States and the Soviet Union.

CAMP DAVID Relations improved again by 1959. Khrushchev visited the United States, and he and Eisenhower held lengthy talks at Camp David, the presidential retreat near Washington, D.C. The spirit of goodwill that grew at these talks encouraged the leaders to announce another summit meeting in Paris in 1960.

THE U-2 INCIDENT The Paris summit proved a disaster. Shortly before it opened, the Soviet military shot down an American U-2 aircraft deep in Soviet territory. The pilot admitted that he had been spying on Soviet military bases.

Eisenhower said that he had approved the U-2 flights and promised to suspend them. Khrushchev denounced the United States and demanded an apology. Eisenhower refused, and the summit collapsed before it really started.

In summary, Eisenhower's foreign policy was primarily a continuation of Truman's containment policy. Many of the events of the 1950s can be compared to kettles ready to boil over in the 1960s. In later years, the Eisenhower administration was criticized by some as not being aware enough of the struggles of developing nations and of their desires to end colonial rule.

AN IMPROVING ECONOMY AT HOME

When Dwight Eisenhower became President in 1953, he was the first Republican President since 1933—the year Herbert Hoover left office during one of the worst years of the Great Depression. Since that time, Democrats Franklin D. Roosevelt and Harry S Truman had called for

KEY THEMES AND CONCEPTS
Foreign Policy
Relations between the United States and the Soviet Union changed several times during the 1950s. Following the death of Soviet leader Joseph Stalin in 1953, the new Soviet leader Nikita Khrushchev focused more on improving conditions within his nation. This eased cold war tensions.

• What event rekindled the Cold War in 1956?

TURNING POINT

Why is the U-2 incident considered a turning point in U.S.-Soviet relations?

**? KEY THEMES AND
CONCEPTS**

**Presidential Decisions
and Actions**
President Eisenhower
believed that what was
good for business benefited
the United States as a
whole. He attempted to
limit the federal govern-
ment's power but expanded
several social programs,
including Social Security.

• Why did farm conditions
present a problem for
Eisenhower?

• How did Congress
resolve the problem?

New Deal and New Society policies that had vastly increased both the federal government's spending and its role in society.

Eisenhower's Economic Policies

Eisenhower had a deep dislike for strong centralized government. In addition, he generally believed policies that were good for big business were good for the nation as a whole.

EISENHOWER'S DOMESTIC POLICIES Eisenhower attempted to cut back on the federal government's size and power. He reduced spending for defense and foreign aid.

Eisenhower did recognize that many social programs begun under the New Deal were very popular. He extended some of these and, in some cases, started new programs. The Social Security program was expanded to include seven million more people, and a new cabinet post, the Department of Health, Education, and Welfare, was created.

THE FARM PROBLEM Conditions on the nation's farms pulled Eisenhower between his desire to cut government spending and his wish to extend some social programs. Farm production had been increasing while prices for agricultural products had been declining.

Farmers had been receiving payments from the federal government to make up for changes in market conditions. Eisenhower's secretary of agriculture wanted to be able to cut such payments. Farmers protested, and in 1956, Congress approved a new program that paid farmers for not planting crops. Both types of payments are called subsidies, or direct payments by a government to private individuals.

"Eisenhower Prosperity" and Consumer Spending

Despite the problems noted above, the American people commonly prospered during the 1950s. There were several reasons for this.

• During World War II, Americans had worked hard and generally earned good wages. Because of rationing and shortages, however, they could usually only spend their money on basic necessities.

• By war's end, Americans had accumulated huge amounts of capital—wealth in the form of money or property. They were ready to spend this capital on consumer goods.

• By the 1950s, wartime price controls were over, and factories had converted from the production of military supplies to the production of consumer goods.

NEW HOMES The postwar years saw the start of a "baby boom." The growth in family size, the accumulation of capital, and the avail-ability of government loans to veterans brought a rapid increase in home building.

SUBURBS Much new home building was done in areas surrounding major cities (urban areas). These areas are called suburbs. The suburbs

Refrigerator-Freezers!

THE FINAL FROST BARRIER!

IT'S HERE!
A FROST-PROOF
FOOD FREEZER!
NO FROST!
NO FROST-LOCKED
FOODS!
NO DEFROSTING!

You'll feel like a queen...

DESIGNED WITH YOU IN MIND!

ANALYZING DOCUMENTS

Examine the advertisement at left, then answer the questions.

• What product is the advertisement promoting?

• Who is the advertisement targeting? What clues lead you to this conclusion?

• What does this advertisement suggest about the U.S. economy at the time?

• How is this advertisement similar to ads you see today? How is it different?

READING STRATEGY

Reinforcing Main Ideas
How did the growth of suburbs contribute to the decline of many cities?

READING STRATEGY

Formulating Questions
The increase in demand for cars benefited many industries, such as the steel and oil industries. Increased automobile ownership also made it possible for people to live in suburbs without public transportation, because the government provided funding for an extensive highway network.

• What were some of the negative consequences of this increased reliance on cars?

offered limited jobs and services for their residents, most of whom worked in the cities. The suburbs grew rapidly. Levittown, New York, for example, became a symbol of **suburbanization,** with some 17,000 tract houses built in four years. By the 1960s, almost a third of all Americans lived in suburbs.

The growth of suburbs contributed to the decline of many cities. As people moved out of cities to suburbs, fewer taxpayers remained to help pay for essential services. At the same time, a greater concentration of poorer people in the cities increased the demand for many social services.

AUTOMOBILES Cars made the growth of suburbs possible, and suburbs increased the demand for cars. Since public transportation systems grew more slowly than suburbs, people in suburbs relied increasingly on their cars. Increased demand for automobiles benefited many areas of the nation's economy. Factories turned out the steel, glass, and rubber that went into new cars. Refineries also produced oil and gas that powered them.

The federal government stepped into the transportation picture with passage of the Federal Highway Act of 1956. This provided funding for what became a 44,000-mile network of interstate highways.

**GEOGRAPHY
IN HISTORY**

In which areas of the United States did the population grow most quickly during in the 1950s? Give examples of three states that experienced rapid growth.

1.

2.

3.

**ANALYZING
DOCUMENTS**

Examine the bar graph at right. Between which two years did the number of homes with television sets increase most dramatically?

A NATION ON THE MOVE Americans moved from central cities to suburbs. They also moved to new areas of the country. Many people moved from the industrialized but decaying cities of the Northeast and Midwest and from the farms of the Midwest to the Sun Belt. This was the name given to the states of the South and West—including Florida, Texas, Arizona, and California—that experienced a faster than average population growth beginning in the postwar years.

The sun and warm climate of these states enticed both retirees and businesses that wished to relocate. As this region grew, it attracted more industry and prompted both population and job loss in what came to be called the Rust Belt. This region included the states of the Northeast (including New York and Massachusetts) and Midwest (including Ohio and Michigan).

Homes with Television Sets, 1948–1960

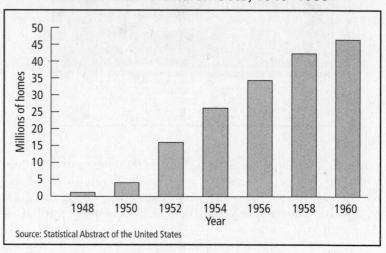

Source: Statistical Abstract of the United States

TELEVISION After limited broadcasting in 1939, national broadcasting began in 1946. Television became the leading form of popular entertainment, and its growth, both as a source of amusement and a tool for learning, has continued to the present day.

A RENEWED STRUGGLE FOR CIVIL RIGHTS

Since the period of Reconstruction after the Civil War, African Americans faced discrimination, especially in southern states. Jim Crow laws limited the freedoms of African Americans. For generations, white southerners continued to maintain economic, social, and political control over the South.

Beginnings of Change

Until well into the twentieth century, much of the South was segregated, or separated by race. Although such segregation was less apparent in the North, African Americans were generally restricted to poorer neighborhoods and lower-paying jobs. Although African Americans fought for change, until the 1950s their gains were limited.

Not until 1947, for example, were African Americans permitted to play on major league baseball teams in this country. In that year, Jackie Robinson joined the Brooklyn Dodgers. This was one sign that public attitudes on segregation were beginning to change.

TRUMAN'S POLICIES ON CIVIL RIGHTS President Truman appointed a presidential commission on civil rights in 1946. Based on its report, Truman called for the establishment of a fair employment practices commission. Congress, however, failed to act on the idea.

Using his powers as commander in chief, Truman issued an executive order banning segregation in the armed forces. He also strengthened the Justice Department's civil rights division, which aided blacks who challenged segregation in the courts.

TURNING POINT

Why is it considered a turning point in the struggle for civil rights when Jackie Robinson joined the Brooklyn Dodgers?

READING STRATEGY

Organizing Information
The struggle to secure African American civil rights required the efforts of countless dedicated activists, organizers, and political leaders. What are two changes that President Truman made that had an impact on civil rights?

1.
2.

Civil Rights Milestones

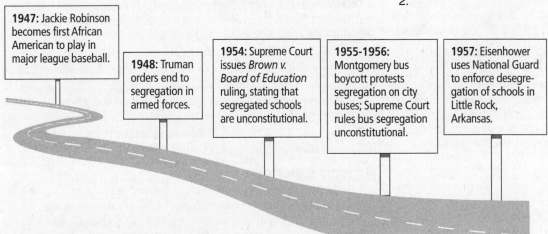

1947: Jackie Robinson becomes first African American to play in major league baseball.

1948: Truman orders end to segregation in armed forces.

1954: Supreme Court issues *Brown v. Board of Education* ruling, stating that segregated schools are unconstitutional.

1955-1956: Montgomery bus boycott protests segregation on city buses; Supreme Court rules bus segregation unconstitutional.

1957: Eisenhower uses National Guard to enforce desegregation of schools in Little Rock, Arkansas.

Civil Rights and the Courts

In the 1950s, the Supreme Court made several important decisions concerning the civil rights of African Americans.

THE WARREN COURT In 1953, a vacancy occurred on the Supreme Court. President Eisenhower then appointed Earl Warren, former governor of California, as chief justice. Warren presided over the Supreme Court until 1969. During that period, the Court reached a number of decisions that deeply affected many areas of American life. Among the most far-reaching of the Warren Court's decisions were those dealing with civil rights for African Americans.

KEY THEMES AND CONCEPTS
Constitutional Principles
Brown v. *Board of Education of Topeka, Kansas* (1954) established that facilities separated by race were unequal. The decision reversed *Plessy* v. *Ferguson* (1896) and made integration of schools possible.

• How did the governor of Arkansas respond to *Brown* v. *Board of Education of Topeka, Kansas*?

KEY THEMES AND CONCEPTS
Government
President Eisenhower was acting in his role as Chief Executive when he sent troops to Little Rock.

BROWN V. *BOARD OF EDUCATION* Only a year after he became chief justice, Warren presided over the court as it reached a landmark decision in *Brown* v. *Board of Education of Topeka, Kansas.* Linda Brown, a young African American student, requested the right to attend a local all-white school in her Topeka neighborhood, rather than attend an all-black school that was further away.

The 1896 *Plessy* v. *Ferguson* decision had held that separate but equal public facilities were legal. Schools were such public facilities, and Brown was refused admittance to the all-white school.

The National Association for the Advancement of Colored People (NAACP) joined the case and appealed it all the way to the Supreme Court. In a unanimous decision, the Court reversed its ruling in *Plessy* v. *Ferguson* and held that in the field of public education, "the doctrine of separate but equal has no place."

LITTLE ROCK Although the Brown case opened the door for desegregation, integration did not follow immediately. Many Americans were shocked by the decision. In the South, whites began campaigns of "massive resistance" to public school desegregation.

Although the Supreme Court had ordered that school integration go forward "with all deliberate speed," many school systems openly defied the ruling. In 1957, the governor of Arkansas ordered the state's National Guard to prevent nine African American students from attending Central High School in Little Rock.

President Eisenhower was reluctant to step in, but the governor's defiance was a direct challenge to the Constitution. Eisenhower placed the Arkansas National Guard under federal control and then used it to enforce integration. At the end of the school year, the governor continued his defiance by ordering all city high schools closed for the following year. The tactic failed, however, and in 1959 the first racially integrated class graduated from Central High School.

African American Activism

Public facilities of all kinds were segregated in the South—schools, movie theaters, lunch counters, drinking fountains, restrooms, buses, and trains. Rather than wait for court rulings to end segregation, in the 1950s African Americans began to organize a **civil rights movement.**

THE MONTGOMERY BUS BOYCOTT In Montgomery, Alabama, in 1955, an African American seamstress named Rosa Parks refused to give up her seat to a white man and move to the back of the bus, as was required by law. She was arrested for violating the law, and her action inspired a boycott of the city's buses.

Martin Luther King, Jr., a young Baptist minister, emerged as a leader of the protest. King had studied the nonviolent methods of Mohandas Gandhi and Henry David Thoreau. His dynamic speaking style drew the attention and support of large numbers of people.

Major Civil Rights Protests, 1954–1965

Year	Event	Outcome
1954	*Brown* v. *Board of Education*	Supreme Court ruled that separate educational facilities for whites and African Americans are inherently unequal.
1955–1956	Montgomery Bus Boycott	Alabama bus company was forced to desegregate its buses. Martin Luther King, Jr., emerged as an important civil rights leader.
1961	Freedom Rides	Interstate Commerce Commission banned segregation in interstate transportation.
1963	James Meredith sues University of Mississippi for admission	Supreme Court upheld Meredith's right to enter the all-white institution.
1963	Protest marches in Birmingham, Alabama	Violence against peaceful demonstrators shocked the nation. Under pressure, Birmingham desegregated public facilities.
1963	March on Washington	More than 200,000 people demonstrated in an impressive display of support for civil rights.
1965	Selma March (Alabama)	State troopers attacked marchers. President Johnson used federal force to protect route from Selma to Montgomery and thousands joined march.

ANALYZING DOCUMENTS

The table at left outlines some of the major civil rights protests from 1954 to 1965.

- Which protest led to the rise of Dr. Martin Luther King, Jr., as an important civil rights leader?

- Which three key protests occurred in Alabama?

♀ KEY THEMES AND ⌐ CONCEPTS

Individuals, Groups, Institutions

African Americans began to take direct action to end segregation following *Brown* v. *Board of Education*. Boycotts of schools, lunch counters, and buses, for example, began.

- How did the actions of Rosa Parks and Martin Luther King, Jr., change attitudes toward segregation?

The boycott lasted 381 days. In the end, the Supreme Court ruled that segregation of public buses was illegal. Although Parks had not planned her action that day, her stand against injustice led the way for others.

Civil Rights Legislation

Congress also made some moves to ensure civil rights for African Americans. In August 1957, it passed the first civil rights act since Reconstruction. The bill created a permanent commission for civil rights and increased federal efforts to ensure blacks the right to vote. Another bill in 1960 further strengthened voting rights.

Although these bills had only limited effectiveness, they did mark the beginning of change. Martin Luther King, Jr., once remarked that it was impossible to legislate what was in a person's heart, but that laws can restrain the heartless. During this time some southern Senators attempted to delay passage of civil rights legislation by using a filibuster. This is an effort by one or more senators to speak continuously on the floor of the Senate until support for their view can be gained or until the Senate leaders decide to delay the proposed bill. Filibusters may last several weeks and can only be ended by a special vote called cloture which can close debate.

2 Decade of Change: the 1960s

⭐ **THE BIG IDEA**

The 1960s were a tumultuous era in American society. During this period

- the struggle for civil rights continued.
- the women's rights movement organized.
- other groups, including Native Americans, struggled for equality.
- New Frontier and Great Society programs expanded upon the New Deal of the 1930s.
- the Cold War affected foreign policy in Latin America.

🔑 **KEY TERMS**

civil disobedience
Civil Rights Act of 1964
Voting Rights Act of 1965
Equal Rights Amendment
affirmative action
United Farm Workers
American Indian Movement
mainstreaming
Americans with Disabilities
   Act of 1990
New Frontier
Great Society
Cuban missile crisis
Berlin Wall

SECTION OVERVIEW

In the early 1960s, the continuing pressure of African American civil rights groups, plus growing public sympathy, forced the passage of new legislation. Women, Latino Americans, Native Americans, and disabled Americans adapted civil rights tactics to achieve their own goals of equality. Meanwhile, the cold war tensions between the United States and the Soviet Union continued, as the two nations came into conflict in Germany and Cuba.

KEY THEMES AND CONCEPTS

As you review this section, take special note of the following key themes and concepts:

Citizenship How did the African American civil rights movement inspire others to struggle to achieve greater equality?

Government How did Presidents Kennedy and Johnson continue and expand upon traditions from the New Deal of the 1930s?

Foreign Policy How did the antagonism between the United States and the Soviet Union bring the two nations to the brink of war?

KEY PEOPLE

James Meredith
Medgar Evers
Lyndon B. Johnson
Malcolm X
Cesar Chavez

KEY SUPREME COURT CASES

Heart of Atlanta Motel v. *United States*
Roe v. *Wade*
Regents of the University of California v. *Bakke*

The Sixties

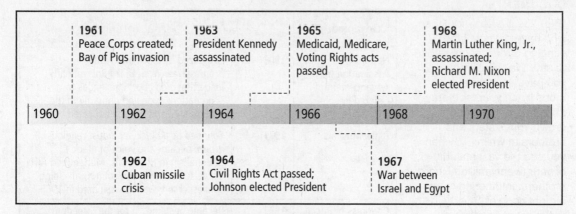

1961
Peace Corps created;
Bay of Pigs invasion

1963
President Kennedy
assassinated

1965
Medicaid, Medicare,
Voting Rights acts
passed

1968
Martin Luther King, Jr.,
assassinated;
Richard M. Nixon
elected President

| 1960 | 1962 | 1964 | 1966 | 1968 | 1970 |

1962
Cuban missile
crisis

1964
Civil Rights Act passed;
Johnson elected President

1967
War between
Israel and Egypt

THE STRUGGLE FOR CIVIL RIGHTS CONTINUES

During the 1960s, the struggle of African Americans to win equality before the law grew more intense. In their fight, African Americans were seeking to overcome a heritage of racism that had been a part of American thought and tradition for more than 300 years.

By the 1960s, however, many African Americans were working together for the common goal of justice and equality. The successes they gained would deeply affect many parts of American society.

African Americans Organize

African Americans formed a number of different groups that used a variety of approaches in the attempt to achieve justice and equality. In the early 1960s, many groups followed the nonviolent methods introduced by Dr. Martin Luther King, Jr., and the Southern Christian Leadership Conference (SCLC), an organization of clergy who shifted the leadership of the civil rights movement to the South.

Many civil rights activists used a form of protest called **civil disobedience.** This means the deliberate breaking of a law to show a belief that the law is unjust. For example, they attempted to use segregated facilities at interstate train stations and bus depots. Usually they were arrested for such acts; often they were beaten.

JAMES MEREDITH The push to integrate education continued. In 1962, James Meredith, an African American Air Force veteran, made headlines when he tried to enroll at the all-white University of Mississippi. The governor of the state personally tried to stop Meredith from enrolling. Riots broke out, and federal marshals and the National Guard were called up. Although he had to overcome continued harassment, Meredith did finally enter and eventually graduate from the university.

Election of 1960

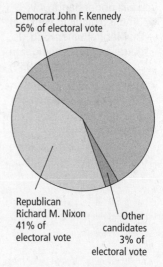

Democrat John F. Kennedy
56% of electoral vote

Republican
Richard M. Nixon
41% of
electoral vote

Other
candidates
3% of
electoral vote

ANALYZING
DOCUMENTS

"Perhaps it is easy for those who have never felt the stinging dark of segregation to say, 'Wait.' But when you have seen vicious mobs lynch your mothers and fathers at will and drown your sisters and brothers at whim; . . . when you see the vast majority of your twenty million Negro brothers smothering in an airtight cage of poverty in the midst of an affluent society; when you suddenly find your tongue twisted . . . as you seek to explain to your six-year-old daughter why she can't go to the public amusement park . . . and see tears welling up in her eyes when she is told that Funtown is closed to colored children, . . . then you will understand why we find it difficult to wait."
—Dr. Martin Luther King, Jr., "Letter from a Birmingham Jail" (1963)

- How does King justify the immediate need for direct action to end discrimination?

Major African American Organizations

Organization	Date of Founding	Background
National Association for the Advancement of Colored People (NAACP)	1909	Organized by black and white progressives; W. E. B. Du Bois an early leader; favored court challenges to segregation; appealed primarily to the professional and college-educated.
Black Muslims	1931	Founded as a black separatist religious group; became the voice of black nationalism in the 1960s; Muhammed Ali converted in 1965; Malcolm X, a leading spokesperson, was assassinated in 1965.
Congress of Racial Equality (CORE)	1942	Became best known for the "freedom rides" of the 1960s, efforts to desegregate interstate transportation.
Southern Christian Leadership Conference (SCLC)	1957	Founded by Martin Luther King, Jr., to encourage nonviolent passive resistance; organized black Christian churches.
Student Nonviolent Coordinating Committee (SNCC)	1960	In early days, used nonviolent civil disobedience in sit-ins and boycotts; later supported the idea of "black power" put forward by Stokely Carmichael.

GREENSBORO Practicing civil disobedience, demonstrators protested such discrimination as segregated lunch counters and buses. Sit-ins at lunch counters—the 1960s version of fast-food restaurants—began at Greensboro, North Carolina, in 1960. There a group of African Americans sat at a "whites only" lunch counter and refused to leave until served. As such protests became popular, some sympathetic whites often joined the sit-ins.

BIRMINGHAM In 1963, Dr. Martin Luther King, Jr., and the SCLC began a campaign to bring integration to Birmingham, Alabama, which many considered to be the most segregated city in the South. At a protest march, police used dogs and fire hoses to break up the marchers and arrested more than 2,000 people. One of those jailed was King, who then wrote his famous "Letter from a Birmingham Jail," in which he defended his methods of nonviolent civil disobedience and restated the need for direct action to end segregation.

Television cameras had brought the scenes of violence in Birmingham to people across the country. This helped build support for the growing civil rights movement. In Birmingham, the protests eventually resulted in the desegregation of city facilities.

MEDGAR EVERS White reaction to African American protests sometimes turned deadly. Medgar Evers, field secretary of the NAACP, had been working to desegregate Jackson, Mississippi. In June 1963, Evers was murdered by a sniper outside his home.

UNIVERSITY OF ALABAMA Also in June 1963, Governor George Wallace of Alabama vowed to stop two African American students from registering at the state university. Pressure from President Kennedy and the later arrival of the National Guard forced Wallace to back down. The two students enrolled peacefully.

THE MARCH ON WASHINGTON The growing civil rights movement moved President Kennedy to deliver a televised speech to the nation in June 1963 on the need to guarantee the civil rights of African Americans. This marked the first speech by a President specifically on this issue. Eight days later, he sent the most comprehensive civil rights bill in the nation's history to Congress.

Civil rights groups organized a huge march on Washington, D.C., in August 1963, to show support for the bill. At the march, Dr. Martin Luther King, Jr., delivered his famous "I have a dream" speech to a crowd of more than 200,000 participants. In the speech, he eloquently expressed his hopes for a unified America.

Not all Americans shared King's dream, however. Just a few weeks after the March on Washington, white terrorists bombed an African American church in Birmingham, killing four young girls.

JOHNSON AND THE CIVIL RIGHTS ACT After the assassination of John F. Kennedy in November 1963, the new President, Lyndon Johnson, recognized the urgency of pushing forward with civil rights legislation. Johnson worked tirelessly for the passage of the bill, and in July 1964, he signed the **Civil Rights Act of 1964,** the most sweeping civil rights law in American history. The bill called for

- protection of voting rights for all Americans.
- opening of public facilities (restaurants, hotels, stores, restrooms) to people of all races.
- a commission to protect equal job opportunities for all Americans.

Passage of the Civil Rights Act came just months after ratification of the Twenty-fourth Amendment to the Constitution, which abolished the poll tax in federal elections. A poll tax was a fee that had to be paid before a person could vote. The poll tax had prevented poorer Americans—including many African Americans—from exercising their legal right to vote.

The Civil Rights Act of 1964 outlawed race discrimination in public accommodations, including motels that refused rooms to African Americans. In the landmark Supreme Court case *Heart of Atlanta Motel* v. *United States* (1964), racial segregation of private facilities engaged in interstate commerce was found unconstitutional.

TURNING POINT

Why is the Civil Rights Act of 1964 considered a turning point in the struggle for civil rights?

READING STRATEGY

Organizing Information
In the space below, list three provisions of the Voting Rights Act of 1965. Which do you think is the most significant? Why?

1.

2.

3.

⚷ **KEY THEMES AND CONCEPTS**

Individuals, Groups, Institutions
In the 1960s, many African Americans felt that they should take more control over the political and economic conditions in their lives. A new leader named Malcolm X emerged and began to attract attention from more militant individuals.

How were Malcolm X's beliefs different from those of Martin Luther King, Jr.?

TURNING POINT

Why is the assassination of Martin Luther King, Jr., in 1968 considered a turning point in history?

THE VOTING RIGHTS ACT OF 1965 Many southern states continued to resist civil rights legislation and Supreme Court rulings. Southern resistance to civil rights laws angered Johnson. He proposed new legislation, which was passed as the **Voting Rights Act of 1965.** This bill

- put an end to literacy tests—tests of a person's ability to read and write that had often been misused to bar African American voters.
- authorized federal examiners to register voters in areas suspected of denying African Americans the right to vote.
- directed the attorney general of the United States to take legal action against states that continued to use poll taxes in state elections.

CHANGES IN THE CIVIL RIGHTS MOVEMENT The summer of 1964 was known as "Freedom Summer" for its many demonstrations, protests, voter registration drives, and the March on Washington. Freedom Summer and the passage of the Voting Rights Act a year later marked highpoints of the civil rights movement.

By the mid-1960s, some civil rights activists became frustrated that the new legislation had not improved conditions enough. Some demanded "Black Power," stressing that African Americans should take total control of the political and economic aspects of their lives. Some advocated the use of violence. Meanwhile, more moderate leaders continued to call for nonviolent methods of protest. These splits weakened the effectiveness of the civil rights movement.

A new, more militant leader, Malcolm X, began to attract a following from African Americans who were frustrated by the pace of the civil rights movement. Malcolm X spoke against integration, instead promoting black nationalism, a belief in the separate identity and racial unity of the African American community. A member of the separatist group Nation of Islam until 1964, Malcolm X broke with that group to form his own religious organization, called Muslim Mosque, Inc. After a pilgrimage to the Muslim holy city of Mecca in Saudi Arabia, during which he saw millions of Muslims of all races worshipping peacefully together, he changed his views about integration and began to work toward a more unified civil rights movement. He had made enemies, though, and in February 1965, he was assassinated at a New York City rally.

In 1964 and 1965, frustration at the discrimination in housing, education, and employment boiled over into riots in New York City, Rochester, and the Watts neighborhood of Los Angeles. In Watts alone, 34 people were killed, and more than a thousand were injured.

The federal government set up the Kerner Commission to investigate the cause of the rioting. It concluded that the riots were a result of the anger that had been building in many of America's inner cities.

ASSASSINATIONS Dr. Martin Luther King, Jr., had been awarded the Nobel Peace Prize in 1964 "for the furtherance of brotherhood among men." He remained a leading speaker for African American rights, even as splits developed in the civil rights movement.

As a supporter of the underprivileged and the needy, King went to Memphis, Tennessee, in April 1968 to back a sanitation workers' strike. There he was shot and killed by a white assassin. The death of the leading spokesperson for nonviolence set off new rounds of rioting in American cities.

Just two months after King's death, Senator Robert F. Kennedy, brother of the late President and now a presidential candidate committed to civil rights, was assassinated. The shock of these deaths and the increasing urban violence made the goals of King and the Kennedys seem far off to many Americans.

THE WOMEN'S RIGHTS MOVEMENT

Like African Americans, women had long been denied equal rights in the United States. The successes of the African American civil rights movement in the 1960s highlighted the need for organized action by women to achieve similar goals.

Past Successes, New Goals

The women's rights movement was not just a product of the 1960s. The struggle for equality had been a long one. Some of the key events in the struggle are listed below.

1848   The Seneca Falls Convention marked the beginning of the organized women's rights movement in this nation.

1868   Passage of the Fifteenth Amendment granted the vote to African American men but not to any women. Susan B. Anthony arranged to have a women's suffrage amendment introduced in Congress. It was defeated there, but Anthony and others continued the fight.

1920   Ratification of the Nineteenth Amendment gave women the right to vote.

1940s   Thousands of women took jobs in war-related industries.

By the 1960s, women had exercised the right to vote for 40 years, yet women still had not achieved equal status with men economically and socially. Women's groups renewed demands for a variety of goals including more job opportunities, equality of pay with men, and an end to discrimination based on sex.

Presidents Kennedy and Johnson appointed no women to major posts in their administrations. Yet in those years, fundamental changes occurred.

- More and more women entered fields that men had traditionally dominated, such as law, medicine, engineering, and the sciences.

- In 1963, Betty Friedan wrote *The Feminine Mystique,* a book arguing that society had forced American women out of the job market and

ANALYZING DOCUMENTS

According to the line graph below, between which years did the number of women working outside the home first exceed 50 percent?

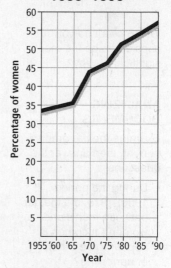

Women Working Outside the Home, 1955–1990

Source: *Statistical Abstract of the United States*

READING STRATEGY

Organizing Information

In the space below, list five important events of the women's rights movement of the 1960s and early 1970s.

1.

2.

3.

4.

5.

Which event do you consider to be the most significant? Why?

ANALYZING DOCUMENTS

Examine the bar graph at right, then answer the questions.

• During the period 1950–1975, did the gap between men's and women's incomes appear to be widening or narrowing?

• What might explain this trend?

back into the home after World War II. She said that not all women were content with the role of homemaker and that more job opportunities should be open to women.

• Title VII of the Civil Rights Act of 1964 barred job discrimination on the basis of sex as well as race.

• The National Organization for Women (NOW) formed in 1966 to push for legislation guaranteeing equality for women.

• Congress approved the **Equal Rights Amendment** (ERA) in 1972 and sent it to the states for ratification. The amendment stated "equality of rights under the law shall not be denied or abridged by the United States or any state on account of sex."

• The Equal Opportunity Act of 1972 required employers to pay equal wages for equal work.

• Title IX of the Educational Amendments Act of 1972 gave female college athletes the right to the same financial support as male athletes.

Median Incomes of Men and Women, 1950–1975

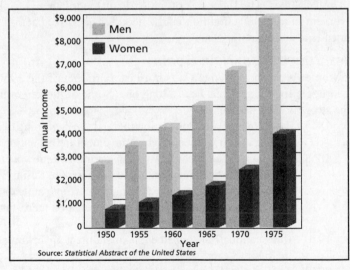

Source: *Statistical Abstract of the United States*

In the landmark case of *Roe* v. *Wade* (1973), the Supreme Court ruled that a woman's right to terminate a pregnancy is constitutionally protected. Laws making abortion a crime were overturned because they violated a woman's right to privacy; the Supreme Court held that the states could only limit abortion after the first six months of pregnancy. Challenges to the decision in *Roe* v. *Wade* continued for decades afterward.

AFFIRMATIVE ACTION Some of the laws guaranteeing equal opportunities for women, African Americans, and other minority groups called for **affirmative action.** This meant taking positive steps to eliminate the effects of past discrimination in hiring. In practice, it often meant giving preference to members of such groups when hiring workers or accepting applicants to schools. These affirmative action programs were begun during the Johnson administration of the 1960s.

Adapted from The New Yorker

"Founding Fathers? How come no Founding Mothers?"

WOMEN'S RIGHTS VOCABULARY The term *feminism* refers to the belief that women should have the same economic, social, and political rights as men. The women's rights movement is sometimes called the feminist movement.

The term *sexism* refers to beliefs or practices that discriminate against a person on the basis of sex. The women's movement directed its efforts at removing sexist terminology, practices, and literature from American business and education.

The term *glass ceiling* was used to describe a mid-level position to which women might be promoted in many jobs but which allowed women to see upper-level, better-paying positions that were held by men and were not open to women. This type of unspoken discrimination occurred in all types of employment and can still be found today.

Setbacks for the Women's Rights Movement

Not all Americans supported the women's rights movement. Some argued that women already had equal rights. Others claimed that those goals undermined "traditional" values. In 1971, President Nixon vetoed a bill that would have provided for a national system of day care for the children of working mothers. His reason for vetoing the bill was that he believed that the family rather than the government should be responsible for the care of children.

Critics also charged that affirmative action programs were a kind of reverse discrimination, in which white males lost chances at jobs to less-qualified women and members of minority groups. In 1979, the Supreme Court ruled in *Regents of the University of California* v. *Bakke* that the school used racial quotas when deciding

PREPARING FOR THE EXAM

Why did the proposed Equal Rights Amendment cause controversy?

ANALYZING DOCUMENTS

According to the graphic organizer below, how did Latinos gain political strength at a national level in the 1960s?

on applicants to medical school. This meant that Allan Bakke was rejected admission to the medical school in favor of less-qualified applicants. The Court ruled that Bakke had been denied equal protection under the Fourteenth Amendment. It nevertheless found that other affirmative action programs may be constitutional.

The proposed ERA generated tremendous controversy. Opponents claimed that the women's rights movement had led to rising divorce rates, increasing numbers of abortions, and the growing acceptance and recognition of homosexuality—all threats to traditional values, said critics. Ratification of the ERA, they argued, would cause still more problems for American society. By the 1982 deadline, the ERA was three states short of ratification and thus was defeated.

In the late 1980s and 1990s, women's groups began to demand legal protection against physical and mental abuse directed toward both women and children. Lawsuits began to occur to protest sexual harassment, especially in the workplace.

OTHER GROUPS STRUGGLE FOR THEIR RIGHTS

In addition to the African American and women's civil rights movements, Latinos, Native Americans, and disabled Americans fought for equality and justice.

Latino Victories in the 1960s

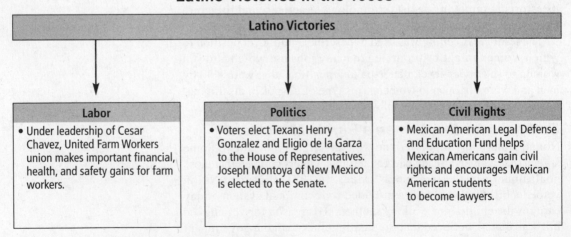

Latino Victories

Labor	**Politics**	**Civil Rights**
• Under leadership of Cesar Chavez, United Farm Workers union makes important financial, health, and safety gains for farm workers.	• Voters elect Texans Henry Gonzalez and Eligio de la Garza to the House of Representatives. Joseph Montoya of New Mexico is elected to the Senate.	• Mexican American Legal Defense and Education Fund helps Mexican Americans gain civil rights and encourages Mexican American students to become lawyers.

Latinos began to organize against discrimination in the 1960s.

Latinos

Latinos—people whose family origins are in the Spanish-speaking nations of Latin America—have often been denied equal opportunities in employment, education, and housing. The largest group of Latinos is Mexican Americans, often known as Chicanos.

By the early 1960s, large numbers of Chicanos were employed as farm workers, often migrants. They faced problems of discrimination, poor pay, and hazardous working conditions. In 1962, a Chicano named Cesar Chavez emerged as a labor leader, starting a union for migrant farm workers, a union that became the **United Farm Workers.** Chavez's work was especially helpful to grape and lettuce pickers in their struggle for higher wages and better working conditions.

Chavez, like Dr. Martin Luther King, Jr., believed in nonviolent methods. Chavez continued to serve as spokesperson for farm workers until his death in 1993. He helped raise the self-esteem of the nation's growing Latino population by making their contributions to the American economy and culture more visible.

Native Americans

In the twentieth century, some conditions for Native Americans had improved. They were granted full citizenship in 1924, and Franklin Roosevelt's Indian New Deal of the 1930s had changed earlier government policies and aimed to rebuild tribes and promote tribal cultures. As the circumstances of the Native Americans improved, their population began to increase.

Nevertheless, conditions remained poor for many Native Americans. The per capita income of Native Americans was well below the poverty level. Rates of alcoholism and suicide were the highest of any ethnic group in the United States. Unemployment rates were far higher than the national average, and the high-school dropout rate was near 50 percent.

NATIVE AMERICANS ORGANIZE In the early 1950s, Congress had enacted legislation to lessen government control over reservations, but this led to the loss of property by many Native Americans and forced some onto welfare. During the Johnson administration, the government tried to improve conditions by starting new programs to raise the standard of housing and to provide medical facilities, educational institutions, and vocational training.

Native Americans began demanding greater responsibility in making decisions that affected their lives. Native Americans took inspiration from the African American civil rights movement. They began to call for "Red Power" and formed the **American Indian Movement** (AIM) to further their goals.

In 1969, a group of militant Native Americans seized Alcatraz Island in San Francisco Bay with the demand that it be turned into an Indian cultural center. In 1972, members of AIM occupied the Bureau of Indian Affairs in Washington, D. C., demanding rights and property they said were guaranteed to them under earlier treaties. In 1973, AIM members occupied the reservation village of Wounded Knee, South Dakota, site

READING STRATEGY

Organizing Information
Latinos also faced problems of discrimination. What are two ways that they fought for equal rights?

1.

2.

 KEY THEMES AND CONCEPTS

Government
How did the federal government change its policies toward Native Americans in the early 1900s? What were the effects of these changes?

PREPARING FOR THE EXAM

- What problems did Native Americans face in the 1960s and 1970s?

- How did they draw attention to their plight?

of the last battle in the Indian wars of the 1800s. The takeover lasted two months, with the militants demanding changes in policies toward Native Americans.

Although these actions did not always achieve Native Americans' goals, the agitation did draw attention to their problems. Throughout the 1970s, court decisions tried to remedy earlier treaty violations. By 1989, Native Americans had been awarded more than $80 million as compensation for lost land.

In addition, government policies changed again. The Indian Self-Determination and Education Assistance Act of 1975 gave Native Americans more control over reservations. Also, the post of Assistant Secretary of the Interior for Indian Affairs was created in 1975 to protect Native American interests.

NEW YORK STATE AND NATIVE AMERICANS   Some major court cases involving Native American rights have taken place in New York State. For example, in *County of Oneida* v. *Oneida Indian Nation of New York State* (1985), the Supreme Court ruled that Native Americans had a right to sue to enforce their original land rights. The Court further stated that New York's purchase of 872 acres from the Oneida Indians in 1795 was illegal, because it was neither witnessed by federal agents nor approved by Congress. Both these steps were required under the federal Indian Trade and Non-Intercourse Act of 1793. Such court decisions have encouraged other Native American groups in New York State and across the nation to sue for return of lost lands.

More recent controversies have arisen in northern New York regarding the St. Regis Indian Reservation, or Akwesasne Mohawk Reservation as it is also known. Violence erupted on the 14,000-acre reservation, which stretches into southern Canada, in the spring of 1990. At issue was gambling on the reservation. The incident involved questions of which Native American group controlled reservation policy as well as the role New York State has in dealing with the reservation.

Disabled Americans

Americans with disabilities have endured a long struggle to gain their full rights in American society. In the nation's early years, care of the handicapped was usually left to their families, often resulting in the neglect or abuse of the disabled. Reformers began to work for change in the early 1800s. For example, in Massachusetts, Dorothea Dix led a campaign to improve conditions for mentally ill people, resulting in the founding of more than 30 state institutions to care for them.

Educational opportunities for hearing-impaired students were gradually widened. Gallaudet College in Washington, D.C., was founded in 1857, and today that institution is internationally recognized for its educational programs for hearing-impaired students. In the late 1980s, its students successfully demonstrated to win appointment of a hearing-impaired person as president of the college. In New York

---

♀ KEY THEMES AND CONCEPTS

Constitutional Principles
The Supreme Court case *County of Oneida* v. *Oneida Indian Nation of New York State* (1985) established that Native American tribes had the right to sue state governments to reclaim their tribal lands.

• Why is *County of Oneida v. Oneida Indian Nation of New York State* important in the struggle for Native American equality?

READING STRATEGY

Reinforcing Main Ideas
How has the view of people with handicaps changed from the nation's early years to today?

State, the National Technical Institute for the Deaf at the Rochester Institute of Technology is another school for the hearing impaired whose programs have won wide recognition. The school provides deaf students with college training in technical and scientific fields.

Educational opportunities were also widened for visually-impaired students. In 1829, the Perkins School for the Blind opened in Boston and quickly became a model for schools elsewhere. Although such schools still exist and serve important functions, many visually-impaired students today attend regular schools under a practice called **mainstreaming.** The idea behind mainstreaming is to bring handicapped students out of the isolation of special schools and into the "mainstream" of student life.

NEW PROGRAMS FOR PEOPLE WITH DISABILITIES The federal government has been especially active in setting out new programs and policies for people with disabilities.

- President Kennedy established the Presidential Commission on Mental Retardation to study and highlight the problems of the mentally handicapped individuals in American society.
- President Kennedy also backed the establishment of the Special Olympics to provide both a showcase and encouragement for athletes with handicapping conditions.
- The Rehabilitation Act of 1973, Section 504, barred discrimination against people with disabilities in any programs, activities, and facilities that were supported by federal funds.
- The Education for All Handicapped Children Act of 1975 ensured a free, appropriate education for children with disabilities, including special education and related services.
- The **Americans with Disabilities Act of 1990** prohibited discrimination in employment, public accommodation, transportation, state and local government services, and telecommunications. Benefits of the act included greater accessibility to public buildings and transportation for people who use wheelchairs and the availability of electronic devices to allow hearing-impaired people to use telephones and enjoy movies.

Activism by disabled veterans, especially from the Vietnam War, drew increased attention to the needs of people with disabilities. Celebrities have also taken up the cause of working for increased congressional funding of medical research. Some examples include Elizabeth Taylor for AIDS research, Christopher Reeve for spinal cord injuries research, and Michael J. Fox for Parkinson's disease.

Schools began to mainstream students with disabilities into regular classrooms. Students who previously might have attended special schools with other students with similar disabilities have begun to attend regular public schools in a major attempt at deinstitutionalization. These efforts are known as programs of inclusion.

KEY THEMES AND CONCEPTS
Diversity
What is the purpose behind the practice of mainstreaming?

READING STRATEGY
Analyzing Cause and Effect
How did the Americans With Disabilities Act (1990) change the lives of people with handicaps?

PREPARING FOR THE EXAM

On the examination, you will need to understand the major domestic programs of the 1960s.

In the space below, give two provisions of President Kennedy's "New Frontier" program and the reasons for these provisions.

1.

2.

⚷ **KEY THEMES AND CONCEPTS**

Government
Johnson's domestic programs are an example of the concept of change. He often referred to his efforts as the War on Poverty. Today, forty years later, Medicare is changing as it struggles to meet the needs of the growing senior citizen population.

THE NEW FRONTIER AND THE GREAT SOCIETY

Not all legislation on domestic issues during the 1960s concerned civil rights. Kennedy's programs, known as the **New Frontier,** and Johnson's, known as the **Great Society,** continued and expanded upon traditions begun during Franklin Roosevelt's New Deal of the 1930s.

Kennedy

- *The space program* Following the successful launch of a Soviet cosmonaut in 1961, the first man in space, President Kennedy committed the nation to a space program with the goal of landing a person on the moon by the end of the 1960s. In July 1969, six years after Kennedy's death, that goal was met when astronaut Neil Armstrong stepped onto the moon's surface. The effort had cost some $25.4 billion.
- *The Peace Corps* This program sent thousands of American volunteers to developing nations where they trained local people in technical, educational, and health programs. The Peace Corps program was intended to offset the growth of communism in such nations. The program is still in existence.

Johnson

- *The VISTA program* The Volunteers in Service to America (VISTA) program was meant as a domestic Peace Corps, aiding poor citizens in rural and impoverished areas.
- *The Office of Economic Opportunity* Set up in 1964, this was the directing agency in President Johnson's War on Poverty. Its branches included Project Head Start (to provide education for preschoolers from low-income families), Project Upward Bound (to assist high-school students from low-income families to attend college), and the Job Corps (to provide vocational training for high-school dropouts).
- *The Elementary and Secondary Education Act* This 1965 measure provided more than $1 billion in federal aid to education, with the greatest share going to school districts with large numbers of students from low-income families. Sections of the bill required that schools accepting the money be integrated.
- *Medicare* Amendments to the Social Security Act provided health insurance and some types of health care to those over the age of 65. A Medicaid program provided states with funds to help the needy who were not covered by Medicare.
- *Department of Housing and Urban Development* This cabinet post was meant to oversee federal efforts to improve housing and aid economic development of cities. Its first head, Robert C. Weaver, was the first African American to hold a cabinet post.

FOREIGN POLICY IN THE 1960S

United States foreign policy under Kennedy and Johnson continued Truman's cold war policy of containment of communism. In Section 3, you will review how this policy led the nation into the **Vietnam War.** In this section, you will see how cold war concerns affected other aspects of the United States foreign policy in the 1960s.

A History of Involvement

As you remember, the United States has been deeply involved in the affairs of Latin America since early in its history. Latin American nations often resented such intervention, and United States policies have left a legacy of anger and hostility.

Some of the key events in United States-Latin American relations are listed on the next page. For additional discussion of these events, see Unit 3, Section 2.

Key Developments in United States— Latin American Relations

The Monroe Doctrine	In 1823, President Monroe warned the nations of Europe not to interfere with the nations of the Western Hemisphere, thus assuming the role of protector of the Western Hemisphere. However, this policy earned the United States a negative image in much of Latin America.
Spanish-American War (1898)	Victory in a war with Spain brought the United States an overseas empire. It also increased the nation's role in Latin America by giving it possession of Puerto Rico and much control over the government of Cuba.
Panama Canal (1901–1914)	The United States gained control over land where it wanted to build a canal by interfering in the internal affairs of Colombia. As a result, the United States made many enemies in Latin America.
Roosevelt Corollary (1904)	Under this addition to the Monroe Doctrine, President Theodore Roosevelt claimed the United States had the right to intervene in the affairs of Latin American nations guilty of "chronic wrongdoing."
"Dollar Diplomacy" (early 1900s)	This term describe President Taft's plan of increasing U.S. influence in Latin America through economic investment backed by military force.
"Good Neighbor" Policy (1933)	This was President Franklin Roosevelt's effort to improve relations with Latin America by stressing increased cooperation.

⚷ KEY THEMES AND CONCEPTS

Examine the table at left, then answer these questions.

• Which event resulted in the United States becoming an imperial nation?

• Which development was intended to improve relations with Latin American nations?

Kennedy and Latin America

Some of President Kennedy's most significant foreign policy decisions involved Latin America.

THE ALLIANCE FOR PROGRESS Kennedy hoped to improve relations with Latin America and stop the spread of communism there through the Alliance for Progress, which pledged $20 billion to help economic development in the region. However, funds often went to aid repressive governments simply because they were anticommunist.

THE BAY OF PIGS After President Kennedy took office, he approved a CIA plan to overthrow Fidel Castro, the communist leader of Cuba. The plan called for Cuban exiles—supplied with U.S. arms, material, and training—to invade Cuba and set off a popular uprising against Castro. The invasion took place on April 17, 1961, at a location called the Bay of Pigs, about 90 miles from Havana. No uprising followed, and Castro's troops quickly crushed the invading forces, to the embarrassment of Kennedy and the United States government.

THE CUBAN MISSILE CRISIS Fearing another U.S. invasion attempt, Castro agreed to a Soviet plan to base nuclear missiles aimed at the United States in Cuba. Kennedy learned of the plan while the bases were under construction. On October 22, 1962, he announced a naval blockade of Cuba and demanded that the Soviets withdraw the missiles. The **Cuban missile crisis** brought the United States and the Soviet Union to the brink of war, but the Soviets backed down and withdrew their missiles.

Kennedy had clearly demonstrated that the United States would not tolerate a Soviet presence in the Western Hemisphere just 90 miles from its shores. By doing so, Kennedy also helped the nation recover some of the prestige it had lost in the failed Bay of Pigs invasion.

U.S. - Soviet Tensions, 1961–1963

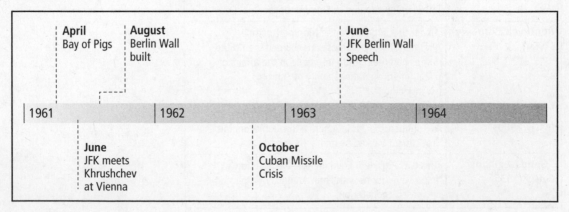

In 1963, the United States, Soviet Union, and Great Britain signed a nuclear test ban treaty in which they agreed not to test nuclear weapons in the air, in outer space, or under the sea. Underground testing was permitted.

Kennedy and Berlin

Since World War II, the division of Germany into a Communist East Germany and a democratic West Germany had added to cold war tensions. President Kennedy and Soviet Premier Nikita Khrushchev met in Austria in June 1961 to discuss relations between the United States and the Soviet Union. Khrushchev thought that the Bay of Pigs disaster revealed American weakness, and he tried to threaten Kennedy into removing NATO troops from Europe. Instead, Kennedy increased U.S. military and financial commitment to West Germany.

Response to the American moves came in August 1961, when the East German government built a wall between East and West Berlin. The **Berlin Wall** was meant to stop the flood of East Germans escaping to freedom in the West and quickly became a symbol of tyranny. In June 1963, Kennedy visited West Berlin, renewing the American commitment to defend that city and Western Europe. In a famous speech, he said that he and all people who wanted freedom were citizens of Berlin.

The Berlin Wall stood as a strong cold war symbol until 1989. In that year, political change sweeping through Eastern Europe led East Germany to tear down the wall. By October 1990, the rapid political changes in the region had led to the reunification of the two Germanys as a single nation for the first time since the end of World War II.

IMPACT OF KENNEDY'S DEATH Kennedy's energetic voice for world democracy and his multilingual wife, Jacqueline, helped to make friends for the United States in many areas of the world. His tragic and unexpected assassination in November 1963 caused an outpouring of grief from around the world as dozens of foreign heads of state came hurriedly to Washington, D.C., for Kennedy's funeral.

ANALYZING DOCUMENTS

Examine the timeline on page 316, then answer these questions.

- How many years passed between the fall of the Berlin Wall and the reunification of Germany?

- Which event occurred first: the meeting between President Kennedy and Soviet Premier Khrushchev, or the building of the Berlin Wall?

Limits of Power: Turmoil at Home & Abroad: 1965–1972

⭐ THE BIG IDEA

Fears of Communist expansion in Southeast Asia led to the United States' involvement in the Vietnam War. During this period

- President Johnson escalated the war.

- student protests became part of the anti-war movement.

- the political and social upheaval of the 1960s divided Americans.

- President Nixon oversaw a cease fire agreement that allowed for U.S. withdrawal from Vietnam.

🔑 KEY TERMS

Gulf of Tonkin Resolution
hawks
doves
Vietnamization
War Powers Act

SECTION OVERVIEW

The fear of communist expansion led the United States to become increasingly involved in Southeast Asia. This involvement led to the Vietnam War—the longest war in United States history. As the war dragged on, American support began to erode. The combination of negative public opinion and the inability of the military to achieve clear-cut victory led to a gradual withdrawal from the war. Meanwhile, great social and cultural changes were taking place in many parts of American society.

KEY THEMES AND CONCEPTS

As you review this section, take special note of the following key themes and concepts:

Foreign Policy Why did the United States become involved in Vietnam?

Presidential Decisions and Actions How did the decisions made by Presidents Johnson and Nixon affect how the Vietnam War was conducted?

Change What social and cultural changes developed in the 1960s?

Constitutional Principles How did Congress limit the power of the President in wartime?

KEY PEOPLE

Lyndon B. Johnson
Richard Nixon
Henry Kissinger

Fear of communist expansion led the United States to become deeply involved in Southeast Asia. Review the chart below to learn about the growing involvement of the United States in this region.

Unrest in Asia, 1945–1960

Date	Event
September 1945	World War II ends in Asia; Ho Chi Minh, a member of the Communist party since 1920, proclaims the Democratic Republic of Vietnam.
1946–1949	France, which had controlled Vietnam since the nineteenth century, appoints a "puppet leader" named Bao Dai, who is ineffective against the power of Ho Chi Minh.
1949	Mao Zedong declares the (Communist) People's Republic of China; recognizes the Vietnamese government of Ho Chi Minh in 1950.
1950–1953	United States fights the Korean War and provides the French with financial aid in their struggle to hang onto Vietnam.
1953–1954	President Eisenhower debates how far the United States should go in backing the French.
1954	The forces of Ho Chi Minh defeat the French at Dienbienphu; Geneva Accords divide Vietnam at the 17th parallel; North and South Vietnam agree to hold elections in 1956 to reunite the country; the United States joins with seven Asian and European nations in the Southeast Asia Treaty Organization (SEATO), an anticommunist pact which extends protection to Vietnam.
1955	United States under Eisenhower increases aid to South Vietnam.
1956	South Vietnamese President Ngo Dinh Diem, fearing the popularity of Ho Chi Minh, refuses to hold elections scheduled under the Geneva Accords.
1960	Ho Chi Minh recognizes the Vietcong, Communist guerrillas in South Vietnam, as the National Liberation Front (NLF) of Vietnam; President Kennedy sends Vice President Johnson to study the crisis in Vietnam.

KENNEDY AND VIETNAM

President Kennedy shared Eisenhower's belief in the domino theory. He, therefore, continued to support the Diem regime. By 1963, the number of United States "advisers" in South Vietnam totaled about 17,000. That year, 489 Americans died in the fighting in Vietnam.

Debate Over Involvement

American advisers urged Diem to adopt reforms to broaden his support. Diem, however, brutally suppressed all opponents and ruled as a dictator. On November 2, 1963, the South Vietnamese military overthrew Diem, with the knowledge and approval of the United States. Around the same time, the White House announced that it intended to withdraw all United States military personnel from

GEOGRAPHY IN HISTORY

Laos shares a long border with North Vietnam. During the Vietnam War, the dense jungle terrain made it difficult for U.S. and South Vietnamese forces to cut off the supply lines that ran between Laos and North Vietnam.

• How might this role as supplier have an impact on Laos later in the war?

KEY THEMES AND CONCEPTS

Presidential Decisions and Actions

Without a formal declaration of war by Congress, Presidents Eisenhower, Kennedy, and Johnson all sent U.S. military forces to Vietnam.

• What authorized these Presidents to take these actions?

Vietnam, 1968

Vietnam by 1965. Kennedy was unable to keep this promise, because he was assassinated in 1963.

JOHNSON AND ESCALATION

Under the Constitution, only Congress can declare war. However, by 1964, three Presidents—Eisenhower, Kennedy, and Johnson—had sent United States aid and troops into Vietnam. Each did so by acting as the commander in chief of the nation's military forces.

The Tonkin Gulf Resolution

On August 4, 1964, President Johnson escalated the war dramatically. He announced on television that American destroyers had been the victim of an unprovoked attack by North Vietnamese gun boats. (It later appeared that the ships might have been protecting South Vietnamese boats headed into North Vietnamese waters.) The next day, Johnson asked Congress for the authority to order air strikes against North Vietnam. With only two dissenting votes, Congress passed the **Gulf of Tonkin Resolution.** The resolution empowered "the President, as commander in chief, to take all necessary measures to repel any armed attack against the forces of the United States and to prevent further aggression." Johnson used the resolution to justify expansion of the war. By April 1965, U.S. planes regularly bombed North Vietnam.

A GUERRILLA WAR At first, United States military leaders expected that the nation's superior technology would guarantee victory. However, they soon found themselves bogged down in a guerrilla war fought in the jungles of Southeast Asia. The enemy did not wear uniforms, and no clear battlefront emerged. Thousands of Vietnamese casualties occurred each month as the United States dropped more bombs on Vietnam, an area about twice the size of New York State, than it had used on Nazi Germany during the heaviest months of fighting during World War II.

REASONS FOR WAR The massive commitment in Vietnam raised questions in the minds of many Americans about why the United States got involved in Vietnam and why it stayed there. The administration argued that the United States was involved in Vietnam to prevent the fall of Vietnam to communism, to stop the rise of aggressor governments, and to protect the nation's position as a superpower and defender of democracy. However, as the war dragged on, many Americans began to question these motives.

Resistance to the War

By late 1965, an antiwar movement had begun to take shape in the United States.

HAWKS AND DOVES In Congress, there were differences of opinion concerning the war. Some stood solidly behind the President and argued in favor of victory at any cost. These members were known as **hawks.** Those who favored immediate withdrawal and an end to the war were known as **doves.**

STUDENT PROTESTS College campuses became centers of political protest against the war. Students organized a new form of protest called teach-ins, or meetings in which speakers, usually promoting unconditional American withdrawal from Vietnam, held study sessions and rallies. The strongest antiwar group in the 1960s was Students for a Democratic Society (SDS), founded in 1960. SDS was antiestablishment, or against big business and government. It led demonstrations, sit-ins, draft-card burnings, and protests against universities with "pro-establishment" regulations.

By 1969, the organization had collapsed into a number of splinter groups. However, SDS's legacy of protest against authority remained a strong force into the 1970s.

⚲ KEY THEMES AND CONCEPTS

Reform Movements

College campuses became centers of the antiwar movement in the United States. Students organized teach-ins and other protests aimed at getting the Johnson administration to end U.S. involvement in Vietnam. Protest marches featuring people of all ages took place in major cities.

- In what different ways did young people respond to the draft?

PROTEST MARCHES People of all ages joined in protest marches against the war. The first huge march took place in Washington, D.C., in 1965. In 1967, some 300,000 Americans marched in New York City. That same year, another 50,000 tried to shut down the Pentagon.

DRAFT RESISTERS By 1968, about 10,000 draft resisters, people unwilling to serve in the military after being drafted, had fled the country for Canada. The nation's youth became increasingly divided as some chose to fight for the United States in Vietnam, while others sought deferments to go to college. A large number of minorities, who could not afford the cost of college, responded to the draft and went to Vietnam. The attitude of American youth became increasingly hostile toward the Johnson administration and all war-related issues.

THE 1960S—POLITICAL AND SOCIAL UPHEAVAL

Some political analysts who studied the events of 1968 believed the nation had survived one of the biggest tests to its political institutions since the Civil War. The 1960s had been shaped by two movements: the civil rights movement and the antiwar movement. The political turmoil of the decade helped produce great social upheaval, especially among the nation's youth.

Cultural Changes

Some young people became disillusioned with traditional American values. For the first time in United States history, thousands of Americans flaunted the use of illegal drugs, often popularized in rock music.

Many young Americans referred to themselves as hippies or flower children. They claimed to be searching for a freer, simpler way of life. Communal living attracted thousands of youths who adopted lifestyles foreign to older Americans. Some spoke of a generation gap between youth and people over 30.

The civil rights movement and the Vietnam War also divided Americans. The assassinations of Robert Kennedy and Dr. Martin Luther King, Jr., heightened emotions.

NIXON AND VIETNAM

By 1969, President Nixon faced a national crisis. The Vietnam War had turned into the nation's most costly war. American support for the war was at an all-time low.

Winding Down the War

Nixon did not bring an end to the war right away. In fact, for a time, he widened American military activities, attacking North Vietnamese supply routes out of Laos and Cambodia.

Key Events of 1968

Month	Event
January	• North Vietnam launches the Tet (New Year's) offensive, using Soviet-made jets and weapons for the first time.
March	• Eugene McCarthy, a peace candidate and leading "dove," wins the Democratic presidential primary in New Hampshire.
	• Robert Kennedy announces his candidacy for the presidency.
	• President Johnson announces that he will not seek reelection and that he will devote the remainder of his term to trying to end the war. The war had hurt his popularity with voters.
April	• American forces in Vietnam reach 549,000; combat deaths climb to 22,951.
	• North Vietnam announces its willingness to enter into peace talks.
	• An assassin claims the life of Dr. Martin Luther King, Jr.
May	• Preliminary peace talks with the North Vietnamese begin, but serious negotiations do not take place for several years.
June	• An assassin claims the life of Robert Kennedy shortly after his victory in the California Democratic presidential primary.
August	• The Democratic National Convention nominates Hubert Humphrey amid the worst political rioting and demonstrations any convention has ever experienced; Humphrey (Johnson's Vice President) inherits a divided party and seeks election in a divided nation.
	• The Republican National Convention nominates Richard Nixon, whose only serious challenger is Ronald Reagan.
	• The American Independent party nominates Governor George Wallace of Alabama, showing that a third party could attract white-backlash voters who opposed the civil rights movement.
November	• Nixon wins the 1968 election with 43.4% of the popular vote; Humphrey claims 42.7%; Wallace takes 13.5%.

VIETNAMIZATION Nixon called for **Vietnamization** of the war, or a takeover of the ground fighting by Vietnamese soldiers. Both Kennedy and Johnson had favored this approach, but neither had been able to make it work. While Nixon promoted Vietnamization, he also bombed neighboring Cambodia, which he claimed served as a base for North Vietnamese guerrillas.

The bombings triggered a large student protest at Kent State University in Ohio. By the time the National Guard broke up the demonstration, four students lay dead and nine others wounded. More

♀ KEY THEMES AND
⌐ CONCEPTS
Presidential Decisions and Actions
What impact did President Nixon's decision to bomb Cambodia have on student protests?

and more Americans were questioning the role of the United States in Vietnam, yet President Nixon increased bombing raids on North Vietnam throughout 1970.

PEACE WITH HONOR Henry Kissinger, Nixon's chief foreign policy adviser, met in Paris with North Vietnamese officials seeking an end to the war. For several years, negotiations remained deadlocked. Finally, on January 15, 1973, Nixon announced that "peace with honor" had been reached and that a cease-fire would soon take effect.

The War Powers Act

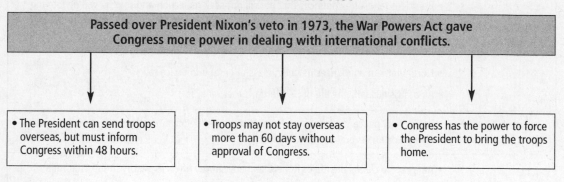

Passed over President Nixon's veto in 1973, the War Powers Act gave Congress more power in dealing with international conflicts.

- The President can send troops overseas, but must inform Congress within 48 hours.

- Troops may not stay overseas more than 60 days without approval of Congress.

- Congress has the power to force the President to bring the troops home.

The War Powers Act

READING STRATEGY

Problem Solving
Why do you think Congress passed the War Powers Act over President Nixon's veto?

In November 1973, Congress passed the War Powers Act over Nixon's veto. This law helped reverse the precedent set by the Gulf of Tonkin Resolution, which gave the President sweeping powers in Vietnam. The **War Powers Act** included the following provisions:

- The President had to notify Congress within 48 hours of sending troops into a foreign country. At that time, the President would have to give Congress a full accounting of the decision.
- The President had to bring the troops home within 60 days unless both houses voted for them to stay.

Vietnam and Limits on United States Power

When the United States finally withdrew from Vietnam, the North Vietnamese overran South Vietnam. For two years, the United States poured billions of dollars of aid into South Vietnam. However, on April 30, 1975, the government in Saigon collapsed. Bitterness over the war still persisted. When the President asked for funds to evacuate the South Vietnamese who had helped the United States, Congress refused. In the end, some 100,000 people fled the country.

The United States had tried for 20 years to guarantee freedom to the people of South Vietnam. However, the United States ultimately could not count its efforts as a success. In the conflict, some 58,000 Americans died, and another 300,000 were wounded. The United States spent over $150 billion on the war effort. Not only did Vietnam fall to communism, but so did its neighbors Cambodia (Kampuchea) and Laos. Throughout the late 1970s and 1980s, the United States sought to understand the Vietnam experience. It was the subject of films, books, and national monuments such as the Vietnam Veterans Memorial in Washington, D.C.

Conclusions Drawn from U.S. Involvement in Vietnam

The following is a list of conclusions drawn from the Vietnam War era.

- The American political system acts in response to a variety of public pressures.
- Modern war technology is not always powerful enough if an opponent is armed with a determined spirit of nationalism.
- Successful military efforts require a well-prepared and supportive public. (Compare, for example, the differing experiences in Vietnam and World War II.)
- The United States was committed to a foreign policy that supported the global nature of United States involvement in foreign affairs.

 PREPARING FOR THE EXAM

For the examination, it will be important to understand the *significance* of historical events, not just the dates of and participants in those events.

- Overall, was the Vietnam War a success or a failure? Why?
- What enduring lessons were learned from the war?
- How has the Vietnam War continued to be remembered in American society?

4 The Trend Towards Conservatism: 1972–1985

Beginning in the early 1970s, conservatism replaced liberalism in American politics. During this period

- President Nixon opened diplomatic relations with China and shaped a policy of détente toward the Soviet Union.

- President Ford pardoned President Nixon following his resignation over the Watergate affair.

- President Reagan supported a domestic program of New Federalism during the 1980s that was begun by President Nixon.

⚷ KEY TERMS

détente
Watergate affair
stagflation
Camp David Accords
supply-side economics
"Star Wars"
Iran-Contra affair

SECTION OVERVIEW

After the upheaval of the 1960s, Richard Nixon tried to take the nation into a new direction, but the Watergate affair led to his resignation. His successors, Gerald Ford and Jimmy Carter, struggled with lingering economic troubles. In the 1980s, conservatives Ronald Reagan and George Bush came to power. After the cold war ended, the United States struggled to determine its new role in international relations.

KEY THEMES AND CONCEPTS

As you review this section, take special note of the following key themes and concepts:

Presidential Decisions and Actions How did President Nixon shape a new policy toward China and the Soviet Union?

Economic Systems How did economic problems of the 1970s present unique challenges to the Nixon, Ford, and Carter administrations?

KEY PEOPLE

Mao Zedong   Jimmy Carter
Warren Burger   Ronald Reagan
Gerald Ford   Mikhail Gorbachev

KEY SUPREME COURT CASES

Engel v. *Vitale* (1962)
Gideon v. *Wainwright* (1963)
Escobedo v. *Illinois* (1964)
Miranda v. *Arizona* (1966)
Tinker v. *Des Moines Community School District* (1969)
New York Times v. *United States* (1971)
Roe v. *Wade* (1973)

An Era of Conservatism, 1972–1990

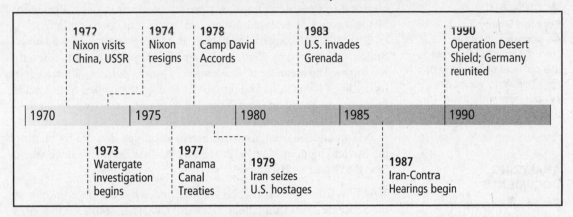

1972 Nixon visits China, USSR

1974 Nixon resigns

1978 Camp David Accords

1983 U.S. invades Grenada

1990 Operation Desert Shield; Germany reunited

1970 — 1975 — 1980 — 1985 — 1990

1973 Watergate investigation begins

1977 Panama Canal Treaties

1979 Iran seizes U.S. hostages

1987 Iran-Contra Hearings begin

FROM COLD WAR TO DETENTE

Although Nixon's main foreign policy objective was ending the Vietnam War, he had other foreign policy interests as well.

Nixon Doctrine

In 1969, Nixon announced what became known as the Nixon Doctrine. This doctrine stated that the United States would no longer provide direct military protection in Asia. Even though the Vietnam War was not yet concluded, Nixon promised Americans that there would be no more Vietnams for the United States.

A New Policy Toward China

Nixon also adopted a new foreign policy towards China. The United States had not had diplomatic relations with the People's Republic since the 1949 Communist revolution.

PRESIDENTIAL VISIT In 1971, Nixon stunned Americans by announcing that he had accepted an invitation to visit China. On February 21, 1972, Nixon arrived in China. National Security Adviser Henry Kissinger accompanied the President on his peace mission.

OPENING THE DOOR After more than 20 years of hostility, Nixon and Chinese leaders Mao Zedong and Premier Zhou Enlai agreed to open the door to normal diplomatic relations. Nixon's visit cleared the way for economic and cultural exchanges. American manufacturers, for example, now had a new market for their products. By following a policy toward China that was separate from the Soviet Union, Nixon underscored the splits that had occurred within communism.

A New Policy Toward the Soviet Union

Nixon balanced his openness with China by looking for ways to ease tensions with the Soviet Union, China's communist rival.

DÉTENTE Nixon and Kissinger shaped a policy called **détente.** The

TURNING POINT

Why is President Nixon's visit to China considered a turning point in U.S. foreign policy?

⚷ **KEY THEMES AND CONCEPTS**

Foreign Policy

As secretary of state, Henry Kissinger favored the political philosophy of *Realpolitik.* In your own words, how would you define *Realpolitik?*

ANALYZING DOCUMENTS

Based on the graphic organizer at right and your knowledge of social studies, would you characterize Nixon as a conservative or a liberal President? Provide two reasons to justify your answer.

1.

2.

goal of détente was to bring about a warming in the cold war. In contrast to President Truman's policy of containment, President Nixon's policy of détente was designed to prevent open conflict.

During the Nixon administration, the foreign policy of the United States was shaped by *Realpolitik,* a political philosophy favored by Kissinger. The meaning of *Realpolitik* is power politics. Therefore, in its dealings with China and the Soviet Union, the United States made its decisions based on what it needed to maintain its own strength— regardless of world opinion.

Nixon underscored his willingness to pursue détente by visiting the Soviet Union in May 1972. He was the first President since World War II to make such a journey.

SALT While in Moscow, Nixon opened what became known as the Strategic Arms Limitations Talks (SALT). These talks led to a 1972 agreement called the SALT Agreement. The agreement set limits on the number of defensive missile sites and strategic offensive missiles each nation would keep.

Nixon's Domestic Policies

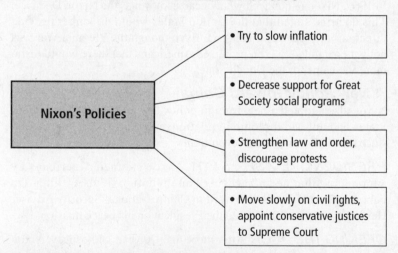

Nixon's Policies

- Try to slow inflation
- Decrease support for Great Society social programs
- Strengthen law and order, discourage protests
- Move slowly on civil rights, appoint conservative justices to Supreme Court

NIXON'S DOMESTIC POLICIES

Nixon was mainly interested in foreign affairs. He knew that he faced a Congress controlled by a Democratic majority. Because of the system of checks and balances, Nixon realized that it would be almost impossible to push Republican policies through Congress. Therefore, he limited his domestic policy goals.

Nixon's Domestic Initiatives

In 1970, the Occupational Safety and Health Administration (OSHA) was created to ensure safe and healthful working conditions for all working Americans. OSHA assists states in providing research, information, education, and training in the field of occupational safety and health.

The Environmental Protection Agency (EPA), established in 1970, coordinated federal programs to combat pollution and protect the environment.

The Clean Air Act of 1970 was a major comprehensive federal law addressing topics related to air pollution. It was amended in 1977 to set new goals since many parts of the country did not meet the standards set by the 1970 act, it was amended again in 1990 to address problems such as acid rain, ground level ozone, stratospheric ozone depletion, and air toxins.

On July 12, 1973, President Nixon united several existing federal drug agencies into the Drug Enforcement Administration (DEA), which enforced federal drug laws and conducted investigations of illegal drugs overseas.

In 1974, the Energy Reorganization Act created the Nuclear Regulatory Commission to regulate the nuclear power industry and the Energy Research and Development Administration to manage the nuclear weapon, nuclear reactor, and energy development programs of the federal government. In 1977, under President Carter, the Department of Energy was established. Today, the department ensures energy security and safety.

New Federalism

Like Eisenhower, Nixon wanted to reduce the role of the federal government and turn over more activities to the states. Nixon called this policy the New Federalism. He criticized Johnson's Great Society as too costly and tried to reduce involvement of the federal government in social welfare programs. To achieve this goal, Nixon instituted revenue sharing, a policy in which the federal government gave part of its income to the states to spend on social welfare as they saw fit.

Curbing Inflation

The Vietnam War had helped trigger inflation, which was one of Nixon's biggest domestic problems. During the 1968 election, Nixon had promised to end inflation and balance the budget. By the time he took office, prices were rising faster than they had in 20 years. Unemployment was rising too. At the same time, the nation's gross national product (GNP) was declining. To bring the economy under control, Nixon implemented a 90-day wage-price freeze in August 1971. He was the first President to impose mandatory wage-price controls in peacetime.

Nixon, Civil Rights, and the Supreme Court

Each President hopes to influence the decisions of the Supreme Court through the appointment of justices. However, the appointees do not

PREPARING FOR THE EXAM
- What did Nixon intend to accomplish with his policy of New Federalism?
- To what previous presidential policy was he reacting?

⚲ **KEY THEMES AND CONCEPTS**
Constitutional Principles

- Did these landmark Supreme Court cases provide more protection for individual rights or less protection?

- What effects did *Gideon v. Wainwright, Escobedo v. Illinois,* and *Miranda v. Arizona* have on people who were accused of a crime?

always rule as a President might expect. For example, President Eisenhower regretted his appointment of Earl Warren to the Supreme Court, because Warren made many liberal decisions that opposed Eisenhower's conservative political views.

NIXON APPOINTEES In 1969, Warren retired, and Nixon appointed Warren Burger as chief justice. During his administration, Nixon also had the opportunity to appoint three other justices. Nixon's appointees were all strict constructionists, believing that Congress and the President have only those powers specifically given to them by the Constitution. The "Nixon Court," however, did not overturn many of the liberal rulings of the 1960s, as Nixon had expected.

OTHER DOMESTIC EVENTS UNDER NIXON

Advances in the space program, an increase in the electorate, and additional rights movements occurred in the 1970s.

The Space Program

In 1969, American astronaut Neil Armstrong became the first person to walk on the moon. The triumph of seeing Armstrong plant a United States flag on the moon's surface marked a bright spot in an otherwise troubled decade.

⚲ **KEY THEMES AND CONCEPTS**
Science and Technology
Why was it significant that an American was the first person to set foot on the moon?

The Twenty-sixth Amendment

In 1971, the Twenty-sixth Amendment to the Constitution was ratified. This amendment extended the vote to people ages 18 and older. By lowering the voting age from 21 to 18, this amendment added almost 12 million new voters to the American electorate.

⚲ **KEY THEMES AND CONCEPTS**
Change

- How did passage of the 26th Amendment affect the number of voters in the United States?

- Would you say that this amendment made the United States more democratic or less democratic?

Women's Rights Movement

In the 1970s, more and more women enrolled in schools of law, medicine, engineering, and business, fields that had been traditionally reserved for men. However, full-time working women in 1971 were paid only 59 percent as much as men. Many of them also did not hold positions equal to their talents. As you read in Section 2, the Equal Rights Amendment failed to win ratification.

Consumer Rights Movement

A strong consumer rights movement also developed in the early 1970s to address abuses by major American industries. The movement was led by Ralph Nader, a young Washington lawyer who organized a protest in the 1960s against the automotive industry. Nader attracted a number of young volunteers, known as "Nader's Raiders," to his cause. They championed environmental and consumer protection.

THE WATERGATE AFFAIR

In 1972, the Republicans nominated Nixon for reelection. The Democrats selected George McGovern. Nixon claimed credit for bringing down inflation and scoring foreign policy triumphs abroad. He swept to victory, carrying the largest popular majority in United States history. Yet less than two years later, Nixon resigned from office.

- **What happened** An illegal break-in to wiretap phones in the Democratic Party headquarters with electronic surveillance equipment
- **Where** Watergate Towers, an apartment complex in Washington, D.C.
- **When** June 17, 1972
- **Who** The Committee to Reelect the President, acting with the knowledge of several high-level Nixon advisers
- **Why** To secure information to undermine the Democratic campaign against Nixon

The Cover-Up

Police captured the "burglars," who carried evidence linking them to the White House. Nixon did not know about the plan until after it happened. However, he then ordered a cover-up, which was a crime under federal law.

THE INVESTIGATION Reporters from the *Washington Post* probed into the case, now known as the **Watergate affair,** but their reports did not hinder Nixon's reelection. Then in 1973, the Senate set up a committee to look into "illegal, improper, or unethical activities" in the 1972 election. For more than a year, the Senate committee came closer and closer to implicating the President.

RESIGNATION OF AGNEW While the Watergate hearings were under way, the Justice Department charged Vice President Spiro Agnew with income tax evasion. Agnew resigned, and Nixon

KEY THEMES AND CONCEPTS

Reform Movements
The consumer rights movement of the 1960s, led by Ralph Nader, achieved important reforms, such as improved safety features in U.S.-built automobiles.

- What earlier movement in American history championed the cause of improving products available to the American people?

READING STRATEGY

Reinforcing Main Ideas
The Watergate affair was a serious scandal that brought down a President.

- What was the reason behind the Watergate break-in?
- What was Nixon's role?
- How did Nixon's involvement in the Watergate affair lead to his resignation?
- How did the Watergate affair prove that the system of checks and balances works?

appointed Gerald R. Ford, the minority leader in the House of Representatives, as Vice President.

THE TAPES In mid-1973, the Senate committee learned that the White House had kept tape recordings of key conversations between Nixon and his top aides. Nixon refused to turn over the tapes. During the summer, the committee opened the hearings to television. The televised proceedings had the appeal of a soap opera as millions of Americans watched.

NIXON RESIGNATION The situation ended when the Supreme Court ordered Nixon to surrender the tapes in its ruling in *United States* v. *Richard Nixon.* Based on evidence in the tapes, the House Judiciary Committee began voting on articles of impeachment against the President. To avoid impeachment, Nixon resigned on August 9, 1974, becoming the first President to do so. On noon of that day, Gerald Ford took the oath of office.

Gerald Ford became the first nonelected President. To fill the office of Vice President, Ford named Nelson Rockefeller, the former governor of New York. From 1974 until 1977, the United States had both a President and Vice President who had not been elected to their offices but had been appointed. Such a situation had not occurred before and has not occurred since.

Significance of Watergate

Although Nixon was never charged with any specific crimes, President Ford pardoned him. Ford hoped to end what he called "our long national nightmare." Many of Nixon's advisers, however, were found guilty of crimes and sentenced to prison. The incident showed, as Ford put it, that "the Constitution works." The system of checks and balances had stopped Nixon from placing the presidency above the law. However, one impact of the Watergate Scandal was a decline in the public's trust in government.

TURNING POINT

Why is the Watergate affair considered a turning point in U.S. history?

THE FORD ADMINISTRATION

Many people called Nixon's administration the "Imperial Presidency" because of his disregard of the Constitution. Ford tried to rebuild the image of the President. However, the Watergate affair had disillusioned many Americans.

Ford's Domestic Policies

From the start, Ford faced a number of domestic problems.

- *Nixon's Pardon* Many Americans questioned Ford's decision to pardon Nixon when so many of his advisers stood trial, were convicted, and were jailed.
- *Amnesty Plan* Ford stirred bitter debate when he offered amnesty to thousands of young men who avoided military service in Vietnam by violating draft laws, fleeing the country, or deserting the military.
- *Inflation* In 1973, the Organization of Petroleum Exporting Countries (OPEC) placed an oil embargo on the United States for its support of Israel. The price of oil and gasoline more than doubled, setting off a new round of inflation. Temporary rationing of gasoline and federal incentives to research energy alternatives helped ease shortages. Even so, Americans remained highly dependent on foreign oil. Inflation topped 10 percent, and the nation entered into its worst recession since World War II.

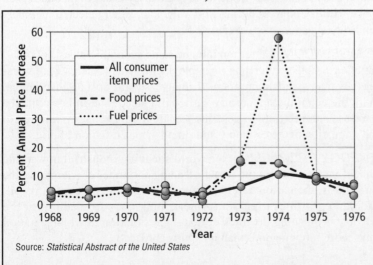

Rate of Inflation, 1968–1976

Source: *Statistical Abstract of the United States*

KEY THEMES AND CONCEPTS

Presidential Decisions and Actions

Following a Senate investigation into the Watergate affair, President Nixon resigned on August 9, 1974. Vice President Gerald Ford became the first non-elected President in U.S. history. Although President Nixon was never charged with any crime, President Ford issued a pardon to him.

- Why do you think President Ford pardoned President Nixon?

ANALYZING DOCUMENTS

Based on the chart at left and your knowledge of social studies, answer the following questions.

- What happened to fuel prices in 1973 and 1974?
- What caused the change in fuel prices in those years?
- How might the change in fuel prices and in all consumer item prices be related?

Ford's Foreign Policies

Henry Kissinger continued working with the Ford administration. Kissinger helped

- negotiate a cease-fire agreement between Egypt and Israel, thus ending the 1973 Yom Kippur War and OPEC oil embargo
- continue the policy of détente with the Soviet Union, including the sale of tons of grain to the Soviets and a hookup of Soviet and American space capsules
- oversee the end of the Vietnam War, including the withdrawal of the last American personnel from Saigon in 1975

Election of 1976

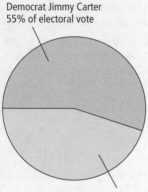

Democrat Jimmy Carter
55% of electoral vote

Republican Gerald R. Ford
45% of electoral vote

The Election of 1976

The nation's bicentennial (200th anniversary) in 1976 gave the Ford presidency a boost. However, it was not enough to help Ford completely shake off his negative association with the Nixon years. He lost a close election to the Democratic candidate, James (Jimmy) Earl Carter, former governor of Georgia.

THE CARTER ADMINISTRATION

Jimmy Carter won the 1976 election, in part, because of his appeal to the American sense of honesty and integrity. He stated a desire to return to basic American "down home" values. He wanted to prove that an "outsider" could make government more responsive to the people. However, Carter's unfamiliarity with Washington politics proved a disadvantage. First Lady Rosalynn Carter became his most trusted adviser.

Carter's Domestic Policies

Carter's presidency was made more difficult by changes that had taken place within Congress because of Watergate. Newly elected members tended to question every executive act.

"STAGFLATION" Carter ran into the same economic woes as Ford—inflation coupled with rising unemployment. The problems were worsened by many welfare programs that increased the cost of government. With the economy apparently stalled in place, economists coined a new term, **stagflation,** to describe the situation. (The term referred to the stagnation of the economy and simultaneous inflation of prices.)

ENERGY PROBLEM As the world's leading industrial power, the United States was also the world's leading consumer of energy. By the late 1970s, the nation had to import more than 40 percent of its oil. OPEC kept prices high, and American dollars flowed out of the country, worsening the trade deficit—the situation in which a nation buys more foreign goods than it exports abroad.

⚲ KEY THEMES AND CONCEPTS

Presidential Decisions and Actions

As you know from your study of United States history, all events are influenced by decisions, actions, and outcomes of earlier times.

- How was Carter's presidency influenced by the shadow of Nixon's presidency?

CORPORATE BAILOUTS Some American corporations were hard hit by stagflation and the decline in purchasing power at home. Foreign imports undersold some American goods, especially automobiles. The Chrysler Corporation and Lockheed Aircraft faced possible bankruptcy. Fearing the effect of massive layoffs on the economy, the federal government authorized huge loans to both corporations to keep them in business.

ENVIRONMENTAL PROBLEMS Acid rain, created by toxic air pollution, continued to threaten forests, lakes, and wildlife in the United States. President Nixon had taken steps to end harmful industrial pollution by creating the Environmental Protection Agency. Carter supported environmental programs as well, but inflation and energy shortages prevented him from undertaking ambitious programs to protect the environment. Coal polluted the air, but the nation needed coal to offset oil shortages. The nation needed to clean up the air, but emission devices for cars and factories pushed up prices.

NUCLEAR ENERGY Carter supported nuclear energy as an alternative to coal and oil. However, in 1979, an accident occurred at the Three Mile Island nuclear plant near Harrisburg, Pennsylvania. Although the problem was brought under control, the incident highlighted the hazards of the nuclear power industry, which by the late 1970s supplied about 4 percent of the nation's energy.

Carter's Foreign Policy

During his presidency, Carter faced a number of foreign-policy challenges.

HELSINKI ACCORDS In 1975, the United States and other nations signed the Helsinki Accords, promising to respect basic human rights. Carter believed that the United States should withhold aid from nations that violated human rights.

CAMP DAVID ACCORDS In 1977, Egyptian President Anwar el-Sadat surprised the world by visiting Israeli Prime Minister Menachem Begin. President Carter seized the opportunity for bringing peace to the Middle East by inviting the two leaders to Camp David, the President's retreat in Maryland. There, Sadat and Begin hammered out the terms for a peace treaty known as the **Camp David Accords.** The two leaders signed the treaty in 1979. Other Arab nations, however, still refused to recognize Israel.

PANAMA CANAL TREATIES In 1977, President Carter signed two treaties promising to turn over control of the Panama Canal to Panama in 1999. The treaties aroused bitter debate, but the Senate narrowly ratified them in 1978.

KEY THEMES AND CONCEPTS

Environment

In the 1970s, the United States faced a number of environmental problems.

- What steps did Nixon and Carter take to resolve some of these problems?

- Do any of these problems persist today? If so, which ones?

PREPARING FOR THE EXAM

What reasons led the American people to elect Ronald Reagan as President in 1980?

Election of 1980

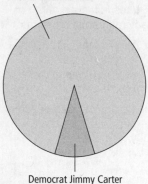

Republican Ronald Reagan 91% of electoral vote

Democrat Jimmy Carter 9% of electoral vote

♀ KEY THEMES AND CONCEPTS

Presidential Decisions and Actions

President Reagan supported the policy of New Federalism that had been begun by President Nixon. New Federalism turned over government control of some social programs to the states. As part of New Federalism, Reagan also supported tax cuts for businesses, a balanced federal budget, and increased spending for national defense.

- Why do you think President Reagan supported New Federalism?

PROBLEMS WITH DÉTENTE In June 1979, Carter met with Soviet leader Leonid Brezhnev to negotiate the SALT II Treaty. However, a Soviet invasion of Afghanistan later that year ended détente. Carter cut off grain shipments to the Soviet Union and boycotted the 1980 summer Olympic games held in Moscow. Carter's tough line spurred debate at home.

HOSTAGE CRISIS The biggest foreign policy crisis for Carter came in Iran. In 1979, a revolution led by Islamic fundamentalists toppled the pro-American shah, Reza Pahlavi. The shah, suffering from terminal cancer, requested treatment in the United States, and Carter agreed. Islamic rebels struck back by seizing the United States embassy in Teheran and holding more than 50 Americans hostage.

The 1980 Election

During the 1980 presidential campaign, Carter was haunted by the continuing hostage crisis, persistent energy shortages, and lingering inflation. The conservative Republican candidate, former California governor Ronald Reagan, promised Americans a "new beginning" and a restoration of confidence at home and abroad. Reagan swept to victory, and on the day of his inauguration, Iran released the hostages after more than a year of captivity.

REAGAN AND THE CHALLENGES OF THE 1980s

A former actor, Reagan appealed to many Americans with his references to the "good old days" and his patriotic speeches. He used his prepared speeches to promote a conservative approach to government and the economy. He targeted inflation as his top priority and argued that big government was the cause of inflation. "In the present crisis," said Reagan, "government is not the solution to our problem; government is the problem."

Reagan's First-Term Domestic Policies

During his first term in office, Reagan supported a domestic program backed by both Eisenhower and Nixon. Like his Republican predecessors, he supported New Federalism, a policy that turned over federal control of some social welfare programs to the states.

SUPPLY-SIDE ECONOMICS Reagan called for cuts in taxes on businesses and individuals, especially those with large incomes. Reagan believed that they would reinvest in more businesses. These businesses would hire more workers and increase the supply of goods and services. Reagan argued that **supply-side economics** would end inflation without increasing the national debt. His ideas later became known as Reaganomics.

BALANCED BUDGET Reagan tried to balance the budget by reducing many social welfare programs. He also made sharp cuts in the Environmental Protection Agency. Despite such efforts, however, the national debt climbed throughout Reagan's presidency.

"STAR WARS" Reagan felt national security rested on defense and made every effort to fight off cuts in the military budget. He pushed for increased spending on missiles, ships, and bombers. He also asked for funding for the Strategic Defense Initiative (SDI), a massive satellite shield designed to intercept and destroy incoming Soviet missiles. SDI became popularly known as **"Star Wars."**

FARM AID In the 1980s, farmers experienced their worst economic problems since the Great Depression. A worldwide recession made it impossible for farmers to sell their surpluses—and to repay their loans. The Reagan administration responded by paying farmers not to plant millions of acres of land to reduce the supply and raise prices. However, prices did not rise, and the national debt grew.

IMMIGRATION In an effort to cut down on the number of undocumented workers living in the United States, Congress passed the 1986 Immigration Reform and Control Act, which forbade employers from hiring illegal immigrants. This new legislation did not solve the problem of the thousands of people who enter the United States illegally every year. These immigrants often work in sweatshop type factories, live in substandard housing, and are paid very low wages.

Origin of Immigrants, 1982–1995

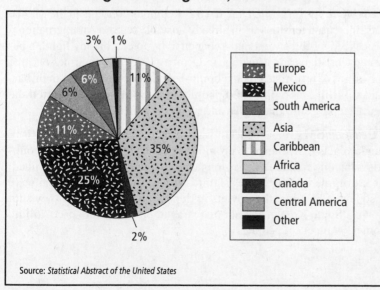

Source: *Statistical Abstract of the United States*

ANALYZING DOCUMENTS

Use the graph at left and your knowledge of social studies to answer the following questions.

- From 1982 to 1995, where did the largest group of immigrants to the United States come from?

- How is this different than the origin of most immigrants in the 19th century?

Reagan's First-Term Foreign Policy

Reagan adopted a tough stand toward communism, describing the Soviet Union as an "evil empire."

QUESTIONING DÉTENTE Reagan's attitude hardened toward communism in December 1981, when the Polish government cracked down on Solidarity, an independent labor party. Reagan called for economic sanctions to force the communist-backed government to end martial law. A renewal of détente did not take place until Reagan's second term.

INTERVENTION IN CENTRAL AMERICA Reagan believed that unstable economic conditions opened the door to communism. He asked for aid to Latin American groups fighting communist takeovers and approved limited military intervention in some nations.

- *El Salvador* Reagan sent arms and military advisers to El Salvador to back anticommunist forces in a civil war. He also pressured the government to hold democratic elections.
- *Nicaragua* In 1979, Marxist guerrillas called the Sandinistas overthrew anticommunist dictator Anastasio Somoza. Because the Sandinistas accepted aid from Cuba and the Soviet Union, Reagan approved aid to the contras, rebels seeking to oust the Sandinistas. Actions by the CIA to help the contras angered Congress, and it cut off aid to the contras in 1987.
- *Grenada* In October, 1983, a rebellion in the Caribbean island nation of Grenada raised fears that it might become a communist base in the Caribbean. To prevent such a possibility, Reagan ordered a surprise United States invasion.

TURMOIL IN THE MIDDLE EAST Religious conflicts in the Middle East increased tensions in an already unstable region. An international peacekeeping force went into Lebanon to try to end bloody fighting between Christians and Muslims. In October 1983, U.S. marines became the target of terrorists when a bomb-laden truck drove into their barracks, killing more than 300 people. In 1984, Reagan admitted the peacekeeping effort had failed and withdrew American troops.

TERRORISM Global concern was raised by an increase in terrorism, random acts of violence to promote a political cause. In some countries, Islamic fundamentalists engaged in terrorism as part of a jihad, or a struggle to protect the Islamic faith. Charges of terrorism were also leveled against the Soviets in September, 1983, when they shot down a South Korean airliner that strayed into their air space, killing some 269 innocent people.

READING STRATEGY

Analyzing Cause And Effect

What factors contributed to United States military interventions in El Salvador, Nicaragua, and Grenada?

 PREPARING FOR THE EXAM

Terrorism is random acts of violence that promote a political cause. Terrorist acts raised global concern during the 1980s.

- Why do you think terrorists bombed an American marine barracks in Lebanon in 1983?
- What effect did this bombing have on Reagan's policy in Lebanon?

The Election of 1984

In the presidential election of 1984, Walter Mondale won the Democratic nomination over several contenders including Jesse Jackson, an influential African American minister. Mondale selected Representative Geraldine Ferraro as his running mate. Reagan campaigned for reelection, with George Bush as his running mate. Reagan won the election and became the first President since Eisenhower to serve two full terms in office.

Reagan's Second-Term Domestic Policy

Reagan, nicknamed the Great Communicator by some journalists, used his charm and persuasive talents to convince many Americans to support a plan aimed at creating a balanced budget by the early 1990s.

Reagan and his supporters promised to make deep cuts in federal programs. Only a few select programs, such as Social Security and defense, were to be spared. Reagan also called for simplification of tax laws and tax cuts for about 60 percent of Americans. Some people charged that the cuts favored the rich. In fact, by the late 1980s, wealth was more unevenly distributed than at any time since the end of World War II.

TRADE IMBALANCE Despite drastic actions by the federal government, the national debt climbed. This was due, in part, to a huge trade imbalance, a situation in which a nation imports more goods than it exports. At the start of Reagan's second term, the trade deficit approached $150 billion.

Reagan's Second-Term Foreign Policy

Reagan redirected his foreign policy to meet changes taking place in the Soviet Union. However, an issue that arose out of the United States dealings in the Middle East and Latin America took up much of his attention.

THE IRAN-CONTRA AFFAIR In 1986, the American public learned that several top presidential aides had sold weapons to Iran in exchange for Iranian help in freeing American hostages held in Lebanon. The money from the sale of arms was then channeled to Nicaragua to support the contras.

Reagan had vowed never to bargain with terrorists or kidnappers. Also, Congress had banned aid to the contras. A congressional committee cleared the President of any wrongdoing in the Iran-Contra affair and concluded that the actions had been illegally undertaken at the direction of Colonel Oliver North and members of the CIA.

In March 2007 Lewis "Scooter' Libby, former Chief of Staff to Vice President Cheney was convicted of lying and obstruction of justice. He was the highest ranking White House official convicted in a government scandal since the Iran-Contra affair during the Reagan administration.

Election of 1984

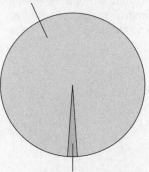

Republican Ronald Reagan
98% of electoral vote

Democrat Walter Mondale
2% of electoral vote

⚲ KEY THEMES AND CONCEPTS

Presidential Decisions and Actions
Later in 2007, George W. Bush (43) commuted Libby's sentence of 30 months in jail, stating that the sentence was too harsh. Libby avoided any jail time.

**PREPARING FOR
THE EXAM**
How did Soviet leader
Mikhail Gorbachev work to
improve relations with the
United States?

RENEWAL OF DÉTENTE In 1985, Mikhail Gorbachev became the new charismatic leader of the Soviet Union. Gorbachev criticized Reagan's policy of "Star Wars" and called for a renewal of détente.

Gorbachev helped further relations by announcing his new policies of *glasnost* and *perestroika*. Glasnost called for greater openness, including increased political freedom in the Soviet Union and Eastern Europe. Perestroika allowed a measure of free enterprise to improve economic conditions within the Soviet Union.

ARMS REDUCTIONS In 1987, the United States and Soviet Union reached an agreement to eliminate short-range and medium-range land-based missiles.

TROUBLES ELSEWHERE Troubles over other foreign policy issues were not so easily resolved. These included
- *Continuing terrorism* Terrorists continued to claim some American lives. In 1985, for example, Palestinian terrorists killed an American passenger aboard the Italian cruise ship, the *Achille Lauro.* In 1988, a bomb destroyed a Pan Am jet over Scotland.
- *Battling the drug trade* First Lady Nancy Reagan launched an antidrug campaign with the slogan, "Just say no!"
- *Ending apartheid* Many people demanded that Americans divest, or get rid of, investments in South Africa to protest that nation's policy of apartheid, or strict racial segregation and discrimination. In 1986, Congress overrode Reagan's veto and imposed strict economic sanctions against South Africa until it ended apartheid.

**KEY THEMES AND
CONCEPTS**
Economic Systems
How did Americans protest
South Africa's policy of
apartheid?

The End of the Cold War

Causes		Results
• Anticommunist movements gain force in Eastern Europe • Soviet leader Mikhail Gorbachev encourages Eastern European leaders to adopt more open policies		• Reform leaders come to power after free elections in Poland and Czechoslovakia • New governments take charge in Bulgaria, Hungary, Romania, and Albania • Berlin Wall falls, East and West Germany are reunified • Soviet Union breaks apart

5

Approaching and Beginning the 21st Century

SECTION OVERVIEW

In 1988 George H.W. Bush(41), a conservative Republican from Texas defeated the Democratic candidate, Michael Dukakis for thePresidency. After serving one term, President Bush was defeated by Arkansas Governor Bill Clinton. President Clinton served from 1993 until President Bush's son George W. Bush(43) was inaugurated in 2001 after he defeated President Clinton's Vice President Al Gore in the race for the White House.

KEY THEMES AND CONCEPTS

Conflict What domestic and international conflicts caused problems for the United States during this time?

Culture How did values of other cultures clash with values of the United States?

Power In what ways did the United States government use its power at home and abroad?

THE GEORGE H. W. BUSH (41) ADMINISTRATION

Domestic Events

ECONOMIC TROUBLES During the election campaign, Bush had promised voters no new taxes. However, as the budget deficit mounted, Bush was forced to break this promise in 1990. By 1992, an economic recession caused increased layoffs and rising unemployment.

SAVINGS AND LOAN SCANDAL In 1990, the misuse of funds by savings and loan institutions surfaced. American taxpayers would pay hundreds of billions of dollars to bail out the savings and loan industry.

SUPREME COURT APPOINTMENTS President Bush appointed two new justices to the Supreme Court: David Souter in 1990 and Clarence Thomas in 1991. Thomas was confirmed by the Senate after

THE BIG IDEA

- President George H.W. Bush (41) served during the end of the Cold War.

- President Clinton promoted many ambitious domestic programs during the 1990's.

- President Clinton was only the second President to experience an impeachment trial.

- President George W. Bush (43) leads the nation in the War on Terrorism following the attacks of September 11, 2001.

very controversial hearings in which he was charged with sexual harassment by Anita Hill, a former employee. See page A-15 for court cases during this time.

Events Abroad

END OF THE COLD WAR In November 1989, the world watched in amazement as Germans tore down the Berlin Wall—a symbolic reminder of the division between the communist and democratic worlds. Throughout the winter of 1989, communist governments in Eastern Europe crumbled. In 1990, Gorbachev received the Nobel Peace Prize for relaxing control over former Soviet satellites. In October of that year, East and West Germany were formally reunited. A failed coup by hard-line communist leaders in 1991 led to the dissolution of the Soviet Union and the 1992 formation of a Commonwealth of Independent States.

INVASION OF PANAMA As President, Bush continued Reagan's war on drugs. He ordered United States troops into Panama to capture General Manuel Noriega, the dictator of Panama, and return him to the United States to face drug charges. In 1992, Noriega was sentenced to serve 40 years in federal prison.

PERSIAN GULF WAR In August 1990, Iraqi leader Saddam Hussein invaded the oil-rich nation of Kuwait. Bush responded by sending United States troops into Saudi Arabia, with the agreement of Saudi leaders. The United Nations condemned Iraq's actions and approved economic sanctions against Iraq. The UN also authorized a joint military buildup in Saudi Arabia, called Operation Desert Shield.

Operation Desert Shield became Operation Desert Storm in January 1991 when the United States with a troop force of over 500,000 (the largest American military commitment since Vietnam) and Allied troops from a number of other nations began a total air assault on Iraq. By the end of February, Bush ordered a cease-fire, and Iraq accepted all UN demands to end the **Persian Gulf War.** More than 300 Allied lives were lost, but the Iraqi death toll was estimated at 100,000.

BOSNIA AND THE BALKANS The end of the Bush administration was marked by the outbreak of violence in the Balkans. In 1991, Slovenia and Croatia declared their independence from Yugoslavia, and fighting broke out throughout the area. Millions became refugees during the fighting. Bosnian Serbs, led by Slobodan Milosevic, carried out ethnic cleansing, or genocidal warfare, killing thousands of innocent civilians.

The 1992 Election

In the 1992 presidential election, George Bush ran as the Republican candidate with Dan Quayle as his running mate. The Democrats selected Arkansas governor Bill Clinton as their candidate, with Al Gore as his running mate. An independent challenger, Texas billionaire Ross Perot, also entered the race. The major issues of the campaign

Election of 1992

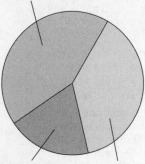

Democrat Bill Clinton
43% of popular vote

Independent
Ross Perot
19% of
popular vote

Republican
George Bush
38% of
popular vote

📝 PREPARING FOR THE EXAM

Was Bill Clinton's victory in the 1992 Presidential election decisive? Why or why not?

concerned the state of the American economy. In the election, Clinton made Bosnia an issue and promised to take strong action there.

Clinton carried 32 states with a total of 370 electoral votes. Although Perot did not earn any electoral votes, he received over 19 million popular votes. Women, African Americans, and Latino Americans were elected to Congress in record high numbers in 1992.

THE CLINTON ADMINISTRATION

Domestic Issues

HEALTH-CARE REFORM In 1993, Clinton presented to Congress a health-care reform plan that would ensure health insurance for all Americans. Critics of the plan complained it was too expensive, complex and would limit choice in health care. In 1994, Congress rejected Clinton's plan.

SOCIAL SECURITY It became clear that the Social Security program, begun during the Great Depression, would run into trouble because of changing demographics. The number of recipients is increasing rapidly due to longer life spans and the aging baby boomer generation. Several plans to fund Social Security have been considered, but no plan has been agreed upon.

SUPREME COURT APPOINTEES Clinton's nominations of Ruth Bader Ginsburg and Stephen Breyer made him the first Democratic President in 26 years to name a Supreme Court justice. See page A-15 for the landmark court case of 1995.

THE 1994 CONGRESSIONAL ELECTIONS In 1994, Republicans took majority control of Congress for the first time in 40 years.

THE 1996 AND 1998 ELECTIONS At the end of 1995, disagreements between Republicans and Clinton over the budget led to a shutdown of the federal government. During the 1996 presidential campaign, Clinton focused public attention on the Republicans' role in the shutdown. He also adopted several Republican issues by signing welfare reform into law and supporting a balanced budget. Clinton easily won re-election. Republicans maintained their congressional majority after both elections, but Democrats gained five House seats in 1998.

SCANDAL AND IMPEACHMENT Many of President Clinton's activities were the subject of investigations, including the Whitewater affair, which accused him and his wife Hillary Rodham Clinton of involvement with an illegal real estate scheme in Arkansas. The Clintons were never formally charged.

In 1998, a special prosecutor accused President Clinton of several offenses, including lying under oath about his relationship with a White House intern. On December 19, 1998, the House impeached

🔍 **KEY THEMES AND CONCEPTS**

Government

How did the 1994 Congressional elections shift the balance of power in Congress?

ANALYZING DOCUMENTS

Examine the cartoon below, then answer the questions.

- What does the book represent?
- What does the black spot stand for?
- What is the meaning of the title of the cartoon?
- What is the opinion that this cartoon is trying to convey?

⚲ **KEY THEMES AND CONCEPTS**

Presidential Decisions and Actions

In the early 1990s, war erupted in the Balkans as the former Yugoslavia fell into a bitter civil war.

- How did President Clinton handle tensions between ethnic groups in the former Yugoslavia in the 1990s?

- What gave Clinton the authority to take this action?

⚲ **KEY THEMES AND CONCEPTS**

Economic Systems

By the 1990s, the economies of many nations had become more interdependent.

- Name two organizations or agreements designed to improve trade among member nations.

- To which of these does the United States belong?

Election of 2000

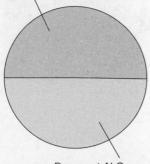

Republican George W. Bush 50.5% of electoral vote

Democrat Al Gore 49.5% of electoral vote

President Clinton on charges of perjury and obstruction of justice. The Senate acquitted the President two months later.

ECONOMIC PROSPERITY In the 1990s, the United States enjoyed the longest period of economic growth in its history.

Foreign Issues

THE MIDDLE EAST The Arab-Israeli conflict has long focused attention on the Middle East. Since 1948, Arabs and Israelis have waged four wars. In 1993, the Palestine Liberation Organization and Israel agreed to a measure of Palestinian self-government. However, incidents of violence slowed the peace process.

THE FORMER YUGOSLAVIA Tensions between ethnic groups in the former Yugoslavia led to war in Bosnia in the early 1990s. The United States helped win an agreement between the two sides in 1995. In 1998, violence erupted in Kosovo, where Serbian forces massacred ethnic Albanian civilians. A brief bombing campaign by NATO forced the Serbs to withdraw. Many Serbian leaders then were arrested for war crimes and tried.

LATIN AMERICA In 1994 President Clinton ordered U.S. troops to lead a multinational force in Haiti to restore a legitimate government after years of dictatorships and unrest. During the rest of the decade millions of dollars in aid was pledged to Haiti by many countries but little has been sent due to the continuing lack of a stable government in that area.

GLOBAL ECONOMY In 1992, the United States, Canada, and Mexico signed the North American Free Trade Agreement (NAFTA) in an effort to break down trade barriers among the three nations. American trade in Europe continued to be strong, despite the formation of the **European Union,** a trade organization designed to break down trade barriers within Europe. The General Agreement on Trade and Tariffs (GATT) was formed in 1945 to encourage international trade. In 1995 the World Trade Organization was formed from GATT and included other nations as well.

THE 2000 ELECTION

In the 2000 presidential election, Texas Governor George W. Bush ran as the Republican candidate against the Democrat, Vice President Al Gore. In one of the closest presidential races in history, Florida emerged as the key state. The Florida vote was so close, a recount of ballots was ordered by law. The election ended when the Supreme Court ruled to discontinue the recounts. Although Gore won the popular vote, Bush won the electoral vote. The election marked the first time the Supreme Court intervened in a presidential election.

THE GEORGE W. BUSH (43) ADMINISTRATION

Domestic Issues

TAXES AND THE ECONOMY President Bush attempted a tax cut and rebates to taxpayers earlier in his administration and in 2008 taxpayers will receive rebate checks of $300.00 to $1200.00. Since 2007 the economy has shown signs of a possible recession with severe difficulties especially in the housing market as thousands of homeowners struggled to meet mortgage payments and others faced bank foreclosures. In 2007 Congress approved an increase in the minimum wage from $5.15 to $5.85 with increases to $7.25 by 2009. The Federal Reserve Board has lowered its interest rate several times, including a drop of .75%, the largest in the history of the Fed. All of these actions are an effort to reverse what appears to be the threat of a recession.

EDUCATIONAL REFORM On January 8, 2002 President Bush signed into law a major educational reform bill called No Child Left Behind. The plan called for increased student and teacher accountability and targets funds for improving schools. Critics have said that it does not accomplish what it needs to do to improve American education.

MASS ACTS OF VIOLENCE Following several years of mass acts of violence in schools and on college campuses, 2007 was the year of the most deadly shooting rampage in United States history with 33 students, including the killer, dead at Virginia Tech in Blacksburg, Virginia. Later in 2007 a sniper in an Omaha, Nebraska shopping mall killed eight while in February of 2008 another gunman killed five students as well as himself at Northern Illinois University. Each incidence of this type of violence renews the debate between Americans with regard to gun control.

IMMIGRATION ISSUES The Bush administration has had to deal with several issues relating to immigration, some of which became more serious after 9/11. The most recent legislation is the Real ID Act of 2005 which strengthened security requirements at U.S. borders and gave the Director of Homeland Security additional powers. There are currently several proposals before both houses of Congress about border patrols and protection, restricting illegal immigration, and anti-terrorism. Since that time there also has been extensive discussion with some preliminary funding bills to construct a wall along the U.S. border between Mexico and the United States. This has met with very mixed reactions on both sides of the border.

It is estimated that the number of illegal immigrants in the United States today numbers more than ten million and may be far in excess of that. Immigration has been a discussion topic for the 2008 presidential candidates.

SOCIAL SECURITY In his first term President Bush wanted to make Social Security reform a primary agenda item. The President's plan to allow younger workers to choose private accounts for a portion of their Social Security contributions drew praise as well as equally strong criticism. The President has also tried to reform the Medicare program. A major concern with these programs is that the number of Americans eligible for them is growing at an increasing rate every year. There is an increasing senior citizen population due to the "aging of the Baby Boomer" generation. At the same time there are fewer workers contributing to the system due to declining American birth rates of the 1970's and 1980's.

ELECTION 2004 In November 2004, George W. Bush, the Republican incumbent won a very close race against challenger, Massachusetts Senator and Vietnam War veteran, John Kerry. The popular vote was Bush, 62,040,606 (51%) to Kerry's 59,028,109 (48%). The state of Ohio ultimately gave the President the needed Electoral votes to win, 286 to 252.

Vice President Dick Cheney continued for a second term. Dr. Condoleeza Rice, former National Security Advisor, became the first African American woman to hold the position of Secretary of State. Within the first few months of being appointed Secretary of State Rice made important trips to Europe, the Middle East and parts of Asia.

The Congressional elections of 2006 were a major upset for both President Bush and the majority Republican Party. Democrats took control of both the House of Representatives and the Senate. Nancy Pelosi, a Representative from California was elected by her party to be the first female Speaker of the House of Representatives. This makes Speaker Pelosi the highest ranking woman in the history of the United States government. According to the constitution the Speaker of the House is second only to the Vice President in succession to the Presidency.

Preparing for the Presidential Election of 2008

Early in 2007 there were already several announced candidates for the Presidential Election of 2008. Some of these were particularly historic because they represent "firsts" in American history. New York Senator Hillary Clinton is both the first former First Lady and the first female from a major Political Party (Democratic) to declare her intention to run for President. Illinois Senator Barack Obama, also a Democrat, is the first African American to be considered a serious Presidential candidate from a major Party.

In the fall of 2007 there were several declared presidential candidates from both the major parties. Please refer to the chart on page 53 of this text which details the steps in becoming a presidential candidate. A series of debates involving candidates from both parties occurred throughout the fall. Gradually several candidates withdrew their names. The primaries began on January 3, 2008 with the Iowa caucus, which was followed shortly by the New Hampshire Primary. Obama won in Iowa and Clinton won in New Hampshire for the Democrats, setting the stage for weeks of continuing debates and campaign travel for both.

John McCain, the Republican front runner, took a strong lead over his opponents and several withdrew from the race. In February 2008, Ralph Nader announced that he would run again for president as a third party candidate. In the 2000 election when Nader ran as a third party candidate he was blamed for taking votes from the Democratic candidate, Al Gore, who won the popular vote but lost the election due to a decision of the Supreme Court involving the electoral vote.

Throughout the spring of 2008, the Democratic frontrunners, Hillary Clinton and Barack Obama, each sought to win primary after primary. Each candidate attracted different groups of voters and each of them continued to build large numbers of delegate votes. As the spring and primary season continued, Senator Clinton gradually fell behind both in convention delegates and in campaign money raised. Many sources ranging from party officials to politicians to the media urged her to leave the race. Senator Obama took the position that she had worked hard and should stay in the race as long as she wanted to do so. Hillary Clinton refused to quit, stayed on the primary ballot and continued to win states until the very last day of the primaries, June 3, 2008. That evening, Barack Obama clinched the Democratic nomination with the required number of delegate votes and he chose to address his supporters in Minneapolis to assume the title of "Presumptive Democratic Nominee" until the convention actually votes and makes him the official candidate. Senator Clinton spoke in New York that evening and both candidates congratulated each other on their efforts and success at bringing so many new voters into the political process during the primary season. Their candidacies caused thousands of new voters representing several groups, such as younger voters, African Americans, and Hispanics, within the general electorate to be registered to vote. The increase in eligible Democratic voters has been of interest to the Republican party leadership as well as they strive to retain control of the White House following declining popular support for President George W. Bush (43).

As this text goes to press, the Vice Presidential choices of both parties remain undetermined. In both parties there is especially high interest in the choice of these candidates for the 2008 election. Senator Clinton received millions of votes across the United States during the primaries and there are many Americans who would like to see her be offered and accept the position of candidate for the Democratic Vice President. In fact the possibility of an Obama/Clinton ticket has been referred to as the "Dream Team" by some, as it would bring together the first African American and the first female candidate to reach such a political position in American history.

Republican presumptive nominee John McCain's choice of a running mate holds equally high interest as McCain, if elected, would be the oldest person to be elected President. He is also a cancer survivor with other health issues.

The official presidential candidates from both parties will not be chosen until their National Political Conventions. The Democratic Political Convention will be held in Denver, Colorado, August 25–28, 2008. The Republican Convention is not until September 1–4, in Minneapolis-St. Paul, Minnesota.

Foreign Issues

SEPTEMBER 11, 2001 AND RESULTING EVENTS Bush focused largely on foreign policy after the September 11, 2001 attacks on the World Trade Center in New York City and the Pentagon in Washington, D.C. Bush called the attacks "acts of war" and committed the country to a campaign against terrorists. American forces attacked military sites and terrorists training camps in Afghanistan. Bush urged Americans not to "expect one battle but a lengthy campaign unlike any other we have ever seen."

THE MIDDLE EAST Problems between the Israelis and Palestinians continue with repeated incidents of suicide bombers and cross border attacks by both sides. Attempts have been made by the United States to develop compromise solutions but episodes of violence delay peace keeping efforts.

In November 2004, Yasir Arafat the leader of the Palestine Liberation Organization and recipient of the Nobel Peace Prize died at 75 after an almost 50 year struggle to gain a permanent homeland for the Palestinian people.

In November 2007 President Bush hosted a Middle East Peace Conference in Annapolis, Maryland which brought together Israeli Prime Minister Ehud Olmert and Palestinian President Mahmound Abbas as well as representatives from 49 other countries. The leaders agreed to work on details of a peace treaty. By the spring of 2008 the area continues to be troubled with violence and disagreeing factions.

WAR IN IRAQ In late 2002 and early 2003, the Bush Administration warned Saddam Hussein to eliminate Iraq's weapons of mass destruction (WMD). Hussein claimed not to have any WMD. The United Nations sent an inspection team, which reported little success finding these weapons. The United States worked to gain United Nations support for

○ KEY THEMES AND ⌐ CONCEPTS

Presidential Decisions and Actions
How have President Bush's actions during the War in Iraq demonstrated his use of Presidential power?

an invasion of Iraq. Failing to gain this support, a small number of countries led by the United States and Great Britain attacked Iraq in March 2003. This campaign is known as Operation Iraqi Freedom. More than 200,000 American troops were sent to the area. For the first time the United States military allowed reporters to be "embedded" with the troops. Bush declared an official end to the war on May 1, 2003.

In July 2003 both sons of Saddam Hussein were killed in a shootout by U.S. forces in Mosul, Iraq. Hussein himself continued to escape capture until December 2003. An Iraqi Governing Council was established during 2003 with the goal of allowing Iraq to be an independent, democratic nation when the United States military completes its transfer of political powers. American casualties continue to rise as the military meets with pockets of resistance. President Bush has defended the War on the grounds that a brutal dictator has been removed, that Hussein had terrorist links and that he was hiding Weapons of Mass Destruction. Given the rising human and financial costs to the United States and the failure to find WMD, critics have questioned the Bush Administration's activites in Iraq and it's long term plan for that country.

During 2004 President Bush and Secretary of Defense Donald Rumsfeld had to answer serious questions about the treatment of Iraqi prisoners when reports of abuse by American troops was disclosed. Some of the responsible soldiers have been found guilty and sentenced to prison terms themselves. In January 2005 with American and Coalition Forces support the new Iraqi government held its first democratic elections under extremely tight security. Insurgents who oppose the new government and the American presence in Iraq continue to cause violent attacks on both military and civilians in Baghdad and elsewhere. By the spring of 2007, over 150,000 American troops continued to serve in Iraq with a goal of training Iraqis soldiers to eventually be able to replace the Americans. Over 3900 American servicemen and women have been killed in Iraq and thousands more have been seriously wounded. In 2006 President Bush replaced the Secretary of Defense with Robert Gates. Early in 2007 they have been forced to answer questions about the poor conditions for health treatment for many returning war wounded. By the end of 2007 several Army leaders had been dismissed from their jobs as a result of the conditions at Walter Reed Medical Center in Washington.

Although the new Iraqi government is making some progress at establishing democracy for themselves, the two most powerful Islamic sects, the Shiites and the Sunnis, have continued to have difficulties in working together. The trial of Saddam Hussein concluded with his being found guilty of multiple murders. He was hanged on December 30, 2006. By 2007 the violent actions of the insurgents have moved Iraq into a civil war. Daily violence and loss of life have increased as American and coalition troops have tried to maintain order. With these events President Bush's popularity ratings with the American public have continued to decline to the lowest levels of his Presidency. There is growing anti-war pressure from numbers of mainstream Americans as the number of American dead and very seriously wounded continued to grow. Early in 2007 Great Britain, America's strongest ally in the Iraqi War announced it will begin to withdraw its troops from Iraq.

Despite the attempts of Congress to limit the increase of troops in Iraq, President Bush announced a new strategy called a "Surge" in which American troop strength increased to over 160,000. This plan was an effort to control the number of suicide bombers, car bombs and roadside attacks by Iraqi insurgents that have caused thousands of Iraqi deaths. The Surge did meet with some success but American war deaths in 2007 also increased to their highest level since 2003. It is estimated that the war in Iraq has cost over $440 billion.

AFGHANISTAN The war in Afghanistan continues as part of the war on terror just as the war in Iraq continues but with somewhat less publicity. In 2006 President Bush visited the area under very heavy security to emphasize the desire of the United States to cooperate with that part of Asia. In 2007 Vice President Cheney visited Afghanistan and suicide bombers attempted to attack the secured compound where the Vice President was staying. It is generally believed that Osama bin Laden, the head of the terrorist group al-Qaeda responsible for the September 11, 2001 attacks, remains at large there or in the rugged mountains of neighboring Pakistan. Bin Laden released his first video in three years in September 2007 and stated that he and al-Qaeda would "continue to escalate the killing and fighting in Iraq." Continued American involvement in Afghanistan is considered crucial to American goals and interests in that part of Asia. Approximately $127 billion has already been spent on the war in Afghanistan.

NORTH KOREA 2007 was a major year for improved relations between the United States and North Korea. For the first time in five years U.S. representatives visited North Korea. North Korea agreed to dismantle its nuclear production facilities and to allow international inspectors to visit the country. This was in exchange for a multi-million dollar aid package. The Bush administration also agreed to begin the process of removing North Korea from its list of nations sponsoring terrorism.

IRAN American foreign policy towards Iran has continued to be a difficult problem. Iranian President Mahmoud Ahmadinejad spoke in New York City at Columbia University in September of 2007 as well as at the United Nations. The ability of Iran to produce nuclear weapons is of primary concern to the United States. President Bush has repeatedly taken a hard line position against this possibility.

PAKISTAN During the years since 9/11, Pakistani President Pervez Musharraf had generally supported the United States in its efforts in the war on terror. In the fall of 2007 former Pakistani leader Benazir Bhutto returned to Pakistan after eight years of exile. This was followed by political upheaval and the eventual death of Bhutto at a campaign rally. By early 2008 when elections were held Musharraf's party lost and a new coalition government was formed. It will be crucial to American efforts in this area that favorable diplomatic relations may be continued with the new government.

AFRICA Early in 2008 President and Mrs. Bush made a visit to several African nations. Throughout the Bush Presidency aid to Africa has been a major goal with much of those funds being directed to the widespread problem of AIDS throughout the continent. The civil war in Kenya caused thousands of deaths and the situation of starvation and mass murders in Darfur has drawn world wide attention.

CUBA The relationship between the United States and Cuba, the island nation ninety miles from southern Florida, has been a troubled one since 1959 when Fidel Castro became the Communist leader. On February 19, 2008 Castro announced that he would be stepping down from the Cuban Presidency and that he would be succeeded by his brother Raul. The United States will be watching closely to determine if this will be an opportunity for democracy to return to Cuba.

KOSOVO Since the Clinton Administration the United States has been part of a United Nations peace keeping force in Kosovo, a province of Serbia in the Balkan peninsula. On February 17, 2008 Kosovo declared its independence from Serbia. The following day the United States formally recognized the new nation, along with several other Western nations. Russia, in a move suggestive of the Cold War days, sided with Serbia and stated that Kosovo's declaration was a violation of international law.

6

Towards a Postindustrial Society: Living in a Global Age

★ THE BIG IDEA
Since the end of World War II, the rapid pace of change has turned the world into a "global village." Today

- technology and growing corporations have helped to increase job growth.

- most people have longer life expectancies, despite diseases such as AIDS.

- population growth and environmental concerns challenge the United States as well as other countries.

⚷ KEY TERMS
alternative energy sources
Internet
multinational corporations
Earth Day

SECTION OVERVIEW

The United States began as a nation of farmers. Today it is one of the leading economic and political powers in the world. Because of the advanced technology of the postindustrial age, the world has become what some call a "global village." Because of increased interdependence, major events in one part of the world have an impact upon the rest of the world.

KEY THEMES AND CONCEPTS

As you review this section, take special note of the following key themes and concepts:

Change What effects did technological change have on American society?

Places and Regions How did the United States play a unique role in helping resolve conflicts in other regions of the world?

Environment How are concerns about the environment being addressed by activist groups?

Interdependence How has the emergence of a global economy strengthened the interdependence of nations?

RAPID PACE OF CHANGE

Every generation since the Civil War has experienced the effects of the Industrial Revolution. However, the pace of technological change has picked up dramatically since World War II. Today, the United States is moving into a postindustrial age. That is, the American economy no longer rests on the development of new factories and heavy industries, such as the production of steel or coal. Instead, because of technological changes, service-related industries now occupy a larger sector of the economy.

Technology—What Is It?

Technology is the application of scientific knowledge to commerce and industry. To appreciate the effect of technological change, think of the following situations out of the past.

- George Washington, the nation's first President, never called a member of Congress on the telephone, never rode in a limousine, and never saw his photograph in a newspaper.
- Abraham Lincoln, President during the Civil War, never called generals on the telephone and never listened to battle reports on the radio.
- Franklin Roosevelt, President during World War II, never had a speech transmitted by satellite to Europe and never watched a program on television.
- John F. Kennedy, President in the early 1960s, never wrote a speech on a computer and never ate a snack heated up in a microwave.
- All recent Presidents have supported the American space program, but none has yet traveled into space. It is difficult even to imagine the changes that await future Presidents.

The Post-World War II Era

Since the end of World War II, a number of forces have had a great impact upon the economy and upon the lifestyles of Americans.

SCARCE ENERGY SOURCES Scarce oil supplies have led scientists to research **alternative energy sources,** such as solar power. Nuclear power is being used in some parts of the world. However, the hazards associated with nuclear energy, such as the storage of nuclear waste, have created controversy. The accident at a nuclear power plant at Chernobyl, Ukraine, in 1986 has increased debate even more.

USE OF NEW MATERIALS Inventions since World War II have replaced wood and steel in many jobs with synthetics, such as plastic. In some cases, these new materials are lighter and more durable than traditional materials.

SPREAD OF COMPUTERS The prevalent use of computers in American homes and businesses since the 1980s has revolutionized record keeping and the storage of information. Advocates of computers praise their ability to process and store large volumes of information. Critics charge that computers have increased the chances for the invasion of privacy as people access private records without permission, particularly as **Internet** use becomes increasingly widespread.

SECURITY CONCERNS The global increase in acts of terrorism, especially the attacks on the Pentagon and the World Trade towers, made some Americans fear that they were not safe. In response, the government took a number of measures. Airport security was tightened, as was security at bridges, tunnels, nuclear power plants, courthouses, and other vulnerable places. The Patriot Act of 2001 gave sweeping new powers to government agencies. To coordinate federal government efforts, the Homeland Security Act created a new Cabinet-level department, Homeland Security. Its job was to coordinate the efforts of more than 40 federal agencies fighting terror. These agencies include the CIA, FBI, and the National Guard.

KEY THEMES AND CONCEPTS

Change

The United States faced a rapid pace of change during the Industrial Revolution, but that pace increased dramatically after World War II.

- How did the American economy change after World War II?

KEY THEMES AND CONCEPTS

Science and Technology

Bill Gates, as founder of Microsoft, became one of the world's richest individuals. Huge fortunes have been made and lost in the computer industry in the last fifteen years. Bill and Melinda Gates (his wife) administer the charitable Gates Foundation that has given millions of dollars in aid for education and medical research, among other causes.

In 2002 President Bush and Congress created the independent, bipartisan National Commission on Terrorist Attacks on the United States. After extensive hearings by the Commission it released in the summer of 2004 a detailed public report. One of its major recommendations was to unify the United States Intelligence community under the leadership of a new National Intelligence Director. President Bush named John Negroponte, U.S. Ambassador to Iraq to this position in February 2005. The Commission made a number of other recommendations to improve the security of the United States.

GROWTH OF MULTINATIONAL CORPORATIONS Since the 1800s, the organization of American businesses has changed from single ownership and partnerships to corporations. In the post-World War II period, many corporations have become **multinational corporations,** or businesses with bases of operation in many nations.

INCREASED JOB OPPORTUNITIES The greatest increases in jobs in the early 2000s promise to be in the service fields. The largest declines will occur in agricultural employment. Technological advances have made it possible for fewer farmers to produce more food, which will continue to reduce the need for agricultural labor.

NEW LIFESTYLES AND LONGER LIFE SPANS American attitudes toward family size and divorce have changed since the 1950s. Average family size has declined. After years of expansion, many school districts throughout the nation, including New York's, experienced declining school enrollments in the 1980s. Divorce rates first rose and then remained constant. This created the largest number of single-parent households in the nation's history. At the same time, health-care improvements resulting from new technologies, such as laser surgery and organ transplants, have increased average life spans. This has increased the number of older Americans, who in recent years have organized to protect their rights and improve their lives.

EXPANSION OF PUBLIC EDUCATION Access to free public education has helped many Americans improve their standard of living. As individuals complete higher levels of education, they have the chance to secure better-paying jobs and more desirable housing. Thus, education helps further social mobility.

INCREASINGLY DIVERSE POPULATION If current trends continue, it is projected that the population of the United States will grow increasingly diverse over the next half century. More of the newest immigrants to the United States come from Asian and Latin American countries, compared with earlier waves of immigration that came from Europe.

DEALING WITH THE AIDS CRISIS Since the 1980s, medical researchers have gathered more information about AIDS, or Acquired Immune Deficiency Syndrome. Even so, AIDS has spread through some sectors of the American population at an alarming rate. Without a known

KEY THEMES AND CONCEPTS

Change

Changes in technology frequently have an impact on the availability of certain jobs. For example, early telephones did not have a dial or push buttons to make a phone call directly. Instead, a caller would have to place a call through an operator, who made the phone connections at a switchboard. Once technology improved and direct dialing became commonly available, the need for telephone operators decreased.

- In the 1990s and early 2000s, what impact did technological improvements have on agricultural job opportunities?

PREPARING FOR THE EXAM

How have Americans' lifestyles been influenced by each of the following since the end of World War II?

- average family size
- longer life spans
- expansion of public education

The Changing Ethnic Composition of the United States

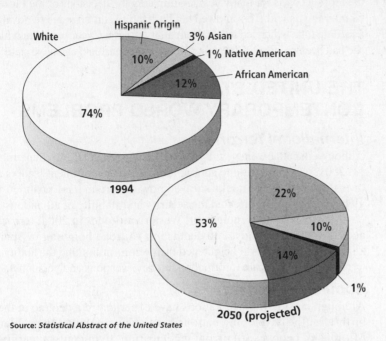

White — 74%
Hispanic Origin — 10%
3% Asian
1% Native American
African American — 12%

1994

53%
22%
10%
14%
1%

2050 (projected)

Source: *Statistical Abstract of the United States*

cure, scientists and public health officials have tried to increase public awareness and prevention of the disease. Many critics have condemned the federal government for not acting faster to find a cure for AIDS.

HELPING THE HOMELESS Not everyone enjoyed the prosperity of the post-World War II years. President Johnson's Great Society programs in the 1960s tried to reduce poverty in the United States. However, cuts in social programs during the 1980s caused a significant rise in the number of Americans living below the poverty line. Local communities and private charitable organizations tried to provide relief, but the issue of homelessness has remained a troubling issue.

GUN CONTROL The issue of gun control became hotly debated in the late 1990s. Urban violence, as well as a number of highly publicized school shootings, caused millions of Americans to reconsider attitudes toward and the availability of guns in this nation. In May 2000, thousands of American mothers marched in the Million Mom March in Washington, D.C., to focus attention on the need to curb gun violence.

The National Rifle Association continues to be one of the strongest lobbyist groups and remains very vocal about the rights of gun owners. This topic will continue to be a controversial one for years to come.

RIGHT TO LIFE ISSUES The United States continues to be a very divided society on the topics of abortion and the right to life/the right to die. In March 2005 President Bush and the Congress took unprecedented actions by involving themselves in the case of Terri Schiavo. She was a terminally ill Florida woman whose right to die had been debated in the Florida courts for many years. Ultimately the decisions of the Florida courts were upheld. This allowed her husband to authorize the removal of a feeding tube which led to her death after a fourteen year period in which she had been medically determined to be in a persistent vegetative state.

THE UNITED STATES AND CONTEMPORARY WORLD PROBLEMS

International Terrorism

Although the attack on New York and Washington, D.C., on September 11, 2001, was aimed at one nation, it mobilized government leaders all over the world. The attacks showed how terrorism has expanded its global reach and has affected the security and stability of all nations.

As the War in Iraq fueled anti Western attitudes in 2004, terrorist activities caused almost 200 deaths in a railroad bombing in Spain. Other areas of the world heightened their efforts at limiting the ability of terrorist groups to share information, money, weapons and personnel.

Population Growth

Although most developed nations have experienced a decline in their birthrates, the developing nations have an overpopulation problem. Millions of people suffer from malnutrition, living only a marginal existence. Foreign aid from the United States has become of vital economic importance in combating world hunger.

Environmental Concerns

Because of increased interdependence, an environmental problem in one nation frequently raises global concerns. An example includes the destruction of the Brazilian tropical rain forests.

ENVIRONMENTAL ACTIVISTS A number of groups have organized to reduce and clean up pollution on the land, in the water, and in the air. Other activist groups work to save endangered species of animals.

Recycling efforts have been organized to reuse paper, glass, plastic, and aluminum. Community organizers are opposing plans to convert vacant lands into dumpsites. Communities are studying the effects of industrial pollution on the groundwater that people drink. In response to public pressure, the federal government has enacted laws requiring automobile manufacturers to put antipollution devices on their cars. Since the first **Earth Day** celebration in 1970, the American people, along with the rest of the world, have begun to realize their obligation to protect the environment for future generations. In 2007, former Vice President Al Gore won a Nobel Peace Prize for his efforts to increase public understanding of issues related to global warming. This followed his widely viewed documentary film, "An Inconvenient Truth," which was about the topic.

KEY THEMES AND CONCEPTS

Interdependence
The concept of a global community means that the United States can not isolate itself from problems in other countries. Population growth in developing nations and environmental concerns in nations with essential ecosystems are two issues that affect the entire world.

- Why should the destruction of tropical rain forests be a concern to people in other nations, including the United States?

READING STRATEGY

Organizing Information
List three ways that environmental activists have raised public awareness about environmental issues.

1.

2.

3.

NATURAL DISASTERS In December 2004 a tsunami, a giant destructive wave, caused upwards of 200,000 deaths and left as many as 5,000,000 homeless in parts of South East Asia, the Indian subcontinent and East Africa. It was the worst natural disaster in modern history and the international community joined together in a massive outpouring of financial aid. President Bush committed the United States to $350 million in aid and millions more were donated by Americans directly to private relief agencies. The President also requested his father, former President George H.W. Bush and former President Bill Clinton to work together to draw attention to the extent of disaster damage in the stricken areas, to visit the area and to solicit private funds to help in the immediate and long term needs of the people of the area.

2005 would continue as a year with very unsettled weather patterns and one of the worst hurricane seasons in United States history. In August Hurricane Katrina caused major flooding in New Orleans, Louisiana and along the Gulf coast states of Mississippi and Alabama. Over two thousand people died, thousands of homes were destroyed and many thousands of people were evacuated. Millions of dollars in property damage occurred throughout the area. Businesses, schools, hospitals, hotels and stores were forced to close, many indefinitely. Media coverage of the hurricane exposed the depth of misery being experienced by all in the area but especially the poverty of large numbers of African Americans. The Bush Administration had to work hard to defend the slow and inadequate response of the Federal govenment lead by FEMA, the Federal Emergency Management Agency. Shortly after Hurricane Katrina, Hurricane Rita inflicted more damage on the already devasted area and Hurricane Wilma caused major damage in Florida. In November 2007 Congress passed the Water Resource Bill for 900 programs for a total of $23 billion, with $3.5 billion specifically earmarked for areas destroyed by Hurricane Katrina. This bill was the first bill to be passed by Congress after a veto by President Bush (43). 2007 continued as another year with multiple natural disasters including tornadoes, snow and ice storms and high winds that took over 115 deaths. Wildfires were so extensive in California that at one point over one half million residents were evacuated.

Foreign Policy After the Cold War

Offered $2.5 billion aid package to Russia to help nation move toward democracy and capitalism.

Sent troops to Bosnia as part of United Nations peacekeeping effort.

Tried unsuccessfully to control violence and civil war in Somalia and other African nations.

Tried to help Israeli and Palestinian leaders negotiate a peace treaty.

Helped Irish and British leaders negotiate a peace agreement.

Troops to Afghanistan and Iraq in followup to terrorist attacks of September 11, 2001.

U.S. leads small group of coalition nations in War in Iraq, 2003–__.

Questions for Regents Practice

For online Questions for Regents Practice,
visit the Prentice Hall Web site at www.phschool.com.

MULTIPLE CHOICE

Directions

Review the Test-Taking Strategies section of this book. Then answer the following questions, drawn from actual Regents examinations. Each question is followed by four choices. Read each question carefully. Decide which choice is the correct answer. Then on a separate piece of paper, mark your answer for each question.

1 The quotations below are from two United States Supreme Court decisions.

I. "Separation of the races does not place a badge of inferiority upon one group over another, thus it is not a violation of the 14th amendment." (1896)

II. "To separate [children in grade school and high school] from others of similar age and qualifications solely because of their race generates a feeling of inferiority as to their status . . . that may affect their hearts and minds in a way unlikely ever to be un-done." (1954)

The difference in opinion between these two rulings best shows
1 a change in judicial philosophy and public attitudes
2 the persistent efforts of the major political parties to increase equal opportunity
3 a recognition that democracy depends on economic equality for all citizens
4 the refusal of the Supreme Court to deal with controversial issues

2 The successful launching of *Sputnik* by the Soviet Union in 1957 signaled the beginning of
1 American fears that the Soviets had achieved technological superiority
2 the Cold War with the United States
3 Soviet aggression in Afghanistan and China
4 disarmament discussions between the superpowers

3 Which development contributed most to the expansion of suburbs since the 1950s?
1 construction of interstate highways
2 invention of the computer
3 completion of transcontinental railroads
4 development of jet aircraft

4 When President Dwight D. Eisenhower sent federal troops to Little Rock, Arkansas, during the 1957 school integration crisis, he was exercising his constitutional power as
1 chief legislator
2 commander in chief
3 chief diplomat
4 head of state

5 Which is a valid conclusion based on United States involvement in the Korean War?
1 The policy of containment was applied in Asia as well as in Europe.
2 United Nations economic sanctions are more effective than military action.
3 The American people will support United States participation in any war, whether declared or undeclared.
4 United States cooperation with a wartime ally ends when the war ends.

6 What was the significance of the use of federal marshals to protect African American students in Little Rock, Arkansas, in 1957?
1 It was the first time martial law had been declared in the United States.
2 It led to federal takeover of many southern public schools.
3 It strengthened control of education by state governments.
4 It showed that the federal government would enforce court decisions on integration.

7 "We conclude that in the field of public education the doctrine of 'separate but equal' has no place. Separate educational facilities are inherently unequal."

This quotation expresses the Supreme Court decision in the case of
1 *Plessy* v. *Ferguson*
2 *Engel* v. *Vitale*
3 *Tinker* v. *Des Moines Independent Community School District*
4 *Brown* v. *Board of Education of Topeka, Kansas*

8 The Supreme Court under Chief Justice Earl Warren had a major impact on the United States in that this Court
1 became involved in foreign affairs by reviewing the constitutionality of treaties
2 weakened the judiciary by refusing to deal with controversial issues
3 supported the idea that states could nullify acts of Congress
4 followed a policy of judicial activism, leading to broad changes in American society

9 Segregation in public schools was declared unconstitutional because it violated the
1 reserved powers provision
2 due process of law provision
3 principle of equal protection under the law
4 principle of a clear and present danger

10 Base your answer to question 10 on the song below and on your knowledge of social studies.

"It isn't nice to block the doorway,
It isn't nice to go to jail,
There are nicer ways to do it,
But the nice ways always fail,
It isn't nice, it isn't nice,
You told us once, you told us twice,
But if that's freedom's price, we
    don't mind."

—Malvina Reynolds, "It Isn't Nice"

This song from the 1960s is most likely referring to the movement to
1 liberalize immigration laws
2 expand civil rights
3 allow women to serve in combat roles in the military
4 grant voting rights to 18-year-old citizens

11 "There are two types of laws: There are *just* laws and there are *unjust* laws. I would be the first to advocate obeying just laws. One has not only a legal but a moral responsibility to obey just laws. Conversely, one has a moral responsibility to disobey unjust laws."

—Martin Luther King, Jr.

This statement is a justification of the concept of
1 cultural pluralism
2 ethnic assimilation
3 reverse discrimination
4 civil disobedience

12 The women's movement was strengthened in the 1960s chiefly because
1 women became increasingly dissatisfied with their status and their roles in society
2 women were angered by the failure of the voters to elect them to Congress
3 job discrimination against women and minorities was eliminated
4 the radical liberation movements of the 1950s had failed

13 "And so my fellow Americans—ask not what you country can do for you—ask what you can do for your country."

When President John F. Kennedy made this statement, he was encouraging the American people to develop
1 a personal commitment to work for national ideals
2 an awareness of environmental hazards
3 a concern for national defense
4 an appreciation for the contributions of immigrants to American society

14 Which statement about the Cuban missile crisis (1962) is most accurate?
1 The crisis showed that the United States and the Soviet Union could agree on total disarmament.
2 The crisis brought the two major world powers very close to war.
3 The United States wanted to establish missile sites in Cuban territory.
4 The communist government in Cuba was overthrown.

15 President Lyndon B. Johnson's Great Society was an effort to solve the problem of
1 poverty
2 drug trafficking
3 overpopulation
4 illegal immigration

16 One similarity between the actions of President Franklin D. Roosevelt and Lyndon B. Johnson is that both
1 led the United States to victory in war
2 expanded the role of government in citizens' lives
3 vetoed legislation on the issue of rights for minorities
4 achieved a balanced federal budget during their terms in office

17 **"Four Students Killed at Kent State University"**

"Gulf of Tonkin Resolution Passed"

"Radical Protesters Disrupt Democratic Convention in Chicago"

These headlines relate to which even in United States history?
1 Civil War
2 World War II
3 Vietnam War
4 Persian Gulf War

18 During the Vietnam War, serious
    questions were raised in the Untied States
    concerning the
    1 authority of the Supreme Court in regard
       to national security
    2 extent of the President's powers as
       commander in chief
    3 loyalty of United States military leaders
    4 role of the North Atlantic Treaty
       Organization (NATO) in international
       peacekeeping

19 A major long-term effect of the Vietnam
    War has been
    1 an end to communist governments
       in Asia
    2 a change in United States foreign policy
       from containment to imperialism
    3 a reluctance to commit United States
       troops for extended military action
       abroad
    4 a continued boycott of trade with Asia

20 The outcome of the Watergate scandal
    reinforced the principle that
    1 national security takes precedence over
       freedom of the press
    2 the power of executive privilege is greater
       than the rule of law
    3 the law applies equally to all citizens,
       including government officials
    4 impeached government officials are
       immune from criminal prosecution

21 The Camp David accords promoted by
    President Jimmy Carter were significant
    because they represented
    1 the first peace agreement between Israel
       and an Arab nation
    2 the establishment of a worldwide human
       rights policy
    3 a lasting arms-reduction treaty
    4 the end of the Vietnam War

22 The "trickle down" economic theory of
    President Herbert Hoover and the "supply
    side" economic policies under President
    Ronald Reagan were based on the idea that
    1 balanced budgets are essential to
       economic success
    2 the federal government needs to assume
       more responsibility for solving economic
       problems
    3 economic growth depends on making
       increased amounts of capital available to
       businesses
    4 economic stability is the responsibility of
       federal monetary agencies

23 The North American Free Trade Agreement
    (NAFTA) between the United States,
    Mexico, and Canada is meant to
    1 increase commerce and eliminate tariffs
    2 encourage lower labor costs
    3 raise environmental standards
    4 allow citizens to move freely from one
       nation to another

24 **"Clinton Offers Economic Aid to Russia"**
    "U.S. Sends Peacekeeping Troops to Bosnia"
    "U.S. Airlifts Food and Medicine to Somalia"

    These headlines illustrate that United States
    foreign policy during the 1990s stressed
    1 containment
    2 collective security
    3 global involvement
    4 neutrality

25 How does the present-day United States
    economy differ from the nation's economy
    of 1900?
    1 Immigrants are no longer a source
       of labor.
    2 Today's government plays a less active
       role in the economy.
    3 The United States is less dependent on
       oil imports.
    4 The growth of service industries is
       greater today.

THEMATIC ESSAY

In developing your answers to the essay, be sure to keep these general definitions in mind:

(a) <u>discuss</u> means "to make observations about something using facts, reasoning, and argument; to present in some detail"

(b) <u>describe</u> means "to illustrate something in words or to tell about it"

(c) <u>evaluate</u> means "to examine and judge the significance, worth, or condition of; to determine the value of"

Directions

Write a well-organized essay that includes an introduction, several paragraphs addressing the task below, and a conclusion.

Theme: Technological Change

Many aspects of United States society have been greatly affected by technological changes.

Task

Identify three aspects of United States society that have been affected by technological change since the beginning of the twentieth century. Explain how that aspect was affected by a specific technological change. Discuss the extent to which the impact of the change was positive or negative.

Suggestions

You may use any example from your study of the United States in the twentieth century. Some suggestions you might wish to consider include: environment, politics, agriculture, urbanization, individual rights, or cultural pluralism.

You are *not* limited to these suggestions.

Guidelines

In your essay be sure to:

- Address all aspects of the *Task*
- Analyze, evaluate, or compare and/or contrast issues and events whenever possible
- Fully support the theme of the essay with relevant facts, examples, and details
- Write a well-developed essay that consistently demonstrates a logical and clear plan of organization
- Introduce the theme by establishing a framework that is beyond a simple restatement of the *Task*
- Conclude your essay with a strong summation of the theme

DOCUMENT-BASED ESSAY

For online Document-Based Essays,
visit the Prentice Hall Web site at www.phschool.com.

This task is designed to test your ability to work with historical documents and is based on the accompanying documents (1–6). Some of the documents have been edited for the purposes of this question. As you analyze the documents, take into account both the source of each document and any point of view that may be presented in the document.

Directions

This document-based question consists of two parts: Part A and Part B. In Part A, you are to read each document and answer the question or questions that follow the document. In Part B, you are to write an essay based on the information in the documents and your knowledge of United States history.

Historical Context

The Preamble to the United States Constitution reads: "We the people of the United States, in order to form a more perfect union, establish justice, insure domestic tranquility, provide for the common defense, promote the general welfare, and secure the blessings of liberty to ourselves and our posterity, do ordain and establish this Constitution for the United States."

Task

Using the information from the documents and your knowledge of American history and geography, write an essay in which you discuss whether the America government, since 1950, has achieved the goals established for our nation in the preamble to the Constitution of the United States.

PART A: SHORT ANSWER

DOCUMENT #1

> *"I have a dream that one day this nation will rise up and live out the true meaning of its creed, 'We hold these truths to be self-evident, that all men are created equal.' I have a dream that one day on the red hills of Georgia, sons of former slaves and the sons of former slave owners will be able to sit down together at the table of brotherhood. . . . I have a dream that my four little children will one day live in a nation where they will not be judged by the color of their skin, but by the content of their character. . . . When we allow freedom to ring, when we let it ring from every village and every hamlet, from every state and every city, we will be able to speed up that day when all of God's children, black men and white men, Jews and Gentiles, Protestants and Catholics, will be able to join hands and sing in the words of the old Negro spiritual: 'Free at last. Free at last. Thank God Almighty, we are free at last.'"*
>
> **—Martin Luther King, Jr., "I Have a Dream" speech, 1963**

1 What does Dr. King's dream suggest about the United States government's success in achieving "the blessings of liberty" for all Americans?

_____

_____

_____

_____

DOCUMENT #2

> *"One thing became clear: that in the black movement I had been fighting for someone else's oppression, and now there was a way that I could fight for my own freedom, and I was going to be much stronger than I ever was."*
>
> **—Cathy Cade, women's rights activist**

2 What experience motivated Cathy Cade to work for the delivery of the "blessings of liberty" to women?

_____

_____

_____

_____

DOCUMENT #3
Selected Great Society Legislation, 1964-1966

Legislation	Purpose
Economic Opportunity Act, 1964	Created to combat causes of poverty, such as illiteracy and unemployment
Volunteers in Service to America (VISTA), 1964	Sent volunteers to help people in poor communities and set up community action programs to give the poor a voice in defining local housing, health, and education policies
Medicare, 1965	Provided hospital and low-cost medical insurance for most Americans aged 65 and older
Medicaid, 1965	Provided low-cost health insurance for low-income Americans of any age who could not afford private health insurance
Elementary and Secondary Education Act of 1965	Provided education aid to states based on the number of children from low-income households
Department of Housing and Urban Development (HUD), 1965	Established to oversee the nation's housing needs and to develop and rehabilitate urban communities. HUD also provided money for rent subsidies and low-income housing.
Water Quality Act, 1965 Clean Water Restoration Act, 1965	Established water and air quality standards and provided funding for environmental research
National Traffic and Motor Vehicle Safety Act, 1966	Established safety standards for all vehicles to protect consumers.

3 How did Lyndon Johnson's Great Society "promote the general welfare"?

_____

_____

_____

_____

DOCUMENT #4

4 What opinion does this cartoon express about how the American government should "provide for the common defense"?

_____

_____

_____

_____

DOCUMENT #5

"Nixon acts as if the kids had it coming. But shooting into a crowd of students, that is violence. They say it could happen again if the [National] Guard is threatened. They consider stones threat enough to kill children. I think the violence comes from the government."

**—Mother of Jeffrey Glenn Miller,
a student killed at Kent State University, quoted in *Life* magazine, May 15, 1970**

5   What opinion did this speaker have about the actions of the National Guard at Kent State University?

_____

_____

_____

_____

6   Who did this speaker blame for the events at Kent State?

_____

_____

_____

_____

DOCUMENT #6

"He told me they didn't fire those shots to scare the students off. He told me they fired those shots because they knew the students were coming after them, coming for their guns. People are calling my husband a murderer; my husband is not a murderer. He was afraid."

—Wife of a member of the National Guard, quoted in *Newsweek* magazine, May 18, 1970

7   What opinion did this speaker have about the actions of the National Guard at Kent State University?

_____

_____

_____

PART B: ESSAY

Directions
Using information from the documents provided, and your knowledge of United States history, write a well-organized essay that includes an introduction, several paragraphs, and a conclusion.

Historical Context
The Preamble to the United States Constitution reads: "We the people of the United States, in order to form a more perfect union, establish justice, insure domestic tranquility, provide for the common defense, promote the general welfare, and secure the blessings of liberty to ourselves and our posterity, do ordain and establish this Constitution for the United States."

Task
Using the information from the documents and your knowledge of American history and geography, write an essay in which you discuss whether the America government, since 1950, has achieved the goals established for our nation in the preamble to the Constitution of the United States.

Guidelines
When writing your essay, be sure to
- Address all aspects of the *Task* by accurately analyzing and interpreting at least <u>four</u> documents
- Incorporate information from the documents in the body of the essay
- Incorporate relevant outside information throughout the essay
- Richly support the theme with relevant facts, examples, and details
- Write a well-developed essay that consistently demonstrates a logical and clean plan of organization
- Introduce the theme by establishing a framework that is beyond a simple restatement of the *Task* or *Historical Context* and conclude the essay with a summation of the theme.

Important People in United States History and Government

The following list highlights the key people other than Presidents who are included in the New York State Core Curriculum for United States History and Government and therefore may be tested on the Regents Examinations. They represent the pluralism that is America.

Ansel Adams	• Photographer whose natural landscapes of the West are also a statement about the importance of the preservation of the wilderness
Samuel Adams	• Bostonian American Revolutionary War leader, political organizer, and journalist who helped to organize the Sons of Liberty and the Massachusetts Committee of Correspondence • Associated with the Boston Massacre and the Boston Tea Party • Member of the Continental Congress and signer of the Declaration of Independence
Jane Addams	• Progressive Era reformer in the social settlement house movement • Founder of Hull House, a Chicago settlement house • Cofounder and first president of Women's International League for Peace and Freedom • Corecipient of the Nobel Peace Prize (1931) • Involved in organizing of the NAACP
Susan B. Anthony	• Women's rights leader from 1851 until her death in 1906 • Most active for women's suffrage, but also worked for women's property rights and rights of married women
Yasir Arafat	• Palestinian leader involved in efforts to negotiate peace in the Middle East during President Clinton's administration • Led Palestinians during a number of violent clashes with Israel
Osama bin Laden	• Leader of the al-Qaeda terrorist network • Directed the September 11, 2001, attacks against the World Trade Center and the Pentagon
John Brown	• Extreme abolitionist who believed in use of violence to promote his cause • Became nationally known after his antislavery group killed proslavery settlers at the Pottawatomie Creek Massacre • His raid against a federal arsenal at Harper's Ferry led to his trial and execution. • Considered a martyr by some antislavery groups and was immortalized by Ralph Waldo Emerson in *John Brown's Body*
William Jennings Bryan	• Unsuccessful Democratic presidential candidate in 1896 and 1900 • Populist who supported farmers and free silver • Orator, religious fundamentalist (Scopes Trial), and anti-imperialist

John C. Calhoun	• Outspoken southern leader and advocate of states' rights • Favored nullification and the extension of slavery into the territories • Vice President under Presidents John Quincy Adams and Andrew Jackson; resigned over nullification issue • Secretary of state under President Tyler; successfully pressed for Texas annexation; opposed Mexican War and California statehood
Andrew Carnegie	• Industrialist and philanthropist who built Carnegie Steel Company, later part of U.S. Steel • In an article, *The Gospel of Wealth* (1889) he defended Social Darwinism, but also stated that the rich had a duty to help the poor, and improve society in areas they deemed important.
Rachel Carson	• Writer, scientist, and environmentalist whose book, *Silent Spring* (1962), identified the hazards of agricultural pesticides • Inspired the environmental movement and legislation
Fidel Castro	• Won Cuban revolution against dictator Batista; headed Cuba 1959–2008; limited civil liberties, nationalized industries • Allied with Soviet Union in 1962 Cuban Missile Crisis • U.S. trade embargo against Cuba under Castro in place since 1962
Willa Cather	• Pulitzer Prize winning writer of stories and novels about the struggle and the strength of the pioneers settling the frontier • Best known for *O Pioneers!* (1913), *My Antonia* (1918), *One of Ours* (1922), and *Death Comes to the Archbishop* (1927)
Cesar Chavez	• Latino leader of California farm workers from 1962 until his death in 1993 • Organized the United Farm Workers (UFW) to help migrant farm workers gain better pay and working conditions
Winston Churchill	• Prime minister of Great Britain during World War II
Father Charles Coughlin	• Roman Catholic priest who used his weekly radio program to attack President Franklin D. Roosevelt and his New Deal programs • Lost popularity because of his pro-fascist, anti-Semitic views; ordered by the Roman Catholic Church in 1942 to stop his political actions
Eugene V. Debs	• Union organizer and Socialist presidential candidate in every election from the 1890s until World War I
Dorothea Dix	• Nineteenth-century social reformer who revolutionized mental health reform; Superintendent of U.S. Army nurses in Civil War
Stephen Douglas	• Illinois Senator whose Kansas-Nebraska Act included his idea of popular sovereignty, which increased sectional tensions. • Lincoln-Douglas debates (1858) made Lincoln nationally known. • Candidate of northern faction of Democratic party in 1860 election
Frederick Douglass	• Former slave, abolitionist, lecturer, active in Underground Railroad • Supported Women's Suffrage, attended Seneca Falls Convention

W.E.B. Du Bois	• African American civil rights leader, historian, writer, sociologist • Cofounder of Niagara Movement and of NAACP • Influenced Harlem Renaissance by publishing African Americans in *The Crisis*. • Opposed Marcus Garvey's "back to Africa" movement and disagreed with Booker T. Washington by pressing for civil and political, not just economic equality for African Americans
John Foster Dulles	• Secretary of state under President Dwight Eisenhower • Made famous the concept of brinkmanship, a foreign policy that brought the United States just to the brink of war
Duke Ellington	• Songwriter, band leader, jazz composer, pianist, and a leading figure of the Harlem Renaissance • Famous songs include "Take the A Train" and "Mood Indigo."
Medgar Evers	• African American activist and NAACP field secretary • Murdered in Mississippi in 1963 by a sniper outside his house
F. Scott Fitzgerald	• Novelist whose works reflect climate of the "roaring twenties" • Novels include *The Great Gatsby,* and *Tender Is the Night*.
Henry Ford	• Industrialist who headed Ford Motor Company • His innovative production methods reduced the cost of producing cars, making it possible for the average person to own an automobile.
Benjamin Franklin	• Philadelphia statesman, diplomat, scientist, writer in revolutionary period • Drafted the 1754 Albany Plan of Union • Member of Second Continental Congress; served on committee to write the Declaration of Independence, which he signed • Helped persuade France to sign the 1778 Treaty of Alliance against England and helped negotiate the Treaty of Paris of 1783, ending American Revolution; delegate to Constitutional Convention
Betty Friedan	• Women's rights activist whose book, *The Feminine Mystique* (1963), encouraged women to find their own identity outside marriage • Helped found National Organization for Women (1966) and National Women's Political Caucus (1971)
William Lloyd Garrison	• Abolitionist editor of newspaper called *The Liberator,* published 1831–1865 demanding immediate end to slavery
Marcus Garvey	• African American nationalist leader who advocated pride and self-help as a means of empowerment • Founder of the Universal Negro Improvement Association, a nationalist and separatist group that wanted a separate black economy and urged African Americans to emigrate to Africa • Ideas influenced the 1960s Black Power movement

Bill Gates	• In 1975 co-founded Microsoft with vision of "a computer on every desk and in every home;" believed "personal computers would change the world" • Philanthropist committed to improving education and public health
Samuel Gompers	• Organizer and president of American Federation of Labor, a craft union for skilled workers; stressed issues such as wages and hours
Alexander Hamilton	• New York delegate at Constitutional Convention who worked for a strong central government • Wrote 51 of *The Federalist Papers* supporting ratifying the Constitution • First secretary of the treasury; promoted U.S. economic development
William Randolph Hearst	• Newspaper publisher whose yellow journalism style helped create public pressure for the Spanish-American War
Ernest Hemingway	• Novelist whose writings expressed conflict and concern created by changing American values; 1954 Nobel Prize for Literature winner
Patrick Henry	• Leader in the American Revolution in Virginia • As a member of Virginia House of Burgesses, introduced resolutions opposing the Stamp Act • Member of Continental Congress; supporter of independence • Opposed Constitution because of belief that it gave too much power to the federal government • Led movement for addition of the Bill of Rights to the Constitution
Langston Hughes	• Poet, playwright, and novelist who wrote about the African American experience, especially that of the poor and working class • A leading figure of the Harlem Renaissance
Saddam Hussein	• Long-time, ruthless Iraqi dictator • Invaded Kuwait causing Persian Gulf War in 1991; removed from power in 2003 during Iraq war. In 2006 hanged for mass murders.
Chiang Kai-shek	• Leader of the Chinese Nationalists in civil war; when defeated by Mao Zedong in 1949 left China and established a government in Taiwan
Robert Kennedy	• Attorney general (1961–1963) and brother of President John F. Kennedy • Assassinated in June 1968
Martin Luther King, Jr.	• Civil rights leader who advocated civil disobedience and nonviolent demonstrations as methods for achieving change • Founded Southern Christian Leadership Conference in 1957 • Led bus boycott in Montgomery, Alabama • Led march from Selma to Montgomery for voting rights • Gave "I Have a Dream" speech in Washington, D.C. • Won Nobel Peace Prize • Assassinated in 1968

Henry Kissinger	• Secretary of state under Presidents Nixon and Ford • Deeply involved in foreign policy in Vietnam, China, the Soviet Union, and the Middle East • Advised Presidents Reagan, Bush, and Clinton
Robert La Follette	• Governor of Wisconsin whose program, the "Wisconsin Idea," became the model for progressive reform • Served as United States senator and Progressive leader • Ran for President as the Progressive party candidate in 1924
Meriwether Lewis and William Clark	• Explorers who led the 1804–1806 expedition to survey lands included in the Louisiana Purchase • Documented the land, plants, animals, and other natural resources from Missouri to Oregon in maps, diaries, and drawings
Sinclair Lewis	• Novelist whose work *Main Street* attacked middle class values • First American to win Nobel Prize for Literature (1930)
John Locke	• British Enlightenment writer whose ideas influenced the Declaration of Independence, state constitutions, and the United States Constitution • Believed that people are born free with certain natural rights, including the rights to life, liberty, and property and must consent to be governed.
Henry Cabot Lodge	• Massachusetts Republican senator whose support of American imperialism and of a powerful navy strongly influenced Theodore Roosevelt • As chairman of Senate Foreign Relations Committee and Senate Majority leader, led successful fight against ratification of the Treaty of Versailles and entry of the United States into the League of Nations • Served as a U.S. representative to Washington Conference
Huey Long	• Populist governor of Louisiana and U.S. senator • Proposed that income and inheritance taxes on the wealthy be used to give each American a $2,500 income, a car, and a college education • Planned to challenge FDR for President, but was assassinated in 1935
Douglas MacArthur	• Led U.S. troops in the Pacific in World War II • Commander of U.S. occupation forces in Japan after World War II • Relieved of command by Truman after publicly disagreeing with him about the conduct of the Korean War
Malcolm X	• Leader of the 1960s Black Power movement • Assassinated in 1965
Horace Mann	• Nineteenth century educator, lawyer, and public official whose support helped create tax-based, nonsectarian public schools free to all children as well as better teacher-training institutions
George C. Marshall	• Army chief of staff during World War II and secretary of state under President Truman promoted the Marshall Plan, which assisted the economic recovery of Europe after World War II

John Marshall	• Chief justice of the United States (1801–1835) • Established prestige of the Supreme Court and strengthened power of federal government in cases such as *Marbury* v. *Madison, McCulloch* v. *Maryland,* and *Gibbons* v. *Ogden.* • First stated the right of judicial review in *Marbury* v. *Madison* (1803).
Thurgood Marshall	• African American attorney who argued *Brown* v. *Board of Education* before the Supreme Court in 1954 and was appointed to that Court in 1967—the first African American to serve on the Supreme Court
Cotton Mather	• New England Puritan associated with the concept of the Puritan work ethic (meaning that hard work is its own reward) and an appreciation of thrift and industry • Supported the Salem witch trials
Joseph R. McCarthy	• Republican Senator of the late 1940s and early 1950s who led a campaign to root out suspected Communists in American life • The term *McCarthyism* came to be associated with an era of government investigation of the private lives of many in public service and in the entertainment industry.
Baron de Montesquieu	• French Enlightenment philosopher who admired the British system of republican government • Influence is seen in separation of powers and in the checks and balances provisions in the Constitution.
John Muir	• Naturalist, conservationist, and writer; influenced President Theodore Roosevelt to protect more land; founded the Sierra Club
Ralph Nader	• Consumer rights crusader; wrote *Unsafe at Any Speed* (1965) to expose the lack of safety standards for cars • Third party presidential candidate (1996, 2000, 2004, 2008)
Frank Norris	• Naturalist writer whose 1901 novel, *The Octopus,* told of the struggle between the railroad and California wheat growers
Robert Oppenheimer	• Physicist who led the American effort to build the first atomic bomb
Thomas Paine	• English-born writer and political philosopher whose influential pamphlet *Common Sense* (1776) pressed for independence from Great Britain
Rosa Parks	• African American civil rights activist whose 1955 refusal to give up her seat to a white person led to the Montgomery, Alabama, bus boycott and helped launch the civil rights movement.
Frances Perkins	• Social reformer and political leader • Named secretary of labor under President Franklin D. Roosevelt in 1933, becoming the first woman to serve in a cabinet position

H. Ross Perot	• Third-party candidate and billionaire businessman who challenged George Bush and Bill Clinton for the presidency in 1992 with new ideas about balancing the federal budget and about other economic issues
Matthew Perry	• Led 1853–1854 naval mission to open Japan to world trade and negotiated U.S. trading rights with Japan (Treaty of Kanagawa)
Gifford Pinchot	• Conservationist and politician who led the Division of Forestry of the Department of Agriculture under President Theodore Roosevelt • Dismissed by Taft after attacking the Secretary of the Interior for removing from federal protection about a million acres of land
Joseph Pulitzer	• Publisher of the *New York Journal,* whose "yellow journalism" in a circulation war with William Randolph Hearst helped provoke the Spanish-American War
Jacob Riis	• Journalist, photographer, and social reformer of the Progressive Era • Used writings and photographs to show the need for better housing for the poor, such as in his 1890 book *How the Other Half Lives*
Jackie Robinson	• Professional baseball player • Became the first African American to play in major league baseball when he joined the Brooklyn Dodgers in 1947
John D. Rockefeller	• Industrialist and philanthropist • Founder of the Standard Oil Company
Nelson A. Rockefeller	• Former governor of New York who was appointed Vice President by President Gerald Ford in 1974 • Only nonelected Vice President to serve with a nonelected President
Eleanor Roosevelt	• Political activist and First Lady • Early and long-time activist for rights for African Americans and women during the New Deal as First Lady and as political activist on her own • Played a key role in creation of United Nations Declaration on Human Rights (1948) and heading the UN Commission on Human Rights (1961) • Chaired the Presidential Commission on the Status of Women during the Kennedy Administration
Julius and Ethel Rosenberg	• Convicted and executed for treason in 1953 during the era of McCarthyism; innocence is still debated
Jean-Jacques Rousseau	• French Enlightenment philosopher • Influenced the Declaration of Independence with his arguments in support of government by the consent of the governed
Sacajawea	• Native American guide for part of the Lewis and Clark expedition • Honored in 2000 with her image on a dollar coin

Nicola Sacco and Bartolomeo Vanzetti	• Italian immigrants and anarchists executed for armed robbery and murder at the height of the antiradical, anti-immigrant feelings of the 1920s • Cleared by the Massachusetts governor in 1977, some 50 years later
Margaret Sanger	• Pioneering advocate of birth control • Organized first American birth control conference in 1921 • Founder of a birth-control lobbying group that became Planned Parenthood in 1942
Upton Sinclair	• Muckraking journalist of the Progressive Era • Influenced the passage of the 1906 Meat Inspection Act with his novel *The Jungle,* which deals with the exploitation of the poor and the factory conditions that led to contaminated meat
Adam Smith	• In *The Wealth of Nations* (1776), this Scottish political economist rejected mercantilism and advocated a free enterprise system, the basis of modern capitalism. • He argued for free trade, the division of labor, competition, individual freedom, supply and demand, and *laissez-faire* as necessary for a sound economy.
Alfred E. Smith	• Reform governor of New York and first Catholic to run for President • Lost to Hoover in the 1928 election, largely because voters did not want a Catholic President and because Smith favored repeal of the Eighteenth Amendment • Right-wing conservative Democrat who helped organized American Liberty League (1934) and opposed New Deal
Bessie Smith	• Harlem Renaissance blues singer known as the "Empress of the Blues" • Recorded with prominent jazz musicians, such as Louis Armstrong and Benny Goodman
Elizabeth Cady Stanton	• Leading crusader for women's rights; also for abolition and temperance • Began women's rights movement with Seneca Falls Convention in New York in 1848; wrote Declaration of Sentiments (1848) • With Susan B. Anthony, cofounded the National Woman Suffrage Association and coedited *Revolution,* a women's rights journal
Lincoln Steffens	• Muckraking journalist, editor, and reformer; wrote about corruption in government and business in his 1906 novel, *The Shame of the Cities*
John Steinbeck	• Author whose novels often deal with problems of the working class during the Great Depression • *The Grapes of Wrath* (Pulitzer Prize, 1939) describes the effect of the drought that created the Dust Bowl on a group of farmers forced to leave Oklahoma and work as migrant laborers in California.
Harriet Beecher Stowe	• Writer whose emotional, controversial, and best selling novel, *Uncle Tom's Cabin* (1850), focused attention on slavery and contributed to the start of the Civil War

Ida Tarbell	• Muckraking journalist whose *History of Standard Oil Company* exposed Rockefeller's unfair and often ruthless business practices.
Norman Thomas	• Political leader, minister, pacifist who ran six times as Socialist party candidate for President • Supporter of moderate social reforms, strongly anticommunist • Helped organize the American Civil Liberties Union and urged nuclear disarmament
Dr. Francis Townsend	• Opponent of the New Deal who promoted a financially impossible plan to provide government pensions for the elderly
Mark Twain	• Author and humorist of the late nineteenth and early twentieth centuries, famous, in part, for his homespun stories about life along the Mississippi River • Mark Twain was the pen name of Samuel L. Clemens.
Voltaire	• French Enlightenment philosopher who praised British institutions and rights and influenced framers of the Constitution • Wrote against religious intolerance and persecution
Earl Warren	• Chief justice of the Supreme Court (1953–1969) • Landmark cases such as *Brown* v. *Board of Education* and *Miranda* v. *Arizona* marked his tenure.
Booker T. Washington	• African American educator, author, and leader • Founded Tuskegee Institute (1881) and wrote *Up from Slavery* (1901) • Urged vocational education and self-improvement rather than confrontation as the way for African Americans to gain racial equality
Ida Wells-Barnett	• African American journalist, suffragist, and reformer • Launched a national crusade against lynching in the 1890s • Cofounder of the NAACP and of the National Association of Colored Women
Edith Wharton	• 1920s novelist who expressed concern about old versus new values in books such as *The Age of Innocence* (1921)
Mao Zedong	• Leader of the communist Chinese government from 1949 until 1976 • Met with President Nixon on Nixon's historic trip to China in 1972
John Peter Zenger	• German immigrant, printer and journalist • Tried for criminal libel for criticizing New York governor in his paper; jury found him not guilty on the grounds that he had printed the truth. • His case was an early step in establishing freedom of the press.

Landmark Supreme Court Cases

Every Supreme Court case deals with important **constitutional principles.** Some cases have had such an enduring impact on United States history and government that they require greater examination. The lasting significance and central constitutional principles of 32 landmark Supreme Court cases are outlined briefly in this section. For more information about the meaning of the constitutional principles, review Unit 2, Section 1, Part 4.

Year	Name of Case	Constitutional Principle	Why Decision is Important
1803	*Marbury* v. *Madison*	• Separation of Powers: Checks and Balances • the Judiciary	• Established the Supreme Court's right of *judicial review*—the right to determine the constitutionality of laws. • Strengthened the judiciary in relation to other branches of government.
1819	*McCulloch* v. *Maryland*	• Federalism: Federal Supremacy • National Power: *Necessary and Proper* Clause • the Judiciary	• Said no state could tax a federally chartered bank because *the power to tax involves the power to destroy.* • Ruling established the principle of national supremacy—that the Constitution and federal laws overrule state laws when the two conflict. • Expanded national power by supporting use of *necessary and proper* clause to carry out constitutional powers.
1824	*Gibbons* v. *Ogden*	• Federalism: Federal Supremacy • Property Rights/ Economic Policy: Interstate Commerce • the Judiciary	• States may regulate only what is solely intrastate commerce (within a state). • Congress has power to regulate interstate commerce, including commerce that involved intrastate-interstate activity. • Ruling established the basis of congressional regulation of interstate commerce.
1832	*Worcester* v. *Georgia*	• Federalism • National Power • Separation of Powers • Equality • Rights of Ethnic/ Racial Groups	• The Constitution gives the federal, not state governments, exclusive jurisdiction over Indian nations. • Treaties between the United States government and Indian nations are the *Supreme Law of the Land;* • Therefore, Georgia laws taking jurisdiction of Cherokee people and land were void. • President Andrew Jackson defied the ruling and the national policy of Indian Removal followed.

Year	Name of Case	Constitutional Principle	Why Decision is Important
1857	*Dred Scott* v. *Sanford*	• the Judiciary • Equality • Civil Liberties • Rights of Ethnic/ Racial Groups	• Ruled that African-Americans were not citizens (overturned by 14th Amendment). • Declared that slaves were property of owners: • As property, protected by 5th amendment, slaves could be taken anywhere; therefore, Missouri Compromise was unconstitutional.
1883	*Civil Rights Cases*	• Equality • National Power: Congress • Rights of Ethnic/ Racial Groups: 13th and 14th Amendments	• Declared 1875 Civil Rights Act unconstitutional. • 14th amendment prohibited states from discrimination, not individual actions in the private sector such as in theaters, hotels, restaurants. • Private discrimination was not a violation of the 13th amendment prohibition against slavery and *involuntary servitude.*
1886	*Wabash, St. Louis & Pacific RR* v. *Illinois*	• Property Rights/ Economic Policy: Interstate Commerce • National Power • Federalism	• Invalidated state law setting railroad rates on that part of an interstate trip within state borders. • By declaring it a federal power to regulate rates and by limiting state regulations, Court strengthened Constitution's interstate commerce clause. • Ruling paved way for creation in 1887 of Interstate Commerce Commission.
1895	*United States* v. *E.C. Knight Co.*	• National Power: Anti-Trust • the Judiciary • Federalism • Property Rights/ Economic Policy: Interstate Commerce	• While federal government did have the right to regulate some parts of economy, states, under 10th amendment, could regulate intrastate economic activities such as manufacturing. • Refineries were *manufacturing operations,* not commerce; therefore, the Sherman Anti-Trust Act could not be applied to American Sugar Refining Co. although company controlled 90% of sugar processing in the nation.
1895	*In Re Debs*	• National Power: Commerce Clause • Property Rights/ Economic Policy: Commerce Clause and Labor	• Ruled that federal government under commerce clause of Constitution had right to halt 1894 Pullman strike. • Said strike hurt *general welfare* of nation by disrupting commerce and mail delivery.

Year	Name of Case	Constitutional Principle	Why Decision is Important
1896	*Plessy* v. *Ferguson*	• Equality • Rights of Ethnic/Racial Groups: 14th Amendment Equal Protection Clause • the Judiciary	• Upheld Louisiana law providing for *equal but separate accommodations for white and colored races*. • Said law did not conflict with 13th or 14th amendments, nor with commerce clause. • 14th amendment was not intended to enforce what Court called *social equality*. • Provided legal justification for *separate but equal* segregation policy until overturned in 1954 by *Brown* v. *Board of Education*.
1904	*Northern Securities Co.* v. *United States*	• National Power: Anti-Trust, Commerce Clause • Property Rights/Economic Policy	• Federal suit (part of T. Roosevelt's trust-busting) using Sherman Antitrust Act. Court ruled that the Northern Securities • Company was formed only to eliminate competition and ordered it to be dissolved. • Congress under commerce clause had authority to regulate any *conspiracy* to eliminate competition.
1905	*Lochner* v. *New York*	• Property Rights/Economic Policy: Contracts • Civil Liberties: 14th Amendment	• Ruled that a New York law limiting bakers to 10-hour days and 60-hour weeks in order to protect public health was unconstitutional. It violated the *right and liberty of an individual to contract*. • New York law went beyond *legitimate* police powers of a state.
1908	*Muller* v. *Oregon*	• Civil Liberties: 14th Amendment • Federalism: 10th v. 14th Amendments • Equality • Rights of Women	• Upheld an Oregon law that limited women to a 10-hour work day in laundries or factories in order to protect women's health. • Cited the physical differences between men and women when ruling that need to protect women's health outweighed the liberty to make a contract that was upheld in *Lochner*.
1919	*Schenck* v. *United States*	• Civil Liberties: Limited in Wartime • the Judiciary	• Established limits on free speech; right is not absolute but dependent on circumstances, i.e. person is not protected if falsely shouts fire in a crowded theatre. • In this case saw defendants' actions as a *clear and present danger* to security of the nation in wartime.

Year	Name of Case	Constitutional Principle	Why Decision is Important
1935	*Schechter Poultry Corporation* v. *United States*	• Separation of Powers • Property Rights/ Economic Policy: Commerce Clause	• Placed limits on the ability of Congress to delegate legislative powers to President. • By narrowly defining interstate commerce also restricted congressional powers to regulate commerce. • Declared the New Deal's National Industrial Act unconstitutional.
1944	*Korematsu* v. *United States*	• Civil Liberties: Equal Protection • Presidential Power in Wartime • Rights of Ethnic/ Racial Groups	• Upheld the power of the president in wartime to limit a group's civil liberties. • Ruled that forcible relocation of Japanese Americans to Wartime Relocation Agency Camps during World War II was legal.
1954	*Brown* v. *Board of Education*	• Equality: Equal Protection • Federalism • Rights of Ethnic/ Racial Groups	• In this school segregation case, Court overturned *Plessy* v. *Ferguson separate but equal* doctrine. • Ruled that *separate educational facilities are inherently* (inseparably) *unequal* and violate the 14th amendment's *equal protection* clause.
1957	*Watkins* v. *United States*	• Criminal Procedures: Due Process • National Power: Congressional Investigations • Civil Liberties	• Congressional investigations must spell out their legislative purpose and jurisdiction. • The Bill of Rights is applicable to congressional investigations. • Watkins was within his rights to refuse to testify to matters beyond scope of House Committee on Un-American Activities.
1961	*Mapp* v. *Ohio*	• Criminal Procedures: 4th Amendment • Civil Liberties: 14th Amendment	• Ruled that 4th and 14th Amendments protected citizen from illegal searches. • Applied *exclusionary rule* to state courts, i.e. evidence obtained unconstitutionally—in this case without a search warrant—could not be used in federal or state courts.
1962	*Baker* v. *Carr*	• Avenues of Representation: Voting Rights; Equal Protection • Federalism	• Court has jurisdiction over apportionment of seats in state legislatures. • Overrepresentation of rural voters and under representation of urban voters was a violation of 14th amendment's *equal protection* clause. • Ruling led to other court cases that established *one person-one vote* concept.

Year	Name of Case	Constitutional Principle	Why Decision is Important
1962	*Engel* v. *Vitale*	• Civil Liberties: Establishment Clause, 1st and 14th Amendments	• Reciting of an official prayer in the schools violated the 1st amendment's *establishment of religion* clause, which was applied to the states by the 14th amendment. • Although students were not required to say the non-denominational prayer, its recitation in class put them under pressure.
1963	*Gideon* v. *Wainwright*	• Civil Liberties • Criminal Procedures: 6th and 14th Amendments	• Ruled unanimously that the 6th amendment right to an attorney, which was applied to the states by the 14th amendment, required that a state provide lawyers for poor people accused of felony crimes, not just capital crimes.
1964	*Heart of Atlanta Motel* v. *United States*	• National Power: Commerce Clause • Civil Liberties: Equal Protection Clause	• Upheld constitutionality of 1964 Civil Rights Act's use of Congressional interstate commerce powers to prohibit discrimination in private facilities whose operations affect interstate commerce.
1966	*Miranda* v. *Arizona*	• Criminal Procedures: Due Process, Self-Incrimination • Civil Liberties: Equal Protection	• Established the requirement prior to questioning to inform those accused of crimes that they have the right to remain silent, the right to a lawyer, and that what they say can be used against them in court. • Evidence obtained without this warning may not be used in court under the *exclusionary rule*.
1969	*Tinker* v. *Des Moines Independent Community School District*	• Civil Liberties: 1st Amendment, Student Rights/ Safe School Environment	• While recognizing the authority of schools *to prescribe and control conduct in the schools,* the court ruled that *neither students or teachers shed their constitutional rights to freedom of speech or expression at the schoolhouse gate.* • Symbolic, silent expression of opinion in absence of any disorder (wearing of black armbands to protest Vietnam War) is protected under the 1st amendment.
1971	*New York Times Co.* v. *United States*	• Civil Liberties: Freedom of the Press • National Power	• Court narrowly upheld 1st amendment right to Freedom of the Press. • Ruled that government had not met the *heavy burden of prior restraint* i.e. not made a strong enough case to stop publication of *The Pentagon Papers* on the grounds that national security would be hurt.

Year	Name of Case	Constitutional Principle	Why Decision is Important
1973	*Roe* v. *Wade*	• Civil Liberties: Right to Privacy • Rights of Women	• Declared state laws making abortions illegal to be unconstitutional while stating certain limits and conditions. • Basis of decision was right to privacy, citing primarily the *due process* clause of 14th amendment.
1974	*United States* v. *Nixon*	• Separation of Powers: Due Process, Executive Power	• By 8-0 vote, Court ruled that Nixon had to turn over the Watergate Tapes to the Special Prosecutor. • No president was above the law; *executive privilege* (confidentiality) was not absolute. • Separation of powers does not protect a president from judicial review of *executive privilege,* nor from the needs of the judicial process.
1985	*New Jersey* v. *T.L.O.*	• Civil Liberties: 4th Amendment, Student Rights/ Safe School Environment	• Affirmed that 4th amendment prohibition on *unreasonable searches and seizures* applied to school officials. • But, necessity of maintaining discipline allowed for searches when there are *reasonable grounds* that the law or school rules have been broken compared to police requirement of *probable cause*.
1990	*Cruzan* v. *Director, Missouri Department of Health*	• Civil Liberties: Due Process	• Ruled that under *due process* clause, a competent person has the right to refuse life-sustaining treatment. • Evidence of the wishes of an incompetent person must be *clear and convincing;* evidence not presented in this case. • Cruzan's parents then gathered what Missouri Court agreed was *clear and convincing* evidence and the life support system was removed.
1992	*Planned Parenthood of Southeastern Pennsylvania et al.*v. *Casey*	• Civil Liberties • Rights of Women	• Upheld *Roe* decision. • Determined that Pennsylvania law with provisions such as 24 hour waiting period and parental consent to a minor's abortion did not create *undue burden or substantial obstacles* to abortion. • Struck down requirement of husband notification.
1995	*Vernonia School District* v. *Acton*	• Civil Liberties: 4th Amendment, Student Rights/ Safe School Environment	• Ruled that a school's practice of testing athletes randomly for drug use did not violate their rights under 4th and 14th amendments. • Cited schools need to maintain student safety and fulfill its educational mission.

Presidents of the United States

George Washington (1732–1799) *Years in office:* 1789–1797 No political party *Elected from:* Virginia *Vice Pres.:* John Adams	• Commanded the Continental army during the American Revolution • President of the Constitutional Convention • Set precedents that were followed by other Presidents, such as forming a cabinet • Strengthened new government through support of Hamilton's financial policies and use of force against the Whiskey Rebellion • Kept peace through Proclamation of Neutrality and Jay Treaty • Set basis of U.S. foreign policy in his Farewell Address
John Adams (1735–1826) *Years in office:* 1797–1801 Federalist *Elected from:* Massachusetts *Vice Pres.:* Thomas Jefferson	• American Revolution leader who protested Stamp Act • Helped draft Declaration of Independence • President during times of war in Europe • Alien and Sedition Acts contributed to his unpopularity and the fall of his party.
Thomas Jefferson (1743–1826) *Years in office:* 1801–1809 Democratic-Republican *Elected from:* Virginia *Vice Pres.:* Aaron Burr, George Clinton	• Major author of the Declaration of Independence • Opposed Federalists • Favored limited, decentralized government • Opposed Hamilton's financial plan and Alien and Sedition Acts • Approved the Louisiana Purchase from France, which doubled the size of the nation
James Madison (1751–1836) *Years in office:* 1809–1817 Democratic-Republican *Elected from:* Virginia *Vice Pres.:* George Clinton, Elbridge Gerry	• Called the Father of the Constitution • One author of the Virginia Plan; his journals provide a record of events at the Constitutional Convention. • Wrote 29 of the Federalist Papers • Proposed the Bill of Rights to Congress • Lost popularity over lack of leadership in War of 1812
James Monroe (1758–1831) *Years in office:* 1817–1825 National Republican *Elected from:* Virginia *Vice Pres.:* Daniel Tompkins	• Established U.S. foreign policy in the Western Hemisphere with the Monroe Doctrine • Settled boundaries with Canada (1818) • Acquired Florida (1819)
John Quincy Adams (1767–1848) *Years in office:* 1825–1829 National Republican *Elected from:* Massachusetts *Vice Pres.:* John Calhoun	• Elected President after election was decided in the House of Representatives • Secretary of state to James Monroe • After leaving office as President, served in House of Representatives; only President to have done so

Andrew Jackson (1767–1845) *Years in office:* 1829–1837 Democrat *Elected from:* Tennessee *Vice Pres.:* John Calhoun, Martin Van Buren	• Hero of Battle of New Orleans (War of 1812) • Opposed Calhoun and nullification • Vetoed rechartering of Second National Bank • Supported Native American removal policy • Associated with mass politics and nominating conventions • Used spoils system
Martin Van Buren (1782–1862) *Years in office:* 1837–1841 Democrat *Elected from:* New York *Vice Pres.:* Richard Johnson	• First New Yorker to become President • Served as Vice President to Jackson • Opposed Texas annexation • Presidency weakened by economic crisis of the Panic of 1837
William Henry Harrison (1774–1841) *Years in office:* 1841 Whig *Elected from:* Ohio *Vice Pres.:* John Tyler	• While governor of Indiana Territory, led military actions against Native Americans in the Battle of Tippecanoe (1811) • Elected as first Whig candidate on the slogan "Tippecanoe and Tyler Too" • First President to die in office; served only one month
John Tyler (1790–1862) *Years in office:* 1841–1845 Whig *Elected from:* Virginia *Vice Pres.:* none	• Became President after the death of Harrison • Texas annexed largely because of his influence
James K. Polk (1795–1849) *Years in office:* 1845–1849 Democrat *Elected from:* Tennessee *Vice Pres.:* George Dallas	• Foreign policy aimed at fulfilling goal of Manifest Destiny • With slogan "54' 40 or fight!" campaigned for all of Oregon country • Supported Texas annexation and acquisition of California • Mexican Cession added to U.S. as result of war
Zachary Taylor (1784–1850) *Years in office:* 1849–1850 Whig *Elected from:* Louisiana *Vice Pres.:* Millard Fillmore	• West Point graduate and military hero of Mexican War, known as Old Rough and Ready • Supported Compromise of 1850 • Died in office
Millard Fillmore (1800–1874) *Years in office:* 1850–1853 Whig *Elected from:* New York *Vice Pres.:* none	• New Yorker by birth, became President on death of Taylor • Supported and signed Compromise of 1850 • Supported Fugitive Slave Law • Candidate for the Know-Nothings
Franklin Pierce (1804–1869) *Years in office:* 1853–1857 Democrat *Elected from:* New Hampshire *Vice Pres.:* William King	• New Englander who supported Kansas-Nebraska Act • Gadsden Purchase ratified during his presidency • Trade treaty with Japan became effective during his administration, due to the efforts of Commodore Perry

James Buchanan (1791–1868) *Years in office:* 1857–1861 Democrat *Elected from:* Pennsylvania *Vice Pres.:* John Breckinridge	• In office when *Dred Scott* decision and John Brown's raid occurred • Took no action in response to the secession of South Carolina and other southern states
Abraham Lincoln (1809–1865) *Years in office:* 1861–1865 Republican *Elected from:* Illinois *Vice Pres.:* Hannibal Hamlin, Andrew Johnson	• Became nationally known as result of Lincoln-Douglas debates in 1858 • First Republican to be elected President • Used war powers of the presidency during Civil War to achieve his goal of preserving the nation • Gave Gettysburg Address; issued Emancipation Proclamation • Assassinated before he could act on his plans of reconstruction
Andrew Johnson (1808–1875) *Years in office:* 1865–1869 Republican *Elected from:* Tennessee *Vice Pres.:* none	• Impeached by House after bitter disagreements with Congress over Reconstruction; acquitted by a single vote • 13th and 14th Amendments ratified during his presidency
Ulysses S. Grant (1822–1885) *Years in office:* 1869–1877 Republican *Elected from:* Illinois *Vice Pres.:* Schuyler Colfax, Henry Wilson	• Civil War military leader who served as supreme commander of the Union army • Transcontinental railroad completed and 15th Amendment ratified during his presidency • Crédit Mobilier and the Whiskey Ring scandals marred his presidency.
Rutherford B. Hayes (1822–1893) *Years in office:* 1877–1881 Republican *Elected from:* Ohio *Vice Pres.:* William Wheeler	• Election decided through compromise, preventing a constitutional crisis after a dispute over electoral votes • Federal troops removed from the South, marking the end of Reconstruction
James A. Garfield (1831–1881) *Years in office:* 1881 Republican *Elected from:* Ohio *Vice Pres.:* Chester A. Arthur	• Assassinated after four months in office
Chester A. Arthur (1830–1886) *Years in office:* 1881–1885 Republican *Elected from:* New York *Vice Pres.:* none	• Vetoed Chinese Exclusion Act (1882) • Supported Pendleton Act (1883), which enacted civil service reform

Grover Cleveland (1837–1908) *Years in office:* 1885–1889; 1893–1897 Democrat *Elected from:* New York *Vice Pres.:* Thomas Hendricks, Adlai Stevenson	• Expanded the civil service • Only President to serve two nonconsecutive terms • Served as governor of New York
Benjamin Harrison (1833–1901) *Years in office:* 1889–1893 Republican *Elected from:* Indiana *Vice Pres.:* Levi Morton	• Elected President with most electoral but not popular votes • Supported Sherman Antitrust Act
William McKinley (1843–1901) *Years in office:* 1897–1901 Republican *Elected from:* Ohio *Vice Pres.:* Garret Hobart, Theodore Roosevelt	• President during a period of expansionism marked by Spanish-American War • A high tariff and the Gold Standard Act passed during his administration • Assassinated in 1901
Theodore Roosevelt (1858–1919) *Years in office:* 1901–1909 Republican *Elected from:* New York *Vice Pres.:* Charles Fairbanks	• Progressive governor of New York (1899–1900) • Presidential programs called the Square Deal • Known as a trustbuster, conservationist, reformer, and nationalist • Used the power of presidency to regulate economic affairs of the nation and to expand its role in Asia and Caribbean • Issued the Roosevelt Corollary to the Monroe Doctrine
William Howard Taft (1857–1903) *Years in office:* 1909–1913 Republican *Elected from:* Ohio *Vice Pres.:* James Sherman	• Policy of "dollar diplomacy" gave diplomatic and military support to U.S. business investment in Latin America • Continued Progressive Era policies of business regulation, but his tariff and conservation policies, which were conservative, split the party
Woodrow Wilson (1856–1924) *Years in office:* 1913–1921 Democrat *Elected from:* New Jersey *Vice Pres.:* Thomas Marshall	• Progressive Era President whose program was known as New Freedom • Reform regulation included Clayton Antitrust Act, Federal Reserve System, Federal Trade Commission Act, and Underwood Tariff Act (which lowered rates) • Led the nation during World War I • Supported the Treaty of Versailles and League of Nations, which the Senate failed to approve
Warren G. Harding (1865–1923) *Years in office:* 1921–1923 Republican *Elected from:* Ohio *Vice Pres.:* Calvin Coolidge	• Led nation into Roaring Twenties on a call for "normalcy" • Administration known for corruption and scandals, including the Teapot Dome Scandal • Opened Washington Conference on Naval Disarmament in 1921, although he opposed internationalism

Calvin Coolidge (1872–1933) *Years in office:* 1923–1929 Republican *Elected from:* Massachusetts *Vice Pres.:* Charles Dawes	• Presidency marked by conservative, laissez-faire attitudes toward business • Presided over "Coolidge prosperity"
Herbert Hoover (1874–1964) *Years in office:* 1929–1933 Republican *Elected from:* New York *Vice Pres.:* Charles Curtis	• Used government resources against the Great Depression without success • Supported loans through Reconstruction Finance Corporation • Opposed direct relief • Used federal troops against the World War I veterans' "Bonus Army"
Franklin D. Roosevelt (1882–1945) *Years in office:* 1933–1945 Democrat *Elected from:* New York *Vice Pres.:* John Garner, Henry Wallace, Harry S Truman	• New Deal policies and leadership in World War II increased the power of the federal government • Tried to expand number of Supreme Court justices when the Court opposed New Deal programs • Pushed for social welfare legislation, such as the Social Security Act • New Deal programs criticized as both inadequate and too extreme • Urged cooperation in Western Hemisphere under the Good Neighbor Policy • Supported Japanese American internment during World War II • Only President to serve more than two terms
Harry S Truman (1884–1972) *Years in office:* 1945–1953 Democrat *Elected from:* Missouri *Vice Pres.:* Alben Barkley	• Made decision to drop two atomic bombs on Japan in 1945 to end World War II • Began the policy of containment of communism with the Truman Doctrine • Supported economic recovery in Europe through the Marshall Plan • Continued the New Deal philosophy with his Fair Deal • Entered into the Korean War during his presidency
Dwight D. Eisenhower (1890–1969) *Years in office:* 1953–1961 Republican *Elected from:* New York *Vice Pres.:* Richard M. Nixon	• Allied commander of forces in Europe during World War II • Issued Eisenhower Doctrine • Approved Saint Lawrence Seaway and 1956 Federal Highway Act • Sent troops to Little Rock to support school desegregation • In office when Alaska and Hawaii became 49th and 50th states
John F. Kennedy (1917–1963) *Years in office:* 1961–1963 Democrat *Elected from:* Massachusetts *Vice Pres.:* Lyndon B. Johnson	• Promoted the New Frontier program (which centered on containment), the Peace Corps, and the Alliance for Progress • Successfully resolved the Cuban missile crisis • Assassinated in 1963
Lyndon B. Johnson (1908–1973) *Years in office:* 1963–1969 Democrat *Elected from:* Texas *Vice Pres.:* Hubert Humphrey	• Promoted antipoverty programs and civil rights through his Great Society program • Used the Gulf of Tonkin Resolution to expand the Vietnam War • Division over his war policy led to his decision not to seek reelection. • President during a period of active civil rights movements for African Americans and women

Richard M. Nixon (1913–1994) *Years in office:* 1969–1974 Republican *Elected from:* New York *Vice Pres.:* Spiro Agnew, Gerald R. Ford	• "Vietnamization" policy and increased bombing followed by a 1973 cease-fire in Vietnam • Relaxed relations with USSR and the People's Republic of China • Resigned as President because of Watergate affair
Gerald R. Ford (1913–2006) *Years in office:* 1974–1977 Republican *Elected from:* Michigan *Vice Pres.:* Nelson Rockefeller	• Only President not to be elected by the American public; appointed as Vice President under Nixon and succeeded to the presidency after Nixon's resignation • Pardoned Nixon for which he was both criticized and praised • Worked to restore faith in government after Watergate crisis
Jimmy Carter (1924–) *Years in office:* 1977–1981 Democrat *Elected from:* Georgia *Vice Pres.:* Walter Mondale	• Domestic problems included inflation and oil shortages • Supported international human rights and Panama Canal treaties • Opposed the Soviet invasion of Afghanistan • Greatest success was the Camp David Accords, which led to peace between Egypt and Israel
Ronald Reagan (1911–2004) *Years in office:* 1981–1989 Republican *Elected from:* California *Vice Pres.:* George H.W. Bush	• Took a conservative viewpoint on social issues, such as abortion and prayer in school • Based his supply-side economic policy (or "Reaganomics") on the belief that government can destroy individual initiative • Presidency marked by huge trade and federal budget deficits • Arms control agreement signed with the USSR in 1985, 1986, and 1987 • Foreign policy aimed at keeping communism out of Latin America • Popularity damaged and foreign policy weakened by Iran-Contra scandal
George H.W. Bush (1924–) *Years in office:* 1989–1993 Republican *Elected from:* Texas *Vice Pres.:* J. Danforth Quayle	• Inherited the budget deficits, savings and loan scandals, and legacy of Iran-Contra Affair from the Reagan administration • In office when cold war ended, and Communist governments in Eastern Europe and Soviet Union fell • Led the United States in the Persian Gulf War against Iraq
William (Bill) Clinton (1946–) *Years in office:* 1993–2000 Democrat *Elected from:* Arkansas *Vice Pres.:* Albert Gore, Jr.	• Domestic policies centered on health care and social security reform, as well as economic issues, such as reduction of the national deficit • Secured approval of NAFTA (North American Free Trade Agreement) • Participated in air war against Iraq and Serbia • Impeached by the House of Representatives in 1998 on charges of perjury and obstruction of justice, but acquitted by the Senate
George W. Bush (1946–) *Years in office:* 2001– Republican *Elected from:* Texas *Vice Pres.:* Dick Cheney	• Took office after a close election in which a dispute over ballot recounts in Florida was ended by the Supreme Court in *Bush* v. *Gore*. • Conservative President whose early proposals included a tax cut, education reform, new energy policies, and a missile defense plan. • Declared war on international terrorism and ordered U.S. forces into Afghanistan to defeat Taliban and al Qaeda extremists. • Led the United States into a War against Iraq to end the dictatorship of Saddam Hussein

June 2004 Essay Questions

This section contains the essay questions from the Regents Examination in United States History and Government that was given in New York State in June 2004. The information given at the front of the book about thematic essays and document-based essays refers to these questions.

Answers to the essay questions are to be written in the separate essay booklet.

In developing your answer to Part II, be sure to keep these general definitions in mind:

   (a) <u>discuss</u> means "to make observations about something using facts, reasoning, and argument; to present in some detail"

   (b) <u>describe</u> means "to illustrate something in words or tell about it"

Part II

THEMATIC ESSAY QUESTION

Directions: Write a well-organized essay that includes an introduction, several paragraphs addressing the task below, and a conclusion.

   Theme: Geography and United States Government Actions

> Geographic factors often influence United States government actions, both foreign and domestic. Some of these factors include location, physical environment, movement of people, climate, and resources.

   Task:

> Identify *two* actions taken by the United States government that were influenced by geographic factors, and for *each* action:
> • Discuss the historical circumstances that resulted in the government action
> • Discuss the influence of a geographic factor on the action
> • Describe the impact of the government action on the United States

   From your study of United States history, you may use any federal government action that was influenced by geography. Some suggestions you might wish to consider include the Louisiana Purchase (1803), issuance of the Monroe Doctrine (1823), passage of the Homestead Act (1862), decision to build the transcontinental railroad (1860s), acquisition of the Philippines (1898), decision to build the Panama Canal (early 1900s), and passage of the Interstate Highway Act (1956).

You are *not* limited to these suggestions.

   Guidelines:

   In your essay, be sure to
   • Address all aspects of the *Task*
   • Support the theme with relevant facts, examples, and details
   • Use a logical and clear plan of organization
   • Introduce the theme by establishing a framework that is beyond a simple restatement of the *Task* and conclude with a summation of the *Theme*

NAME _____ SCHOOL _____

In developing your answer to Part III, be sure to keep this general definition in mind:

discuss means "to make observations about something using facts, reasoning, and argument; to present in some detail"

Part III

DOCUMENT-BASED QUESTION

This question is based on the accompanying documents (1–8). The question is designed to test your ability to work with historical documents. Some of the documents have been edited for the purposes of the question. As you analyze the documents, take into account both the source of each document and any point of view that may be presented in the document.

Historical Context:

The Civil War and the period of Reconstruction brought great social, political, and economic changes to American society. The effects of these changes continued into the 20th century.

Task: Using information from the documents and your knowledge of United States history, answer the questions that follow each document in Part A. Your answers to the questions will help you write the Part B essay in which you will be asked to

> • Identify and discuss *one* social, *one* political, **AND** *one* economic change in American society that occurred as a result of the Civil War or the period of Reconstruction

Part A

Short-Answer Questions

Directions: Analyze the documents and answer the short-answer questions that follow each document in the space provided.

Document 1

> . . . All persons born or naturalized in the United States, and subject to the jurisdiction thereof, are citizens of the United States and of the State wherein they reside. No State shall make or enforce any law which shall abridge the privileges or immunities of citizens of the United States; nor shall any State deprive any person of life, liberty, or property, without due process of law; nor deny to any person within its jurisdiction the equal protection of the laws. . . .

— 14th Amendment, Section 1, 1868

1*a* How does the 14th Amendment define citizenship? [1]

_____

_____

Score [   ]

b During Reconstruction, how was the 14th Amendment intended to help formerly enslaved persons? [1]

_____

_____

Score [   ]

Document 2

. . . History does not furnish an example of emancipation under conditions less friendly to the emancipated class than this American example. Liberty came to the freedmen of the United States not in mercy, but in wrath [anger], not by moral choice but by military necessity, not by the generous action of the people among whom they were to live, and whose good-will was essential to the success of the measure, but by strangers, foreigners, invaders, trespassers, aliens, and enemies. The very manner of their emancipation invited to the heads of the freedmen the bitterest hostility of race and class. They were hated because they had been slaves, hated because they were now free, and hated because of those who had freed them. Nothing was to have been expected other than what has happened, and he is a poor student of the human heart who does not see that the old master class would naturally employ every power and means in their reach to make the great measure of emancipation unsuccessful and utterly odious [hateful]. It was born in the tempest and whirlwind [turmoil] of war, and has lived in a storm of violence and blood. When the Hebrews were emancipated, they were told to take spoil [goods or property] from the Egyptians. When the serfs of Russia were emancipated [in 1861], they were given three acres of ground upon which they could live and make a living. But not so when our slaves were emancipated. They were sent away empty-handed, without money, without friends, and without a foot of land to stand upon. Old and young, sick and well, were turned loose to the open sky, naked to their enemies. The old slave quarter that had before sheltered them and the fields that had yielded them corn were now denied them. The old master class, in its wrath, said, "Clear out! The Yankees have freed you, now let them feed and shelter you! . . ."

Source: Frederick Douglass, *Life and Times of Frederick Douglass*, Park Publishing Co., 1881

2   According to this document, what did Frederick Douglass identify as a problem with the way the United States government emancipated the slaves?   [1]

_____

_____

_____

Score ☐

Document 3

> . . . We believe you are not familiar with the description of the Ku Klux Klans riding nightly over the country, going from county to county, and in the county towns, spreading terror wherever they go by robbing, whipping, ravishing, and killing our people without provocation [reason], compelling [forcing] colored people to break the ice and bathe in the chilly waters of the Kentucky river.
>
> The [state] legislature has adjourned. They refused to enact any laws to suppress [stop] Ku-Klux disorder. We regard them [the Ku-Kluxers] as now being licensed to continue their dark and bloody deeds under cover of the dark night. They refuse to allow us to testify in the state courts where a white man is concerned. We find their deeds are perpetrated [carried out] only upon colored men and white Republicans. We also find that for our services to the government and our race we have become the special object of hatred and persecution at the hands of the Democratic Party. Our people are driven from their homes in great numbers, having no redress [relief from distress] only [except] the United States court, which is in many cases unable to reach them.
>
> We would state that we have been law-abiding citizens, pay our taxes, and in many parts of the state our people have been driven from the polls, refused the right to vote. Many have been slaughtered while attempting to vote. We ask, how long is this state of things to last? . . .

— Petition to the United States Congress, March 25, 1871, Miscellaneous Documents of the United States Senate, 42nd Congress, 1st Session, 1871

3a Based on this document, identify **one** way the Ku Klux Klan terrorized African Americans.   [1]

_____

Score ▢

b According to this document, how did the actions of the Ku Klux Klan affect African Americans' participation in the political process?   [1]

_____

_____

Score ▢

Document 4

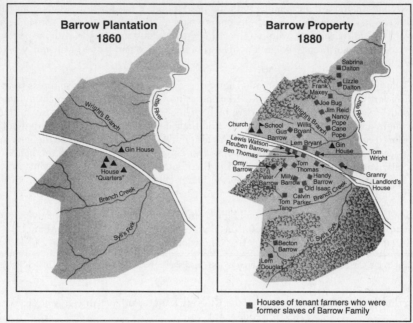

Sources: *Scribner's Monthly*, "A Georgia Plantation," April 1881 and
Graebner and Richards, *The American Record*, McGraw Hill, 2001 (adapted)

4 According to these illustrations, how did the economic role of African Americans change between 1860 and 1880? [1]

_____

_____

Score ☐

Document 5

. . . When we come to the New Industrial South the change is marvellous, and so vast and various that I scarcely know where to begin in a short paper that cannot go much into details. Instead of a South devoted to agriculture and politics, we find a South wide-awake to business, excited and even astonished at the development of its own immense resources in metals, marbles, coal, timber, fertilizers, eagerly laying lines of communication, rapidly opening mines, building furnaces, foundries [workplace where melted metal is poured into molds], and all sorts of shops for utilizing the native riches. It is like the discovery of a new world. When the Northerner finds great foundries in Virginia using only (with slight exceptions) the products of Virginia iron and coal mines; when he finds Alabama and Tennessee making iron so good and so cheap that it finds ready market in Pennsylvania; and foundries multiplying near the great furnaces for supplying Northern markets; when he finds cotton-mills running to full capacity on grades of cheap cottons universally in demand throughout the South and Southwest; when he finds small industries, such as paper-box factories and wooden bucket and tub factories, sending all they can make into the North and widely over the West; when he sees the loads of most beautiful marbles shipped North; when he learns that some of the largest and most important engines and mill machinery were made in Southern shops; when he finds in Richmond a "pole locomotive," made to run on logs laid end to end, and drag out from Michigan forests and Southern swamps lumber hitherto inaccessible; when he sees worn out highlands in Georgia and Carolina bear more cotton than ever before by help of a fertilizer the base of which is the cotton seed itself (worth more as a fertilizer than it was before the oil was extracted from it); when he sees a multitude of small shops giving employment to men, women, and children who never had any work of that sort to do before; and when he sees Roanoke iron cast in Richmond into car irons, and returned to a car factory in Roanoke which last year sold three hundred cars to the New York and New England Railroad—he begins to open his eyes. The South is manufacturing a great variety of things needed in the house, on the farm, and in the shops, for home consumption, and already sends to the North and West several manufactured products. With iron, coal, timber contiguous [adjoining] and easily obtained, the amount sent out is certain to increase as the labor becomes more skillful. The most striking industrial development today is in iron, coal, lumber, and marbles; the more encouraging for the self-sustaining life of the Southern people is the multiplication of small industries in nearly every city I visited. . . .

Source: Charles Dudley Warner, "The South Revisited,"
Harper's New Monthly Magazine (March 1887)

5   According to this passage, what was *one* economic change that had occurred in the South by 1887?   [1]

_____

_____

Score ☐

Document 6

A Public Fountain in North Carolina, 1950

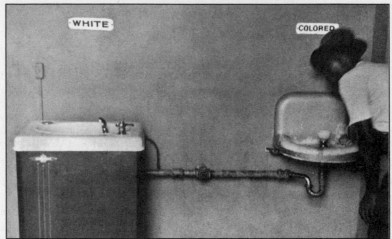

— Photograph by Elliott Erwitt
Source: Steve Kasher, *The Civil Rights Movement: A Photographic History, 1954–68,*
Abbeville Press

6   What does this photograph show about the treatment of African Americans in the South after Reconstruction?   [1]

_____

_____

Score ☐

Document 7

. . . Since 1868 there has been a steady and persistent determination to eliminate us from the politics of the Southern States. We are not to be eliminated. Suffrage is a federal guaranty and not a privilege to be conferred [given] or withheld by the States. We contend for the principle of manhood suffrage as the most effective safeguard of citizenship. A disfranchised citizen [one who is deprived of the right to vote] is a pariah [outcast] in the body politic. We are not opposed to legitimate restriction of the suffrage, but we insist that restrictions shall apply alike to all citizens of all States. We are willing to accept an educational or property qualification, or both; and we contend that retroactive legislation depriving citizens of the suffrage rights is a hardship which should be speedily passed upon by the courts. We insist that neither of these was intended or is conserved [protected] by the new constitutions of Mississippi, South Carolina or Louisiana. Their framers intended and did disfranchise a majority of their citizenship [deprived them of the right to vote] because of "race and color" and "previous condition," and we therefore call upon the Congress to reduce the representation of those States in the Congress as provided and made mandatory by Section 2 of Article XIV of the Constitution. We call upon Afro-Americans everywhere to resist by all lawful means the determination to deprive them of their suffrage rights. If it is necessary to accomplish this vital purpose to divide their vote in a given State we advise that they divide it. The shibboleth [custom] of party must give way to the shibboleth of self-preservation. . . .

— Afro-American Council public statement, 1898
Source: Francis L. Broderick and August Meier, *Negro Protest Thought in the Twentieth Century*,
Bobbs-Merrill Company

7   What political problem is being described in this passage?   [1]

_____

_____

Score [   ]

Document 8

Parade in New York City sponsored by the NAACP in 1917

Source: Robert Divine et al., *America Past and Present,* Addison Wesley (adapted)

8   What was the general goal of the marchers shown in this photograph?   [1]

_____

_____

Score ☐

Part B

Essay

Directions: Write a well-organized essay that includes an introduction, several paragraphs, and a conclusion. Use evidence from at least *five* documents in your essay. Support your response with relevant facts, examples, and details. Include additional outside information.

Historical Context:

The Civil War and the period of Reconstruction brought great social, political, and economic changes to American society. The effects of these changes continued into the 20th century.

Task: Using information from the documents and your knowledge of United States history, write an essay in which you

> • Identify and discuss *one* social, *one* political, **AND** *one* economic change in American society that occurred as a result of the Civil War or the period of Reconstruction

Guidelines:

In your essay, be sure to
- Address all aspects of the *Task* by accurately analyzing and interpreting at least *five* documents
- Incorporate information from the documents in the body of the essay
- Incorporate relevant outside information
- Support the theme with relevant facts, examples, and details
- Use a logical and clear plan of organization
- Introduce the theme by establishing a framework that is beyond a simple restatement of the *Task* or *Historical Context* and conclude with a summation of the theme

Glossary

abolitionist: a person seeking the legal end of slavery

affirmative action: steps taken to increase the representation of women and minorities, especially in jobs and higher education

AFL/CIO: influential labor union consisting of a merger between the American Federation of Labor and the Congress of Industrial Organizations in 1955

agrarian protest: demands by farmers for improvements in areas affecting agriculture, especially in the late 1800s

alien: a citizen of a foreign country

alliance: a group of nations mutually allied by treaty

Allies: the World War I alliance of Great Britain, France, Russia, and later the United States; also the World War II alliance of Great Britain, the United States, the Soviet Union, and other nations

al-Qaeda: world terrorist organization responsible for September 11, 2001 attacks on the World Trade Center and the Pentagon, led by Osama bin Laden

amendment: a change in or addition to a legal document, motion, bylaw, law, or constitution

American system: a plan offered by Henry Clay for internal improvements

annex: to attach new territory to an existing area, such as a country

Antifederalist: a person opposed to the Constitution during the ratification debate of 1787

anti-Semitism: prejudice against Jews

antitrust: opposed to practices and agreements that restrict trade, such as monopolies, price-fixing, and trusts

appeasement: the policy of giving in to an aggressor's demands in order to keep the peace

appellate jurisdiction: the authority of a court to review the decisions of inferior (lower) courts

Articles of Confederation: the first American constitution

assassination: the murder of a public figure

assembly line: a method of production in which automobiles or other items being manufactured move past workers and machines and are assembled piece by piece until completed

assimilation: the process of becoming part of another culture

assumption plan: the taking over of state debts by the federal government after the American Revolution

atomic age: a term used to describe period begun by the explosion of the first atomic bomb in 1945

baby boom: the rapid growth in the population of the United States between 1945 and 1964

balance of power: distribution of political and economic power that prevents any one nation from becoming too strong

balance of terror: a balance of power achieved when opposing sides possess nuclear weapons

balance of trade: the difference in value between a nation's imports and its exports

bankruptcy: a court action to release a person or corporation from unpaid debts

belligerents: nations fighting a war, usually after a declaration of war

bicameral legislature: a lawmaking body composed of two houses

big business: corporations or monopolies seen as having too much control over a society and its economy

bill: a proposal presented to a legislative body for possible enactment as law

Bill of Rights: the first 10 amendments to the U.S. Constitution, dealing mostly with civil rights

bipartisan: supported by two political parties

Black Codes: laws passed, especially by southern states after the Civil War, to control the actions and limit the rights of African Americans

blacklist: a list, circulated among employers, of people who will not be hired because of their views, beliefs, or actions

blitzkrieg: a sudden invasion or "lightning war," first practiced by Germany in World War II

blockade: the shutting off of a port to keep people or supplies from moving in or out

blue-collar worker: someone who holds and industrial or factory job

boycott: an organized refusal to buy or use a product or service, or to deal with a company or group of companies, as a protest or as a means to force them to take some action

brinkmanship: the policy of being willing to go "to the brink" of war to preserve peace

bureaucracy: a collective term for all of the workers who run the agencies that do the everyday business of government

cabinet: the group of officials who head government departments and advise the President

capitalism: the economic system based on private initiative, competition, profit, and the private ownership of the means of producing goods and services

carpetbagger: pejorative name for a Northerner who went to the South during Reconstruction

checks and balances: the system set up by the U.S. Constitution in which each branch of the federal government has the power to limit the actions of the other branches

citizen: a person who by birth or naturalization owes loyalty to, and receives the protection of, a nation's government

citizenship: the duties, rights, and privileges of a citizen

civil disobedience: nonviolent protest against unjust laws

civil liberties: certain rights guaranteed to all citizens of a nation

civil rights: rights guaranteed to citizens by the U.S. Constitution and laws of the nation

civil service: government jobs for which appointments and promotions are now based on merit rather than on political patronage

closed shop: a workplace in which employees must be labor union members in order to be hired

coalition: an alliance of political groups

Cold War: the state of tension between the United States and the Soviet Union after World War II

collective bargaining: the process by which a union negotiates with management for a contract

collective security: a system in which member nations agree to take joint action to meet any threat or breach of international peace

colonialism: the practice under which a nation takes control of other lands for its economic, military, or other use

colony: a settlement of people in a distant land who are ruled by a government of their native land

commerce clause: Article I, Section 8, Clause 3 of the U.S. Constitution, which gives Congress the power to regulate interstate and foreign trade

committee system: method under which members of the legislative branch form into smaller groups to facilitate such business as considering proposed legislation and holding investigations

communism: the economic system based on the collective ownership of property and the means of production, with all individuals expected to contribute to society according to their abilities and to receive from it according to their needs

compromise: the resolution of conflict in which concessions are made by all parties to achieve a common goal

concentration camp: a place where political opponents or other "enemies" of a nation are forcibly confined, especially those established by Nazi Germany before and during World War II

concurrent powers: powers shared by the national and state governments

confederation: an alliance of independent states

conference committee: a temporary joint committee of both houses of a legislature, created to reconcile differences between the two houses' version of a bill

conglomerate: a corporation that owns many different, unrelated businesses

Congress: the legislative, or lawmaking, branch of the United States government, made up of the Senate and the House of Representatives

consent of the governed: principle that says people are the source of the powers of government

conservation: the careful use or preserving of natural resources

conspicuous consumption: public enjoyment of costly possessions done in such a way as to emphasize the fact that one can afford such possessions

constitution: body of fundamental law, setting out the basic principles, structures, processes, and functions of a government and placing limits on its actions; (Cap.) the supreme law of the United States

constitutional: permissible under the Constitution

Constitutional Convention: formal meeting of state delegates in Philadelphia in 1787 at which the Constitution was written

consumer: person who spends money on goods and services

consumer goods: goods produced for use by individuals as opposed to use by businesses

consumerism: the practice of protecting consumers by publicizing defective and unsafe products or misleading business practices

consumer protection: measures to shield buyers of goods and services from unsafe products and unfair or illegal sales practices

containment: the U.S. policy after World War II of trying to keep the Soviet Union from expanding its area of influence and dominance

corporation: business owned by many investors that raises money by selling stocks or shares to those investors

court packing: Franklin Roosevelt's 1937 plan to add justices to the Supreme Court

credit: delayed payment for goods or services

creditor nation: a nation that is owed money by other nations

cultural diversity: many cultures existing in the same society

cultural pluralism: the idea that different cultures can exist side by side in the same society, all contributing to the society without losing their identities

culture: the way of life of a given people

custom: a habit or practice so established that it has the force of law

debtor nation: a nation that owes money to another nation or nations

Declaration of Independence: the 1776 document that stated Britain's North American colonies had become free and independent of the parent country

deficit: the amount by which money spent is greater than money received

deficit spending: government practice of spending more money than it takes in from taxes and other revenues

delegated powers: powers given by the Constitution to the national government and denied to state governments

demagogue: a person who gains political power by rousing the passions of the people

demobilization: the process by which a nation reconverts to peacetime status after a war or the threat of war

democracy: system of government in which supreme authority rests with the people, either directly or through elected representatives

Democratic party: one of the modern political parties, descended from Jefferson's Democratic-Republican party; also one of the oldest continuous political parties in the world

Democratic-Republican party: one of the first political parties in the United States, led by Jefferson and other leaders who were opposed to the Federalists; also known as Jeffersonian Republicans

demography: the study of populations through statistics

depression: a long and severe decline in economic activity

détente: the easing of tension between nations

dictatorship: form of government in which the power to govern is held by one person or a small group

direct democracy: system of government in which the people participate directly in decision making through the voting process

direct election of senators: system put into practice under the Seventeenth Amendment whereby the voters rather than the state legislatures elect members of the U.S. Senate

disarmament: reduction of a nation's armed forces or weapons of war

discrimination: policy or attitude that denies rights to people based on race, religion, sex, or other characteristics

disestablishment: depriving a state church of official support from the government, or never allowing a state church to be founded

diversity: variety

divestiture: a refusal to hold stock in companies that have operations in South Africa

division of powers: basic principle of federalism; the constitutional provisions by which governmental powers are divided between the national and the state governments

dollar diplomacy: President Taft's policy of encouraging United States investment in Latin America

domestic policy: everything a nation's government says and does in relation to internal matters

domino theory: the idea, prevalent during the Vietnam War, that if one Asian nation became Communist, neighboring nations would as well

due process of law: constitutional guarantee that government will not deprive any person of life, liberty, or property by any unfair, arbitrary, or unreasonable action

economic: pertaining to production, distribution, and use of wealth

economic nationalism: policies focused on improving the economy of one's own nation

economic programs: any policies set forward by a government that relate to the workings of its economy

elastic clause: Article I, Section 8, Clause 18 of the Constitution, which is the basis for the implied powers of Congress

electoral college: an assembly elected by the voters that meets every four years to formally elect the President of the United States

electoral vote: the results of the voting by the electoral college

electorate: all the persons entitled to vote in a given election

emancipation: the act of setting a person or people free

Emancipation Proclamation: the Presidential decree, effective January 1, 1863, that freed slaves in Confederate held territory

empathy: the process of sharing and understanding the feelings or thoughts of another person

English Bill of Rights: the 1689 agreement between Parliament and William and Mary which established that representative government and the rule of law outweighed the power of any monarch

Enlightenment: Eighteenth-century movement that emphasized science and reason as key to improving society

entrepreneur: a person who organizes, operates, and assumes the risks of a business enterprise

environment: natural surroundings and all the things that make them up

equal protection under the law: a right guaranteed to American citizens under the Fourteenth Amendment

espionage: spying

ethnic group: people of foreign birth or descent living in another country

European Economic Community: organization, also known as the Common Market, formed in 1957 to ease trade and travel among member European nations

European Union: the economic organization of European nations designed to increase the economic power of Europe in the world economy

excise tax: taxes levied on the production, transportation, sale, or consumption of goods or services

executive branch: part of a government that carries out its laws

executive power: the powers of the head of an executive branch of government to carry out the laws

executive privilege: the right claimed by Presidents to withhold information from the legislative or judicial branches

expansionism: desire to enlarge the territory owned or controlled by one's nation

expatriate: a person who gives up her or his homeland to live in another country

expressed powers: those delegated powers of the national government that are given to it in so many words by the Constitution

farm output: total value of products produced by a nation's farms

fascism: political philosophy that calls for glorification of the state, a single party system with a strong ruler, and aggressive nationalism

federal government: the central or national government

federalism: a system of government in which authority is divided between national and state governments; the belief in or advocacy of such a system

Federalist: supporter of the Constitution in the ratification debate of 1787, favored a strong national government

Federalist Party: one of the first political parties in the United States, organized by those who favored the ratification of the Constitution

Federal Reserve System: the nation's central banking system, established in 1913; a system of 12 regional banks overseen by a central board

feminist movement: the struggle of women for equality

First Amendment: Bill of Rights' guarantee of freedom of religion, speech, press, assembly, and petition

fiscal policy: policies relating to a nation's finances

flapper: nickname for a young woman in the 1920s who declared her independence from traditional rules

foreign policy: the actions and stands that every nation takes in every aspect of its relationships with other countries; everything a nation's government says and does in world affairs

Fourteen Points: President Woodrow Wilson's proposal in 1918 for a postwar European peace

Fourteenth Amendment: "due process" amendment that gave African Americans the right to vote and extended Bill of Rights protections to citizens of the states

free enterprise: an economic system based on private ownership, individual enterprise, and competition

freedom of speech: the right of freedom of expression guaranteed to Americans by the First Amendment

frontier: the border of a country; as defined by the U.S. Bureau of the Census, the edge of settlement beyond which the land was occupied by two or fewer people per square mile

frontier thesis: idea set forth by historian Frederick Jackson Turner that the nation's frontier regions shaped its character and institutions

Fugitive Slave Law: part of the Compromise of 1850, the Fugitive Slave Law required all citizens to help catch runaway slaves.

fundamentalist: one who believes that the Bible is the literal word of God

General Agreement on Tariffs and Trade (GATT): international agreement on reducing tariffs and expanding world trade

genocide: the systematic destruction of a race of people

Gentlemen's Agreement: informal agreement between the United States and Japan in 1907 to limit Japanese immigration to this country

Gettysburg Address: famous speech by President Abraham Lincoln on the meaning of the Civil War, given in November 1863 at the dedication of a national cemetery on the site of the Battle of Gettysburg

ghetto: area in which many members of some minority group live, to which they are restricted by economic pressure or social discrimination

Gilded Age: term used to describe the period from 1865 to 1900

glasnost: a period of "openness" in relations between the United States and the Soviet Union that began in the late 1980s

global interdependence: the idea that the nations of the world must rely on each other in many different ways, including trade, transportation, and communication

Glorious Revolution: the bloodless revolution in 1689 in which the English Parliament overthrew James II and replaced him with William and Mary

gold standard: a system in which a nation's currency is based on the value of gold

Good Neighbor Policy: Franklin D. Roosevelt's policy toward Latin America intended to strengthen relations with the nations of that region

government: that complex of offices, personnel, and processes by which a state is ruled, and by which its public policies are made and enforced

grandfather clause: laws passed in some southern states giving the right to vote only to people who had that right on January 1, 1867, and their descendants; intended to keep blacks from voting

Grangers, The: organization of farmers founded for social reasons in 1867, which later campaigned for state regulation of railroads and other reforms

grass-roots support: political backing from ordinary citizens, especially from rural areas

Great Compromise: the plan for a two-house legislature adopted at the Constitutional Convention in 1787 that settled differences between large and small states over representation in Congress

Great Depression: period of economic hard times from 1929 to 1941

Great Migration: migration of English settlers to the Massachusetts Bay Colony beginning in the 1630s

Great Society: the name given to President Johnson's domestic program in the 1960s

gross national product (GNP): the total value of all the goods and services produced in a nation in a year

guerrilla warfare: fighting by stealth and with small bands, which make surprise raids against stronger forces

hemisphere: half of the earth's surface

holding company: a company that gains control of other companies by buying their stock

Holocaust: name given to Nazi Germany's persecution of Jews before and during World War II; in this time, more than 6 million Jews died

Homestead Act: 1862 law that offered 160 acres of western land to settlers

House of Representatives: lower house of the U.S. Congress in which states are represented according to the size of their populations

humanitarian: one who is concerned with the welfare of all people

human rights: basic rights that should belong to all people including freedom of speech, religion, and the press

immigration: the movement of people from other countries into a country

immigration laws: laws controlling the movement of people into a country

immigration quota: limit on immigration allowing only a certain number of people to move into a country during a specified period

impeachment: the process by which the House of Representatives makes an accusation of wrongdoing against the President or other high federal officials

imperialism: policy by which one country takes control of another either directly or through economic or political dominance

implied powers: those delegated powers of the national government implied by (inferred from) the expressed powers; those powers "necessary and proper" to carry out the expressed powers

income tax: a tax levied on individual and corporate income

incumbent: person currently occupying a political office at the time of a new election

indemnities: money paid by a losing nation to a winning nation after a war

independence: freedom from the control, influence, or support of other people or nations

Indian Removal Policy: under President Andrew Jackson, the policy of moving all Native Americans to lands west of the Mississippi River in the 1830s

individual rights: basic rights that belong to each person

industrialization: process by which a nation begins to develop large industries

inflation: an economic condition in which prices rise substantially over a significant period of time

injunction: a court order prohibiting a given action; used frequently against workers in nineteeth-century labor-management disputes

interdependence: a condition in which parties are reliant on each other

internal affairs: public or business matters within the boundaries of a country

internal improvements: roads, bridges, canals, and other similar projects funded by the national government

internationalism: the belief, held by some Americans in the 1930s, that the United States should aid the victims of international aggression

international law: the norms of behavior generally agreed to and followed by the nations of the world in their dealings with each other

internment camps: places of confinement, especially in wartime

interstate commerce: trade among the states

intervention: interference by one nation in the affairs of another

intrastate commerce: trade within the borders of a state

Iron Curtain: the line between Soviet-dominated Eastern Europe and the West, so-called because the Soviets and their satellite nations prevented the free passage of people, information, and ideas across their borders

isolationism: a policy of avoiding alliances and other types of involvement in the affairs of other nations

isthmus: a narrow strip or neck of land running from one larger land area to another

Japanese-American relocation: policy under which Americans of Japanese ancestry were confined during World War II

Jim Crow laws: laws in the Southern states in the nineteenth and twentieth centuries that forced the segregation of the races

jingoism: aggressive nationalism

joint resolution: legislative measure which must be passed by both houses and approved by the chief executive to become effective; similar to a bill, with the force of law, and often used for unusual or temporary circumstances

judicial activism: broad interpretation of the Constitution leading to court-directed change

judicial branch: part of the government that decides if laws are carried out fairly

judicial restraint: narrow interpretation of the Constitution

judicial review: power of the Supreme Court to determine the constitutionality of acts of the legislative and executive branches of the government

judiciary: judicial branch of a government, its system of courts

jurisdiction: power of a court to hear (to try and decide) a case

jury: a group of people who hear evidence in a legal case and give a decision based on that evidence

justice: fairness; trial and judgment according to established process of the law

Know-Nothing party: common name for the American party, a nativist political organization formed in 1849

Korean War: conflict over the future of the Korean peninsula, fought between 1950 and 1953 and ending in a stalemate

Ku Klux Klan: secret society first formed in the South during Reconstruction to ensure white supremacy over blacks; reformed in the 1920s to express opposition to Jews, Catholics, Bolsheviks, and others considered "un-American"

labor union: workers organized as a group to seek higher wages, improve working conditions, and obtain other benefits

laissez-faire: noninterference; has come to mean a policy by which the government minimizes its regulation of industry and the economy

landslide election: an election in which a victorious candidate gathers an overwhelming percentage of the total votes cast

law: rule recognized by a nation, state, or community as binding on its members

League of Nations: association of nations to protect the independence of member nations, proposed by President Wilson in his Fourteen Points and formed after World War I

legislative branch: the lawmaking agencies of a government

legislature: group of people with the power of making laws for a nation or state

less developed nations: nations that have not fully industrialized, usually Third World nations

lifespan: the lifetime of an individual

limited government: basic principle of the American system of government; belief that government is not all-powerful, and may only do those things the people have given it the power to do

Lincoln-Douglas debates: the series of political debates between Stephen Douglas and Abraham Lincoln during the Senate campaign of 1858, which catapulted Lincoln to the national spotlight

literacy: the ability to read and write

literacy test: test of a potential voter's ability to read and write; once used in several states to prevent blacks and other minorities from voting; now outlawed

lobby: to attempt to influence legislation; also, groups that attempt to do so

lockout: during a labor dispute, the closing of a business (by locking the gates) to keep employees from entering

loose interpretation: a belief that the provisions of the Constitution, especially those granting power to the government, are to be construed in broad terms

Louisiana Purchase: purchase by the United States of the Louisiana Territory from France in 1803

lynch: to execute someone illegally, by hanging, burning, or other means

majority: at least one more than half (e.g., over 50 percent of the votes in an election)

Manhattan Project: secret American program during World War II to develop an atomic bomb

Manifest Destiny: a belief held in the first half of the nineteenth century that the United States had a mission to expand its borders to incorporate all land between the Atlantic and Pacific oceans

margin: a small part of the total price of a stock purchase deposited with a broker at the time of purchase with the promise to pay the full sum at a later date

Marshall Court: the Supreme Court during the tenure of John Marshall as chief justice, in which key decisions were made that strengthened the federal government's role in the nation's economic business

mass circulation: reaching a very large audience

mass production: rapid manufacture of large numbers of a product

Mayflower Compact: agreement signed by Pilgrims before landing at Plymouth

McCarthyism: the use of indiscriminate and unfounded accusations and sensationalist investigative methods to suppress political opponents portrayed as subversive; term taken from the name of Senator Joseph McCarthy, who carried out such practices

melting pot theory: the idea that different immigrant groups in the United States will lose their old identities and that a new American identity will emerge from the blending of cultures

mercantilism: economic theory that a nation's strength came from building up its gold supplies and expanding its trade

merger: a combining of two or more companies into a larger company

Mexican Cession: lands turned over to the United States after the Mexican War in what is now the states of California, Nevada, Utah, and parts of Wyoming, Colorado, Arizona, and New Mexico

Mexican War: conflict between the United States and Mexico from 1846 to 1848, ending with a victory for the United States

militarism: policy of building up strong military forces to prepare for war

minimum wage: the lowest wage that can be paid to certain workers as set by national or state law

minority: less than half

minority group: group within a nation that differs from most of the population in race, religion, national origin, etc.

minor party: one of the less widely supported political parties in a governmental system

missionary: one who attempts to spread the religious ideas of a faith in a foreign land

mobilization: a call-up of military forces, usually in preparation for war

monarchy: government headed by a single ruler, usually a king or queen

monetary policy: actions and positions taken by a government in regard to its system of money

monopoly: dominance in or control of a market for certain goods or services by a single company or combination of companies

Monroe Doctrine: policy statement of President James Monroe in 1823 warning nations of western Europe not to interfere with the newly independent nations of Latin America

moral diplomacy: a term describing President Woodrow Wilson's approach to foreign policy, which emphasized the use of negotiation and arbitration rather than force to settle international disputes

Mormons: members of the Church of Jesus Christ of Latter-day Saints; in the 1840s, thousands moved to Utah seeking freedom from religious persecution

muckraker: early twentieth-century American journalist who tried to improve society by exposing political corruption, health hazards, and other social problems

multilateral action: joint action taken by three or more nations

municipal government: the government of a city, town, or village

National Association for the Advancement of Colored People (NAACP): an organization founded in 1909 to fight for the rights of African Americans

national bank: bank chartered by the federal government

national government: in the United States, the federal government

nationalism: pride in or devotion to one's country

National Organization for Women (NOW): founded in 1966 to work for equal rights for women

national self interest: aim of all foreign policy

nativism: a belief in the superiority of the way of life of one's home country; in the United States, this was often associated with a desire to limit immigration

North Atlantic Treaty Organization (NATO): an alliance formed for mutual defense in 1949 under the North Atlantic Treaty, and now made up of 15 nations stretching from Canada to Turkey

naturalization: the process by which a citizen of one country becomes a citizen of another

natural rights: rights that all people are entitled to from birth

Nazism: belief in the policies of Adolf Hitler

necessary and proper clause: another name for the elastic clause, which is the basis of the implied powers of Congress

negotiation: talking over an issue by two or more parties with the aim of reaching a mutually agreeable settlement

neutrality: the policy of not taking sides in a dispute or a war

New Deal: name given to the programs of President Franklin D. Roosevelt

New Federalism: name given to the attempt to lessen the federal government role in its dealings with states during the presidencies of Nixon and Reagan

New Freedom: name given to the programs of President Woodrow Wilson

New Frontier: name given to the programs of President John F. Kennedy

New Nationalism: plan under which Theodore Roosevelt ran for President in 1912

nominating convention: political gathering at which a party names candidates for office

noninvolvement: policy of taking no side in international disputes, neutrality

nonrecognition: refusal to establish formal diplomatic relations with the new government of a nation

normalcy: President Warren G. Harding's term for the return to peace after World War I

North American Free Trade Agreement (NAFTA): agreement calling for the removal of trade restrictions between the United States, Canada, and Mexico

nuclear freeze: a halt in the manufacture and deployment of nuclear weapons

nuclear power: energy produced from a controlled atomic reaction

nuclear waste: the byproducts of the production of nuclear power

nullification: a state's refusal to recognize a federal law

Nuremberg Trials: post-World War II trials in which German government and military figures were tried for crimes committed during the war

Open Door Policy: policy toward China set out by Secretary of State John Hay allowing any nation to trade in any other nation's sphere of influence

original jurisdiction: the court in which a case is heard firsthand

overproduction: a condition that exists when the supply of a product exceeds the demand for that product

pacifist: a person who is opposed to war and refuses to fight under any circumstances

pardon: a release from the punishment or legal consequences of a crime granted by a President or governor

parliament: the legislature of Great Britain

patent and copyright laws: laws giving rights to inventions, literary, musical, and artistic works to their creators

patriotism: love and support of one's nation

peaceful coexistence: phrase describing the aim of U.S.–Soviet relations during a time of improved relations between those nations in the 1950s

per capita income: income per person

perestroika: the restructuring of the Soviet Union's economy under Mikhail Gorbachev that began a move toward free enterprise

plantation: large estate farmed by many workers

political party: organized group that seeks to control government through the winning of elections and the holding of public office

political system: the way a nation is governed

poll tax: a tax that must be paid before one can vote, often used in Southern states to discourage or prevent blacks from voting and now banned in national elections by the Twenty-fourth Amendment

pool: method of ending competition used by railroads in the late 1800s in which they divided up business in given areas and fixed prices

popular sovereignty: basic principle of the American system of government that the people are the only source of any and all governmental power

popular vote: votes cast by the people for the electors representing candidates in presidential elections

Populist movement: political movement begun by farmers and members of labor unions in the late 1800s seeking to limit the power of big businesses and grant greater say in the governmental process to individuals

power: control, authority, right

preamble: an introduction to a speech or piece of writing

prejudice: unfavorable opinion about people who are of different religion, race, or nationality

President: the chief executive of a modern republic, especially of the United States

primary: election held before a general election in which voters choose their party's candidates for office

Progressive era: the period of 1900–1920 that saw the greatest action by Progressive reformers

Progressive movement: reform movement that worked to correct abuses in American society

Prohibition: the period 1920–1933 when the making and sale of liquor was illegal in the United States

propaganda: spreading of ideas or beliefs that help a particular cause and hurt an opposing cause

protectionism: belief in policies that favor the protection of domestically produced goods

protective tariff: tax on imports designed to discourage their sale and to favor the development of domestic industry

protectorate: a country under the protection and partial control of a stronger country

public opinion: those attitudes held by a significant number of persons on matters of government and politics; expressed group attitudes

purchasing power: the ability to buy goods and services; the value of what money could buy at one time compared to what the same amount could buy at another time

racial equality: a condition in which people are treated in the same manner by law and society regardless of their race

racism: belief that one race is superior to another

Radical Republicans: group of Republicans in Congress who wanted to protect the rights of freedmen in the South and keep rich Southern planters from regaining political power

ratification: formal approval, final consent to the effectiveness of a constitution, constitutional amendment, or treaty

raw materials: natural substances before processing that will in some way increase their value or usefulness

recession: a decline in economic activity usually shorter and less severe than a depression

Reconstruction: the period 1867–1877 when the federal government or local republican governments ruled the Southern states that had seceded

recovery: a restoring to a normal condition; one of the aims of FDR's New Deal

Red Scare: term used to describe periods in the 1920s and 1950s when American fear and suspicion of communism was at its height

reform: change for the better; one of the goals of FDR's New Deal

regulatory agencies: parts of the federal bureaucracy charged with overseeing different aspects of the nation's economy

religious freedom: the ability to worship as one chooses, guaranteed in this nation by the First Amendment

reparations: payments for losses a nation has suffered during a war

representation: condition of being acted and spoken for in government

representative government: system of government in which voters elect representatives to make laws for them

republic: nation in which voters choose representatives to govern them

Republican party: one of the modern political parties, founded in 1854 in opposition to slavery

reservation: limited area set aside for Native Americans by the U.S. government

reserved powers: those powers held by the state in the American federal system

revenue: income

robber baron: terms used to describe large-scale entrepreneurs of the late 1800s

Roosevelt Corollary: expansion of the Monroe Doctrine announced by President Theodore Roosevelt in 1904 that claimed the United States had the right to intervene in Latin America to preserve law and order

rural: in or of the country

salad bowl theory: idea that people of different backgrounds can exist side by side in the United States, maintaining their identities while still contributing to the overall society

salutary neglect: manner in which England governed the American colonies in the late 1600s and early 1700s, marked by weak enforcement of laws regulating colonial trade

scalawag: white Southerner who supported Radical Republicans during Reconstruction

scarcity: too small a supply

secession: the act of formally withdrawing from membership in a group or organization; in the United States, the withdrawing of 11 southern states from the Union in 1861

sectionalism: strong sense of loyalty to a state or section instead of to the whole country

sedition: an attempt to incite a rebellion against a national government

segregation: separation of people of different races

Selective Service: the military draft name first used during World War I

self-determination: right of national groups to their own territories and their own forms of government

Senate: upper house of the U.S. Congress in which each state has two members

separate but equal: principle upheld in *Plessy* v. *Ferguson* (1896) in which the Supreme Court ruled that segregation of public facilities was legal

separation of church and state: principle set out in the First Amendment that the government shall take no actions to establish or interfere with the practice of religion

separation of powers: the principle that gives the powers of making, enforcing, and interpreting laws to separate legislative, executive, and judicial branches of government

settlement house: a private center providing social services for the poor in a needy neighborhood

sharecropper: farmer who works land owned by another and gives the landowner part of the harvest

sitdown strike: work stoppage in which employees refuse to leave the workplace and occupy it in an attempt to force their employer to come to terms

slavery: condition in which one person is the property of another; banned in this country by the Thirteenth Amendment

social contract theory: the idea that people agreed to give up some rights and powers to a government that would provide for their safety and well-being

Social Darwinism: the belief that the evolutionary idea of "survival of the fittest" applied to societies and businesses

socialism: economic and political system based on the public ownership of the means by which goods and services are produced, distributed, and exchanged

social reform: efforts to better conditions within a society

social security: programs of the federal government to provide economic assistance to the disabled, unemployed, poor, and aged

social welfare: programs to promote public well-being

sovereignty: absolute power of a state within its own territory

soviet: elected assembly in the Soviet Union; (Cap.) pertaining to the Soviet Union

speculator: person who invests in a risky business venture in hopes of making a large profit

spoils system: system or practice of giving appointed offices as rewards from the successful party in an election; name for the patronage system under President Andrew Jackson

Square Deal: name given to programs of President Theodore Roosevelt

stagflation: an economic condition characterized by both inflation and recession

states rights: idea that individual states had the right to limit the power of the federal government

stereotype: a fixed, oversimplified idea about a person or group

stock market: place where shares in corporations are traded

strict interpretation: a literal reading of the Constitution holding that the federal government has only those powers explicitly delegated to it in the Constitution

suburbs: smaller towns surrounding large cities

suffragists: people who campaigned for women's right to vote

summit meetings: conferences of the heads of two or more nations

supply-side economics: the theory that the government can best stimulate the economy by cutting taxes and encouraging investment in business

supremacy clause: Article VI, Section 2 of the Constitution, which makes that document and federal laws and treaties the "supreme law of the land"

Supreme Court: the highest federal court and the final interpreter of the Constitution

surplus goods: extra goods

tariff: tax placed on goods brought into a country

technology: the complete body of ways a society provides itself with material objects

temperance: movement: campaign against the sale or drinking of alcohol

tenant farming: system of farming in which a farmer rents land to farm from a landowner

territorial integrity: condition in which a nation's borders are guaranteed against disturbance by other nations

territory: a political division of the United States before it becomes a state; a large area of land

terrorism: the use of violence, intimidation, and coercion to achieve an end, to gain publicity for a cause, or to disrupt the normal functioning of society

Tet Offensive: 1968 attack by Viet Cong and North Vietnamese forces throughout South Vietnam; a turning point in the Vietnam War

Third World: during the Cold war, nations in the modern world that professed not to be allied with the Soviet Union and its allies or the United States and its allies, especially the developing nations of Asia, Africa, and Latin America

three branches of government: the division of the powers of government into legislative, executive, and judicial functions

three-fifths compromise: compromise reached at the Constitutional Convention of 1787 whereby three-fifths of a state's slave population would be figured into the state's total population

totalitarian: form of government in which the power to rule embraces all matters of human concern

tradition: the handling down of beliefs, customs, and practices from generation to generation

Trail of Tears: the forced movement of Cherokee in 1838–1839 to land west of the Mississippi River

transcontinental railroad: railway extending from coast to coast, completed in 1869

treaty: a formal agreement concluded between two or more countries

Treaty of Versailles: treaty marking the end of World War I that the U.S. Senate refused to ratify

Triple Alliance: name of the alliance of Germany, Austria-Hungry, and Italy before World War I

Triple Entente: name of the alliance of Great Britain, France, and Russia before World War I

trust: group of corporations run by a single board of directors

trustbuster: person who wanted to break up some or all trusts

two-party system: political system in which the candidates of only two major parties have a reasonable chance of winning elections

unconstitutional: not permitted by the constitution of a nation

unilateral action: an action taken by one nation only

unitary government: form of government in which all of the powers are held in a single agency

universal suffrage: the right to vote is extended to all adults

urban: in or of the city

urbanization: process by which more of a nation's population becomes concentrated in its cities

venture capital: money invested in a new corporation or other business enterprise

veto: chief executive's power to reject a bill passed by a legislature

Vietnam War: nation's longest war, fought in Southeast Asia from the late 1950s to 1973

void: without legal force or effect

War of 1812: war between the United States and Great Britain

War Powers Act: law passed in 1973 requiring the President to seek congressional approval if troops are sent into action for longer than 60 days

Weapons of mass destruction: WMD, devices used for large scale and total destruction, i.e. nuclear bombs, nerve gas, chemical warfare.

Whig party: one of the first political parties, standing for the limitation of executive power and the defense of liberty; by the 1850s had declined in power

white-collar worker: someone holding a job in business or in a profession

women's rights movement: the struggle of women for equality

work ethic: a belief that hard work is a virtuous end in itself

World War I: conflict between Allied Powers and Central Powers from 1914 to 1918

World War II: conflict between Allied and Axis nations from 1939 to 1945

yellow journalism: sensational style of reporting used by some newspapers in the late 1800s

yellow peril: derogatory term implying that Asian peoples threatened the ways of life of white Americans

Index

Acknowledgments

Staff Credits
Russ Lappa, Baljit Nijjar, Roberto Portocarrero, Paula Wehde, Tracy C. Wilson

Document-Based Essay Question Writers
Fran Legum and Jane Librett
Department of Instructional Programs and Alternative Schools
Nassau BOCES

Note: Every effort has been made to locate the copyright owner of materials reprinted in this book. Omissions brought to our attention will be corrected in subsequent printings.

Illustrations
Page 25, S. Kelley ©1994 San Diego Tribune-Copley News Service; **p. 37, 100,** Library of Congress; **p. 151,** Culver Pictures; **p. 154,** C. Jay Taylor/The Granger Collection; **p. 168,** Prentice Hall photo; **p. 184, 188,** Library of Congress; **p. 193,** Stock Montage; **p. 214,** John Held Jr./The Granger Collection; **p. 229,** Prentice Hall photo; **p. 238,** Library of Congress; **p. 248,** FDR Library; **p. 270,** Roy Justus, The Minneapolis Star, 1947; **p. 284,** E. H. Shepard/The Granger Collection; **p. 297,** The Granger Collection; **p. 309,** Drawing by Dana Fradon ©1972, The New Yorker Magazine, Inc.; **p. 343,** Steve Sack/Star Tribune; **p. 361,** ©Herblock in the Washington Post.

Regents Examination—June 2008

This section contains the Regents Examination in United States History and Government that was given in New York State in June 2008.

Circle your answers to Part I on this exam and write your answers to the thematic essay and document-based essay questions on separate sheets of paper. Be sure to refer to the test-taking strategies in the front of this book as you prepare to answer the test questions.

Part I

Answer all questions in this part.

Directions (1–50): For each statement or question, write on the separate answer sheet the *number* of the word or expression that, of those given, best completes the statement or answers the question.

1 Which geographic factor most helped the United States maintain its foreign policy of neutrality during much of the 1800s?

(1) climate of the Great Plains
(2) oceans on its east and west coasts
(3) large network of navigable rivers
(4) mountain ranges near the Atlantic and Pacific coasts

2 Before 1763, the British policy of salutary neglect toward its American colonies was based on the desire of Great Britain to

(1) treat all English people, including colonists, on an equal basis
(2) benefit from the economic prosperity of the American colonies
(3) encourage manufacturing in the American colonies
(4) ensure that all mercantile regulations were strictly followed

3 A major criticism of the Articles of Confederation was that too much power had been given to the

(1) British monarchy
(2) House of Burgesses
(3) state governments
(4) national government

4 What was the primary reason that slavery became more widespread in the South than in the North?

(1) The abolitionist movement was based in the North.
(2) The textile industry was controlled by southern merchants.
(3) Opposition to slavery by the Anglican Church was stronger in the North.
(4) Geographic factors contributed to the growth of the southern plantation system.

5 Which action can be taken by the United States Supreme Court to illustrate the concept that the Constitution is "the supreme law of the land"?

(1) hiring new federal judges
(2) voting articles of impeachment
(3) declaring a state law unconstitutional
(4) rejecting a presidential nomination to the cabinet

6 Passing marriage and divorce laws, creating vehicle and traffic regulations, and setting high school graduation requirements are examples of powers traditionally

(1) exercised solely by local governments
(2) reserved to the state governments
(3) delegated entirely to the federal government
(4) shared by the national and local governments

7 In the early 1800s, the Mississippi River was important to the United States because it

(1) served as a major highway for trade
(2) led to wars between Great Britain and Spain
(3) divided the Indian territories from the United States
(4) served as a border between the United States and Mexico

8 An example of a primary source of information about the War of 1812 would be a

(1) battle plan for the attack on Fort McHenry
(2) historical novel on the Battle of New Orleans
(3) movie on the life of President James Madison
(4) textbook passage on the naval engagements of the war

9 In the 1840s, the term *Manifest Destiny* was used by many Americans to justify

(1) the extension of slavery into the territories
(2) war with Russia over the Oregon territory
(3) the acquisition of colonies in Latin America
(4) westward expansion into lands claimed by other nations

Base your answer to question 10 on the cartoon below and on your knowledge of social studies.

Source: Rex Babin, *The Sacramento Bee,* June 29, 2004

10 Which constitutional principle is the focus of this cartoon?

(1) individual liberties   (3) freedom of speech
(2) separation of powers   (4) federalism

11 Which term refers to the idea that settlers had the right to decide whether slavery would be legal in their territory?

(1) nullification
(2) sectionalism
(3) popular sovereignty
(4) southern secession

12 The Supreme Court decision in *Dred Scott* v. *Sanford* (1857) was significant because it

(1) allowed slavery in California
(2) outlawed slavery in the Southern States
(3) upheld the actions of the Underground Railroad
(4) ruled that Congress could not ban slavery in the territories

13 What was a common purpose of the three amendments added to the United States Constitution between 1865 and 1870?

(1) extending suffrage to Southern women
(2) reforming the sharecropping system
(3) granting rights to African Americans
(4) protecting rights of Southerners accused of treason

14 The Radical Republicans in Congress opposed President Abraham Lincoln's plan for Reconstruction because Lincoln

(1) called for the imprisonment of most Confederate leaders
(2) rejected the idea of harsh punishments for the South
(3) planned to keep Northern troops in the South after the war
(4) demanded immediate civil and political rights for formerly enslaved persons

Base your answers to questions 15 and 16 on the map below and on your knowledge of social studies.

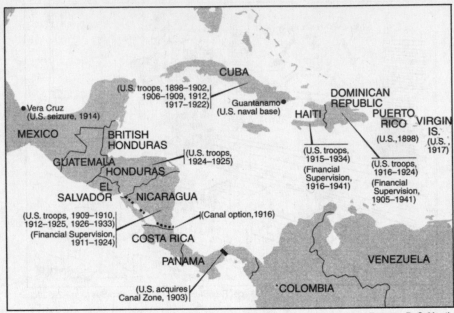

Source: Thomas G. Paterson et al., *American Foreign Policy: A History 1900 to Present*, D. C. Heath, 1991 (adapted)

15 Which title would be the most accurate for this map?

(1) Ending Colonization in Latin America
(2) Promoting Trade with Latin America
(3) Humanitarian Aid in the Western Hemisphere
(4) United States Intervention in the Caribbean Area

16 The United States government justified most of the actions shown on the map by citing the

(1) terms of the Roosevelt corollary to the Monroe Doctrine
(2) threats from Germany after World War I
(3) desire to stop illegal immigration from Latin America
(4) need to protect Latin America from the threat of communism

17 Which statement about the development of the Great Plains in the late 1800s is most accurate?

(1) Great profits could be earned in the steel industry.
(2) Railroads decreased in importance throughout the region.
(3) Immigrants could no longer afford to become farmers.
(4) Mechanized farming became dominant in the region.

18 The Interstate Commerce Act (1887) and the Sherman Antitrust Act (1890) were efforts by the federal government to

(1) regulate some aspects of business
(2) expand the positive features of the trusts
(3) favor big business over small companies
(4) move toward government ownership of key industries

19 In the late 1800s, the Homestead steel strike and the Pullman railcar strike were unsuccessful because

(1) the government supported business owners
(2) most workers refused to take part in the strike
(3) the Supreme Court ruled both strikes were illegal
(4) factory owners hired children to replace the strikers

20 The Supreme Court decision in *Plessy* v. *Ferguson* (1896) upheld a state law that had

(1) banned the hiring of Chinese workers
(2) established racial segregation practices
(3) outlawed the use of prison inmate labor
(4) forced Native American Indians to relocate to reservations

21 The United States promoted its economic interest in China by

(1) intervening in the Sino-Japanese War
(2) passing the Chinese Exclusion Act
(3) encouraging the Boxer Rebellion
(4) adopting the Open Door policy

22 Until the early 20th century, few restrictions on immigration to the United States existed primarily because

(1) industry needed an increasing supply of labor
(2) immigration totals had always been relatively low
(3) labor unions had always favored unrestricted immigration
(4) the Supreme Court had ruled that Congress could not restrict immigration

23 In the early 1900s, the muckrakers provided a service to the American public by

(1) calling for a strong military buildup
(2) lobbying for less government regulation of business
(3) exposing abuses in government and industry
(4) encouraging states to resist federal government authority

Base your answer to question 24 on the chart below and on your knowledge of social studies.

States and Territories Fully Enfranchising Women Prior to the 19th Amendment

State	Date Begun
Territory of Wyoming	1869
Wyoming	1890
Colorado	1893
Utah	1896
Idaho	1896
Arizona	1912
Washington	1910
California	1911
Kansas	1912
Oregon	1912
Territory of Alaska	1913
Montana	1914
Nevada	1914
New York	1917
Michigan	1918
Oklahoma	1918
South Dakota	1918

Source: Alexander Keyssar, *The Right to Vote,* Basic Books, 2000 (adapted)

24 Which conclusion about woman's suffrage is best supported by the information in the chart?

(1) Congress did not allow women to vote in the territories.
(2) Before 1917, many of the western states had granted women the right to vote.
(3) The United States Supreme Court had to approve a woman's right to vote in each state.
(4) Women were permitted to vote only in state elections.

25 After World War I, the United States Senate refused to approve the Treaty of Versailles. This action reflected the Senate's intention to

(1) provide support for the League of Nations
(2) punish the nations that began the war
(3) return to a policy of isolationism
(4) maintain United States leadership in world affairs

Base your answer to question 26 on the poem below and on your knowledge of social studies.

Mother to Son

Well, son, I'll tell you:
Life for me ain't been no crystal stair.
It's had tacks in it,
And splinters,
And boards torn up,
And places with no carpet on the floor—
Bare.
But all the time
I'se been a-climbin' on,
And reachin' landin's,
And turnin' corners,
And sometimes goin' in the dark
Where there ain't been no light.
So boy, don't you turn back.
Don't you set down on the steps
'Cause you finds it kinder hard.
Don't you fall now—
For I'se still goin', honey,
I'se still climbin',
And life for me ain't been no crystal stair.

—Langston Hughes, 1922

26 One purpose of this poem, written during the Harlem Renaissance, was to

(1) explain the advantages of inner-city life
(2) discuss ideas in the language used by immigrant Americans
(3) ask African Americans to accept things as they are
(4) encourage African Americans to continue their struggle for equality

27 The Scopes trial of 1925 illustrated the

(1) desire for new voting rights laws
(2) need for better private schools
(3) conflict between Protestant fundamentalism and science
(4) effects of the Red Scare on the legal system

28 What was a major cause of the Great Depression?

(1) decrease in the production of goods during most of the 1920s
(2) unequal distribution of wealth in the United States
(3) overregulation of the banking industry
(4) low tariffs on foreign goods

29 The National Labor Relations Act of 1935 (Wagner Act) affected workers by

(1) protecting their right to form unions and bargain collectively
(2) preventing public employee unions from going on strike
(3) providing federal pensions for retired workers
(4) forbidding racial discrimination in employment

Base your answer to question 30 on the cartoon below and on your knowledge of social studies.

"We saved thirteen points sending Junior to bed without his supper."

Source: *Esquire Magazine*, 1944 (adapted)

30 Which feature of life on the home front during World War II is most clearly illustrated by this 1944 cartoon?

(1) food rationing
(2) housing shortages
(3) juvenile delinquency
(4) conserving natural resources

31 Prior to the start of World War II, Great Britain and France followed a policy of appeasement when they
(1) rejected an alliance with the Soviet Union
(2) allowed Germany to expand its territory
(3) signed the agreements at the Yalta Conference
(4) opposed United States efforts to rearm

32 The war crimes trials that followed World War II were historically significant because for the first time
(1) nations were asked to pay for war damages
(2) individuals were given immunity from prosecution
(3) nations on both sides were found guilty of causing the war
(4) individuals were held accountable for their actions during wartime

Base your answer to question 33 on the quotation below and on your knowledge of social studies.

. . . I believe that it must be the policy of the United States to support free peoples who are resisting attempted subjugation [control] by armed minorities or by outside pressures.

I believe that we must assist free peoples to work out their own destinies in their own way.

I believe that our help should be primarily through economic and financial aid which is essential to economic stability and orderly political processes. . . .

—President Harry Truman, speech to Congress (Truman Doctrine), March 12, 1947

33 The program described in this quotation was part of the foreign policy of
(1) détente   (3) neutrality
(2) containment   (4) colonialism

34 In both *Schenck* v. *United States* (1919) and *Korematsu* v. *United States* (1944), the Supreme Court ruled that during wartime
(1) civil liberties may be limited
(2) women can fight in combat
(3) drafting of noncitizens is permitted
(4) sale of alcohol is illegal

35 After the end of World War II, many working women left their factory jobs because they were
(1) fired from their jobs due to poor performance
(2) unprepared for peacetime employment
(3) forced to give up their jobs to returning war veterans
(4) dissatisfied with their low wages

36 The Eisenhower Doctrine (1957) was an effort by the United States to
(1) gain control of the Suez Canal
(2) take possession of Middle East oil wells
(3) find a homeland for Palestinian refugees
(4) counter the influence of the Soviet Union in the Middle East

37 During the 1950s and 1960s, which civil rights leader advocated black separatism?
(1) Medgar Evers   (3) Rosa Parks
(2) James Meredith   (4) Malcolm X

38 The term *Great Society* was used by President Lyndon B. Johnson to describe his efforts to
(1) lower taxes for all Americans
(2) win the race for outer space
(3) end poverty and discrimination in the United States
(4) improve the nation's armed forces

39 The Berkeley demonstrations, riots at the 1968 Democratic National Convention, and the Kent State protest all reflect student disapproval of
(1) the Vietnam War
(2) increases in college tuition
(3) the unequal status of American women
(4) racial segregation

40 Which situation in the 1970s caused the United States to reconsider its dependence on foreign energy resources?

(1) war in Afghanistan

(2) oil embargo by the Organization of Petroleum Exporting Countries (OPEC)

(3) meetings with the Soviet Union to limit nuclear weapons

(4) free-trade agreements with Canada and Mexico

Base your answer to question 41 on the cartoon below and on your knowledge of social studies.

Source: Herblock, "I am Not a Crook," *The Washington Post*, May 24, 1974

41 The cartoon is most closely associated with the controversy over the

(1) Watergate affair

(2) war on drugs

(3) Arab-Israeli conflict

(4) Iran hostage crisis

42 One similarity between President Jimmy Carter and President Bill Clinton is that both leaders

(1) attempted to bring peace to the Middle East

(2) supported the federal takeover of public education

(3) testified under oath at United States Senate hearings

(4) proposed treaties to limit trade with Latin America

Base your answer to question 43 on the graph below and on your knowledge of social studies.

More people getting food stamps

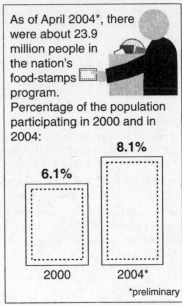

As of April 2004*, there were about 23.9 million people in the nation's food-stamps program.
Percentage of the population participating in 2000 and in 2004:

6.1% — 2000

8.1% — 2004*

*preliminary

Source: *USA Today,* July 28, 2004 (adapted)

43 Which statement is best supported by the information in this graph?

(1) The surplus of food was greater in 2000 than in 2004.

(2) More money was being spent by consumers at the grocery store in 2000.

(3) The government was helping fewer people in 2004 than in 2000.

(4) More people needed financial assistance to feed their families in 2004.

Base your answer to question 44 on the graph below and on your knowledge of social studies.

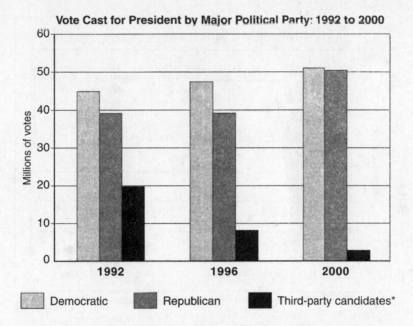

Vote Cast for President by Major Political Party: 1992 to 2000

Democratic   Republican   Third-party candidates*

* Candidates with 1 million or more votes: 1992 – Independent Party, Ross Perot
1996 – Reform Party, Ross Perot
2000 – Green Party, Ralph Nader

Source: U. S. Census Bureau, *Statistical Abstract of the United States: 2004–2005* (adapted)

44 Data from this graph support the conclusion that between 1992 and 2000

(1) the Democrats lost more votes to third-party candidates than the Republicans did
(2) third-party candidates received less support in each succeeding presidential election
(3) less than 50 percent of eligible voters participated in elections
(4) the Republicans received more than 40 million votes in each election

45 In 1990, approximately 12 percent of the United States population was over 65. It is estimated that in 2030 that number will climb to nearly 20 percent.

Source: U.S. Census Bureau

The most likely result of this trend will be an increase in the number of

(1) immigrants from Asia
(2) students attending colleges
(3) people receiving Social Security
(4) members of the House of Representatives

46 An initial response of the United States to the terrorist attacks of September 11, 2001, was to

(1) aid in the overthrow of Taliban rule in Afghanistan
(2) reduce support for Israel
(3) end trade with all Middle Eastern nations
(4) demand an end to communist rule in Iraq

Base your answer to question 47 on the graph below and on your knowledge of social studies.

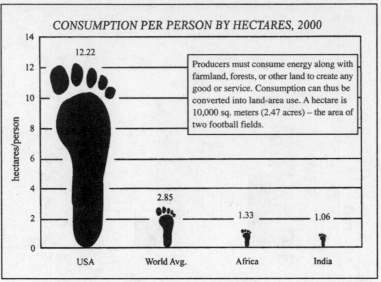

CONSUMPTION PER PERSON BY HECTARES, 2000

Producers must consume energy along with farmland, forests, or other land to create any good or service. Consumption can thus be converted into land-area use. A hectare is 10,000 sq. meters (2.47 acres) – the area of two football fields.

12.22 — USA

2.85 — World Avg.

1.33 — Africa

1.06 — India

hectares/person

Source: Bigelow and Peterson, eds., *Rethinking Globalization,* Rethinking Schools, 2002 (adapted)

47 A conclusion best supported by the information in this graph is that the United States

(1) is more efficient and less wasteful than other nations
(2) shows great concern for lesser-developed countries
(3) consumes several times the world average of many resources
(4) spends more than other nations on environmental protection

48 One way in which the Gold Rush in 1849 and the Dust Bowl of the 1930s are similar is that both resulted in

(1) a war with other countries
(2) the sale of cheap federal land
(3) an increase in westward migration
(4) the removal of Native American Indians to reservations

49 Samuel Gompers, Eugene V. Debs, and John L. Lewis all influenced the American economy by

(1) supporting free trade between nations
(2) encouraging the use of monopolies
(3) advocating laissez-faire capitalism
(4) working to build unions and improve pay

50 Which category most accurately completes the heading for the partial outline below?

I. Supreme Court Cases that Deal With

_____

A. *Engel* v. *Vitale* (1962)
B. *Tinker* v. *Des Moines School District* (1969)
C. *New Jersey* v. *T.L.O.* (1985)
D. *Vernonia School District* v. *Acton* (1995)

(1) Right to Counsel
(2) Student Rights
(3) School Integration
(4) Federal Funding of Education

Answers to the essay questions are to be written in the separate essay booklet.

In developing your answer to Part II, be sure to keep this general definition in mind.

discuss means "to make observations about something using facts, reasoning, and argument; to present in some detail"

Part II

THEMATIC ESSAY QUESTION

Directions: Write a well-organized essay that includes an introduction, several paragraphs addressing the task below, and a conclusion.

Theme: Change

Throughout United States history, individuals other than presidents have played significant roles that led to changes in the nation's economy, government, or society.

Task:

Select *two* important individuals, other than presidents, and the area in which they tried to bring about change, and for *each*
- Discuss *one* action taken by the individual that led to changes in the nation's economy, government, or society
- Discuss changes that came about as a result of the individual's action

You may use any important person from your study of United States history (other than a president). Some suggestions you might wish to consider include Frederick Douglass and slavery, Andrew Carnegie and industrialization, Jacob Riis and urban life, Upton Sinclair and consumer protection, Henry Ford and the automobile industry, Margaret Sanger and reproductive rights, Martin Luther King Jr. and civil rights, Cesar Chavez and migrant farmworkers, and Bill Gates and the software industry.

You are *not* limited to these suggestions. However, you may *not* select a president of the United States.

Guidelines:

In your essay, be sure to:
- Develop all aspects of the task
- Support the theme with relevant facts, examples, and details
- Use a logical and clear plan of organization, including an introduction and a conclusion that are beyond a restatement of the theme

NAME _____ SCHOOL _____

In developing your answers to Part III, be sure to keep these general definitions in mind:

(a) <u>describe</u> means "to illustrate something in words or tell about it"

(b) <u>explain</u> means "to make plain or understandable; to give reasons for or causes of; to show the logical development or relationships of"

(c) <u>discuss</u> means "to make observations about something using facts, reasoning, and argument; to present in some detail"

Part III

DOCUMENT-BASED QUESTION

This question is based on the accompanying documents. The question is designed to test your ability to work with historical documents. Some of the documents have been edited for the purposes of the question. As you analyze the documents, take into account the source of each document and any point of view that may be presented in the document.

Historical Context:

The president of the United States has been granted power as the commander in chief by the Constitution. While the president has used his military powers to commit troops overseas, he has also used this power to respond to domestic crises. Three such domestic crises were the **Civil War (1861–1865)** during the presidency of Abraham Lincoln, the **Bonus March (1932)** during the presidency of Herbert Hoover, and **Little Rock, Arkansas (1957)** during the presidency of Dwight D. Eisenhower.

Task: Using information from the documents and your knowledge of United States history, answer the questions that follow each document in Part A. Your answers to the questions will help you write the Part B essay, in which you will be asked to

Choose **two** domestic crises mentioned in the historical context that led presidents to use their military power as commander in chief and for **each**

- Describe the historical circumstances that led to the crisis
- Explain an action taken by the president to resolve the crisis
- Discuss the extent to which the president's action resolved the crisis **or** had an impact on American society

Part A
Short-Answer Questions

Directions: Analyze the documents and answer the short-answer questions that follow each document in the space provided.

Document 1

> . . . I [President Abraham Lincoln] would save the Union. I would save it the shortest way under the Constitution. The sooner the national authority can be restored the nearer the Union will be "the Union as it was." If there be those who would not save the Union unless they could at the same time *save* slavery, I do not agree with them. If there be those who would not save the Union unless they could at the same time *destroy* slavery, I do not agree with them. My paramount [most important] object in this struggle [the Civil War] *is* to save the Union, and is *not* either to save or to destroy slavery. If I could save the Union without freeing *any* slave I would do it, and if I could save it by freeing *all* the slaves I would do it; and if I could save it by freeing some and leaving others alone, I would also do that. What I do about slavery and the colored [African American] race, I do because I believe it helps to save the Union; and what I forbear [refrain from doing], I forbear because I do *not* believe it would help save the Union. I shall do *less* whenever I shall believe what I am doing hurts the cause, and I shall do *more* whenever I shall believe doing more will help the cause. I shall try to correct errors when shown to be errors; and I shall adopt new views so fast as they shall appear to be true views. . . .

Source: Abraham Lincoln to Horace Greeley, *New York Tribune*, August 25, 1862

1 According to this document, what is President Abraham Lincoln's main objective in fighting the Civil War? [1]

_____

_____

Score ☐

Document 2

> . . . Now, therefore I, Abraham Lincoln, President of the United States, by virtue of the power in me vested as Commander-in-Chief, of the Army and Navy of the United States in time of actual armed rebellion [Civil War] against the authority and government of the United States, and as a fit and necessary war measure for suppressing [stopping] said rebellion, do, on this first day of January, in the year of our Lord one thousand eight hundred and sixty-three, and in accordance with my purpose so to do publicly proclaimed for the full period of one hundred days, from the day first above mentioned, order and designate as the States and parts of States wherein the people thereof respectively, are this day in rebellion against the United States, the following, to wit: . . .
>
> And by virtue of the power, and for the purpose aforesaid, I do order and declare that all persons held as slaves within said designated States [those states in rebellion], and parts of States, are, and henceforward shall be free; and that the Executive government of the United States, including the military and naval authorities thereof, will recognize and maintain the freedom of said persons. . . .

Source: Abraham Lincoln, Emancipation Proclamation, January 1, 1863

2 According to this document, what was President Abraham Lincoln hoping to achieve by issuing the Emancipation Proclamation? [1]

_____

_____

Score ⬜

Document 3a

> Washington, March 26, 1863
> Hon. Andrew Johnson
> My dear Sir:
>
> I am told you have at least <u>thought</u> of raising a negro [African American] military force. In my opinion the country now needs no specific thing so much as some man of your ability, and position, to go to this work. When I speak of your position, I mean that of an eminent [respected] citizen of a slave-state, and himself a slave-holder. The colored population is the great <u>available</u>, and yet <u>unavailed</u> of, force, for restoring the Union. The bare sight of fifty thousand armed and drilled black soldiers upon the banks of the Mississippi, would end the rebellion at once. And who doubts that we can present that sight if we but take hold in earnest? If you <u>have</u> been thinking of it please do not dismiss the thought.
>
> Yours very truly
> A. Lincoln

Source: Abraham Lincoln to Andrew Johnson, March 26, 1863, Abraham Lincoln Papers, Library of Congress

3a According to this document, what role did Abraham Lincoln think African Americans could play in restoring the Union? [1]

_____

_____

Score ☐

Document 3b

> . . . By the end of the Civil War, roughly 179,000 black men (10% of the Union Army) served as soldiers in the U.S. Army and another 19,000 served in the Navy. Nearly 40,000 black soldiers died over the course of the war—30,000 of infection or disease. Black soldiers served in artillery and infantry and performed all noncombat support functions that sustain an army, as well. Black carpenters, chaplains, cooks, guards, laborers, nurses, scouts, spies, steamboat pilots, surgeons, and teamsters also contributed to the war cause. There were nearly 80 black commissioned officers. Black women, who could not formally join the Army, nonetheless served as nurses, spies, and scouts, the most famous being Harriet Tubman, who scouted for the 2nd South Carolina Volunteers. . . .

Source: "The Fight for Equal Rights: Black Soldiers in the Civil War," National Archives & Records Administration

3b Based on this document, state **one** contribution made by African Americans to the war effort. [1]

_____

_____

Score ☐

Document 4

By June 1932, a large group of World War I veterans had gathered in Washington, D.C., to demand the bonus they had been promised for serving their country. These veterans were known as the Bonus Expeditionary Force (B. E. F.) or Bonus Army. The B. E. F. wanted the bonus early as a form of Depression relief.

> Last week the House of Representatives surrendered to the siege of the Bonus Expeditionary Force encamped near the Capitol. It voted (226-to-175) to take up the bill by Texas' [Congressman] Patman for immediate cashing of Adjusted Service Compensation certificates at a cost of $2,400,000,000 in printing-press money. This first test of the Bonus boosters' strength indicated that the House would probably pass the Patman bill and send it to the Senate. In that body 56 Senators—a majority—were said to be lined up against the Bonus. But even should the measure somehow get by Congress an insurmountable veto awaited it at the White House.
>
> Largely ignorant of legislative processes, the B. E. F., bivouacked [camped] some 15,000 strong on the Anacostia mudflats, was delirious with delight at its House victory. Its tattered personnel, destitute veterans who had "bummed" their way to the Capital from all over the country, whooped and pranced about among their crude shelters. Most of them had left hungry wives and children behind. They had gone to Washington because, long jobless, they had nothing better to do. In camp with their A. E. F. [American Expeditionary Force] fellows again, they seemed to have revived the old ganging spirit of Army days as an escape from reality. They convinced themselves that they were there to right some vague wrong—a wrong somehow bound up in the fact that the Government had opened its Treasury to banks, railroads and the like but closed it to needy individuals. When the House voted to take up their bill, they slapped one another on the back and were quite sure they would be getting their money in a few days to take home. . . .

Source: *Time Magazine*, June 20, 1932 (adapted)

4a According to *Time Magazine*, what was likely to happen to the Patman bill when it passed the House of Representatives and was sent to the Senate? [1]

_____

_____

Score ☐

b Based on this *Time Magazine* article, identify **one** part of the economy that had already benefited from government spending. [1]

_____

_____

Score ☐

Document 5

To: General Douglas MacArthur, Chief of Staff, U.S. Army.

The President has just informed me that the civil government of the District of Columbia has reported to him that it is unable to maintain law and order in the District.

You will have United States troops proceed immediately to the scene of disorder. Cooperate fully with the District of Columbia police force which is now in charge. Surround the affected area and clear it without delay.

Turn over all prisoners to the civil authorities.

In your orders insist that any women and children who may be in the affected area be accorded every consideration and kindness. Use all humanity consistent with the due execution of this order.

PATRICK J. HURLEY
Secretary of War.

Source: Patrick J. Hurley, President Hoover's Secretary of War, Washington, D.C., July 28, 1932,
Herbert Hoover Presidential Library

5 According to this document, what was General MacArthur ordered to do by President Herbert Hoover's Secretary of War in response to the march of the Bonus Army? [1]

_____

_____

Score ☐

Document 6

> . . . Clark Booth, of the Veterans of Foreign Wars, declared that he had been a Republican all his life up to four days ago and was vice chairman of the Hoover campaign committee in 1928 for the Mobile district, but that Hoover's action in calling out the troops against the Washington veterans "made me a Democrat and I will take the stump against Herbert Hoover."
>
> William Taylor, a veteran of the World War [I] who is also a member of the Alabama Legislature, delivered the chief attack against President Hoover in offering a resolution which was passed unanimously. He declared that "if Hoover had called out troops to keep lobbyists of Wall Street from the White House there would be no depression," adding that the veterans who had gathered in Washington were there only to "attempt to get that to which they are entitled."
>
> "The Democrats will make Hoover pay on March 4 [Inauguration Day] with the aid of the veterans," Mr. Taylor declared, "the President can go back to his home, or return to England where he belongs.". . .

Source: "Assail Hoover in Mobile, Veterans Score Ousting of Bonus Army and 'Republican Prosperity.',"
New York Times, August 4, 1932

6 According to this *New York Times* article, what was **one** political impact of President Herbert Hoover's actions against the Bonus Army?   [1]

_____

_____

Score [ ]

Document 7a

Source: Photograph by Will Counts for *Arkansas Democrat*

A white student passes through an Arkansas National Guard line as Elizabeth Eckford is turned away on September 4, 1957.

Source: Clayborne Carson, ed., *Civil Rights Chronicle*, Legacy Publishing

A mob surrounds Elizabeth Eckford outside Central High School in Little Rock, Arkansas.

7a Based on these photographs, what happened to Elizabeth Eckford as she tried to attend Central High School on September 4, 1957?   [1]

_____

_____

Score [ ]

Document 7b

> . . . On September 4, after walking a virtual gauntlet of hysterical whites to reach the front door of Central High, the Little Rock Nine were turned back by Arkansas National Guardsmen. The white crowd hooted and cheered, shouted, stomped, and whistled. The segregationist whites of Little Rock did not see the vulnerability or the bravery of the students. Instead, they saw symbols of the South's defeat in the War Between the States, its perceived degradation during the Reconstruction that followed, and the threats to the southern way of life they had been taught to believe was sacrosanct [sacred]. . . .

Source: Clayborne Carson, ed., *Civil Rights Chronicle*, Legacy Publishing

7b According to this document, what was **one** reason some white citizens of Little Rock, Arkansas, did not want the Little Rock Nine to attend Central High School?   [1]

_____

_____

Score [ ]

Document 8a

> . . . This morning the mob again gathered in front of the Central High School of Little Rock, obviously for the purpose of again preventing the carrying out of the Court's order relating to the admission of Negro [African American] children to the school.
>
> Whenever normal agencies prove inadequate to the task and it becomes necessary for the Executive Branch of the Federal Government to use its powers and authority to uphold Federal Courts, the President's responsibility is inescapable.
>
> In accordance with that responsibility, I have today issued an Executive Order directing the use of troops under Federal authority to aid in the execution of Federal law at Little Rock, Arkansas. This became necessary when my Proclamation of yesterday was not observed, and the obstruction of justice still continues.
>
> It is important that the reasons for my action be understood by all citizens.
>
> As you know, the Supreme Court of the United States has decided that separate public educational facilities for the races are inherently [by nature] unequal and therefore compulsory school segregation laws are unconstitutional. . . .

Source: Address by President Dwight D. Eisenhower, September 24, 1957

8a (1) Based on this document, what was *one* action taken by President Dwight D. Eisenhower in response to the crisis in Little Rock? [1]

_____

_____

Score ▢

(2) Based on this document, what was *one* reason President Dwight D. Eisenhower took action in the crisis in Little Rock? [1]

_____

_____

Score ▢

Document 8b

Source: Clayborne Carson, ed., *Civil Rights Chronicle,* Legacy Publishing (adapted)

**On September 25, 1957 federal troops escort the Little Rock Nine
to their classes at Central High School.**

8b Based on this photograph, what was the job of the United States Army troops in Little Rock, Arkansas? [1]

_____

_____

Score ☐

Document 9

President Dwight D. Eisenhower's actions in Little Rock were an important step in enforcing the Supreme Court's 1954 decision regarding school segregation. However, state and local resistance to school integration continued.

> . . . Little Rock and the developments following in its wake marked the turning of the tide. In September, 1957, desegregation was stalemated. Little Rock broke the stalemate. Virginia early felt the impact of the Little Rock developments. By the end of 1958, the "Old Dominion" state had entrenched itself behind some thirty-four new segregation bulwarks [barriers] — the whole gamut of evasive devices that had spread across the South to prevent desegregation. It was a self-styled program of "massive resistance," a program which other states admittedly sought to duplicate. But as the Bristol (Va.) *Herald-Courier* observed in late 1958, when the showdown came, "'Massive resistance' met every test but one. It could not keep the schools open and segregated.". . .

Source: James W. Vander Zanden, "The Impact of Little Rock," *Journal of Educational Sociology,* April 1962

9 According to James W. Vander Zanden, what are *two* impacts of President Dwight D. Eisenhower's decision to enforce desegregation? [2]

(1) _____

_____

Score ☐

(2) _____

_____

Score ☐

Part B
Essay

Directions: Write a well-organized essay that includes an introduction, several paragraphs, and a conclusion. Use evidence from *at least four* documents in the body of the essay. Support your response with relevant facts, examples, and details. Include additional outside information.

Historical Context:

The president of the United States has been granted power as the commander in chief by the Constitution. While the president has used his military powers to commit troops overseas, he has also used this power to respond to domestic crises. Three such domestic crises were the ***Civil War (1861–1865)*** during the presidency of Abraham Lincoln, the ***Bonus March (1932)*** during the presidency of Herbert Hoover, and ***Little Rock, Arkansas (1957)*** during the presidency of Dwight D. Eisenhower.

Task: Using information from the documents and your knowledge of United States history, write an essay in which you

> Choose *two* domestic crises mentioned in the historical context that led presidents to use their military power as commander in chief and for *each*
> * Describe the historical circumstances that led to the crisis
> * Explain an action taken by the president to resolve the crisis
> * Discuss the extent to which the president's action resolved the crisis *or* had an impact on American society

Guidelines:

In your essay, be sure to
* Develop all aspects of the task
* Incorporate information from *at least four* documents
* Incorporate relevant outside information
* Support the theme with relevant facts, examples, and details
* Use a logical and clear plan of organization, including an introduction and conclusion that are beyond a restatement of the theme

Regents Examination—January 2008

This section contains the Regents Examination in United States History and Government that was given in New York State in January 2008.

Circle your answers to Part I on this exam and write your answers to the thematic essay and document-based essay questions on separate sheets of paper. Be sure to refer to the test-taking strategies in the front of this book as you prepare to answer the test questions.

Part I

Answer all questions in this part.

Directions (1–50): For each statement or question, write on the separate answer sheet the *number* of the word or expression that, of those given, best completes the statement or answers the question.

1 The relatively flat, grassy region of the United States between the Mississippi River and the Rocky Mountains is known as the

(1) Great Plains (3) Coastal Plain
(2) Great Basin (4) Piedmont

2 Which geographic feature contributed the most to the development of commerce throughout colonial America?

(1) mountains (3) natural harbors
(2) grasslands (4) interior lakes

3 Which heading best completes the partial outline below?

I._____

   A. Villages with town meetings
   B. Small farms and commercial fishing
   C. First American college

(1) New England Colonies
(2) Middle Colonies
(3) Southern Colonies
(4) Spanish Colonies

4 In the publication *Common Sense,* Thomas Paine argued that the American colonies should

(1) approve the Treaty of Paris (1763)
(2) ratify the Constitution of the United States
(3) end their political relationship with Great Britain
(4) support the policies of King George III

5 The Articles of Confederation and the United States Constitution both provided for

(1) an executive branch
(2) a national legislature
(3) a political party system
(4) a presidential cabinet

6 During the debate over the ratification of the Constitution, Antifederalists argued that

(1) the new Constitution left too much political power to state governments
(2) a strong national government would gain respect from European nations
(3) checks and balances were unnecessary in a federal government
(4) the new Constitution would threaten the rights of individual citizens

7 The conflict over representation in Congress was addressed at the Constitutional Convention of 1787 by

(1) creating a two-house legislature
(2) limiting the terms of lawmakers to four years
(3) giving Congress implied powers
(4) ending the importation of enslaved persons

8 Which action is an example of judicial review?

(1) The president proposes a bill to reduce the powers of the federal courts.
(2) A state court finds a defendant guilty of murder.
(3) The Supreme Court declares a federal law unconstitutional.
(4) The Senate approves a president's nominee for the Supreme Court.

9 "... I know too that it is a maxim [rule] with us, and I think it a wise one, not to entangle ourselves with the affairs of Europe. ..."

— Thomas Jefferson, December 21, 1787,
Library of Congress

Which document most clearly reflects the advice given in this statement?

(1) Albany Plan of Union
(2) Articles of Confederation
(3) Bill of Rights
(4) Washington's Farewell Address

10 Which presidential role resulted from practice and custom rather than from constitutional authority?

(1) commander in chief
(2) chief executive
(3) head of his political party
(4) head of state

11 Extending the right to vote in national elections to formerly enslaved African Americans, women, and all citizens at least eighteen years old was accomplished through

(1) constitutional amendments
(2) congressional laws
(3) presidential executive orders
(4) Supreme Court decisions

12 The foreign policies of President James Polk involving Texas, California, and the Oregon Territory were all efforts to

(1) remain neutral toward western territories
(2) continue traditional American isolationism
(3) weaken the Monroe Doctrine
(4) fulfill the goal of Manifest Destiny

13 The Declaration of Sentiments, adopted at the Seneca Falls Convention in 1848, was significant because it

(1) promoted the idea of equal rights for women
(2) demanded the immediate abolition of slavery
(3) called for the prohibition of alcoholic beverages
(4) asked government to restrict harmful business practices

14 The Reconstruction plans of President Abraham Lincoln and President Andrew Johnson included a provision for the

(1) resumption of full participation in Congress by Southern States
(2) long-term military occupation of the Confederacy
(3) payment of war reparations by Southern States
(4) harsh punishment of former Confederate officials

15 Passage of the Homestead Act and of legislation supporting the construction of transcontinental railroads demonstrated the federal government's commitment to

(1) limits on big business
(2) settlement of western territories
(3) conservation of natural resources
(4) equality for all immigrants

16 Which factor contributed the most to urbanization in the late 1800s?

(1) assimilation   (3) imperialism
(2) industrialization   (4) nullification

17 In the late 1800s, free and unlimited coinage of silver was supported by farmers primarily because they hoped this policy would

(1) make foreign crop prices less competitive
(2) allow farmers to grow a greater variety of crops
(3) increase crop prices and make it easier to repay loans
(4) bring about political equality between rural and urban residents

18 During the late 1800s and early 1900s, the term *robber baron* best defined a person who

(1) controlled large tracts of western lands
(2) used ruthless business tactics
(3) stole from the rich to give to the poor
(4) encouraged the conservation of raw materials

GO ON TO THE NEXT PAGE ⇨

Base your answers to questions 19 and 20 on the newspaper headlines below and on your knowledge of social studies.

Source: "Crucible of Empire," PBS Online (adapted)

19 The headlines in this newspaper are an example of

    (1) yellow journalism   (3) muckraking literature

    (2) investigative reporting   (4) government censorship

20 Publication of this and similar news stories encouraged Congress to

    (1) declare war on Spain   (3) pass antiterrorist legislation

    (2) improve naval safety   (4) conduct a criminal investigation

Base your answers to questions 21 and 22 on the chart below and on your knowledge of social studies.

Immigration Before and After Quota Laws	From Northern and Western Europe	From Southern and Eastern Europe and Asia
Average annual number of immigrants before quotas (1907–1914)	176,983	685,531
Emergency Quota Act of 1921	198,082	158,367
Quotas in Immigration Act of 1924	140,999	21,847

Source: Thomas A. Bailey et al., *The American Pageant,* Houghton-Mifflin (adapted)

21 What was an effect of the immigration laws of 1921 and 1924?

(1) reduction of immigration from southern and eastern Europe and Asia
(2) establishment of equality among ethnic groups seeking entrance to the United States
(3) increase in the total number of immigrants allowed to enter the United States
(4) removal of restrictions from the nations of northern and western Europe

22 One reason for the passage of the laws shown in this chart was to

(1) limit economic growth
(2) protect the jobs of workers in the United States
(3) improve working conditions in American factories
(4) promote non-European immigration

23 In the late 19th and early 20th centuries, the United States became involved in Latin America primarily to

(1) establish new colonies
(2) protect economic and security interests
(3) raise the living standards of Latin Americans
(4) stop the flow of illegal drugs into the United States

24 The Federal Reserve Act of 1913 was intended to

(1) create a national parks system
(2) regulate the stock market
(3) control the nation's money supply
(4) establish homelands for Native American Indians

25 Which geographic feature most influenced the ability of the United States to protect its mainland from attack during World War I?

(1) Gulf of Mexico   (3) Pacific Ocean
(2) Great Lakes   (4) Atlantic Ocean

26 Which argument was used by the Supreme Court in reaching its "clear and present danger" ruling in *Schenck* v. *United States* (1919)?

(1) The military is under civilian control.
(2) Powers are separated between the federal and state governments.
(3) Constitutional rights are not absolute.
(4) The Constitution provides for equal protection under the laws

Base your answer to question 27 on the poem below and on your knowledge of social studies.

I, Too

I, too, sing America.

I am the darker brother.
They send me to eat in the kitchen
When company comes,
But I laugh,
And eat well,
And grow strong.

Tomorrow,
I'll be at the table
When company comes.
Nobody'll dare
Say to me,
"Eat in the kitchen,"
Then.

Besides,
They'll see how beautiful I am
And be ashamed —

I, too, am America.

— Langston Hughes, in Rampersad and Roessel, eds.,
The Collected Poems of Langston Hughes,
Alfred A. Knopf

27 This Langston Hughes poem illustrates a major theme of the Harlem Renaissance by

(1) supporting the creation of colleges operated by African Americans
(2) stressing the need for economic reform
(3) expressing the pride and hope of many African Americans
(4) detailing mistreatment of African Americans by the music industry

28 Which statement about the stock market crash of 1929 is most accurate?

(1) It was the single cause of the Great Depression.
(2) It was caused by the effects of the Great Depression.
(3) It continued long after the Great Depression ended.
(4) It helped lead to the Great Depression.

29 One major way President Franklin D. Roosevelt's New Deal tried to combat the effects of the Great Depression was by

(1) keeping workers' wages low
(2) increasing protective tariff rates
(3) giving states more control over the federal budget
(4) funding public works relief programs

30 In 1937, President Franklin D. Roosevelt was criticized for his proposal to add justices to the United States Supreme Court because these appointments would have

(1) broken earlier campaign promises
(2) violated the constitutional limit on the number of justices
(3) threatened the system of checks and balances
(4) established a more conservative Court

31 Which action by the United States best represents United States foreign policy in the 1930s?

(1) passing the Neutrality Acts
(2) creating the Southeast Asia Treaty Organization (SEATO)
(3) deciding to create the United Nations
(4) joining the Allied powers

Base your answer to question 32 on the telegram below and on your knowledge of social studies.

CLASS OF SERVICE		1201	SYMBOLS

WESTERN UNION

This is a full-rate Telegram or Cablegram unless its deferred character is indicated by a suitable symbol above or preceding the address.

A. N. WILLIAMS
PRESIDENT

NEWCOMB CARLTON
CHAIRMAN OF THE BOARD

J. C. WILLEVER
FIRST VICE-PRESIDENT

DL = Day Letter
NT = Overnight Telegram
LC = Deferred Cable
NLT = Cable Night Letter
Ship Radiogram

The filing time shown in the date line on telegrams and day letters is STANDARD TIME at point of origin.   Time of receipt is STANDARD TIME at point of destination

```
H8N H 37 NT 5 EXA

        QR NEWYORK DEC 7 1941

HIS EXCELLENCY THE PRESIDENT OF THE U.S.
                    WASHDC

WE THE AMERICAN CITIZENS OF  JAPANESE DESCENT OF NEWYORKCITY AND

VICINITY JOIN ALL AMERICANS IN  CONDEMNING JAPANESE AGGRESSION AGAINST

OUR COUNTRY AND SUPPORT ALL MEASURES  TAKEN FOR THE DEFENSE OF

THE NATION.
        X  TOZAI CLUB OF NEWYORK,323 WEST 108 ST NEWYORKCITY
```

Source: New York State Education Department, *Consider the Source: Historical Records in the Classroom,*
State Archives and Records Administration (adapted)

32 This telegram was sent as a response to the

(1) start of World War II
(2) attack on Pearl Harbor
(3) passage of a law to ban Japanese immigration
(4) drafting of Japanese Americans into the military

33 A major purpose of the GI Bill was to provide World War II veterans with

(1) educational opportunities after the war
(2) protection against racial discrimination
(3) civilian jobs in the military
(4) increased Social Security payments

34 The Truman Doctrine, the Marshall Plan, and the North Atlantic Treaty Organization (NATO) were all part of the foreign policy of

(1) isolationism   (3) colonialism
(2) détente   (4) containment

Base your answers to questions 35 and 36 on the program below and on your knowledge of social studies.

MARCH ON WASHINGTON FOR JOBS AND FREEDOM

AUGUST 28, 1963

LINCOLN MEMORIAL PROGRAM

1. The National Anthem — *Led by* Marian Anderson.
2. Invocation — The Very Rev. Patrick O'Boyle, *Archbishop of Washington.*
3. Opening Remarks — A. Philip Randolph, *Director March on Washington for Jobs and Freedom.*
4. Remarks — Dr. Eugene Carson Blake, *Stated Clerk, United Presbyterian Church of the U.S.A.; Vice Chairman, Commission on Race Relations of the National Council of Churches of Christ in America.*
5. Tribute to Negro Women Fighters for Freedom — Mrs. Medgar Evers
   Daisy Bates
   Diane Nash Bevel
   Mrs. Medgar Evers
   Mrs. Herbert Lee
   Rosa Parks
   Gloria Richardson
6. Remarks — John Lewis, *National Chairman, Student Nonviolent Coordinating Committee.*
7. Remarks — Walter Reuther, *President, United Automobile, Aerospace and Agricultural Implement Workers of America, AFL-CIO; Chairman, Industrial Union Department, AFL-CIO.*
8. Remarks — James Farmer, *National Director, Congress of Racial Equality.*
9. Selection — Eva Jessye *Choir*
10. Prayer — Rabbi Uri Miller, *President Synagogue Council of America.*
11. Remarks — Whitney M. Young, Jr., *Executive Director, National Urban League.*
12. Remarks — Mathew Ahmann, *Executive Director, National Catholic Conference for Interracial Justice.*
13. Remarks — Roy Wilkins, *Executive Secretary, National Association for the Advancement of Colored People.*
14. Selection — Miss Mahalia Jackson
15. Remarks — Rabbi Joachim Prinz, *President American Jewish Congress.*
16. Remarks — The Rev. Dr. Martin Luther King, Jr., *President, Southern Christian Leadership Conference.*
17. The Pledge — A Philip Randolph
18. Benediction — Dr. Benjamin E. Mays, *President, Morehouse College.*

"WE SHALL OVERCOME"

Source: March on Washington Program, National Archives and Records Administration (adapted)

35 Which conclusion is most clearly supported by information in this program?

(1) Opponents of racial integration were allowed equal time on the program.
(2) Support for the March on Washington came from a variety of groups.
(3) Freedom of religion was an important goal of the March.
(4) The March was directed at southern state legislators.

36 Rosa Parks was honored at the March on Washington for her part in

(1) bringing about the Montgomery bus boycott
(2) integrating Little Rock Central High School
(3) forming the Student Nonviolent Coordinating Committee
(4) organizing lunch counter sit-ins in Greensboro, North Carolina

Base your answers to questions 37 and 38 on the map below and on your knowledge of social studies.

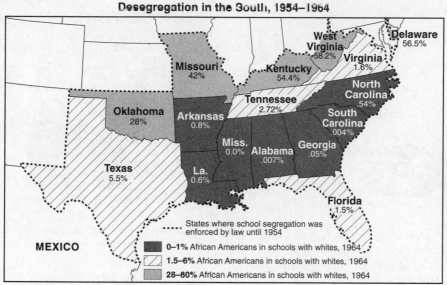

Desegregation in the South, 1954–1964

Source: Mary Beth Norton et al., *A People and a Nation*, Vol. II, 1986 (adapted)

37 Which conclusion about the success of efforts to end segregation in public schools in the 1950s and 1960s can be drawn from the map?

(1) In 1964, a majority of southern states had no integrated schools.

(2) State governments were slow to integrate public school systems.

(3) A higher percentage of African American students attended integrated public schools in Arkansas than in Oklahoma.

(4) Prior to 1964, a majority of African American students attended integrated schools in former Confederate States.

38 The information on the map shows how southern states responded to

(1) demands for affirmative action programs

(2) civil rights legislation to ban segregation in restaurants

(3) state programs to implement school busing initiatives

(4) the Supreme Court decision in *Brown* v. *Board of Education of Topeka*

39 What was the primary reason Richard Nixon resigned his presidency?

(1) He was convicted of several serious crimes.

(2) He was facing impeachment by the House of Representatives.

(3) His reelection was declared invalid by the Supreme Court.

(4) His actions in Cambodia and Laos were exposed in the *Pentagon Papers*.

40 In the late 1990s, increasing public concern about the role of money in politics led to

(1) all candidates receiving an equal amount of money

(2) a ban on all private campaign contributions

(3) attempts to reform campaign financing

(4) the widespread defeat of incumbent congressional candidates

Base your answer to question 41 on the cartoon below and on your knowledge of social studies.

Source: Jeff Parker, *Florida Today*, 2000 (adapted)

41 The cartoon refers to the idea that most candidates for the presidency try to

(1) win the majority of popular votes nationwide
(2) campaign equally in all states
(3) win the electoral vote in certain key states
(4) gain the support of first-time voters

Base your answer to question 42 on the quotation below and on your knowledge of social studies.

. . . There may come a time when we elect a president at age 45 or 50, and then 20 years later the country comes up with the same sort of problems that the president faced before and the people would like to bring that man or woman back, and they'd have no ability to do so. I'd kind of like to see it changed. I don't have terribly strong feelings about it. . . .

— President Bill Clinton, *A Conversation with Former President Bill Clinton*, John F. Kennedy Library and Foundation, May 28, 2003

42 In this statement, President Clinton is commenting on the

(1) presidential primaries
(2) presidential two-term limit
(3) two-party political system
(4) electoral college system

Base your answer to question 43 on the cartoon below and on your knowledge of social studies.

Source: Walt Handelsman, *Newsday*, 2003 (adapted)

43 According to this cartoonist, the problem faced by these college graduates was mainly the result of

(1) slow economic growth
(2) Prohibition
(3) the Great Depression
(4) high rates of inflation

44 The federal government responded to the 2001 attacks on the World Trade Center and the Pentagon by

(1) creating a cabinet-level agency for homeland security
(2) deporting most illegal aliens
(3) decreasing defense spending
(4) expanding the civil liberties of American citizens

45 Cultural pluralism in American society is best characterized by the

(1) existence of ethnic diversity within the population
(2) failure of many immigrants to vote in elections
(3) rejection of United States citizenship by most immigrants
(4) flow of illegal immigrants into California

46 The actions of President Abraham Lincoln during the Civil War and of President Franklin D. Roosevelt during World War II demonstrate that, during times of war, presidents sometimes have

(1) given up control of the military
(2) failed to gain enough public support to win reelection
(3) granted greater independence to state governments
(4) restricted individual freedoms

47 **"President Jackson Signs Force Bill Against South Carolina"**

"Congress Declares Southern States Must Accept 14th Amendment"

"President Eisenhower Sends Federal Troops to Little Rock, Arkansas"

Which principle is illustrated by these headlines?

(1) executive privilege
(2) popular sovereignty
(3) limited government
(4) federal supremacy

48 **"Muhammad Ali Refuses Military Draft Induction"**

"Tet Offensive Forces Troops to Defend Saigon"

"President Johnson Decides Not to Seek Reelection"

Which war is associated with the events mentioned in these headlines?

(1) World War II   (3) Vietnam War
(2) Korean War   (4) Persian Gulf War

49 Frederick Douglass, Malcolm X, and Jesse Jackson are each well known for

(1) helping to end slavery
(2) working for African American rights
(3) organizing the Underground Railroad
(4) supporting Jim Crow laws

50 Which group was the main target of the Palmer Raids of 1919–1920 and the McCarthy hearings of the 1950s?

(1) nativists   (3) communists
(2) industrialists   (4) African Americans

Answers to the essay questions are to be written in the separate essay booklet.

In developing your answer to Part II, be sure to keep these general definitions in mind:

(a) <u>describe</u> means "to illustrate something in words or tell about it"

(b) <u>discuss</u> means "to make observations about something using facts, reasoning, and argument; to present in some detail"

Part II

THEMATIC ESSAY QUESTION

Directions: Write a well-organized essay that includes an introduction, several paragraphs addressing the task below, and a conclusion.

Theme: Change — War

> United States participation in wars has resulted in political, social, and economic changes for various groups of Americans. These changes have had varying impacts on American society both during and after each war.

Task:

> Identify *two* different groups of Americans that were affected by United States participation in a war and for *each*
> - Describe a social, political, *or* economic change the group experienced because of the war
> - Discuss the extent to which that change affected American society

You may use any appropriate group from your study of United States history. Some suggestions you might wish to consider include enslaved persons during the Civil War, Native American Indians during the Indian Wars, women during World War I *or* World War II, Japanese Americans during World War II, and American college students *or* army draftees during the Vietnam War.

You are *not* limited to these suggestions.

Guidelines:

In your essay, be sure to:
- Develop all aspects of the task
- Support the theme with relevant facts, examples, and details
- Use a logical and clear plan of organization, including an introduction and a conclusion that are beyond a restatement of the theme

NAME _____ SCHOOL _____

In developing your answer to Part III, be sure to keep this general definition in mind:

> discuss means "to make observations about something using facts, reasoning, and argument; to present in some detail"

Part III

DOCUMENT-BASED QUESTION

This question is based on the accompanying documents. It is designed to test your ability to work with historical documents. Some of the documents have been edited for the purposes of the question. As you analyze the documents, take into account the source of each document and any point of view that may be presented in the document.

Historical Context:

> Throughout the 1800s and the early 1900s, reformers sought to solve the social, political, and economic problems of the period. Various methods were used by reformers to address these problems.

Task: Using information from the documents and your knowledge of United States history, answer the questions that follow each document in Part A. Your answers to the questions will help you write the Part B essay, in which you will be asked to

> • Discuss the social, political, **and/or** economic problems addressed by reformers in the 1800s and early 1900s. In your discussion, include the methods used by reformers to expose these problems.

Part A
Short-Answer Questions

Directions: Analyze the documents and answer the short-answer questions that follow each document in the space provided.

Document 1

THE LIBERATOR.

VOL. 1.   WILLIAM LLOYD GARRISON AND ISAAC KNAPP, PUBLISHERS.   No. 1.

BOSTON, MASSACHUSETTS.]   OUR COUNTRY IS THE WORLD—OUR COUNTRYMEN ARE MANKIND.   [SATURDAY, JANUARY 1, 1831.

> . . . I am aware, that many object to the severity of my language; but is there not cause for severity? I *will be* as harsh as truth, and as uncompromising as justice. On this subject [abolition of slavery] I do not wish to think, or speak, or write, with moderation. No! no! Tell a man whose house is on fire, to give a moderate alarm; tell him to moderately rescue his wife from the hands of the ravisher; tell the mother to gradually extricate her babe from the fire into which it has fallen; —but urge me not to use moderation in a cause like the present. I am in earnest—I will not equivocate—I will not excuse—I will not retreat a single inch—AND I WILL BE HEARD. The apathy of the people is enough to make every statue leap from its pedestal, and to hasten the resurrection of the dead. . . .

Source: William Lloyd Garrison, *The Liberator,* January 1, 1831, Vol. 1, No. 1

1 Based on this newspaper article, what was **one** goal that William Lloyd Garrison was trying to achieve? [1]

_____

_____

Score ☐

Document 2

"UNCLE TOM'S CABIN." This heart-melting and thrilling work continues to find a demand that can hardly be met by the utmost activity of the press and the bookbinders. We are informed by the publishers, that the eightieth thousand edition [copy] will be published to-morrow, making 160,000 volumes [total copies] in the brief period of eleven weeks!—a sale unprecedented in the country, in any instance, if not in the whole world. English editions of it are rapidly selling—one being printed in London in a cheap form, at the low rate of 2s. 6d., or about 60 cents. It should never be forgotten, that Mrs. H. B. Stowe, its gifted author, was moved to take up the subject of slavery, in the manner, by the passage of the Fugitive Slave Law. So does a just God overrule evil for good.

Source: *The Liberator,* June 11, 1852

2 According to *The Liberator,* how did the public react to the publication of Harriet Beecher Stowe's *Uncle Tom's Cabin?* [1]

_____

_____

Score ☐

Document 3a

The Bosses of the Senate

Source: Joseph J. Keppler, *Puck*, 1889 (adapted)

3a What is **one** political problem identified by Joseph J. Keppler in this cartoon? [1]

_____

_____

Score ☐

Document 3b

> ### People's Party [Populist] Platform
> ### (Omaha Platform)
> ### July 4, 1892
>
> . . .The conditions which surround us best justify our co-operation; we meet in the midst of a nation brought to the verge of moral, political, and material ruin. Corruption dominates the ballot-box, the Legislatures, the Congress, and touches even the ermine [robes] of the bench. The people are demoralized; most of the States have been compelled to isolate the voters at the polling places to prevent universal intimidation and bribery. The newspapers are largely subsidized or muzzled, public opinion silenced, business prostrated [crushed], homes covered with mortgages, labor impoverished, and the land concentrating in the hands of the capitalists. The urban workmen are denied the right to organize for self-protection, imported pauperized labor beats down their wages, a hireling standing army, unrecognized by our laws, is established to shoot them down, and they are rapidly degenerating into European conditions. The fruits of the toil of millions are boldly stolen to build up the fortunes for a few, unprecedented in the history of mankind; and the possessors of these, in turn, despise the Republic and endanger liberty. From the same prolific womb of governmental injustice we breed the two great classes— tramps and millionaires. . . .

Source: *National Economist,* Washington, D.C., 1892

3*b* According to this political party platform, what were ***two*** specific problems that led to the formation of the Populist Party?   [2]

(1)_____

_____

Score [   ]

(2)_____

_____

Score [   ]

Document 4a

An Old Rear-Tenement In Roosevelt Street

Source: Jacob Riis, 1890

Document 4b

. . . It is ten years and over, now, since that line [between rich and poor] divided New York's population evenly. To-day three-fourths of its people live in the tenements, and the nineteenth century drift of the population to the cities is sending ever-increasing multitudes to crowd them. The fifteen thousand tenant houses that were the despair of the sanitarian in the past generation have swelled into thirty-seven thousand, and more than twelve hundred thousand persons call them home. The one way out he saw—rapid transit to the suburbs—has brought no relief. We know now that there is no way out; that the "system" that was the evil offspring of public neglect and private greed has come to stay, a storm-centre forever of our civilization. Nothing is left but to make the best of a bad bargain. . . .

Source: Jacob Riis, *How the Other Half Lives*, Charles Scribner's Sons, 1890

4 Based on these documents, state *two* problems faced by cities in the United States in the late 1800s. [2]

(1)_____

_____

Score ☐

(2)_____

_____

Score ☐

Document 5a

In this Frank Beard cartoon, a saloon owner is wrapped in the protection of the law from the accusations of Themis, the Greek goddess of justice.

Under the Cloak of the Law

● **WORK OF THE SALOON**

The Manufacture and Sale of Liquor
Is Responsible For

70 per cent of our criminals

50 per cent of the inmates
of insane asylums

80 per cent of the inmates
of our poor houses

100 per cent of our troubles

The destruction of
homes

The corruption
of voters

Source: Frank Beard, *Fifty Great Cartoons*,
The Ram's Horn Press, 1899

5a According to Frank Beard, what was *one* reason people supported the temperance movement? [1]

_____

_____

Score ☐

Document 5b

> . . . the manufacture, sale, or transportation of intoxicating liquors within, the importation thereof into, or the exportation thereof from the United States and all territory subject to the jurisdiction thereof for beverage purposes is hereby prohibited.

Source: United States Constitution, 18th Amendment, Section 1, 1919

5b Based on this document, state *one* way reformers tried to stop the sale of intoxicating liquors in the United States. [1]

_____

_____

Score ☐

Document 6

BEEF TRUST BEATEN, BUT ESCAPES EXPOSURE

President's Remarkable Promise Put Inspection Bill Through.

DAMAGING REPORT SHELVED

The President's Agents Described to Him Packing House Conditions Worse Than Those Told of in Sinclair's Story.

Special to The New York Times.

. . .The President Was Indignant.

The President [Theodore Roosevelt] did not send Neill and Reynolds [federal officials] forth merely on the statements made by Upton Sinclair in his novel, "The Jungle." After he had been convinced of the truth of Sinclair's statements he manifested such an interest in the question that other people brought statements to him. He read the proofs of articles on the subject, and everything he read increased his anger. He then asked his two friends to look into the matter, and let him know if the stories told to him were true. They did look into it, and told him that everything he had learned was correct. Immediately upon this, filled with indignation, the President had Senator Beveridge introduce the Meat Inspection bill, and then served a notice that unless it was passed in jig time [very quickly] the report would be made public. . . .

Source: *New York Times,* May 27, 1906

---

6 According to the *New York Times,* how did *The Jungle* and other reports influence President Theodore Roosevelt's actions? [1]

_____

_____

Score ☐

Document 7

PREFACE

Salary—A periodical [regular] allowance made as compensation to a person for his official or professional services or for his regular work. –*Funk and Wagnalls.*

Notice the words, "a person." Here is no differentiation between male persons and female persons.

Yet the City of New York pays a "male" person for certain "professional services" $900, while paying a "female" person only $600 for the same "professional services." Stranger still, it pays for certain experience of a "male" person $105, while paying a "female" person only $40 for the identical experience. These are but samples of the "glaring inequalities" in the teachers' salary schedules. . . .

Source: Grace C. Strachan, *Equal Pay for Equal Work,* B. F. Buck & Company, 1910

7 What is *one* problem addressed by Grace C. Strachan? [1]

_____

_____

Score ☐

Document 8

Source: Library of Congress (adapted)

8 Based on the information on this poster, why is child labor considered a national problem? [1]

_____

_____

Score ☐

Part B
Essay

Directions: Write a well-organized essay that includes an introduction, several paragraphs, and a conclusion. Use evidence from *at least **five*** documents in the body of the essay. Support your response with relevant facts, examples, and details. Include additional outside information.

Historical Context:

Throughout the 1800s and the early 1900s, reformers sought to solve the social, political, and economic problems of the period. Various methods were used by reformers to address these problems.

Task: Using information from the documents and your knowledge of United States history, write an essay in which you

> • Discuss the social, political, ***and/or*** economic problems addressed by reformers in the 1800s and early 1900s. In your discussion, include the methods used by reformers to expose these problems.

Guidelines:

In your essay, be sure to:
- Develop all aspects of the task
- Incorporate information from *at least **five*** documents
- Incorporate relevant outside information
- Support the theme with relevant facts, examples, and details
- Use a logical and clear plan of organization, including an introduction and a conclusion that are beyond a restatement of the theme

Regents Examination—August 2007

This section contains the Regents Examination in United States History and Government that was given in New York State in August 2007.

Circle your answers to Part I on this exam and write your answers to the thematic essay and document-based essay questions on separate sheets of paper. Be sure to refer to the test-taking strategies in the front of this book as you prepare to answer the test questions.

Part I

Answer all questions in this part.

Directions (1–50): For each statement or question, write on the separate answer sheet the *number* of the word or expression that, of those given, best completes the statement or answers the question.

Base your answer to question 1 on the map below and on your knowledge of social studies.

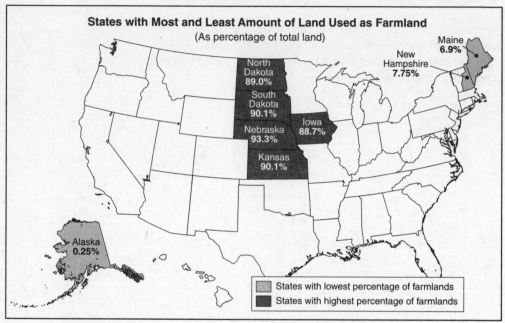

Source: 2002 Census in Agriculture, United States Department of Agriculture

1 The states with the largest percentage of land used for agriculture are located in areas with

  (1) relatively flat terrain   (3) easy access to the West Coast
  (2) the warmest year-round climate   (4) ocean ports

---

2 According to the theory of mercantilism, the principal purpose of the thirteen original colonies was to provide Great Britain with

  (1) naval bases
  (2) raw materials and markets
  (3) workers and manufactured goods
  (4) military recruits

3 The colonists' slogan, "No taxation without representation," expresses a belief in

  (1) free trade
  (2) economic interdependence
  (3) the supremacy of Parliament
  (4) the consent of the governed

Base your answer to question 4 on the quotation below and on your knowledge of social studies.

. . . I challenge the warmest advocate for reconciliation, to shew [show], a single advantage that this continent can reap, by being connected with Great Britain. I repeat the challenge, not a single advantage is derived. Our corn will fetch its price in any market in Europe, and our imported goods must be paid for, buy them where we will. . . .

— Thomas Paine, 1776

4 In this statement, Thomas Paine suggested that the American colonies should

(1) negotiate an end to the conflict with England
(2) form an alliance with England
(3) declare independence from England
(4) boycott goods from England

5 The Great Compromise reached at the Constitutional Convention of 1787 settled a dispute over how

(1) state boundaries would be determined
(2) the states would be represented in Congress
(3) power would be divided between the states and the national government
(4) a leader would be selected for the executive branch

6 The United States Constitution corrected a weakness in the Articles of Confederation by

(1) providing for the abolition of slavery
(2) creating a process for territories to become states
(3) granting Congress sole control over interstate and foreign commerce
(4) banning the possession of guns by citizens during peacetime

7 The adoption of the Bill of Rights (1791) addressed Antifederalist criticism of the new Constitution by

(1) providing for an indirect method of electing the president
(2) protecting citizens from abuses of power by the national government
(3) allowing the national government to coin money
(4) establishing a process for impeaching federal officials

Base your answer to question 8 on the quotation below and on your knowledge of social studies.

. . . He [the President] shall have power, by and with the advice and consent of the Senate, to make treaties, provided two thirds of the senators present concur; and he shall nominate, and by and with the advice and consent of the Senate, shall appoint ambassadors, other public ministers and consuls, judges of the Supreme Court, and all other officers of the United States, whose appointments are not herein otherwise provided for, and which shall be established by law: but the Congress may by law vest the appointment of such inferior officers, as they think proper, in the President alone, in the courts of law, or in the heads of departments.

— Article II, Section 2, Clause 2, Constitution of the United States

8 This portion of the Constitution illustrates the principle of

(1) checks and balances
(2) executive privilege
(3) judicial review
(4) implied powers

9 A major criticism of the electoral college is that it

(1) limits the influence of the two-party political system

(2) allows a president to be elected without a majority of the popular vote

(3) forces each political candidate to campaign in every state

(4) makes the federal election process too expensive

10 Which action is an example of the unwritten constitution?

(1) formation of the first cabinet by President George Washington

(2) admission of Vermont and Kentucky as states

(3) enforcement of the Alien and Sedition Acts by President John Adams

(4) declaration of war by Congress in 1812

11 A major purpose of the Monroe Doctrine (1823) was to

(1) limit European influence in the Western Hemisphere

(2) establish United States colonies in South America

(3) form military alliances with Latin American nations

(4) avoid involvement in Canadian conflicts

12 Most tariffs in the 19th century were intended to

(1) allow access to cheap foreign imports

(2) raise revenue and protect domestic manufacturing

(3) redistribute wealth among the social classes

(4) limit American exports

13 Which Supreme Court case best completes the partial outline below?

> I. _____
>
>   A. Heard under Chief Justice John Marshall
>   B. Established judicial review
>   C. Strengthened the judiciary

(1) *Marbury* v. *Madison* (1803)

(2) *McCulloch* v. *Maryland* (1819)

(3) *Gibbons* v. *Ogden* (1824)

(4) *Dred Scott* v. *Sanford* (1857)

14 Increased immigration from Ireland to the United States during the 1840s was primarily a result of

(1) crop failures in Ireland that led to mass starvation

(2) refugees fleeing the new monarchy in Ireland

(3) unemployment in Ireland caused by industrialization

(4) religious warfare in Ireland between Catholics and Protestants

15 Which situation was the most immediate result of Abraham Lincoln's election to the presidency in 1860?

(1) Kansas and Nebraska joined the Union as free states.

(2) A constitutional amendment was adopted to end slavery.

(3) Missouri entered the Union as a slave state.

(4) Several Southern States seceded from the Union.

Base your answers to questions 16 and 17 on the graphs below and on your knowledge of social studies.

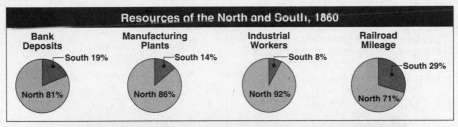

Resources of the North and South, 1860

Bank Deposits — South 19%, North 81%
Manufacturing Plants — South 14%, North 86%
Industrial Workers — South 8%, North 92%
Railroad Mileage — South 29%, North 71%

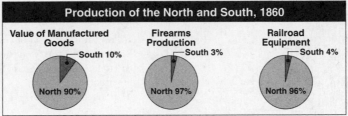

Production of the North and South, 1860

Value of Manufactured Goods — South 10%, North 90%
Firearms Production — South 3%, North 97%
Railroad Equipment — South 4%, North 96%

Source: *The Americans: In-Depth Resources*, McDougal Littell (adapted)

16 The data shown in the graphs best support the conclusion that the North

   (1) was better prepared economically to fight the Civil War
   (2) lagged behind the South in bank deposits
   (3) produced more agricultural products than the South
   (4) lacked several important resources to fight the war

17 The South won many battles and the Civil War lasted four years. These two facts support the conclusion that

   (1) the Underground Railroad was important to the Southern cause
   (2) factors other than those shown in the graphs were important
   (3) the North was more dependent on foreign aid than the South
   (4) personal wealth was a key factor in determining the outcome of the war

18 What was the primary goal of President Abraham Lincoln's post–Civil War policy?

   (1) establishing military districts in the South
   (2) extending land ownership to African American men
   (3) restoring Southern representation in Congress
   (4) arresting military leaders of the Confederacy

19 During the Reconstruction Era (1865–1877), the 15th amendment was adopted to grant African Americans

   (1) educational opportunities
   (2) economic equality
   (3) freedom of speech
   (4) voting rights

Base your answer to question 20 on the cartoon below and on your knowledge of social studies.

The Rising of the Usurpers and the Sinking of the Liberties of the People

Source: Thomas Nast, 1889 (adapted)

20 This cartoonist is expressing
(1) support for new tariffs
(2) encouragement for increased immigration
(3) concern for environmental pollution
(4) dissatisfaction with the power of big business

21 In the late 1800s, the principles of Social Darwinism were most consistent with the ideas of
(1) Populism
(2) laissez-faire economics
(3) trustbusting
(4) utopian socialism

22 During the last quarter of the 19th century, large numbers of immigrants were admitted to the United States primarily because of the economy's need for more
(1) skilled craftsmen
(2) educated professionals
(3) unskilled factory workers
(4) scientists and technicians

23 A major purpose of both the Chinese Exclusion Act (1882) and the Gentlemen's Agreement with Japan (1907) was to
(1) limit immigration of certain ethnic groups
(2) enrich America's cultural diversity
(3) treat all Asian and European immigrants equally
(4) relocate Asians displaced by war

24 In his book, *How the Other Half Lives*, muckraker Jacob Riis exposed the
(1) ruthlessness of the Standard Oil Company
(2) social ills of life in New York City's tenements
(3) unsanitary conditions in the meatpacking industry
(4) abuses of the railroad industry

25 What was a major reason most western states granted women suffrage prior to the adoption of the 19th amendment?
(1) Western states had more college-educated women than the eastern states.
(2) Women outnumbered men in states west of the Mississippi River.
(3) A majority of western states had legislatures controlled by women.
(4) The important roles played by frontier women promoted equality.

26 Progressive Era reformers sought to expand voter participation in government by adopting
(1) the initiative and referendum
(2) tougher literacy tests
(3) additional poll taxes
(4) a civil service system

27 What was the goal of those who supported the constitutional amendment that provided for direct election of United States senators?

(1) expanding the power of the legislative branch
(2) providing equal voting rights to minority groups
(3) making the Senate more responsive to the people
(4) basing Senate representation on state population

28 President Theodore Roosevelt's Big Stick policy is most closely associated with

(1) friendly relations with China after the Boxer Rebellion
(2) conservation of natural resources
(3) court actions to support business monopolies
(4) intervention in Latin American affairs

29 As a result of the Spanish-American War, the United States saw the need to build the Panama Canal because

(1) new colonies had been acquired in Africa
(2) Spanish opposition to the canal had ended
(3) the United States navy could then move more quickly between oceans
(4) United States railroads could not transport enough manufactured goods

30 The United States found it difficult to remain neutral during the first three years of World War I because of its desire to

(1) expand its interests in the Caribbean
(2) control the Suez Canal
(3) maintain freedom of the seas for trade with European nations
(4) obtain migrant workers for American farms

31 One goal of many Harlem Renaissance writers was to

(1) increase pride in African American culture
(2) support existing racial barriers
(3) cut off connections with mainstream American values
(4) encourage African Americans to create their own political party

32 Many farmers failed to share in the general prosperity of the 1920s mainly because they

(1) lacked new farm machinery to increase production
(2) did not have sufficient numbers of farm laborers
(3) had to pay high wages to their workers
(4) received low prices for crops due to overproduction

33 Congress opposed President Franklin D. Roosevelt's plan to increase the number of justices on the Supreme Court because the plan would have

(1) threatened the principle of checks and balances
(2) abolished judicial review
(3) violated the elastic clause of the Constitution
(4) given the federal government too much power over the states

34 The Neutrality Acts of 1935–1937 were primarily designed to

(1) avoid policies that had led to United States involvement in World War I
(2) halt the spread of communism in the Western Hemisphere
(3) promote United States membership in the League of Nations
(4) stop Japan from attacking United States territories in the Far East

35 In *Korematsu* v. *United States* (1944), the Supreme Court said that the removal of Japanese Americans from their homes was constitutional because

(1) most Japanese Americans were not United States citizens
(2) many Japanese Americans refused to serve in the United States Armed Forces
(3) this type of action was necessary during a national emergency
(4) there was strong evidence of significant Japanese sabotage on the West Coast

Base your answer to question 36 on the posters below and on your knowledge of social studies.

Source: Office of War Information, 1943   Source: U. S. Civil Service Commission

36 These posters were used during World War II to encourage women to

(1) serve in the armed forces   (3) buy war bonds
(2) exercise their vote   (4) contribute to the war effort

---

37 Which statement best explains why the United States mainland suffered minimal physical damage in both World War I and World War II?

(1) The United States policy of isolationism discouraged attacks by other countries.
(2) Geographic location kept the United States protected from most of the fighting.
(3) United States military fortifications prevented attacks on United States soil.
(4) Latin America provided a buffer zone from acts of aggression by other countries.

38 The primary reason for the formation of the North Atlantic Treaty Organization (NATO) in 1949 was to

(1) maintain peace in the Middle East
(2) block the German Nazi threat in Europe
(3) protect Western Europe from the Soviet Union
(4) increase United States influence in Asia

39 Most opponents of the Senate hearings led by Senator Joseph McCarthy during the 1950s argued that these investigations

   (1) weakened the armed forces of the nation

   (2) violated the constitutional rights of many people

   (3) undermined the powers of the president

   (4) encouraged the spread of communism

40 When President Dwight D. Eisenhower sent troops into Little Rock, Arkansas, in 1957, he was fulfilling his presidential role as

   (1) chief executive

   (2) chief diplomat

   (3) head of state

   (4) head of his political party

41 What was a major reason President Lyndon B. Johnson decided not to run for reelection in 1968?

   (1) He was ineligible to hold a third term as president.

   (2) He was threatened with impeachment for government scandals.

   (3) His Vietnam War policies had reduced his popularity with voters.

   (4) Most Americans were unhappy with his failure to establish social reforms.

42 The Supreme Court ruling in *United States* v. *Nixon* (1974) was significant because it directly

   (1) increased the power of the legislative branch

   (2) showed that the Court controlled the executive branch

   (3) limited the president's power of executive privilege

   (4) weakened the principle of federalism

43 The Camp David Accords negotiated by President Jimmy Carter were important because they

   (1) reduced tensions in the Middle East

   (2) renewed diplomatic relations between the United States and China

   (3) slowed the pace of the nuclear arms race

   (4) provided for cooperation with the Soviet Union in the exploration of outer space

Base your answers to questions 44 and 45 on the chart below and on your knowledge of social studies.

ESTIMATED PERCENTAGE OF VOTING-AGE AFRICAN AMERICANS REGISTERED IN 1965 AND 1988		
STATE	**March 1965**	**November 1988**
Alabama	19.3	68.4
Georgia	27.4	56.8
Louisiana	31.6	77.1
Mississippi	6.7	74.2
N. Carolina	46.8	58.2
S. Carolina	37.3	56.7
Virginia	38.3	63.8

Source: U.S. Department of Justice, Civil Rights Division (adapted)

44 Which state had the largest increase in the percentage of African Americans registered to vote between 1965 and 1988?

   (1) Alabama   (3) Louisiana

   (2) Georgia   (4) Mississippi

45 Which conclusion is best supported by the changes shown on the chart?

   (1) African American voters would have little impact on presidential elections.

   (2) The income of African Americans had increased between 1965 and 1988.

   (3) Efforts to encourage African American voter registration were successful.

   (4) After 1988, no further effort was made to register African Americans.

46 The Supreme Court decisions in *New Jersey* v. *T.L.O.* (1985) and *Vernonia School District* v. *Acton* (1995) show that

   (1) a student's right to privacy is limited under certain conditions

   (2) prayer in public schools must be limited

   (3) racially segregated schools are unconstitutional

   (4) a student has no guaranteed rights while in school

Base your answer to question 47 on the cartoon below and on your knowledge of social studies.

"OK. You huddled masses. I know you're in here."

Source: Signe Wilkinson, *San Jose Mercury News*, 1984 (adapted)

47 The cartoonist is directing criticism at the

(1) use of unskilled workers
(2) government policy toward illegal immigrants
(3) poor quality of domestic textiles
(4) use of nonunion labor in the workplace

48 One similarity in the policies of President Herbert Hoover and President Ronald Reagan is that both supported

(1) a reduction of military spending
(2) the end of Social Security
(3) appointment of a woman to the Supreme Court
(4) economic changes favoring big business

49 Which sequence shows the correct order of events related to the history of African Americans in the United States?

(1) Radical Reconstruction → Emancipation Proclamation → *Brown* v. *Board of Education* decision → Great Migration
(2) Emancipation Proclamation → Radical Reconstruction → Great Migration → *Brown* v. *Board of Education* decision
(3) Great Migration → Emancipation Proclamation → *Brown* v. *Board of Education* decision → Radical Reconstruction
(4) *Brown* v. *Board of Education* decision → Great Migration → Radical Reconstruction → Emancipation Proclamation

50 Evidence that the United States has become more economically interdependent since 1990 is shown by its

(1) participation in the North American Free Trade Agreement (NAFTA)
(2) change from a service economy to a manufacturing economy
(3) increased dependence on domestic farm products
(4) policy of restricting imports

Answers to the essay questions are to be written in the separate essay booklet.

In developing your answer to Part II, be sure to keep these general definitions in mind:

(a) <u>describe</u> means "to illustrate something in words or tell about it"

(b) <u>discuss</u> means "to make observations about something using facts, reasoning, and argument; to present in some detail"

(c) <u>evaluate</u> means "to examine and judge the significance, worth, or condition of; to determine the value of "

Part II

THEMATIC ESSAY QUESTION

Directions: Write a well-organized essay that includes an introduction, several paragraphs addressing the task below, and a conclusion.

Theme: Contributions of Individuals to American Life

> Throughout the 20th century, individuals attempted to address problems within American society. Their efforts have had a significant impact on American life.

Task:

> Identify *two* individuals who have had a significant impact on American life during the 20th century and for *each*
> • Describe a problem in American society that the individual tried to change
> • Discuss an important contribution made by the individual to address this problem
> • Evaluate the impact of the contribution on American life

You may use any historically significant individual from your study of 20th-century United States history. Some suggestions you might wish to consider include Upton Sinclair, Henry Ford, Langston Hughes, Eleanor Roosevelt, Jackie Robinson, Martin Luther King, Jr., Betty Friedan, Rachel Carson, Cesar Chavez, and Bill Gates.

You are *not* limited to these suggestions.

Guidelines:

In your essay, be sure to:
• Develop all aspects of the task
• Support the theme with relevant facts, examples, and details
• Use a logical and clear plan of organization, including an introduction and a conclusion that are beyond a restatement of the theme

NAME _____ SCHOOL _____

In developing your answer to Part III, be sure to keep this general definition in mind:

> <u>discuss</u> means "to make observations about something using facts, reasoning, and argument; to present in some detail"

Part III

DOCUMENT-BASED QUESTION

This question is based on the accompanying documents. It is designed to test your ability to work with historical documents. Some of the documents have been edited for the purposes of the question. As you analyze the documents, take into account the source of each document and any point of view that may be presented in the document.

Historical Context:

> Between 1800 and 1900, the United States experienced great economic growth. Two factors that contributed to this growth were government policies and technological developments.

Task: Using information from the documents and your knowledge of United States history, answer the questions that follow each document in Part A. Your answers to the questions will help you write the Part B essay in which you will be asked to

> • Discuss how government policies **and** technological developments influenced the growth of the United States economy between 1800 and 1900

Part A

Short-Answer Questions

Directions: Analyze the documents and answer the short-answer questions that follow each document in the space provided.

Document 1a

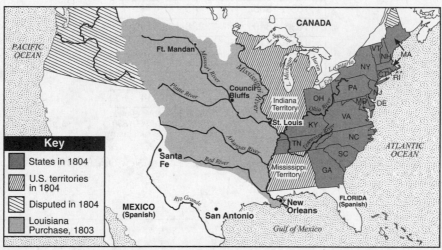

Source: Paul Boyer, *Boyer's The American Nation*, Holt, Rinehart and Winston (adapted)

1a Based on the information on this map, what action did President Thomas Jefferson take to encourage the economic growth of the United States? [1]

_____

_____

Score ▢

Document 1b

Value of Produce From the Interior
Received at the Port of New Orleans, 1816–1860

Time Period	Value in Dollars
1816–1820	61,432,458
1821–1825	75,675,672
1826–1830	107,886,410
1831–1835	143,477,674
1836–1840	220,408,589
1841–1845	266,614,052
1846–1850	425,893,436
1851–1855	671,653,147
1856–1860	827,736,914

Source: Douglass C. North, *The Economic Growth
of the United States, 1790–1860,*
W.W. Norton & Co., 1966 (adapted)

1*b* Based on this chart, what was *one* way that control of the port of New Orleans affected the United States economy? [1]

_____

_____

Score ☐

Document 2

The Effects of the Cotton Gin

. . . After the invention of the cotton gin, the yield of raw cotton doubled each decade after 1800. Demand was fueled by other inventions of the Industrial Revolution, such as the machines to spin and weave it and the steamboat to transport it. By midcentury America was growing three-quarters of the world's supply of cotton, most of it shipped to England or New England where it was manufactured into cloth. During this time tobacco fell in value, rice exports at best stayed steady, and sugar began to thrive, but only in Louisiana. At midcentury the South provided three-fifths of America's exports — most of it in cotton.

However, like many inventors, [Eli] Whitney (who died in 1825) could not have foreseen the ways in which his invention would change society for the worse. The most significant of these was the growth of slavery. While it was true that the cotton gin reduced the labor of removing seeds, it did not reduce the need for [use of] slaves to grow and pick the cotton. In fact, the opposite occurred. Cotton growing became so profitable for the planters that it greatly increased their demand for both land and slave labor. In 1790 there were six slave states; in 1860 there were 15. From 1790 until Congress banned the importation of slaves from Africa in 1808, Southerners imported 80,000 Africans. By 1860 approximately one in three Southerners was a slave. . . .

Source: Joan Brodsky Schur, "Eli Whitney's Patent for the Cotton Gin,"
U.S. National Archives & Records Administration

2*a* According to Joan Brodsky Schur, how did the cotton gin contribute to the growth of the United States economy? [1]

_____

_____

Score ☐

b According to Joan Brodsky Schur, what was **one** *negative* impact of the cotton gin on American society? [1]

_____

_____

Score ☐

Document 3a

> . . . The war [War of 1812] exposed not only weaknesses in defense, but also in transportation. Modes and methods of transportation were totally inadequate. Generals moved troops slowly by carriages, or on foot, on poorly developed roads. President James Madison supported the idea of internal improvements, yet he vetoed an internal improvements bill, which would have provided for the construction of roads. He felt that roads and canals that would benefit local communities should be funded by the respective states and private enterprises. He did, however, approve monies for a National Road, solely on the grounds that it would benefit national defense. This road began in Maryland and stretched all the way to Ohio, joining the Northeast with the western frontier. An equally significant improvement was the completion of the Erie Canal, linking the Great Lakes with New York City and the Atlantic Ocean. . . .

Source: Kerry C. Kelly, "Anti-railroad Propaganda Poster — The Growth of Regionalism, 1800–1860,"
U.S. National Archives & Records Administration

3a According to Kerry C. Kelly, what was **one** government action that improved transportation? [1]

_____

_____

Score [ ]

Document 3b

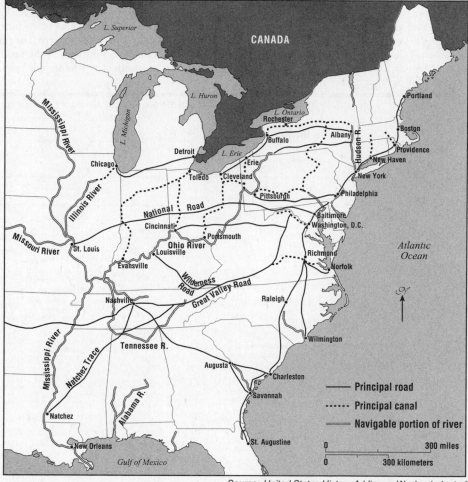

Roads, Canals, and Navigable Rivers, 1850

Source: *United States History*, Addison—Wesley (adapted)

3b Based on the information on this map, state *one* benefit of roads, canals, and/or navigable rivers on the United States economy. [1]

_____

_____

Score ☐

Document 4

. . . And what is this tariff? It seems to have been regarded as a sort of monster, huge and deformed; a wild beast, endowed with tremendous powers of destruction, about to be let loose among our people, if not to devour them, at least to consume their substance. But let us calm our passions, and deliberately survey this alarming, this terrific being. The sole object of the tariff is to tax the produce of foreign industry, with the view of promoting American industry. The tax is exclusively leveled at foreign industry. That is the avowed and the direct purpose of the tariff. If it subjects any part of American industry to burdens, that is an effect not intended, but is altogether incidental, and perfectly voluntary. . . .

Source: Henry Clay debating the Tariff Bill, March 1824, *Annals of Congress, Vol. 42*

4 According to Henry Clay, what was the purpose of the tariff? [1]

_____

_____

Score ☐

Document 5

Federal Land Policy in the 1800s

Grants	Acres
1. Land given as homestead grants	213.9 million acres
2. Land given to support railroad construction	129.0 million acres
3. Land given to states for educational purposes	
– common schools	73.2 million acres
– agricultural & mechanical colleges	11.1 million acres
4. Land given to war veterans (Revolutionary War, War of 1812, Mexican War)	68.2 million acres

Source: Anderson and Martin, "The Public Domain and Nineteenth Century Transfer Policy," *Cato Journal*, Vol. 6, No. 3, Winter 1987 (adapted)

5 Based on this chart, what were *two* examples of federal land policy in the 1800s? [2]

(1) _____

_____

Score ☐

(2) _____

_____

Score ☐

Document 6a

This poster advertised a wheat harvesting machine, one of many McCormick farm machines.

Self Binders
Harvesters
Reapers
Mowers & Droppers

McCORMICK HARVESTING MACHINE CO.

Source: Shober & Carqueville Lithog. Co. for McCormick Harvesting Machine Co.,
Wisconsin Historical Society (adapted)

Document 6b

Year	Wheat Production (in millions of bushels)	Corn Production (in millions of bushels)
1870	260.1	874.3
1875	309.1	850.1
1880	448.8	1,547.9
1885	512.8	1,795.5
1890	490.6	2,112.9
1895	460.2	1,212.8
1900	547.3	2,078.1

Source: *Statistical Abstract of the United States*, 1901

6 According to these documents, what impact did technology have on agricultural production in the United States? [1]

Score

Document 7

... During the post-Civil War decades, such wartime Republican initiatives as the Homestead Act and the Morrill Act for endowing agricultural colleges bore valuable economic fruit in the form of greater agricultural productivity. Federal railroad legislation had even weightier consequences. By 1871, under the terms of the Pacific Railroad Act and subsequent measures, the federal government had given private railroad companies over 130 million acres of land in the trans-Mississippi West, about one-tenth of the entire public domain. Individual states contributed a total of forty-nine million additional acres from their own public lands. This huge mass of real estate—larger than the state of Texas—was a vital source of funds for the railroads. People with savings—especially middle-class folk—who would not buy the stocks and bonds of the railroads, did buy their land. Thousands were attracted west to take up farms in the grants of the Northern Pacific, Union Pacific, Burlington, and other land-rich railroads. Their contribution to the roads' coffers was immense. The average price at which the railroads sold their land was about $3.30 an acre, bringing the promoters about $435 million. ...

Source: Irwin Unger, *These United States: The Questions of Our Past,* Little, Brown, 1978

7 According to Irwin Unger, what was **one** impact of federal land policy on the United States economy?   [1]

_____

_____

Score [ ]

Document 8

> . . . If you find it hard to believe that the Internet is merely a modern twist on a 19th-century system, consider the many striking parallels. For a start, the telegraph, like the Internet, changed communication completely. While the Internet can turn hours into seconds, the telegraph turned weeks into minutes. Before the telegraph, someone sending a dispatch to India from London had to wait months before receiving a reply. With the telegraph, communication took place as fast as operators could tap out Morse code.
>
> . . . Before too long, many telegraph users came to see it as a mixed blessing. Businessmen, who were keen adopters of the technology because it enabled them to keep track of distant markets and overseas events, found that it also led to an acceleration in the pace and stress of life. One harassed New York executive complained in 1868: "The businessman of the present day must be continually on the jump. The slow express train will not answer his purpose, and the poor merchant has no other way in which to work to secure a living for his family. He MUST use the telegraph." Information overload existed even then. . . .

Source: Tom Standage, "The 19th-Century Internet," www.contextmag.com

8 According to Tom Standage, what was *one* effect of the telegraph on American business? [1]

_____

_____

Score ☐

Document 9

> . . . Like information technology [IT] today, railroads in the second half of the 19th century promised to revolutionize society—shrinking distances, dramatically lowering costs, opening new markets, and increasing competition. Railroads were the great transformational technology of the age and promised to change everything. Like IT today, railroads sucked up the bulk of the world's investment capital, creating a speculative bubble that ultimately burst—blowing away much of the capital that investors had poured into the industry. While many investors lost their shirts, railroads did, in the end, deliver the revolution promised. Costs came down, living standards rose, markets expanded, and geography shrank. In fact, the railroad infrastructure, built with so much sweat, blood, and money a century ago, is still serving us today. . . .

Source: Barry Sheehy, "Train Wrecks: Why Information Technology Investments Derail," CPC Econometrics

9 According to Barry Sheehy, what were **two** effects of railroads on the American economy? [2]

(1) _____

_____

Score ☐

(2) _____

_____

Score ☐

Part B
Essay

Directions: Write a well-organized essay that includes an introduction, several paragraphs, and a conclusion. Use evidence from *at least five* documents in your essay. Support your response with relevant facts, examples, and details. Include additional outside information.

Historical Context:

Between 1800 and 1900, the United States experienced great economic growth. Two factors that contributed to this growth were government policies and technological developments.

Task: Using information from the documents and your knowledge of United States history, write an essay in which you

> • Discuss how government policies *and* technological developments influenced the growth of the United States economy between 1800 and 1900

Guidelines:

In your essay, be sure to:

- Develop all aspects of the task
- Incorporate information from *at least five* documents
- Incorporate relevant outside information
- Support the theme with relevant facts, examples, and details
- Use a logical and clear plan of organization, including an introduction and conclusion that are beyond a restatement of the theme

Regents Examination—June 2007

This section contains the Regents Examination in United States History and Government that was given in New York State in June 2007.

Circle your answers to Part I on this exam and write your answers to the thematic essay and document-based essay questions on separate sheets of paper. Be sure to refer to the test-taking strategies in the front of this book as you prepare to answer the test questions.

Part I

Answer all questions in this part.

Directions (1–50): For each statement or question, write on the separate answer sheet the *number* of the word or expression that, of those given, best completes the statement or answers the question.

1 In the pamphlet *Common Sense*, Thomas Paine urged the American colonists to
(1) oppose the French colonization of North America
(2) compromise with the British
(3) reaffirm their loyalty to King George III
(4) declare their independence from Great Britain

2 What was the primary reason for holding the Constitutional Convention of 1787?
(1) outlaw slavery in both the North and the South
(2) place taxes on imports and exports
(3) revise the Articles of Confederation
(4) reduce the power of the federal government

3 Which idea did the Founding Fathers include in the Constitution that allows Congress to meet the needs of a changing society?
(1) federalism
(2) separation of powers
(3) the elastic clause
(4) States rights

4 The major reason Antifederalists opposed ratification of the Constitution was because they believed
(1) amending the Constitution was too easy
(2) too much power was given to the states
(3) a federal court system would be too weak
(4) individual rights were not adequately protected

5 Which power was delegated to the federal government in the United States Constitution?
(1) establishing an official religion
(2) controlling interstate commerce
(3) regulating marriage and divorce
(4) granting titles of nobility

Base your answers to questions 6 and 7 on the quotation below and on your knowledge of social studies.

. . . The Privilege of the Writ of Habeas Corpus shall not be suspended, unless when in Cases of Rebellion or Invasion the public Safety may require it. . . .
— Article I, Section 9, Clause 2, United States Constitution

6 This clause of the Constitution expresses the idea that
(1) civil liberties are not absolute
(2) revolution is essential to democracy
(3) national defense is less important than individual rights
(4) freedom of the press is guaranteed

7 During which war was the writ of habeas corpus suspended by the president?
(1) Revolutionary War   (3) Mexican War
(2) War of 1812   (4) Civil War

8 Which heading best completes the partial outline below?

I. _____
  A. Political parties
  B. Committee system in Congress
  C. Judicial review
  D. President's cabinet

(1) Unwritten Constitution
(2) Constitutional Amendments
(3) Electoral Process
(4) Checks and Balances

9 • The United States government taxes gasoline.
 • New York State law requires a sales tax on many goods.

These two statements best illustrate the principle of

(1) concurrent powers
(2) property rights
(3) reserved powers
(4) popular sovereignty

10 Which statement about the United States House of Representatives is accurate?

(1) Representatives are chosen by the legislatures of their states.
(2) The Constitution allows each state two representatives.
(3) The number of representatives from each state is based on its population.
(4) The political party of the president always holds a majority of House seats.

11 Lobbying groups like the National Rifle Association (NRA) and the National Education Association (NEA) can influence government decisions because they

(1) directly choose the leaders of Congress
(2) work to elect legislators who support their views
(3) pay the salaries of elected officials
(4) become members of third political parties

12 The Mississippi River system was an important economic resource during the first half of the 1800s because it was used to

(1) irrigate desert lands
(2) transport farm goods to market
(3) move immigrants to the Northeast
(4) produce hydroelectric power

13 Washington's Proclamation of Neutrality (1793), Jefferson's Embargo Act (1807), and the Monroe Doctrine (1823) were all efforts to

(1) avoid political conflicts with European nations
(2) directly support European revolutions
(3) aid Great Britain in its war against France
(4) promote military alliances

14 Under the leadership of Chief Justice John Marshall (1801–1835), the United States Supreme Court issued decisions that

(1) declared racial segregation laws unconstitutional
(2) gave states the power to tax the Bank of the United States
(3) increased the ability of Congress to limit the powers of the president
(4) established the supremacy of federal laws over state laws

15 What was a major reason that slavery expanded in the South in the first half of the 1800s?

(1) Federal government regulations favored Southern exports.
(2) New inventions led to an increase in cotton production.
(3) Most early textile mills were built in the South.
(4) The federal government encouraged the importation of enslaved persons.

16 President Andrew Jackson used the spoils system to

(1) veto bills he disliked
(2) enforce Supreme Court decisions
(3) move Native American Indians off their traditional lands
(4) provide jobs to political party supporters

17 The slogan "Fifty-four forty or fight!," the annexation of Texas, and the Mexican War all relate to the

(1) theory of nullification
(2) practice of secession
(3) belief in Manifest Destiny
(4) idea of due process

18 The Homestead Act (1862) attempted to promote development of western lands by

(1) creating a system of dams for crop irrigation
(2) providing free land to settlers
(3) removing all restrictions on immigration
(4) placing Native American Indians on reservations

19 Which two geographic features most influenced United States foreign policy throughout the 19th century?

(1) Atlantic Ocean and Pacific Ocean
(2) Gulf of Mexico and Missouri River
(3) Great Lakes and Hudson River
(4) Appalachian Mountains and Rocky Mountains

20 In the second half of the 1800s, the federal government encouraged the building of transcontinental railroads by

(1) giving land to the railroad companies
(2) purchasing large amounts of railroad stock
(3) forcing convicts to work as laborers
(4) taking control of the railroad trust

21 Which action marked the end of Reconstruction in the United States?

(1) ratification of the 14th amendment
(2) withdrawal of federal troops from the South
(3) creation of the Freedmen's Bureau
(4) impeachment of President Andrew Johnson

22 During the late 1800s, which group strongly supported an open immigration policy?

(1) conservationists   (3) factory owners
(2) nativists   (4) southern farmers

23 What was a major goal of the Dawes Act (1887)?

(1) to provide a tribal legislature to govern all reservations
(2) to remove the Cherokees from the southeastern United States
(3) to strengthen Native American Indian tribal unity
(4) to encourage assimilation of Native American Indians

24 The theory of Social Darwinism was often used to justify the

(1) creation of the Ku Klux Klan
(2) formation of business monopolies
(3) use of strikes by labor unions
(4) passage of antitrust laws

25 The national income tax, free and unlimited coinage of silver, and the direct election of senators were proposals that were included in the

(1) Declaration of Sentiments
(2) Republican plan for Reconstruction
(3) Populist Party platform
(4) Federal Reserve System

26 Prior to entering World War I, the United States protested Germany's use of submarine warfare primarily because it

(1) violated the Monroe Doctrine
(2) discouraged immigration to the United States
(3) posed a direct threat to American cities
(4) violated the principle of freedom of the seas

27 What was a primary reason for the great migration of African Americans to northern cities during World War I?

(1) Job opportunities were available in northern factories.
(2) Jim Crow laws in the South had been repealed.
(3) Voting rights laws had been passed in northern states.
(4) The federal government had guaranteed an end to discrimination.

28 Which characteristic of the 1920s is illustrated by the trial of Sacco and Vanzetti?

(1) hostility toward woman's suffrage
(2) support for segregation
(3) opposition to separation of church and state
(4) intolerance toward immigrants

Base your answers to questions 29 and 30 on the map below and on your knowledge of social studies.

United States Territory and Leases, 1857–1903

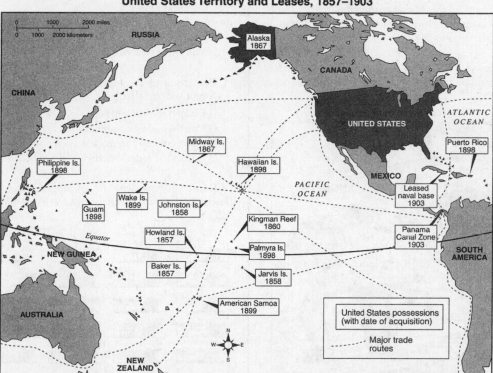

Source: Maps.com (adapted)

29 The main purpose of this map is to illustrate the

(1) sources of important natural resources
(2) development of United States imperialism
(3) growth of the Atlantic slave trade
(4) results of the Spanish-American War

30 The conclusion that can best be supported by the information on this map is that construction of the Panama Canal was motivated by the desire of the United States to

(1) raise the living standards of Latin American people
(2) increase naval mobility and expand overseas markets
(3) improve relations with Latin American and Asian nations
(4) maintain a policy of collective security

31 The national policy of Prohibition ended when the states

(1) strengthened food and drug laws
(2) legalized alcohol for medical purposes
(3) ratified the 21st amendment
(4) banned interstate shipment of alcoholic beverages

Base your answer to question 32 on the cartoon below and on your knowledge of social studies.

The Trojan Horse at Our Gate

Source: Carey Orr, *The Chicago Tribune*, September 17, 1935 (adapted)

32 The main idea of the cartoon is that the New Deal

(1) threatens the Constitution and the American people
(2) threatens the two-party political system
(3) provides American citizens with greater political freedom
(4) provides protection from foreign tyranny

33 President Franklin D. Roosevelt's Good Neighbor policy was designed mainly to

(1) reduce border conflicts with Canada
(2) increase acceptance of minorities within the United States
(3) encourage Germany and the Soviet Union to resolve their differences
(4) improve relations with Latin America

34 One result of President Franklin D. Roosevelt's New Deal was that it

(1) raised the national debt
(2) weakened labor unions
(3) deregulated the stock market
(4) repealed federal antitrust laws

Base your answer to question 35 on the illustration below and on your knowledge of social studies.

Source: Library of Congress (adapted)

35 The main purpose of the World War II coupons shown in this illustration was to

(1) choose men for the draft
(2) conserve essential goods for military use
(3) encourage increased production of consumer goods
(4) pay defense contractors for military hardware

36 In which pair of events is the second event a response to the first?

(1) Truman Doctrine → D-Day Invasion
(2) Manhattan Project → Lend-Lease Act
(3) Holocaust → Nuremberg War Crimes trials
(4) Germany's invasion of Poland → Munich Conference

37 United States foreign policy changed following World War II as the United States

(1) became more involved in world affairs
(2) returned to a policy of isolationism
(3) rejected membership in the United Nations
(4) pursued a policy of appeasement toward the Soviet Union

38 President Harry Truman's order requiring loyalty checks and the Senate hearings led by Joseph McCarthy were both responses to

(1) excessive spending by the armed forces after World War II
(2) racial discrimination against African Americans
(3) fear of communist influence in government
(4) control of labor unions by known criminals

39 As a result of the Interstate Highway Act of 1956, the United States experienced

(1) increased suburban growth
(2) the elimination of urban renewal programs
(3) less air pollution from motor vehicles
(4) a reduction in United States dependence on foreign oil

40 The Supreme Court decisions in *Gideon* v. *Wainwright* (1963) and *Miranda* v. *Arizona* (1966) resulted in

(1) an increase in the power of the police to obtain evidence
(2) a clarification of rules pertaining to cruel and unusual punishment
(3) a limitation of a citizen's right to an attorney
(4) an expansion of rights for persons accused of crimes

41 A major effect of the Watergate scandal of the 1970s was that it

(1) led to the Arab oil embargo
(2) reduced people's trust in government
(3) resulted in term limits for elected officials
(4) increased presidential power

42 In the Camp David Accords (1978), President Jimmy Carter succeeded in

(1) returning the Panama Canal Zone to Panama
(2) suspending grain sales to the Soviet Union and China
(3) providing a foundation for a peace treaty between Egypt and Israel
(4) freeing hostages being held in Iran

43 Which event is most closely associated with the end of the Cold War?

(1) passage of the North American Free Trade Agreement (NAFTA)
(2) establishment of a policy of détente with the Soviet Union
(3) invasion of Afghanistan by the Soviet Union
(4) fall of the Berlin Wall

44 Which event led to the other three?

(1) United States overthrow of the Taliban in Afghanistan
(2) passage of the Patriot Act
(3) September 11, 2001, terrorist attacks against the United States
(4) creation of the Department of Homeland Security

45 Which person's action was most closely associated with the abolitionist movement?

(1) William Lloyd Garrison's publication of *The Liberator*
(2) Booker T. Washington's commitment to African American education
(3) Thurgood Marshall's legal argument in *Brown* v. *Board of Education of Topeka*
(4) Martin Luther King, Jr.'s leadership of the Birmingham march

46 "Neither slavery nor involuntary servitude, except as a punishment for crime whereof the party shall have been duly convicted, shall exist within the United States, or any place subject to their jurisdiction."

This statement is part of the

(1) Missouri Compromise
(2) Kansas-Nebraska Act
(3) Dred Scott decision
(4) 13th amendment to the Constitution

Base your answer to question 47 on the song lyrics below and on your knowledge of social studies.

Brother, Can You Spare a Dime?

. . . Once I built a tower, up to the sun, brick and rivet and lime.
Once I built a tower, now it's done--
Brother, can you spare a dime? . . .
— E. Y. Harburg and J. Gorney

47 These song lyrics are most closely related to

(1) the writers of the Harlem Renaissance
(2) unemployment during the Great Depression
(3) the "Lost Generation" following World War I
(4) business expansion during the 1950s

48 Which pair of events shows a correct cause-and-effect relationship?

(1) secession of South Carolina → election of Abraham Lincoln
(2) United States enters the Spanish-American War → sinking of the USS *Maine*
(3) passage of the Meat Inspection Act → publication of *The Jungle*
(4) Soviets launch *Sputnik* → United States lands astronauts on the Moon

49 The Marshall Plan (1948) and the Cuban missile crisis (1962) are most closely associated with

(1) the establishment of the Peace Corps
(2) the creation of the Alliance for Progress
(3) United States–Soviet relations during the Cold War
(4) an increase in trade between the United States and Cuba

50 Which federal government program has been most affected by the longer life expectancy of people in the United States?

(1) Medicare
(2) Americans with Disabilities Act
(3) War on Poverty
(4) No Child Left Behind Act

Answers to the essay questions are to be written in the separate essay booklet.

In developing your answer to Part II, be sure to keep these general definitions in mind:

(a) <u>explain</u> means "to make plain or understandable; to give reasons for or causes of; to show the logical development or relationships of"

(b) <u>discuss</u> means "to make observations about something using fact, reasoning, and argument; to present in some detail"

Part II

THEMATIC ESSAY QUESTION

Directions: Write a well-organized essay that includes an introduction, several paragraphs addressing the task below, and a conclusion.

Theme: Change — Industrialization

> During the 19th century, the United States experienced tremendous industrial growth. This industrial growth resulted in many changes in American life.

Task:

> Identify *two* changes in American life that resulted from industrial growth in the United States and for *each* change
> - Explain how industrialization contributed to this change
> - Discuss *one* positive *or* one negative effect of this change on American life

You may use any appropriate change in American life that resulted from industrial growth. Some suggestions you might wish to consider include increased immigration, new inventions or technologies, growth of labor unions, growth of monopolies, growth of reform movements, and increased urbanization.

You are *not* limited to these suggestions.

Guidelines:

In your essay, be sure to:
- Develop all aspects of the task
- Support the theme with relevant facts, examples, and details
- Use a logical and clear plan of organization, including an introduction and a conclusion that are beyond a restatement of the theme

NAME _____ SCHOOL _____

In developing your answers to Part III, be sure to keep this general definition in mind:

> <u>discuss</u> means "to make observations about something using facts, reasoning, and argument; to present in some detail"

Part III

DOCUMENT-BASED QUESTION

This question is based on the accompanying documents. It is designed to test your ability to work with historical documents. Some of the documents have been edited for the purposes of the question. As you analyze the documents, take into account the source of each document and any point of view that may be presented in the document.

Historical Context:

> The woman's suffrage movement of the 1800s and early 1900s and the civil rights movement of the 1950s and 1960s had many similar goals and used similar methods to achieve these goals. Yet these movements also had many different goals and used different methods to achieve them.

Task: Using information from the documents and your knowledge of United States history, answer the questions that follow each document in Part A. Your answers to the questions will help you write the Part B essay, in which you will be asked to

> • Discuss the similarities ***and/or*** the differences between the woman's suffrage movement of the 1800s and early 1900s and the civil rights movement of the 1950s and 1960s in terms of
>
>   — the goals of the movements ***and***
>   — the methods used by the movements to achieve these goals

Part A
Short-Answer Questions

Directions: Analyze the documents and answer the short-answer questions that follow each document in the space provided.

Document 1

On November 5, 1872, Susan B. Anthony, along with sixteen other women, went to the local polling booth in Rochester to vote in the general election. She was arrested and made this statement during her trial. In the trial, she was convicted and fined.

> . . . Miss Anthony.[speaking] — May it please your honor, I will never pay a dollar of your unjust penalty. All the stock in trade I possess is a debt of $10,000, incurred by publishing my paper— The Revolution—the sole object of which was to educate all women to do precisely as I have done, rebel against your man-made, unjust, unconstitutional forms of law, which tax, fine, imprison and hang women, while denying them the right of representation in the government; and I will work on with might and main to pay every dollar of that honest debt, but not a penny shall go to this unjust claim. And I shall earnestly and persistently continue to urge all women to the practical recognition of the old Revolutionary maxim, "Resistance to tyranny is obedience to God.". . .

Source: Ida Husted Harper, *The Life and Work of Susan B. Anthony, Vol. I,* The Hollenbeck Press, 1898

1 According to Susan B. Anthony, why did she refuse to pay a fine? [1]

_____

_____

Score ☐

Document 2

Suffragists' Machine

Perfected in All States

Under Mrs. Catt's Rule

**Votes for Women Campaign Is
Now Run with All the Method
of Experienced Men Politicians**

. . . A suffrage publishing company, whose first President was Mrs. Cyrus W. Field, and whose present President is Miss Esther Ogden, is one of the important auxiliaries of the National American Suffrage Association's work. It has proved so successful as a business proposition that in January of this year, after two years of work, it declared a dividend of 3 per cent. This publishing company issues fliers, leaflets, books, posters, and suffrage maps. Incidentally, it produces, as an adjunct of the propaganda work, playing cards, stationery with "Votes for Women" printed on it, calendars, dinner cards, and postcards; also parasols, &c. [etc.], for use in parades. Last year this company issued 5,000,000 fliers. . . .

Source: *New York Times*, April 29, 1917

---

2 According to this *New York Times* article, what was **one** way that the National American Suffrage Association drew attention to its cause? [1]

_____

_____

Score ☐

Document 3a

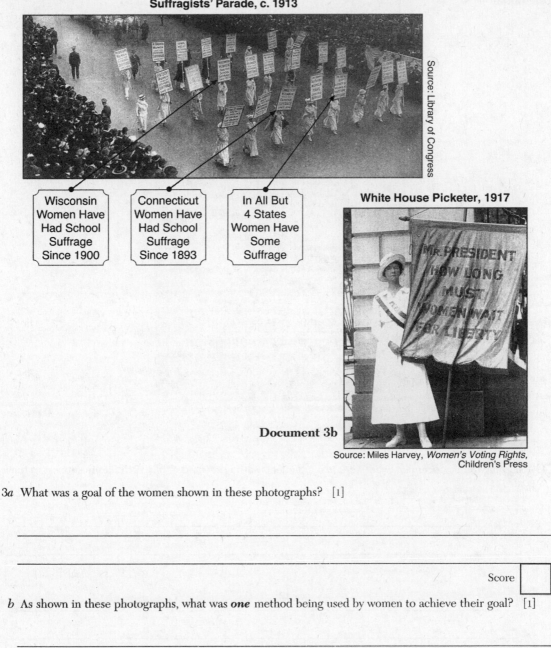

Suffragists' Parade, c. 1913

Source: Library of Congress

Wisconsin Women Have Had School Suffrage Since 1900

Connecticut Women Have Had School Suffrage Since 1893

In All But 4 States Women Have Some Suffrage

White House Picketer, 1917

MR. PRESIDENT HOW LONG MUST WOMEN WAIT FOR LIBERTY?

Document 3b

Source: Miles Harvey, *Women's Voting Rights*, Children's Press

3a What was a goal of the women shown in these photographs? [1]

_____

_____

Score ☐

b As shown in these photographs, what was *one* method being used by women to achieve their goal? [1]

_____

_____

Score ☐

Document 4

Twelve Reasons Why Women Should Vote

1. BECAUSE those who obey the laws should help to choose those who make the laws.
2. BECAUSE laws affect women as much as men.
3. BECAUSE laws which affect WOMEN are now passed without consulting them.
4. BECAUSE laws affecting CHILDREN should include the woman's point of view as well as the man's.
5. BECAUSE laws affecting the HOME are voted on in every session of the Legislature.
6. BECAUSE women have experience which would be helpful to legislation.
7. BECAUSE to deprive women of the vote is to lower their position in common estimation.
8. BECAUSE having the vote would increase the sense of responsibility among women toward questions of public importance.
10. BECAUSE hundreds of thousands of intelligent, thoughtful, hard-working women want the vote.
11. BECAUSE the objections against their having the vote are based on prejudice, not on reason.
12. BECAUSE to sum up all reasons in one—IT IS FOR THE COMMON GOOD OF ALL.

VOTE FOR WOMAN SUFFRAGE
GIVE THIS TO A FRIEND AND ASK HIM TO VOTE FOR IT

MASSACHUSETTS WOMAN SUFFRAGE ASSOCIATION
Headquarters: 585 Boylston St., Boston

Source: Massachusetts Woman Suffrage Association

(Note: The original version of this flier
did not include a Reason 9.)

4 According to this document, what were *two* arguments suffragists used in this 1915 flier in support of their goal? [2]

(1)_____

_____

Score ☐

(2)_____

_____

Score ☐

Document 5

... At these meetings [about the treatment of African Americans on buses], we discussed not only the two women who had been arrested, but also a number of additional bus incidents that never found their way into court, no doubt because the victims were black passengers. Several of the white drivers were determined to harass our people at every opportunity. For example, when the bus was even slightly crowded, they would make blacks pay their fare, then get off, and go to the back door to enter. Sometimes they would even take off with a squeal as a passenger trudged toward the rear after paying. At least once a driver closed the back door on a black woman's arm and then dragged her to the next stop before allowing her to climb aboard. Clearly this kind of gratuitous [unnecessary] cruelty was contributing to an increasing tension on Montgomery buses. We tried to reason with local authorities and with bus company officials. They were polite, listened to our complaints with serious expressions on their faces, and did nothing.

On December 1, 1955, Mrs. Parks took her now-famous bus ride and set events in motion that would lead to a social revolution of monumental proportions. . . .

Source: Ralph David Abernathy, *And the Walls Came Tumbling Down*, Harper & Row

5*a* According to Ralph David Abernathy, what was a goal of African Americans in Montgomery, Alabama? [1]

_____

_____

Score ☐

b According to Ralph David Abernathy, what was **one** method used by African Americans to address their concerns? [1]

_____

_____

Score ☐

Document 6a

College students face a hostile crowd at a southern "Whites Only" lunch counter in 1963.

Source: Juan Williams, *Eyes on the Prize,* Viking

Document 6b

African American college students wait for service or forcible removal from a "Whites Only" lunch counter.

Source: Gary Nash et al., ed., *The American People,* Pearson Longman

6a Based on these photographs, identify **one** method used by these civil rights activists to achieve their goals. [1]

_____

_____ Score ☐

b What was **one** specific goal of the civil rights activists shown in these photographs? [1]

_____

_____ Score ☐

Document 7

April 16, 1963
Birmingham, Alabama

. . . You may well ask: "Why direct action? Why sit-ins, marches and so forth? Isn't negotiation a better path?" You are quite right in calling, for negotiation. Indeed, this is the very purpose of direct action. Nonviolent direct action seeks to create such a crisis and foster such a tension that a community which has constantly refused to negotiate is forced to confront the issue. It seeks so to dramatize the issue that it can no longer be ignored. My citing the creation of tension as part of the work of the nonviolent-resister may sound rather shocking. But I must confess that I am not afraid of the word "tension." I have earnestly opposed violent tension, but there is a type of constructive, nonviolent tension which is necessary for growth. Just as Socrates felt that it was necessary to create a tension in the mind so that individuals could rise from the bondage of myths and half-truths to the unfettered [free] realm of creative analysis and objective appraisal, we must see the need for nonviolent gadflies [activists] to create the kind of tension in society that will help men rise from the dark depths of prejudice and racism to the majestic heights of understanding and brotherhood. . . .

Source: Martin Luther King, Jr., "Letter from Birmingham Jail," 1963

7a According to Martin Luther King, Jr., what was *one* method of achieving the goals of the civil rights movement? [1]

_____

_____

Score ☐

b According to Martin Luther King, Jr., what was a specific goal of the civil rights movement? [1]

_____

_____

Score ☐

Document 8

200,000 MARCH FOR CIVIL RIGHTS IN ORDERLY WASHINGTON RALLY

WASHINGTON, Aug. 28 — More than 200,000 Americans, most of them black but many of them white, demonstrated here today for a full and speedy program of civil rights and equal job opportunities.

It was the greatest assembly for a redress of grievances that this capital has ever seen.

One hundred years and 240 days after Abraham Lincoln enjoined the emancipated slaves to "abstain from all violence" and "labor faithfully for reasonable wages," this vast throng [crowd] proclaimed in march and song and through the speeches of their leaders that they were still waiting for the freedom and the jobs. . . .

Source: *New York Times,* August 29, 1963

8*a* According to this *New York Times* article, what method was used by these activists to achieve their goals? [1]

_____

_____

Score ☐

b According to this *New York Times* article, what was a specific goal of these activists? [1]

_____

_____

Score ☐

Document 9

JERICHO, U.S.A.

Source: Herblock, *Washington Post,* March 21, 1965 (adapted)

9 As shown in this Herblock cartoon, what was a specific goal of these marchers in their effort to gain equal rights? [1]

_____

_____

Score ☐

Part B
Essay

Directions: Write a well-organized essay that includes an introduction, several paragraphs, and a conclusion. Use evidence from *at least five* documents in the body of the essay. Support your response with relevant facts, examples, and details. Include additional outside information.

Historical Context:

The woman's suffrage movement of the 1800s and early 1900s and the civil rights movement of the 1950s and 1960s had many similar goals and used similar methods to achieve these goals. Yet these movements also had many different goals and used different methods to achieve them.

Task: Using information from the documents and your knowledge of United States history, write an essay in which you

- Discuss the similarities *and/or* the differences between the woman's suffrage movement of the 1800s and early 1900s and the civil rights movement of the 1950s and 1960s in terms of
  — the goals of the movements *and*
  — the methods used by the movements to achieve these goals

Guidelines:

In your essay, be sure to:
- Develop all aspects of the task
- Incorporate information from *at least five* documents
- Incorporate relevant outside information
- Support the theme with relevant facts, examples, and details
- Use a logical and clear plan of organization, including an introduction and conclusion that are beyond a restatement of the theme

Regents Examination—January 2007

This section contains the Regents Examination in United States History and Government that was given in New York State in January 2007.

Circle your answers to Part I on this exam and write your answers to the thematic essay and document-based essay questions on separate sheets of paper. Be sure to refer to the test-taking strategies in the front of this book as you prepare to answer the test questions.

Part I

Answer all questions in this part.

Directions (1–50): For each statement or question, write on the separate answer sheet the *number* of the word or expression that, of those given, best completes the statement or answers the question.

Base your answers to questions 1 and 2 on the map below and on your knowledge of social studies.

North America, 1803

Source: *Exploring American History*, Globe Book Company (adapted)

1 Which geographic feature was the boundary line between the United States and French Louisiana in 1803?

  (1) Appalachian Mountains   (3) Mississippi River
  (2) Great Lakes   (4) Rocky Mountains

2 If the Great Plains were shown in this map, they would be located mostly in

  (1) French Louisiana   (3) the Oregon Country
  (2) Spanish Mexico   (4) the original thirteen states

3 Which document included John Locke's idea that people have the right to overthrow an oppressive government?

(1) Mayflower Compact
(2) Northwest Ordinance
(3) Declaration of Independence
(4) Bill of Rights

4 Many colonies objected to the Albany Plan of Union (1754) mainly because

(1) the colonies had just been given representation in Parliament
(2) the plan gave too much power to Native American Indians
(3) threats to colonial safety had ended
(4) colonial assemblies did not want to give up their individual power

5 Thomas Paine's publication *Common Sense* was most influential in persuading American colonists to support

(1) additional British taxes on the colonies
(2) colonial independence
(3) the Whiskey Rebellion
(4) continued ties with Great Britain

6 A major weakness of government under the Articles of Confederation was that

(1) the large states received more votes in Congress than the small states did
(2) the national government could not enforce its laws
(3) too much power was given to the president
(4) state governments could not coin money

7 To address the concerns of many Antifederalists during the debate over ratification of the Constitution, the Federalists agreed that

(1) political parties would be formed
(2) states would retain control of interstate commerce
(3) slavery would be eliminated by an amendment
(4) a bill of rights would be added

8 During the Constitutional Convention of 1787, the Great Compromise resolved a conflict over

(1) presidential power
(2) the issue of nullification
(3) representation in Congress
(4) taxes on imports

9 The United States Constitution requires that a national census be taken every ten years to

(1) provide the government with information about voter registration
(2) establish a standard for setting income tax rates
(3) determine the number of members each state has in the House of Representatives
(4) decide who can vote in presidential elections

10 According to the United States Constitution, the president has the power to

(1) nominate federal judges
(2) declare war
(3) grant titles of nobility
(4) reverse Supreme Court decisions

11 In the 2000 presidential election, which aspect of the electoral college system caused the most controversy?

(1) A state can divide its electoral votes among different candidates.
(2) States with few electoral votes have no influence on election outcomes.
(3) The selection of electors varies among states.
(4) The winner of the popular vote might not get the majority of the electoral vote.

12 In his Farewell Address, President George Washington advised the nation to avoid permanent alliances because he believed that the United States

(1) would risk its security by involvement in European affairs
(2) had no need for the products or markets of Europe
(3) possessed military power superior to any European nation
(4) needed to limit European immigration

13 The decision in *Marbury* v. *Madison* (1803) expanded the power of the Supreme Court by

(1) restricting the use of the elastic clause
(2) establishing the power of judicial review
(3) upholding the constitutionality of the National Bank
(4) interpreting the interstate commerce clause

14 Prior to 1850, what was a main reason the North developed an economy increasingly based on manufacturing while the South continued to rely on an economy based on agriculture?

(1) Protective tariffs applied only to northern seaports.
(2) Geographic conditions supported different types of economic activity.
(3) Slavery in the North promoted rapid economic growth.
(4) Manufacturers failed to make a profit in the South.

15 The *Declaration of Sentiments*, adopted during the Seneca Falls Convention in 1848, is most closely associated with the rights of

(1) immigrants
(2) enslaved persons
(3) Native American Indians
(4) women

16

> I. Actions Taken by President Abraham Lincoln During the Civil War
>
> A. Increased the size of the army without congressional authorization
> B. Arrested and jailed anti-Unionists without giving a reason
> C. Censored some anti-Union newspapers and had some editors and publishers arrested

Which statement is most clearly supported by these actions of President Lincoln?

(1) Wartime emergencies led President Lincoln to expand his presidential powers.
(2) President Lincoln was impeached for violating the Constitution.
(3) Checks and balances effectively limited President Lincoln's actions.
(4) President Lincoln wanted to abolish the Bill of Rights.

17 In the late 1800s, the creation of the Standard Oil Trust by John D. Rockefeller was intended to

(1) protect small, independent oil firms
(2) control prices and practices in the oil refining business
(3) increase competition among oil refining companies
(4) distribute donations to charitable causes

18 Passage of the Dawes Act of 1887 affected Native American Indians by

(1) supporting their cultural traditions
(2) attempting to assimilate them into mainstream American culture
(3) forcing their removal from areas east of the Mississippi River
(4) starting a series of Indian wars on the Great Plains

19 The changes in American agriculture during the late 1800s led farmers to

(1) grow fewer cash crops for export
(2) request an end to agricultural tariffs
(3) demand a reduced role for government in agriculture
(4) become more dependent on banks and railroads

20 The Supreme Court cases of *Wabash, St. Louis & Pacific R.R.* v. *Illinois* (1886) and *United States* v. *E. C. Knight Co.* (1895) were based on laws that were intended to

(1) limit the power of big business
(2) support farmers' efforts to increase the money supply
(3) maintain a laissez-faire approach to the economy
(4) improve working conditions for immigrants

21 The Spanish-American War (1898) marked a turning point in United States foreign policy because the United States

(1) developed a plan for peaceful coexistence
(2) emerged as a major world power
(3) pledged neutrality in future European conflicts
(4) refused to become a colonial power

Base your answers to questions 22 and 23 on the cartoon below and on your knowledge of social studies.

Woman's Holy War
Grand Charge on the Enemy's Works

Source: Currier and Ives,
Library of Congress (adapted)

22 The "Holy War" illustrated in the cartoon was an effort to

(1) recruit women soldiers
(2) promote world peace
(3) ban the sale of alcoholic beverages
(4) spread Christian religious beliefs

23 Women gained a victory in the "war" shown in the cartoon through the

(1) ratification of a constitutional amendment
(2) legalization of birth control
(3) expansion of missionary activities overseas
(4) repeal of national Prohibition

24 A primary reason for the establishment of the Open Door policy (1899) was to

(1) protect United States trade in the Far East
(2) gain control of the Panama Canal Zone
(3) encourage Chinese immigration to the United States
(4) improve relations with Russia

Base your answers to questions 25 and 26 on the statements below that discuss immigration laws in the early 20th century, and on your knowledge of social studies.

Speaker A: A literacy test as a requirement for immigration to the United States is reasonable. Great numbers of uneducated workers take jobs and good wages from our workers.

Speaker B: Requiring literacy of immigrants is unfair. It will keep people out because they lacked the opportunity to gain an education.

Speaker C: A literacy test will allow more people from northern and western Europe to enter. They are similar to the majority of the United States population.

Speaker D: Literacy is not an issue. The real purpose of this law is to discriminate against immigrants from certain parts of the world.

25 Supporters of literacy tests to restrict immigration would most likely favor the views of *Speakers*

(1) *A* and *C*   (3) *B* and *D*
(2) *B* and *C*   (4) *A* and *B*

26 The immigrants referred to by *Speaker D* were mainly from

(1) Canada and Mexico
(2) South America
(3) western Europe
(4) southern and eastern Europe

Base your answer to question 27 on the map below and on your knowledge of social studies.

Suffrage Legislation, 1890–1919

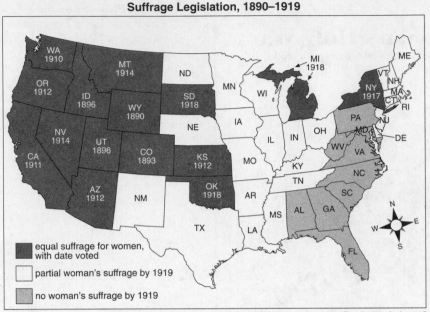

Source: Sandra Opdycke, *The Routledge Historical Atlas of Women in America*, Routledge (adapted)

27 What does the map show about woman's suffrage legislation before ratification of the federal woman's suffrage amendment in 1920?

(1) Opposition to woman's suffrage was strongest in the New England states.

(2) New York was the first state to grant women the right to vote in state elections.

(3) State legislatures never gave women the right to vote.

(4) Many western states granted women suffrage before passage of the 19th amendment.

28 During the Progressive Era, public demands for direct consumer protection resulted in passage of the

(1) Pure Food and Drug Act

(2) Fair Labor Standards Act

(3) Underwood Tariff

(4) income tax amendment

29 The Federal Reserve System helps to regulate

(1) the annual federal budget

(2) state sales tax rates

(3) Social Security payments

(4) the nation's money supply

30 Which issue was the focus of the Supreme Court decision in *Schenck v. United States* (1919)?

(1) freedom of speech for war protesters

(2) relocation of ethnic minority groups

(3) use of detention camps for enemy aliens

(4) integration of military forces

31 During the Harlem Renaissance of the 1920s, African American authors and artists used literature and art to

(1) end segregation of public facilities

(2) promote affirmative action programs

(3) celebrate the richness of their heritage

(4) urge voters to elect more African Americans to political office

32 Which economic condition was a major cause of the Great Depression?

(1) high wages of industrial workers

(2) deficit spending by the federal government

(3) inability of industry to produce enough consumer goods

(4) uneven distribution of income between the rich and the poor

33 The march of the "Bonus Army" and referring to shantytowns as "Hoovervilles" in the early 1930s illustrate

(1) growing discontent with Republican efforts to deal with the Great Depression

(2) state projects that created jobs for the unemployed

(3) federal attempts to restore confidence in the American economy

(4) the president's success in solving social problems

Base your answer to question 34 on the cartoon below and on your knowledge of social studies.

The Galloping Snail

Source: Burt Thomas, *Detroit News* (adapted)

34 The cartoonist is commenting on President Franklin D. Roosevelt's efforts to

(1) veto several bills sent him by Congress

(2) end New Deal programs

(3) gain quick passage of his legislation

(4) slow down the legislative process

35 Critics of the New Deal claimed that the Tennessee Valley Authority (TVA) and the Social Security System threatened the United States economy by

(1) applying socialist principles

(2) imposing unfair working hours

(3) decreasing government spending

(4) eroding antitrust laws

Base your answer to question 36 on the ration card shown below and on your knowledge of social studies.

36 The use of this card, issued by the federal government, was intended to

(1) help the automobile industry

(2) support the troops in wartime

(3) increase the use of gasoline

(4) decrease the cost of automobiles

37 A goal of the Marshall Plan (1948) was to

(1) rebuild Japan after World War II

(2) provide military aid to the Warsaw Pact

(3) establish a Pan-American military alliance system

(4) provide economic aid to European nations threatened by communism

38 Which heading is most appropriate for the partial outline below?

> I._____
>   A. The House Un-American Activities Committee
>   B. Loyalty review boards
>   C. Bomb shelters
>   D. *Watkins* v. *United States* (1957)

(1) Results of World War I
(2) The Cold War at Home
(3) Problems of Urbanization
(4) Reactions to Immigration

Base your answer to question 39 on the statement below and on your knowledge of social studies.

. . . Whenever normal agencies prove inadequate to the task and it becomes necessary for the Executive Branch of the Federal Government to use its powers and authority to uphold Federal Courts, the President's responsibility is inescapable.

In accordance with that responsibility, I have today issued an Executive Order directing the use of troops under Federal authority to aid in the execution of Federal law at Little Rock, Arkansas. This became necessary when my Proclamation of yesterday was not observed, and the obstruction of justice still continues. . . .

— President Dwight D. Eisenhower,
September 24, 1957

39 The situation described in this statement grew out of efforts to

(1) uphold the Voting Rights Act
(2) pass a constitutional amendment ending poll taxes
(3) enforce the decision in *Brown* v. *Board of Education of Topeka*
(4) extend the Montgomery bus boycott to Little Rock

Base your answers to questions 40 and 41 on the cartoon below and on your knowledge of social studies.

Source: Herblock, *Washington Post,* 1974 (adapted)

40 The conflict that was the focus of the cartoon involved President Richard Nixon's attempt to

(1) increase the number of troops in Vietnam
(2) withhold evidence in the Watergate scandal
(3) impose mandatory wage and price controls
(4) improve relations with the People's Republic of China

41 The cartoon illustrates the constitutional principle of

(1) federalism
(2) checks and balances
(3) representative government
(4) civilian control of the military

42 Population increases that resulted from the baby boom of the 1950s and 1960s contributed to a

  (1) housing surplus

  (2) drop in immigration

  (3) reduction in government services

  (4) rise in demand for consumer goods

43 The 1961 Bay of Pigs invasion and the 1962 missile crisis are conflicts directly related to United States relations with which two nations?

  (1) the Dominican Republic and Haiti

  (2) Cuba and the Soviet Union

  (3) China and Japan

  (4) North Korea and South Korea

44 What was a central issue in the Supreme Court cases of *Gideon* v. *Wainwright* (1963) and *Miranda* v. *Arizona* (1966)?

  (1) freedom of religion

  (2) voting rights

  (3) rights of the accused

  (4) property rights

45 The economic policies of President Ronald Reagan (1981–1989) and President George W. Bush (2001–present) are similar in that both

  (1) balanced the federal budget

  (2) expanded welfare programs to end poverty

  (3) used tax cuts to encourage economic growth

  (4) decreased military spending

46 Since the 1990s, the primary issue concerning the health care system in the United States has been the

  (1) increasing cost of medical care

  (2) shortage of prescription drugs

  (3) safety of medical procedures

  (4) reorganization of hospitals

47 Books such as *Uncle Tom's Cabin*, *How the Other Half Lives*, and *The Feminine Mystique* all show that literature can sometimes

  (1) expose government corruption

  (2) cause violent revolution

  (3) begin military conflict

  (4) encourage social reform

48 The Progressive movement (1900–1920) was primarily a response to problems created by

  (1) abolitionists   (3) industrialization

  (2) nativists   (4) segregation

49 The term *Dust Bowl* is most closely associated with which historical circumstance?

  (1) a major drought that occurred during the 1930s

  (2) logging practices in the Pacific Northwest in the 1950s

  (3) an increase in pollution during the 1960s

  (4) the migration to the Sun Belt in the 1970s

50 The Camp David Accords and the Persian Gulf War both show the desire of the United States to

  (1) create stability in the Middle East

  (2) expand trade with Asian nations

  (3) maintain friendly relations with Europe

  (4) provide economic stability in Latin America

Answers to the essay questions are to be written in the separate essay booklet.

In developing your answer to Part II, be sure to keep these general definitions in mind:

(a) <u>describe</u> means "to illustrate something in words or tell about it"

(b) <u>discuss</u> means "to make observations about something using facts, reasoning, and argument; to present in some detail"

Part II

THEMATIC ESSAY QUESTION

Directions: Write a well-organized essay that includes an introduction, several paragraphs addressing the task below, and a conclusion.

Theme: Influence of Geographic Factors on Governmental Actions

> Actions taken by the United States government have often been influenced by geographic factors. Some of these factors include location, climate, natural resources, and physical features.

Task:

> Identify *two* actions taken by the United States government that have been influenced by geographic factors and for *each*
> * State *one* reason the United States took the action
> * Describe how a geographic factor influenced the action
> * Discuss the impact of the action on the United States

You may use any action taken by the United States government that was influenced by a geographic factor. Some suggestions you might wish to consider include the Lewis and Clark expedition (1804–1806), issuance of the Monroe Doctrine (1823), Mexican War (1846–1848), Commodore Perry's opening of Japan (1853), passage of the Homestead Act (1862), purchase of Alaska (1867), construction of the Panama Canal (1904–1914), entry into World War II (1941), passage of the Interstate Highway Act (1956), and involvement in the Persian Gulf War (1991).

You are *not* limited to these suggestions.

Guidelines:

In your essay, be sure to:
* Develop all aspects of the task
* Support the theme with relevant facts, examples, and details
* Use a logical and clear plan of organization, including an introduction and a conclusion that are beyond a restatement of the theme

NAME _____ SCHOOL _____

In developing your answer to Part III, be sure to keep these general definitions in mind:

(a) <u>explain</u> means "to make plain or understandable; to give reasons for or causes of; to show the logical development or relationships of "

(b) <u>discuss</u> means "to make observations about something using facts, reasoning, and argument; to present in some detail"

Part III

DOCUMENT-BASED QUESTION

This question is based on the accompanying documents. It is designed to test your ability to work with historical documents. Some of the documents have been edited for the purposes of the question. As you analyze the documents, take into account the source of each document and any point of view that may be presented in the document.

Historical Context:

> Since World War II, conflicts in Asia have played a major role in the Cold War. One of these conflicts arose in Vietnam. United States involvement in this conflict was sometimes controversial. The decision to send troops to Vietnam had a major impact on American society and on United States foreign policy.

Task: Using information from the documents and your knowledge of United States history, answer the questions that follow each document in Part A. Your answers to the questions will help you write the Part B essay, in which you will be asked to

---

- Explain the reasons for United States involvement in Vietnam
- Discuss the impact of the Vietnam War on American society
- Discuss the impact of the Vietnam War on United States foreign policy

---

Part A
Short-Answer Questions

Directions: Analyze the documents and answer the short-answer questions that follow each document in the space provided.

Document 1

> . . . At the present moment in world history nearly every nation must choose between alternative ways of life. The choice is too often not a free one.
>
> One way of life is based upon the will of the majority, and is distinguished by free institutions, representative government, free elections, guarantees of individual liberty, freedom of speech and religion, and freedom from political oppression.
>
> The second way of life is based upon the will of a minority forcibly imposed upon the majority. It relies upon terror and oppression, a controlled press and radio, fixed elections, and the suppression of personal freedoms.
>
> I believe that it must be the policy of the United States to support free peoples who are resisting attempted subjugation [control] by armed minorities or by outside pressures.
>
> I believe that we must assist free peoples to work out their own destinies in their own way. . . .

Source: President Harry Truman, Address to Congress (Truman Doctrine), March 12, 1947

1a According to President Harry Truman, what is **one** problem when governments are controlled by the will of a minority? [1]

_____

_____

Score ☐

b According to President Truman, what policy must the United States support? [1]

_____

_____

Score ☐

Document 2a

> . . . Communist aggression in Korea is a part of the worldwide strategy of the Kremlin to destroy freedom. It has shown men all over the world that Communist imperialism may strike anywhere, anytime.
>
> The defense of Korea is part of the worldwide effort of all the free nations to maintain freedom. It has shown free men that if they stand together, and pool their strength, Communist aggression cannot succeed. . . .

Source: President Harry Truman, Address at a dinner of the Civil Defense Conference, May 7, 1951

2a According to President Harry Truman, why was it important for the United States to help defend Korea? [1]

_____

_____

Score ☐

Document 2b

Another Hole in the Dike

Source: Fred O. Seibel, *Richmond Times-Dispatch*,
May 5, 1953 (adapted)

2b Based on this cartoon, what problem did the United States face in Asia by 1953? [1]

_____

_____

Score ☐

Document 3

THE NATURE OF THE CONFLICT

. . . The world as it is in Asia is not a serene or peaceful place.

The first reality is that North Viet-Nam has attacked the independent nation of South Viet-Nam. Its object is total conquest.

Of course, some of the people of South Viet-Nam are participating in attack on their own government. But trained men and supplies, orders and arms, flow in a constant stream from north to south.

This support is the heartbeat of the war. . . .

WHY ARE WE IN VIET-NAM?

Why are these realities our concern? Why are we in South Viet-Nam?

We are there because we have a promise to keep. Since 1954 every American President has offered support to the people of South Viet-Nam. We have helped to build, and we have helped to defend. Thus, over many years, we have made a national pledge to help South Viet-Nam defend its independence.

And I intend to keep that promise. . . .

Source: President Lyndon B. Johnson, Speech at Johns Hopkins University, April 7, 1965

3 According to President Lyndon B. Johnson, why was the United States involved in Vietnam? [1]

_____

_____

Score ☐

Document 4a

> . . . When the country looks to Lyndon Johnson these days, it gains the inescapable impression that Vietnam is America's top priority. Mr. Johnson uses the bully pulpit [power] of the Presidency (not to mention the Rose Garden) time and again to tell a painfully divided nation why it is fighting and must continue to fight in Southeast Asia. No amount of resistance—and it is growing—can blunt [lessen] his resolve. Few question his personal resolve on the Negro [African American] problem (he is, after all, the President who proclaimed "We Shall Overcome!" in a speech three years ago). But his public posture [position] here projects none of the sense of urgency that marks his Vietnam crusading. . . .

Source: "The Negro in America: What Must Be Done," *Newsweek*, November 20, 1967

Document 4b

Source: Charles Brooks,
Birmingham News (adapted)

4 According to these documents, what were *two* effects of the Vietnam War on American society? [2]

(1)_____

_____

Score ☐

(2)_____

_____

Score ☐

Document 5a

Anti-Vietnam War protesters march down Fifth Avenue in New York City on April 27, 1968. The demonstration attracted 87,000 people and led to 60 arrests. Also on the 27th, some 200,000 New York City students boycotted classes.

Source: *The Sixties Chronicle*, Legacy Publishing

Document 5b

This article appeared in the *New York Times* three days after the Kent State shootings.

Illinois Deploys Guard

More than 80 colleges across the country closed their doors yesterday for periods ranging from a day to the remainder of the academic year as thousands of students joined the growing nationwide campus protest against the war in Southeast Asia.

In California, Gov. Ronald Reagan, citing "emotional turmoil," closed down the entire state university and college system from midnight last night until next Monday. More than 280,000 students at 19 colleges and nine university campuses are involved.

Pennsylvania State University, with 18 campuses, was closed for an indeterminate [indefinite] period.

In the New York metropolitan area about 15 colleges closed, some for a day, some for the week, and some for the rest of the term.

A spokesman for the National Student Association said that students had been staying away from classes at almost 300 campuses in the country. . . .

Source: Frank J. Prial, *New York Times*, May 7, 1970

5 Based on these documents, state *two* ways the Vietnam War affected American society. [2]

(1)_____

_____

Score ☐

(2)_____

_____

Score ☐

Document 6

After the Vietnam War ended in 1975, large numbers of Vietnamese refugees settled in Westminster, California.

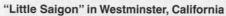

"Little Saigon" in Westminster, California

Source: Bailey and Kennedy, *The American Pageant,* D. C. Heath and Co., 1991

6 According to this photograph, how have Vietnamese immigrants contributed to American society? [1]

_____

_____

Score ☐

Document 7

> . . . Within sixty calendar days after a report is submitted or is required to be submitted pursuant to section 1543(a)(1) of this title, whichever is earlier, the President shall terminate any use of United States Armed Forces with respect to which such report was submitted (or required to be submitted), unless the Congress (1) has declared war or has enacted a specific authorization for such use of United States Armed Forces, (2) has extended by law such sixty-day period, or (3) is physically unable to meet as a result of an armed attack upon the United States. Such sixty-day period shall be extended for not more than an additional thirty days if the President determines and certifies to the Congress in writing that unavoidable military necessity respecting the safety of United States Armed Forces requires the continued use of such armed forces in the course of bringing about a prompt removal of such forces. . . .

Source: War Powers Act, 1973

7 Based on this document, state *one* way in which the War Powers Act could limit United States involvement in foreign conflicts. [1]

_____

_____

Score ▢

Document 8

> . . . Fourteen years after the last United States combat units left Vietnam, at least 15 men who were there have made their way into Congress.
>
> ### Each Draws His Own Lesson
>
> Some are Republicans, like Representative David O'B. Martin of upstate New York; some are Democrats, like Representatives H. Martin Lancaster of North Carolina and John P. Murtha of Pennsylvania; some are conservatives, and some are liberals. Each has drawn his own lesson from having participated in the war, and each applies the experience in his own way to the issues of foreign policy he confronts as a legislator.
>
> Some support military aid to the Nicaraguan rebels, some oppose it. A few favored sending the Marine contingent to Beirut in 1982, though most say they had grave reservations. Some see the Soviet threat in larger terms than others.
>
> But the Vietnam experience has given almost all of them a sense of seasoned caution about using American military power without having the broad support of the American people. And this translates into some sober views on the limitations of force, especially in impoverished countries torn by internal strife. . . .

Source: David K. Shipler, "The Vietnam Experience and the Congressman of the 1980's," *New York Times*, May 28, 1987

8 According to this article, how has the experience of many Congressmen who served in Vietnam affected their views on when to use American military force? [1]

_____

_____

Score ☐

Document 9

Comments on United States participation in Operation Desert Storm and Persian Gulf War, 1991

"By God, we've kicked the Vietnam syndrome once and for all!" So said President George Bush in a euphoric [joyful] victory statement at the end of the Gulf War, suggesting the extent to which Vietnam continued to prey on the American psyche more than fifteen years after the fall of Saigon. Indeed the Vietnam War was by far the most convulsive and traumatic of America's three wars in Asia in the 50 years since Pearl Harbor. It set the U.S. economy on a downward spiral. It left America's foreign policy at least temporarily in disarray, discrediting the postwar policy of containment and undermining the consensus that supported it. It divided the American people as no other event since their own Civil War a century earlier. It battered their collective soul.

Such was the lingering impact of the Vietnam War that the Persian Gulf conflict appeared at times as much a struggle with its ghosts as with Saddam Hussein's Iraq. President Bush's eulogy for the Vietnam syndrome may therefore be premature. Success in the Gulf War no doubt raised the nation's confidence in its foreign policy leadership and its military institutions and weakened long-standing inhibitions against intervention abroad. Still it seems doubtful that military victory over a nation with a population less than one-third of Vietnam in a conflict fought under the most favorable circumstances could expunge [erase] deeply encrusted and still painful memories of an earlier and very different kind of war. . . .

Source: George C. Herring, "America and Vietnam: The Unending War," *Foreign Affairs*, Winter 1991/92

9 According to this document, what was *one* impact of the Vietnam War on United States foreign policy? [1]

_____

_____

Score [   ]

Part B
Essay

Directions: Write a well-organized essay that includes an introduction, several paragraphs, and a conclusion. Use evidence from *at least **five*** documents in the body of the essay. Support your response with relevant facts, examples, and details. Include additional outside information.

Historical Context:

Since World War II, conflicts in Asia have played a major role in the Cold War. One of these conflicts arose in Vietnam. United States involvement in this conflict was sometimes controversial. The decision to send troops to Vietnam had a major impact on American society and on United States foreign policy.

Task: Using information from the documents and your knowledge of United States history, write an essay in which you

- Explain the reasons for United States involvement in Vietnam
- Discuss the impact of the Vietnam War on American society
- Discuss the impact of the Vietnam War on United States foreign policy

Guidelines:

In your essay, be sure to:
- Develop all aspects of the task
- Incorporate information from *at least **five*** documents
- Incorporate relevant outside information
- Support the theme with relevant facts, examples, and details
- Use a logical and clear plan of organization, including an introduction and conclusion that are beyond a restatement of the theme

Regents Examination—August 2006

This section contains the Regents Examination in United States History and Government that was given in New York State in August 2006.

Circle your answers to Part I on this exam and write your answers to the thematic essay and document-based essay questions on separate sheets of paper. Be sure to refer to the test-taking strategies in the front of this book as you prepare to answer the test questions.

Part I

Answer all questions in this part.

Directions (1–50): For each statement or question, write on the separate answer sheet the *number* of the word or expression that, of those given, best completes the statement or answers the question.

Base your answer to question 1 on the map below and on your knowledge of social studies.

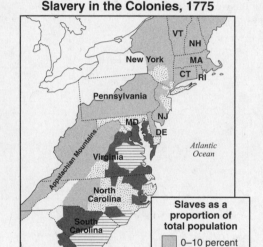

Slavery in the Colonies, 1775

Slaves as a proportion of total population

- 0–10 percent
- 10–30 percent
- 30–50 percent
- 50–70 percent

Source: James A. Henretta et al., *America's History*, Dorsey Press (adapted)

1 A conclusion supported by the information on the map is that slavery in the American colonies was

(1) declining by the start of the Revolutionary War
(2) concentrated in areas suitable for large plantations
(3) becoming illegal in the northern colonies
(4) growing fastest in the New England colonies

2 Judicial review, as practiced by the federal courts, resulted directly from

(1) the decisions of colonial governors
(2) the Articles of Confederation
(3) the Bill of Rights
(4) a Supreme Court decision

3 John Locke's theory of natural rights, as reflected in the Declaration of Independence, states that

(1) government is the source of all individual rights
(2) power should be concentrated in the monarchy
(3) power to govern belongs to the people
(4) individual liberties are best protected by a strong government

4 The Northwest Ordinance of 1787 set a precedent for other western territories by

(1) allowing slavery
(2) including voting rights for women
(3) providing a method for the creation of new states
(4) setting aside land for churches

5 The government created by the Articles of Confederation was unsuccessful at solving many major problems because

(1) unlimited power was given to the Supreme Court
(2) most power remained with the state governments
(3) members of Congress were elected according to each state's population
(4) political parties prevented the passage of legislation

6 The first amendment guarantee of freedom of speech was added to the United States Constitution primarily because its supporters believed it was essential to

(1) discourage criticism of government policies
(2) ensure the functioning of democracy
(3) limit political debate in Congress
(4) encourage more candidates to run for office

7 Which change within the federal government results from the census that is taken every ten years?

(1) The Supreme Court gains new justices.

(2) Members of Congress face new term limits.

(3) Large states gain additional seats in the Senate.

(4) Some states lose or gain members in the House of Representatives.

8 A major foreign policy success of President Thomas Jefferson's administration was the

(1) purchase of the Louisiana Territory

(2) support for the Alien and Sedition Acts

(3) victory in the war of 1812

(4) passage of the Embargo Act

9 *Federalism* is a term used to define the division of power between the

(1) president and the vice president

(2) Senate and the House of Representatives

(3) national and state levels of government

(4) three branches of the federal government

10 The major purpose of the Monroe Doctrine (1823) was to

(1) create a military alliance for the defense of North America

(2) guarantee democratic governments in Latin America

(3) secure new colonies in the Caribbean

(4) limit European influence in the Western Hemisphere

11 In the Compromise of 1850 and the Kansas-Nebraska Act of 1854, popular sovereignty was proposed as a way to

(1) allow northern states the power to ban slavery

(2) deny southern states the legal right to own slaves

(3) allow settlers in new territories to vote on the issue of slavery

(4) overturn previous Supreme Court decisions on slavery

Base your answers to questions 12 and 13 on the cartoon below and on your knowledge of social studies.

The "Strong" Government, 1869–1877

Source: J. A. Wales, *Puck*, May 12, 1880 (adapted)

12 What is the main idea of this cartoon from the Reconstruction Era?

(1) Southern society was oppressed by Radical Republican policies.

(2) Military force was necessary to stop Southern secession.

(3) United States soldiers forced women in the South to work in factories.

(4) Sharecropping was an economic burden for women after the Civil War.

13 Which congressional action led to the Southern viewpoint expressed in this cartoon?

(1) passage of the Homestead Act

(2) strengthening of the Fugitive Slave Laws

(3) military occupation of the former Confederate States

(4) ending the Freedmen's Bureau

14 In an effort to resolve conflicts with the frontier settlers in the 1870s, the federal government forced Native American Indians to

(1) move west of the Mississippi River
(2) live on reservations with definite boundaries
(3) relocate to urban industrial centers
(4) help build the transcontinental railroad

15 After 1880, a major new source of labor for American factories was

(1) western farmers who moved back to eastern cities
(2) young women who worked until they married
(3) formerly enslaved persons fleeing from the South
(4) immigrants from southern and eastern Europe

16 During the 19th century, the completion of the Erie Canal and the transcontinental railroads contributed to the industrial growth of the United States by

(1) making the movement of goods easier and cheaper
(2) protecting the United States from low-priced foreign imports
(3) encouraging subsistence farming
(4) connecting the United States to markets in Mexico and Canada

17 During the late 1800s, the principles of Social Darwinism were used to justify

(1) support for unlimited immigration
(2) desegregation of public facilities
(3) the use of strikes by organized labor
(4) the accumulation of great wealth by industrialists

18 What was the decision of the Supreme Court in *Plessy* v. *Ferguson* (1896)?

(1) Black Codes were unconstitutional.
(2) The citizenship principle established in *Dred Scott* v. *Sanford* was repealed.
(3) The 15th amendment failed to guarantee the right to vote to all males.
(4) Racial segregation did not violate the equal protection provision of the 14th amendment.

Base your answers to questions 19 and 20 on the cartoon below and on your knowledge of social studies.

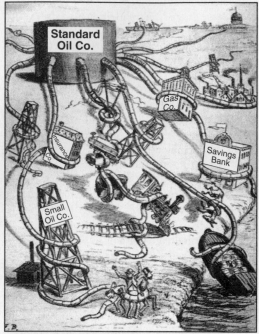

Source: Frank Beard, *The Judge,* July 19, 1884 (adapted)

19 Which type of business organization is being criticized in this cartoon?

(1) monopoly
(2) multinational corporation
(3) partnership
(4) proprietorship

20 Which government policy would this cartoonist most likely support?

(1) adopting antitrust laws
(2) easing regulations regarding mergers
(3) giving government subsidies to financial institutions
(4) encouraging large companies to relocate overseas

Base your answer to question 21 on the cartoon below and on your knowledge of social studies.

"A suggestion for the 53-cent dollar."

Source: Mark Sullivan, *Our Times, Vol. 1, The Turn of the Century* (adapted)

21 This cartoon from the 1896 presidential election campaign attacked William Jennings Bryan's proposal for
(1) free coinage of silver
(2) lower tariffs on farm goods
(3) strengthening the gold standard
(4) government regulation of the railroads

22 By proclaiming the Open Door policy in 1899, the United States was attempting to
(1) keep Japan from attacking and colonizing China
(2) increase trade between Russia and the United States
(3) ensure equal trading opportunities in China
(4) prevent European countries from colonizing the Western Hemisphere

Base your answer to question 23 on the speakers' statements below and on your knowledge of social studies.

Speaker A: It is more important now to focus on vocational training and economic opportunities than on removing obstacles to social equality for African Americans.

Speaker B: The Constitution is color-blind and recognizes no superior class in this country. All citizens are equal before the law.

Speaker C: The American Negro [African American] must focus on the achievement of three goals: higher education, full political participation, and continued support for civil rights.

Speaker D: African Americans should return home to Africa to establish their own independent nation free from white control.

23 During the early 1900s, reform leaders tried to advance the goals of *Speaker C* by
(1) supporting passage of Jim Crow laws
(2) forming the Tuskegee Institute in Alabama
(3) avoiding attempts to overturn racial segregation in the courts
(4) creating the National Association for the Advancement of Colored People (NAACP)

24 The photographs of Jacob Riis are most closely associated with the
(1) battlefields of the Civil War
(2) living conditions of the urban poor
(3) plight of sharecroppers in the South
(4) victims of the Dust Bowl on the Great Plains

25 In the 1920s, both Langston Hughes and Duke Ellington made major contributions to
(1) economic growth   (3) the creative arts
(2) educational reform   (4) political leadership

26 President Theodore Roosevelt's Big Stick policy was used by the United States to

(1) police the Western Hemisphere
(2) expand its colonial empire in Africa
(3) isolate itself from European conflicts
(4) settle a dispute between Russia and Japan

27 In the years before the United States entered World War I, President Woodrow Wilson violated his position of strict neutrality by

(1) secretly sending troops to fight for the democratic nations
(2) openly encouraging Mexico to send troops to support the Allies
(3) supporting economic policies that favored the Allied nations
(4) using United States warships to attack German submarines

28 Which Progressive Era political reform allows voters to choose party candidates to run for elected public offices?

(1) referendum   (3) initiative
(2) recall   (4) direct primary

29 In *Schenck* v. *United States* (1919), the Supreme Court upheld the right of government to protect national security during wartime by

(1) nationalizing important industries that supported the war effort
(2) limiting speech that presented a clear and present danger to the nation
(3) suspending the writ of habeas corpus for illegal aliens
(4) expelling enemy aliens who had favored the Central Powers

30 The changing image of women during the 1920s was symbolized by the

(1) passage of an equal pay act
(2) drafting of women into the army
(3) popularity of the flappers and their style of dress
(4) appointment of several women to President Calvin Coolidge's cabinet

Base your answer to question 31 on the graph below and on your knowledge of social studies.

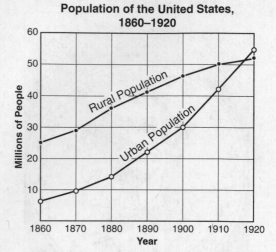

Source: United States Bureau of the Census (adapted)

31 Which statement about population distribution in the United States between 1860 and 1920 is best supported by the graph?

(1) Rural population declined after 1910.
(2) Many Americans migrated from urban to rural areas.
(3) Immigration played a limited role in urban growth.
(4) The population of cities grew at a faster rate than that of rural areas.

32 The economic prosperity of the 1920s was mainly the result of the

(1) adoption of lower tariff rates
(2) stricter enforcement of antitrust laws
(3) success of most United States farmers
(4) development of new industries for consumer goods

33 The Harlem Renaissance was important to American society because it

(1) highlighted the cultural achievements of African Americans

(2) isolated African Americans from mainstream society

(3) provided new political opportunities for African Americans

(4) brought an end to racial segregation in the North

34 The New Deal programs of President Franklin D. Roosevelt changed the United States economy by

(1) restoring the principle of a balanced budget

(2) expanding the trustbusting practices of Progressive Era presidents

(3) encouraging greater production of agricultural goods

(4) increasing government involvement with both business and labor

35 Which statement most accurately describes the foreign policy change made by the United States between the start of World War II (1939) and the attack on Pearl Harbor (1941)?

(1) The traditional isolationism of the United States was strengthened.

(2) The nation shifted from neutrality to military support for the Allies.

(3) War was declared on Germany but not on Japan.

(4) Financial aid was offered to both the Allied and Axis powers.

36 In 1948, President Harry Truman showed his support for civil rights by issuing an executive order to

(1) end the immigration quota system

(2) assure equal status for women in military service

(3) ban racial segregation in the military

(4) guarantee jobs for Native American Indians

Base your answer to question 37 on the poster below and on your knowledge social studies.

Source: Alfred T. Palmer, *Office of War Information*, 1943

37 During World War II, posters like this were used to

(1) prevent antiwar protests

(2) recruit more women workers

(3) convince women to enlist in the military services

(4) gain acceptance for wartime rationing programs

Base your answer to question 38 on the photograph below and on your knowledge of social studies.

Source: Bailey and Kennedy, *The American Pageant*, 9th edition, D.C. Heath and Co.

38 This photograph shows the post–World War II growth that was typical of

(1) tourist resorts
(2) suburban communities
(3) inner cities
(4) public housing projects

39 The United States began a trade embargo against Cuba in the 1960s to

(1) encourage political change in Cuba
(2) promote domestic industries in Cuba
(3) motivate Cubans to immigrate to the United States
(4) end the domination of the banana industry by Cuba

40 One goal of President Lyndon Johnson's Great Society was to

(1) improve the quality of life for the poor
(2) privatize many government programs
(3) send additional troops to Vietnam
(4) reduce the number of nuclear weapons

41 The Civil Rights Act of 1964 was intended to end

(1) loyalty oaths for federal employees
(2) affirmative action programs in education
(3) unfair treatment of the elderly
(4) discrimination based on race or sex

Base your answers to questions 42 and 43 on the passage below and on your knowledge of social studies.

You have the right to remain silent. Anything you say can and will be used against you in a court of law. You have the right to speak to an attorney, and to have an attorney present during any questioning. If you cannot afford a lawyer, one will be provided for you at government expense.
— www.usconstitution.net

42 The requirements included in this passage are part of the Supreme Court's effort to protect the rights of

(1) individuals accused of crimes
(2) students from unreasonable searches
(3) defendants from double jeopardy
(4) criminals from cruel and unusual punishment

43 This passage resulted from which Supreme Court decision?

(1) *Mapp* v. *Ohio* (1961)
(2) *Gideon* v. *Wainwright* (1963)
(3) *Miranda* v. *Arizona* (1966)
(4) *Tinker* v. *Des Moines* (1969)

44 • Announcement of Eisenhower Doctrine (1957)
• Operation Desert Storm (1991)
• Operation Iraqi Freedom (2003 – present)

These events involve attempts by the United States to

(1) protect human rights in Europe
(2) protect its interests in the Middle East
(3) deliver humanitarian aid to Africa
(4) contain the spread of communism in Asia

Base your answer to question 45 on the cartoon below and on your knowledge of social studies.

Teamwork

Source: Jim Morin, *The Miami Herald*,
King Features Syndicate, 1989

45 What is the main idea of this cartoon?

(1) The global economy is on the verge of collapse.
(2) Rich nations should help poor nations improve their economic conditions.
(3) One nation's economic problems affect many other nations.
(4) Each nation controls its own economic destiny.

46 During the 1990s, an increase in Mexican immigration to the United States was caused by the immigrants' desire for

(1) greater political freedom
(2) bilingual education
(3) better economic opportunities
(4) religious freedom

47 A major goal of the women's movement over the past twenty years has been to gain

(1) full property rights
(2) the right to vote
(3) equal economic opportunity
(4) better access to Social Security

48 A similarity between the Bank of the United States, created in 1791, and the present-day Federal Reserve System is that both were established to

(1) set tariff rates
(2) regulate the money supply
(3) achieve balanced budgets
(4) restrict the gold supply

49 The Supreme Court decisions in *Gibbons* v. *Ogden* and *Northern Securities Co.* v. *United States* were based on the federal government's power to

(1) issue patents
(2) control the stock market
(3) regulate interstate commerce
(4) encourage technological development

50 One similarity shared by President Andrew Johnson and President Bill Clinton is that both

(1) served only one term as president
(2) were impeached but not convicted
(3) had no vice president
(4) came to office after the death of a president

Answers to the essay questions are to be written in the separate essay booklet.

In developing your answer to Part II, be sure to keep this general definition in mind:

discuss means "to make observations about something using facts, reasoning, and argument; to present in some detail"

PART II

THEMATIC ESSAY QUESTION

Directions: Write a well-organized essay that includes an introduction, several paragraphs addressing the task below, and a conclusion.

Theme: Migration of Peoples

> Throughout our nation's history, important migrations or movements of people within the United States have occurred. These migrations have had a significant impact on both the people who moved and on American society.

Task:

> Identify *two* migrations or movements of people within the United States and for *each*
> - Discuss the historical circumstances that led to the migration of these people
> - Discuss the impact of the migration on the people who moved *and/or* on American society

You may use any important migration or movement of people from your study of United States history. Some suggestions you might wish to consider include the forced migration of Native American Indians (1800–1880), the westward movement (1840–1890), the migration of African Americans from the South to cities in the North (1900–1929), the Puerto Rican migration to the North after World War II (1945–1960), the westward migration from the Dust Bowl (1930s), suburbanization (1945–present), and the migration to the Sun Belt (1950–present).

You are *not* limited to these suggestions.

Guidelines:

In your essay, be sure to
- Develop all aspects of the task
- Support the theme with relevant facts, examples, and details
- Use a logical and clear plan of organization, including an introduction and a conclusion that are beyond a restatement of the theme

NAME _____ SCHOOL _____

In developing your answer to Part III, be sure to keep this general definition in mind:

discuss means "to make observations about something using facts, reasoning, and argument; to present in some detail"

PART III

DOCUMENT-BASED QUESTION

This question is based on the accompanying documents. The question is designed to test your ability to work with historical documents. Some of the documents have been edited for the purposes of the question. As you analyze the documents, take into account the source of each document and any point of view that may be presented in the document.

Historical Context:

> Following World War II, the United States and the Soviet Union emerged as rival superpowers. This rivalry led to a period known as the Cold War. During the first fifteen years of the Cold War (1945–1960), the threat of communism presented many different challenges to the United States.

Task: Using information from the documents and your knowledge of United States history, answer the questions that follow each document in Part A. Your answers to the questions will help you write the Part B essay, in which you will be asked to

> • Discuss how the threat of communism during the Cold War affected the United States in the period from 1945 to 1960

Part A
Short-Answer Questions

Directions: Analyze the documents and answer the questions that follow each document in the space provided.

Document 1

Source: Justus, *Minneapolis Star,* 1947 (adapted)

1 According to this cartoon, why was Congress rushing to the aid of Western Europe? [1]

_____

_____

Score ☐

This excerpt is from a telegram sent to the Soviet Ambassador to the United States from the Acting Secretary of State in September 1948. A copy of this telegram was sent to President Harry Truman on September 27, 1948.

> 1. The Governments of the United States, France and the United Kingdom, conscious of their obligations under the charter of the United Nations to settle disputes by peaceful means, took the initiative on July 30, 1948, in approaching the Soviet Government for informal discussions in Moscow in order to explore every possibility of adjusting a dangerous situation which had arisen by reason of measures taken by the Soviet Government directly challenging the rights of the other occupying powers in Berlin. These measures, persistently pursued, amounted to a blockade of land and water transport and communication between the Western Zones of Germany and Berlin which not only endangered the maintenance of the forces of occupation of the United States, France and the United Kingdom in that city but also jeopardized the discharge by those governments of their duties as occupying powers through the threat of starvation, disease and economic ruin for the population of Berlin. . . .

Source: Telegram from United States Department of State to President Truman, September 27, 1948

2a According to this passage, what action taken by the Soviet Union created tensions between the Soviet government and the governments of the United States and its Allies?   [1]

_____

_____

Score ☐

Document 2b

Source: Eric Morris, *Blockade*, Stein & Day (adapted)

2b According to this graph, what action was taken by the United States and its Allies in response to the events described in Document 2a?   [1]

_____

_____

Score ☐

Document 3

> ... NATO was simply a necessity. The developing situation with the Soviet Union demanded the participation of the United States in the defense of Western Europe. Any other solution would have opened the area to Soviet domination, contrary to the interests of the United States and contrary to any decent world order. At the time of the signing of the pact, April 4, 1949, I do not believe that anyone envisaged [imagined] the kind of military setup that NATO evolved into and from which de Gaulle withdrew French forces in 1966. It [NATO] was, rather, regarded as a traditional military alliance of like-minded countries. It was not regarded as a panacea [cure] for the problems besetting [affecting] Europe, but only as an elementary precaution against Communist aggression. . . .

Source: Charles E. Bohlen, *Witness to History, 1929–1969,* W. W. Norton & Company, 1973

3 According to this document, why was the North Atlantic Treaty Organization (NATO) necessary? [1]

_____

_____

Score ☐

Document 4

Initial newspaper stories concerning Senator McCarthy's speech in Wheeling, West Virginia, reported that the Senator said he knew of 205 communists in the State Department. Senator McCarthy later told the Senate he had used the number 57 in Wheeling. He placed this account of his Wheeling speech in the *Congressional Record*.

> . . . This, ladies and gentlemen, gives you somewhat of a picture of the type of individuals who have been helping to shape our foreign policy. In my opinion the State Department, which is one of the most important government departments, is thoroughly infested with Communists.
>
> I have in my hand 57 cases of individuals who would appear to be either card carrying members or certainly loyal to the Communist Party, but who nevertheless are still helping to shape our foreign policy.
>
> One thing to remember in discussing the Communists in our government is that we are not dealing with spies who get 30 pieces of silver to steal the blueprints of a new weapon. We are dealing with a far more sinister type of activity because it permits the enemy to guide and shape our policy. . . .

Source: Senator Joseph R. McCarthy, Speech, February 9, 1950, Wheeling, West Virginia, in *Congressional Record*, 81st Congress, 2nd Session

4 According to this document, what did Senator McCarthy suggest about communist influence in the United States government? [1]

_____

_____

Score [ ]

Document 5

> . . . The attack upon Korea makes it plain beyond all doubt that Communism has passed beyond the use of subversion to conquer independent nations and will now use armed invasion and war. It has defied the orders of the Security Council of the United Nations issued to preserve international peace and security. In these circumstances the occupation of Formosa [Taiwan] by Communist forces would be a direct threat to the security of the Pacific area and to United States forces performing their lawful and necessary functions in that area.
>
> Accordingly I have ordered the Seventh Fleet to prevent any attack on Formosa. As a corollary of this action I am calling upon the Chinese Government on Formosa to cease all air and sea operations against the mainland. The Seventh Fleet will see that this is done. The determination of the future status of Formosa must await the restoration of security in the Pacific, a peace settlement with Japan, or consideration by the United Nations. . . .

— President Harry Truman, Press Release, June 27, 1950

5*a* Based on this document, state **one** reason given by President Truman to justify his concern about communism. [1]

_____

_____

Score ☐

b According to this document, state **one** action President Truman took after the attack on Korea. [1]

_____

_____

Score ☐

Document 6a

> . . . Our unity as a nation is sustained by free communication of thought and by easy transportation of people and goods. The ceaseless flow of information throughout the Republic is matched by individual and commercial movement over a vast system of inter-connected highways criss-crossing the Country and joining at our national borders with friendly neighbors to the north and south. . . .

Source: President Dwight D. Eisenhower, message to Congress, February 22, 1955

Document 6b

> . . . In case of an atomic attack on our key cities, the road net must permit quick evacuation of target areas, mobilization of defense forces and maintenance of every essential economic function. But the present system in critical areas would be the breeder [cause] of a deadly congestion within hours of an attack. . . .

Source: President Dwight D. Eisenhower, message to Congress, February 22, 1955 (adapted)

6 Based on these documents, state **two** reasons President Eisenhower believed that the Interstate Highway System was important to national defense.   [2]

(1)_____

_____

Score ▢

(2)_____

_____

Score ▢

Document 7

. . . When the air-raid siren sounded, our teachers stopped talking and led us to the school basement. There the gym teachers lined us up against the cement walls and steel lockers, and showed us how to lean in and fold our arms over our heads. Our small school ran from kindergarten through twelfth grade. We had air-raid drills in small batches, four or five grades together, because there was no room for us all against the walls. The teachers had to stand in the middle of the basement rooms: those bright Pittsburgh women who taught Latin, science, and art, and those educated, beautifully mannered European women who taught French, history, and German, who had landed in Pittsburgh at the end of their respective flights from Hitler, and who had baffled us by their common insistence on tidiness, above all, in our written work.

The teachers stood in the middle of the room, not talking to each other. We tucked against the walls and lockers: dozens of clean girls wearing green jumpers, green knee socks, and pink-soled white bucks. We folded our skinny arms over our heads, and raised to the enemy a clatter of gold scarab bracelets and gold bangle bracelets. . . .

Source: Annie Dillard, *An American Childhood,* Harper & Row

7 According to this document, state *one* way schools were affected by the threat of communism.   [1]

_____

_____

Score ☐

Document 8

... Our safety, and that of the free world, demand, of course, effective systems for gathering information about the military capabilities of other powerful nations, especially those that make a fetish [obsessive habit] of secrecy. This involves many techniques and methods. In these times of vast military machines and nuclear-tipped missiles, the ferreting [finding] out of this information is indispensable to free world security.

This has long been one of my most serious preoccupations. It is part of my grave responsibility, within the over-all problem of protecting the American people, to guard ourselves and our allies against surprise attack.

During the period leading up to World War II we learned from bitter experience the imperative [absolute] necessity of a continuous gathering of intelligence information, the maintenance of military communications and contact, and alertness of command.

An additional word seems appropriate about this matter of communications and command. While the Secretary of Defense and I were in Paris, we were, of course, away from our normal command posts. He recommended that under the circumstances we test the continuing readiness of our military communications. I personally approved. Such tests are valuable and will be frequently repeated in the future.

Moreover, as President, charged by the Constitution with the conduct of America's foreign relations, and as Commander-in-Chief, charged with the direction of the operations and activities of our Armed Forces and their supporting services, I take full responsibility for approving all the various programs undertaken by our government to secure and evaluate military intelligence.

It was in the prosecution [carrying out] of one of these intelligence programs that the widely publicized U-2 incident occurred.

Aerial photography has been one of many methods we have used to keep ourselves and the free world abreast of major Soviet military developments. The usefulness of this work has been well established through four years of effort. The Soviets were well aware of it. Chairman Khrushchev has stated that he became aware of these flights several years ago. Only last week, in his Paris press conference, Chairman Khrushchev confirmed that he knew of these flights when he visited the United States last September. ...

Source: President Dwight D. Eisenhower, Address, May 25, 1960,
Public Papers of the Presidents of the United States: Dwight D. Eisenhower 1960–1961

8 Based on this document, state **two** reasons given by President Eisenhower for gathering information about the Soviet military. [2]

(1)_____

_____

Score ☐

(2)_____

_____

Score ☐

Part B
Essay

Directions: Write a well-organized essay that includes an introduction, several paragraphs, and a conclusion. Use evidence from *at least five* documents in your essay. Support your response with relevant facts, examples, and details. Include additional outside information.

Historical Context:

Following World War II, the United States and the Soviet Union emerged as rival superpowers. This rivalry led to a period known as the Cold War. During the first fifteen years of the Cold War (1945–1960), the threat of communism presented many different challenges to the United States.

Task: Using information from the documents and your knowledge of United States history, write an essay in which you

> • Discuss how the threat of communism during the Cold War affected the United States in the period from 1945 to 1960

Guidelines

In your essay, be sure to
- Develop all aspects of the task
- Incorporate information from *at least five* documents
- Incorporate relevant outside information
- Support the theme with relevant facts, examples, and details
- Use a logical and clear plan of organization, including an introduction and conclusion that are beyond a restatement of the theme